MW00769137

Geo. Squier

Critical Studies in the History of Anthropology

Series Editors: *Regna Darnell, Stephen O. Murray*

Ephraim George Squier

and the Development of

American Anthropology

Terry A. Barnhart

University of Nebraska Press

Lincoln and London

Copyright © 2005 by the Board of Regents of the University of Nebraska. All rights reserved. Manufactured
in the United States of America. Set in Quadraat by Kim
Essman. Book design by Richard Eckersley. Printed by
Thomson-Shore, Inc.

Portions of chapter 2 previously appeared as "A Question of Authorship: The Ephraim George Squier–Edwin
Hamilton Davis Controversy," Ohio History 92 (Annual
1983), 52–71. Portions of chapter 5 previously appeared
as "The Iroquois as Mound Builders: Ephraim George
Squier and the Archaeology of Western New York," New
York History 77, no.2 (Spring 1996), 125–50. Portions
of chapter 11 previously appeared as "Toward a Science
of Man: European Influences on the Archaeology of
Ephraim George Squier," in New Perspectives on the Origins
of Americanist Archaeology, eds. David L. Bowman and
Stephen Williams (Tuscaloosa: University of Alabama
Press, 2002), 87–116.

♾

Library of Congress Cataloging-in-Publication Data
Barnhart, Terry A., 1952–
Ephraim George Squier and the development of American anthropology / Terry A. Barnhart.
p. cm. – (Critical studies in the history of anthropology)
Includes bibliographical references and index.
ISBN 0-8032-1321-2 (hardcover : alkaline paper)
1. Squier, E. G. (Ephraim George), 1821–1888.
2. Anthropologists – United States – Biography. 3. Anthropologists – Latin America – Biography. 4. Mound-
builders – Ohio River Valley. 5. Mound-builders –
Mississippi River Valley. 6. Ohio River Valley – Antiquities. 7. Mississippi River Valley – Antiquities.
8. Latin America – Antiquities. 9. Davis, E. H. (Edwin
Hamilton), 1811–1888. I. Title. II. Series
GN21.S68B37 2005   301′.092–dc22   2004019927

The study of man, physiologically and psychically, is confessedly the noblest which can claim human attention. . . . The study of man, in this comprehensive sense, constitutes the science of Ethnology. The elements of this science are the results, the ultimates of all other sciences; it begins where the rest stop. . . . [It] presupposes a general high attainment in all other departments of knowledge. It is essentially the science of the age; the offspring of that prevailing mental and physical energy which neglects no subject of inquiry. — E. G. Squier, "American Ethnology," *American Review* (April 1849)

CONTENTS

ILLUSTRATIONS

ACKNOWLEDGMENTS

While writing this book, I accumulated debts and obligations to many people. Some assisted me directly by reading and critically commenting on portions of earlier stages this work. Others provided invaluable reference and research services by locating or verifying fugitive sources. Still others helped indirectly by precept, example, and encouragement. Their efforts on my behalf have been conspicuous and indispensable. I am particularly indebted to Richard M. Jellison, professor emeritus at Miami University, who first sparked my interest in Squier and other early anthropologists and introduced me to an absorbing field of historical inquiry.

Others have helped me along the way by encouraging me to continue my research on Squier or by offering their insights on his place in the history of American anthropology. Notable among them are William Stanton, formerly at the University of Pittsburgh; Reginald Horsman, professor emeritus at the University of Wisconsin at Milwaukee; David Browman at Washington University in St. Louis; and Steven Williams, emeritus Peabody Professor of American Archaeology and Ethnology and formerly curator of North American archaeology for the Peabody Museum at Harvard University. The writings of David M. Oestreicher and Charles Boewe on the Walam Olum helped me clarify my own thinking about Squier's use of Rafinesque's Walam Olum manuscript and its place in Squier's anthropological thought. John A. Strong, professor emeritus at the Southampton College of Long Island University in Southampton, New York, generously shared his insights and knowledge of Squier's contributions to the archaeology of Central America and encouraged me to continue my study of Squier into the Central American phase of his anthropological career.

Thanks also to John W. Kicheloe of Meredith College, who graciously provided me with a copy of the earliest known letter by Squier describing his investigations in Ohio. Both Keith McElroy and Lawrence G. Desmond patiently answered my inquiries regarding Squier's use of photography in Peru and his relationship with Augustus Le Plongeon. Bradley K. Lepper and Martha Potter Otto at the Ohio Historical Society taught me much about anthropological concepts of culture and some of the intellectual traditions in which American archaeology gradually developed as a field of anthropological inquiry. They have also shared with me their own research on more than one occasion. I am equally indebted to my Peruvian colleague at Eastern Illinois University, José Deustua, who patiently answered my many questions about the cultural history of Peru and the works of Peruvian scholars.

Acknowledgments

The assistance of Donna L. Davey and Jan Hilley of the Manuscripts Department at the New-York Historical Society was particularly valuable in the verification of citations in the society's Squier Family Papers and the Ephraim George Squier Papers. David Dressing at the Latin American Library of Tulane University, Thomas G. Knoles at the American Antiquarian Society, Glenn L. McMullen at the Indiana Historical Society, John C. Dann at the William L. Clements Library of the University of Michigan, and Patrick Kerwin at the Library of Congress have placed me under similar obligations for helping me with the Squier Papers at those repositories. Charlene Peacock assisted me with the Samuel George Morton Papers at the Library Company of Philadelphia, Anne Kling with the James McBride Papers at the Cincinnati Historical Society, Sandra B. Neyman with the Samuel P. Hildreth Papers at Marietta College, Mary M. Huth with the Lewis Henry Morgan Papers at the Rush Rhees Library of the University of Rochester, and William Stingone and Wayne Furman with special collections at the New York Public Library. William E. Cox and Alan L. Bain provided me with copies of incoming letters from Squier and Edwin Hamilton Davis in the Joseph Henry Papers at the Smithsonian Institution Archives, and Tracy Elizabeth Robinson helped me secure permission to cite them. The photographic services of Beverly J. Cruse at the Media Center of Eastern Illinois University's Booth Library and the good offices of the Interlibrary Loan Department at Booth Library were likewise essential. A 2003 Summer Research Award from Eastern Illinois University aided the completion of the last chapters.

Several staff members of the University of Nebraska Press contributed directly to the editing of this work. Gary Dunham, editor in chief of the University of Nebraska Press, had faith in the project and had patience with a historian's preoccupation with documentation. The critical readings of Regna Darnell and Stephen O. Murray, editors of the Critical Studies in the History of American Anthropology series, have placed me under numerous obligations for their invaluable recommendations. Jeremy Hall in acquisitions worked with me from the acceptance of the manuscript for publication through the copyediting and printing. The copyediting of Jonathan Lawrence has made this work more coherent from first page to last. Linnea Fredrickson and Alison Rold made the final stages of production a painless and efficient process.

Thanks to my family can scarcely repay them for the assistance they have given me in many ways and over many years. My mother, Helen Barnhart, and my late father, Russell A. Barnhart, gave me love, support, and an education, debts I will never be able to repay. My wife, Jo Ellen Barnhart, has enabled and supported all I have ever done in life that is personally and professionally meaningful and has given me shelter from the storm in ways she will never know. Our sons, Adrian and Andy, have enriched our lives and have mercifully learned, like their mother, to tolerate my mobile and intrusive boxes of research notes and papers and the seemingly endless hours spent immersed in them and at the word processor. Your understanding, tolerance, and support have been an essential part of this endeavor. I hope your faith in me has been partially justified by the appearance of this work.

When Ephraim George Squier is remembered today, it is usually for his research on Ohio Valley prehistory. Yet Squier's investigations encompassed much more. It is the breadth and duration of his career that make him the most important figure in the nineteenth-century establishment of American archaeology, long before the beginning of professional training and professional associations.

The Mound Builder synthesis of Squier and his coauthor Edwin Hamilton Davis was judged sufficiently important for it to be the subject of the first scientific publication of the then-new Smithsonian Institution. Terry A. Barnhart's fine biography of Squier shows how that work came into being and recounts some of the less well remembered but very considerable ethnological and linguistic writing Squier did, particularly on Central and South American vocabularies, migrations, and iconographies. Squier was a political partisan as well as a scientist and was rewarded with U.S. consular positions in Nicaragua, Honduras, and Peru. Along with his light consular duties in Peru, he undertook mapping the ruins of the (pre-Columbian, pre-Inca) Chimú capital of Chan Chan as well as writing a travel book on his explorations in the "land of the Incas."

Squier is an interesting figure in the history of Whig politics in general and of nineteenth-century American expansionism and the projection of United States power under the aegis of its "manifest destiny" in particular. As was the case for the Wilkes expedition analyzed in Barry Joyce's earlier book in our series, *The Shaping of American Ethnography*, Squier's anthropology beyond the borders of the United States provided rationales for rescuing benighted aliens – in Squier's case, Latin Americans whose European superiority had degenerated through mestizoization (in the white American view of his time, "miscegenation") – and providing tutelage from the vigorous young United States for backward peoples.

The major metatheoretical issue in the preprofessional anthropology of Squier's day was whether humankind had a single origin (monogenism, with Native Americans often assumed to be one of the "lost tribes of Israel" or other people mentioned in the Bible) or whether the races had multiple origins (polygenism, with various kinds of nonwhites viewed as being created separately and comprising inferior species). Among Americans interested in a science of mankind before Squier, Albert Gallatin and Henry Rowe Schoolcraft championed monogenism, while the physician and physical anthropologist Samuel George Morton, leader of the "American School," contended that distinct human races could be ranked by cranial size (itself a presumed marker of intelligence).

Squier put forth a softer polygenism, combining Gallatin's (and Humboldt's) position of mankind's psychic unity with the by then dominant scientific belief of separate origins and parallel (if retarded and/or backsliding) sociocultural evolution. That is, Squier argued that the similarities found among cultures – particularly nature worship – did not depend on a common origin. For Squier, separate origins of races did not preclude progress to "civilization," though "degeneration" was a constant danger, even for the apex of "civilization," the northeastern United States.

Squire's version of the question of human origin allowed culture to override biology under some circumstances. Such a position, especially in the ante- and postbellum United States, where matters of scientific racism were fraught with immediate and contentious implications, helped to mitigate the general quick slide from race to racism in mid-nineteenth-century anthropology.

Barnhart admirably shows the interconnections of nineteenth-century American science and popular racist beliefs and reveals how elite and mass discourses dovetailed with and rationalized the geopolitics of a United States that was expanding and extending influence over the whole of the Western Hemisphere. He also shows Squier as advocating and attempting to produce holistic anthropology. Squier himself undertook archaeological, ethnological, and linguistic researches, although he was most active as an archaeologist.

Stephen O. Murray and Regna Darnell

Ephraim George Squier

and the Development of

American Anthropology

Prologue

Ephraim George Squier and the History
of American Anthropology

The anthropological career of Ephraim George Squier is an intriguing mixture of exploration, adventure, and original scholarship. Whether investigating the prehistoric Indian mounds and earthen enclosures of Ohio and New York, the stone idols once worshiped by the indigenous groups of Nicaragua, the vocabularies and migrations of the Nahua-speaking peoples of Central America, or the ruins of ancient Peru, Squier pursued his researches of aboriginal America with audacity, enthusiasm, and seemingly boundless energy. Beginning with the publication of *Ancient Monuments of the Mississippi Valley* in 1848 and ending with the appearance of his long-awaited *Peru* in 1877, his writings earned the accolades of contemporaries and made him a valued correspondent of scholars and learned societies throughout the United States and Europe. Over the course of thirty years, Squier zealously promoted the study of the American Indian through his fieldwork, publications, and activities in the American Ethnological Society.

Squier and his contemporaries conducted their archaeological and ethnological inquiries in an era when American anthropology lacked an infrastructure. There were no paid positions, reliable sources of funding for research, specialized journals, professional associations, or standards of professional training and practice. The boundaries between ethnology and archaeology were imprecisely drawn, and the idea of anthropology as an integrated approach to the study of man was just beginning to emerge. The term *anthropology* itself occasionally appears in the literature of the early and mid-nineteenth century, even though its occurrence is rare and its meaning subsumed under the period's largely undifferentiated banner of historical and natural sciences. Constantine Samuel Rafinesque, for instance, described anthropology in 1832 as the philosophical basis for the study of philology and ethnology.[1]

The term *ethnology* was, however, more commonly used in the early and mid-nineteenth century to describe what is today known as anthropology. Luke Burke, editor of the *Ethnological Journal* in London, defined ethnology in

1848 as "a science which investigates the mental and physical differences of Mankind, and the organic laws upon which they depend; and which seeks to deduce from these investigations, principles of human guidance, in all the important relations of social existence." The terms *ethnology* and *ethnography* were often used synonymously, but in their broadest sense they were understood to mean "the natural history of man." While the science of ethnology sought to know everything organically connected with the natural history of man, its historical branch inquired into all facts of the past that illustrated the physical characteristics and the presumed moral and intellectual traits of the various races. Historical ethnology concerned itself with determining the early seats, migrations, amalgamations, modifications, and social conditions of the races and with establishing their "position in the social scale."[2]

Ethnologists in the United Sates and Europe in the mid-nineteenth century saw the need for a more comprehensive and integrated science that examined humankind in all of its physical, psychological, material, historical, and linguistic characteristics as well as its corresponding social relations and institutions. The disciplinary specialization and professionalization that gradually reconfigured American anthropology in the last quarter of the nineteenth century occurred as the avocational anthropologists of Squier's generation were rapidly passing from the scene. Several of the leading points of inquiry that define ethnology and archaeology as anthropological disciplines were, nonetheless, being advanced and strenuously debated both in the United States and Europe from the 1840s through the 1870s. Squier was at the center of many of those debates and developments. He consistently articulated the need for a more holistic and integrated approach to the study of man, and he did so explicitly as early as 1849.[3] His views were part of a larger discourse about the direction of ethnological investigations in the United States and Europe, within which are to be found the germs of ideas and methods that later defined and gave structure to physical and cultural anthropology and their various subfields and areas of specialization.[4]

American anthropology during Squier's era was far more democratic than it would ever be thereafter. The specialization, professionalization, and consolidation of the discipline in the late nineteenth and early twentieth century changed those conditions significantly, even though the avocational tradition in archaeology is still alive and well. Anthropology in Squier's day was a great commons in which anyone could declare oneself to be an archaeologist or ethnologist. As William R. Stanton has noted, "America, with its Indians, its Negro slaves, and its varied populations of whites, tended to make every citizen, if not an ethnologist, at least a speculator on matters of race."[5] But the more empirical and systematic of the early investigators certainly merit close attention. Squier was often critical of the unsubstantiated speculations that passed for archaeological and ethnological inquiry, and he devoted a good deal of ink and energy in combating popular notions about the pre-Columbian colonization of America by Europeans.[6]

Squier's pious affirmations of the need for a more scientifically exacting approach to the study of man were neither hollow rhetoric nor mere posturing. He sought to remove the leaden thrall of biblical ethnology from American archaeology and ethnology. Anthropologists, moreover, would continue to wrestle with some of the same issues and problems that confronted Squier and his contemporaries for years to come, albeit on different terms and a far different set of assumptions. The preprofessional figures in anthropology's past "shared the attributes that characterize the discipline of anthropology in any age – a reliance on systematic explanations constructed with a self-assurance that masks the fact that its foundation and conclusions are period- and culture-dependent."[7] Few anthropologists in the mid-nineteenth century were more self-assured than Squier, and few produced works that provide more insight into the socially and culturally bound constructions that defined the anthropology of his day.

A distinct set of ideas and concerns guided Squier's analysis of archaeological and ethnological evidence and shaped the theoretical dimensions of his writings over his long career. Unity of thought and recurrence of theme link *Ancient Monuments of the Mississippi Valley* (1848), *Aboriginal Monuments of the State of New York* (1851), *The Serpent Symbol, and the Worship of the Reciprocal Principles of Nature in America* (1851), and his related minor writings. Squier took an enlarged view of his subject in all three of those works, and he regarded them as intimately connected. His subsequent fieldwork in Central America and Peru resulted in several publications that are as distinct from his earlier works in tone and character as they are in setting. The two-volume *Nicaragua* (1852), *Notes on Central America* (1855), *The States of Central America* (1858), and *Peru* (1877) were significant departures from his earlier works in many ways. His writings on Central America in particular are encyclopedic in their scope and a mixture of empiricism and polemics. Yet in his anthropology Squier continued to develop a common set of ideas, interests, and themes, even though the continuities between the earlier and later phases of his career have yet to be integrated into an in-depth analysis.

The American anthropological community as an organized network of professionals did not begin to emerge in the United States until the late nineteenth century, while professionally trained anthropologists did not arrive on the scene until the early twentieth century. Squier's investigations and those of his compeers in the American School of Ethnology occurred within a comparatively inchoate network of intellectual relationships and institutional affiliations. But the emerging discipline of anthropology in the United States was well on its way toward differentiating itself from history and natural history as a scientific study of man in the 1840s and 1850s, when advocates advanced anthropology's claim to social utility based on a distinctive subject matter and methodology. The establishment of the American Ethnological Society in 1842, the Smithsonian Institution in 1846, and the American Association for the Advancement of Science in 1848 contributed to the organization of the American scientific community and the infant science of American anthropology.[8]

Specialization, integration, and consolidation were transforming American culture from the mid- to the late nineteenth century as a by-product of the emerging urban and industrial order. Those changes had a profound impact on the organization of knowledge in all areas of scholarly endeavor.[9] The American scientific community began to organize during those formative years, and the emerging disciplines of archaeology and ethnology were no exception. Squier's activities and writings reflect the distinctive character and direction of American anthropology from the 1840s through the early 1870s, and they were an essential part of the process of disciplinary self-definition. The assumptions about human nature that shaped his anthropological thought, the problems and issues he thought important, and the kinds of evidence he used to support his arguments tell us much about Squier and the history of American anthropology from the mid- to the late nineteenth century.

It may be objected that use of the term *anthropology* in connection with Squier's career and those of his contemporaries is anachronistic – a term of convenience inappropriately imported into the past. If the American anthropological community did not begin to coalesce as a professional community until the 1870s and 1880s, that does not mean that earlier investigators were not practicing anthropology. The elements of the four-field approach to the study of man (the anthropological subdisciplines of physical anthropology, archaeology, ethnology, and linguistics) that later came to define the discipline of anthropology existed in embryo at an earlier day, however imprecise and rudimentary the boundaries and definitions. That is particularly true of the work of Squier and the other members of the American School. Josiah Clark Nott and George Robins Gliddon self-consciously referred to Samuel George Morton as the founder of their "cis-Atlantic School of Anthropology" as early as 1854,[10] while in 1869 Squier spearheaded the movement that transformed the American Ethnological Society into the short-lived Anthropological Institute of New-York.

4

The American School's contributions to the development of anthropology were, moreover, recognized in England and France from the 1840s to the 1860s. The *Anthropological Review* of London, for example, observed of Squier's friend and correspondent Josiah Clark Nott in 1868 that to give an extended notice of Nott's work and its importance to the development of anthropological science in the United States "would be practically to write a history of transatlantic anthropology, from the death of Dr. Samuel George Morton [in 1851] to a very recent period."[11] The passing of time has decidedly changed our opinion about many of the assumptions, attitudes, and conclusions of the American School, but their contemporaries held their works in high regard. Squier and his cronies attempted to make the older and more fragmented ethnology in the United States conform to recent developments within the emerging anthropological community of Europe.

Squier articulated the need for American ethnologists to take a more comprehensive and integrated approach to the study of man, one that examined the American Indian physiologically, psychologically, linguistically, archaeologically, and historically. Squier's own works embody that approach and draw upon a wide array of supporting evidence. Anthropology as a concept and approach to the study of man can be properly historicized within the context of Squier's life. His study of archaeological and ethnological problems exemplifies an anthropologically oriented approach to American prehistory that is consonant with later developments, especially in his use of ethnographic analogies to interpret archaeological artifacts and sites.[12] If anthropology is essentially "a generalizing and comparative discipline,"[13] then Squier is indeed a worthy intellectual ancestor. He is a transitional figure in the history of American anthropology in many ways.

The ethnocentrism and scientific racism that informed many of the writings of the American School represent the least useful aspects of its legacy and go against the grain of latter-day sensibilities. A virulent racism permeated all aspects of American society and culture in the early and mid-nineteenth century and was reflected in both American and European anthropology. The racial determinism of the American School is a forceful reminder of the social construction of knowledge and of how much has changed in our basic assumptions and attitudes about race from an anthropological point of view. But the approach to the study of man and the methods employed by the members of the American School, however flawed or erroneous, were essentially anthropological. The research interests and methodologies of the American School are still of interest from a historical point of view.

I treat Squier's diplomatic and entrepreneurial activities in Central America here only to the extent that they affected the objectivity of his scholarship, and to the degree necessary to establish the political context of his archaeological and ethnological fieldwork in the region. The observations recorded in *Nicaragua, Notes on Central America, The States of Central America*, and related contributions to periodicals amply illustrate how his political and social views, diplomatic activities, and entrepreneurial interests affected his anthropology. Squier's earlier archaeological investigations in Ohio and later fieldwork in Peru have tended to overshadow the significance of his contributions to the ethnology, ethnography, and ethnohistory of Central America. Scholars have noted the polemical and propagandistic aspects of his treatment of the Miskito Indians, for example, but have tended to either ignore or minimize the original contributions he made to Central American archaeology and ethnology between 1849 and 1869.

Intellectual biography concerns itself with the origin and development of ideas and with their embodiment in the works of particular writers and in the collective discourse of their era. I have endeavored to more clearly delineate Squier's efforts at comprehending the contours of American prehistory and the presumed origins, migrations, and affinities of aboriginal peoples on the American continent. Both his original contributions to knowledge and the unresolved issues and problems with which he grappled are examined, while particular attention is given to topics and little-known writings that fill gaps in previous treatments of his work. Squier's anthropological interests and activities are positioned within the larger contours of his life, the broader background of American society and culture, and in relation to those of his predecessors, his contemporaries, and his successors in the field of American anthropology. Both the private and public spheres of his life are examined together with the psychological dimensions of his personality and character. Although I have stopped short of a psychoanalytic approach, I am sensible of the need for biographers to seek insights into the psychological motivations of their subjects.[14]

The multitalented Squier possessed one of the best minds of his generation. He was largely self-educated and relentlessly driven by an overweening ambition. He is a complex and engaging figure, one that represents both the best and the worst attributes of his day. His historical significance rests on the fact that his writings and activities reflect so many of the normative attitudes in the nascent field of American anthropology. The interplay of personality and experience, the wellsprings of ambition, the sources of conflict and rivalries, and the influence of intellectual affiliations all find a place in the chapters that follow. As David Byron Davis has noted, "By showing how cultural tensions and contradictions may be internalized, struggled with, and resolved within actual individuals, biography offers the most promising key to synthesis."[15] There were many such cultural tensions and contradictions in Squier's anthropological career, while the depth and breadth of his scholarly interests and activities provide synthesis in understanding the anthropological concerns of his generation.

Those who attempt to construct what Jacob Gruber has called "intellectual biography" in the history of anthropology must be cognizant of the intellectual and cultural barriers they will encounter.[16] Coming to grips with timebound meanings and usages is particularly important, since the intellectual traditions and assumptions that informed the early periods of anthropological inquiry faded from view long ago. As historians and anthropologists have distanced themselves from the work of their avocational predecessors (often called "antiquaries"), their ability to perceive the texture, symbolism, and language of that lost world has likewise been diminished. Biographers must be intellectual and cultural historians as well as chroniclers. They must discern their subjects' intellectual habits and cast of mind, must know the individuals with whom they interacted, the institutions that influenced their activities, and the aims of their research. In a word, they must anchor themselves within the intellectual tradition in which their subjects read, spoke, and wrote.

Making those connections when dealing with preprofessional figures in anthropology's past is particularly crucial. One of the benefits of studying earlier periods of archaeological and ethnological investigations is, indeed, that it may provide anthropologists with a salutary "distance from their own theoretical and methodological preoccupations."[17] Stepping outside present-day concerns, interests, and agendas may have a salutary effect by adding useful historical perspectives to contemporary anthropology – a true linkage of past and present that makes neither one serve the other and allows each to more fully speak on its own terms. The anthropology of one era should not define that of another but should rather be presented synchronically and diachronically within a developmental sequence. The intellectual lineages and schools of thought in anthropology's past were nurtured within personal and institutional networks that individually and collectively comprise a historical sociology of anthropological knowledge.[18] Contemporary practice has its own intellectual lineages and schools of thought that have likewise followed a historical trajectory to the present, thus making the history of anthropology an important field of professional concern and area of specialization.[19]

The intellectual and cultural distance that separates professional anthropology from its avocational origins dictates caution lest we lapse into presentist perspectives. The baneful effects of presentism intrude themselves into all historical studies, as Herbert Butterfield so aptly noted in *The Whig Interpretation of History* (1931).[20] History is too often written as affirmation of the present, giving rise to certain fallacies within the underlying assumptions of historians, the historical process, and the rendering of moral judgments. The judgments that historians make about the past are essentially presentist, since they use values, attitudes, understandings, and standards of their own time as benchmarks to interpret the past. The historiographical dimensions of the problem are formidable. The difficulties involved in divorcing oneself from presentist perspectives take the full measure of all students of the past. It is, indeed, far easier to draw attention to the problem of presentism than to free oneself of it.

David Hackett Fischer defines the fallacy of presentism as "a complex anachronism, in which the antecedent in a narrative series is falsified by being defined or interpreted in terms of the consequent. . . . [I]t is the mistaken idea that the proper way to do history is to prune away the dead branches of the past, and to preserve the green buds and twigs which have grown into the dark forest our contemporary world."[21] Presentism distorts and falsifies the actual configurations of the past by dressing it in ill-fitting clothes of later date. The history of ideas often comes wrapped in many such anachronisms. Understandings, attitudes, and values imported into the past from the present must be stripped away in order to encounter the past unencumbered by the backward projections of our own time- and culture-bound assumptions. But presentism also robs us of historicized perspectives on our own time, for it precludes an understanding of the present and possible trajectories of the future in other than self-referential terms.

Presentism does not bring the past forward to us as it would stand and speak were it possible for it to do so. Thomas S. Kuhn perceived the misrepresentations that can arise from presentist perspectives in the history of science, when the "normative science" of one era is interpreted from the normative values of another.[22] The scientific paradigms of the present (backward projections) obscure those of the past, creating cognitive dissonance. Kuhn's deft conceptualization of how scientific revolutions originate as anomalies and finally emerge as normative science through consensus building is most instructive as an interpretive strategy in the history of American anthropology. It helps us better understand the processes by which the scientific truths of one generation come to be the myths and fictions of another.

Numerous scholars working in the history of anthropology have directed attention to the dichotomy between historicism and presentism and to the pitfalls awaiting investigators who do not attempt to abandon their presentist assumptions and perspectives.[23] The dangers of looking for contemporary ideas and understandings in old places are many, especially when working with the time-bound meanings of words such as *race, culture, evolution,* and *civilization,* which have far more restricted and precise meanings today than in the nineteenth century. The indiscriminate and often incorrect use of the word *race* is particularly problematic in the early literature, since it was commonly used to make biological, ethnic, and cultural distinctions. The terms *savage, barbarous,* and *semi-civilized* are likewise problematic. They are not only jarring today but were often invoked within a particular set of assumptions regarding the place of peoples within the "scale of civilization" (to use a period phrase) – a pre-Darwinian developmentalist scheme that found wide expression in the early and mid-nineteenth century. A failure to properly historicize those usages not infrequently causes confusion as to the actual opinions and conclusions being expressed by nineteenth-century writers. I give due consideration to this problem in the pages that follow.

The present distorts the past in other ways as well. The orthodox views of one generation often determine who is remembered and who forgotten in history, and the past is made to serve the present by reaffirming existing paradigms. All too frequently, nineteenth-century works are quoted with little or no regard for the actual context in which they were developed or for the larger cultural discourse of which they were an integral part. The aphorism that history is the story of winners as written by the winners is given further affirmation by the intellectual history of anthropology. The losers – those whose ideas were part of previous paradigms – are frequently ignored or dismissed out of hand, while those to whom we wish to lay claim as intellectual ancestors are inducted into anthropology's pantheon of right thinkers. Looking too diligently for either correctness or error in the past is poor historical method and tends to obscure more than it clarifies. As one historian of archaeology has commented, "A knowing superiority from hindsight is the easiest and most pernicious attitude to fall into."[24] Judgmental histories that attack discarded notions with little or no effort to understand them on their own terms are poor servants indeed. Paradigms come and go, yet certain anthropological problems remain unresolved or only partially understood.

Such is precisely the case in a good deal of the historical literature dealing with anthropology's preprofessional past, which has frequently been written from the perspectives of post-Boasian anthropology. Under that view, the significant benchmarks of anthropology's past are those which lead inexorably to consensus about what anthropology is or is not. Ideas and events in anthropology's past that do not fit into normative practice are avoided or relegated to the dustbin of exploded hypotheses and discarded theory. The figures in anthropology's past whose ideas and values are out of the mainstream of current practice tend to be either dismissed or else unduly minimize in terms of their contributions to the development of anthropology. There were many dead ends in nineteenth-century anthropology, but only a narrow parochialism reduces the complexity and ambiguities of past arguments about the nature of man to a linear march of progress from the darkness of the preprofessional past to the enlightened present. As has been noted regarding the history of American anthropology, "There are lessons in the failures as well as the successes."[25] Squier and other anthropologists of his era had their fair share of both.

The history of archaeology in particular has greatly benefited from the perspectives of several scholars who have called for more contextually and methodologically rigorous treatments of archaeology's past. Andrew L. Christenson has articulated the need for archaeologists who write the history of their discipline to be more aware of historical method and to more critically question "the theoretical biases that archaeologists may bring to the interpretation of archaeology's past."[26] Christenson's observation is similar to that of Bruce G. Trigger, who has commented on "the natural tendencies for archaeologists to view the history of their discipline from presentist and provincial viewpoints that the professional historian is trained to avoid."[27] It has even been suggested that there is an ingrained prejudice against the history of pre-Boasian figures within the subculture of professional anthropology.[28]

Historians who presume to write the history of any episode or era of American archaeology or ethnology, however, must master more than the methodological rigors of their own craft. They must also know something of the anthropological theory and method of the period under investigation. Once again, Trigger has succinctly identified the problem as it relates to the history of archaeology:

> The history of any scientific discipline requires intimate familiarity with at least two separate fields. Substantive knowledge is needed of the science being investigated, together with knowledge of historical methodology and a detailed understanding of the history of Western thought and culture that has given rise to the science. Only rarely do individual scholars achieve equal proficiency in both fields. This is one reason why much mutual benefit might be gained from more regular interaction between professional historians who are committed to studying the development of archaeology and archaeologists who are studying the history of their own discipline.[29]

Anthropological inquiry in the early and mid-nineteenth century is often depicted in negative terms, as a period to be glossed over or avoided when possible, memorable only for its racial stereotypes, pseudo-science, episodes of archaeological fraud, grave robbing, or the role that archaeology and ethnology played as agents of colonialism in the dispossession of American Indian peoples. The exploitative aspects of anthropology's past are not to be minimized. The racial theories of the American School were used in the 1840s and 1850s to justify Manifest Destiny, an exploitative Indian policy, and the institution of slavery. But an imposing attitude that assumes the period to be beneath serious consideration represents a distinct historiographical problem.

Historians of American archaeology in particular have, as Thomas Gilbert Tax has observed, "underplayed the achievements of earlier years" and over-emphasized archaeology's romantic and unscientific origins."[30] This is certainly true of the period prior to the establishment of the Smithsonian's Bureau of American Ethnology in 1879 and the work of Frederic Ward Putnam at Harvard University's Peabody Museum of American Archaeology and Ethnology from the 1870s to the turn of the century. But we should not have historical amnesia about the concerns of earlier periods. As Gordon R. Willey and Jeremy A. Sabloff have noted, the "follies and foibles" of archaeology's preprofessional past are also part of the story. Those who endeavor to avoid them as being unscientific or non-anthropological (which they often are) should think more historically, since "no individual, no institution, no intellectual tradition can ever fully escape from its genetic forbears, and archaeology is no exception."[31] Contemporary concerns and preoccupations should not induce us to minimize or ignore the achievements of the more empirical investigators of the early and mid-nineteenth century.

The arguments advanced in the following pages developed in stages as I worked my way across the distinct chronological periods of Squier's career. One cannot live with a subject of research over the span of several years without forming an attachment – misplaced or otherwise. I readily confess an admiration for Squier's many talents and accomplishments, of which I have been repeatedly reminded while plodding through the extensive range of his correspondence, manuscripts, and publications. I have attempted, nonetheless, to render an account of his contributions to American anthropology that is neither encomium nor detraction, that draws attention to both his accomplishments and his shortcomings as a scholar, and that distinguishes between the countervailing tendencies of empiricism and polemics which characterized many of his writings.

One can well be critical of Squier's penchant for self-laudation, his shabby treatment of Edwin Hamilton Davis, his animus toward Henry Rowe Schoolcraft, his strident embrace of Manifest Destiny in Central America, and the corollary doctrine of scientific racism. His racist assumptions and attitudes were shared by many of his contemporaries and were an integral part of a larger discourse about race and the maintenance of social hierarchy. However, we do not have to endorse all of Squier's assumptions, attitudes, and conclusions in order to recognize his achievements and significance in the history of American anthropology. I expect that Squier, who leveled many harsh criticisms against his contemporaries, would be somewhat comfortable with that judgment.

1. Literary Ambitions

The Genesis of an Anthropologist

Ephraim George Squier came to the study of anthropology through earlier experiences as a schoolteacher, a student of civil engineering, a poet, and, most importantly, a journalist. Each of those undertakings greatly contributed to his later work as an archaeologist and ethnologist. His formative years from 1840 to 1845 chronicle his development as a writer, display his emerging organizational abilities, and reveal his flamboyant personality and salient traits of character. A relentless ambition to gain fame as a writer consumed Squier from an early age, and he developed an entrepreneurial talent to turn most situations to his advantage in pursuit of that objective. It was Squier the aspiring poet, lecturer, and journalist who first confessed the burning ambition that propelled all aspects of his multifaceted career and gave free rein to the literary romanticism and cultural nationalism that were such a conspicuous part of American letters in the early and mid-nineteenth century.

Squier's early years as a struggling writer at Albany, New York, and Hartford, Connecticut, are an important prelude to his later career as an anthropologist. It was then that he launched his journalistic career, lectured before several mechanics' associations about the importance of self-culture as the only true means of social advancement for the American working classes, and formulated the rudiments of ideas about the origin and progress of civilization that later influenced his anthropological thought. As a journalist he continued to hone his writing skills, declared his political allegiance to the Whig Party, and vigorously campaigned for Henry Clay as president. Squier was alive to the literary, social, and political movements of his era, and his writings mirror the main currents of American thought. His genesis as an anthropologist may seem indirect, but in a preprofessional era there was no certain path or formula for him and his contemporaries to follow in the study of man.

Squier was born in Bethlehem, New York, on June 17, 1821. His father, Joel Squier (1798–1891), was licensed as a Methodist minister in 1829, became a member of the Troy Conference of the Methodist Episcopal Church in 1832, and rode circuit at eight towns and eighteen preaching stops in Vermont and northern New York. Little is known of Ephraim's mother, Katherine Kilmer Squier (1797–1833), who died in the twelfth year of her son's life. After her death, Rev. Squier married Katherine's sister Maria Kilmer (1802–86). Maria and Joel had two children, Charles Wesley Squier (1836–69) and Frank Squier (1840–1908). Ephraim's half brother Charles served as a captain and chief engineer of the Third Army Corps during the Civil War and died in 1869 from injuries sustained in a train accident on the Erie Railway. His other half brother, Frank, a New York paper merchant, was destined to play an important role in the closing years of Ephraim's life.[1]

Because of the modest means of his itinerant father, Ephraim was denied the opportunity of obtaining a formal education. He attended local common schools wherever his father's circuit took him and largely educated himself. From 1836 to 1839, however, he received the rudiments of a liberal arts education at the Troy Conference Academy in West Poultney, Vermont. There he also began a short-lived teaching career in the local common schools. Squier made better progress in his studies at West Poultney in mathematics than in Greek and Latin, a circumstance he impudently attributed to the ineptitude of his teachers rather than to his own "dumbness." His Latin instructor, Squier said, knew as much of that language as he did of Choctaw, while he regarded the "cross-petulant-impatient" pedagogy of his Greek teacher as entirely detrimental to learning. With characteristic confidence, Squier never doubted that in the end he would "overhaul" his classmates.[2] He proved himself a quick study at the Troy Academy, as he would throughout his adult life.

Squier's career as a teacher lasted little longer than his own school days at West Poultney. Although teaching was the calling that his father continually urged upon him, Squier had no intention to "live and die, a despised and miserable pedagogue – the most illy paid and thankless of all employments."[3] Determined to find another occupation, the increasingly restless Squier qualified himself as a civil engineer. Although he possessed an aptitude for mathematics and geometry, his aspirations as a civil engineer ended with the temporary suspension of public works construction during the economic panic of 1837 to 1839.[4] Significantly, however, that skill would later serve him well as a surveyor of Indian mounds, the proposed Honduras Interoceanic Railway, and the ancient monuments of Peru.

Disenchanted with teaching and civil engineering, Squier turned to poetry. At the tender age of nineteen, he became the contributing editor of *The Literary Pearl: And Weekly Village Messenger*. Henry W. Underhill printed and published the *Literary Pearl* at Charlton, New York, as a magazine of original and selected prose and poetry. It appeared in thirteen numbers between November 18, 1840, and February 13, 1841.[5]

> Little "Pearl" late emerged from obscurity's deep
> For a voyage on Fame's sea of commotion!
> Good speed to thy course! far and wide may it sweep,
> O'er that trackless and changeable Ocean![6]

Although otherwise deserving of oblivion, the *Pearl* possesses the dubious distinction of containing several of Squier's earliest-known writings (see fig. 1).[7]

Squier announced in the last number of the *Literary Pearl* his intention of publishing a more attractive magazine from a more attractive place. The new publication was the *Lady's Cabinet Magazine* and the place Albany, New York. The *Lady's Cabinet*, apparently also known as the *Parlor Magazine*, was first issued in May 1841, a hapless union of the *Philadelphia Visiter* [sic], the *Literary Pearl*, and the *Poughkeepsie Casket*. Devoted to "polite literature," the *Lady's Cabinet* was edited by Squier and originally owned and published by Squier and James H. Chappell at Albany and Philadelphia. Through most of its numbers, however, the *Lady's Cabinet* was published and solely printed at Albany by Joel Munsell. Thus began a journalistic association between Squier and Munsell that continued throughout Squier's years at Albany.[8]

Although Squier received compliments on "the bright array of contributors" found among the pages of the *Lady's Cabinet*, the magazine ultimately fared no better than the obscure periodicals it had replaced, sinking unpitied and unmourned into oblivion with the appearance of the March number in 1842. It had been a typical production, Squier later recalled, of "the Millennium of Millinery Literature."[9] Nonetheless, the autobiographical nature of Squier's poem "What's In a Name?" is worthy of remembrance. Here we see a consuming desire for literary recognition – to leave a name to the world – and his struggle to overcome his humble origins.

> Is there a man above all others great?
> 'Tis he who burst the fetters of a low estate,
> And strongly struggling, triumphs over fate!
> But is there one who meanly creeps the earth,
> And though with honors crown'd, yet without worth,
> Mark ye the man – *he boasts a lofty birth.*[10]

A more ambitious project was *The Poet's Magazine: A Repository of Original and Selected Poetry.* The *Poet's Magazine* was published at Albany and would be Squier's last undertaking as a publisher and editor of poetry. It appeared in

1. Ephraim George Squier (1821–88) by Maria Louisana Wagner, 1840. Miniature on ivory. Signed and dated. Squier's literary ambitions and talents manifested themselves at an early age, as seen in this portrait made at age nineteen. (Accession no. 1960.52/negative no. 41306. Collection of the New-York Historical Society. Reprinted with permission.)

two numbers only. Munsell later summarized its fate in words that epitomize all of Squier's early ventures as a poet: "Work never completed – never sold was never paid for."[11] Nevertheless, Squier's unsuccessful efforts to make the *Poet's Magazine* a repository for the American muse illustrate his nationalistic sentiments and early intellectual qualities. In professing the originality, self-reliance, and energy that characterized the poetic imagination of America, for instance, Squier presents a full and accurate description of himself as an aspiring poet:

> There is no nation on the globe among which exists a more genuine poetic feeling. It is true we have no national standard of poetry worthy of the name, for the imagination has been trained in no school, it has no particular turn of bent in imitation of any admitted master. It possesses an originality and strength which is seldom found among any people, except at the early periods of the national existence; when the mind is yet unfettered, before free fancy is shorn of its pinions and trammeled by artificial rules and restraints. . . . The American, physically and mentally, is active and energetic; and when he steals a moment from the pressing occupations of his busy life, and banishes care for a little space, the imagination is on the wing, and he gazes on the earth and sky with that wild and enthusiastic feeling which characterizes his poetry.[12]

The *Poet's Magazine* also reflects the romanticism that significantly colored Squier's later conception of the mounds and their mysterious builders. In the New World, he said, nature abounded in all the romantic themes necessary to stimulate the poet's fancy. Americans need not apologize for the lack of a remote or heroic past. "There are, indeed, no associations of olden time, no hallowed recollections of long-past days linger around some consecrated spot, but the creative Fancy can people the silent and gloomy ruins that frown amid the mighty forests of America; can invest every secret dale, and silver lake and mountain pass with its story – can weave the fairy web of the elfin loom over every spot, and tinge, with a pencil dipped in the rainbow hues of imagination, every scene on this vast continent."[13] Such was the romanticism that would later "people the gloomy ruins" of Ohio with an ancient and presumably perished race that was then known only as the Mound Builders. Squier's romanticism would later be bridled, but it was never entirely absent from his anthropology.

Squier's own contributions to these and other periodicals of poetry merit little consideration save for the contemplative musings of "The Past." Here his early preoccupation with achievement and reputation are again readily apparent as he ponders the vain, illusive, and fleeting nature of reputation.

"The Past," solemn and foreboding, conveys the spiritual restlessness and anxiety of Squier's early years as a struggling poet. It constitutes one of his better poems and suggests a fear that the "midnight waters" of oblivion would one day claim him before he had achieved the illusive prize of fame:

Hail Monarch of the Mighty Past, all hail!
Dim broods thy form upon a murky sea,
Whose awful surges heave with noiseless swell,
Whose distant bounds thine eye alone can see.

All hail! dark Spirit of that Fearful Deep,
Upon whose crumbling shore I, trembling stand,
The midnight waters eddying at my feet;
I watch the waving of thy shadowy hand.

Perchance among the crowd that wait thy beck,
When some more noble victim leaves the shore,
A voice of praise a moment sounds, but ere
The echo rings, it dies – 'tis heard no more!

And thus the everlasting surge pours on –
On sweep the myriads to thy stern domain –
Vain, vain the short, illusive voice of fame,
The struggles of the Soul, all, all are vain!

I come, dread Spirit of Eternal Sea –
Above, around the midnight waters roll –
Oh Mystic Shadow! is there not but thee,
None mightier to save the Human Soul?[14]

Squier later described his early efforts at poetry as an infantile "attack" comparable to "measles."[15] Nonetheless, his poems filled an early intellectual void. They were an important outlet for his creative energies and ambitions, however equivocal his talents as a poet. They met a need not satisfied by teaching school, by the prospects of civil engineering, or by his father's theology. Squier's poems reveal the inner man seeking recognition in an indifferent world. The poet's only "boon," said Squier, was the opportunity to establish a name that would be remembered beyond the pale of the grave. "Little pleasure awaits him [the poet] in this world in his intercourse with his fellow men, he lives in his own thoughts and communes with himself, looking forward without fear to that rest which knows no waking."[16] Squier's longing for fame would continue throughout his long and productive career as a scholar, but it first expressed itself through his poetry. [17]

Moving from poetry to social causes, Squier continued his association with Joel Munsell as coeditor of the *New York State Mechanic*. At this time he helped to make ends meet by reporting news as the Albany correspondent for the *New York Journal of Commerce*, [18] but working for Munsell at the *Mechanic* laid claim to most of his time and talents. The *Mechanic*, an eight-page weekly published and printed at Albany, was the official organ of the New York Mechanics' Association. It promoted the interests, rights, and social advancement of the laboring classes of America. The *Mechanic* championed the dignity of honest work and exhorted its readers "to break the bonds of *caste* and the barriers of prejudice" associated with the laboring classes of America. "It is a mean unworthy idea to regard the mass of mankind as beasts of burthen, never destined to intellectual or moral greatness." Those whom necessity required to toil for their daily bread had neither time nor incentive to pursue the spiritual qualities of self-culture – the only true means of social advancement. The mass of society must be able to elevate themselves above the burden of daily toil and "animal wants" and given the means to cultivate the "heart and mind." [19] Action was the watchword of the day as laborers were encouraged to utilize their intellectual and political strengths to promote their rights and interests.

Apart from its wider aims and class-conscious rhetoric, the *Mechanic*'s primary objective was to end the evil of unfair competition resulting from the use of state prison labor in the mechanical trades. State penitentiary contracts, it was argued, placed prison-made manufactures in competition with those made by independent mechanics and resulted in large profits for penitentiary contractors. Employed as coopers, shoemakers, and other like trades, convicts labored for a few cents a day and allegedly flooded the market with goods sold at lower costs than those made in fair competition. Although the extent of this injury may have been exaggerated, mechanics were convinced that it placed their livelihoods in jeopardy. It was further argued that the employment of criminals in the mechanical trades degraded independent laborers by attaching a stigma to their vocations in general. [20] The editors of the *Mechanic* urged readers to petition the state legislature requesting the repeal or modification of existing state prison laws that allowed such abuses to continue. The Albany Mechanics' Association appointed Squier and Munsell to a committee charged with investigating alleged abuses of the convict labor laws passed by the New York legislature in 1835 and 1842. Those enactments related to the employment of convicts in the mechanical trades at Sing Sing prison, where violations were said to continue. The investigative committee visited Sing Sing prison in October 1843, and Squier was one of the authors of its published report. [21]

Besides the convict labor controversy, the editors of the *Mechanic* also engaged in the debate then raging over Fourierism and temperance. Albany was a leading center of the workingman's movement, and Squier and Munsell were sensitive to the social causes associated with it. As an observer in the *Mechanic* noted: "The world is full of plans of reform. . . . They keep a constant din about us. . . . They are the glory of our age and country." [22] That was certainly true in 1842 when a group of mechanics from Albany and New York City established the Sylvania phalanx in western Pennsylvania. Articles on Fourierism then became a regular column of the *Mechanic*. Unlike some journalists, however, Squier and Munsell were unwilling to embrace the phalanx as the great panacea of the workingman. Although agreeing with the philanthropic goals of Fourierism, they regarded the methods adopted to achieve those ends as untenable. Squier also remained aloof from the "equivocal reputation" of the temperance crusade and "the thousand asses" who promoted it at the lectern and in the press. [23] Drink may have been the curse of the working class, but Squier found temperance crusaders to be an affliction in their own right.

Instead, Squier's cause was "of a higher stamp." As a lecturer he promoted the social and intellectual advancement of the American laborer by advocating the twin virtues of self-culture and self-reliance. Here a new field, philanthropy, presented itself before him. The social and intellectual advancement of the American laboring classes was a cause "sanctified," he said, by such great men as William Ellery Channing and William Leggett. An admiring Squier sought to boldly follow in their footsteps in a cause he later characterized as "creditable to head and heart." [24] He prepared "Two Lectures on the Origin and Progress of Modern Civilization" at Albany during the winter of 1841–42, [25] and he presented another on the "Laboring Classes of Europe and America Compared" to the mechanics associations of Brooklyn, Baltimore, New York City, Poughkeepsie, Jersey City, and Albany. [26] The lecture on the laboring classes appeared serially in the *New York State Mechanic* [27] and as the first number of Munsell's *Working Man's Miscellany*. [28]

Squier's discursive lectures not only defined the principles of his philanthropy but also provide further insight into his own aspirations and character. His views on the importance of self-culture for the social advancement of the American laborer, for instance, are as much a reflection of his own experiences and thought as they are a statement of the conventional rhetoric of middle-class philanthropy. Squier's lectures on the origin and progress of modern civilization are a case in point. If not for the life of the mind, he asked, why did man exist at all? "But is he placed here merely as a machine, superior indeed to the brute that cowers before his gaze, but like that brute to live, to see the light, to breath the air, to propagate his species and die? Is this all?"[29] Man's intellect defined him as man, gave meaning to his otherwise brutish existence, and provided the only true means for elevating his station in society. Squier gave the mechanics a résumé of European history from the fall of Rome through the French Revolution, attributing the emergence of civilization from a state of savagism to the fundamental need for social order and improvement. Europe had undergone difficult periods of adjustment and decline across those centuries, but civilization and social progress inevitably, it seemed, triumphed over adversity. Indeed, periodic disorders in what Squier called "the social body" appeared to be a prerequisite to human progress. Adversity had always been a spur to social progress. Squier's view of history, society, and man's capacity for intellectual progress allowed for both progress and decline, but the later was not a fixed condition.

Like social crises and watershed events, environmental conditions also shaped the course of civilization, leaving indelible imprints upon human character. Climate and topography at all times and in all places required man to adapt to local circumstance. Adaptations, in turn, imparted what were generally recognized as distinguishing national characteristics. Did not the course of European civilization illustrate the influence of circumstances on human character? "Who doubts that the vivacious Frenchman and the free Switzer, have had their character much modified by condition or course of life which the peculiarities of their several countries compelled them to adopt[?]" Environmental influences, said Squier, had shaped the national characteristics of Europeans and the course of modern civilization. European civilization itself was nothing more than the aggregate of human progress, which Squier defined as "the melioration" of the great social body and the improvement of the mental faculties among all members of society.[30] Faith in man's capacity for progress was a bequest of the Enlightenment and one fully shared by Squier. It would be a short step for him to translate these early ideas about social progress into his later writings on archaeology and ethnology. Indeed, Squier's optimistic faith in intellectual and moral progress became a defining features of his anthropological thought – a faith he would only gradually and reluctantly come to question in the face of supposedly new scientific evidence to the contrary that emerged in the 1840s and 1850s.

But no such doubts clouded Squier's thoughts during his crusading days at Albany. Intellectual improvement through self-culture was the path to true social progress for the laboring classes of America and to the amelioration of the invidious and divisive social distinctions that sprang from disparities in education and wealth. Mechanics must be made to realize that the cultivation of native intellect was far too important to their interests to be taken for granted or not to be pursued with vigor. Neither the nostrums of political parties nor the panaceas of social reformers could do for mechanics what they could do for themselves.

> Awake! ye have slumbered long enough! Your mighty energies have long enough been bound down by the leaden thrall of inaction; and it is now time, high time that you assert your rights and privileges, and assume your own exalted station in society. And what is the first great object to be attained? We answer, the improvement of the mind. . . . The mind of man is a mine: it must be worked if its treasures are ever to be developed. Study, conversation and observation bring to light the stores of pure intellectual wealth. SELF TRAINING makes the man of vigorous and sound mind, the original man, the noblest word of God.[31]

Squier's highly critical comments on the value of a formal education compared to the proclaimed virtue of self-culture suggest that they are at least partly autobiographical in nature. Squier's own experiences and character are seldom absent from his writings. As editor of the *Lady's Cabinet*, for example, Squier had lampooned the literary pretensions of the "college neophyte" who was miraculously transformed from "the plodding schoolboy . . . into the profound and erudite graduate, with the magnificent appendage of 'A.B.' "[32] He returned to this theme with much vigor in his lectures before the mechanics associations of New York. Although admittedly prepared for a sympathetic audience, these sentiments were doubtless based on Squier's own school experiences and a nagging sense of inadequacy about his own education. Self-culture, he maintained, would instill an intellectual strength "to which the pampered and effeminate son of wealth can never arrive, although thousands may have been lavished with a profuse hand in his education or in the purchase of finely gilded books to line the walls of his library." Only self-culture would inculcate original thought in lieu of the fashionable canons of received opinion that were uncritically ingested at school.

> Our modern system of education, without enlarging the mind or its capacity, fills it with scraps and disconnected ideas, confused and indigested, and without giving time for thought and reflection, bewilders it in an intricate maze; making the man but a mere walking receptacle of other men's ideas, facts without order, and knowledge without the power of combining and deducing, or rendering it in any way subservient or useful. Thought and *reflection* can only bring out the hidden characters of the mind, and strengthen and improve it.[33]

Lack of formal education was no excuse for complacency and ignorance. Self-educated individuals of humble origins and modest means could also aspire to greatness. "Wisdom does sometimes, but not commonly, feed her children with a silver spoon." It was not social station but self-culture and self-reliance alone that ennobled the soul, elevated the mind, and refined the intellect. The self-educated mechanic had no cause to apologize. "Let him rejoice that his mind has never been trammelled by the egotism and self-satisfaction which the accumulation of good-for-nothing classical lore in our 'institutions' seldom fails to engender; and that the mind is yet untrammelled and free to be used as the God of nature designed, in searching deep in that comprehensive philosophy which extends through the universe, and embraces 'All thinking things, the objects of all thought.' "[34] True knowledge was not to be found in cloistered and ivied halls, "where the student muses over superfluous annotations, where subtle polemics are vainly discussing their narrow dogmas." Knowledge must be cultivated through original and bold thinking: "A vigorous native intellect, improved by self-culture, and enriched by the development of its own exhaustless resources, is more to be desired than one trammelled by the false rules of art, and feeble, because merely imitative."[35] Squier remained the embodiment of the self-culture and independent thought he so ardently advocated in his lectures at Albany.

Squier's crusade for the interests of the American laborer seems to have been at least partly encouraged by his own humble origins. Squier worked at the *Mechanic* for trifling pay, and his Albany years were a period of "poverty and privation."[36] As he confided to his parents, indebtedness to others, including his father, was the bête noire of his early life. "If there is a degrading slavery above all others it is this." He had learned firsthand that "no man can be a *philanthropist* but one of wealth."[37] This was an early lesson never forgotten. Squier later pursued wealth not only to rid himself of indebtedness but as a means of supporting his anthropological researches. Although he eventually came to live a comfortable life, the independent means that sometimes seemed within his reach ultimately eluded him. Indeed, it was his quest for financial independence that later led to his entrepreneurial activities in Central America.

Apart from promoting the benefits of self-culture, Squier's lectures also echoed the words of William Leggett (1801–39) on the importance of "associate action" in promoting the social advancement of the American worker. Leggett was "one who spoke as seldom has man spoken – as a free, independent thinker – a champion of the rights of the laborers of our country: a man whose name and whose memory they should ever cherish – the name, the memory of William Leggett."[38] Squier informed the mechanics' auxiliary at

Poughkeepsie that Leggett's associate action should be the guiding principle of their cause:

> Before the mechanics of this country will sustain their proper and natural relation to the great social body, they must abjure their allegiance to the despotism of party, throw aside those too long cherished prejudices which have stood like spectres between them and their interests, meet as bretheren [sic] upon the broad platform of fellowship, and move together with unity of purpose toward their rights and privileges as men. Betrayed, dishonored, disgraced, by their tenacious adherence to party – like whipped spaniels they become more docile, more servile tools in the hands of the unprincipled demagogue, at every new instance of his utter disregard of their interests and welfare. [39]

Squier's lectures are also interesting as early expressions of his strident nationalism. When comparing American and European society, Squier articulated the same nationalistic sentiment that characterized his rhetoric in the *Poet's Magazine* on the originality and genius of the American muse. After drawing a melancholy picture of degradation among the lives of European laborers, Squier contrasted their unhappy lot with that of American workers. In America, he asserted, the supporting principles of society had always been original, natural, and therefore correct. These principles began spontaneously with the arrival of the first English immigrants and provided the New World with an appropriately new society. "American society then began. It has had no infancy; it has passed through no centuries of darkness, nor ages of twilight and scarce perceptible advancement, but like Minerva from the head of Jove, sprung forth full armed and glorious in the proud strength of manly vigor." [40]

Continuing his paean to American uniqueness, Squier drew attention to the "special providence" that had guided the origin and development of American society. The teachings of American history were clear: separation from Europe in all things great and small. "This is the voice of nature, which did not in vain disjoin our continent from the old world, nor reserve it beyond the ocean for fifty centuries, only that it might become a receptacle for the exploded principles, the degenerate, and the remediless corruptions of other states. This is the voice of our history, which traces every thing in our character, and prosperous in our fortune, to dissent, non-conformity, departure, resistance, [and] revolution." [41]

America's "peculiar and happy" society, however, contained a potentially self-destructive paradox. The institution of slavery in the South represented a regressive social element. The presence of slavery challenged Squier's personal faith in the capacity of American society for progressive and enlightened development. "Oh, how sad the thought that I must make this reservation how melancholy the fact! Oh America, land of my birth, land of my hopes and pride! America, to whose glory the world is witness would to God that the last dark stain upon thy garments of purity was washed away; that the last remnant of oppression were consigned to oblivion."[42] Squier was never an active abolitionist, but neither his philanthropic nor his political ideals would allow him to accept the perpetuation and extension of slavery.

Squier's early commitment to social reform and his journalistic association with Munsell came to an abrupt end when the *New York State Mechanic* issued its last number on June 17, 1843. The state legislature passed a new convict labor law in 1842, and the paper at last succumbed to a declining subscription. Although short-lived, the assertive and class-conscious *Mechanic* had firmly established Squier as a journalist. He continued to regard it fondly as the most effective paper of its kind ever published in the United States.[43] Squier's editorial "ardor" in promoting the *Mechanic's* mission and his abilities as a lecturer and organizer of local mechanic associations earned him much-needed recognition. The paper's publishing committee acknowledged him as a gifted writer and recommended him to local mechanics auxiliaries as a thoroughly entertaining speaker who possessed "a happy fancy in illustration." Squier enviously fumed to his parents, however, that Munsell had "carried away" most of the honors for the *Mechanic's* favorable reputation.[44]

The demise of the *New York State Mechanic* left Squier temporarily unemployed. It was then that he completed work on an abridged American edition of George Tradescent Lay's *The Chinese as They Are*.[45] Squier had developed a serious interest in Chinese history and opportunities in China for American enterprise, an interest that even included an unsuccessful application for appointment as an American commissioner to China.[46] The Chinese trade and the military and economic activities of the British in Canton were then commanding worldwide attention, and Squier's edition of Lay's work was prepared to gratify popular interest. His edition of *The Chinese as They Are* contains his own corroborative notes and additional chapters on Chinese history, population, government, civilization, education, literature, and commerce, which were derived from his library readings at Albany. *The Chinese as They Are* proved an eminently forgettable and profitless undertaking, but Squier was consoled by the fact that the entire edition of five thousand copies had sold out.[47] This work was his first foray, vicariously at least, as an explorer of an exotic culture, and it provides additional evidence of his desire for literary recognition and the opportunistic bent of his character.

Squier's journalistic talent, along with the recommendation of Horace Greeley of the *New York Tribune*, next took him to Connecticut, where he worked as coeditor of the *Hartford Journal* from November 1, 1843, until January 25, 1845. The official organ of the Whig Party in Connecticut, the *Hartford Journal* stood squarely behind the protection of American industry and Henry Clay of Kentucky for the presidency of the United States: "our *first*, Last and ONLY choice." The *Journal* was owned, published, and coedited by the Hartford printer and politico Elihu Geer, whom Squier found to be the most energetic man he had ever met. The decidedly Squierish tone and style of the unsigned Squier-Geer editorials, however, suggests that Squier primarily edited the *Journal*. Finding his prospects as favorable as could be desired, he wrote home that Hartford was "*just the spot* where I am wanted." [48] He threw himself with characteristic enthusiasm into the gall and wormwood of campaign journalism.

Despite the declared political neutrality of Squier's former paper, the *New York State Mechanic*, his editorials in support of a discriminating tariff on imported manufactures and his censure of the "fallacy" of reciprocity in international trade made his Whig sympathies manifestly clear. Those sympathies became even more apparent in 1843 when editors and publishers of the press learned that he had authored several other political pieces. Squier thus acquired the reputation as an "inflexible Whig," [49] an inflexibility he more than amply demonstrated as coeditor of the *Hartford Journal*. As a watchman for the Whig press, Squier pummeled the Democratic Party at every turn. Taking his lead from the aggressive campaign journalism of Francis P. Blair and Amos Kendall in the Democratic *Extra Globe*, he advocated the principles and policies of the Whig Party through the vituperative presidential campaign of 1844.

In contrast to the polite restraint and "mistaken sense of dignity" shown by many of his "antiquated bretheren [sic]," Squier brashly announced the birth of a new generation of Whig journalist. The new Whig was willing to engage the Democratic Party with "a fearlessness and energy, promptness and perseverance, which the conflict with a reckless and unscrupulous foe demanded." He credited this style of journalism with having already transformed the once brazen Locofoco press in Connecticut into "craven whimperers – and made them cower like snivelling school boys under the well earned lash." Squier's intemperate editorials on the "treachery" of Tylerism, the alleged malfeasance of Locofoco officeholders, and the unconstitutionality of the annexation of Texas were so "provocative" that they not only offended the sensibilities of his opponents but also astonished the fainthearted within his own party. [50] "If the lash has at last reached the quick," he answered, "let it be plied with renewed vigor."[51] It was in this school of invective that Squier learned the piquant repartee that sometimes appeared in his later writings.

Apart from advocating the principles and policies of the Whig Party in the *Hartford Journal*, Squier also proved himself an equally effective party organizer. He rallied Connecticut Whigs to action by preaching the necessity of local organization in the forthcoming election. The office of the *Journal* became a clearinghouse of information for the organization of Clay Clubs, with Squier heading the formation of chapters in Hartford, New Haven, and surrounding communities. As a result of those efforts he was elected secretary of the Connecticut Clay Club Convention held at New Haven in November 1843.[52] He was also among the nearly one hundred Connecticut delegates who raised the banner for Clay and Frelinghuysen at the Whig Young Men's Convention held concurrently with the national convention at Baltimore on May 1, 1844.[53]

It is little wonder that Clay's national defeat left Squier a devastated partisan. Although he correctly predicted Clay's victory in Connecticut, he was at a loss to explain how the majority of Americans could have been persuaded to vote against him. Squier venerated Clay as "a brilliant type of the self-made American"[54] and was certain that his astonishing defeat would result in "the prostration of industry and the extension of slavery." Moreover, when Geer sold the *Hartford Journal* to the *Hartford Courant*, Squier feared that his "political and personal enemies" would seize the occasion to undermine his position as editor. It was then that he began to seriously consider editorial opportunities with Whig papers at Baltimore and in Ohio. "Baltimore," he decided, "is out of the question. I will not live where there are slaves!"[55] In early 1845, Squier made his decision and accepted a position as editor of the *Scioto Gazette* in Chillicothe, Ohio. Little could he then have suspected that the lasting reputation he so earnestly sought would be found at Chillicothe among the prehistoric Indian mounds of the Scioto Valley.

Such was the uncertain odyssey that brought Ephraim George Squier to the study of Ohio's prehistoric Indian mounds. He had left his family circle at Charlton, New York, sure of his own capabilities as a writer and determined to earn his place "in that small and lightly freighted bark, which will survive the general wreck and outride the storms that agitate the gloomy seas of oblivion."[56] At Albany the youthful Squier confessed "an ambition that burns like fire in my veins" and he resolved "to leave at least a name to the world."[57] Despite parental concern over his "hair brained" and profitless literary aspirations, he had chosen his path and let nothing deter him – not even his empty pockets. As he once assured his skeptical father, "if success in life depends on enterprise I shall gain it." [58] True to his word, Squier was the very embodiment of enterprise and energy throughout his years at Albany and Hartford. He established himself as a capable journalist under often disappointing and difficult circumstances that might have disheartened less resilient, self-assured, and ambitious spirits. Those essential qualities of character continued to manifest themselves in all of Squier's later enterprises. The rough-and-tumble of the editorial business had not only proven "congenial" to his "nature and turn of mind" [59] but had afforded him the opportunity to develop the literary and organizational skills that were such a boon to his later career as a scholar.

Squier got his start in life during his years at Albany and Hartford. There he wrote for room and board and persevered against his father's strictures to abandon his literary endeavors for the more practical vocation of teaching. He had unsuccessfully launched his literary ambitions with the *Literary Pearl* in 1840, but by 1845 he had matured into a first-rate journalist. Sensing the end of innocence occasioned by the passing of those years, he penned a song to the carefree and sunlit days of his youth:

Oh the days of our happy Youth are o'er!
When the cloudless skies were bright
And we gaily launched from the fairy shore,
In the flashing water's light.
And our gilded bark, like a meteor spark,
Danced lightly on its way,

And the curling wave a murmur gave,
When fossed in rainbow spray –
Oh, then for the days, the sunny days,
The days that no more shall be;
Ere the cares of life, its storm and strife,
Disturbed the sleepy sea!

Oh, the days are gone of our sunny youth!
Its days of song and mirth,
And from the frown of Care o'er the smile of Truth,
Like the storm shade on the earth,
Rest dim and dark, the fatal mark,
Of the ills that years entail –

Nor can the smile, though bright the while,
To hide their trace avail.
Oh, then for the days, the merry days,

The days of our sunny youth,
Ere falsehood's guile had dimmed the smile,
The angel smile of truth.[60]

Ambition, strife, and worldly care were Squier's constant companions during his years at Albany and Hartford. He would have no further occasion to wax nostalgic about a youth that could be no more. The innocence of those sunny days no longer served him, and his days as an aspiring and idealistic poet were behind him. But the literary ambitions, romanticism, and cultural nationalism that first manifested themselves during his early years would be constant companions in later life.

2. In Search of the Mound Builders

The Squier-Davis Association

Squier arrived at Chillicothe, Ohio, in the early spring of 1845 eager for new adventure as editor of the *Scioto Gazette*. The *Gazette* was Whig in persuasion, the oldest surviving newspaper in the state, and politically one of the most influential. Squier edited the paper until December 6, 1846, when the members of the Ohio House of Representatives elected him to a single term as the house clerk. His duties at the *Gazette* were considerably less demanding than those at the *Hartford Journal*, a circumstance that provided him with ample leisure to investigate the enigmatic Indian mounds and geometric earthworks abounding in the vicinity of Chillicothe.[1] The romanticism that earlier expressed itself in Squier's poetry embraced these remains as works of monumental grandeur – ancient icons of a nameless and presumably perished people. Archaeology then became his new passion. It would be archaeology and not political journalism that soon catapulted Squier to international prominence. As an archaeologist he would soon achieve the recognition and lasting reputation for which he had unsuccessfully striven as a poet and journalist.

Squier's earliest known description of the mounds and earthworks near Chillicothe is contained in a letter written to the Albany journalist and publisher Joel Munsell, a friend and former associate in the newspaper business.[2] In the letter, Squier expresses astonishment at the extent, size, and number of the remains found in the fertile valleys of the Scioto, Muskingum, and Miami Rivers. He reports the existence of "geometrically perfect" circles, mysterious squares, and parallel walls running miles in length. What he presumes to be works of defense and large mounds were found on hilltops. No less amazing was the indifference of many local residents to the preservation and study of the mounds and enclosures that were increasingly threatened with destruction. "The people don't seem to care a damn for them, and what with the plough, and grading turnpikes, and making bricks, they are fast passing away!" He describes for Munsell the excavation of a mound on a fork of Paint Creek (the north fork of Paint Creek at a site today known as the Hopewell Mound Group), which Squier and Davis knew as Clark's Work. Squier's curiosity about the mounds had been piqued by the writings of Caleb Atwater and Josiah Priest, but upon opening one of the mounds at Clark's Work he discovered that much was yet to be learned about the nameless people known as the Mound Builders. "Here I found some wonderful carvings more perfect and more bewildering than any I ever before head of! It is strange how these things have been overlooked!"

The mounds of Ohio had been erected, said Squier, by a people inhabiting the area "prior to our existing race of Indians." He said much the same thing in announcing his recent discoveries to his parents a little more than a month later. The mounds were built by a "race" that had been "highly advanced in the arts" but was "now extinct." The only records of that ancient people were the thousands of mounds they left behind. "That they were long anterior to our present race of Indians is certain." [3] Squier had stumbled upon a new field of endeavor and one of absorbing interest. "I dream of the old works by night and I think of them by day." [4] He was determined to write a book on the subject of American antiquities that would make all previous work pale by comparison. Confident and brash he most certainly was, but he was also quite capable.

Squier's entry into this new field was greatly assisted by his early acquaintance at Chillicothe with Edwin Hamilton Davis, the first of several colleagues who would play an instrumental role in fostering Squier's career as an anthropologist. Davis was a practicing physician, surgeon, and self-declared "moundologist" who had contracted "the antiquarian malady" at an early age. [5] He was ten years Squier's elder and his opposite in personality, educational attainments, and physical presence. Davis was reticent and distinguished in bearing, Squier diminutive but audacious. [6] Davis introduced Squier into a fraternity of Ohio antiquaries who made the study of local archaeology an impassioned avocation. All about them were cabinets of curiosities and incurable enthusiasm for an absorbing field of inquiry.

Edwin Hamilton Davis was born in Hillsboro, Ohio, on January 22, 1811. [7] He was the eldest son of Henry Davis, a Dartmouth-educated merchant and banker, and Avis Slocum (Towne) Davis. Raised in an area abounding with prehistoric Indian remains, he early on acquired an interest in their origin, purposes, and preservation, hoping "to arrest from destruction the works of a former age and a peculiar people . . . as hundreds are yearly ploughed into the earth by our money loving tillers of the soil." [8] Davis began his mound researches in 1831 while still a student at Kenyon College in Gambier, Ohio. He presented his early archaeological observations before the Philomathesian Society at Kenyon, remarks he later gave as his 1833 commencement address on the "Antiquities of Ohio." Those researches were further encouraged, according to Davis, after his introduction to Daniel Webster, who visited Kenyon that same year. Webster lamented the rapid destruction of American antiquities by the plow and reportedly even proposed to Davis the establishment of a society to purchase and preserve the more important examples for future investigation. It was then, Davis later said, that he first resolved to record information about these remains through accurate surveys and descriptions.[9]

After graduating from Kenyon, Davis continued his antiquarian avocation while preparing himself as a physician and surgeon at Cincinnati Medical College. He became an avid collector of "Indian antiquities" found near the ancient works of Ross County, an interest that proved to be a lifelong and expensive pursuit. After graduating from Cincinnati Medical College on March 3, 1838, he established a successful practice at Chillicothe. In 1841 he married Lucy Woodbridge, the daughter of a prominent Chillicothe banker, a marriage that resulted in nine children. That same year, Davis's performance of the operation for strabismus (an eye affliction or squint) secured his reputation as a surgeon. He claimed that this was the first such surgery ever performed in Ohio and only the second in the nation. Davis was thus settled into his medical and antiquarian pursuits at Chillicothe when he was "assisted" in mound researches by his new "friend and associate" Ephraim George Squier.[10] "Permit me to introduce to your notice," Davis wrote Samuel P. Hildreth in May 1846, "Mr. E. G. Squier, my associate in Mound researches; a subject which has also engaged your attention. He is desirous of seeing your collection, and of exhibiting a few of our specimens to you."[11] Squier was definitely an associate of Davis's, and presumably a friend, but it is unlikely that he ever considered himself an assistant (see fig. 2).

The prehistoric Indian mounds and earthen enclosures of the Mississippi Valley were first encountered at the beginning of Euro-American expansion into the trans-Appalachian frontier in the late eighteenth century. The spread of western settlement and the creation of new states in the early nineteenth century presented new opportunities for the study of local remains, which resulted in detached and incidental notices of works in travel accounts, newspapers, gazetteers, literary and scientific periodicals, and the transactions of learned societies. Much of that literature was superficial and poorly documented. Little regard was given to classifying the structural differences of these remains or to the possibility that they were built by different peoples, in different eras, and for different purposes. Descriptive accounts based on actual surveys and excavations were far too sporadic and few in number to support a systematic and comprehensive study. When Caleb Atwater of Circleville, Ohio, published the first general survey of western antiquities in the

2. Edwin Hamilton Davis (1811–88), ca. 1850. Davis's contributions to the Squier-Davis investigations earned him coauthorship of *Ancient Monuments of the Mississippi Valley*, but only after a significant controversy with Squier over their relative contributions to the investigations. (National Portrait Gallery, Smithsonian Institution, Washington DC. Reprinted with permission.)

Transactions of the American Antiquarian Society in 1820, he commented on the unsatisfactory nature of most existing accounts on the subject. The mooted questions concerning the origin, era, and assumed purposes of these works in large measure remained "lost in a labyrinth of doubt" and idle speculation. [12] Those who sought to decipher the riddle of the mounds through the often erroneous and contradictory literature on the subject were often more bewildered than enlightened. As Benjamin Silliman Jr. observed to Squier in December 1845, "The history of the mounds of the west is one full of interest and no doubt capable of much elucidation. Much has been written on this subject by those who have formed only speculative opinions, without much knowledge of facts and with no principle of interpretation." [13]

While much of the existing literature on the mounds was overly speculative and prone to exaggeration, there were notable exceptions. The more empirical observers were primarily concerned with describing the actual character of the works in question and only secondarily with conjecture. We also need to make a clear distinction between informed conjecture based on firsthand observation and the reveries of armchair antiquaries with no field experience. The archaeological value of some of these early accounts endures, as many of the sites they describe have since been destroyed or greatly altered in their original configurations. Speculation is not absent but is kept subordinate to facts. The more descriptive and accurate of the earlier accounts of the mounds were, moreover, absolutely essential for making a comparative survey of archaeological remains found throughout the Mississippi Valley. Several of the more useful accounts appeared in Silliman's *American Journal of Science and Arts,* which was the first scientific periodical to devote serious attention to the subject of American antiquities. Richard C. Taylor and S. Taylor contributed notices on the effigy mounds of Wisconsin, and C. G. Forshey gave an account of some mounds in Louisiana. [14] The accounts of Daniel Drake, William Henry Harrison, James McBride, Charles Whittlesey, Samuel P. Hildreth, and John Locke are also notable in this regard. Squier and Davis's debt to these worthy predecessors and contemporaries was a conspicuous one.

When Squier and Davis began their investigation in 1845, the intellectual climate and institutional settings in which archaeological and ethnological inquiries were conducted were rapidly changing. Romantic and fanciful speculation on the origin of the mounds would continue until the end of the nineteenth century, but idle conjecture was beginning to give way to the more exacting demands of scientific inquiry. The 1840s were an exciting and expansive period in the development of American anthropology. The establishment of the American Ethnological Society in 1842 gave impetus to archaeological and ethnological researches, while the founding of the Smithsonian Institution in 1846 promoted all branches of scientific inquiry, including the rather nebulous subjects of American archaeology and ethnology. Anthropological inquiry in the United States was further stimulated by the exploration of prehistoric remains and the assimilation of new sources of ethnographic information. As the United States expanded beyond the Mississippi, new regions were opened to exploration and new Indian groups came under study. Interest in aboriginal peoples and archaeological remains from around the globe also increased as American merchants, missionaries, and explorers penetrated new foreign markets and cultures. The publication of John Lloyd Stephen's *Incidents of Travel in Central America, Chiapas, and Yucatan* in 1842 stimulated interest in the antiquities of Central America and the hope that similar explorations would one day be undertaken among the mounds and earthworks of the Mississippi Valley. Particularly notable were the ethnological collections, vocabularies, and publications resulting from the first United States Exploring Expedition of 1838 to 1842. The publication of Charles Wilkes's five-volume narrative of the expedition in 1845 continued to expand the frontiers of geographic and ethnographic knowledge.[15]

Scientific interest in American Indians advanced further with the publication, in 1841, of George Catlin's two-volume *Letters and Notes on the Manners, Customs, and Condition of the North American Indians*, which described and visually represented the Indian tribes encountered in his travels beyond the Mississippi between 1832 and 1839. Similar interest attended John C. Frémont's expeditions to the Rocky Mountains in 1842 and to Oregon and California in 1843 and 1844, the report of which appeared in 1845.[16] American archaeology and ethnology were expanding fields of inquiry as a consequence of those developments.[17] Archaeologists and ethnologists in the early and mid-nineteenth century, moreover, conducted their explorations as part of a much larger geographical reconnaissance within the settled and unsettled portions of the United States.[18] The publication of Squier and Davis's *Ancient Monuments of the Mississippi Valley* in 1848 was a significant part of those larger developments.

Squier and Davis began their investigations in the spring of 1845 and conducted them at intervals until the spring of 1847. The investigations were conducted mostly, if not entirely, at the expense of Davis, who accompanied Squier in the field whenever his medical practice allowed. Excavating mounds was an expensive business and one that Davis said had cost him over five thousand dollars.[19] Davis's interests centered primarily on the excavations and in the patient and painstaking restoration of pipe and pottery fragments recovered from the clay basins or "altars" of the mounds, but he also participated in the surveying. Davis's name appears with Squier's as surveyor on twenty-eight of the survey maps published in *Ancient Monuments*, on one as the sole surveyor, and on the survey of the Newark Earthworks by Charles Whittlesey, Squier, and "E.H.D." dated 1837–1847. Squier appears as the sole surveyor on one map and on two others with surveyors other than Davis. There is no way to determine how many of the excavations were supervised by Davis, by Squier, or by both, but Davis's letters to Samuel George Morton and to Samuel Foster Haven clearly indicate that he possessed detailed knowledge of the internal structure of the mounds and of the different classes of materials found within them. Davis often assumed a paternalistic tone in his letters to the younger Squier. While Davis referred to Squier as a "friend and associate" who "assisted" him in mound research, the ambitious and capable Squier clearly thought otherwise.[20]

Squier and Davis claimed to have excavated approximately two hundred prehistoric Indian mounds, surveyed some one hundred earthen enclosures, and amassed what was then one of the largest archaeological collections in the United States. The scene of their surveys and explorations was the Scioto Valley of southern Ohio. The number and variety of Indian mounds and enclosures in the Scioto Valley presented an unrivaled field for archaeological inquiry. With pick, mattock, and shovel their workmen explored the interiors of local mounds through vertical shafts dropped from summit to base, while Squier and Davis carefully recorded their internal structure, relationship to the surrounding topography, and the exact conditions under which they found artifacts and human remains. By July 1846, Squier and Davis's crews had reportedly opened eighty mounds, made numerous surveys of local enclosures, and recovered no less than six thousand articles of stone, bone, and metal.[21] Squier and Davis's fieldwork was crude by later standards of archaeological investigation, but the number and relative thoroughness of their surveys and excavations made them the most extensive and complete that had yet been attempted. Even today they remain a monument to individual enterprise. Squier and Davis indeed accomplished much in a relatively short period of time. Squier boasted to his clerical father as early as the spring of 1846: "I will show you some things you never dreamed of in your philosophy."[22]

Squier and Davis hoped to expand their work into a systematic survey of the entire Mississippi Valley, but the cost of conducting such fieldwork was manifestly prohibitive. An expanded field of investigation would require financial support from eastern scientific and antiquarian societies. Squier traveled east in search of such assistance in June 1846, presenting ambitious proposals to learned societies in New York, Worcester, Boston, and New Haven.

He presented his researches with Davis as a model for conducting further archaeological investigations. He proposed to establish guidelines for future fieldwork and to direct the investigations of local antiquarians throughout the Mississippi Valley. Once adequate financial assistance was obtained for their labors, Squier was certain that his counterparts in the region would cooperate in furthering the study of the antiquities found in their localities. He hoped that the learned societies funding the research would also publish the results. Squier believed that such a survey would take no more than three years to complete if properly directed. [23]

Squier first made his proposal to the American Ethnological Society of New York. There he presented examples of the artifacts recovered in his excavations with Davis along with maps, plans, and sectional views of the mounds and earthworks of the Scioto Valley. The society promoted the study of ethnology in its widest accepted meaning: "inquiries into the origin, progress, and characteristics of the various races of man." The papers read before its eclectic members embraced archaeology, philology, and ethnography. The first volume of the society's highly regarded *Transactions* contained an article by Henry Rowe Schoolcraft on the excavation of the Grave Creek mound in western Virginia and another by Gerard Troost on the antiquities of Tennessee. [24] The society encouraged additional investigations into the origin and character of the earthworks of the Ohio and Mississippi Valleys, noting that "there are few individuals in our western country who may not obtain interesting materials for their elucidation." [25] Few individuals were better situated to obtain such materials than Squier and Davis.

Squier's presentation understandably generated considerable interest among the society's members – so much so that the society's secretary, New York publisher John Russell Bartlett, and its venerable founder and president, Albert Gallatin, offered to publish a full account of the Squier-Davis researches in the next volume of the *Transactions*. Gallatin and Bartlett endorsed Squier's plan for extending his explorations with Davis and used their influence in promoting interest in their investigations among other members of the eastern scientific community. Squier received no financial assistance for conducting an expanded field of explorations, but his relationships with Bartlett, Gallatin, and other members of the society introduced him into a transatlantic community of scholars and the larger world of anthropological theory. He remained an active member of the American Ethnological Society for the next twenty-five years and became its most influential member after Gallatin's death in 1849.

Squier next sought aid from the American Antiquarian Society in Worcester, Massachusetts. The society had published Caleb Atwater's account of the

Ohio mounds in the first volume of its *Transactions* in 1820, and its members shared the hope of their counterparts in the American Ethnological Society that the obscurity still surrounding the origin of these remains would be brought under further study. Squier's presentation and application for assistance at Worcester generated no less interest. Since Davis had previously written the society concerning his investigations with Squier, he suggested that Squier include his name along with Gallatin's letter of introduction. Such an omission, he cautioned, might lead them to "think there was some collision or competition otherwise." Squier, meanwhile, sought to "strike while the iron is still hot" despite Davis's caution. The result was a tentative offer of financial assistance. [26]

Squier next approached the American Academy of Arts and Sciences in Boston. He presented the same plan of investigation submitted to the American Ethnological Society and the American Antiquarian Society, apparently in the hope of receiving more than one sponsor and source of financial assistance. More than fifty members of the academy warmly received him at the home of John Collins Warren, professor of anatomy and surgery at Harvard and a serious student of ethnology. Also present at the meeting were Jared Sparks, Edward Everett, and William Hickling Prescott, all of whom would later sponsor Squier's diplomatic appointment to Central America on scientific grounds. Squier's presentation resulted in an honorary membership in the academy, yet another offer to publish his findings, and at least the prospects of future financial assistance. [27] Such recognition was heady wine for the ambitious and vain Squier.

Squier's eastern campaign continued at the New Haven home of Benjamin Silliman, professor of chemistry and mineralogy at Yale and editor and publisher of the *American Journal of Science and Arts*. Established in 1818, the journal was one of the first scientific periodicals to seriously examine the subject of American antiquities. Silliman introduced Squier at a special meeting of the Connecticut Academy of Arts and Sciences and the faculty of Yale held on July 7, 1846. The latter proved so enthusiastic about Squier's accomplishments that they made him an honorary member of the college. Squier also made arrangements with Silliman to publish brief notices of his ongoing fieldwork with Davis and a more substantial account that would explain the rationale of their classification of mounds and enclosures. [28]

In Chillicothe, meanwhile, Davis monitored Squier's eastern movements with mixed emotions. He congratulated Squier on his conquest of great men but also expressed disappointment that Squier had not given Davis proper acknowledgment for his contributions to the investigations. "Upon reflection Mr. E. G. S. I am convinced that all papers should appear under our joint signatures – author['s] name first. This will be no more than justice to each, as we expect to conduct the whole matter jointly." He wished Squier continued success but pointedly reminded him not to "forget your friend at home. Meet [sic] out to him equal credit and a due share of the honours, etc." Regarding Squier's preliminary article for Silliman, Davis cautioned him to give only enough general information as to attract attention and to excite interest. It would be important for them to "reserve our ammunition for the main fire" – the account of their findings that was to be published in the *Transactions of the American Ethnological Society*. [29]

Davis further cautioned Squier against being "too sanguine" in his efforts to obtain financial assistance. He disagreed with Squier's tactic of approaching several societies at once, believing it more prudent to concentrate on one or two. Squier's approach, Davis feared, would lessen their chances of receiving financial aid from the American Antiquarian Society and could result in jealousies of interest. He advised Squier "to cool down a degree or two, – and concentrate your mighty energies." After the support of a single society was secured and further investigations made, it would then be appropriate to seek the patronage of others. Davis also believed that Squier was prematurely rushing the publication of their findings, which precluded the possibility of closer examination and verification. He specifically asked Squier to contact a geologist to identify the composition of the stone effigy pipes they had recovered from the Mound City site near Chillicothe, and to find a naturalist to identify the species of birds and animals represented in the effigies. Davis also sought assistance in the identification of the animal teeth and shell beads in their collection. Such analyses required far more time than Squier was allowing in his plans for publication.

Davis strongly disagreed with Squier's proposed plan for extending the scope of their investigations and the time frame he allowed for its completion. Soliciting archaeological information from correspondents far and wide, he advised, would probably prove a disappointing and untrustworthy venture: "Don't attempt too much predicated upon the hope of exciting the same enthusiasm professed by yourself in a hundred antiquaries scattered over the U. States by pen and ink batteries. My God! You might as well expect information from the moon by addressing the man there, as to get anything of value from most correspondents." [30] Davis believed that a field of investigation conducted on a scale as large as that proposed by Squier would, even under ideal circumstances, take at least five years to properly complete. Only then would they be able to produce a work that "would do justice to the subject, ourselves, and the country." Certainly such an undertaking could not be satisfactorily accomplished in the two to three years allowed for by Squier.

Davis's concerns about Squier's proposed plan of investigation were well founded. The expense of such a large-scale undertaking was simply too great to attract sponsors, and the reliability of correspondents was too uncertain to inspire confidence. The American Academy of Arts and Sciences found itself unable to assist in the matter due to insufficient funds, while the American Antiquarian Society deferred the final decision on its tentative offer of support until the spring. Much as Davis surmised, the society was reluctant to fund investigations that were already being sponsored by the American Ethnological Society. The council of the American Antiquarian Society did not see what could then be "usefully" accomplished, and it postponed further action in the matter of financial assistance until the publication of the account of the Squier-Davis surveys and excavations in the forthcoming volume of the *Transactions American Ethnological Society*. That account, it was argued, would suggest what type of additional investigations the American Antiquarian Society could effectively support.[31]

The reception of that news was certainly discouraging, but Squier and Davis did not yet despair. They still hoped to secure aid from the American Antiquarian Society after the publication of their findings by the American Ethnological Society. Since Squier's promotional efforts had directed an unprecedented amount of scholarly interest, encouragement, and expectation toward their researches, they had every reason to remain optimistic about their prospects. Samuel Foster Haven, librarian of the American Antiquarian Society, told Squier that there could be no doubt as to the value of his researches with Davis or the reputation they would confer on them as "originators and pioneers" in the field of archaeology. Their labors were certain to serve as a model for future inquiry. John Collins Warren thought that even the American Academy of Arts and Sciences might yet be persuaded to do something, and he invited Squier to deliver a course of lectures on America antiquities before the academy that winter. Such lectures, Warren said, would direct public attention to the subject and greatly increase Squier's chance of securing assistance. Squier seriously considered Warren's offer, but at length he decided that the account he was preparing for the American Ethnological Society would serve the same purpose.

Squier and Davis resumed their investigations with renewed vigor in the fall of 1846.[32] Squier at the same time hastened to complete the accounts of the investigations he was preparing for the *Transactions of the American Ethnological Society* and for Silliman's *American Journal of Science and Arts*. Bartlett urged him to forge ahead with the account for the American Ethnological Society, which would be "the best feeler we can throw out and will show the world that we have antiquarian treasure among us." Since the American Antiquarian Society had deferred its decision on Squier's application for financial assistance until after the publication of this account, Bartlett emphasized its importance for Squier's newly launched career as an archaeologist. Adverse reaction to the publication would undoubtedly hurt his chances of continuing the investigations on a larger scale. Bartlett's continued attentions in these matters undoubtedly flattered Squier's vanity, just as certainly as they aroused his ambition by drawing attention to the scholarly reputation that loomed eminently before him.[33] Squier forged ahead with energy and perseverance in preparing the account for the American Ethnological Society.

His progress in writing was temporarily interrupted in the winter of 1846 and 1847 when he resigned his position at the *Scioto Gazette* and began new duties as the clerk of the Ohio House of Representatives. Squier sought the position at the suggestion of political friends in Ohio, but his motives for doing so at that particular time are not entirely clear. Perceived prestige, political ambition, and dissatisfaction with his position at the *Gazette* appear to be the most plausible explanations. As he informed his parents, the clerkship was a less lucrative position than reporting, but it conferred a certain amount of "Éclat, which is sometimes worth more than money." He was elected to the position on December 7, 1846, and served in that capacity until February 8, 1847. Although his assistants were saddled with most of the drudgery of preparing the index to the *House Journal*, he found his duties as clerk to be considerably heavier than those at the *Gazette*. The clerkship required long hours of tedious work that interrupted his researches with Davis at a critical juncture in their efforts to obtain financial assistance.[34]

Squier's decision to leave the *Gazette* certainly suggests that he was less than satisfied with his position there. He apparently found the views of some of the Whigs in Chillicothe not to his liking.[35] His departure may have been prompted at least in part by the heated political contest over the repeal of the Ohio black codes, which denied blacks in Ohio the right to testify in court. As editor of the *Scioto Gazette*, Squier joined those in the Whig Party who supported the repeal of the black codes, regarding them as but another form of slavery. Not all of the Ohio Whigs, however, supported their repeal, and this eventually led to a personal encounter between Squier and a supporter of the black codes at a convention of the Whig Party held in Ross County, Ohio.[36] That incident may well have soured Squier's attitude toward continuing his editorship at the *Gazette*. He may also have harbored political ambitions that led him to seek the clerkship as a springboard to higher political office. The clerkship certainly placed him at the elbow of the leaders of the Whig Party, but he found the mundane task of compiling the *House Journal* to be an altogether unpleasant one.

Whatever his reasons for resigning his position at the *Gazette*, Squier's determination to continue his archaeological researches in the spring had not diminished. He still hoped to obtain financial support that would enable him to extend the scope of the investigations of the perishable remains that were fast disappearing in a "utilitarian age." He believed such an "arduous" undertaking would fully occupy him for two to three years, but the results would be well worth the labor. As he noted to his parents, "The field is a wide and rich one and holds out a bright prospect of reputation and remuneration to the person who engages in it, in the right spirit and with a proper determination." Although he did not for a moment doubt that he was that person, Squier was haunted by the prospect of having to abandon the researches he had so ably begun. He saw himself at a pivotal and precarious moment in his chosen field of endeavor and was determined to somehow continue. [37] Squier's inability to fund his researches continued to handicap his chosen career as an archaeologist. It did not help that his father scolded him for not being "sufficiently provident" with what little money he had. [38]

It was during Squier's absence in Columbus that Davis received a visit at Chillicothe from the celebrated Montroville Wilson Dickeson. Dickeson had opened some 150 to 200 mounds in Mississippi and Louisiana between 1837 and 1844 and had gathered a large number of artifacts that he temporarily deposited in the Museum of the Academy of Natural Sciences in Philadelphia. Included in his collection were examples of mound pottery, copper ornaments, beads, stone idols, terra-cotta figures of the human head, engraved clay tablets, mica, and some sixty human crania. Dickeson, like Squier, gave an account of his explorations and archaeological collection before the American Ethnological Society in 1846, and in the same year the Academy of Natural Sciences of Philadelphia provided him with financial assistance for continuing his investigations. Samuel George Morton was particularly interested in the crania Dickeson was uncovering from southern mounds, supposing them to be the remains of the Natchez Indians. Morton believed the Natchez were an intermediate link between the "semi-civilized" and "barbarous" tribes that comprised his Toltecan and Barbarous divisions of the American race. He thought it likely that the Natchez were the descendants of the Mound Builders of the Mississippi Valley. Dickeson had unwittingly become Squier and Davis's rival for the attentions of the American Ethnological Society and in their attempt to secure financial assistance for further investigations. [39]

Davis learned during Dickeson's visit that his colleague had accomplished much. Davis was not, however, uncritical of Dickeson's work, observing that the latter knew "more of osteology than mounds." Davis found Dickeson's notebooks and sketches to be of great interest and "some wonderful," but he concluded that Dickeson conducted his explorations over too wide a field and embraced too many subjects. Certainly Dickeson had something yet to learn of to "moundology." Davis found his field methods to be "too loose," at times unreliable, and based on many "hearsay facts." Davis also criticized the manner in which Dickeson used black slave labor in opening mounds: "The negroes dig and he sketches." Davis found the use of slaves to be a "very cozy" and inexpensive arrangement but regarded the exactness of that method to be inferior to that used in his explorations with Squier. Dickeson reportedly expressed great admiration for the work of Squier and Davis and much regretted that he had missed Squier during his brief stay. Dickeson proposed an exchange of artifacts with Davis from what were then the two largest archaeological collections in the United States. [40] Dickeson, like Davis, was constantly in search of artifacts for his collection, which he displayed publicly at various places between the 1840s and 1870s. [41]

Squier regretted having missed Dickeson during his visit at Chillicothe. Had they met he would have proposed to him a plan to determine whether the antiquities of the northern and southern Mississippi Valley were contemporaneous in origin. The larger and more regular truncated pyramidal mounds in the South were particularly intriguing, since Squier believed them to more nearly resemble the teocalli of Mexico than those in the Ohio Valley. Inconsistent with the idea that the southern remains marked an advance in social development, however, was "the fact" that copper, silver, and lead were found in northern mounds, but none of those metals had yet been found in the South (Squier was then unaware that Dickeson had recovered copper ornaments in his investigations). The absence of large enclosures in the Gulf States, works that were so conspicuous in the Ohio Valley, was another important consideration of inquiry. Squier regarded many of the northern enclosures to be defensive in origin. He accepted their absence in the South as supporting the hypothesis that the Ohio Mound Builders were driven south by pressure from their enemies. Once they were removed from a state of constant warfare, their need to erect defensive works disappeared. [42] The relative age and character of the southern mounds were important problems of research – problems he would address should he afforded the means of continuing his investigations southward.

Squier's attitude toward Dickeson, however, was far more critical than deferential. He was suspicious of both Dickeson's claims and his methods and was impatient with the amount of attention Dickeson received from Bartlett and Morton. Bartlett in particular was impressed with Dickeson's account of his explorations and archaeological collection given before the American Ethnological Society in 1846. Squier admitted that Dickeson appeared to have accomplished a great deal in his mound explorations but dismissed his greatly touted collection of sixteen thousand arrowheads as being of little consequence. Displaying a trace of jealously, perhaps, he asserted that he could produce an "infinite number" of arrowheads but that the quantity of such specimens was far less important archaeologically than a representative sampling: "An hundred specimens illustrating their various forms are just as good as a wagon load." Dickeson's collection of mound pottery, however, was an entirely different matter. Squier wanted to compare Dickeson's specimens with those recovered by himself and Davis from Mound City. The crania recovered in Dickeson's investigations were of no less interest. Squier wondered if it was possible that Dickeson had recovered the remains of the Natchez Indians from the mounds, but because he knew very little of the character of aboriginal remains in the South, he refrained from making such a conjecture. [43]

Squier wanted to know about the aboriginal remains in the lower Mississippi Valley and continued his strategy of simultaneously soliciting several learned societies for financial support as a means toward that end. Jared Sparks advised that it was unwise to do so until Squier had first published his findings, noting that "the public mind will then be more enlightened, and more easily drawn to the enterprise." Sparks seconded Gallatin's suggestion that the larger work could be funded by subscription, in which case Squier would be well advised to survey the entire range of the Indian antiquities found within the United States. A work of that scope would be a monumental undertaking yet one that would bring its author a liberal subscription if properly conducted and brought forward by a responsible publisher. Sparks further counseled Squier to keep clear of theory, speculation, and exaggeration, instead allowing the novelty of his findings to speak for itself. Sparks, like Bartlett, believed the account Squier was preparing for American Ethnological Society would be important in generating interest in the prosecution of further investigations, which Sparks assured Squier that he would promote within the learned circle at Boston. [44]

Squier returned to Chillicothe and resumed his researches with Davis after the adjournment of the Ohio legislature in February 1847. Archaeology then became his sole occupation – though for how long remained a nagging question. It was at this moment of uncertainty that George Perkins Marsh, a member of the American Ethnological Society and regent of the recently established Smithsonian Institution, offered the timely suggestion that Squier submit his account of the investigations to Joseph Henry, the Smithsonian's secretary. Marsh knew Henry to be interested in Squier's work with Davis and, given the Smithsonian's liberal endowment, thought it likely that Henry would publish their findings in full. If published by the Smithsonian, the manuscript would appear in the best type and illustration possible and would likely earn its authors liberal remuneration for their labors. Publication by the Smithsonian, Marsh assured Squier, would be "a better *honorarium* for your labors than you can hope for in any other way."[45] Acting on Marsh's advice, Squier and Davis turned to the Smithsonian.

Henry confirmed his interest in the Squier-Davis researches in April when he contacted Squier and convinced him to submit the finished manuscript for consideration. Henry was determined to launch the Smithsonian on a proper footing and had definite opinions as to the type of scientific inquiry the Smithsonian would promote. Assuming that the manuscript was based on original research and judged of value, he was prepared to publish it in the first volume of the *Smithsonian Contributions to Knowledge*. Although it was not his intention to publish separate volumes outside that series, after a reasonable period of time he would permit the authors to republish their materials in private editions with free use of the lithographs, engravings, and type owned by the Smithsonian. Authors could in this manner be remunerated for some of the expenses incurred in their investigations.

Henry advised Squier that the Smithsonian's publication of the work would draw the favorable attention of the world scientific community and ensure the authors' lasting reputation. He convincingly argued that the alternative of publishing their work in a commercial edition by the authors' private arrangement might produce a prejudiced response among scholars. Popular science often received a cool reception in scholarly circles, Henry cautioned, since "reputation was the privilege of only the learned few to grant." As a further inducement he promised to provide Squier and Davis with additional copies of their work, to be used as the authors saw fit. A private edition could at that time be appropriately published.[46] Such arguments were persuasive and prompted Squier to push his researches with Davis to their conclusion. That spring they made their final surveys and excavations, after which Squier devoted himself exclusively to writing, to the delineation of survey maps and other illustrations, and to the verification of measurements.

It was at the conclusion of the Squier-Davis investigations in May 1847 that Squier first met the expatriated Englishman and popular lecturer on Egyptology George Robins Gliddon. Gliddon became one of several intellectual mentors who greatly influenced Squier's anthropological thought and who aggressively promoted interest in his researches in Europe. Gliddon, a former U.S. consul at Cairo and a twenty-three-year resident of Egypt, established himself as an American authority on Egyptian archaeology with a course of twenty-four lectures delivered at the Lowell Institute of Boston in 1843 and 1844 – twice the number announced to the public.[47] Those lectures formed the basis of his *Ancient Egypt*, published in 1844. Eighteen thousand copies of this work sold in the United States within three years, and it eventually appeared in at least thirteen editions. Gliddon provided the 137 Egyptian and Nubian skulls that formed the basis of Morton's highly regarded *Crania Aegyptiaca*, published the same year, which compared those skulls to representations of physical types found on Egyptian monuments.[48] Encouraged by the success of *Ancient Egypt*, Gliddon launched a new lecture series on Egyptian archaeology in 1846.[49] Neither American scholars nor the public knew much of ancient Egypt, but the subject's remote and exotic nature appealed to the romantic mood of the mid-nineteenth century. Others were drawn to the subject owing to their interest in the Old Testament. J. G. Wilkinson's three-volume *Manners and Customs of the Ancient Egyptians* (1837) and Gliddon's lectures and books promoted popular interest in Egyptian archaeology in the United States and stimulated a cognate interest in the infant science of American archaeology.

Gliddon and Squier were introduced to Gliddon through correspondence by their mutual acquaintance John Russell Bartlett. Bartlett suggested that Squier invite Gliddon, who was then lecturing in Cincinnati, to speak in Chillicothe.[50] Gliddon wrote Squier that he would welcome an opportunity to explain his "hieroglyphical discoveries" to the citizens of Chillicothe and to get a firsthand account of Squier's investigations with Davis. "We will then discuss all the antiquarian subjects that form our several labors: some *books* I have will be very opportune to you as they exist no where but in my custody – whilst I shall derive much instruction from the extraordinary exhumations you have effected from the tumuli of a forgotten yet civilized race."[51] Gliddon was eager to initiate Squier in the meaning of Champollion's discoveries and the "Nilotic mysteries" and novelties of Egyptology. "We have *two* worlds to talk about!"[52] He eagerly accepted Squier's invitation and in early May gave a course of four well-received lectures on Egyptian history, religion, arts, sciences, and customs.

Gliddon's lectures were high drama conducted by a practiced hand. He employed artists to paint canvas tableaux that covered the four walls of a lecture hall, enveloping his audience within a panorama of pyramids, temples, hieroglyphic inscriptions, and portraits illustrating Egyptian costume and physical type. The animated Gliddon discussed the latest findings on the chronology and ethnography of ancient Egypt. His audiences learned that Egyptologists were then carrying the era of Menes to four and even five thousand years before Christ, an antiquity that could not be accounted for within the restrictions of biblical chronology. The craniological evidence offered in Morton's *Crania Aegyptiaca* together with the representations of "national characteristics" (physical types) found on Egyptian monuments demonstrated that the various racial elements comprising Egyptian society were radically distinct in 2000 BC and had not changed since. The physical characteristics distinguishing the various races were as old as the oldest human records. The implications of those findings were clear enough for those willing to pursue them to a logical conclusion. The time necessary for Egyptian civilization to have reached the stage of development it had attained by 2000 BC could not be reconciled with the Hebrew chronology. Nor could the ancient diversity and radical distinctiveness of the different races within that society be explained by deriving all of mankind from a single pair of human beings. The various races of man must have originated in separate creations.

The theory of separate origins was certainly not a new one. In the mid-nineteenth century, however, it took on new trappings of respectability based on new interpretations of evidence provided by physical anthropology and archaeology. It became known as the doctrine of polygenesis and was endorsed by many eminent scientists in the United States and Europe. Advocates of polygenesis argued that each of the human races had a separate origin and was a distinct species. Did not the racial distinctiveness of the American Indian and the apparently remote antiquity of the mounds lead to similar conclusions? Gliddon and others certainly thought so. Squier's friendship and correspondence with Gliddon associated him with what the *Ethnological Journal* of London referred to as "the school of American Ethnologists." The fascinating and seemingly incongruous members of the American School of Ethnology were loosely bound together by the theory of separate origins.[53] Squier, the impious son of clergyman, was a curious member indeed.

Gliddon and his "Mound Digger" Squier became fast friends and confidential correspondents. Squier found in Gliddon a personality as audacious, gregarious, and irreverent as his own. Gliddon's enthusiasm for all branches of anthropological inquiry and his rather sycophantic attentions to the results of Squier's researches formed the basis of their friendship. Gliddon's self-conscious paganism and his embrace of Squier as a "brother in sanctity and colleague in iniquity" humored Squier and played to his vanity.[54] Gliddon trod lightly on the religious sensibilities of his audiences in his lectures, but Davis noted that privately he took an impish delight in "knocking the Bible into a cocked hat."[55] Gliddon, Josiah Clark Nott of Mobile, Alabama, Samuel George Morton of Philadelphia, and Squier came to form a veritable coterie of iconoclasm. Although Squier was far too cautious to openly align himself with the controversial racial theories of the American School, his tentative endorsement of its major tenets is apparent in his correspondence with Gliddon, Morton, and Nott and in some of his later writings. Gliddon's racial theory and his correspondence with Squier were unquestionably major influences on his anthropological thought. He did more than anyone else to promote interest in Squier's researches in Europe.

Squier's association with Morton further cemented his relationship with the American School. Whereas the pugnacious Nott and Gliddon were the school's polemicists, Morton was its acknowledged founder and spiritual leader. Respected at home and abroad, Morton had established himself as the leading voice of American anthropology in his *Crania Americana* (1839). He took a deep interest in the Squier-Davis research almost from the very beginning. As early as October 1845 be began to solicit information from Davis concerning the crania exhumed in the excavations and directed their attention to the results of his comparative study of mound crania. Morton maintained a correspondence with Squier and Davis through the remainder of their collaboration, made substantial contributions to their investigations by lending manuscript material to Squier that he had collected in his own studies of the American Indian, and helped promote interest in their labors among others. Morton's influence on the archaeology of Squier and Davis was pervasive.

Squier and Davis's relationship with Morton centered on their efforts to recover an "authentic" Mound Builder skull for Morton's examination. Although numerous crania were found during the excavations at Mound City in 1846, Squier and Davis recognized that the comparatively well preserved remains located near the surface of the mounds were of a later era than those deposited in the original interments at the base. The crania recovered from original burials were either too decomposed to be of use for comparative study or had been crushed by the weight of the earth above them. Squier and Davis's initial efforts at finding a well-preserved cranium in an original interment resulted only in the recovery of two lower jawbones. Squier sent sketches of these to Morton: "They are heavy, wide, and much flattened, presenting in all these respects a marked contrast to the jaw of a modern Indian." Given such meager results, Squier thought the prospect of finding an authentic Mound Builder skull to be "entirely hopeless."[56]

Squier's interest in finding such a skull was to have Morton compare it to the aboriginal crania of Mexico, Central America, and Peru, precisely as he had done in *Crania Americana*. Morton's mutual interest in making such comparisons stemmed not only from a desire to corroborate the findings set forth in his earlier work but also from his subsequent examination of the crania recovered during Dickeson's mound excavations in Mississippi and Louisiana. Dickeson, like Squier and Davis, also made temporal distinctions between the burials found at different levels of the mounds. The examples of crania in Dickeson's archaeological collection provided Morton with new evidence in support of his theory that the Mound Builder and the American Indian were of the same race and that, whether ancient or contemporary, the American Indian was radically distinct from other types of mankind. As Morton remarked to Squier, the results of Dickeson's investigations showed "the same links of connection between the demi-civilized & barbarous tribes which everywhere prove a common and indigenous origin for all the American nations." Regardless of whether the various groups of American Indians were descended from a single pair of progenitors or fifty, said Morton, they were sufficiently alike in their physiognomy, intellect, moral habits, and archaeological remains as to form "a vast homogeneous group of mankind." The American Indian was "*aborigine*, distinct and separate from all others."[57]

Morton was confident that the results of the Squier-Davis researches would provide similar evidence of the racial unity of the ancient Mound Builders and later groups of American Indians. That confidence was fully confirmed in the early spring of 1847. While excavating an unobtrusive mound some four miles south of Chillicothe, Squier and Davis were finally successful in their efforts to recover a well-preserved Mound Builder skull. They found the cranium under conditions that left no doubt that it belonged to the original builders of the mound. An elated Squier informed Morton of their find: "Eureka! My Dear Doctor. Give us joy. We have recovered one genuine skull of the Mound Builders at last!" Squier submitted four views of the skull along with preliminary measurements of its diameter, arch, periphery, and facial angle: "Did you ever observe a more *compact* head?" Squier gave Morton a full account of the circumstances and conditions under which the cranium had been found. Such details were necessary to properly authenticate the skull as an original rather than an intrusive deposit. The fact that this was the only well-preserved cranium they had been able to recover from an original burial led Squier to believe that "ninety nine out of every hundred skulls" found in the mounds belonged to "the recent Indians."[58]

Morton rejoiced with Squier over the discovery of his Mound Builder skull and made a careful examination of the drawings and measurements sent him by Squier. He found the Scioto Valley skull to be "a truly *aboriginal* skull[,] in fact a 'perfect type.'" It represented in every way "that race which is indigenous to the American continent, having been planted here by the hand of Omnipotence, and which, in all its numberless localities, conform with more or less precision." Squier and Davis interpreted their Mound Builder skull as confirming Morton's earlier opinion that "the Indian population of all epochs have belonged to a single homogeneous race." Morton thought that the features of the Scioto Valley skull most nearly conformed to the Peruvian heads figured in his *Crania Americana*: "how admirably they correspond with yours." Morton wanted to make a plaster cast of the skull to serve as "the type of Indian confirmation," which he would use in the identification of crania belonging to that race. [59] His findings directed the thoughts of Squier and Davis southward in their search for the elusive Mound Builder. Their views on the probable ethnic affinities of the Mound Builders with the aboriginal peoples of Mesoamerica owed much to Morton and provide the context for correctly interpreting the theoretical aspects of Squier and Davis's archaeology. The characteristically reserved Davis, for example, found the arguments presented in Morton's *An Inquiry into the Distinctive Characteristics of the Aboriginal Race of America* (1842) to be "quite conclusive."[60] Squier's relationship with Morton would continue until Morton's death in 1851, and Morton's writing continued to be the template in which Squier's thoughts on race would develop over the next decade.

3. Archaeology and the Smithsonian Institution

Editing and Publishing the Squier-Davis Manuscript

The Congress of the United States founded the Smithsonian Institution on August 10, 1846, based on an earlier bequest of $500,000 by the English benefactor James Smithson.[1] The Smithson bequest provided for the founding at Washington of an establishment for "the increase and diffusion of knowledge among men." His motives for the endowment are not entirely clear, but as a result the United States possessed a scientific establishment that promised to be as prestigious as any in Europe. The nature of the Smithson bequest, the relationship of the Smithsonian Institution to the national government, and the assumptions and expectations of the public were, however, inherently problematic and often contested. A clear tension existed between the cultural nationalism of many Americans and the transnational views of the Smithsonian's first secretary, Joseph Henry, who had definite views on what type of organization the Smithsonian actually was and ought to be.

In implementing the plan of organization adopted for Smithsonian in December 1847, Henry consistently reminded government officials, the regents of the Smithsonian, and the public at large that the Smithsonian was not a national institute but rather the bequest of an individual that had merely been entrusted to the care of the U.S. government. The bequest of Smithson, a foreigner, had been for the establishment at Washington of an institute for the increase and diffusion of knowledge that would benefit all mankind – not just American scientists, researching American subjects, and in the name of American science. The U.S. government was a trustee of the bequest and the agent for carrying out the original intentions of Smithson's will. As Henry said in presenting the plan of the organization to the public, "The institution is not a national establishment as is frequently supposed, but the establishment of an individual and is to bear and perpetuate his name."[2]

Henry shared the conviction of many scientists then and now that science and the origination and dissemination of knowledge should transcend nationalism, but cultural nationalists were not so disposed. Henry's views and opinions were too finely shaded for most Americans who regarded the Smithsonian as being national in its origin and purpose, and continued to do so from that day to this. The Board of Regents was composed of politicians and elected official of the U.S. government who themselves harbored nationalistic aspirations for the fledgling institute, while the Smithsonian's plan of organization itself called for the establishment at the Smithsonian of a "National Museum" as directed under the act of Congress establishing the institute. That provision ran counter to Henry's transnational view of science and explained his uneasiness about touting the Smithsonian as an American establishment – a contradiction not lost on Henry, who consistently showed a reluctance to spend the Smithsonian's annual appropriations on the projected national museum at the expense of publishing original contributions to knowledge. Henry kept the Smithsonian out of the museum business for as long as he could, but he was fighting a losing battle.

Henry consistently stated his concern over the potentially deleterious effects of nationalism on the program of the Smithsonian and its future reputation among learned societies. While finalizing the arrangements for publishing Squier and Davis's work as the first volume of the *Smithsonian Contributions to Knowledge*, for example, Henry effected a change in the language of the report of the evaluative committee of the American Ethnological Society recommending its publication. He did not want it to appear that the work was being presented as a national work by a national institute. Henry might have been troubled, or at least bemused or resigned to inevitability, when an advertisement in the *Literary World* hailed *Ancient Monuments of the Mississippi Valley* as a "Great American Work." Reviewers of *Ancient Monuments* expressed similar sentiments and commented on the appropriateness of launching the *Smithsonian Contributions to Knowledge* with a work on the ancient inhabitants of North America – a quintessentially American subject. But even Henry took pardonable pride in the quarto edition of the work, noting that its state-of-the-art typography, engravings, and lithography favorably compared to any similar work ever published in Europe.

The new institute was to inaugurate a series of monographs based on original research in order to meet the requirement of Smithson's bequest. It is indeed significant in the history of American anthropology that Henry decided to publish the results of the Squier-Davis investigations as the first volume of the *Smithsonian Contributions to Knowledge*. The association of archaeology with the newly established Smithsonian Institution unquestionably promoted its legitimacy more effectively than could otherwise have been the case. Editing and publishing the Squier-Davis manuscript, however, proved to be a difficult and controversial process that delayed publication and threatened serious consequences for the reputation of its authors and the Smithsonian.

The publication of the Squier-Davis manuscript began a productive program of anthropological research at the Smithsonian.[3] It also firmly established the reputations of the authors, just as Samuel Foster Haven had predicted, as true pioneers of archaeological investigation. Henry, a physicist, had no interest in anthropology per se, but he was determined that the Smithsonian would promote all departments of knowledge equally. The originality of the Squier-Davis investigations and the significant amount of attention they had already generated favorably disposed him to begin publication of the *Smithsonian Contributions to Knowledge* series with the Squier-Davis manuscript. Henry used the work as a model for the submission of future monographs and established a high standard of scholarship for the Smithsonian and for Squier and Davis.[4] Anthropological researches, including "explorations and accurate surveys of the mounds," were thereafter conspicuous subjects among the Smithsonian's programs for the increase and diffusion of knowledge. George Perkins Marsh had advised Squier and Davis well. They could not have hoped for a better honorarium than to have the results of their investigations published by the Smithsonian Institution.

Squier and Davis submitted their manuscript to the Smithsonian under joint signature in May 1847. Squier wrote the manuscript and prepared the accompanying engravings and lithographs of sites and artifacts based on the excavations and surveys he jointly conducted with Davis. Squier met with Henry at Princeton in order to finalize arrangements for publication, reporting to his parents that he was "anxious to publish my book [no mention of Davis], and will pay liberally for it." Accordingly, Squier now sought to be released from any obligation to publish exclusively with the American Ethnological Society. Gallatin readily consented to Squier's request. An additional year of investigations had greatly extended the scope of the Squier-Davis manuscript, and it was obvious that the cost of publishing it in a suitable manner was well beyond the society's resources. The estimated cost of making the necessary lithographs and engravings alone was prohibitive. Bartlett was quite startled when Squier informed him that the finished work would be three hundred to four hundred printed pages.[5]

It was then that Squier and Davis renewed their application for aid to the American Antiquarian Society. They submitted to the society's council an account of their fieldwork that included drawings of the effigy pipes, articles of wrought metal, and the clay "altars" at the base of the mounds upon which they were found. The council, however, still desired further information. No decision on the expediency of funding additional explorations or of underwriting the substantial cost involved in publishing the results of the researches already conducted would be made until it received "a reasonable promise of creditable results." The council sent Samuel Foster Haven on a fact-finding tour to their field of operations in June 1847. While Squier remained in New York to arrange matters with Henry, Haven spent three days with Davis inspecting local works near Chillicothe. Haven also examined the works at Marietta, Portsmouth, and Newark described by Caleb Atwater in the first volume of the *Transactions of the American Antiquarian Society*.[6] Jared Sparks informed Squier in July 1847 that the question of aiding his researches had been fully discussed at a recent meeting of the society and that there seemed to be "a unanimous opinion" that such assistance would be an appropriate expenditure of the society's funds. He also thought the society was prepared to publish the larger work he had already prepared. Future developments, he supposed, would depend on the nature of Haven's report on his fact-finding tour.[7]

Haven reported the results of his trip to the council of the American Antiquarian Society on August 1, 1847. He drew attention to the manner in which Squier and Davis's method of surveying and mapping the mounds differed from that of Atwater. Since the society had published Atwater's pioneering surveys of Ohio mounds in 1820, they wanted to be certain that Squier and Davis's work was both accurate and original. Such caution was justified because Squier and Davis were investigating some of the same sites earlier reported on by Atwater. Davis gave Haven drawings of earthworks and artifacts during his visit to Chillicothe and allowed him to make copies of others as illustrations for his report to the council. Haven attested to both the originality and accuracy of Squier and Davis's work, which he found superior to Atwater's in every way. He discovered, for example, that Atwater had apparently taken his plan of the "Fortification on the East Bank of the Little Miami River" in Warren County, Ohio, from the drawing and description of the work published in the *Port Folio* in 1809 and 1810. Atwater's account, said Haven, "is about word for word the same."[8] Haven was not disappointed in either the extent or the fidelity of the Squier-Davis investigations, but based on his own observations he soberly concluded that

the apparent superiority of the "mound builders" to the Eastern tribes whose history is better known, in the arts of civilized life, was not as great as I supposed would be the case. I should like to make a particular comparison between them, and think I shall attempt it. . . . The difference in habits of life, arising from agricultural pursuits, fixed habitations, and denser population, may afford sufficient explanations of the superior advancement of one portion of the same people over another portion[,] not only contemporary but equal in intellectual endowments. We know the difference that mere locality, greater or less fertility of the soil, and facility of supporting life make among our own race. My wonder is less that the occupants of the rich valleys of the West should have left such remains behind them, than that they should have left no more and none of a higher order, supposing them to have possessed permanent settlements in so temperate as well as so productive a region.[9]

Notwithstanding that caveat, Haven expressed unqualified admiration for "the science, industry, and judgment displayed by yourself and the Doctor."

Despite Haven's favorable report, the council would still not commit to financial assistance. Henry's interest in publishing the Squier-Davis manuscript in such circumstances was timely indeed. Owing to the expense of executing its numerous woodcut engravings and lithographic plates, it is unlikely that any sponsor other than the Smithsonian would have published the work in full or in a suitable manner. Final consideration of the Squier-Davis manuscript by the Smithsonian, however, required that a committee of recognized authorities favorably appraise the manuscript and recommend its publication. Gallatin formed such a committee from the ranks of the American Ethnological Society at Henry's request. It consisted of Edward Robinson, John Russell Bartlett, William W. Turner, Samuel George Morton, and George Perkins Marsh, all sponsors and promoters of Squier's researches. A favorable judgment was a foregone conclusion. Gallatin forwarded Henry a copy of the committee's report and resolutions on the Squier-Davis manuscript that was originally entitled "Archaeological Researches: An Inquiry into the Origin and Purposes of the Aboriginal Monuments and Remains of the Mississippi Valley."

Gallatin judged the work as far superior to Atwater's. He found it a welcome departure from the vague accounts and groundless theories that all too often pandered to the popular taste for the sensational and the imaginative. The authors of the work were entitled to high commendation for their effective labors: "Though ardent, Messrs. Squier and Davis are animated by that thorough love of truth which renders their researches worthy of entire confidence." The members of the evaluative committee fully concurred. They regarded the manuscript to be an original and valuable contribution to knowledge and were particularly impressed with its "scientific arrangement, simplicity and directness of statement, and legitimate deduction of facts." Marsh judged the work to be the first systematic study of American archaeology and praised its philosophical spirit. He thought that the Smithsonian could not begin its publications with a more appropriate or commendable monograph. Morton considered it the single most important contribution to American archaeology that had yet been compiled. As a work of both scholarly and general interest the committee highly recommended its publication. The Smithsonian officially accepted the Squier-Davis manuscript for publication in June 1847. The American Ethnological Society, as the original sponsors of Squier and Davis, would publish an abstract of the work in the second volume of its *Transactions*, while the Smithsonian would publish a fully illustrated folio edition of the entire manuscript. [10]

Henry agreed to promote interest in the work by publishing the committee's report and resolutions, provided they were first amended in several particulars. He did not want to divulge the actual manner in which the arrangements for publication had been made. He feared that if it were known that the manuscript had first been submitted to the American Ethnological Society for publication it might establish a precedent for having manuscripts submitted to the Smithsonian that already bore the endorsements of other learned societies. If such a precedent were established, the Smithsonian would be inundated with similarly endorsed submissions from throughout the country. Henry insisted that the committee's report be revised. He wanted it clearly understood that the Smithsonian had solicited the evaluation of the manuscript from the American Ethnological Society and that their appraisal had not been volunteered to the Smithsonian, as he thought the original draft of the report incorrectly implied.

The rules of the Smithsonian required that an impartial committee selected by the Smithsonian evaluate all manuscripts submitted for publication, and not, Henry added, by a committee selected by the author or his friends. He was also reluctant to promote the work as "an American production," as was done in the committee's original resolutions, which might imply that only American works would be presented by the Smithsonian. Henry reminded Squier that the Smithsonian was founded upon the largesse of a foreigner whose sole aim was to increase and disperse knowledge among men. The committee, he said, erred in supposing the Smithsonian to be an establishment of the national government instead of an individual patron. [11] As Henry would soon discover, however, both scholars and the public continued to regard the Smithsonian as a national establishment.

It was precisely at the moment of their success that the Squier-Davis association ironically came to an acrimonious end. The two colleagues traveled east in Gliddon's company after the completion of their researches in May 1847 and then met with Henry at Princeton to finalize matters concerning the publication of the manuscript. [12] Squier remained in New York at the

Smithsonian's expense to supervise the printing and engraving, while Davis returned to his medical practice in Chillicothe. Davis afterward grew anxious when Squier failed to answer some of his inquiries. He also urged Squier to be generous in acknowledging the works of their predecessors. "Don't be too hard upon the poor Devils (The Antiquaries) that have gone before us," he advised, "as we may have followers too." Davis also remained apprehensive over receiving recognition for his own contributions. He reported that he noticed Squier's name mentioned in connection with the mounds in every eastern paper he read: "I shall have to do something to keep up my end of the rope."[13] The final break in their increasingly estranged relationship came on September 22, 1847, when Davis first read the resolutions of the American Ethnological Society.[14] Davis "was not only disappointed, but grieved to find they [the committee] had stepped out of their way to inflict severe injury on my character." The object of his resentment was the original wording of the committee's second resolution: "we agree the work prepared by Mr. Squier on the subject is an object of general interest . . . worthy of the subject and highly creditable to the Author." Davis challenged the committee's authority to determine the authorship of a manuscript submitted under joint signature, and in his last known letter to Squier he charged him with foul play:

> To say the least, I must consider it a breach of our *private understanding* (an arrangement of your own proposing as your letters show), and that too, without the slightest cause on my part to justify the course. I have never publicly nor privately claimed the literary honours of the work; yet more, I personally informed Messrs. Gliddon, Bartlett, and Prof. Henry (as they will testify) that you were entitled to the credit in that particular. But my dear sir, there are many other considerations no less worthy of honour; connected with the authorship of such a work. For instance, the scientific portion, requiring so much patient research into all branches of geology, mineralogy, conchology, and even natural history together with many subjects too numerous to mention here. Yet requiring that archaeological acumen which is alone the result of long experience in conducting investigations. . . . I can't conceive that you desire to appropriate the whole credit of the work, as the resolution does to yourself; nor will I as yet permit myself to believe it was intended – I should regret very much the occurrence of anything that should disturb that friendship which has sprung from several years of constant intercourse.[15]

Squier expressed astonishment at the implications made in Davis's letter. He saw nothing objectionable about the report and denied having any influence upon the committee's actions or language: "I suggested nothing, asked nothing, knew nothing of it." [16] Such feuding caused concern to the ever-cautious Henry, who worried about the possible consequences of a public fray over Davis's contributions to the investigations. He grew even more concerned in November 1847 when the preliminary account for the American Ethnological Society, first published as a pamphlet, appeared under Squier's name only. [17] Davis is identified as Squier's "associate," and in a footnote it is implied that Davis would be coauthor of the larger work forthcoming from the Smithsonian. Since this account was an abstract of that work, Henry regretted that Davis's name had not appeared as coauthor. He was also concerned over the timing of its appearance. [18] Davis later maintained that the controversy following the publication of this account under Squier's name only prompted the regents of the Smithsonian to cancel their pledge of one thousand dollars as remuneration for publishing the Squier-Davis manuscript. In further consequence of this article, Davis said, the regents threatened to stop publication of the larger work unless Davis came to New York during its printing and engraving. His presence in New York during this time allegedly resulted in the loss of an entire year's medical practice at Chillicothe in addition to the cost of his residence in New York. [19]

Squier became increasingly truculent in response to Henry's concern over the Squier-Davis dispute. He bluntly informed Henry that he did not regard the publication of the account for the American Ethnological Society to be any of the Smithsonian's business. He also angrily delivered the "ultimatum" to Henry that the title page and preface of the forthcoming work from the Smithsonian must clearly reflect that the literary responsibility for the work was entirely his own. Squier claimed that it had always been his intention to grant Davis equal credit for the larger work forthcoming from the Smithsonian, even though the manuscript was completely and exclusively his own in design and execution. He claimed to have "made *every* drawing, written *every* paragraph, personally surveyed *every* mound, and superintended the examination of *every* mound." Davis's sole contributions, Squier asserted, were the perfunctory tasks of carrying the surveying chain and the cleaning and arranging of the artifacts recovered in the excavations. Such tasks were "capable of being performed by any boy in the country possessing ordinary intelligence." Squier regarded Davis's only reasonable claim to coauthorship to be his payment for a portion of the expenses involved in the explorations. He found it an "excess of impudence" that Davis would suggest that his name should appear first on the title page, as he understood was the case. Squier was also infuriated by the accusations made by Davis in his letters to others, letters that impugned his character by claiming be was attempting "to rob him of honours which he never earned." [20]

Accusations, to be sure, there most certainly were. Writing to Samuel Foster Haven of the American Antiquarian Society, Davis railed against the unequal apportionment of honors in the society's resolutions: "Nice distinction indeed! To denominate me a mere explorer, while the whole credit of preparing the work is given to another." Davis painfully recalled Haven's earlier prescience regarding who would receive the most credit for their joint investigations. "I have often thought of your prediction 'that my little friend would run off with the lion's share.' It has been verified to the letter and even further. He is now first in research; all in preparing the work." Davis held that Squier had known little or nothing of the mounds before his arrival in Chillicothe and that he had never even seen an earthwork before that time. Given Squier's duties as editor of the *Scioto Gazette* and then as clerk of the Ohio House of Representatives, the incredulous Davis asked: "Where has he had the time to do everything?" As for himself, Davis claimed to have accumulated considerable knowledge of the mounds before ever having met his erstwhile partner.[21]

The beginning of that partnership, Davis reiterated, was exclusively Squier's proposal. Squier had asked to join him as a "junior partner" in explorations. Elated at having met a kindred spirit, Davis accepted the proposition without hesitation: "He came into the firm bringing a ready pen and skillful pencil, with some knowledge of surveying." Together they had excavated and surveyed the mounds and earthworks for the two years of their association, "almost entirely at the expense of the senior partner." At the end of their fieldwork, "the junior partner takes up his abode in the library and cabinet of the senior, where both toil almost day and night for many months producing the work in question. Now who is entitled to the most credit? I am of a temperament to bear most things, but this is beyond all forbearance. . . . I conceive myself wronged by the last one who should have inflicted an injury upon me." With such an open breach in their relationship, all that remained of the Squier-Davis association was publication of their manuscript. The continuation of their dispute, however, delayed publication and threatened severe consequences for both the authors and the Smithsonian.

Davis was not the only one concerned about receiving due credit for his contributions to the Squier-Davis investigations. Equally disconcerting for Henry was the related issue of acknowledging other investigators who had agreed to have their own original materials incorporated into the manuscript. Squier and Davis had solicited the use of the archaeological surveys and field notes made by James McBride of Hamilton and Charles Whittlesey of Cleveland, and a smaller number by Samuel P. Hildreth of Marietta and John Locke of Cincinnati.[22] All of those investigators had distinguished themselves in their archaeological avocations, but Squier and Davis were particularly impressed with McBride's work. McBride made his first known archaeological survey in 1828 and continued to survey the mounds and enclosures of the Miami Valley over the next two decades. Although he occasionally excavated mounds, surveying constituted his greatest contribution to archaeology. McBride published an account of some of his early surveys in 1838,[23] and by 1845 he had completed about twenty-five survey maps. He thought it would take at least two or three more years to complete the survey of all known works in the Miami Valley. His intention was to compile these data into an archaeological map of the Miami Valley and present them to a learned society for publication. His first preference was the Ohio Historical and Philosophical Society, an organization of which he was a charter member and through which he had already published some of his surveys.[24]

Both Squier and Davis visited McBride on various occasions in 1846 when they reported on the progress of their investigations at Chillicothe. In January 1846 McBride generously lent his bound volumes of surveys and drawings to Squier, who presented them before the American Ethnological Society along with the surveys and drawings made by himself and Davis. The investigators proposed McBride's name as a corresponding member of the society in recognition of what he had accomplished in his own investigations. Davis was particularly keen on examining his surveys, drawings, and field notes, hoping to publish selections from them together with the results of his own investigations with Squier. He solicited the use of these materials, assuring McBride that he would receive full credit for his contributions. McBride agreed to Davis's proposition and gave him free use of his manuscript drawings and field notes.[25] Davis later cautioned Squier to be certain that McBride's name was placed on all his surveys being prepared for publication, understanding that McBride had expressed concern over receiving due credit for his contributions. Davis's concern proved well founded. Shortly after his own break with Squier, the issue of granting due credit to McBride for his contributions to the investigations became a matter of contention.

Once again the controversy centered on the publication of Squier's preliminary account for the American Ethnological Society. McBride, after reading the pamphlet version published by Bartlett and Welford in November 1847, wrote Squier that in the larger work forthcoming from the Smithsonian "I should be pleased if you would either in the description of the work, or in a conspicuous manner on the map, state on what date and by whom surveyed."[26] McBride also wanted Squier to acknowledge the frequent assistance he had received from John W. Erwin in making his surveys. "If the names of those who aided in making the surveys are not mentioned," he cautioned Squier, "I fear that fault will be found with myself or you for the omission." He asked Squier to identify his contributed surveys as having been made by "*James McBride & John W. Erwin.*"[27] Unfortunately, McBride's advice to Squier came too late. Erwin wrote a stinging letter to the editors of the *Cincinnati Gazette* in December 1847 that charged Squier with appropriating the credit due to McBride for his years of original research. Erwin, a civil engineer on the Miami Canal, was probably the most experienced surveyor then in Ohio. He had earlier been an assistant engineer on the National Road and was also the surveyor in charge of laying out numerous turnpike roads in western Ohio. Erwin shared McBride's interest in preserving accurate information about the works that were being threatened with destruction throughout the Miami Valley, and he frequently assisted McBride in surveying "the only memorials of a former people, now only known by those remains of their skill and industry."[28] The McBride and McBride-Erwin surveys made between 1836 and 1847 were among the most accurate that had yet been made.

Erwin charged Squier with failing to properly credit McBride for his survey of an earthwork located on the Great Miami River in Butler County. "Had I not been acquainted with this work, I should have taken it for granted that it was among the number of *one hundred* or *more* which Mr. Squier had surveyed at his expense." Even though Squier had dated the survey in question and placed McBride's name on it, Erwin complained that the credit was so small and indistinct that finding it required the "aid of good glasses."[29] Squier had also failed, said Erwin, to properly identify McBride as the surveyor of another mound in Butler County that was mentioned in the text but not figured. Erwin's understanding was that when McBride generously placed his bound volumes of surveys and drawings in Squier's hands, it was with "an *express understanding*" that he would receive full recognition for his original investigations. "This would have been done by a noble minded man without such an understanding, but some men have no other way to bring themselves into notice than upon the labor of others." Erwin knew how much time and money McBride had spent collecting the materials lent to Squier and how anxious McBride was that they someday be published. "Those who know Mr. M. are satisfied that would *scorn* to *appropriate* to *himself* credit which justly belonged to *another*, and that he has no desire to acquire *fame* at the *expense* of others, without giving due credit therefore." Erwin hoped that the situation would be rectified in the larger work forthcoming from the Smithsonian.[30]

The serious charges made in Erwin's letter were deeply troubling to George Perkins Marsh, a regent of the Smithsonian and a promoter of Squier's investigations. If McBride had made his surveys independently of

Squier, said Marsh, then he had every right to expect that his name should appear as delineator as well as surveyor. McBride eased tensions by solemnly assuring Squier that he had full confidence in his integrity. He disclaimed any previous knowledge of the letter in the *Cincinnati Gazette* and said he was unaware that his name was mentioned or in any manner connected with it until the arrival of Squier's letter. He solemnly assured Squier that he knew nothing of the letter or who had written it, but given his earlier statement of concerns he surely must have suspected that Erwin was the author in question. McBride denied having ever doubted that Squier would do anything other than give him proper credit for all his contributions. McBride did ask his son-in-law, however, to call on Squier during his visit to New York in January 1848 in order to inspect the engraved maps that were being made from his surveys and to see how the engraving and printing of the work was progressing. [31] One may infer from that request that McBride wanted to ensure that both his name and Erwin's appeared on the engravings, but McBride at no time appears to have been involved with the accusations that Erwin leveled against Squier. One must conclude that Erwin's animus was motivated more by his own anonymity at Squier's hands than by any alleged ill use of his friend McBride. Squier had, in fact, placed McBride's name on the survey in question, albeit in a manner unacceptable to Erwin.

McBride did acknowledge that Charles Whittlesey had written him stating his fear that Squier would not give McBride due credit for his surveys. Whittlesey, as Squier soon discovered, also harbored serious doubts as to whether he would receive proper acknowledgment for his own contributions to the Squier-Davis researches. Whittlesey had surveyed more than thirty ancient works as the topographic engineer on the first Ohio Geological Survey of 1837–38. His surveys, like those of McBride and Erwin, set a high standard for Squier and Davis to equal. His surveys gave the elevation and depression of embankments through vertical profiles and showed each in relation to the adjacent topography. The 1837 survey of the Marietta earthworks, made for Whittlesey by Samuel R. Curtis, [32] is an example of the general method that Whittlesey proposed to use in platting the archaeological surveys made during the Ohio Geological Survey. [33] Once published, those surveys would be a lasting record of a vanishing landscape.

Many of these ruins of a lost race are to this day without a description, while their forms and dimensions are fast disappearing under the operation of the plough and the spade. For it is in the rich valleys of the Miami, the Scioto, and the Muskingum, where the modern agriculturist now cultivates the soil, that an ancient people, more numerous than the present occupants, pursued the same peaceful avocation at least ten centuries ago. And upon the sites of modern towns within these valleys, as at Cincinnati, Chillicothe, Circleville, Piketon, Portsmouth and Marietta, the ancients located their cities, of which distinct traces [yet] exist. . . . The evidences of remote population and labor, now apparent within the State of Ohio, will, when collected in one mass, surprise all who have not bestowed attention upon the subject of Western Antiquities. [34]

Whittlesey further observed that future research and inquiry were certain to reveal "a connected system of antique structures, upon all the tributaries of the Scioto, and its kindred streams, leading to the Ohio." [35] It was just such "a connected system" that Squier and Davis attempted to demonstrate as a result of their own surveys and explorations.

Whittlesey initially intended to include the archaeological surveys made during the Ohio Geological Survey as part of the survey's final report. Those plans were forestalled, however, when the geological survey unexpectedly ended without the completion of a final report. It was then that Joseph Sullivant of Columbus proposed that Whittlesey continue his investigations at Sullivant's expense. The surveys were to be jointly published and the expense again to be incurred by Sullivant. Whittlesey made additional surveys toward that end in 1839 and 1840, but due to Sullivant's ill health the project was never completed. [36] Squier requested the use of those surveys in 1847 in order to make the Smithsonian monograph as comprehensive as possible. Since Ohio's antiquities were fast disappearing, Squier noted, Whittlesey's surveys would greatly assist him in recording their location and true character. "Once carefully surveyed etc., and whatever maybe the fate of the originals, their peculiarities will be preserved for the inspection of the curious which may follow us." [37] Whittlesey obliged Squier's request by contributing at least twenty surveys of ancient works that were mostly of sites located in northern Ohio. After the appearance of Squier's account for the American Ethnological Society, however, Whittlesey had second thoughts about contributing his surveys to the larger work to be published by the Smithsonian.

Whittlesey, like Erwin, also objected to the ungenerous "spirit" of Squier's account for the American Ethnological Society and his annoying tendency of ignoring the contributions made by his predecessors. "A reader not otherwise acquainted with the fact would infer that before you there were none worthy of notice," he wrote Squier, "[and] that you are the original and principal source of information." Such worthy investigators as Rufus Putnam, Thaddeus Mason Harris, Daniel Drake, Caleb Atwater, John Locke, and James McBride deserved far better than anonymity at Squier's hands. Fear-ing that his own contributions might go unrecognized, Whittlesey informed Squier that be could not be so obliging as to allow his labors to be appropriated by another. He requested the return of his plans and descriptions to "abide future events." It was only after he had received a full explanation of Squier's intentions that he again agreed to their use and apologized for any injury he might have made to Squier's feelings or reputation. He nevertheless regretted that Squier and Davis had not joined with him in producing, with the aid of the American Ethnological Society and the Smithsonian, a full and complete account that would omit none of the works that had yet been surveyed in the state of Ohio.[38]

Both Marsh and Henry, meanwhile, remained apprehensive over the possible consequences of Squier's continuing feud with Davis. Marsh was aware that Squier had actually drafted the manuscript but had assumed the existence of an understanding with Davis relative to coauthorship in recognition of his contributions to the investigations. He further assumed that Squier had made collaborative excavations and surveys with Davis but was not aware that Squier claimed exclusive authorship as he now understood was the case. He was of the opinion that the Smithsonian's willingness to support Squier's plan for extending his investigations rested entirely on the favorable public acceptance of this work and the elimination of hard feelings with Davis. Generosity was the only acceptable course, he wrote Squier, since "the whole of the literary credit will in the end redound to you, and that you can well afford to spare a crumb to those who have occupied a humbler rank than yourself in the field of labor." Squier should arrange the title page, preface, and plans of contributors so as to give full credit to all parties concerned.[39]

Henry likewise desired a speedy and equitable settlement of grievances. Taking a carrot-and-stick approach to the problem, he delayed publication of the Squier-Davis manuscript on the one hand while appealing to Squier's obvious ambition and vanity on the other. "I consider your present prospects superior to those of any other young man of my acquaintance," he wrote, "and with proper prudence and continued and laborious use of your talents you will secure a lasting reputation and command not only respect but funds sufficient to providing your researches over the whole american [sic] continent." Such success, however, depended entirely on a change in Squier's manner of dealing with Davis: "You must make up your mind to act not only justly but perhaps generously to Dr. D. I can assure you that nothing will be lost by this course."[40] Privately, however, Henry confided his exasperation with Squier to the American botanist Asa Gray: "The attention which Squier has received from some of the great men in Boston and New York has nearly turned his head and caused him to give me considerable trouble."[41]

Squier's ill humor toward Henry intensified with the latter's elimination of certain "theoretical matter" from the manuscript just prior to its printing. Henry was determined to establish the highest standard of scholarship for the works published by the Smithsonian, and he insisted that theorizing be eliminated or at least kept subordinate to facts. He also eliminated several engravings that Squier had garnered from other sources, restricting him to original illustrations relating to the Squier-Davis surveys, excavations, and artifacts and those of their collaborators. [42] Henry's editorial prerogative in this matter infuriated Squier, who denied that he had any theories to propound and declared that he was just as "competent" as Henry to decide what should and should not be eliminated from the manuscript. He chided Henry's timidity as an editor: "It will be quite time enough to get frightened and cry 'wolf' when the wolf is seen." [43] Although the theoretical matter alluded to was not specified in Squier's letter, it no doubt related to Squier's preoccupation with inferring the religious conceptions and practices of the Mound Builders through cultural analogies with the known beliefs of other groups of American aborigines and the early cultures of the Old World. The development of such analogies was a salient feature of his anthropological thought.

Squier's difficulties with the Smithsonian were far from over. He became even more agitated toward Henry when Davis suddenly appeared in New York during the printing and engraving of the manuscript. It was quite inconceivable to him why Henry had demanded Davis's presence: "He had done nothing, will do nothing, can do nothing." [44] Squier also learned that the regents had decided to give the authors 250 of the 1,000 copies of their work printed in lieu of money, as previously arranged with Henry. They justified the decision based on the fear that monetary remuneration would establish a poor precedent for Smithsonian publications. The remaining 750 copies of the work were to be donated to learned societies that published their transactions and further circulated through exchanges with libraries. The donated copies were to be distributed immediately after printing, while the authors' copies were to be withheld for two months.

Whether the regents' decision in this matter was related to Squier's dispute with Davis (as Davis later claimed) is not known, but whatever the motive, Squier did not accept the action with equanimity. Such "grasping avarice" led him to consider legal action against the Smithsonian for violation of contract. He wisely abandoned the notion, however, realizing that such recourse would cost him as much as it would win. Nonetheless, Squier believed that by changing the arrangements of publication the "cautious regents" had "forfeited their reputation as honest men." As he informed his parents, "I fancy my 'golden expectations' are not of a remunerable nature. They are not very golden at any rate. I do not, however, choose to throw away the only remunerable opportunity I have ever had to make something handsome."[45]

Squier had been at odds with Henry and the regents almost from the beginning. He was more than pleased to have his manuscript published by the Smithsonian, but he was disappointed that Henry and the regents would not provide him with financial assistance for continuing his fieldwork or reimburse himself and Davis for some of the expenses incurred in their investigations. His friend Gliddon was outraged by the brick-and-mortar mentality of the regents, who were willing to pay $240,000 for buildings and only $1,000 for publications.[46] Gliddon commiserated with Squier over "the blank prospect" offered him by Henry and encouraged Squier to sue the Smithsonian if the regents did not abide by the original arrangements of publication. He lampooned Henry's affiliation of Princeton, which he uncharitably characterized as "that manufactory of inarticulation and moonstricken piety." He thought Henry to be an exception since his actions marked him as a man of science, but he agreed with Squier that Henry did not understand the first thing about archaeology. The regents were "benighted and obtuse devils" whose "aristocratic tendencies" belied their democratic pretensions. He hoped that they would still publish Squier's findings, but "were I you, I would see them d——d before I would abate one iota of my rights to profit and fame." Gliddon later concluded that "Prof. Henry must be a brick" after all.[47]

Squier also had to contend with Davis, who continued to press his claims for equal credit. The dispute finally exhausted Henry's patience. He informed Squier that the manuscript would not be published until he and Davis had reached an agreement on that part of the preface describing their respective contributions.[48] It was then that the beleaguered and belligerent Squier gave his own account of his association with Davis. Not surprisingly, it was the antithesis of that earlier given to Haven by Davis. Squier claimed to have had an inchoate interest in American antiquities before his arrival at Chillicothe. Dissatisfied with existing accounts of the mounds, he had decided to conduct his own inquiry. Davis's small collection of artifacts and mutual interest in archaeology fostered a working relationship. Squier maintained that Davis had previously made no surveys, maps, or plans, "nor has he opened a single mound, or if he had, certainly could tell nothing of their contents." Squier was "gratified" when Davis agreed to accompany him in the field, and he claimed to have allowed Davis to make copies of his notes and plans. Davis's medical practice had allowed him little time to do more than clean and arrange the collection of artifacts resulting from the excavations, the contents of which Squier claimed half ownership.[49]

Although the Squier-Davis dispute was far from over, Henry's intercession finally forced them to an uneasy agreement on the content of the manuscript's controversial preface. Only then did *Ancient Monuments of the Mississippi Valley* make its belated public appearance. [50] The preface of the work, greatly extended beyond its original scope, acknowledges the authors' many debts to members of the eastern scientific establishment and to kindred spirits throughout the country who had contributed the results of their own researches. The "minute fidelity" and primary importance of the McBride-Erwin surveys, McBride's years of investigations in the Miami Valley, and the "generous liberality" with which he gave Squier and Davis unrestricted use of his materials are fully acknowledged. The "liberality" of Charles Whittlesey, his years of research, and the value of his contributed surveys and notes are likewise recognized. Davis also receives kinder treatment than in Squier's letters to Henry and Marsh. Davis's long-standing interest in the mounds, his activities as a collector, and his contributions to that part of the research embracing the natural sciences are duly acknowledged. He is also credited with having incurred the larger portion of the expenses attending the investigations and with the restoration and classification of the resulting collection of artifacts.

Such recognition was little comfort to an embittered Davis. Soon after the publication of *Ancient Monuments* the Squier-Davis dispute became a matter of litigation. [51] Ownership of the archaeological collection resulting from their investigations remained an unresolved issue. Squier claimed half ownership of the artifacts, even though they remained in Davis's sole possession. There was also the issue of Squier's alleged indebtedness to Davis, an allegation that Squier flatly denied. Davis and his "jackass lawyers," he said, were to be given no quarter for making so outrageous a charge. He threatened to sue Davis for $2,500 as compensation "for services rendered" unless he desisted in prosecuting the "trumped up" charge of indebtedness. Squier remained agitated at Henry's willingness to meet with Davis, coolly dismissing Henry as a "nervous old lady!" and a "noodle." He summarily dismissed Davis as a "poor jealous devil" whose "envious disposition" kept him living "in a little private hell." [52]

Davis informed Samuel George Morton in June 1849 that he regarded *Ancient Monuments of the Mississippi* as the partial fulfillment of "the great objective of his life" but that he resented that "misinformed or prejudiced persons" had awarded most of the honors for the work to Squier. He could only hope that time would correct the "injury." Davis wanted to continue his investigations, he said, due to "the imperious necessity" of ensuring his future reputation. He was preparing an ethnological map for Henry that indicated the character and relative location of mounds in the United States with an explanation of their classification. Davis continued to work on that project for many years, but his responsibilities at the New York Medical College (Davis left Chillicothe in 1850 following his appointment to the chair of materia medica and therapeutics at the college) and his later medical practice in New York forestalled its completion. Davis's portfolio of archaeological drawings and his correspondence with Henry do indicate, however, that he made some progress toward completing this map.[53] Davis also charged Squier with appropriating his own research regarding the sculptured rocks and in his article on Rafinesque's translation of the Walam Olum manuscript published in the *American Review*.[54]

There is clear evidence that Davis had a serious interest in these subjects, but absolutely none to suggest that he would have ever published anything on them himself, or that Squier had unfairly appropriated his materials. Squier was the scholar, Davis the collector and classifier. Recognition of that fact in no way denigrates the importance of the contributions made by Davis. One must take his incessant protestations about the injustices done to him with a grain of salt. Davis had legitimate grievances against Squier but also a penchant for overstating them, and he seldom missed an opportunity to sardonically comment on Squier's character.[55] Davis said he regretted his "ill-starred" and vexatious association with Squier and remained bitter over the manner in which Squier had "monopolized most of the glory as well as the proceeds of the publication (if there were any) leaving me little else than my collection to remunerate me for my time and money." He continued to fear for his future reputation "because efforts have been made to appropriate the results of my labors for the benefit of others."[56] Davis proved a good judge of history. His contributions to the Squier-Davis researches have received scant attention, thus confirming his greatest fear. The Davis of "Squier and Davis" has largely remained in the shadows of history as he did among his contemporaries.[57] It would have been difficult for it to be otherwise, however, given the extent of Squier's contributions to the investigations, his subsequent achievements in Central America and Peru, and his corresponding prominence in the history of American anthropology. Davis might say that he regretted his former association with Squier, but most certainly we know more and not less of him as a consequence.

The judgments of posterity have been unkind to Davis, but on balance it was he who owed the greater of the mutual debts. Squier was the animating spirit who transformed their collaboration into the first systematic study of American archaeology. He wrote the manuscript, arranged for its publication, and prepared the survey maps and drawings. Squier collaborated with

Davis in the supervision of the excavations and in making the surveys, but he appears to have contributed far more to both than did Davis. The good doctor's medical practice, by his own admission, often kept him from accompanying Squier in the field. [58] Davis acknowledged, however begrudgingly, Squier's skill as a writer, draftsman, and delineator. Only though his brief but productive association with the multitalented Squier was Davis able to share his archaeological interest and knowledge with a larger audience and secure his reputation as a pioneer in the field of archaeology. Acknowledgment of Davis's contributions to the Squier-Davis association is not to minimize those made by Squier but rather to give Davis his due. It is doubtful that Squier could have accomplished so much in so short a time without Davis's assistance. Most certainly Davis's scientific training, knowledge of the natural sciences, willingness to invest time and money into the investigations, interest in describing and classifying archaeological materials, and knowledge of Ohio antiquities and antiquaries prior to Squier's arrival in Chillicothe must be taken into account in evaluating this significant period in Squier's career. Squier and Davis would later frequent the same circles of the American Ethnological Society in New York, but they remained estranged and sensitive over their former relationship for the rest of their lives. [59]

4. Interpreting the Mound Builders

The Archaeology of Squier and Davis

Ancient Monuments of the Mississippi Valley is a remarkable synthesis of what was known about the prehistoric Indian mounds and earthworks of the United States at the time of its publication in 1848. It is reserved, cautious, and judicious in its generalizations and offers the most complete and comprehensive view of the subject that had yet appeared. Squier and Davis's deductions are confined to what could be legitimately inferred from the supporting evidence, at least so far as they understood that evidence, and largely to the exclusion of speculation and theory. The authors professed to have rid themselves of all preconceived notions at the outset of their researches and to have entered the field "*de novo*, as if nothing had been known or said concerning the remains to which attention was directed. It was concluded that if these monuments were capable of reflecting any certain light upon the grand archaeological questions connected with the primitive history of the American continent, the origin, migrations, and early state of the American race, that then they should be more carefully and minutely, and above all, more systematically investigated."[1]

That statement was pro forma and a little disingenuous. Squier and Davis never succeeded in entirely divesting themselves of preconceived notions. Squier admitted to Samuel George Morton in January 1847 the impossibility of conducting an inquiry free of some hypothesis.[2] Theoretical assumptions were part and parcel of the archaeology of Squier and Davis, as they were in the researches of their predecessors and successors. Nevertheless, the results of the investigations recorded in *Ancient Monuments* were a significant departure from the more unsubstantiated and fragmented accounts of the past. The authors understood the rules of evidence and logic, and they further benefited from the superb editing of Joseph Henry. The work established a high standard of archaeological reporting and was a model of its era. Its documentary and descriptive qualities are still of interest today, while the theoretical dimensions have aged less well.

The comprehensive scope of *Ancient Monuments* is one of its most original and enduring features. The work surveys the general structural features and geographical distribution of the effigy mounds of the upper Great Lakes region, especially Wisconsin; the conical mounds, geometric enclosures, and less common truncated pyramidal mounds of the Ohio Valley; and also the larger, more numerous, and frequently more regularly formed truncated pyramidal mounds and less numerous enclosures in the states bordering the Gulf of Mexico. Most of the authors' original observations, however, center on the mounds and enclosures of Ohio, the scene of their original investigations and those of their colleagues James McBride and Charles Whittlesey. Squier and Davis estimated at the time of their investigations that there were no less than ten thousand mounds and between one thousand and fifteen hundred enclosures in the state of Ohio alone. In Ross County, where most of the Squier-Davis surveys and all of the excavations were undertaken, the researchers put the number at nearly one hundred enclosures and five hundred mounds.[3]

The existence of such a large number and variety of works in so localized an area enabled Squier and Davis to make the first detailed attempt at the classification of Ohio mounds and their comparison to similar works found in the lower Mississippi Valley. The investigators classified and interpreted the mounds according to their position, form, structure, contents, and assumed purposes. Although antiquated and problematic in several respects, Squier and Davis's effort to categorize these remains is an essential component of their work. The functional assumptions of this typology have direct bearing on several of the authors' leading conclusions on the probable ethnic affinities, presumed migrations, and social conditions of the Mound Builders. The subordinate divisions of Squier and Davis's structural typology firmly established, contrary to popular opinion, that not all mounds were burial places, nor were all enclosures defensive in their origin. Although Squier and Davis were not the first observers to make these distinctions,[4] they were the first to develop them into a larger explanatory model. Their classifications continued to be cited as authority on the composition and purpose of the mounds until the 1880s, when their functional assumptions were superseded by the classifications made by the Smithsonian's Bureau of American Ethnology.

Squier and Davis's typology divides enclosures into three classes and the mounds into four. Each division, however, still formed part of a "single system" and was the work of "the same people." Enclosures, sites bounded by embankments of earth or stone, are classified as "Works of Defense," "Sacred Enclosures," and those of a miscellaneous character. The mounds are identified as "Altar Mounds" (or "Sacrificial Mounds"), "Mounds of Sepulture," "Temple Mounds," and "Anomalous Mounds." Altar mounds were found in or near sacred enclosures, possessed stratified soil features, and were erected over symmetrical basins or "altars" of burned clay or stone. Squier and Davis associated the basins or altars with human sacrifices or thought them to have been somehow connected with the religious beliefs and customs of their builders. They found the largest deposits of aboriginal art within this type of mound. Temple mounds were thought to have been platforms for religious structures. They receive close attention from Squier and Davis due to perceived structural similarities between them and the more elaborate teocalli of Mexico and Central America. [5]

The structural typology of Squier and Davis assigns a religious origin to a large number of remains. They were convinced that the form and position of many of the geometric enclosures in the Mississippi Valley established that they had not been constructed for defensive purposes. The fact that many of the presumably sacrificial or altar mounds were frequently found inside or near what the authors regarded as sacred enclosures led them to conclude that the areas within them had been set off as "tabooed" or consecrated ground.

> We have reason to believe that the religious system of the mound-builders, like that of the Aztecs, exercised among them a great, if not a controlling influence. Their government may have been, for aught we know, a government of the priesthood; one in which the priestly and civil functions were jointly exercised, and one sufficiently powerful to have secured in the Mississippi valley, as it did in Mexico, the erection of many of those vast monuments, which for ages will continue to challenge the wonder of men. . . . It is a conclusion which every day's investigation and observation has tended to confirm, that most, perhaps all, of the earthworks not manifestly defensive in their character, were in some way connected with the superstitious rites of their builders, – though in what precise manner, it is, and perhaps, ever will be, impossible satisfactorily to determine. [6]

Many of the rectangular, circular, and elliptical enclosures of the Ohio Valley are consequently classified as sacred enclosures, and the mounds found within them are likewise attributed to a religious purpose. The magnitude and obvious design of these works gave Squier and Davis pause for reflection and comment on the possible symbolic meaning of their various forms and combinations. "We can find their parallels only in the great temples of Abury and Stonehenge in England, and Carnac in Brittany, and must [by reason of analogy] associate them with sun worship and its kindred superstitions." [7] As indicated in this brief but suggestive passage, Squier had seized upon "sun worship and its kindred superstitions" as the underlying principle of the various religious and mythological systems of the American Indian. He was convinced that a comparative analysis of those systems and those found among the early cultures – "nations," as Squier would say – nations of the Old World at a similar stage of development would lead to important results. Such an inquiry would involve an analysis of archaeological remains in the Old World, the principles upon which they were constructed, and the degree to which a symbolic meaning could be deduced from their designs.[8] Squier was convinced that a comparative study of this kind would provide a rationale for interpreting the symbolism of archaeological remains throughout the American continent.

Squier's early interest in cross-cultural analogies is further evident in his observations on the Great Serpent Mound of Brush Creek. The discovery of the Serpent Mound in 1846 engendered in Squier a cultlike fascination with serpent symbolism and the problem of explaining its presence in the New World. As he observed in *Ancient Monuments*,

> The serpent, separate or in combination with the circle, egg, or globe, has been a predominant symbol among many primitive nations. It prevailed in Egypt, Greece, and Assyria, and entered widely into the superstitions of the Celts, the Hindoos, and the Chinese. It even penetrated into America; and was conspicuous in the mythology of the ancient Mexicans, among whom its significance does not seem to have differed materially from that which it possessed in the old world. The fact that the ancient Celts, and perhaps other nations of the old continent, erected sacred structures in the form of the serpent, is one of high interest. Of this description was the great temple of Abury, in England, – in many respects the most imposing ancient monument of the British islands.[9]

Such analogies, if fully investigated, were certain to shed much light on the development of "the primitive superstitions of remotely separated peoples, and especially upon the origin of the American race."[10] Just how it was that the serpent symbol had "penetrated into America" and how its presence here was significant in terms of "the origin of the American race," Squier did not say. He would, however, continue to wrestle with this question for several more years. Did the existence of serpent symbolism in America denote cultural diffusion or independent invention? What did the existence of these analogies suggest about the psychic unity of man? Squier's pursuit of these questions ultimately led him to write *The Serpent Symbol, and the Worship of the Reciprocal Principles of Nature in America*, published in 1851. It is significant to note here, however, that the origin of that work can be found in a few of the more suggestive passages of *Ancient Monuments* (see fig. 3).

Squier and Davis's comparative analysis of the truncated pyramidal

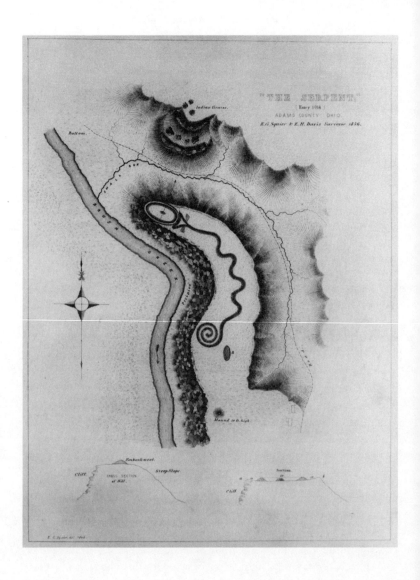

3. The Serpent Mound at Brush Creek in Adams County, Ohio. The discovery of the Serpent Mound in 1846 began Squier's cultlike fascination with serpent symbolism in aboriginal America and its presumably analogous and cognate forms of worship among early peoples throughout the globe. (Plate xxxv of Squier and Davis's *Ancient Monuments of the Mississippi Valley*, facing page 96.)

74

mounds and enclosures of the Ohio Valley and those found further south is an important component of their archaeology. It is here that the authors gave several of their leading conclusions on the presumed migrations of the Mound Builders, their theoretical connection with the aboriginal peoples of Mexico and Central America, and the possible symbolic significance of the circular and square enclosures they surveyed in the Scioto Valley. Squier and Davis possessed relatively little information concerning the content, character, and general distribution of the southern works, yet they were keenly aware of the need to make a careful comparison of those remains to like structures in the Ohio Valley. The desire to continue their fieldwork south of the Ohio Valley had prompted their unsuccessful attempts to obtain financial assistance. With no opportunity to continue their investigation south, however, they relied upon the work of other investigators to draw what comparisons they could. Squier and Davis provided detailed accounts of mounds and enclosures in Kentucky, Tennessee, South Carolina, Alabama, Louisiana, and Mississippi that were based on the surveys, plans, and descriptions of William Blanding, Constantine Rafinesque, [11] R. Morris, C. G. Forshey, and James Hough.

Squier and Davis were particularly intrigued with the structural similarities between the numerous pyramidal mounds of the South and those less commonly found in the Ohio Valley. The "elevated squares" at Marietta and the Cedar-Banks Works were cited as examples in this connection. These structures appeared to have served the same purpose as the more elaborate stone teocalli of Mexico and Central America [12] to which they presumably bore a close resemblance. The Ohio works, like those in Mesoamerica, were probably the sites of temples or had served as "high places" devoted to the performance of unknown ceremonies. Squier also drew attention to the resemblance between the Marietta works and those in the Gulf States in his article on the classification of the mounds that he prepared for the American Ethnological Society. [13] There he juxtaposed vertical and horizontal plans of a pyramidal mound at Marietta and a similar structure at Madison Parish, Louisiana, to better illustrate the "connection" between this class of works in Ohio and those in the lower Mississippi Valley and Mexico. Squier and Davis believed that such structural similarities established an ethnic connection between the Mound Builders and the aboriginal peoples of Mesoamerica.

The theory that the Mound Builders were somehow connected with the aboriginal peoples of Mexico and Central America was already established. [14] Samuel P. Hildreth, for example, also believed that the pyramidal mounds at Marietta had served as platforms for temples or other public buildings. Hildreth likened them to works described by Stephens at Palenque and to those existing at other Central American sites. Hildreth regarded the architects of the Central American works as being further advanced in the arts than were the northern Mound Builders, but he maintained that a people possessing similar habits and a common type of government had constructed the mounds and stone teocalli.

> It may be objected that they are too distant from each other ever to have been built by the same race. Allowing they were not of the same nation; yet similar wants, and similar habits of thinking would probably lead to very similar results. But there can be no reasonable objection to their being erected by a colony from Mexico, where the same works are found as in Central America. Neither is there any serious objection to their being the parent tribe of the Mexicans, driven away southerly by the more northern and warlike tribes. [15]

Of these alternative hypotheses, Hildreth thought it more likely that the Mound Builders had been the ancestors of the ancient Mexicans. Squier and Davis were doubtless influenced by these observations, even though they tentatively advanced this theory on the results of their own investigations.

Squier and Davis admitted that much more research was necessary before anything conclusive could be said regarding the origin and era of the southern mounds or their resemblance to those in the Ohio Valley. Only a systematic investigation of the contents of the southern mounds in relation to their form and position would provide further clues to these important questions. It remained to be seen whether the same people whose remains were found north of the Ohio River also erected the southern works, and if so, whether they were contemporaneous in origin. If it was determined that they were the work of the same people but of different eras, the question then arose as to whether their builders had migrated from the north to the south or vice versa. These questions were then unanswerable, but the importance that Squier and Davis attached to them clearly indicates the direction they believed future investigations should take. The authors suggestively note that a proper study of such problems might "disclose the curious and important fact, that upon the Ohio and Mississippi first originated those elements which afterwards, in a regular course of progress, developed themselves into the gorgeous semi-civilization of Mexico and Peru. Or it may, on the contrary, make known the no less interesting fact, that from these centres radiated colonies, which sustained themselves for a period, and finally disappeared, leaving perhaps only a few modified remnants in the region bordering upon the Gulf." [16] It is clear that Squier and Davis regarded the southern remains as important clues to unraveling the riddle of the Ohio mounds and the supposed migrations of their builders.

Squier and Davis's interests in the aboriginal remains of the lower Mississippi Valley were further peaked in 1847 when Samuel George Morton placed in the authors' possession a manuscript by William Bartram (1739–1823). Bartram traveled through the Carolinas, Georgia, and East and West Florida between 1773 and 1776.[17] His manuscript, written in 1789, is an account of the history, religion, and customs of the tribes composing the Creek confederacy. It consists of his observations given in response to a series of questions on the Muscogulges or Creek Indians. An unidentified party, who in all likelihood was Dr. Benjamin Smith Barton of Philadelphia, submitted these questions to Bartram.[18] Squier and Davis incorporated excerpts and illustrations from Bartram's manuscript into their own just prior to its printing.[19] Squier subsequently published the Bartram manuscript in full in the third volume of the *Transactions of the American Ethnological Society*, adding his own prefatory and supplemental notes.[20] Bartram's descriptions and sketches of truncated mounds and rectangular enclosures established that the Creeks occupied these remains in the mid-eighteenth century. Those observations, together with those made in Bartram's *Travels* (1791),[21] provided Squier and Davis with important information on the character of these structures and "the secondary if not the primary purposes to which the southern monuments were applied."[22]

Squier and Davis hastened to point out that Bartram did not attribute the actual construction of those works to the Creek Indians. The Creeks used the structures in their war and religious ceremonies and as the site of their village council house, but Bartram believed an earlier people had built them. Squier and Davis accepted as eminently plausible Bartram's belief that "the ancients" who originally constructed these works had probably used them for the same purposes as had the later Creeks.[23] Based on Bartram's descriptions and the accounts of other early observers, Squier and Davis were even willing to attribute the origin of at least some of the mounds of the lower Mississippi Valley to the annual bone burials of the Cherokee and other southern tribes. Squier would also later cite examples of the construction of mounds by historic Indian groups in the appendix of his work on the aboriginal remains of New York.[24] He remained convinced, however, that an earlier aboriginal people who had preceded the known groups of North American Indians in the possession of the Mississippi Valley had built the vast majority of the mounds.

Bartram's descriptions of the circular and rectangular housing structures in the Creek towns he visited were of no less interest. Regardless of the date or origin of the aboriginal remains located within these settlements, Squier and Davis regarded the Creeks' "singular attachment" to the circular and rectangular designs of their village structures as a circumstance of great importance. The Great Winter Council House of the Creeks was a circular structure built atop a truncated circular mound. It was the only place where the Creeks were said to keep the "eternal fire" – presumably a symbol of the sun. Since the Creeks were known to worship the sun, Squier and Davis extrapolated that the circular forms of the Creek council houses were probably symbolic of the sun. Thus, they argued, "the inferences drawn by analogy are therefore sustained by collateral facts." Taking the analogy one step further, they inferred that the combination of the circle and square found in the village structures of the Creeks probably indicated the symbolic meaning of the frequent combinations of these forms among the enclosures surveyed by the authors in Ohio. "In their [the Creeks'] less imposing structures may we not discern the type of the great circles and squares of Ohio – the traces of a system of idolatry which dotted the valleys of the West with giant temples symbolizing in their form the nature of the worship to which they were dedicated?" [25] Based on the analogy of the Creek Indians, Squier and Davis reasoned that the Mound Builders had probably worshiped the sun and that their circular enclosures were symbolic of that devotional purpose. The attempts made in *Ancient Monuments* to use analogy to infer the supposed religious beliefs and practices of the Mound Builders owes far more to Squier than to Davis. The analogies cautiously drawn in *Ancient Monuments* would be more boldly elaborated in Squier's later writings.

There can be no question of Squier's desire to extend his investigations southward or that his persistent efforts at obtaining financial assistance were directed toward that end. He solicited information about local works from Benjamin L. C. Wailes of Washington, Mississippi; Rev. R. Morris of Mount Sylvan, Mississippi; and J. G. M. Ramsey of Mecklenburg, Tennessee – all of whom had conducted their own investigations of local works and possessed collections of associated archaeological materials. Wailes was an avid collector of archeological and geological specimens that he deposited in the cabinet of Jefferson College. He also surveyed and sketched local mound groups. M. W. Dickeson, another investigator of southern mounds, had made "a few superficial excavations" in some of the same work examined by Wailes, but he had recovered nothing from them. Dickeson was an enterprising collector who, like Wailes, had gathered a large collection of Indian antiquities from local farmers who plowed them up in the vicinity of the mounds and former habitation sites. He obtained stone axes, arrowheads, discoidal stones, and earthen pottery from direct excavations. The iron implements and glass beads contained in some cemetery sites indicated contact with Europeans.

Wailes planned to continue his investigations of the mounds, hinting that he might join Squier in such an undertaking if he could obtain the necessary funds. He assured Squier: "Nothing would afford me more gratification than a systematic examination of those [works] I am acquainted with[,] could I afford the expense of travel and excavating, etc. – and would like to give the results of my labours to any Society or Institution of a public character for any aide that might be afforded adequate to the expense."[26] Wailes's aims were quite compatible with the plan of investigation that Squier had proposed in June and July 1846 to the American Ethnological Society, the American Antiquarian Society, and the American Academy of Arts and Sciences at Boston. Squier still believed in the feasibility of that proposal if only he could obtain the necessary funding. He could then direct the inquiries of local investigators such as Wailes, reimburse them for their expenses, and assure them that their findings would be published by the learned societies funding the research.

Despite Davis's cynicism about obtaining anything of worth from most correspondents, Squier received valuable information from Wailes and Morris, both of whom provided Squier with drawings and descriptions of the antiquities in their cabinets.[27] Morris, a native of New York City, responded to Squier's written inquires about local works and declared himself eager to contribute whatever information he could for inclusion in the manuscript soon to be published by the Smithsonian. He sent Squier surveys and descriptions he made of two enclosures and associated mounds in Lafayette County, Mississippi. These works especially interested Squier and Davis given their resemblance to similar structures in the Ohio Valley.[28] Morris's investigations promised important results. He had recently opened four mounds in Lafayette County with the assistance of his students at Mount Sylvan Academy. Morris's "museum" at the academy consisted of both archaeological and natural history specimens, the most significant part of which included arrowheads, spear points, ornaments, discoidal stones, and pipe fragments.[29] It is not surprising that Squier wanted to continue his investigations in the South, where he would have undoubtedly received valuable assistance from Wailes and Morris.

Squier also solicited information from J. G. M. Ramsey, corresponding secretary of the East Tennessee Historical and Antiquarian Society. Ramsey regretted that Squier had not extended his explorations into Tennessee and urged him to do so at the first opportunity. He responded to Squier's inquires about the character of local remains and offered to assist him if he would come to Tennessee. Ramsey was himself an archaeological investigator and had gathered an archaeological cabinet. He sent Squier drawings of some of the articles in his collection, some of which strongly resembled those described in Squier's previous accounts of the mounds and their contents. Ramsey reported that the mounds of Tennessee were of every variety of size, form, and purpose. The largest number, as well as those of the largest size, he believed to be temples or structures used for civil and religious purpose. "Do not all nations passing from a state of barbarism to one of great improvement (I do not say civilization) erect such structures as we now call Druidical? Are their civil and religious rites and the altars and buildings necessary for their exercise not always and necessarily identical or similar? Are the barrows in England dissimilar from the mounds of one description in America?" [30] Squier inquired about the sculptured stone images with representations of the male reproductive organ described by Gerard Troost and contained in Ramsey's collection. [31] One of them was of an adult in the state of erection and the other of an infant in miniature. Ramsey did not believe that the sculptures furnished any evidence of aboriginal phallic worship, as Squier appears to have suggested. Squier clearly thought otherwise and continued to collect evidences of phallic worship in the United States over the next several years.

Squier's inability to obtain financial aid for continuing his investigations in the South was one of the biggest disappointments of his career. His lack of success, however, was not for want of trying. He approached the American Antiquarian Society, the Smithsonian Institution, and even floated the idea of a congressional appropriation for that purpose with James Henry Hammond (1807–64), a former congressman and governor of South Carolina. [32] Francis L. Hawks, a member of the American Ethnological Society and a resident of New Orleans, wanted to help Squier find a means by which he could explore mounds in the South but was unable to do more than give him encouragement. It even appears that Squier at one point considered raising funds by selling what was presumably his half of the archaeological materials recovered during his investigations with Davis. [33] That idea was not feasible, however, since Davis would never have agreed to such a sale. The collection, with the exception of a few items that remained in Squier's possession, became Davis's exclusive property. He never recognized Squier's claim to half ownership of the collection, which he regarded as his sole recompense for the expenses incurred in his investigations with Squier.

Morton also encouraged Squier to extend his investigation southward, although he thought Squier would be competing "in vain" with Dickeson in exploring southern mounds. Dickeson claimed to have already opened 150 of them in Mississippi and Louisiana. Nevertheless, Morton supposed that

Dickeson had left something for others to do. He wanted Squier to investigate the southern works, to give "a truthful account of them," and to avoid archaeological "quackery" – apparently a backhanded reference to the work of Dickeson. Morton believed that the Smithsonian Institution should, at least in part, provide Squier with the means for conducting the proposed investigations.[34]

Squier thought his chances of getting such assistance from the Smithsonian, or any other learned society, were extremely slim. He had earlier enlisted the influence of George Perkins Marsh, a regent of the Smithsonian and a firm supporter of Squier's investigations, to see if such an appropriation could be made. Marsh, who was doubtless tiring of Squier's feud with Davis and his truculent attitude toward Joseph Henry, told him plainly that he did not think such assistance would be forthcoming from the Smithsonian. He advised Squier to again take his request for aid to the American Antiquarian Society.[35] Samuel Foster Haven laid Squier's new request for assistance before the council of the American Antiquarian Society, but it still declined to enter into any arrangement for new investigations. Jared Sparks wrote the council in support of Squier's request for aid, but its members refused to consider the matter further until the Smithsonian had published the full account of the Squier-Davis investigations.[36] Even Sparks now doubted whether the cautious council members would ever support Squier.[37]

Squier's interest in investigating the monuments in the lower Mississippi Valley partly explains his attitude toward Dickeson, whom he regarded as both a competitor and a charlatan. Given Squier and Davis's interest in obtaining authentic information about archaeological remains south of the Ohio Valley, it is interesting to note that Dickeson's exploration rated no more than a polite footnote in *Ancient Monuments*:

> The inability to add very largely to our stock of information respecting the monuments of the Southern United States, is less a matter of regret, since it is ascertained that Dr. M. W. Dickeson of Philadelphia, whose researches in natural science have created no little interest, has devoted much of his time to their investigation. His inquiries have been conducted on a large scale, and will serve to reflect much new light upon our antiquities. It is hoped the public will soon be put in possession of the results of his labors.[38]

Dickeson barely rates recognition as an archaeological investigator in the preface of *Ancient Monuments*, and he is mentioned only one other time in connection with the excavation of the great mound at Seltzertown, near Washington, Mississippi. There he is again relegated to a footnote and only indirectly cited through Bartlett's essay on the "Progress of Ethnology."[39] It is interesting to note that Charles Eliot Norton, who reviewed *Ancient Monuments* in the *North American Review*, wondered why Squier gave so little attention to Dickeson's extremely interesting investigations as reported in Bartlett's "Progress of Ethnology." It remained to be seen, Squier replied, whether Dickeson's work was reliable: "Many things which Dr. D. affirms to exist, *may* exist, – but whether they *do* exist, is quite another question."[40]

Squier was less restrained in his characterizations of Dickeson to Morton. He charged Dickeson with exaggerating the number of mounds he had excavated, which supposedly had grown from 492 to 1,000. "This has certainly been a good *growing* season for the Dr.'s crops!"[41] Squier expressed disbelief at Dickeson's claim to have discovered a fossilized human bone (*os innominata*) at Grand Bayou near Natchez, Mississippi. Dickeson further claimed to have found other human bones associated with the fossilized remains of the extinct mammoth at the same location. Squier could not believe that Dickeson actually intended to publish such "fictions." The publication of Dickeson's purported discoveries would do "infinite mischief" and bring discredit to archaeology, "for the mass of men prefer the wonderful and extravagant to the simple and true." Archaeological pretenders, a class of investigators that presumably included Dickeson, should be publicly crucified by way of "wholesome example," Squier wrote Morton.[42] Dickeson never completed his contemplated work on American antiquities, but a partially completed manuscript of the projected work and a manuscript catalog of his collection are in the archival holdings of the Free Museum of Science and Art at the University of Pennsylvania. The manuscripts describe his mound explorations and document his archaeological collection.[43]

Squier and Davis spoke with the greatest authority when describing the artifacts and human remains recovered in their excavations. Like their major predecessor, Caleb Atwater, the investigators recognized that the ornaments, implements, and human remains found in the mounds were frequently of different eras.[44] The lengths to which they went in making these distinctions, however, signaled a new departure in archaeological investigations. Repeatedly in *Ancient Monuments* and in Squier's related writings, the reader is reminded of the need to discriminate between the artifacts and skeletal materials found in original mound deposits, those found at the base of the mounds, and those of "the more recent races of the aborigines" found in the intrusive deposits nearer the surface. A failure to make those temporal distinctions easily led to false conclusions concerning the actual era of the mounds and the customs and condition of the people who built them.[45]

Squier and Davis characterized the ornaments, implements, and ceremonial artifacts recovered from the earlier mound deposits as being more numerous, made of finer materials, and more skillfully crafted than those attributed to "the modern race of Indians" found in later burials and other intrusive deposits. They favorably compared the fragments of ornamental pottery vessels recovered from Mound City to the most elegant Peruvian examples to which they reputedly bore a striking resemblance. The sculptured effigy pipes from Mound City and the sculptured stone tablets from Clark's Work were similarly regarded as belonging to "a higher grade of art." Such remains, the authors argued, could only have been produced by a people who were considerably skilled in the decorative or minor arts, a people presumably more advanced than any known group of North American Indians. [46] Those who labored to establish that the prehistoric ancestors of one or several groups North American Indians had built the mounds later censured their arguments for the superiority of Mound Builder art over that of the historic North American Indian. That interpretation connected archaeological and ethnological inquiry to a common purpose, the study of the North American Indian, and freed investigators of the need to attribute the mounds to a presumably lost race of Toltecs or the more absurd theories that they had been built by a non-Indian people.

As repositories of aboriginal art, the mounds of the Scioto Valley provided Squier and Davis with abundant evidence of the artistic attainments, the burial customs, and the presumed "connections and communications" of their ancient makers with other parts of the American continent. They made their most important explorations at Mound City, a thirteen-acre enclosure containing some twenty-three mounds. There, in 1846, they recovered a cache of nearly two hundred stone effigy pipes from Mound no. 8, also known as "the pipe mound." The admirable workmanship and apparent antiquity of these pipes, which depicted various species of birds, mammals, reptiles, and four representations of the human head, were the source of much comment. These sculptures pay mute testimony to the artistic attainments of their makers, while the human head effigies indicate hairstyle, ornamentation, and facial markings. Regarding the "predominant physical features" represented by these pipes, Squier and Davis observed that they did not essentially differ from that of "the great American family, the type of which seems to have been radically the same through the extent of the continent, excluding, perhaps, a few of the tribes at the extremes." [47]

Squier and Davis's lost race of Mound Builders were, therefore, physiologically American Indians, notwithstanding their misuse of the word "race" when making distinctions between the Mound Builders and later Indian peoples. But the authors did not regard the Mound Builders as the ancestors of any of the groups of North American Indians living in the Ohio Valley during the historic era. Squier and Davis were not arguing that the Mound Builders were a non-Indian race in a biological sense but rather in a cultural one. Their presumably lost or extinct "race of the mounds" were neither the lost tribes of Israel, Phoenician colonizers, or the Welsh followers of Prince Madoc. They belonged to same division of the human family as the later Indian groups known to history, but they were not believed to be the ancestors of any of the groups residing in Ohio at the earliest knowledge of Europeans. Those are cultural and ethnic distinctions and not racial ones as we employ the term today, but the context is confused by the indiscriminate use of the term *race* in much of the early literature. Squier and Davis clearly believed that the Mound Builders and Indians belonged to Morton's "American race," which included all American aborigines ancient and modern, but they made numerous chronological and cultural distinctions to show that they were not the same peoples. The interrelationships among race, culture, and ethnicity (independent variables) are obfuscated in the archaeology of Squier and Davis, just as they were in that of their contemporaries.

Squier and Davis's analysis of the animals and birds represented in Mound City effigy pipes is among the most problematic aspect of their work. The investigators' faulty zoological knowledge misled them in their identification of seven of the effigy pipes as representations of tropical lamantins, also known as manatees or sea cows, and of several bird pipes as tropical toucans. Their attempt to explain the presence of these effigies in an Ohio mound consequently led them to erroneous conclusions. The presumed manatee pipes were at first regarded as "monstrous creations of fancy," but later Davis announced to Squier his singular "discovery" that they were a specific variety of lamantin known as the "round-tailed manitus, *Manitus Senigalensis*, DESM." Since manatees were only found a thousand miles south of Ohio, they concluded that there had been "a migration, a very extensive intercommunication, or a contemporaneous existence of the same race of over a vast extent of country." In any event, the representations of manatee were "too exact" to have been made by someone poorly acquainted with them and their habits.[48] Henry W. Henshaw overthrew these conclusions in 1880, showing that the supposed manatees and toucans were probably indistinct representations of indigenous otters and raptorial birds.[49]

Squier and Davis devoted considerable attention to the sculptured stone tablets that had been periodically recovered from the mounds. Some of these tablets were reputed to bear hieroglyphic or alphabetic inscriptions, and there was much speculation concerning their origin and presumed meaning. The most celebrated of these finds were the engraved stone recovered from the Grave Creek mound in 1838 and the sculpture tablet recovered during the removal of a mound at Cincinnati in 1841. Squier initially accepted Henry Rowe Schoolcraft's opinion that the Grave Creek stone was an alphabetic inscription, as well as Erasmus Gist's view that the Cincinnati tablet was a hieroglyphic engraving. He did so in a brief account appearing in the *Scioto Gazette* in October 1845, where he specifically cited the Grave Creek stone as evidence that the Mound Builders had possessed letters and stated that the Cincinnati tablet was a "hieroglyphical stone."[50] Davis expressed his opinion to Morton that parts of Squier's article in the *Gazette* were possibly "premature,"[51] which, in fact, they proved to be.

The results of Squier's later inquiries into the Grave Creek stone led him to a different set of conclusions regarding its true character. Notwithstanding Squier's initial opinion on the subject, both he and Davis were quick to note that they had discovered nothing of a hieroglyphic or alphabetic nature in the course of their investigations. They had been unable to find any credible evidence that the Mound Builders had possessed anything even remotely approximating an alphabet or hieroglyphic system of writing.

> The earthworks, and the mounds and their contents, certainly indicate, that prior to the occupation of the Mississippi Valley by the more recent tribes of Indians, there existed here a numerous population, agricultural in their habits, considerably advanced in the arts, and undoubtedly, in all respect, much superior to their successors. There is, however, no reason to believe that their condition was anything more than an approximation towards that attained by the semi-civilized nations of the central portion of the continent, – who themselves had not arrived at the construction of an alphabet. . . . It would be unwarrantable therefore to assign to the race of the mounds a superiority in this respect over nations palpably so much in advance of them in all others. It would be a reversal of the teachings of history, an exception to the law of harmonious development, which it would require a large assemblage of well-attested facts to sustain. Such an array of facts, it is scarcely necessary to add, we do not possess.[52]

It is certainly understandable in the light of those views that Squier and Davis would take exception to the alleged discoveries of stone tablets bearing "strange and mystical inscriptions." The credence sometimes given to the reports of such finds is largely explained by the romantic view of the Mound Builders as a lost civilization. Fanciful minds little doubted that the Mound Builders had possessed letters and that written records would be someday be discovered in the mounds. One of Squier's correspondents spoke for many in this regard when be observed, while speaking on the probable connection between the mounds and the antiquities of Mexico and Central America, that from the mounds' remains "perhaps some American 'Rosetta Stone' may yet be exhumed to discover to the astonished savants of the Old Continent that on our side of the 'great Water' nations of civilized human beings with Arts, Science, and religion have existed in the valleys, and peopled the banks of the American 'Nile' thousands of years gone by; and probably prior to the 'Nilotic' events themselves." [53]

Schoolcraft first aroused scholarly interest in the Grave Creek inscription by communicating facsimiles to the Royal Geographical Society of London in 1841 and to the Royal Society of Northern Antiquaries at Copenhagen in 1842. He directed further attention to the inscription after visiting the Grave Creek mound in August 1843. The site had then become a macabre museum of dangling bones and artifacts. Abelard Tomlinson, the proprietor, built a three-story observatory on the summit of the mound, bricked the lower excavation tunnel into a Gothic arch, and plastered the walls of its lower chamber. There the contents of the Grave Creek mound were exhibited in candlelit array. Schoolcraft examined the stone's parallel lines of markings and presented his findings before the American Ethnological Society. He discounted the inscription's earlier identification as hieroglyphic but was struck by the resemblance that twenty-two of its twenty-four characters seemed to share with several ancient alphabets: Phoenician, Celtic, Anglo-Saxon, Runic (Norse), Etruscan, Gallic, Greek, and Erse. He was particularly impressed with their greater similarity to ancient Celtic writings known as the Bardic alphabet, as exhibited in the so-called "Stick-Book." [54]

Despite such a conglomeration of alphabetic elements, Schoolcraft still regarded the Grave Creek inscription as genuine. He speculated that its probable authors were either wayfaring Celts from Spain or their equally intrepid counterparts from Britain, who had migrated to the New World sometime before the end of the tenth century. Though offering no clues that would explain the stone's presence in the Grave Creek mound, he implied that the translation of its inscrutable inscription would doubtless reveal a new chapter in the history of the American continent. As he noted in a paper presented before the New-York Historical Society, the Grave Creek inscription promised "to address posterity in an articulate voice." He attributed the find to what he fancifully called the "MEDITERRANEAN PERIOD" of the American past, "the earliest and most obscure" of several periods comprising the "European branch" of American prehistory. Obscure indeed. The inscription appeared to him to bear a family resemblance to the ancient Mediterranean alphabet that had spread westward throughout Europe before the adoption of the Roman alphabet. [55] Since several ancient peoples wrote in that early script, it should be no matter of surprise that it would resemble the symbols used by several ancient societies in the Old World.

In the light of those views, it is no surprise that the Grave Creek stone was a subject of deep interest to Squier and Davis. Both were suspicious of the inscription's singularity and of the veracity of the accounts reporting its appearance. Davis thought the stone "a hoax in toto," while Gliddon, Squier's confidant and intellectual fellow traveler, also regarded it a spurious find. Gliddon privately lampooned the gullibility of those who accepted it as an alphabetic inscription and was particularly critical of Schoolcraft. [56] He once boasted that he "could annihilate his [Schoolcraft's] archaeology in three pages!!! He is one of the Grave Creek Flats!" [57] Squier and Davis believed that a critical appraisal of the circumstances attending the discovery of the Grave Creek stone threw considerable doubt upon its authenticity.

> The fact that it is not mentioned by intelligent observers writing from the spot at the time of the excavation of the [Grave Creek] mound, and that no notice of its appearance was made public until after the opening of the mound for exhibition, joined with the strong presumptive evidence against anything of the kind occurring, furnished by the antagonistic character of all the ancient remains of the continent, so far as they are known, – are insuperable objections to its reception. Until it is better authenticated, it should be entirely excluded from a place among the antiquities of our country. [58]

It was Squier alone, however, who became the first scholar to publicly denounce the Grave Creek inscription as a fraud. As a champion of his newly adopted field, Squier assumed the "disagreeable and ungrateful task . . . of brushing away the rubbish which impedes the progress of sound investigation." [59] He regarded the attention given the Grave Creek stone as the worst of such rubbish and spared none of his satirical talents in attempting to demolish its claims to further notice. Although Squier originally accepted Schoolcraft's opinion on the authenticity and alphabetic nature of the inscription, he now turned his invective squarely against that view. His intemperate attack on the Grave Creek stone earned him the enmity of those who later championed its authenticity. [60] Schoolcraft never forgave him for having fun at his expense. Squier chided the acceptance of the stone as an alphabetic inscription and, tongue-in-cheek, compared the various attempts made at identifying its origin to Hamlet's exercise in indecision with Polonius:

Polonius: By the Mass! And it is like a camel, indeed!
Hamlet: Me thinks it is like a weasel.

CHAPTER 4

Polonius: It is backed like a weasel.
Hamlet: Or like a whale?
Polonius: Very much like a whale!

Squier dismissed the stone as a calculated find, a commercial promotion typical of "an immense attraction" in theater. Positively pleased that the mound's museum had proven a pecuniary failure, he provided an enthusiastic account of its demise: "The 'rotunda' has fallen in, the bolts and bars have vanished, and the gate to the enclosure no longer requires the incantation of a *dime* to creak a rusty welcome to the curious visitor. Sic Transit Gloria Moundi!"[61]

The rattlesnake tablets recovered by Squier and Davis from Mound no. 1 of Clark's Work provided further evidence of the Mound Builders' "higher grade of art" and probable religious conceptions. As Davis observed to Bartlett shortly after the discovery of the tablets in 1846, "My friend, Mr. Squier, is so enthusiastic upon this subject, that he goes off half-cocked sometimes (as the Western phrase is)."[62] Squier little doubted that serpents were highly venerated within the proscriptions of the Mound Builders' religion and was enthralled in speculation concerning the possible significance of the serpentine design of the tablets from Clark's Work.

> The serpent entered widely into the superstitions of the American nations, savage and semicivilized, and was conspicuous among their symbols as the emblem of the greatest gods of their mythology, both good and evil. And wherever it appears, whether among the carvings of the Natchez (who, according to Charlevoix, placed it upon their altars as an object of worship), among the paintings of the Aztecs, or upon the temples of Central America, it is worthy of remark that it is invariably a *rattlesnake.* . . . As such it appears in the crown of *Tezcatlipoca*, the Brahman of the Aztec pantheon, and in the helmets of the warrior priests of that divinity. The feather-headed rattlesnake, it should be observed, was in Mexico the peculiar symbol of *Tezcatlipoca*, otherwise symbolized as the sun.[63]

The serpent symbol, associated here with sun worship, seemed to link the mythological system of the Mound Builders with those of the Natchez, the Aztecs, and the aboriginal inhabitants of Central America. Squier later explained that association in *The Serpent Symbol*, where he argued that the worship of the sun or fire – the universal symbol of the procreative power in nature – was the underlying principle of all the religious systems of the American Indian. Here was a germ of an idea he would continue to develop for several more years.

Besides the various classes of artifacts recovered by Squier and Davis, the researchers also unearthed numerous examples of human crania. These remains are carefully compared in *Ancient Monuments* to the mound crania figured in Morton's *Crania Americana*. Although this aspect of the Squier-Davis research has attracted considerable attention, much confusion exists regarding the authors' actual findings. Squier and Davis unearthed several burials during their excavations at Mound City in 1846. Those interments were found near the surface in areas where the convex stratigraphy of the mounds had been disturbed. The crania recovered from those burials were invariably well preserved and were attributed by Squier and Davis to the Indian tribes occupying the Scioto Valley during the fifteenth century and later periods. They were indistinguishable, the authors asserted, from the skulls found in the local burials grounds of the Shawnee and "other late Indian tribes." The investigators sent one of those crania to Morton, who found it to conform to the skulls of "the recent Indians" represented in his unparalleled collection. Skulls found in the original burials at the base of the mounds, by contrast, were so severely decomposed as to crumble at the slightest touch, or else they had been flattened and broken into fragments by the weight of the earth above them. Squier and Davis were able to recover but a single example of a skull from an original interment that was sufficiently intact as to allow for a comparative examination. That circumstance induced them to believe that few of the crania previously recovered from the mounds were actually those of their original builders. [64]

Squier and Davis readily acknowledged that nothing conclusive about the cranial conformation of the Mound Builders could be deduced from a single skull, but they postulated that a comparative study of its features was nonetheless worthy of consideration. They provided an engraving of the side, vertical, and frontal views of the cranium, along with Morton's meticulous measurements of its various dimensions. Squier and Davis provide a detailed account of the circumstances of the recovery of the skull, including a cross-section of the structural features of the mound in which it was found. Since the various layers of the mound were found entirely undisturbed, there was no doubt that the cranium had been deposited in the mound by its original builders. "Either, therefore, we must admit that the skull is a genuine relic of the mound-builders proper, or assume the improbable alternative that the mound in question does not belong to the grand system of earthworks of which we have been treating." [65] Having established the position of the cranium within an original mound burial, the authors then presented Morton's identification of its ethnic affinities. Given the frequent misrepresentations on this point, it is important to note that Squier and Davis presented Morton's conclusions without reservation or qualification. "The vertical oc-

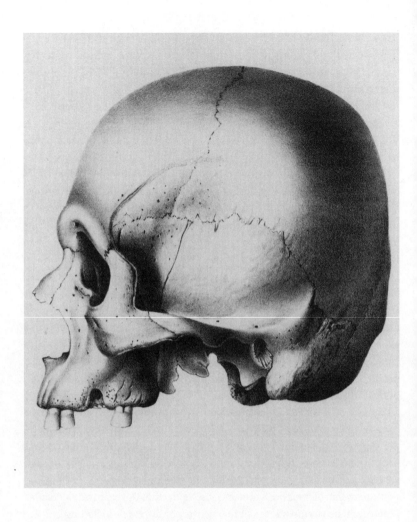

4. Mound Builder cranium from the Scioto Valley. Squier and Davis submitted this celebrated skull to the expert opinion of Samuel George Morton, who pronounced it a "perfect type" of an American aboriginal cranium, but more particularly of the Toltecan family of which the Peruvian head could be taken as the type. (Plate XLVII of Squier and Davis, *Ancient Monuments of the Mississippi Valley*, facing page 288.)

ciput, the prominent vertex, and great inter-parietal diameter, all of which are strongly marked in this skull, are, according to Dr. Morton, features characteristic of the American race, but more particularly of the family he denominates Toltecan, and of which the Peruvian head may be taken as the type" (see fig. 4).

The characteristics of Squier and Davis's Scioto Valley skull further confirmed Morton's views on the Toltecan cranial type of the North American Mound Builders he had earlier presented in *Crania Americana*. In that work, Morton paid particular attention to mound crania, which he compared with skulls of known Indian peoples to determine whether the prehistoric and historic aborigines of America belonged to one or to several races. The results of his analysis were based on examples of eight crania: five reported to have been recovered from burial mounds within the United States and three from Peru. Of the five North American skulls, one was recovered from a mound in Circleville, Ohio, one from a mound on the upper Mississippi, one from the lower chamber of the Grave Creek mound in present-day West Virginia, one from a mound on the Alabama River, and another from Tennessee. [66] After comparing these skulls to numerous other examples of aboriginal crania from North and South America, Morton identified the Mound Builders as having been a Toltecan subgroup of the American Indian. He believed the Toltecs were an aboriginal family that once ranged from Chile as far north as the Great Lakes of North America. It was likely, Morton significantly observed, that future investigations of the mounds would verify that the North American Mound Builders were of "Toltecan stock." Whether they had originally migrated from Mexico to the Mississippi Valley or vice versa was an open question. Morton was reasonably certain, however, that the Alligewi of Algonquian Indian tradition were the Mound Builders of the Mississippi Valley, who had been driven southward by "barbarous" groups of Iroquois and Algonquians. [67] Many nineteenth-century observers, and some of them among the more informed, subscribed to that theory.

The influence of Morton's views on the archaeology of Squier and Davis was indeed significant. It is important to note that while *Crania Americana* established the racial unity of prehistoric Mound Builders and historic American Indians, Morton also divided the American race into two distinct families: first, the "American Family" or "barbarous nations" of North America, except the Eskimo, whom he considered to be of Mongolian origin; and second, the Toltecan family or semi-civilized tribes, whom he identified as the ancient aboriginal populations of Mexico and Peru. Morton regarded those Toltecan peoples as having a distinctive cranial type and to have been intellectually superior to the American or Barbarous family, as shown by their attainments in art and architecture.[68] In order to understand the underlying assumptions of Squier and Davis's analysis of mound crania, it is necessary to note the Toltecan-Barbarous dichotomy within Morton's classification of the American race.

Squier and Davis accepted only two of the five North America mound skulls figured and described in Morton's *Crania Americana* "as genuine remains of the mound-builders." The other three they attributed to "the recent Indians," who were known to appropriate the mounds as burial places and whose remains they had often encountered during their excavations. Because of the particular conditions of its recovery, they accepted the Grave Creek skull as that of a Mound Builder, as they did the cranium exhumed by Gerard Troost from a mound at the junction of the French, Broad, and Holston Rivers in eastern Tennessee. The latter skull was entirely intact when recovered, but the rest of the skeleton was greatly decomposed. Troost also made a distinction between it and "the skulls of modern Indians" in the drawings he sent to Morton. The ancient skull, said Troost, differed so much from the other examples of American crania figured in Morton's *Crania Americana* that he at first doubted the accuracy of the drawing. Only after examining it next to the original skull did Morton accept the drawing's accuracy. That circumstance led Troost to identify the Mound Builders as an ancient and "wholly extinct race."[69]

Morton's theory of racial unity allowed for significant anatomical differences between the ancient Mound Builders and the later groups of "barbarous nations" who had presumably succeeded them in possession of the Mississippi Valley. That was precisely the point Squier and Davis were trying to establish by contending that three of the five mound skulls in Morton's *Crania Americana* were referable to "the recent Indians." They attempted to establish this distinction by giving the measurements of four "modern skulls" recovered during their excavations in the Scioto Valley in a comparative table of mound crania. Their table is based on Morton's statistical data and includes the measurements of Squier and Davis's genuine Mound Builder cranium, the skulls discussed in *Crania Americana* (including the Peruvian crania), and two additional skulls removed from Mammoth Cave in Kentucky. Squier and Davis then reaffirmed their opinion that three of the five North American mound skulls in Morton's *Crania Americana* were from intrusive burials based on "the general coincidence in measurements between them and those indubitably of recent date."[70]

Squier and Davis's interpretation of the Mound Builders as a lost race was clearly predicated upon Morton's projection of an ancient Toltecan subgroup of the American Indian. The only corrective of *Crania Americana* was the authors' attempt to demonstrate that three of the mound skulls measured and figured in that work were of intrusive origin, which they attributed to the Indian peoples inhabiting the Mississippi Valley at a later date. They raised no objection to Morton's opinion that their Scioto Valley skull was as a "perfect type" of an American aboriginal cranium or that it most closely resembled the Peruvian type of the Toltecan skull. Although they refer to "the remarkable" facial angle and internal capacity of the skull in comparison to others, they made no suggestion that these characteristics were incompatible with Morton's findings. They also state their opinion that the inferior maxillary bones recovered from original mound burials during their investigations were more massive and less projecting than those belonging to skeletons of a later date. Once again, however, this hardly constitutes an attempt to refute Morton's findings.

It simply does not follow, as has been suggested, that Squier and Davis's views on the cranial characteristics of the "race of the mounds" were somehow at variance with Morton's craniology.[71] Nor were their distinctions between original and intrusive mound crania an attempt to "throw out" Morton's supporting evidence on the racial unity of the historic American Indians and the ancient Mound Builders.[72] There was no "conflict" between the research of Morton and the "theories" of Squier and Davis, nor did the latter attempt to present their Scioto Valley cranium as evidence that the Mound Builders possessed a cranial type more distinct from that of other native groups than Morton allowed.[73] Various writers have incorrectly attributed all of these statements to Squier and Davis. The authors' "race of the mounds" and Morton's Toltecan Mound Builders were one and the same people. When Squier and Davis refer to "the race of the mounds" and to their Scioto Valley skull as "the only skull incontestably belonging to an individual of that race," the distinction being made is that the Mound Builders were a different and presumably extinct aboriginal group that had been driven from the Mississippi Valley by the ancestors of the Indians residing there at earliest knowledge. That the "race of the mounds" had belonged to Morton's "American race" they never doubted. Indeed, Squier and Davis were hardly in a position to challenge Morton's authority on Indian skulls even if they had desired to do so.[74] They deferred to him in all things pertaining to craniology. As Davis later observed regarding a skull removed from the center of a mound near Madison, Wisconsin, in 1859, "No marked difference is observable between the [mound] crania and those of our Indians."[75]

The number, magnitude, and extensive geographical distribution of these remains suggested to the investigators that the elusive Mound Builders were a numerous, widespread, and essentially homogeneous people. They inferred the homogeneity of their customs, religious beliefs, and social organization from the "uniformity" of position, form, and contents displayed by the mounds and enclosures throughout the Mississippi Valley. "This opinion can be in no way affected," said Squier and Davis, "whether we assume that the ancient race was at one time diffused over the entire valley, or that it migrated slowly from one portion of it to the other, under the pressure of hostile neighbors or the attractions of a more genial climate." They regarded the structural differences among the aboriginal remains located in the various geographical divisions of the region as being insufficiently pronounced to warrant their attribution to different peoples.[76] The authors clearly favored, however, the hypothesis of a contemporaneous occupation of the Mississippi Valley, an occupation that presumably continued until Mound Builders' mysterious disappearance. Squier and Davis had found, lying "side by side in the same mounds," native copper from the Lake Superior region, mica from the Alleghenies, marine shells from the Gulf of Mexico, and obsidian that they attributed to a Mexican source (the source has since proven to be the Yellowstone region of Wyoming). The widely separated sources of these exotic materials seemed to indicate "the contemporaneous existence of communication between these extremes. . . . This fact seems seriously to conflict with the hypothesis of a migration, either northward or southward." Little more could be said concerning the supposed migrations and disappearance of the "extinct race, whose name is lost to tradition itself, and whose very existence is left to the sole and silent attestation of the rude but often imposing monuments which throng the valleys of the West."

As for the origin and ethnic affinities of that nameless people, Squier and Davis allowed their readers to arrive at their own conclusions. Indeed, on the question of origins they are altogether silent. The clues to the authors' guarded views on the ethnic affinities of the Mound Builders were, nonetheless, abundantly apparent to those who carefully followed the threads of analysis woven into *Ancient Monuments*. Morton's Toltecan identification of Squier and Davis's Mound Builder cranium, the apparent structural similarities existing between the truncated pyramidal mounds of the Mississippi Valley and those of Mesoamerica, the presence of serpent symbolism, and the assumption that the Mound Builders were socially and artistically more advanced than known groups of North American Indians (and by extension their prehistoric ancestors) led Squier and Davis to but one conclusion. The evidence of their investigations indicated "a connection more or less intimate between the race of the mounds and the semi-civilized nations which formerly had their seats among the sierras of Mexico, upon the plains of Central America and Peru, and who erected the imposing structures which from their number, vastness, and mysterious significance, invest the central portions of the continent with an interest not less absorbing than that which attaches to the valley of the Nile."[77]

Evidence supporting the antiquity of the mounds receives considerable attention throughout *Ancient Monuments*. Squier and Davis found mounds and enclosures located on all but the first or most recent river terraces of the Scioto Valley. That circumstance suggested that the most recent terraces were formed after the practice of mound building had been abandoned and that the works located on the superior terraces were of remote antiquity. "The formation of each terrace forms a sort of semi-geological era in the history of the valley; and the fact that none the ancient works occur on the lowest or latest-formed of these, while they are found indiscriminately upon all others, bears directly upon the question of their antiquity." Squier and Davis attempted to form a rough estimate of that age by calculating the erosive powers of the adjacent rivers and streams. Assuming that the excavating power of these waterways decreased as the square of their depth increased (an inverse ratio), they believed that the deposit of the most recent terraces must have taken a much longer period of time to form than the older terraces above them. A further consideration in this regard was the tendency of rivers and streams to wander from their original channels. Sometimes they approached and even partially destroyed the works located on the older terraces where this occurred and then receded anywhere from a quarter- to a half-mile distant. At the High Banks Works in Ross County, for example, the Scioto River had cut its way as high as the third river terrace, receding nearly three-quarters of a mile away from its original channel near which these works are located. Since the recession of the Scioto and the subsequent succession of the forest on the intervening bottomland must have occurred subsequent to this encroachment, the High Banks Works had to be of a remote antiquity.[78]

Additional evidence of the remote antiquity of the mounds and the earthen embankments of the enclosures were the mature trees that covered their sides and summits. The trees were of the same variety and size as those found in the primitive forests surrounding them. At the Fort Hill enclosure in Highland County, Ohio, a large chestnut tree on the embankment of that work measured twenty-one feet in circumference, while a fallen and decayed oak tree also on the embankment measured twenty-three feet. Tree-ring dating at the site indicated "a positive antiquity of from six to eight hundred years." Adding to this age the indeterminate time elapsing between the construction and abandonment of the enclosure and the time needed for the succession of the forest after its abandonment, the authors were irresistibly drawn to the conclusion that the Fort Hill enclosure was at least a thousand years old.

All around the site, however, were the decayed remains of other trees which doubtless had been of equal dimensions and that attested an even remoter age. In the light of such evidence, the authors assigned the mounds an antiquity that unquestionably had to be measured in centuries.[79]

The implications of such antiquity were not elaborated in *Ancient Monuments*, but Squier had earlier stated them forthrightly in the *Scioto Gazette*. He believed the mounds were at least two thousand years old and had been erected before the construction of the more elaborate aboriginal remains of Mexico and Central America.

> We think evidences of the final migration of the race southwards, from either the pressure of hostile tribes, or from the attractions of a more genial climate, may be traced in their works, which, as a general rule, increase in magnitude, regularity of structure, and in number as they descend the rivers tributary of the Mississippi, and as they go down that giant stream. They are few, and small, and rude, on the Allegheny; they are larger, and more numerous, and more symmetrical on the Ohio; they swell to immense dimensions, and increase to almost incalculable numbers on the Mississippi; and, by a gradual transition, pass from the rude earth Mound[s] of New-York, to the immense cut stone Pyramids of Mexico – from the fortified villages and the rude sacrificial altars of the Scioto Valley, to the magnificent cities and imposing places of sacrifice in Central America.[80]

These were far from novel views, but their validity seemed to be confirmed by what Squier termed the "Grand Law of Development." The premises of that maxim required the presumably older remains of the Mississippi Valley to be regarded as the ruder prototypes of the more elaborate stone structures of Mesoamerica. The mounds were of a remote but uncertain antiquity, yet they were sufficiently old to give the coup de grâce to biblical chronology and ethnology. The iconoclastic Josiah Clark Nott, for instance, congratulated Squier for having "the hardihood to assert that the Indians were making potato hills in the [Mississippi] *Valley* before Eve was convicted and punished for stealing apples."[81] The archaeology of Squier and Davis provided polygenists like Nott, Gliddon, and Morton with new and seemingly conclusive evidence that the American Indian was of ancient origin and indigenous to the New World.

Ancient Monuments of the Mississippi Valley endures as an archaeological classic because of its scientific arrangement, scope, and originality, but the work had a larger cultural significance to contemporary readers and reviewers. Its publication in the fall of 1848 was a literary as well as a scientific event. Discussions of the prehistoric past were part of the literary culture of antebellum America and were infused with the same romanticism and nationalism that characterized the work of American historians, poets, and novelists. George Bancroft, William Hickling Prescott, and Francis Parkman all wrote in the romantic tradition of American letters.[82] Those same intellectual and cultural concerns informed Squier's approach to the prehistoric past. The search for native sources of inspiration permeated American arts and letters in the early and mid-nineteenth century, and appeals to the American past played an important role in the self-conscious movement to create a distinctively national literature. In his "American Scholar" address at Harvard in 1837, Ralph Waldo Emerson challenged his literary-minded countrymen to seek inspiration in American subjects: "We have listened too long to the courtly muses of Europe." What subject provided romantic and nationalistic imaginations with more native grounds than the subject of American antiquities? The prehistoric Indians mounds of the Mississippi Valley were part of a picturesque and vanishing landscape, ancient icons of a presumably "lost race." Squier and Davis's work struck a responsive chord among cultural nationalists who sought to promote the work of American writers who wrote on American themes. Empiricism, romanticism, and nationalism were concurrent intellectual traditions that informed the historical and anthropological literature of the period.

The appearance of this "Great American Work" as the first volume of the *Smithsonian Contributions to Knowledge* immediately conferred respectability upon the authors, upon the recently established Smithsonian, and upon the emerging field of American archaeology. Although there were scattered criticisms that the Smithsonian had begun the series with an "ethnological" work instead of a treatise on physical or practical science, these comments were more than drowned out by the accolades. The Smithsonian spared no expense in printing the monograph, and only the most accomplished lithographers and engravers were employed in preparing the work's copious illustrations. Joseph Henry favorably compared the work with pardonable pride to any similar study that had yet been published.[83] Squier's explorations and surveys with Davis were an auspicious beginning to a long and distinguished career as an anthropologist. They even earned him, thanks to Joseph Henry, an honorary A.M. degree from Princeton College. Henry arranged for the degree to be conferred so that Squier's "A.M." could appear on the title page with Davis's "M.D." Henry sought to lend added prestige to their work and further ensure its favorable reception among the learned.[84]

Reviewers of the *Ancient Monuments* expressed strong nationalistic sentiment in singing the work's praises. Theodore Dwight Woolsey, president of Yale and a member of the American Ethnological Society, thought it appropriate that the Smithsonian had chosen to commence its publications with "proper national feeling, at home." What subject of research was more American than the ancient Mound Builders of the Mississippi Valley? Henry had chosen wisely in inaugurating the *Smithsonian Contributions to Knowledge* series with the work of Squier and Davis: "Instead of inaugurating themselves by accounts of dodos on the other side of the globe, or of extinct volcanoes in Asia, or by vocabularies of the Papuan islanders, they chose for the subject of their first volume the antiquities of those mysterious races within our own borders, who may be called human fossils, and whose last vestiges are fast disappearing before the labor of civilized man." [85] The ornaments, implements, and stone sculptures recovered in the Squier-Davis excavations, said Woolsey, "introduced a new era in the knowledge of Indian art." He hoped that Congress or the Smithsonian would make an appropriation for the support of additional mound explorations in order to rescue such remains from the destruction that otherwise awaited them. Such explorations would soon result in "a comparative museum of antiquities" worthy of the nation. Woolsey thought it would be a shame if such collections of ancient American art went to private collections or foreign countries rather than to a national museum at Washington. [86]

An anonymous reviewer in the *Literary World* also saw "a very great historical propriety" in beginning the Smithsonian series with a record of the earliest traces of civilization in America. The researches of Squier and Davis showed that the America discovered by Columbus was a continent in disguise, one possessed of its own remote and "eventful history."

> After sitting down in silence under the reproach, if reproach it be, of the excessive modernness and newness of our country, which has been described over and over again by foreign and native journals, as being bare of old associations as though it had been made by a journeyman potter day before yesterday, we find we have what no other nation on the known globe can claim: a perfect union of the past and present; the vigor of a nation just born walking over the hallowed ashes of a race whose history is too early for a record, and surrounded by the living forms of a people hovering between the two. [87]

The most penetrating analysis of *Ancient Monuments* was a thirty-page abstract by Charles Eliot Norton that appeared in the *North American Review*. [88] Norton credited the work with shedding new light on old questions concerning the origin of the ancient semi-civilization of Mexico. His general comments on the "race" or ethnic affinities of the Mound Builders and the aboriginal inhabitants of Mexico succinctly summarize the suggestions of such a Toltecan connection presented by Squier and Davis. The similarity in shape between the "temple" mounds of the Mississippi Valley and the teo-calli of Mexico, the existence of serpent symbolism among both the Mound Builders and Mexicans, the presence of obsidian in the mounds (incorrectly believed to be from a Mexican source), the presumed representations of tou-cans among the sculptured effigy pipes from Mound City, and the presence of pearls attributed to the Gulf of Mexico all seemed to establish an ethnic connection between the Mound Builders and the ancient Mexicans.[89] "The question now arises," Norton wrote, "how intimate was this connection? Was it that of two distinct races, or was it that of branches of the same family? Resting our conclusion upon the character of the sculptured beads, and of the skull found in the mounds, setting aside all facts with regard to which a doubt might exist, we are led to the belief that the ancient inhabitants of Mexico and the ancient inhabitants of the United States belonged to the same family; that is to the Toltecan family of races."[90]

Norton endorsed the theory, at least as a probability, that the Mound Builders were the original stock of the Toltecan family that subsequently mi-grated southward into Mexico. If that view was correct, "we must ascribe to their remains in the United States, an equal antiquity with those of the Toltecs in Mexico and Central America, if not, indeed, a higher one." He was also willing to accept Squier and Davis's corollary of this theory: that American agriculture had a northern origin and that the climate and rich alluvial soils of the Mississippi Valley were just as conducive to the indigenous cultivation of maize as were the plains of Mexico.[91] To say that Squier concurred with Norton's assessment of his views on these questions is an understatement. He enthusiastically informed his friend and correspondent Francis Parkman that Norton was "a glorious fellow" who "enters more fully into the philosophy of my studies than any man I have met, excepting perhaps, Dr. Morton and Gliddon."[92] Norton understood better than any other reviewer the premises upon which Squier and Davis worked and the implications of their findings.

Ancient Monuments also received a laudatory reception in England. Luke Burke, editor of the London *Ethnological Journal*, echoed the refrain of the *Literary World*. "The time has past for looking upon this continent as a new world," he wrote. "Every step in investigations reveals some impress of the remotest times, and the question will soon be, whether it was the *first*, or only *one of the first* centres of high civilization."[93] The mound researches of Squier and Davis in the Ohio Valley and those of Dickeson in the lower Mississippi Valley led to but one conclusion:

that the civilization of the era of the mounds was long anterior to that to which we owe the great stone monuments of Central America, while we look upon this latter civilization as rivaling in antiquity that of ancient Egypt. The more facts accumulate around us, the vaster became [sic] the proportions of primeval civilization and empire, and the farther do they stretch out into the night of time. America presents a noble field for research, and we doubt not that one department of it, at least, will be well and vigorously cultivated; but when may we expect labourers who will do for Yucatan, Mexico, and Peru, what Squier, Davis, and Dickeson are doing for the great Mississippi region?[94]

Just as George Perkins Marsh and Joseph Henry had advised, and just as Davis had feared, Squier received most of the credit for *Ancient Monuments*. Several accounts of the Squier-Davis investigations, such as Norton's review in the *American Review*, mentioned Davis only in passing if at all. It was Squier's literary abilities and promotional talents that brought their work to the attention of the American Ethnological Society and the Smithsonian Institution, and in turn to the attention of the scientific community in the United States and Europe.

Gliddon was particularly instrumental in promoting interest in Squier's work among his acquaintances in Europe. It was through him that Squier's researches first came to the attention of Luke Burke of the *Ethnological Journal* and Edme-François Jomard, president of the Geographical Society of Paris. Jomard gave notices of Squier's discoveries in the *Bulletin de la Société de Geographie*.[95] The German naturalist and world traveler Baron Alexander von Humboldt, perhaps the most respected scientist of his day, was no less impressed by Squier's researches. "With Dr. Morton's *Crania Americana*," he is reported as saying, "the work of Mr. Squier constitutes the most valuable contribution ever made to the archaeology and ethnology of America."[96] Similar praise came from the Swiss archaeologist Aime Nicolas Morot, who later called *Ancient Monuments* as glorious a monument to American science as Bunker Hill is of American bravery. He was impressed by the scientific "spirit" of the work and credited its authors with discovering the Copper Age in America.[97]

Such was the general consensus on the Squier-Davis researches until the founding of the Smithsonian's Bureau of American Ethnology in 1879. Indeed, the reverence with which the views of Squier and Davis were generally received placed an enormous burden on the next generation of archaeologists who labored to overthrow the "lost race" theory. Henry W. Henshaw of the Bureau of American Ethnology began the task of debunking the honored authors in 1880. Henshaw's re-analysis of the animal effigy pipes from

Mound City corrected their exotic zoological identifications of tropical manatees and toucans and the theory of a southern connection for the Mound Builders based upon that evidence. [98] Cyrus Thomas, the bureau's director of mound explorations, rejected the functional assumptions of the authors' "imperfect and faulty" classification of mounds and enclosures in favor of a less theoretical nomenclature. The sacrificial "altars" of Squier and Davis, for example, are now known to have been crematories and not places of human sacrifice.

Thomas's field agents in Ohio, James D. Middleton and Gerard Fowke, demonstrated the relative inaccuracy of some of the Squier-Davis surveys after re-surveying several Scioto Valley sites in 1887. [99] Much to Thomas's surprise, however, he also found that Squier and Davis's estimates of the geometric regularity of these sites were borne out by the more accurate surveys of Middleton and Fowke. It should be noted in regard to Thomas's critique of the Squier-Davis surveys, however, that the government-supported fieldwork of the Bureau of American Ethnology directed by Thomas was conducted by teams of field assistants and with resources that far exceeded those available to Squier and Davis. The surveys of the latter, conducted under limiting circumstances and far from ideal conditions, appear to be no more and no less accurate than other amateur surveys conducted in the same period. Significantly, however, in some instances the Squier-Davis survey maps and descriptions are the sole surviving records of sites since destroyed or greatly altered in their original configurations.

Archaeologists have remained respectful of the pioneering researches of Squier and Davis notwithstanding these important correctives. Even though the extinct "race of the mounds" has since been proven to be distinct cultures of North American Indians and not Toltecs, Ancient Monuments has lost none of its interest as a descriptive account of archaeological sites and artifacts. The Johnson Reprint Company of New York photographically reproduced the work in 1965, while AMS Press reprinted it for Harvard's Peabody Museum of Archeology and Ethnology in 1973. In 1998, The Smithsonian reissued a 150th-anniversary edition of Ancient Monuments that includes a valuable introduction by David J. Meltzer, an index, and a bibliography of references cited by Squier and Davis. [100] By documenting the artifacts recovered in their excavations, by carefully discriminating between intrusive and original mound deposits, and by promoting the systematic surveying and mapping of prehistoric sites threatened with destruction, the work of Squier and Davis long served as a model of empirical observation and reporting. Ancient Monuments directed popular and scholarly interest to the subject of American antiquities as had no previous work. In the final analysis, this is the legacy of Squier and Davis.

5. Revisiting the Mounds

The Iroquois and the Archaeology of Western New York

No sooner had the results of the Squier-Davis investigations been put to press than Squier finalized arrangements to continue his search for the Mound Builders into the western counties of New York. He conducted those investigations under the joint auspices of the New-York Historical Society and the Smithsonian Institution with the combined support of two hundred dollars. That meager assistance was as close as Squier ever came to realizing his ambitious plan for extending the range of his archaeological investigations. Modest as that support was, it at least came at a propitious moment. Squier was residing in New York City in 1848 in order to supervise the printing and distribution of *Ancient Monuments of the Mississippi Valley*. The precarious financial circumstances that tormented him throughout his early career were at that moment particularly acute. The pursuit of science, he reported to John Russell Bartlett, had so far left his pockets quite empty. [1]

It was then that Squier's friends and promoters within the New-York Historical Society and the Smithsonian came to his assistance. Bartlett and George Henry Moore raised one hundred dollars from the members of the New-York Historical Society to help Squier defray the cost of continuing his investigations into the state's western counties. Joseph Henry, secretary of the Smithsonian Institution and publisher of Squier's first monograph, could only offer an equal amount, since half the income from the Smithsonian's founding bequest had been devoted for the next three years to the erection of a suitable building. [2] Squier was disappointed that the Smithsonian did not provide more assistance, but the limited scope of the proposed fieldwork was at least something that a determined individual could accomplish with dispatch and thoroughness. More importantly, Henry agreed that the Smithsonian would publish the complete results of his investigations in the second volume of its *Contributions to Knowledge*, with a preliminary account to appear in the *Proceedings of the New-York Historical Society*. The publication of a second Smithsonian monograph would further confirm Squier's reputation as a pioneer of archaeological investigations in the United States. It is indeed a testament to Henry's objectivity and patience that he would continue to work with Squier given the difficulties he had with him during the Squier-Davis dispute. Henry recognized Squier's talent and ambition and the significance of his investigations, and he wanted the Smithsonian to continue to publish archaeological monographs based on original research.

Squier's fieldwork in western New York has largely remained a footnote in treatments of his early career.[3] His surveys and explorations in New York and the circumstances leading to the publication of *Aboriginal Monuments of the State of New York* are significant in their own right. Those investigations were a logical extension of his work in Ohio and were regarded as such by the learned societies that promoted his researches. The unity of thought and recurrence of theme that connect *Aboriginal Monuments of the State of New York* and *Ancient Monuments of the Mississippi Valley* isolate important components in Squier's anthropological thought. Moreover, the extent to which Squier modified and elaborated his earlier views on the subject of American antiquities in his second Smithsonian monograph has remained largely unknown. In reporting his findings in *Aboriginal Monuments of the State of New York*, Squier met the same high standard of critical inquiry established by his first Smithsonian monograph. His use of historical documentation and ethnological analogies in the comparative study of archaeological evidence in New York was in keeping with his earlier work in Ohio and with later anthropological practice.[4] No assessment of Squier's early anthropological career is complete without reference to the questions raised by his investigations in western New York.

Although the aboriginal remains of western New York were smaller and fewer in number than those in the Mississippi Valley, they had been the subject of much interest and speculation. The existence of burial mounds and earthen enclosures in the region became generally known with the beginning of Euro-American settlement in the area during the late eighteenth century. De Witt Clinton gave the first connected view of their extent and character in a paper read before the Literary and Philosophical Society of New-York in 1817 and published at Albany the following year. Clinton gave brief accounts of enclosures he examined in Onondaga and Chenango Counties and raised important questions relating to the antiquity of the works and their proximity to others in the same region. The first volume of John V. N. Yates and Joseph W. Moulton's *History of the State of New-York* (1824) also noted the presence of archaeological remains and speculated about their place in the aboriginal annals of New York. Further notice of the subject appeared in James Macauley's *Natural, Statistical, and Civil History of the State of New York* (1829) and, more importantly, in Henry Rowe Schoolcraft's *Notes on the Iroquois* (1847).[5]

Those early accounts were not based on original surveys. Actual surveys were necessary before a comparative study could be made and legitimate conclusions drawn about their origin, antiquity, and probable relationship to remains found elsewhere in the eastern United States. If these works were found to be geometric in form – that is, true circles, ellipses, and squares – a common origin with those found in the Mississippi Valley would be implied. If their dimensions were irregular in form, a different origin and, perhaps, a different era would likewise be suggested. Such spatial and temporal considerations loomed large in Squier's fieldwork. The relative situation, number, range, and form of works in western New York could only be determined through a county-by-county survey. No less important was determining the characteristics of associated artifacts and other evidences of occupation. Descriptive fieldwork and the systematic classification of data alone could offer clues to the origin, antiquity, and assumed purposes of the works in question. Squier's fieldwork in western New York was a significant first step in that direction.

Squier initially assumed that the earthworks in New York were the northeastern termini of a larger defensive network extending diagonally through northern and central Ohio to the Wabash River in Indiana. Squier and Davis classified the works falling within that range as defensive structures. They attributed the enclosures and mounds of New York to the Mound Builders of the Mississippi Valley and drew attention to their close resemblance in position and form to those of northern Ohio.[6] Thus the initial problem Squier's New York fieldwork addressed was to determine whether the aboriginal remains of the state were built by a frontier colony from the Ohio Valley or represented the "ruder beginnings" of a people who subsequently migrated south and erected the more elaborate antiquities of the Mississippi Valley.[7] The results of Squier's investigation in western New York, however, led him to an entirely different conclusion regarding the origin and era of the earthworks of New York and those in northern Ohio.

Few individuals were better suited than Squier to undertake such an investigation at that time. His recent work with Davis in Ohio had brought him an unprecedented amount of attention as a pioneer of American archaeology. As he had in Ohio, however, Squier received invaluable assistance from several individuals during the course of his investigations in New York. Letters of introduction from officers and members of the New-York Historical Society and the American Ethnological Society preceded him in the field. The letters solicited assistance and information from the enlightened and public-spirited antiquaries who resided in areas containing aboriginal remains.[8] Squier received, in turn, other letters of introduction from kindred spirits at

Syracuse, Rochester, Lancaster, Niagara Falls, Buffalo, and Manlius to their counterparts elsewhere in western New York. The cooperation of local informants, some of whom accompanied him to the field, was of inestimable value to Squier, since such assistance enabled him to determine the exact locations of works whose existence was often unknown outside their immediate vicinity.[9] Junius H. Clark of Manlius in Onondaga County, Dr. T. Reynolds of Brockville in St. Lawrence, County, Augustus Porter of Niagara, and Moses Long of Rochester all eased Squier's way. Especially valuable was the assistance received from Lewis Henry Morgan of Rochester and Orsamus Holmes Marshall of Buffalo. With such able assistance, Squier could indeed accomplish much.

The cooperation of Lewis Henry Morgan is particularly noteworthy. Morgan shared Squier's interest in making accurate surveys of the state's antiquities before they were destroyed by the farmer's plow. He had personally made surveys of several works with accompanying drawings or ground plans with the intention of submitting a brief report on the subject to the Board of Regents of the State University of New York at Albany. It was indeed a "singular coincidence" that he met Squier at Rochester only ten days after having prepared those drawings. Morgan gave Squier the locations of works near Geneva and Cayuga, and they appear to have made a joint survey of a work located near Victor.[10] Morgan provided Squier with Iroquois place-names for some of the sites examined and suggested that he incorporate them into his completed work. He even agreed to contribute an ethnological map of the state of New York, with accompanying text on "aboriginal geography" and the principles of the Iroquois League.[11] The appearance of Morgan's map in Squier's forthcoming Smithsonian monograph received advance notice but never materialized. Because of Squier's diplomatic appointment to Central America in 1849 and his departure for Nicaragua, he and Morgan could never complete the arrangements for the map to be engraved. Francis Parkman regretted that Morgan's map was not incorporated into Squier's finished work,[12] but the map did appear in Morgan's *League of the Iroquois* published the same year.[13]

Squier conducted his investigations in western New York over eight weeks from October to December 1848. The delays and difficulties involved in getting his first Smithsonian monograph printed and distributed prevented him from beginning fieldwork in the spring and summer as he had originally planned. Despite drenching rains, "oceans of mud," and snowstorms that frequently slowed his progress, he located some one hundred enclosures, surveyed about fifty or sixty of those works, excavated a small number of mounds, and collected a large number of artifacts. Following the meanders of river roads and bridle paths, he took careful note of the relationship between natural features and the location of archaeological remains. His fieldwork embraced seventeen western counties but was mostly confined to Jefferson, Monroe, Livingston, Genesee, and Erie Counties. He found a far greater number of remains in these localities than he had at first supposed. Indeed, he learned of the existence of far more works than his funds and the lateness of the season would allow him to examine. He hoped the regents of the State University of New York at Albany might aid in the continuation of his fieldwork the following spring.[14] Unfortunately, that assistance was not forthcoming.

Squier made a preliminary report of his findings before the New-York Historical Society at the conclusion of his fieldwork in December 1848.[15] The Smithsonian Institution accepted the larger work for publication on October 20, 1849, upon the recommendations of Brantz Mayer and William W. Turner of the American Ethnological Society, and *Aboriginal Monuments of the State of New York* made its public appearance in 1851 as part of the second volume of the *Smithsonian Contributions to Knowledge*.[16] The cost of producing the lithographic plates, engravings, and text in this work made it far too expensive to be generally accessible. In order to promote public interest in the importance of the subject, the Smithsonian allowed a more affordable edition to be republished at Buffalo by George W. Derby the same year. The privately printed edition contains a revised text and stereotyped copies of the original plates and engravings. Squier added collateral materials and appended a supplemental or "synoptical view" of the ancient remains in the Mississippi Valley in order to facilitate comparisons between them and those in western New York.[17]

The findings presented in *Aboriginal Monuments of the State of New York* were indeed significant. Squier estimated that between 200 and 250 earthworks had formerly existed in the state as a whole, probably half of which had been obliterated or greatly defaced. Many of the sites he visited had met precisely that fate. "It is a little discouraging and a good deal to be regretted that nearly all the ancient works," he wrote Bartlett during his research, "and many of the most interesting ones, which have for any length of time been exposed to the plough are entirely obliterated or so much broken in upon, that their outlines can no longer be traced. I have just come in time to save a number, which will exist only on paper in a very few years."[18] The enclosures for the most part were smaller than those in Ohio, and their embankments were lower in elevation. Almost all were found in high places such as the bluffs of lake terraces and the summits of limestone ledges. They were occasionally found in the lowlands but were always positioned on a hill, a dry knoll, or the bank of a stream. Almost invariably the earthworks were built near a source of water, and their gateways or openings faced those sources.

This uniformity of position indicated to Squier that such works were built for defensive purposes. Some of the remains had previously been thought to be true circles, ellipses, and accurate squares, suggesting a common origin with works in the Mississippi Valley, but Squier's surveys showed them to have been constructed not on geometric principles but in conformity with the topography of the land on which they stood. It had also been previously assumed that none of the works were found on the first terrace of the central lakes. That belief gave rise to the widely received opinion that works situated on the second and third terraces were built after the lakes had subsided and the first terraces formed, a circumstance suggesting a remote antiquity. In attempting to verify that assumption, Squier found works located indiscriminately upon the first and the upper terraces as well as on the islands of the lakes and rivers of western New York.[19]

Squier found further uniformity in the evidences of habitation at those sites and in the character of associated artifacts. He located numerous excavated pits, or caches, where the former inhabitants had kept stores of parched corn. Caches were invariably dug in the most elevated and dry points of land, and many of them still held bushels of carbonized corn and the remains of bark and slips of wood used to line them. The sites of lodges could yet be traced at many enclosures, where burned stones, charcoal, and ashes were found mixed with animal bones, pottery fragments, broken pipes, and occasional ornaments of beads, stone, bone, and shell. Fragments of quartz and shell-tempered pottery were abundant, while the pipes were mostly made of clay and often fashioned into effigies of animals, the human head, or otherwise ornamented. Most of the artifacts resembled those in use among the Iroquois and other tribes who formerly resided in western New York. Such evidence suggested that these sites were permanently occupied as fortified villages and were of comparatively recent origin.[20] Squier wrote to Bartlett: "I have seen no works yet which I feel disposed or warranted to ascribe to the race of the mounds."[21]

Squier remained enamored of the idea that an earlier and presumably a more skilled people had erected the mounds of the Mississippi Valley. Nowhere is this more apparent than in his discussion of artifacts. In contrast to his enthusiasm for the "higher grade of art" claimed for the Mound Builders of the Mississippi Valley, he did not regard the materials recovered during his investigations in New York of sufficient importance to warrant a detailed notice. He valued the aboriginal art of New York only "as relics of a race fast disappearing, and whose existence will soon be known to history alone. It is to be hoped that, however insignificant they may seem, they may be carefully preserved and treasured for public inspection, in places or institutions designed for the purpose." [22] That wish was partially fulfilled. The Board of Regents of the State University of New York established a State Cabinet of Natural History in 1848 that included a Historical and Antiquarian Collection. The regents issued a circular soliciting the donation of archaeological, ethnological, and historical specimens to the cabinet, and they were interested in the materials recovered during Squier's fieldwork. They purchased those materials from Squier in May 1849 for fifty dollars, when they became a part of the state collection at Albany. [23]

Burial mounds were other key indicators in Squier's investigations. Squier examined several "bone mounds" that were occasionally found in association with earthen enclosures. He attributed those mounds to the practice, common among several groups of North American Indians, of periodically gathering the bones of their ancestors. Bartram, Charlevoix, Brébeuf, Creuxius, and other early observers described the ceremony as the "Festival of the Dead." Charlevoix described the ceremony in detail among the Huron and Iroquois. Families that had lost members during the previous eight years collected their bones and reburied them in a common grave. A small number of other burial mounds in western New York were of a different character than the bone mounds that Squier attributed to the Festival of the Dead. He found that most of those mounds had already been opened under the "idle curiosity" of local inhabitants known as "money-diggers" – those who looted mounds in search of hidden treasure. The money-diggers, said Squier, were "a ghostly race of which, singularly enough, even at this day, representatives may be found in almost every village." Squier was fortunate enough to find a mound on Tonawanda Island in the Niagara River that had escaped their "midnight attentions." He did not think that the mounds he explored in western New York resembled those of the Mississippi Valley (see fig. 5). [24]

Squier directed most of his attention to the earthen enclosures of western New York, which were far more numerous than burial mounds. His surveys of these sites implied a defensive origin. [25] The evidence of long habitation found within many of the enclosures suggested that most were fortified villages. Nothing positive about their date could be affirmed, even though heavy forests covered many. Squier thought that too much emphasis had been placed on this circumstance, since a heavy forest in itself was not necessarily an indication of great age: "We may plausibly suppose that it was not essential to the purposes of the builders that the forests should be removed." Even so, he found trees of one to three feet in diameter growing on the embankments of works. If they had grown there subsequent to the construction

5. Burial mound on Tonawanda Island in the Niagara River. Squier found this mound to be one of the few in western New York that had escaped the "idle curiosity" and "midnight attentions" of "money-diggers"—those who looted local mounds in search of hidden treasure. (From Squier, "The Ancient Monuments of the United States," *Harper's New Monthly Magazine*, May 1860, 737.)

of the works, their origin would date beyond the era of the European discovery in the fifteenth century. He did not, however, regard this circumstance as in any way justifying the inference that the tribes who had built the mounds and earthen enclosures of Western New York were earlier than those found residing in the area by the first European explorers.

Squier saw further evidence of a historic or late-prehistoric origin for these sites in associated artifacts and human remains. The clay pipes, pottery, and ornaments he found in situ were "absolutely identical" to those identifying the village sites occupied by the Cayuga and Seneca in the seventeenth century. Human remains likewise suggested a comparatively recent origin. Squier found cemeteries located near many of the enclosures that contained well-preserved skeletons. Save for the absence of European trade goods, the remains did not essentially differ from skeletal materials found at abandoned Indian villages. Squier concluded that if the earthworks of western New York could be shown to be of ancient origin, they must have been "not only *secondarily* but *generally* occupied by the Iroquois or neighboring and contemporary nations, or else – and this hypothesis is most consistent and reasonable – they were erected by them."

Squier bolstered this hypothesis with historical evidence. In all probability, the Iroquois had erected the embankments of the enclosures as earthen supports for palisades used in fortifying their villages. The disappearance of embankments shortly after contact with Europeans he attributed to the introduction of iron implements that enabled the palisades to be secured in the ground without the need for earthen embankments. Contact with Europeans introduced new forms of warfare after the acquisition of firearms, which no doubt accounted for the absence of palisades at later villages. With the lapse of time, the origin of the earthworks disappeared from the living memories of the Indian peoples whose ancestors had built them.

Squier argued that the manner in which the Iroquois palisaded their early villages, as described in David Cusik's *History of the Six Nations*, for example, undoubtedly applied to the erection of the more ancient embankments examined during his fieldwork. Early accounts describing the stockaded villages of the Iroquois made this conclusion seem all the more plausible. Squier interrogated these sources in support of his opinion that all the earthworks of western New York marked the sites of stockaded villages once inhabited by the Iroquois. Henry Rowe Schoolcraft, Lewis Henry Morgan, Orasamus Holmes Marshall, and Francis Parkman were all conversant in the Iroquois practice of stockading their villages in the seventeenth century. The location and design of the earthworks together with historical documentation that the Iroquois once inhabited stockaded villages satisfactorily explained the origin of the older earthworks examined in the course of Squier's investigations.[26]

The preponderance of archaeological and historical evidence bearing upon this subject led Squier to a conclusion little anticipated when he began his investigations in New York. He had no doubt

> that the earth-works of western New York were erected by the Iroquois or their western neighbors, and do not possess an antiquity going very far back of the Discovery. Their general occurrence upon a line parallel to, and not far distant from the Lakes, favors the hypothesis that they were built by frontier tribes – an hypothesis entirely conformable to aboriginal traditions. Here, according to these traditions, every foot of ground was contested between the Iroquois and the Gah-kwas [either the Erie or the Neutral Indians][27] and other western tribes; and here, as a consequence, where most exposed to attack, were permanent defenses most necessary.[28]

Squier concluded that the antiquities of western New York were significant illustrations of the aboriginal means used by the Iroquois in fortifying their villages. They further established that the Iroquois were more sedentary and agricultural in their habits than previously supposed and that they had occasionally built mounds. He regarded them otherwise as possessing little relevance to "the grand ethnological and archaeological questions involved in the ante-Columbian History of the Continent." He still believed that the elusive Mound Builders of the Mississippi Valley were an earlier aboriginal people whose intellectual and social attainments were superior to the "savage or hunter tribes of North America." The architects of the mounds in the Mississippi Valley, he confidently asserted, had not erected the earthworks and mounds of western New York. More than ever, he was convinced that his search for the origin, migrations, and affinities of the ancient Mound Builders had to be directed southward of the Ohio Valley.

Squier's investigations in western New York also led him to change his earlier opinion regarding the origin and era of the enclosures of northern Ohio. He no longer attributed those works to the Mound Builders but rather thought them to be of comparatively recent date and probably of a common origin with those of western New York.[29] Charles Whittlesey of Cleveland, long a student of the aboriginal remains of northern Ohio, accepted that conclusion. He had no doubt that the earthworks of western New York described by Squier were part and parcel of the system of similar structures found along the southern shore of Lake Erie. Whittlesey always regarded the works in northern Ohio to be of a more recent origin than those in central

Ohio. He further acknowledged that Squier made a strong case for attributing the works in western New York to "the present Indians," which he had not previously believed.[30] Whittlesey must have harbored doubts on that point, however, for in 1868 he changed his mind. He then postulated the presence of a third earth-building people who were distinct from the Indians and the Mound Builders and possibly intermediate in point of time. "Mr. Squier in his 'Antiquities of Western New York' attributes them [the earthworks] to the Indians, but upon grounds that do not seem to me sufficient."[31]

The findings embodied in *Aboriginal Monuments of the State of New York* significantly modify Squier's earlier views on the origin and era of the archaeological remains of northern Ohio and western New York, and they clarify his views on the presumed character of the Mound Builders. Moreover, in reporting these findings be met the same high standards for archaeological inquiry established by *Ancient Monuments of the Mississippi Valley*. In commenting on the large amount of unprofitable and unphilosophical speculation about the origin and purposes of aboriginal remains in New York, for example, he launched what was by then a quintessential refrain:

> Rigid criticism is especially indispensable in archaeological investigations, yet there is no department of human research in which so wide a range has been given to conjecture. Men seem to have indulged the belief that here nothing is fixed, nothing certain, and have turned aside into this field as one where the severer rules which elsewhere regulate philosophical research are not enforced, and where every species of extravagance may be indulged in with impunity. . . . The Indian who wrought the rude outlines upon the rock at Dighton, little dreamed that his work would ultimately come to be regarded as affording indubitable evidence of Hebrew, Phoenician and Scandinavian adventure and colonization in America; and the builders of the rude defenses of Western New York, as little suspected that Celt and Tartar, and even the apocryphal Madoc, with his "ten ships," would, in this the nineteenth century of our faith, be vigorously invoked to yield paternity to their labors![32]

Squier's second Smithsonian work is also important for the content of its elaborate appendix, which is longer than the monograph proper. A good portion of the subject matter is intimately connected with *Ancient Monuments of the Mississippi Valley*, while the remainder elaborates upon the central issues and problems raised in the text of *Aboriginal Monuments*. Here Squier continued to take an enlarged view of his subject by developing cultural analogies between the Old and New Worlds as he had more circumspectly done in *Ancient Monuments*. Those analogies are the connecting links between Squier's

Smithsonian monographs. In making those extended comparisons, however, Squier hastened to note that no connection or common origin between the aboriginal remains of the Old and New Worlds should be inferred. Such similarities were logically explained as "the inevitable results of similar conditions" existing among distinct and widely separated peoples.

> Human development must be, if not in precisely the same channels, in the same direction, and must pass through the same stages. We cannot be surprised, therefore, that the earlier, as in fact the later monuments of every people, exhibit resemblances more or less striking. What is true physically, or rather *monumentally*, is not less so in respect to intellectual and moral development. And it is not to be denied that the want of a sufficient allowance, for natural and inevitable coincidences, has led to many errors in tracing the origin and affinities of nations.[33]

One need not look for common origins and mysterious cultural dependencies to explain the similarities existing between the aboriginal remains of America and those in other parts of the world. This thread of logic runs through all of Squier's early anthropological writings and reflects the developmentalist assumptions of American ethnology in the mid-nineteenth century.

The appendix of *Aboriginal Monuments* also contains Squier's overview of known mound-building practices among existing groups of North American Indians. He drew upon those examples to support his attribution of the mounds in western New York to the bone burials of the Iroquois or their neighbors. He recognized that some of the mounds in the South, like those in New York, were of comparatively recent origin and directly attributable to tribes still residing there in the historic era. Bartram's account of the Florida Indians heaping earthen mounds over the remains of family members in the Festival of the Dead was called to witness as an explanation of their probable origin. Squier also accepted Thomas Jefferson's belief that the burial mounds described in his *Notes on Virginia* were built by recent tribes of Indians, but he regarded the existence of these mounds to be of little importance. He was still unwilling to attribute the vast majority of the mounds in the Mississippi Valley to a similar origin.

> We have no satisfactory evidence that the race of the mounds passed over the Alleghenies; the existence, therefore, of a few tumuli to the east of these mountains, unless in connection with other and extensive works, such as seem to have marked every step of the progress of that race, is of little importance, and not at all conclusive upon this point; especially as

it will hardly be denied that the existing races of Indians did and still do occasionally construct mounds of small size. [34]

Squier was cognizant of the fact that some of the historic North American tribes had at one time built mounds. Nevertheless, he remained convinced that the ancient Mound Builders of the Mississippi Valley were an "extinct" aboriginal group. The venerable Mound Builders were unconnected with any of the historic tribes of eastern North America. The only possible exceptions were the more sedentary Natchez and Florida tribes bordering the Gulf of Mexico. Squier regarded the Florida groups as "the connecting link between the gorgeous semi-civilization of Mexico and the nomadic state of the Northern families," while the Natchez had "assimilated more nearly to the central American and Peruvian stocks [of] the Toltecan family than had the other eastern tribes." [35] He was willing to theoretically accept that some of the southeastern groups might be the descendants of the enigmatic "race of the mounds," but certainly not the Iroquois or, apparently, any other group north of the Gulf.

Not all of Squier's contemporaries concurred with his views on the origin of the earthworks of western New York. Most notably, Lewis Henry Morgan disagreed with his general attribution of "Trench Enclosures" to the Iroquois. "There is no fact in Indian history more certain than that they are not," he wrote Squier in March 1849. [36] Some of those works could be assigned such an origin, but others, he believed, were works of the earlier Mound Builders and not the Iroquois. Morgan accepted the remains at Geneva, Pompey, and Levonia as Iroquoian works of a comparatively recent date. The "Palisade Fortification" near Geneva in Ontario County he identified as a Seneca work, but the presence of bastions indicated that the Seneca had erected the earthwork with the assistance of either the English or the French. Sullivan destroyed the structure during his expedition against the Seneca in 1779. A fragment of a palisade at one of the openings was still above ground when Morgan surveyed the site in 1847, and it was among the items he contributed to the state's Historical and Antiquarian Collection at Albany. Morgan attributed the remainder of the aboriginal remains in New York to the earlier period of the "Mound Builders." Those works marked the presence of "a race, whose name we know not: neither know we the era of their departure." [37]

Morgan interpreted aboriginal art as further evidence of different Mound Builder and Iroquois occupations in New York. He saw two distinct classes of remains and eras. The first class of remains belonged to the pre-Columbian period, or "the era of the 'Mound Builders,' whose defensive works, mounds, and sacred enclosures are scattered so profusely throughout the west." The second class were of a later date and attributable to the Iroquois and to "the fugitive races, who, since the extermination of the 'Mound Builders' have displaced each other in succession, until the period of the Iroquois commenced." Morgan regarded the remains of the Mound Builders as evidence that they possessed "a semi-civilization and considerable development in the art of agriculture." Implements of copper, chert, stone, porphyry, and earthen materials of elaborate and ingenious workmanship identified the former habitations of the Mound Builders apart from their mounds and enclosures. "The fugitive specimens belonging to this period [Morgan's Mound Builder period], which are occasionally found with the limits of our State, are much superior to any of the productions of the earlier Iroquois" (the "earlier Iroquois" were the remote ancestors of the existing Iroquoian groups, in distinction to the more ancient and presumably "semi-civilized" Mound Builders).[38]

Morgan further bolstered his case by drawing on aboriginal traditions. Since the Iroquois had preserved the names of several of their ancient localities, he saw no reason to doubt the veracity of historical traditions as to which works had been built by their ancestors and which had not. When he commenced his studies of Indian lore, he wrote Squier, he looked upon such traditions as mere vagaries. He later changed his mind. The historical traditions of the Iroquois, in contrast to fables designed to merely instruct or entertain, were capable of explication.[39] Morgan elaborated upon that point in *League of the Iroquois*:

> Mingled up with this mass of fable, were their historical traditions. This branch of their unwritten literature is both valuable and interesting. These traditions are remarkably tenacious of the truth, and between them all there is a striking harmony of facts. Any one who takes occasion to compare parts of these traditions with concurrent history, will be surprised at their accuracy, whether the version be from the Oneida, the Onondaga, the Seneca, or the Mohawk. The embellishments gained by their transmission from hand to hand are usually separable from the substance and the latter is entitled to credence.[40]

Squier had no quarrel with the importance that Morgan placed on historical traditions, for no one had a keener interest in collecting them than he. He was more cautious than Morgan, however, when calling upon them to explain archaeological problems. However interesting and important oral traditions were in many particulars, they were not conclusive. Notwithstanding Morgan's faith in Iroquois traditions, Squier saw no evidence of a Mound Builder presence in western New York.

Orsamus Holmes Marshall, another New York antiquarian of the right sort, disagreed with Morgan and agreed with Squier. Marshall saw no evidence of an occupation of western New York earlier than the Iroquois:

There is no satisfactory evidence of the existence in this vicinity, of a race preceding the Indians. The "mound-builders": that mysterious people who once spread in countless multitudes over the valleys of the Ohio, the Mississippi, and their tributaries, never, so far as diligent research has been able to discover, dwelt in this locality. The ancient fortifications, tumuli, and artificial structures that abound in Western New York can all be referred to a later date and a modern race. But at what precise period, and by what particular people they were constructed, are questions which have hitherto eluded the most diligent historical research. The Senecas are equally ignorant on the subject.[41]

The opposing views of Morgan and Marshall epitomize the diversity of opinion on the subject of the Mound Builders in the mid-nineteenth century. In the face of such uncertainty, it is not surprising that Squier's guarded views were received as authority for many years to come. Archaeologists have remained respectful of Squier's pioneering contribution to the archaeology of western New York, despite the incorrectness of certain of his conclusions. The distinction that he and his contemporaries made between the Mound Builders and Indians as distinct "races" was a false dichotomy. What they were actually describing were ethnic, cultural, and chronological differences among prehistoric sites and artifacts. Indeed, the consistent misuse of the term *race* for culture and ethnicity is a problem found throughout the early archaeological literature.

Squier's survey maps and descriptions, by contrast, represent original and enduring contributions to knowledge. William M. Beauchamp's *Aboriginal Occupation of New York* (1900) is respectful of what Squier accomplished as a surveyor with the limited means and time available to him. Later investigators, such as William A. Ritchie, continued to appreciate his efforts. Ritchie credited Squier with having produced survey maps that were in most cases generally reliable. That may sound like damning with faint praise, but in many instances his surveys are the only record of sites subsequently destroyed. As Ritchie further commented,

No serious exception will be taken to his conclusion that the earth-walled structures of western New York were erected by the Iroquois not long before the discovery, although it is now clear that Owasco culture groups, preceding the Iroquois, were the authors of some. His limited experience with New York burial tumuli, however, evidently concealed, even from his experienced eye, the connection with the vastly more numerous Hopewellian mounds of Ohio, in whose exploration he had pioneered.[42]

Squier never resumed his fieldwork in New York. He was entirely without the means to do so, even though he knew of other archaeological sites that the lateness of the season had prevented him from examining.[43] Instead of returning to the field in the spring as he had hoped, he accepted a diplomatic appointment to Nicaragua in April 1849. It would be the antiquities and Indian peoples of Central America that would command his anthropological interests for years to come. Squier would never again be an original investigator of archaeological remains in the United States, but what he accomplished in the field between 1845 and 1849 is truly remarkable. His fieldwork in New York, like his investigations with Davis in Ohio, represents the best of the amateur tradition in American archaeology during the nineteenth century. Squier's investigations in New York were not as comprehensive, as sustained, or as significant as those in Ohio, but they were still systematic and led to important results.

6. The Burden of Proof

American Indian Traditions and the Walam Olum

Squier was one of several writers in the early and mid-nineteenth century to note the importance of the traditions of American Indians in the study of their origin, affinities, and presumed connections. His research initially resulted in the publication of three articles dealing with Algonquian legends and traditions that appeared in Wiley and Putnam's *American Review* in 1848 and 1849.[1] Two of the articles were based on Ojibwa legends, and the third is a more substantive account of the historical and mythological traditions of the Lenape or Delaware Indians based on the Walam Olum ("painted sticks" or "painted record") manuscript of Constantine Rafinesque. While the originality, humor, and romantic allure of these legends greatly appealed to Squier's romanticism and cultural nationalism, Squier the anthropologist argued for their importance as a branch of ethnological inquiry.

The Harvard-educated Ojibwa chief, missionary, and lecturer George Copway (Kah-ge-ga-gah-bowh: "Firm Standing") verbally related to Squier the Ojibwa legend of "Ne-She-Kay-Be-Nais, or the 'Lone Bird' " and the Algonquian tradition of "Manabozho and the Great Serpent." In the Ojibwa tradition related to Squier, Ne-She-Kay-Be-Nais is the daughter of Wha-bon and Me-ge-seek who was taken from the lodge of her parents and transformed into the familiar face on the moon – she is the Ojibwa "Lone Bird." In the traditions of many Algonquian peoples, Manabozho is a cultural hero and protector who engaged in a titanic struggle with the evil Manitou known as the Great Serpent. Squier obtained the migration tradition of the Lenape related in the Walam Olum from Brantz Mayer in 1846. Mayer lent Squier the Rafinesque manuscripts he acquired after Rafinesque's death in 1840, which include both the Walam Olum and Rafinesque's surveys and notes on archaeological sites in Kentucky, Tennessee, and Alabama. Squier's assessment of Rafinesque, his attempt to corroborate the authenticity of the Walam Olum, and his use of Rafinesque's ethnological and archaeological materials are significant not only in terms of his own career but particularly in regard to the controversy that has since surrounded the uncertain origin of Rafinesque's Walam Olum.

Squier's interest in Algonquian traditions represents a significant aspect of his anthropological thought. He saw certain uniformities in these traditions that seemed to link them with the mythological beliefs of other American Indian groups – yet further evidence of the essential unity and distinctiveness of the American race. He was convinced that a comparative study of mythological and historical traditions of aboriginal groups on the American continent would go far toward establishing both their relationship to each other and the rank of the American race within the "scale of human development."[2] If such original materials could be collected, "they would open to the world a new view of the aboriginal mind."[3] Squier saw in American Indian traditions further evidence of parallels in the intellectual development of early peoples throughout the world, and he concluded that there was "not only a wonderful uniformity and concurrence in their elements and more important particulars, but also an absolute identity, in many essential respects, with those which existed among the primitive nations of the old world, far back in the monumental and traditional periods."[4]

Squier's explanation of this "absolute identity" goes to the heart and soul of his anthropological theory. The "predominant" religious ideas of aboriginal America appeared to him to be based on what was usually known as sun worship, but which he thought should more properly be called "the adoration of the powers of Nature." He believed this to be the underlying principle of early religious or mythological systems throughout the world. It was found in aboriginal America in its simplest and most vague forms through all intermediate stages of development. He saw no difficulty in accounting for these similarities "without claiming a common origin for the nations displaying them." Mankind, he noted, was everywhere the same in regard to certain fundamentals of intellectual development. "Alike in the elements of their mental and moral constitutions; having common hopes and aspirations, moved by the same impulses, and actuated by similar motives, is it surprising that there exist among nations of men the most widely separated, a wonderful unity of elementary beliefs and conceptions? All have before them the suggestions of Nature, the grand phenomena of which are everywhere the same; and all from the observance would be apt to arrive at similar results."[5] Similarities in religious symbolism among widely separated and distinct peoples were natural and predictable phenomena. Since the development of a symbolic system to convey abstract religious ideas was a necessity among all nonliterate peoples, the presence in aboriginal America of religious symbols and associated observances that were essentially the same as those that had at one time existed among the peoples of the Old World could be logically explained. Such similarities were entirely attributable to universals in human reasoning. Squier and other ethnologists of the period knew these universals as the "psychic unity" of man.

Squier's interest in Algonquian myths and historical traditions was part of a larger research agenda. He believed he had discovered the underlying principles of the religious and mythological systems of aboriginal groups throughout the American continent, and, indeed, among the early religions of the Old World as well. A systematic and comparative study of those beliefs would, he was certain, demonstrate the psychological unity and distinctiveness of the American race no less conclusively than would its physical characteristics and languages. His research led him to see certain similarities in the diverse religious and mythological systems of aboriginal America. Although the religious beliefs of the North American Indians, the Aztecs, the Central Americans, and the Inca were outwardly different, he perceived them to be rooted in a common set of ideas, related practices, and conventional symbols.

The religious beliefs and legends of the Algonquians included what Squier referred to as the well-defined idea of "a Supreme Unity, a great and beneficent Creator and Preserver." There were also lesser mythological beings who protected humans and who warred against, and usually prevailed over, the evil beings that would do them harm. "Like the pastoral Sabians [sun worshipers] of central Asia, the Algonquians were close observers of nature and its manifestations. In the sun they saw the symbol of that Great Spirit from whom they believed all life preceded." The sun was the home of the Creator and Preserver, the Milky Way the "path of souls" leading to the spirit-land, and the northern lights (aurora borealis) the "dance of the dead."[6] Commonalities in the religious beliefs and traditions of the Algonquian peoples were important in their own right, but they also pointed to themes shared in the belief systems of other American aborigines.

Squier saw further evidence of the psychological unity of the American Indian in the Algonquian tradition of Manabozho and the Great Serpent, who had his parallel incarnation among the aboriginal peoples of Mexico, Columbia, and Peru. "In almost every primitive mythology we find a character partaking of a divine and human nature, who is the beneficent teacher of men, who instructs them in religion and the arts, and who, after a life of exemplary usefulness, disappears mysteriously, leaving his people impressed with the highest respect for his institutions, and indulging in the hope of his final return among them." Such cultural heroes were universal. In India the great teacher and founder of religion appeared as Buddha, in China as Fo-hi, in Persia as Zoroaster, in Egypt as Osiris, in Phoenicia as Taut, and in Greece as Hermes. "In the mythological systems of America, this intermediate demi-god was not less clearly recognized than in those of the old world; indeed, as these systems were less complicated, because less modified from their primitive forms, the Great Teacher appears with more distinctness."[7]

The origin and character of this supernatural being was well defined among the aboriginal nations of Mexico, Columbia, and Peru. Among the ancient Mexicans the great teacher was Quetzalcoatl ("Feathered Serpent"), the son of Tonacatlecoatl ("Serpent Sun") and the principal being of the Aztecs. The Aztecs venerated Tonacatlecoatl through festivals and at the great temple of Cholula. Tonacatlecoatl sent a message to a virgin of Tulan, informing her that it was his desire that she should conceive a son, which she did without knowing any man. An analogous being exists in the traditions of Peru as Manco Capac. Once again he is the son of the sun and the great teacher of Incan religion, government, and art. According to La Vega, the inhabitants of Peru lived a brutish existence before Manco Capac came among them. The sun took pity on them and sent his son Manco Capac and his daughter Mama Cora, who was both the sister and wife of Manco Capac. The sun placed them on an island in Lake Titicaca, which afterward remained a sacred place to the Inca. Manco Capac and Mama Cora eventually left the island in search of a new home. Traveling north they founded the imperial city of Cuzco, where they taught their followers to worship the sun, cultivate the practical arts, and govern themselves and teach others the arts of living. Manco Capac did not leave his people but died a natural death among them. The Inca claimed their descent and sovereignty from him and worshiped his memory in the Festival of the Sun during the summer solstice.

Similar figures appeared in the traditions of North American Indians. According to John Howard Payne, who devoted considerable time and attention to collecting Cherokee traditions and religious customs, the great prophet and teacher of the Cherokee was Wasi. It was he who told the Cherokee of the past since the beginning of the world and he who foretold their future. Wasi instructed the people in their feasts, their fasts, and the ceremonies of their religion. He told them how they were to select their shamans and chiefs and that the people should follow his directions from generation to generation. A tribal elder among the Cherokee was traditionally referred to as a Wasi singer – one who sang or chanted the song of Wasi.[8] Among the Iroquois traditions recorded by Henry Rowe Schoolcraft was that of another great instructor known as Hiawatha or Tarengawagan, from whom they learned the arts of hunting, gardening, and medicine. Hiawatha conveyed to the Iroquois the laws of the Great Spirit, established their forms of government, and consolidated the five tribes into a confederacy before departing from the earth in a white canoe.[9]

The corresponding figure in the cosmological traditions of the Ojibwa was Manabozho, a being known by various dialectal variations of his name. Nanabohzo, Nanabush, Michabou, and Michabozho are among them, while the Recollect friar and explorer Louis Hennepin knew him as Messou. As Nanabush he was the cultural hero of the Ojibwa, as noted by Thomas L. McKenny in his *Sketches of a Tour to the Lakes* (1827) and in John Tanner's *Narrative* of his captivity among the Ojibwa (1830). [10] Most traditions represent Manabozho as the son of a supernatural Manitou and an earthly mother. He was the protector and provider of the people from whom they learned their religion and how to cultivate vegetables. The Potawotomie knew him as Nanaboojoo, who interceded with the Great Spirit in the creation of animals for food and clothing. He taught them to grow the roots and herbs used in their medicinal cures and allowed them to hunt the animals he entrusted to the care of Mesakkummikokwi, the great-grandmother of the human race. [11] Schoolcraft noted in his *Algic Researches* (1839), a study of Algonquian ("Algic") traditions, that the heroic and superhuman exploits of Manabozho assumed a prominent place in Algonquian traditions: "Interwoven with their leading traits are innumerable tales of personal achievement, sagacity, endurance, miracle, and trick, which place him in almost every scene of deep interest that can be imagined." Narratives of his wonderful deeds and personality were often vague or disconnected concerning particulars, but the larger fabric of the tradition of Manabozho was ubiquitous. "Scarcely any two persons agree in all the minor circumstances, and scarcely any omit the leading incidents." [12] The substance of the tradition of Manabozho and the Great Serpent had often been presented, but according to Squier it had not previously been published in its complete and pure form. [13]

Squier's discussion and explanatory notes in "Ne-She-Kay-Be-Nais" and "Manabozho and the Great Serpent" indicate his efforts at compiling the documented traditions of American Indians. The rudiments of two important themes emerge here: sun worship was the basis of the religious systems of American Indian groups throughout the American continent, and the serpent entered widely into their symbolic representations of cosmological ideas. The serpent appeared as a symbol of the sun in Mexico and as an evil force among the Algonquians. The enemies of Algonquians were sometimes referred to as "snakes" or "snake people," whereas the major deity of the Aztecs was Tonacatlecoatl ("Serpent Sun") and his son Quetzalcoatl ("Feathered Serpent"). The symbolic significance of the serpent among the Mexicans, said Squier, more nearly approximated that assigned to it in some Eastern mythologies. "It symbolized the greatest of the gods of the Aztec pantheon, and, in some combination or other, was interwoven with the whole fabric of Aztec superstition." [14] Squier also thought it significant that, according to Edwin James, the Menominee word for the Manitou of the Chippewa translated as Ahwahtoke ("a snake"). The German naturalist and explorer Prince Maximilian of Wied-Neuwied recorded in his *Travels in the Interior of North America* (1843) that the Mandan people also had a tradition of a serpent-being. The Mandan serpent resided in a lake and received offerings from the people. [15] The prominence of serpent symbolism in the mythological systems of American Indians would continue to lay claim to Squier's time and attention for several more years.

Squier lamented that opportunities for studying the historical and mythological traditions of aboriginal America were severely handicapped by the circumstances in which Europeans had encountered and colonized the New World, but the surviving traditions still indicated common ideas. The discovery of America in the fifteenth century was a momentous event that lifted "the veil of night from a vast continent, . . . teeming with a strange people, divided into numberless families, exhibiting many common points of resemblance, yet differing widely in their condition, manners, customs, and civil and social organization." Amid that mosaic of Indian cultures were the so-called Floridian tribes bordering the Gulf of Mexico, which in many respects Squier regarded as one of the most interesting groups of North America. When first known to Europeans, the Florida tribes were more sedentary and agricultural than the Algonquian and Iroquoian groups to their north and east. More importantly for Squier, they possessed a more "systematized religion" and consolidated form of social organization. He considered the Gulf tribes to be "the connecting link between the gorgeous semi-civilization of Mexico and the nomadic state of the Northern families." The Natchez in particular, said Squier, had "assimilated" more nearly to the Central American and the Peruvian stocks of the Toltecan family than any other North American group, and they too, according to Le Page du Pratz, who resided in lower Louisiana from 1718 to 1734, had worshiped the sun. [16]

Further to the south were the ancient Aztecs and their dependents, "nations rivalling in their barbarous magnificence the splendors of the oriental world," who possessed an elaborate but sanguinary religion. The architectural monuments of the Central American groups compared favorably with the best examples of the Old World, while south of the equator the Spanish encountered the Inca, who practiced a "primitive Sabianism" or sun worship. Everywhere he looked in aboriginal American, Squier saw sun worship and its kindred ideas and customs, which he believed were the basis of all American Indian religious conceptions. It was a matter of regret that authentic accounts of the institutions, religions, traditions, and customs of the Mexicans and Peruvians were not made when first known to the Spanish, for it was among those groups that one could expect sun worship to have been the most fully developed. He did not go easy on the Spanish conquerors for the manner in which they treated aboriginal religious ideas and practices in Mexico and Peru. He was particularly critical of the clergy.

> Actuated by a fierce bigotry, and eager only to elevate the symbol of their intolerance over the emblems of a rival priesthood, [Spanish clerics] misrepresented the religious conceptions of the Indians, and exaggerated the bloody observance of the aboriginal ritual, as an apology, if not a justification, for their own barbarism and cruelty. They threw down the high altars of Aztec superstition, and consecrated to their own mummeries the solar symbols of the Peruvian temples. They burned the pictured historical and mythological records of the ancient empire in the public square of Mexico; defaced the sculptures on her monuments, and crushed in pieces the statues of her gods. Yet the next day, with an easy transition, they proclaimed the great personification of the female, or productive principle of Nature, who in the Mexican, as in every other system of mythology, was the consort of the Sun, to be none other that the Eve of the Mosaic record, or the Mother of Christ; they even tracked the vagrant St. Thomas in the person of the benign Quetzalcoatl, the Mexican counterpart of the Hindoo Buddah and the Egyptian Osiris![17]

The tragic consequences of those actions for the study of the religious conceptions and symbols of the Mexicans and Peruvians were immediate and devastating. Permanent doubt had been cast on the Spanish accounts of aboriginal nations.

The circumstances surrounding the exploration and colonization of North America by the English and the French were only slightly more favorable for the recording of unprejudiced and reliable information. Here too, much had been lost. English colonists on the whole took little interest in the native peoples they dispossessed. The Puritan divine Cotton Mather confessed that he was entirely ignorant of when and how the Indians had come to America, but he surmised that the devil had sent them hither to ensure that the gospel would never be propagated among them. Squier credited the Jesuits with being more observant and accurate than other "propagandists of the Catholic faith," but he found their accounts disappointing in matters relating to the history and religion of the Indian peoples with whom they were intimately acquainted. "All treated the religious conceptions and practices and transmitted traditions of the Indians with little regard." The information recorded by the early European observers among the Indians was fragmentary and meager, providing latter-day investigators with but little that would aid their researches into "the history of mind and man."[18]

In his search for the origins of American Indians and a rationale for interpreting the symbolism and design of their archaeological remains, Squier had several guides. Benjamin Smith Barton noted in the second edition of his *New Views of the Origin of the Tribes and Nations of America* (1798) that the traditions of American Indians were often perpetuated in great purity and were entitled to much consideration by those interested in their origin, migrations, and affinities. Barton believed that certain religious beliefs and practices were "extremely permanent" and resistant to change. "The mythology of Asia is still preserved in America" and could be traced with confidence. He attributed the rapid disappearance of aboriginal beliefs in America to constant contact with Europeans, not to the passage of time. Barton lamented that even the most sentimental defenders of American Indians did not recognize the inherent importance of their arts, religions, and moral values, and he regretted that his countrymen did not manifest more zeal in collecting materials concerning their history.[19] Those views fit well into Squier's conceptual universe and his interest in collecting materials relating to the religious conceptions and practices of American Indians.

James H. McCulloh Jr. of Baltimore shared Barton's opinion on the importance of studying the known religious traditions and customs of American Indians. In his well-respected work on the history of aboriginal America, McCulloh observed of the religion of the ancient Mexicans that

> of all researches that most effectively aid us to discover the origin of a nation or people, whose history is unknown or deeply involved in the obscurity of ancient times, none perhaps are attended with such important results, as the analysis of their theological dogmas, and their religious practices. In such matters mankind adheres with greatest tenacity, and though both modified and corrupted in the revolutions of ages, they still preserve features of their original construction, when language, arts, sciences, and political establishments no longer retain distinct lineaments of their ancient constitutions.[20]

The American historian William Hickling Prescott further attested the value of such studies in the first volume of his *History of the Conquest of Mexico*. "The existence of similar religious ideas in remote regions," he wrote, "inhabited by different races, is an interesting subject of study; furnishing as it does, one of the most important links in the great chain of communication which binds together the distant families of nations."[21] The British diplomat and traveler in India James Tod (1782–1835), another of Squier's authorities, stated in his two-volume *Annals and Antiquities of Rajasthan* (1829–32) that "however important may be the study of military, civil, and political history, the science is incomplete without mythological history; and he is little imbued with the spirit of philosophy, who can perceive in the fables of antiquity nothing more than the extravagances of a fervid imagination. Mythology may be considered the parent of History." [22] The observations of Barton, McCulloh, Prescott, and Tod were points of departure for Squier's inquiries into religious conceptions and traditions of the American Indian.

A more significant inquiry centered on the Walam Olum manuscript of Constantine Samuel Rafinesque (1783–1840). The Walam Olum purports to be an authentic migration tradition of the Lenape or Delaware Indians, and discussion of its origin, authenticity, and meaning holds a conspicuous and controversial place in the history of American anthropology. Squier presented his findings on the Walam Olum in a paper read before the New-York Historical Society in June 1848. The account appeared in the *American Review* the following year and was subsequently reprinted in William Beach's *Indian Miscellany* (1877) and Samuel G. Drake's *Aboriginal Races of North America* (1880). [23] Squier's account reproduces Rafinesque's symbols (more or less accurately) for the first two songs, the accompanying Lenape songs, Rafinesque's English translations, and his own paraphrases. Squier gives paraphrases only for Rafinesque's translations of songs three through six. But it is Squier's analysis of the traditions of the Walam Olum and his efforts to corroborate them through other ethnographical and historical sources that are important. He accepted the genuineness of the Walam Olum, but like many investigators who followed him, he was painfully aware of the burden of proof relating to their origin and claims to attention (see fig. 6).

In 1836, in the first volume of his *American Nations*, Rafinesque published his English translations for ten of the Lenape songs of the Walam Olum, the fragment on the history of the Lenape from about 1600 to 1820 obtained from a "John Burns," and the single-page "specimen" of the original Lenape text. But he published none of the mnemonic symbols. The omission of the pictographs probably had more to do with printing costs than anything else. The text was printed, for whatever reason, before he had an opportunity to revise it. That Rafinesque intended to publish the symbols and songs together with his translations is indicated in the text of *American Nations*: "The translation will be given of the songs annexed to each" painted record. "The Walam Olum contained the connected annals of the Lenape nation, he said, and in illustrating that history the "original glyphs or symbols" were to be figured together with the original songs. And in another place he says: "the whole text and all the symbols will be given hereafter." [24] It is unfortunate

SONG II.—THE DELUGE.

1. Wulamo   maskan-ako-anup   lennowak   makowini   essopak.
   Long ago   powerful snake when   men also   bad beings   had become.

2. Maskanako   shingalusit   nijini-essopak   shawalendamep
   Strong snake   enemy   beings had become   became troubled
   ekin-shingalan.
   together hating.

3. Nishawi   palliton,   nishawi   machiton,   nishawi   matta
   Both   fighting,   both   spoiling,   both   not
   lungundowin
   peaceful (or keeping peace.)

4. Mattapewi   wiki   nihanlowit   mekwazuan.
   Less men   with   dead keeper   fighting.

5. Maskanako   gichi   penauwelendamep   lennowak   owini
   Strong snake   great   resolved   men   beings
   palliton.
   to destroy (fight).

6. N'akowa   petonep,   amangam   petonep   akopehella
   Black snake he brought,   monster   he brought   rushing snake water
   petonep.
   he brought.

7. Pehella-pehella,   pohoka-pohoka,   eshohok-eshohok,
   Much water rushing,   much go to hills,   much penetrating,
   palliton-palliton.
   much destroying.

8. Tulapit   menapit   Nanaboush,   maska-boush,
   At Tula (or turtle land)   at that island   Nanabush   (strong)
   owinimokom   linowimokom.
   of beings the grandfather   of men the grandfather.

6. Mnemonic symbols of the Walam Olum. Squier both admired and criticized Rafinesque's archaeological and ethnological researches and the manuscript collections he compiled over an extraordinary career. He was the first scholar to reproduce Rafinesque's symbols, the Delaware text of the accompanying songs, and Rafinesque's English translation of the controversial Walam Olum manuscript. Squier concluded that both internal and collateral evidence indicated that the Walam Olum was an authentic Delaware tradition, but he regretted that Rafinesque had not taken steps to document his sources. (From Squier, "Historical and Mythological Traditions of the Algonquins, with a Translation of the 'Walum-Olum,' or Bark Record of the Lenni-Lenape," *American Review*, n.s., 3 (February 1849): 278–79.)

that the symbols were not published and that only a single specimen of the accompanying Lenape words was given, for "each symbol applies to a verse of many words." Had Rafinesque published the symbols, the Lenape songs, and his translations together as he clearly had planned, the Walam Olum probably would have received more attention than it did before his death in 1840. As it was, however, the tradition of the Walam Olum seems to have gone largely unnoticed until Squier published his account in 1849.

Rafinesque was a prolific writer, and his manuscripts were scattered and passed into several hands after his death. [25] Brantz Mayer of Baltimore acquired Rafinesque's Walam Olum manuscript, his notes and plans relating to archaeological sites in Kentucky, Tennessee, and Alabama, and his manuscript entitled "The Ancient Monuments of North and South America." [26] Mayer, a corresponding member of the American Ethnological Society, took a deep interest in the Squier's investigations and lent him the Rafinesque manuscripts sometime in 1846. [27] Curiously, however, Squier tells us that he came into possession of the Rafinesque manuscripts "through the hands of the executors of the lamented Nicollet" and that among them was the Walam Olum. [28] That statement seems altogether inexplicable unless it suggests, rightly or wrongly, that Mayer had himself obtained the manuscripts from the estate of the scientific explorer Joseph Nicola Nicollet (1786–1843). Possibly Nicollet acquired the manuscripts after Rafinesque's death in 1840 and then Mayer obtained them through Nicollet's executors after 1843. I have been unable to learn anything further regarding Nicollet in that connection.

The five divisions of the manuscript consist of traditions regarding the creation of the world and a deluge, the various migrations of the Lenape or Delaware Indians, and the succession of tribal leaders coming down to the time of contact with Europeans. The traditions are recorded through mnemonic symbols (pictographs) with accompanying phrases or songs in the Lenape language and English. Rafinesque says in the first volume of *American Nations* that he received the original wooden sticks from "the late Dr. Ward of Indiana," who had himself obtained them in 1820 from the Lenape living on the White River in Indiana as a favor for a medical cure. Rafinesque obtained the corresponding songs or chants in the Lenape language from an unidentified source in 1822. [29] But on the first page of the Walam Olum manuscript (which does not appear in *American Nations*) he appears to further confuse the question of provenance when he says that both "This Mpt [manuscript] & the wooden original was procured in 1822 in Kentucky but was inexplicable until a deep study of the Linapi [sic] enabled me to translate them, with explanations." What happened to Dr. Ward of Indiana and the date of 1820? The two statements are not contradictory, however, since Rafinesque did not say that he actually came into possession of the original Walam Olum in 1820, only that Dr. Ward did. It would appear from Rafinesque's ambiguous statements that he did not come into possession of either the painted sticks or the songs until 1822.

Equally obscure is the source of the additional songs that bring the Walam Olum manuscript into the historical period. Rafinesque refers to them as a "Fragment on the History of Linapis since abt 1600 when the Wallam-olum closes." The fragment appears in the manuscript after the symbols and Rafinesque's translations end. They purport to relate the history of the Lenape down to the 1820s, when they were living in Indiana. Rafinesque says only that a "John Burns" translated the fragment into English from the Lenape. It is unclear whether Rafinesque also acquired the Burns translation in 1822 or subsequently, but he translated the songs into English in 1833 with the aid of David Zeisberger's manuscript dictionary of the Delaware language in the library of the American Philosophical Society. He claimed to have copied the symbols from the original wooden sticks, placing his transcriptions of them in two notebooks alongside the accompanying Lenape and English texts of the songs. The notebooks were among the Rafinesque manuscripts lent to Squier by Mayer in 1846.

Though far from being an expert on the Lenape language, Squier accepted the accuracy of Rafinesque's translations to the extent that he was able to verify the traditions embodied in the narrative. He concluded that "there is slight doubt that the original is what it professes to be, a genuine Indian record. The evidence that it is so is however rather internal and collateral than direct." [30] Squier would not be the last scholar to accept the genuineness of the Walam Olum – a somewhat qualified embrace, it will be shown – while also drawing attention to unanswered, and perhaps now unanswerable, questions relating to its origin. He found that the traditions embodied in the Walam Olum for the most part coincided with those still existing in modified form among the Lenape and other Algonquian tribes. The manner in which they were recorded seemed to conform to the system of picture writing used by those groups in recording events and communicating intelligence. The symbols in the Walam Olum did not seem to Squier to be in any way anomalous.

To record chants or songs, various American Indian groups used mnemonic symbols that conveyed abstract ideas about creation, the power of nature, and religion. The Moravian missionary John Heckewelder noted among the Lenape the widespread use of such symbols, which were easily understood by those knowledgeable of their conventional meanings. The use of symbols was so common that members of different tribes were said to be able to read each other's markings. [31] George Henry Loskiel noted in his

History of the Mission of the United Brethren, based on information provided to him by the Moravian missionary David Zeisberger, that the Delaware carved these symbols into pieces of wood, trees, and stones to give warning and as a means of commemorating important events, and that their meaning was universally understood. [32] Heckewelder and other sources corroborate Loskiel's description of how the Lenape used carved symbols to communicate.

The content of the Lenape songs and the style of picture writing recorded in the Walam Olum appeared to Squier to be sufficiently corroborated by similar Algonquian traditions and mnemonic symbols as documented in the writings of Loskiel, George Catlin, Heckewelder, Henry Rowe Schoolcraft, John Tanner, and Edwin James. The *Metai* song of the Ojibwa, for example, contained about thirty symbols and took nearly an hour to sing or chant. James described the manner in which the recorded songs were perpetuated: "They are usually carved on a flat piece of wood, and the figures suggest to the minds of those who have learned the songs, the ideas and the order of their succession." Tribal shamans were entrusted with the teaching of the songs as a means of perpetuating oral traditions similar to those recorded in the Walam Olum. Tanner said it took him more than a year to learn the song for medicine hunting. In the face of such testimony, Squier had no reason to doubt that the songs or chants recorded in the Walam Olum had been perpetuated in like manner. "Admitting then, as we must do upon the evidence, that the Algonquins had the means of imperfectly recording their traditions, songs, etc., we can readily understand how these might be taught by father to son, and perpetuated in great purity through a succession of priests. . . . The very fact that tribal traditions were recorded through the use of conventional symbols and songs would give them a degree of fixedness, and entitles them to a consideration which they would not possess if handed down in a simple oral form." [33]

Squier published the Walam Olum manuscript as an authentic tradition of the Delaware Indians based on what he believed was strong internal and collateral evidence. It appeared to him to be a series of traditional songs recorded in the original mnemonic signs. Someone conversant in the Delaware language had written out the accompanying words from the recitations of the Lenape themselves, precisely as was done with some of the songs recorded by James in his appendix to Tanner's captivity narrative. Unfortunately, we get no help from Rafinesque in answering the question of who had written them down.

Internal evidence suggested to Squier that the Walam Olum was what it claimed to be. That evidence was sufficiently strong, in his estimation, "to settle [the question of] its authenticity." But he did not rely solely on his as-

sessment. He also submitted the Walam Olum manuscript, "without explanation," to the opinion of George Copway, who did not hesitate in declaring
the symbols, the accompanying explanations in Delaware, and the general
ideas transmitted in the narrative to be authentic. Copway also attested to
the fidelity of Rafinesque's translation. Copway, an Ojibwa, was fluent in his
native dialect and knowledgeable of the traditions of the Ojibwa and other
Algonquian groups such as the Lenape, but he was certainly not an expert on
the traditions and language of the Delaware.[34] And yet it is easy to understand
how Squier would accept Copway's opinion – he spoke the Algonquian dialect of the Ojibwa and was quite familiar with the tradition of pictographic
writing. Copway was so impressed with the symbols of the Walam Olum,
moreover, that he appears to have used them as a model for about a dozen of
the pictographs appearing in his *Traditional History and Characteristic Sketches of
the Ojibway Nation* (1850).[35]

The testimony of Heckewelder, Loskiel, Schoolcraft, and James agreed
that all the Algonquian tribes used symbols to record their traditions, while
Copway's opinion regarding the authenticity of the symbols and songs
seemed to Squier to be conclusive. Squier made a reasonable effort to authenticate the Walam Olum based on the available evidence, even though his
effort stopped well short of the lengths to which later investigators would
go in their study of its origin and presumed meaning. As Squier himself said
about presenting his paraphrases of these extraordinary annals to the public,
"I feel I am not obtruding the coinage of a curious idler, nor an apocryphal
record, but presenting [a] matter deserving of attention, and of important
bearing upon many interesting questions connected with the history of our
aboriginal nations."[36] Squier's paraphrases of Rafinesque's translations of
the songs in many instances use forms of expression that were not literal
translations – or even reinterpretations, for that matter – but rather literary
licenses taken in order to make the songs more intelligible and smooth. But
he was confident that his paraphrases on the whole had done no violence to
the original tradition.

For the sake of convenience, Squier divided Rafinesque's Walam Olum
manuscript into two parts. The first part consists of traditions relating to the
creation of the world, and the second part consists of those that could be
regarded as historical. He presented only the first two songs as they appear
in the original as a means of illustrating how Rafinesque had written the
manuscript. Such sampling was suitable to his purposes, but it would be
found wanting by later investigators who would bring forward more complete, accurate, and authoritative editions of the original manuscript.

The Walam Olum embodies several religious concepts that further affirmed Squier's assumptions about the underlying principles of all native religions. In the first song the idea of a "Supreme Unity" (a good, infinite, and eternal Creator) stood boldly forth, a conception that some might regard as a comparatively late engraftment of a Christian idea upon Algonquian tradition. Squier conceded that contact with Christian missionaries had probably influenced their conceptions, but if so it was merely enlarging and modifying a preexisting belief. Early travelers and missionaries offered conclusive evidence that the idea of a supreme Creator of the universe was aboriginal in its origin. Loskiel noted the prevalence of the belief in a single God who had created the universe, controlled the elements, and provided the earth's bounty.[37]

The Creator or Supreme Being was known among various Algonquian groups as Kitchi-Manitou or Gitchy-Monedo (the Supreme and Good Being). Kitchi-Manitou was superior to the evil being known as Mitchi-Manitou or Mudje-Monedo. The bad Manitou also possessed great power, although he was inferior to the good and almighty Creator. He was placated with offerings and sacrifices so that his anger and evil could be avoided. The powers of the evil Michi-Manitou, according to Jonathan Carver, were entirely earthbound and did not follow into the future life.[38] The bad Manitou in the Walam Olum was the creator of flies, gnats, and all annoying insects. "While the symbol of the Good Spirit was the Sun, that of the Evil Spirits was the Serpent, under which form he appears in the tradition of Manabozho and the Great Serpent."[39] In Squier's estimation, the identification of serpents as evil beings and the specific mention of Nanaboush (another name for Manabozho) lent further credence to the Walam Olum's claims for authenticity.

The Walam Olum's specific allusion to the turtle was not entirely clear to Squier, but he noted that the turtle figured prominently in Algonquian mythology and reviewed the available supporting evidence. Both Pierre-François Charlevoix and Louis Hennepin observed that the Ojibwa had a tradition that the mother of the human race, after falling from heaven, seated herself on the back of a turtle. Around the turtle and the great mother, the earth gradually formed.[40] Alexander Henry observed that the Ojibwa regarded the Great Turtle as a spirit being who never lied, and he gives an account of one of their ceremonies dedicated to the Great Turtle. The island of Michilimakanac (literally, "the Great Turtle") was believed to shelter the spirit of the Great Turtle, probably because a large hill near the center of the island was thought to resemble a turtle's back.[41] Heckewelder observed that the Turtle tribe of the Delaware claimed a superior position among other Delaware groups because of its association with the Great Turtle who bore the earth on its back. He further says that earthquakes were attributed to the movements of the Great Turtle.[42] The combined testimony of those authorities seemed to Squier to corroborate the authenticity of the Walam Olum – it made the right associations.

Squier was no less intrigued with the historical part of the tradition relating to Lenape migrations. The details concerning the Delaware migration across the Mississippi River, their encounter with the strange people known as the Tallegwi (or Allegwi), their protracted war with them, and the final exile of the Tallegwi to the south generally coincided with traditions known to have existed among the Delaware. "It may be suggested," said Squier, "that the account of the second migration, across frozen waters, is so much in accordance with popular prejudice, as to the mode in which the progenitors of the American race arrived in America, that it throws suspicion on the entire record. It is not impossible, indeed, that the original tradition may have been slightly modified here, by the dissemination of European notions among the Indians."[43] And yet he hastened to note that a tradition of the northern Ojibwa related by Alexander McKenzie generally corresponded with the Delaware idea of an icy crossing into a new land. "The Indians [Ojibwa] say that they originally came from another country, inhabited by a wicked people, and had traversed a great lake, which was shallow, narrow and full of islands, where they suffered great hardships and much misery, it being always winter, with ice and deep snows. . . . They describe the deluge when the waters spread over the whole earth, except the highest mountain, on the top of which they were preserved."[44]

The theory that the Indians had come to America from Asia across the Bering Strait was well established by the mid-nineteenth century, but speculation in this regard dated from a much earlier period.[45] Samuel Foster Haven speculated in 1856 that linguistic and physiological evidence indicated that American Indians were of great antiquity and probably Asian in their origin. "With all their characteristics affinities are found in the early condition of Asiatic races," he wrote, "and a channel of communication is pointed out through which they might have poured into this continent before the existing institutions and national divisions of the parent country were developed."[46] Haven did not mention the Bering Strait by name, but it had been recognized as the most logical route from Asia to the American continent since Captain Cook discovered the narrowness of the strait between Siberia and Alaska on his final voyage in 1778. Europeans did not discover the Bering Strait until 1728, but José de Acosta speculated on the existence of polar land bridges connecting the continents as early as 1590 in his *Historia Natural y moral de las Indias*.[47]

Squier regretted, as would a long train of scholars after him, that the circumstances under which the Walam Olum was found, transcribed, and translated by Rafinesque could not be authenticated beyond the shadow of doubt. He recognized that in the absence of such an explicit account, the authenticity of the Walam Olum as an aboriginal record would always be an open question. Rafinesque's failure to provide such important details and his tendency toward what Squier called "carelessness and often extravagant assumptions" has cast permanent doubt on the manuscript's actual origin. "Still, upon neither of these grounds may we reject these records. As already observed, they have the internal evidence of genuineness, and are well supported by collateral circumstances."[48]

It was known, for example, that the Delaware and other Algonquian groups used symbolic signs and songs as a means of perpetuating historical traditions like those found in the Walam Olum. As Loskiel observed,

> The Delawares delight in describing their genealogies, and are so well versed in them, that they mark every branch of the family with the greatest precision. They also add the character of their forefathers: such an one was a wise and intelligent counselor; a renowned warrior, or a rich man, etc. But though they are indifferent about the history of former times, and ignorant of the art of reading and writing, yet their ancestors were well aware that they stood in need of something to enable them to convey their ideas to a distant nation, or preserve the memory of remarkable events. To this end they invented something like hieroglyphics, and also strings and belts of wampum, etc.[49]

The similarity between the Delaware traditions recorded in the Walam Olum and those existing among other Algonquian groups made that document appear less anomalous and suspect to Squier than it would otherwise be. But that was particularly true in the case of the Delaware concerning their contest with the Tallegwi. As Squier noted: "The name of this people is still perpetuated in the word *Alleghany*, the original significance of which is more apparent, when it is written in an unabbreviated form, *Tallegwi-henna*, or *Tallegwi-hanna*, literally 'River of the Tallegwi.'"[50] The Delaware or Lenape word *Allegheny* referred to the Ohio River and was still used as the designation of the northern and principal tributary of the Ohio River. The fact that Heckewelder recorded the traditional account of the contest between the Lenape and the Tallegwi added further testimony to the concurrence between the events chronicled in the Walam Olum and those documented independently of Rafinesque. The possibility that Heckewelder's earlier account had inspired Rafinesque and had been engrafted by him upon the narrative of the

Walam Olum did not seem to have overly concerned Squier as it would later skeptics.

Heckewelder recorded a Lenape migration legend in his account of the history and customs of the Lenape that appeared in the *Transactions of the American Philosophical Society* in 1819.[51] The details in his account differed from those in the Walam Olum in some particulars, Squier noted, but he was inclined to give priority to the tradition as given in the Walam Olum because it was more simple and consistent. The details related by Heckewelder generally correspond with those found in the Walam Olum, but he does not mention the existence of the Walam Olum glyphs or songs. Squier gives condensed quotations from Heckewelder's "diffuse account" of that tradition, omitting the part relating the Delaware's wars with the Cherokee. Since Rafinesque was intimately familiar with Heckewelder's account, one cannot rule out the possibility that he simply used the tradition as the basis of the more elaborate narrative of the Walam Olum. The Heckewelder account does not validate the authenticity of symbols or songs in the Walam Olum; it only supports the idea that a portion of the migration tradition related in the Walam Olum existed among the Lenape. Rafinesque's mnemonic symbols, his translations of the accompanying songs, and his failure to adequately document the provenance of the symbols and songs are still problematic.

The Lenape migration tradition related by Heckewelder derives the Lenape from a distant western country where they resided for many hundreds of years. Their eastward migrations occur over a long but indeterminate period of time, eventually bringing them to the Mississippi River. After crossing the Mississippi, they encounter a very powerful people who live in large towns and who call themselves the Tallegwi or Talligewi. A Colonel John Gibson, whom Heckewelder credits with speaking several Indian dialects, was of the opinion that they were actually called Alligewi. It is unclear from Heckewelder's account whether Alligewi was the name given them by the Lenape or was rather what the people called themselves. The Tallegwi or Alligewi, as the case may be, were said to have built defensive entrenchments or "fortifications." The Lenape and their allies the Mengwe (Iroquois) go to war with the Alligewi, and after many years they drive them southward down the Mississippi. Given Squier's investigations of earthworks in Ohio and New York, it is curious that he makes no comment on the fact that the Tallegwi were said to have built defensive entrenchments. His silence is even more curious in the light of the fact that one of his most influential mentors, Samuel George Morton, thought it likely that the Alligewi of Delaware tradition were the Mound Builders of the Mississippi Valley, who had been driven southward by groups of Iroquois and Algonquians.[52]

Squier was deeply impressed by the fact that the traditions of almost all the tribes on the Atlantic coast allude to an earlier migration from the west. John Lawson recorded the tradition among the Indian peoples of North Carolina (he did not say which ones) in his account of his travels through that colony published in 1709: "When you ask them whence their Fore-Fathers came, that first inhabited the Country, they will point to the westward and say, *Where the Sun sleeps, our Forefathers came thence.*" [53] The Natchez, who Squier thought more nearly resembled the Central American and Peruvian groups of a presumably Toltecan origin, informed Antoine Simone Le Page Du Pratz that they had formerly lived "under the sun" to their southwest. William Bartram reported that the Creek had formerly lived west of the Mississippi but moved east after having a dream that told them they were to travel to the country where the sun rises. The Cherokees had a similar tradition. They believed that countless years ago all of the Indians traveled a great distance until they came to a great body of water, at which point one part of them continued north and the other south. [54] The concurrence of Indian traditions regarding a western origin and migration seemed to lend further credence to the veracity of the Walam Olum. Though differing from other traditions in its remarkable amount of detail, it agreed with them in general. "Whatever their historical value," said Squier, "they posses the highest interest, as coming to us through the medium of a rude system of representation, which may be taken as the first advance beyond a simple oral transmission of ideas." [55]

Schoolcraft took a different view of the Walam Olum and became the first in a long line of writers who expressed skepticism about its genuineness as an aboriginal record. His *Algic Researches* had established his authority on the subject. He read Squier's "Historical and Mythological Traditions of the Algonquins" with attentive curiosity, and in a long and important letter to Squier he critically commented on the alleged significance of the Walam Olum and on Squier's discussion of its symbols. [56] Schoolcraft expressed regret that such a record should have passed into the hands of Rafinesque, a man "who spoiled, *historically and scientifically,* everything he touched." While Schoolcraft was far less certain than Squier of the Walam Olum's "absolute historical value," he admitted that it generally corresponded with the Algonquian traditions and picture writing he had himself recorded from bark rolls and tabular pieces of wood known as song boards. He was less impressed with Rafinesque's explanation of the Walam Olum's symbols than Squier. "They fail in fullness and point," he noted, "and appear to lack the acquaintance with the Olum idiom, and the system of pictorial interpretation, which must be supplied by induction and memory."

Schoolcraft had nowhere been able to find historical records with "the extent and continuity" of those presented in the Walam Olum. He could not cite a single instance, with the possible exception of the Dighton rock, when known Algonquian records attempted to perpetuate traditions of more than one or two centuries' duration, while most went back no further than fifty years. In the ideographic and mnemonic writing with which Schoolcraft was familiar, the aboriginal writer frequently recorded but a single event: a battle, the deeds of a brave warrior or hunter, the number of scalps taken in a raid, or the number of animals killed on a hunt. More commonly they recorded ritualistic medicine, hunting, and war songs. The remarkable series of events recorded in the Walam Olum were anomalies that could only be accepted with great caution. Some of the symbols were also problematic. The symbols for the sun and moon were common, but Schoolcraft had never seen its triangle and combinations before. He attributed these anomalies to Rafinesque's eccentricities: "It is not improbable that Mr. Rafinesque was better acquainted with the doctrines of Zoroaster, and the early oriental nations of a triune power, than the ancient Delawares, to whom these particular figures are ascribed."

Schoolcraft saw nothing in the Walam Olum that would carry the date of its recorded events beyond the introduction of Christianity among the Delaware by the Moravian missionaries in the eighteenth century. In fact, he regarded that event as the probable inspiration for much of the Walam Olum's content, suggesting that it may have represented an idealization of a "golden age" in their remote past. It was abundantly evident that when Christianity was introduced to the Delaware they saw allegories in their own traditions that were similar to the biblical account of creation and the deluge. The Walam Olum was probably a mixture of Delaware traditions and Christian teachings. Since few Indian converts ever became so completely Christianized as to completely abandon their traditional beliefs, it was not difficult for Schoolcraft to comprehend how readily the biblical accounts of Jonah and Noah could be seen as the counterparts to the exploits of their own Manabozho. "In this manner, and upon the banks of the Muskingum or White River of Indiana, I think the Walam Olum was drawn." How much Rafinesque had to do with the transcription of the original sticks and who had provided the interpretation of its symbols were unanswered questions that alone could determine the historical significance of the Walam Olum, notwithstanding the enthusiasm that Squier exhibited in bringing the Walam Olum before the public.

The next scholar to critically investigate the Walam Olum was Daniel Garrison Brinton, professor of ethnology and archaeology at the Academy of Natural Sciences of Philadelphia, whose career contributed significantly to the professionalization of American anthropology.[57] Brinton embodied the results of his own inquiries into the origin, authenticity, and meaning of the Walam Olum in The Lenape and Their Legends (1885). He did so, however, with not a little trepidation. "Not without hesitation do I send forth this volume to the learned world," he wrote. "Regarded as an authentic memorial, the original text of the WALAM OLUM will require a more accurate rendering than I have been able to give it; while the possibility that a more searching criticism will demonstrate it to have been a fabrication may condemn as labor lost the pains that I have bestowed upon it." But at least he was confident that his own inquiry would allow his successors to better determine "its true positions in American archaeology, whatever that may be."[58] His 262-page investigation of the subject was nothing if not thorough.

Brinton acquired the Walam Olum notebooks from the Mayer family sometime between 1879 and 1885 and deposited them in the Museum of the University of Pennsylvania. They are today part of the Daniel G. Brinton Papers in the Van Pelt Library of the University of Pennsylvania. His account of the Walam Olum contains the symbols, the complete text (except for the fragment translated for Rafinesque by John Burns), and a new translation and inquiry into its authenticity. He made his translation with the assistance of "several educated native Delawares" (Rev. Albert Anthony, Rev. John Kilbuck, and Chief Gabriel Tobias), all of whom agreed that the Walam Olum manuscript was authentic, even if problematic in certain particulars of native syntax.[59] Brinton concluded that the Walam Olum manuscript was "a genuine native production, which was repeated orally to some one indifferently conversant with the Lenape language, who wrote it down to the best of his ability." As an aboriginal record it could claim neither antiquity nor linguistic purity, but it could be accepted as "an authentic modern version" of ancient Lenape traditions that had been influenced by European teachings. The narrator of the Walam Olum was most likely a shaman or chief who had spent his life in the Lenape villages of Ohio and Indiana, someone who had been influenced by Christian ideas but wanted to preserve "the pagan rites, legends, and myths of his ancestors." Certain lines and passages of the Walam Olum were probably "repeated in the archaic form in which they had been handed down for generations."[60]

As for the crucial question of whether the Walam Olum was a forgery by Rafinesque, Brinton concluded that it was not. "It is necessary to ask and to answer this question, though its seems, at first sight, an insult to the memory of the man to do so." But Rafinesque's character and reputation invited the question, for "an air of distrust and doubt shadowed Rafinesque's scientific reputation during his life, and he was not admitted on a favorable footing to the learned circles of the city where he spent the last fifteen years of his life. His articles were declined a hearing in its societies; and the learned linguist, Mr. Peter Stephen Duponceau, whose specialty was the Delaware language, wholly and deliberately ignored everything by the author of 'The American Nations.' "[61] Brinton was too critical and careful a scholar to accept Rafinesque's assertions at face value, but his textual analysis of the Walam Olum had at least convinced him of its authenticity.

Brinton agreed with Squier that the Walam Olum was authentic, but he criticized him for publishing a careless copy of Rafinesque's text and mnemonic symbols. Squier had omitted words, had made no attempt to determine the accuracy of Rafinesque's translations, and had reproduced imperfect facsimiles of symbols, in several instances even reversing them. How many of the discrepancies in the symbols were attributable to errors in stereotyping during the printing of Squier's article or to mistakes made by Squier during transcription is unknown. [62] As a critical study of the Walam Olum, however, Brinton regarded Squier's article to be of little worth. [63] Brinton was certainly justified in identifying the discrepancies found in Squier's transcriptions, but his assertion that his article was of little worth was both self-serving and misleading. Brinton passes over in silence Squier's attempt to compile corroborative evidence from other sources, even though Brinton accepted the document as an authentic Lenape tradition based on some of the same grounds earlier taken by Squier. Brinton's inquiry into the authenticity and meaning of the Walam Olum went far beyond anything attempted by Squier, but it is not without problems of its own.

Brinton's account omits the fragment of the tradition translated for Rafinesque by John Burns, which is present in the published accounts of both Rafinesque and Squier. Brinton omitted the fragment because it had no Lenape text and because nothing was known of John Burns. Even if the fragment was reasonably authentic, Brinton did not think it had any historical value. And yet the fragment is what brings the narrative into the historic era. It is the only part of the Walam Olum manuscript, as has been noted, that admits of some direct corroboration from historical sources.[64] That omission was unfortunate, for it opened Brinton to criticism for an otherwise substantive work. Brinton's *Lenape and Their Legends* is still worth reading as a study of the history and culture of the Lenape quite apart from the conclusions he arrived at concerning the authenticity of the Walam Olum – a saving grace to be certain – but even those are no worse for the comparison. Both Brinton and Squier found much in the traditions of the Walam Olum to recommend them to the attention of scholars, but Brinton's labors are particularly noteworthy.

As substantive as Brinton's inquiry was, it pales in comparison to the 379 pages of *Walam Olum, or Red Score: The Migration Legend of the Lenni Lenape or Delaware Indians*, published by the Indiana Historical Society in 1954. *Walam Olum or Red Score* was the fruit of a twenty-year research project funded by Eli Lilly, with contributions by Glenn A. Black, Lilly, George K. Neumann, Joe E. Pierce, Carl F. Voeglin, Ermine W. Voeglin, and Paul Weer. The work provided a new translation of the songs by Carl F. Voeglin, photographically reproduced the Walam Olum manuscript in its entirety, and presented new linguistic, historical, archaeological, ethnological, and physical anthropological evidence bearing on the supposed authenticity and meaning of the tradition. It remains the most critical and authoritative work on the Walam Olum, notwithstanding negative judgments as to its intrinsic worth by its critics. Like Brinton and Squier before them, the research team accepted the genuineness of the Walam Olum, but in the final analysis they could not establish its authenticity beyond a reasonable doubt. Nor has anyone since.

Archaeological evidence casts further doubt on Rafinesque's Walam Olum as a genuine aboriginal record. The pictographs are in no way comparable to the figures found on the stone carvings or petroglyphs found in Lenapehoking, the traditional homeland of the Lenape. The archaeological record in New Jersey and eastern Pennsylvania does not support the idea of a new aboriginal group's sudden appearance at a certain point in time as related in the migration tradition of the Walam Olum. The historic Lenape appear to have evolved locally from ancestral groups that lived in the region for many thousands of years. Genetic, linguistic, and archaeological evidence indicates that American Indians originated in central Asia and migrated to the American continent via the Bering Strait, which supports Rafinesque's theory of how the Lenape and other Indian groups originally arrived on the American continent. But it would have to be assumed that the traditions of the Walam Olum refer to the arrival of the Paleolithic ancestors of the Lenape in order to account for the vast amounts of time necessary for Lenape culture to have developed in situ in New Jersey and Pennsylvania with no apparent break in the archaeological record. That assumption does not seem warranted based on available archaeological evidence.[65]

Further compounding the problem of establishing the authenticity of the Walam Olum is that fact that the original painted and inscribed sticks, or song boards, have never been found. There is, in fact, no evidence whatsoever that they ever existed except for Rafinesque's passing mention of them. So far as is known, Rafinesque first mentioned their existence in a letter written in December 1834 in a supplement to his essay on the grammar of Algonquian languages submitted in consideration of Prix Volney in linguistics. Rafinesque explicitly states in that letter that the painted tablets were at Philadelphia (presumably in his possession but possibly that of someone else). "There is in Philadelphia among several fragments of Neobagan [Ojibway] and Wampum figures . . . a manuscript on tablets of cedar wood the sacred tree of the Linnique [Lenape] peoples." The tablets offered "new philological and also graphic materials" for the study of the American languages. "The name of the manuscript merits attention, it is WALLAM OLUM."[66]

Clinton Alfred Weslager has shown that the Maryland Historical Society's records indicate that Brantz Mayer, who came into possession of the Walam Olum manuscript after Rafinesque's death, deposited some nondescript bark records in the holdings of the society that he withdrew in 1875. It is only speculation based on circumstantial evidence that those bark records were the painted records of the Walam Olum. It is a moot point, however, since the bark records that Mayer withdrew from the Maryland Historical Society have never been found, nor were they listed among the items in Mayer's estate records in 1879.[67]

It is doubtful that Rafinesque's painted records were ever in Mayer's possession, for if they had been he most certainly would have given them to Squier when he loaned him the Walam Olum manuscript. The fact that he did not do so and that both Mayer and Squier are silent as to their existence suggests that the original painted records – assuming that they once existed and were not a forgery – were lost by 1846 if not before. It is difficult to understand why Rafinesque would not have taken steps to ensure the survival of the original symbols, for the uncertainty surrounding the origin of the Walam Olum tradition and the painted sticks has cast permanent doubt on its authenticity. The only possible explanation is that Rafinesque never had the originals in possession, or only did so long enough to make transcriptions of them. Under that assumption, the originals may well have remained in the possession of his mysterious Dr. Ward or someone else.

There is, of course, no way of determining whether Mayer's birch-bark records were Rafinesque's Walam Olum tablets without seeing the originals, the whereabouts of which are also unknown. But the presumptions are decidedly against their being one and the same. Rafinesque said in his supplemental letter to the Prix Volney Committee that the symbols of the Walam Olum were painted and inscribed on tablets of cedar wood, not on birch bark. It is also unlikely, if not inconceivable, that Mayer would not have taken pains to both identify and preserve the wooden tablets of the Walam Olum if he ever had them in his possession, and there is simply no evidence that he ever did. Mayer was an accomplished scholar and well aware of the issues Squier raised about the authenticity of the Walam Olum in the *American Review*. Even though Squier accepted its genuineness, he had not done so uncritically. Having lent the Walam Olum manuscript to Squier in 1846, Mayer most certainly would have taken steps to further legitimize its genuineness by preserving the original symbols upon which the songs were allegedly based. It seems unlikely that the unidentified birch-bark records that he deposited and then removed from the Maryland Historical Society in 1875 were those of the Walam Olum.

There are those who still argue, as Squier did before them, that there is compelling circumstantial evidence supporting the authenticity of the Walam Olum. Charles Boewe, after a lifetime of painstaking research into the life of Rafinesque, concluded that it was not a hoax: "He did not invent it – rather, he was pleased to see it so closely paralleled in Heckewelder's account – and he believed in its essential veracity himself. Yet, until reliable correlative evidence appears – evidence from someone contemporaneous with Rafinesque – there always will be doubts so long as his is the only testimonial available."[68] Squier would have agreed with that opinion completely, but the question of Rafinesque's character and motives still begs to be addressed. Was he a dishonest charlatan whose conscious intent was to misrepresent? Is the Walam Olum a pure hoax after all? Some scholars have answered that question in the affirmative and some in the negative. August C. Mahr, for example, defended Rafinesque's integrity in the *American Anthropologist* in 1957. Mahr argued that the text of the Walam Olum, far from being a forgery, was written by Rafinesque as it was related to him by a Unami (Lenape) informant.[69] But that confident assertion is far from a majority opinion.

Nor does the fact that similar pictographic records existed among earlier and contemporary Algonquian groups preclude the possibility that those in the Walam Olum are forgeries. Squier had been too impressed with such correspondences and not sufficiently skeptical of the possibility that Rafinesque copied the into the Walam Olum. After all, Rafinesque was well aware that such records existed and had studied them carefully. David Oestreicher, who has delved the deepest into Rafinesque's sources, has determined that the symbols in the Walam Olum are hybrid compounds drawn from an eclectic array of sources, not all of which are American Indian in origin. The symbols of the Walam Olum bear the closest resemblance to pictographs on the bark records used in the Midewiwin ceremonies of the Ojibwa. Indeed, the Midewiwin pictographs reproduced in the appendix of Tanner's captivity narrative appear to have been one of Rafinesque's sources.[70] Squier also noted those similarities but thought they strengthened rather than weakened the Walam Olum's claims to authenticity.

Notwithstanding lingering doubts about the authenticity of the Walam Olum, there are still those who accept it for what it claims to be – an authentic

Lenape migration tradition. Some of the Delaware have come to accept it as authentic, while other Delaware and Munsee groups have rejected its validity because they had never heard the Walam Olum mentioned by their parents or tribal elders. [71] Those outside the discipline of anthropology have tended to be less cautious and critical in embracing the Walam Olum. One student of American poetry described it as an ancient saga of classic proportions, "possibly as great as the Iliad."[72] The Walam Olum has been published in anthologies of American Indian poetry, literature, and folklore as an authentic chronicle of the Lenape without further qualification or critical commentary. One compiler of American Indian literature called it "the Bible and Aeneid of the Delawares" and "the closest thing we know of in Indian Literature to the European epic." [73] For some enthusiasts, embracing the Walam in unqualified terms appears to be more an act of faith than anything else. Accepting its claims to attention at times seems tantamount to redressing grievances and expatiating guilt for past prejudices and indiscretions committed against American Indians by Euro-Americans. [74] Those who are convinced of its fraudulence, meanwhile, must continue to combat the romantic cachet and cultlike reverence that often attaches to the Walam Olum.

William W. Newcomb took the position that the Walam Olum may be an authentic Lenape tradition, but if so it dates to a period subsequent to contact with Europeans. It may be an alteration of a traditional folk belief that reflects the far-reaching changes at work among the Lenape Indians in the early nineteenth century. Under this view, the Walam Olum may have been the expression of a nativistic revival among Lenape traditionalists who were trying to maintain or resurrect part of their rapidly vanishing culture. [75] The most recent textual analysis of the Walam Olum and investigation of Rafinesque's sources, however, find that its claims to genuineness are entirely wanting. After years of linguistic and historical research, Oestreicher has concluded that the Walam Olum is unquestionably a forgery by Rafinesque. [76] He suggests that Rafinesque fabricated the Walam Olum in order to support his previously stated theory about the origins of the American Indians. In his "Ancient Annals of Kentucky" (1824), Rafinesque stated that the Lenape had reached the American continent by crossing the Bering Strait on ice. Continuing an intermittent migration eastward, they at length crossed the Mississippi River into the land of the "Talegan" (i.e. Tallegwi). [77]

A common concern in all of these studies is identifying Rafinesque's "Dr. Ward." Brinton attempted to do so but found no such person in the medical records of Indiana that would allow him to make the necessary connection. He did, however, find a Ward family residing in the neighborhood of Cynthiana, Kentucky. That same family, moreover, had resided there in 1820, the year in which Rafinesque's Dr. Ward had acquired the original Walam Olum from the Lenape. A member of that family had also been a friend of Rafinesque's and appears to have shared with Rafinesque what was probably nothing more than a passing interest in archaeology. Rafinesque says of him in his *A Life of Travels and Researches:* "My friend, Mr. Ward, took me to Cynthiana in a gig, where I surveyed other ancient monuments." [78] But the suggestion that Rafinesque's "Mr. Ward" and his "Dr. Ward" are one and the same is problematic: the Ward from Cynthiana was not identified as being a physician, nor was he from Indiana. Both the time period and the association with Rafinesque in Kentucky are suggestive but inconclusive. Even so, Brinton made a huge leap of faith. Understandably excited at the discovery of a "Mr. Ward" in Rafinesque's autobiography, he goes on to say: "It was there (at Ward's house), no doubt, that he [Rafinesque] copied the signs and the original text of the Walam Olum." [79] That surmise is entirely circumstantial and conjectural.

Paul Weer conducted an even more thorough investigation into the identity of the "late Dr. Ward" as part of the research team that presented its findings in *Walam Olum, or Red Score*. Weer concluded that Rafinesque's Dr. Ward was Dr. John Russell Ward, who resided at Carlisle, Kentucky, even though Rafinesque said he was from Indiana. John Russell Ward lived at Carlisle until 1829, when he moved to Fulton, Missouri. He died there in 1834 and thus qualifies as a candidate for being the "late Dr. Ward." [80] William Barlow and Davis O. Powell, however, have more recently suggested that circumstantial evidence identifies Dr. Malthus A. Ward as the probable source of Rafinesque's Walam Olum. [81] Dr. Malthus A. Ward practiced medicine in the White River Valley in 1820, whereas there is no evidence that John Russell Ward ever lived in Indiana. Dr. Malthus A. Ward was at least at the right place at the right time, but he lived until 1863 and could not have been "the late Dr. Ward" mentioned by Rafinesque in 1836.

Charles Boewe presents two candidates for Rafinesque's "Dr. Ward." He might have been William Ward, a medical student at Transylvania College from 1823 to 1826 who graduated with a medical degree on February 20, 1826. But both William Ward and John Russell Ward were Kentuckians with no known connection with Indiana. There was also a Rev. John Ward of Lexington, who married the sister of Rafinesque's best friend and promoter, John D. Clifford. [82] Either one of these Wards could be the Ward in question, even though they too were residents of Kentucky and not of Indiana. The identity of Rafinesque's Dr. Ward thus remains unproven. It is curious, even tragic, that Rafinesque did not make an effort to fully identify the respective sources of the symbols and songs of the Walam Olum or to preserve the original pictographs that came into his possession. He must have anticipated the skepticism that would arise from the lack of unambiguous and unequivocal evidence supporting his transcriptions of the symbols and translations of the songs.

Rafinesque once likened his ethnological inquiries to the investigations of Jean-François Champollion, the celebrated decipherer of Egyptian hieroglyphics. He published two letters to Champollion in his short-lived *Atlantic Journal* in 1832, where he declared in the first letter that "I am going to follow in your footsteps on another continent, and [pursue] a theme equally obscure; to none but yourself can I address with more propriety, letters on a subject so much alike in purpose and importance, and so similar to your own labors." [83] Rafinesque referred to his method of linguistic reconstruction as "Historical Palingenesy or the restoration of ancient nations and languages presumed lost" in the second edition of his pamphlet on the *Ancient Monuments of North and South America*. There he compares his study of extinct languages and nations to the manner in which Georges Cuvier and other paleontologists restored knowledge of extinct animals from mere fragments of their scattered bones. [84] He said much the same thing about his "Historical and Ethnographical Palingenesy" two years later in *The Good Book, and Amenities of Nature, or Annals of Historical and Natural Sciences* (1840), published in the last year of his life: "I take scattered words of extinct Nations and Languages, and out of a few or any number, I restore them to our historical knowledge. Therefore I imitate or rather emulate Cuvier; he has been greatly praised! shall I be?" [85] Unfortunately, he did little to create favorable opinion about himself with the careless manner in which he presented the Walam Olum to the opinion of a candid world.

Squier made extensive use of the Rafinesque manuscripts that came into his possession in 1846. He was particularly interested in Rafinesque's archaeological field notes and plans. Rafinesque made several surveys and descriptions of southeastern mounds and earthworks and published several accounts of the character of those in Kentucky. [86] Squier published Rafinesque's plans and descriptions of mounds and earthworks in Kentucky, Tennessee, and Alabama in *Ancient Monuments of the Mississippi Valley* and in an article on ancient sites in Kentucky that appeared in the *American Journal of Science and Arts* in July 1849. [87] He characterized Rafinesque's descriptions of archaeological sites as "brief, crude, and imperfect," but it may certainly be said that his plans are generally accurate in the sense that they locate sites and indicate their salient features. [88] Squier certainly recognized their value notwithstanding his reservations about their accuracy. It has been noted, moreover, that in some instances the engraved versions of Rafinesque's site plans appearing in

Squier and Davis's *Ancient Monuments* differ in detail from Rafinesque's original drawings, suggesting that they were either embellished or even redrawn during the engraving process. Rafinesque's original plans in those instances are more accurate than the engraved versions of them published by Squier.[89] Here is yet another example of the value of examining archival materials relating to published accounts of archaeological sites, since liberties were often taken in the process of printing engravings.

Squier mined a rich vein in his use of Rafinesque's ethnological and archaeological manuscripts, but the charge that he was "less than candid" in acknowledging that Rafinesque was his source in publishing those materials, or that he sometimes credited Rafinesque's field sketches and sometimes not, is overstated and decidedly unfair.[90] This is a curious assertion, since quite the opposite is true. Squier clearly and consistently acknowledged that he was publishing original Rafinesque manuscripts as part of his own works. He did so in the preface, in the text, and on the published surveys appearing in *Ancient Monuments*. He also acknowledged that Rafinesque was his source of information in "A Monograph of the Ancient Monuments of the State of Kentucky," which appeared in the *American Journal of Science and Arts* in July 1849, clearly indicating that portion of the account which is based on Rafinesque manuscripts. It seems difficult to argue that Rafinesque is somehow more of a neglected or forgotten archaeologist because Squier published his original materials.[91] Most certainly the contrary is true. Rafinesque's contributions to American archaeology became better known *precisely because* they appeared in *Ancient Monuments*, where they are consistently credited to Rafinesque.

I know of only one instance in which Squier did not credit Rafinesque as his source. Figure 78 of Squier and Davis's *Ancient Monuments* is the "representation of an article of clay, found a number of years ago, in a mound near Nashville, Tennessee. It has the form of a human head, with a portentous noise and unprecedented Phrenological developments."[92] Nothing further is said as to source of the engraving, which appears on a very crowded page of woodcuts. Squier did not in that particular instance acknowledge that a Rafinesque manuscript was the source of the drawing, but he was otherwise consistent in acknowledging Rafinesque's descriptions and plans of archaeological sites. That single omission does not obviate the numerous credits of Rafinesque's other contributions. Squier gave due credit to Rafinesque, assertions to the contrary notwithstanding. One can object to Squier's characterization of the manuscripts as "crude" and "imperfect" but not to the manner in which he credited them.

One further example will show the manner in which Squier used and credited the Rafinesque manuscripts that had been lent him by Mayer. Rafinesque's account of six mound groups and enclosures in Montgomery County, Kentucky, near Mount Sterling is of particular interest owing to its association of the site with sun worship. His discussion of the site originally appeared as the second of three letters on American antiquities by Rafinesque written to Thomas Jefferson that appeared in the *Kentucky Reporter* in August and September 1820.[93] Squier reprinted the second Rafinesque letter in his "A Monograph of the Ancient Monuments of the State of Kentucky" in the *American Journal of Science and Arts* in July 1849, which is mostly based on the Rafinesque manuscripts that were lent him by Mayer. Squier uses the letter "R" in the text of that account to denote when he is quoting from Rafinesque, certainly an acceptable attribution given the fact that he identifies Rafinesque as his source of information at the beginning of the article.

Rafinesque ventured the hypothesis in that letter that the works in Montgomery County had been part of a town and that the circular enclosures with outward parapets were probably temples dedicated to sun worship, such as those erected by the Natchez Indians. He thought the square enclosures might have been council houses or the residences of chiefs, who were called children of the sun, as among the Natchez and the Indian peoples of Florida and Peru.[94] Squier must have been intrigued by that passing observation, even though he then made no comment. He too attributed at least some of the earthworks of the Mississippi Valley to sun worship, and he had concluded that sun worship was the underlying principle of all the aboriginal religious systems on the American continent. He may have borrowed that idea from Rafinesque in the first instance, but it is more likely that he did not. All those familiar with Du Pratz's *History of Louisiana* would associate sun worship with the Natchez and their temple mounds. Neither Rafinesque nor Squier was the first observer to equate circular earthworks with sun worship.[95]

Rafinesque accomplished much in his scientific investigations, but many of his contemporaries distrusted him. Learned societies in Philadelphia, where he lived from 1826 until his death in 1840, refused to publish his work, while the linguist and specialist in the Lenape language Peter Stephen DuPonceau, secretary of the American Philosophical Society, appears to have purposely shunned him. If Rafinesque's contemporaries were uncertain about him, later observers have been even more so. His character, personality, and reputation have been subjects of frequent comment. He has been described as an eccentric, an erratic genius, an errant naturalist, an egocentric, and even a lunatic. Rafinesque's strangeness is the stuff of legend in the history of the natural sciences, prompting Victor Wolfgang von Hagen to once refer to him as an "unnatural naturalist."[96] More is the pity to his defenders, who regard him as a misunderstood genius whose scientific contributions as a naturalist deserve more recognition than they have received.[97]

Rafinesque's extravagant archaeological and ethnological theories, as opposed to his descriptive fieldwork, have fared little better at the hands of historians. Samuel Foster Haven, the librarian of the American Antiquarian Society, placed Rafinesque's conjectures about the peopling of America set forward in his "Ancient Annals of Kentucky" under the head of "vagaries." He acknowledged him as a man of considerable scholarly and scientific attainments – a "laborious student in almost every conceivable department of knowledge" – adding that he only lacked "the faculty of judicious discrimination to secure him a distinguished name among men." Brinton's opinion of Rafinesque's theories was equally unfavorable: "Ancient Annals of Kentucky" was "an absurd production" based on "the flimsiest foundations," while the pages of *American Nations* were "filled with extravagant theories and baseless analogies." R. J. Farquharson, a student of American Indian languages, said of Rafinesque in 1879 that he had "eaten of 'the insane root,' " but he credited him with being correct about the presence of phonetic elements in the aboriginal languages of America. American historian Justin Winsor noted Rafinesque's "eccentricities and unstableness of head" but said that his works were not entirely worthless, owing to his "acute observation."[98] Squier had rendered a very similar judgment.

Rafinesque is a complex and enigmatic figure, an unorthodox genius who alienated himself from many of his contemporaries and placed himself on the margins of the American scientific community. He was much maligned in his own day, and opinion about his character and trustworthiness has been divided over the years. Clio on the whole has not been kind to the memory of Rafinesque. An impartial evaluation of Rafinesque's accomplishments and failings as a scholar is difficult, since a well-defined wall of impressions and prejudice stands between that tortured soul and our distant perceptions of him. His remarkable life and intriguing character must be evaluated cautiously. It has been well said on that score: "It remains difficult to render justice to Rafinesque 150 years after the death of this complex individual."[99] Anthropologists' negative opinions regarding the genuineness of the Walam Olum manuscript have only added to negative impressions and prejudices against Rafinesque as a scholar. The Walam Olum, it has been noted, has "brought him whatever fame – or notoriety – he now enjoys in prehistory."[100] Alas, for poor Rafinesque, that is most certainly true.

Squier was the first of a long procession of scholars who attempted to assess the authenticity and significance of the Walam Olum. He concluded that the traditions of the Walam Olum were genuine, but significantly he noted that the supporting evidence was internal and collateral and not direct. We simply cannot surmount the threshold of supposition, conjecture, and circumstantial evidence relating to the origin and presumed meaning of the Walam Olum that in any way warrants a dissenting opinion. The burden of proof has not changed with the passage of time. Squier would not be surprised to learn that subsequent opinion on the value of the Walam Olum has been divided, but he certainly would be disappointed to know that some regard it as a patent fraud. But whatever one's position on the Walam Olum, its controversial place in the history of American anthropology is most definitely secure.

7. Idols and Indians

The Archaeology and Ethnology of Nicaragua

Squier could little have imagined at the beginning of 1849 that circumstances and the engine of personal ambition were about to take him to Nicaragua as a diplomatic agent of the United States. He resided in Nicaragua from June 1849 until June 1850, during which time he negotiated a treaty for the construction of an American canal, incessantly tweaked John Bull's nose as he aggressively promoted American interests in the region, and conducted archaeological and ethnological investigations with great enthusiasm and bravado. His partner in those investigations was James McDonough, an American artist who sketched the people, scenery, and antiquities encountered during their travels. Squier reconnoitered the countryside in search of stone idols, collected Indian vocabularies, and studied sixteenth-century Spanish accounts of the aboriginal groups of Nicaragua. Based upon the available archaeological, ethnological, and ethnohistorical evidence, he demonstrated that Nahual-speaking peoples from Mexico had migrated to Nicaragua prior to the arrival of the Spanish, where their descendants were still to be found. He considered this to be among his most significant contributions to American ethnology.

Squier submitted a colorful narrative of his investigations of *piedras antiguas* (ancient stones) to the American Ethnological Society in New York on March 2, 1850, which appeared serially in the *Literary World* as "Ancient Monuments in the Islands of Lake Nicaragua, Central America."[1] Those archaeological discoveries, together with his inquiries into the aboriginal languages and ethnohistory of the region, were more fully described in the narrative chapters and appendix of his two-volume *Nicaragua: Its People, Scenery, Monuments, and the Proposed Interoceanic Canal*, published in 1852, and in his "Observations on the Archaeology and Ethnology of Nicaragua," which appeared in the third volume of the *Transactions of the American Ethnological Society* in the following year.[2] His account in the *Transactions* is mostly taken verbatim from the two-chapter appendix to *Nicaragua* on the "Aborigines of Nicaragua" and a portion of one of the narrative chapters.[3] But there are significant differences between these two accounts, as we will see. Assessments of the value of Squier's archaeological and ethnological and ethnological fieldwork in that country have been mixed, ranging from festschrifts to indictments of his scholarship as nothing more than anthropological propaganda.

Strange to say, however, those who have been most critical of Squier's anthropological investigations in Nicaragua make no mention of the considerable range of the archaeological, ethnological, and ethnohistorical evidence presented in *Nicaragua* and in his account in the *Transactions*. The polemical and ethnocentric aspects of his writings have received the lion's share of attention, while the leading objectives of his archaeological and ethnological investigations and the methods he used to pursue them are not generally known. This is an unfortunate omission, for no subjects laid fuller claim to his interests than the monumental remains of Central America and the presumed relations and ethnic affiliations of its little-known Indian peoples. Squier's contributions to the archaeology and ethnology of Nicaragua remains are among the least known of his anthropological career.

The conclusion of Squier's fieldwork in New York in December 1848 marked a turning point in his life. The paltry pecuniary circumstances that dogged him throughout his early years were particularly acute at that time. The financial assistance he received for supervising the printing and engraving of the Squier-Davis manuscript at New York and the two hundred dollars he received for his fieldwork in western New York had been his only sources of income since he left Ohio. He feared that empty pockets would force him to abandon the field of archaeological investigations he had so recently and successfully entered. His unsuccessful efforts at securing financial assistance from the Smithsonian Institution and the American Antiquarian Society for continuing his fieldwork elsewhere in the United States offered him little hope of future success. It was then that he fixed upon the suggestion of Albert Gallatin and other members of the American Ethnological Society that he seek a diplomatic appointment to Central America as a means of furthering his researches among the region's elaborate archaeological remains. There was clear precedent for such an assignment, for Martin Van Buren had appointed John Lloyd Stephens as the American ambassador to the Central American Federation in 1839. Stephens's diplomatic post enabled him to explore Mayan sites in Yucatán and to publish his findings in his two-volume *Incidents of Travel in Central America, Chiapas, and Yucatan* in 1841.[4]

Squier's prospects of receiving such an appointment brightened considerably in February 1849, when some of his Whig friends in Washington informed him that a diplomatic position in Guatemala was likely to be open soon and that Squier could probably secure the appointment. A diplomatic appointment would provide Squier with the governmental aid and protection necessary for promoting his investigations in a politically troubled region. Only through such indirect means could he ever afford the expense of conducting archaeological researches in such a remote area. Squier had every reason to believe that his prospects for securing a diplomatic appointment were bright, and he sought to bring "the big guns" to bear in support of his efforts. He secured the influential recommendations of Albert Gallatin, William Hickling Prescott, John Lloyd Stevens, Edward Everett, Jared Sparks, Washington Irving, Francis Leiber, officers and members of the New-York Historical Society and the American Ethnological Society, and many more besides.[5] Squier sought to follow in Stephens's footsteps and to conduct archaeological investigations and American foreign policy in double harness.[6] Those endorsements, combined with his solid credential as a Whig partisan, carried the day (see fig. 7).

On April 2, 1849, Squier became the first diplomatic appointment of the Zachary Taylor administration, even though it appears that he had refused to support Taylor's nomination on the Whig ticket in 1848.[7] The *National Intelligencer* roundly approved of the appointment and the scientific objectives on which it was largely based, calling for a special congressional appropriation to aid Squier in his proposed archaeological investigations in Central America. "The remains of the ancient inhabitants of this country – connected as they undoubtedly are in one system with those of the North – have, as yet, been very imperfectly studied. *Stephens* saw a portion of them; but the most interesting and important yet remain unexamined."[8] The congressional appropriation called for by the *National Intelligencer* never materialized. Given the U.S. government's reluctance to appropriate money for the support of scientific enterprises in the mid-nineteenth century, it would have been truly remarkable if Congress had done so. When Representative James H. Hammond of South Carolina informed Squier that he did not think Congress had any right to appropriate money for supporting scientific explorations, he doubtless spoke for the majority.[9] Even though the government had sponsored and supported the United States Exploring Expedition of 1838 to 1842, it had done so begrudgingly and not without controversy.[10]

Squier's attention had been constantly directed to perceived similarities between some of the works in the Mississippi Valley and the ancient remains in Central America described by Antonio Del Rio, Guillaume Du Paix, Frederick de Waldeck, and John Lloyd Stephens. How far the antiquities of Central America would shed light on the early history of man throughout the Americas was an open question, but Squier was confident that a properly conducted system of investigations would lead to important results. He had arrived at a stage in his inquiries when it seemed indispensable that he should

7. "E. Geo. Squier, Charge d'Affaires of the United States to the Republics of Central America." Mezzotint engraving by E. M. Whelply, from a photograph by Mad. Whernert for the *American Review* (1850). Squier received his diplomatic appointment to Nicaragua as a means of conducting archaeological investigations, but soon he became embroiled in the politics of Anglo-American intrigue to a greater extent than he initially anticipated. (National Portrait Gallery, Smithsonian Institution, Washington DC. Reprinted with permission.)

continue his explorations further southward. "The manifest connections between some of the ancient monuments of Mexico and Central America and those of the United States are eminently suggestive, and demand further investigation," he wrote. "It will be curious and important to know how far they may serve mutually to illustrate and explain each other." Here was a largely unexplored field that promised to be richer than any other in objects of archaeological and historical interest. "It is not impossible indeed that there yet exist monuments of the original stock which built and occupied the vast structures of Yucatan, Palenque, and Copan, secluded in the fastness of the interior, and like the *Moquis* in the unexplored regions above the Gila, still retain their original habits and institutions but slightly impaired."[11]

The initial archaeological objectives of Squier's trip to Central America were, however, compromised from the start. Instead of securing a post in Guatemala, he obtained a regional appointment to León, Nicaragua, as chargé d'affaires of the United States to the Republics of Central America.[12] His prime directive was to secure the American right-of-way for an interoceanic canal across Nicaragua. One can well imagine that Squier received news of the appointment with mixed emotions. His diplomatic appointment to León placed him south of the archaeological sites in Guatemala, a major center of Mayan civilization. If Squier was disappointed in that assignment, as one can well imagine he might have been, he gave no indication of the fact. He had little time to reflect upon the matter, however, for he soon immersed himself in his new responsibilities. Although he initially assumed that his diplomatic duties would be nominal, they quickly proved otherwise. With characteristic pluck and confidence, he immediately thrust himself into the midst of Anglo-American intrigue in Central America. Anglo-American interests and ambitions in Central America at the time of Squier's diplomatic appointment focused on the construction of an isthmian canal. The design of American foreign policy was to secure a diplomatic foothold in Central America that would enable the construction of an American-built canal across the Central American isthmus at the expense of British commercial interests in the region. The idea of a trans-isthmian canal was not a new one. The Spanish had mentioned the desirability of the project in the mid-sixteenth century, while Henry Clay advanced American interest in such an undertaking during the Congress of Panama in 1826.

A series of events in the late 1840s led to the rediscovery of Central America by American policy makers. The settlement of the Oregon boundary dispute with Great Britain in 1846, the discovery of gold at Sutter's Mill in California on January 24, 1848, and the cession of California to the United States by Mexico under the Treaty of Guadalupe Hidalgo the following month focused

the nation's attention on the Pacific coast as never before. The California
gold rush attracted perhaps as many as one hundred thousand prospectors
over the next five years – not only Americans but also immigrants from Europe, Asia, and South America. European gold-seekers traveled to the new
Promised Land by one of two routes: either they made the trip entirely by ship
around Cape Horn or partly by ship to Central America. There they traveled
overland across either the Panama or the Nicaragua routes to the Pacific,
from whence they sailed to California. The Panama and Nicaraguan routes
were the best means of reaching the Pacific for Americans too, and control
of those strategically important routes had become an issue of some importance to American policy makers by the time Squier assumed his diplomatic
duties in 1849.[13] Squier would do more than any other writer of the period to
direct attention to the region's strategic and economic importance as a direct
route between the Atlantic and Pacific Oceans.

Squier succeeded Elijah Hise as the United States chargé d'affaires in Central America in May 1849. He departed from New York aboard the brig *Francis* on May 11 and arrived at San Juan on June 8. The novel and picturesque
scenes of Central American life, the magnificence of its geography, the salu-
briousness of the climate, and the habits and customs of its diverse population made a deep impression. It was "particularly beautiful," Squier wrote
home, that an "entire equality" existed among the Indians, Negroes, mesti-
zos, "sambos," whites, and Spanish.[14] He would later modify that opinion,
but for the moment he could do nothing but marvel at the relaxed state of
social relations in Central America relative to those in the United States. The
salient characteristic and latent potentialities of the region appealed to his
romantic proclivities, economic ambition, and scientific curiosity in equal
measure. Thereafter, Central America never fully relinquished its hold upon
Squier's time and attentions.

Squier soon emerged as a self-assured apostle of American Manifest Destiny in Central America. He doubted not that the coming of the *americanos del
norte* would establish social order and progress, by instituting the beneficent
blessings of American civilization, enterprise, and commerce in place of the
torpor he attributed to Central American societies. He sought to awaken the
America people to "the great truth" of their mission in Nicaragua: "that the
United States is the natural head of the great American family, and that it is a
duty which it owes, alike to God and man, to extend its advice, its encouragement, and its support to the oppressed and struggling Republics of Central
America." The difficulties and instability that had beset the Spanish American republics were not to be attributed so much to "the insensate passions
of their people," he observed, as to foreign intervention in their internal af-

fairs and the unfortunate and unfavorable conditions in which they had been forced to exist. There were patriots in Central America who were struggling against "the machinations and unscrupulous policy of monarchists and oligarchists, at home and abroad, to vindicate the principles of self-government and free institutions, and who deserve, and should receive, the support and encouragement of the American people and government."[15]

The nationalism that had earlier expressed itself so vividly in Squier's poetry and journalism now embraced the mission of the United States to spread republican ideas and institutions throughout Central America. "The fortune of war has planted our eagles on the Pacific: across the entire continent from ocean to ocean, for twenty-five degrees of latitude, our Republic is supreme. . . . To gird the world as with a loop, to pass a current of American republicanism, vivifying dead nations and emancipating mankind, over the continents of the earth, it [the United States] needs but that one small spot [Central America] should be left free from foreign threats and aggression, to exercise for itself its inherent sovereign rights." Squier regarded Central America as the key to controlling the commercial riches and political destinies of the entire American continent. He believed it was the United States' duty to preserve the political autonomy and territorial integrity of the region against the encroachments of Great Britain and to open its latent commerce to the world through the construction of an interoceanic canal. Only then could Americans realize "that commercial and national preeminence to which their elastic institutions and their individual superiority amongst races of lesser vitality, invites and enables them to aspire."[16] Squier had no monopoly on smug arrogance and ethnocentrism among nineteenth-century travelers in Central America, but most certainly he had his share.

American economic, political, and cultural intervention in Nicaragua would most certainly bring dramatic changes. As a representative of the U.S. government sent to Nicaragua to negotiate the construction of an American canal, Squier was an agent of those changes – a fact of which he was fully aware. Nicaragua was a country in transition, and the dramatic contrast between continuity with the past and the imminent arrival of a different future was much in his thoughts. As he observed soon after his arrival in San Juan, Nicaragua was a land of extreme contrasts:

There was a strange blending of objects pertaining to the extremes of civilization. The boiler of the steamer was side by side with the graceful canoe, identical with that in which the simple natives of Hispaniola brought fruits to Columbus; and men in stiff European costumes were seen passing among others, whose dark, naked bodies, protected only at the loins, indicated their descent from the aborigines who had disputed the possession of the soil with the mailed followers of Cordova, and made vain propitiations to the symbolical sun to assist them against their enemies.[17]

As he floated along the far shore of the harbor at San Juan, Squier imagined that the habits of the natives had not changed over the course of three hundred years, that their thatched huts were the same, and that the scenes he gazed upon were the same as those witnessed by the Spanish explorers. Such conditions moved him to reflect upon the dramatic changes that would soon descend upon Nicaragua's native inhabitants. "They little thought that the party of strangers, gliding silently before them, were there to prepare the way for the clanging steamer, and that the great world without was meditating the Titanic enterprise of laying open their primeval solitudes, grading down their hills, and opening, from one great ocean to another, a gigantic canal, upon which the navies of the world might pass, laden with the treasures of two hemispheres!"[18] Squier thought those changes were both inevitable and desirable, but the romantic in him harbored ambivalent feelings about their impact on Nicaragua's exotic scenes and aboriginal peoples.

Squier came to Nicaragua to prepare the way for a canal that would bring the world to Nicaragua. He little doubted that the changes following in the wake of that event would make places like the Indian pueblos of Jinotepec, Nindiri, and Nandyme little more than a fond and dreamy memory. He never doubted that he was a harbinger of social progress and order in Nicaragua, but the romantic in him held fast to the sights, sounds, and smells of a vanishing landscape and way of life. American cultural influence in the region preceded his arrival in Nicaragua and would become more pronounced after his departure, but his activities in Central America were part and parcel of a larger process of cultural change. The opinions and attitudes expressed in his writings, moreover, shaped perceptions of the region and influenced the historiography on Central America for years to come.[19]

Almost from the moment of his arrival, Squier became a lightning rod of American interests and ambitions in Nicaragua. The Mosquito Coast was then a British protectorate, a state of affairs he regarded to be but a flimsy pretext for the British aggrandizement of the entire region. British "insolence," Squier immodestly asserted, had placed Nicaraguans in such a state of suspense about their future sovereignty that he would have to deliver them from their anxieties at the first opportunity.[20] Diplomatic relations between the United States and Great Britain in Central America were severely strained over British encroachments on the sovereignty of Belize and the Honduras

Bay Islands and by the British decision to seize the port of San Juan in Nicaragua in payment of a debt. Possession of the port of San Juan gave Great Britain control of access to the San Juan River, the best route for a proposed interoceanic canal. Cornelius Vanderbilt, Joseph L. White, Nathaniel H. Wolfe, and their fellow investors founded the American Atlantic and Pacific Ship-Canal Company at New York in 1849 and sought the assistance of Secretary of State John Middleton Clayton in securing the necessary concessions from the Nicaraguan government. Clayton instructed Squier to bring his influence to bear upon the government of Nicaragua in securing a contract for Vanderbilt's company.[21]

Squier embraced those instructions with a reckless abandon that surprised Clayton and occasionally gave him cause to complain of Squier's impetuousness. Even Squier's friends and supporters were astonished at his impassioned affirmations of the Monroe Doctrine and the zeal with which he advocated American interests. As his friend and correspondent Francis Parkman cautioned him, "Don't let Politics swallow up Science. They will pull together well enough and make a strong team."[22] Parkman nonetheless marveled at Squier's grit and energy. "I am rather inclined to envy you less for your success and your prospects, than for your power of activity." He cautioned that "Nature has made you tough as a pine knot, but a pine knot won't stand fire."[23] Parkman advised well. Squier became so deeply embroiled in Anglo-American intrigue in Central America that he had precious little time to conduct the archaeological investigations that had prompted him to seek a diplomatic appointment in the first place. Squier moved aggressively to stem the tide of British encroachments in Central America, be they real or imagined, and in August 1849 he recommended that the United States purchase the Isle of Tigre as the western terminus of the proposed Nicaraguan canal. When Clayton balked at this provocative suggestion and the British seized Tigre in October of that year, Squier fumed over the timidity of his government and condemned the actions of Great Britain.

The Anglophobia exhibited in Squier's harangues made Clayton's job of dealing with the British government all the more difficult. Clayton could well disapprove of Squier's belligerent attitude toward Great Britain, but not of the singular dispatch with which he fulfilled his diplomatic mission. Squier negotiated a formal agreement with the Nicaraguan government on August 27, 1849, granting the American Atlantic and Pacific Ship-Canal Company the exclusive right to construct and maintain a Nicaraguan canal. The U.S. government was not part of the contract but rather the means of effecting it. Nicaragua ratified the accord on September 23, 1849, causing much celebration on the part of the elated Squier and much consternation on the part of the British government. Squier also negotiated a commercial treaty with Nicaragua that allowed the government of the United States and American citizens free transit across Nicaragua, in return for which the United States recognized Nicaragua's sovereignty and the property it possessed along the line of the proposed canal. The line of the proposed canal, problematically, included San Juan on the Atlantic coast, a city that was then under the protection and control of Great Britain.

The Nicaraguan assembly ratified the Squier treaty on September 27, 1849, but the U.S. Senate was reluctant to do so, since it would have presented a formal challenge to Great Britain. Squier and the administration he served were at odds. The Senate never ratified the Squier treaty, but the agreement prompted the British minister to the United States, Sir Henry Bulwer, to seek an American-British accord that would allow for the joint construction and mutual control of the proposed canal. The result of those negotiations was the Clayton-Bulwer Treaty, ratified by the U.S. Senate in 1850. Squier was highly critical of the Clayton-Bulwer Treaty and of Clayton's role in securing it. He had accomplished what he had been asked to do, only to be undermined (in his point of view) by the very one who had asked it of him. The United States settled for a joint canal agreement when an exclusive one had already been obtained. Yet Clayton believed that compromise was better than continued confrontation and that Squier's aggressive posture toward British interests in Nicaragua, if left unchecked, would further strain an already frayed relationship. There can be little doubt, however, that Squier's singular success in securing the consent of the Nicaraguan government to the canal contract and a favorable commercial treaty had given Clayton the upper hand in his negotiations with Bulwer. The Clayton-Bulwer Treaty lessened diplomatic tensions between the United States and Great Britain in Central America, but the proposed canal was never built because the construction costs proved to be prohibitive. The American Atlantic and Pacific Ship-Canal Company chose instead to provide those traveling from New York to California across Nicaragua with transportation by steamship and stagecoach.

Squier was the personification of American expansion in Central America, and his nationalistic sentiments and sense of personal mission frequently informed his archaeology and ethnology in significant ways. The same ethnocentrism and strident nationalism that animated his diplomatic activities likewise provided the political context in which his archaeological and ethnological inquiries were conducted. During the year and a half of his diplomatic appointment, Squier gathered a significant amount of archaeological, ethnological, and ethnohistorical information about Nicaragua. Diplomatic affairs left no time for the large-scale archaeological investigations he had hoped to conduct, yet he still found time, he informed his parents, to prosecute his studies with "signal success." [24] Squier struck out in search of archaeological remains in Nicaragua on several different occasions between July and December 1849, during spare moments stolen from his diplomatic duties. Those forays into the field took him to the island of Momotombita in Lake Managua, to the Cerro Santiago region southwest of Subtiaba, to the cliff-lined shores of Lake Nihapa, and to the islands of Pensacola and Zapatero in Lake Nicaragua. [25]

Squier conducted each of those colorful episodes with great relish and bravado and under far from favorable circumstances. The diminutive Squier positively swaggered among his crews and the tropical undergrowth, barking out orders with machete in hand and the butt of his Colt revolver calculatingly visible at his hip. His fieldwork was neither as systematic nor as sustained as that earlier conducted in Ohio and New York, but his contributions to the archaeology and ethnology of Nicaragua are not insignificant. Squier led his first archaeological expedition to the island of Momotombita in Lake Managua. Shortly after his arrival in León he observed a stone statue standing in the city's main plaza. The figure was sculptured in the form of a man who sat upon what appeared to be a pedestal with his hands clasped across his breast. Squier acquired the idol and sent it to the Smithsonian Institution, the first of several he would deposit in the Smithsonian over the next several months. Upon learning that the monolith came from the island of Momotombita in Lake Managua, he immediately proposed an expedition. He set out for Momotombita on July 26 in the company of his artist, James McDonough; Dr. Joseph W. Livingston, the U.S. consul at León; the Spanish-born priest Padre Paul, editor of the government newspaper El Correo del Istmo; and their guide or "patron," Victorino. On the shore of Lake Managua, Squier hired a crew that took his company of adventurers to the island in a "bongo" – a large dugout canoe fitted with a sail. [26]

The party arrived at Momotombita and proceeded to a "natural amphitheater" where the underbrush gave way to high grass. There, one by one, Squier's crew found the stone monuments lying hidden beneath the grass around the periphery of the open area. Unknown parties had already carried away many of the figures, while those that remained were badly broken and defaced. Squier's guide recalled that at one time there were as many as fifty statues facing the opening, some of which were still standing. According to Squier, the idols were still venerated by some of the local Indians. Most of the monoliths on Momotombita were representations of males, lesser numbers of females, and a few in which the sex could not be determined. The depiction of male and female genitalia on the statues was a matter of some importance to Squier: "The reason for these distinctions may be found in the fact that the doctrine of the Reciprocal Principles of Nature, or Nature Active and Passive Male and Female, was recognized in nearly all the primitive religious systems of the New as well as the Old World, and in none more clearly than in those of Central America."[27] Squier made no further comment about the significance of the reciprocal principles of nature in the iconography of aboriginal America, but he elaborated his views on the subject in The Serpent Symbol (1851).

Squier examined the monoliths on Momotombita while McDonough made sketches. The undergrowth at the site was so thick that Squier soon despaired of undertaking a systematic investigation or of looking for more statues. He had neither the time nor the resources to do so. Nonetheless, he was determined to remove one of the larger figures at Momotombita for shipment to the Smithsonian. His resolve stiffened when he learned that only a few years earlier the English Council had reportedly made an unsuccessful attempt to remove the very same figure for shipment to the British Museum. Squier, ever the nationalist, was determined to succeed where his British predecessor had failed. His crew, after considerable effort and exhortation, used skids and ropes to drag the statue to the shore of Lake Managua and loaded it across the reinforced seats of their bongo. After they negotiated a hazardous return passage across the lake with his precious cargo, Squier reported, the statue broke down three carts on the road to León. He sent the idol and fragments of others to the port of Realejo, from where they were shipped around Cape Horn for deposit in the Smithsonian. Archaeology has often been the handmaiden of imperialism, as the holdings of museums in Europe and the United States readily attest. Squier's shipment of the idol from Momotombita to the Smithsonian is a classic example. His party also carried away from the site a colossal head which at one time had been attached to an idol. He donated other archaeological materials he obtained from Nicaraguan Indians to the New-York Historical Society.[28] Squier planned to revisit Momotombita during the dry season for a more careful examination, but he never returned (see figs. 8 and 9).

Squier's next excursion took him to an undisclosed area southwest of the Indian pueblo of Subtiaba. The circumstances leading to that expedition are worth noting, for they indicate the manner in which Squier ingratiated himself with Indian informants regarding the location of archaeological remains. One of the most satisfying incidents associated with his arrival in León was a formal visit he received from the community leaders of Subtiaba. The contingent consisted of José de la Cruz Garcias, Francisco Luis Antan, and Simon Roque. Roque presented Squier with an address of welcome both in Spanish and in his native dialect, which Squier characterized as a good

8. Idol from the island of Momotombita. Squier led his
first archaeological expedition to the island of Momotombita in Lake Managua in July 1849. There he examined the monoliths while his artist James McDonough
made sketches, among them Head of Idol no. 2 from
Momotombita. He sent one of the larger figures and
fragments of others to the port of Realejo, from where
they were shipped around the Cape Horn for deposit in
the Smithsonian. (From Squier, *Nicaragua*, 1:313.)

9. Colossal head from Momotombita. Squier's exploring party also carried away from Momotombita a colossal head that had once been attached to an idol. Squier
was informed by his guide that other *piedras antiguas* were
to be found on the island, but he despaired of making
any further headway in the long grass and bushes. He
proposed to resume his search on the island in the dry
season, but he never returned. (From Squier, *Nicaragua*,
1:314.)

specimen of Indian eloquence (he did not identify the specific language in which he spoke). Squier and Roque remained close friends during Squier's three-month residence at León, and Roque was among the local informants who assisted Squier in his search for Nicaraguan antiquities. The Subtiaba delegates were curious to learn about conditions among the Indian population of the United States, and an embarrassed Squier confessed: "I was ashamed to tell them the truth." They had heard that Squier was "a great friend of the Indians" and on the lookout for *piedras antiguas*. The party would only share information with him on the subject in private. Roque informed Squier that they knew the location of some of the ancient stones that their ancestors had buried long ago. They were willing to make Squier a gift of some of them on the condition that their exact location remained a strict secret. Squier agreed to the condition, whereupon the delegates from Subtiaba agreed to excavate some of the statues and send them to his residence in León. He parted company with his Indian friends with the understanding that he would soon visit them in Subtiaba.[29]

Two days later, Squier awoke to find two of the statues at the doorstep of his residence in León. A few nights later a cart brought two more.[30] One or two of the statues were among those that Squier sent to the Smithsonian. Some of the features of the stones were mutilated, a condition he attributed to "the zeal" of the priests who followed in the wake of the armies of Pedro Arias de Avila and Cordova. He subsequently learned that more of these idols still lay hidden in the forest between León and the coast, and he was told that local Indian groups secretly visited the site for the performance of dances and other religious rituals.[31] He wrote Francis Parkman that no Spaniards were permitted to be present during the recovery of the statues that had been brought to him at León, nor were they allowed to know the location of where they were found. "The Spirit of the Chiefs who resisted Cordova to the death, is not yet wholly broken, and they look forward with exultation to the time when the conquering race shall be swallowed up by the 'sons of Washington' as they call all Americans."[32] Whether Squier's Indian friends at Subtiaba were as anxious to exchange Spanish colonialism for American colonialism as he suggests is unknown. Squier may have been told what he wanted to hear, or he may have chosen to interpret it that way for his own purposes, but he did not for a moment question that it was the destiny of the United States to displace Spanish influence throughout the hemisphere and to revive "dead nations."

Squier visited Subtiaba as promised, where he collected an Indian vocabulary of some two hundred words. The manner in which he ingratiated himself with the leaders of the community is as instructive as it is colorful. He met them at the *cabildo* (council chamber), where all the elders of the community were gathered to assist him with his task of compiling a vocabulary of their native language. His attempts at filling out a blank vocabulary caused a good deal of amusement among his informants and generated animated discussions between the village elders as to the meaning of certain words and phrases. At the conclusion of his inquires, he was presented with a poem, "Una Decima," that had been written by one of the local schoolmasters. As he bade his farewell to Subtiaba he received three cheers for the "El Ministro del Norte" followed by three more for "El Amigo de los Indios."[33] Squier no doubt thought of himself as the friend of his congenial Indian hosts, and in a relative sense he certainly was. The interest he took in their languages and in the monuments of their ancestors seemed to confirm their confidence in him. They would have been troubled to know many of the ethnocentric assumptions that colored his views of Indian peoples in Central America, but he was not unsympathetic to their interests, conditions, and aspirations.

Squier was more favorably disposed toward Indian peoples generally than were many of his contemporaries, and he clearly held reservations about the racial determinism of those who dismissed them as a congenitally defective and irredeemable race. The Indian tribes of Central America were capable of "high improvement," he noted, and had shown themselves to be quite adept at assimilation and adaptation. "They constitute, when favorably situated, the best class of citizens, and would anywhere make what in Europe is called a good rural population. In brief, the better I become acquainted with the various aboriginal families of the continent, the higher position I am disposed to award them, and the less I am disposed to assent to the relative rank assigned them by the systematic writers."[34] That attitude probably explains why Indian groups warmed to Squier throughout his travels in Nicaragua. His views on race were in the process of changing, however, and they became darker and less optimistic only a few years later.

Squier knew nothing of the idols that the Indians of Subtiaba had sent to him at León except that they were excavated from a site near the base of the Cerro Santiago to the southwest of Subtiaba, a location at which they had been buried for centuries. He set out in that direction in search of more idols in the company of an unnamed guide obtained for him by General Don José Guerro, a former minister of state in Nicaragua and commander of the military garrison at León at the time of Squier's residence there. Squier and his guide traveled southwest of Subtiaba toward the ocean, and at length they found the idols hidden in a forest amidst a tangled mass of vines and underbrush. The ground was scattered with fragments of idols, suggesting that it had once been a ceremonial site, but Squier could find only a single sandstone figure that remained intact. It was partially buried and stood at a severe angle nearby the remains of a stone platform. As in most instances, the face of the idol had been mutilated, but the rest remained clearly defined. Squier cited the activities of the Fray Francisco de Bobadilla, of the Order of Mercy, as probably accounting for the destruction and defacement of those idols and others. Bobadilla reportedly converted forty thousand natives to Christianity in three months in the cazique of Nagrando, whose principal town stood upon the site that later became León. Bobadilla destroyed the idols at the aboriginal temple located in the town and replaced them with the cross. He shattered their faces with a mace and threw them unceremoniously to the ground. During the night, however, some of the Indians of the district reportedly took them away and buried them so that Spanish would not find them. Squier thought it likely that those were the very same idols that had been exhumed for him by the Indians of Subtiaba and brought to him at León, two of which he sent to the Smithsonian (see fig. 10). [35]

Squier next visited Lake Nihapa near Grenada in September 1849 in the company of an unidentified guide. He had heard at León about the antiquities said to exist in the vicinity of Managua, and later he learned that rock paintings (piedras pintadas) were to be found near Managua on the cliffs overlooking Lake Nihapa. Nothing was known of the origin of the drawings except that they had been made before the Spanish Conquest. Squier found a variety of figures painted in bright red on the face of cliffs that lined the shores of the lake, just as he had been informed. Nearly all of them had been effaced by long exposure to the elements, but some retained their distinct outlines. Conspicuous among those figures was that of a coiled serpent plumed with feathers, which the Indians in the vicinity knew as "el Sol" (the sun). Serpent symbolism in aboriginal America held particular interest and significance for Squier, for it was often associated with sun worship and sometimes corresponded with the idea of a supreme deity. The plumed serpent figured in the rock painting at Lake Managua, significantly, combined both symbols in one. Squier did not further comment upon the significant of serpent symbolism in Nicaragua, but he did direct the attention of those interested in the subject of religious symbolism to his work on The Serpent Symbol. Squier found traces of hundreds of other painted rocks at the site, but the style and character of this one in particular attracted his attention because of its resemblance to certain figures found in the painted historical records of the ancient Mexicans. [36]

Squier also learned of the existence of inscribed rocks (piedras labradas) located in a ravine not far from Masaya. The figures found there were outlines of animals, men, and unknown representations cut into the smooth rock walls of the ravine. A few were yet discernible, but most had been obliter-

10. Idols of Subtiaba no. 4. Squier traveled southwest of Subtiaba toward the ocean and at length found the *piedras* (idols) he sought hidden in a forest amidst a tangled mass of vines and underbrush. The ground was scattered with fragments of idols, suggesting that it had once been a ceremonial site, but Squier could find only a single sandstone figure that remained intact. It was partially buried and stood at a severe angle nearby the remains of a stone platform. (From Squier, *Nicaragua*, vol. 1, plate 11, facing page 321.)

ated to the point that they could no longer be traced. The figures covered the face of the cliff for more than a hundred yards. Similar rock sculptures were found all over the American continent from New England to Patagonia. Squier attributed most of those inscriptions to "savage tribes," who were known to make such pictorial representations as commemorations of important events. He thought the inscriptions were too rude to be of much archaeological value, other than as illustrations of a rudimentary pictorial system that gradually lead to hieroglyphic and alphabetic forms of writing among some early societies and not in others. The presence of the drawings suggested that the secluded ravine, known locally as the Quebrada de las Inscripciones, had once been a sacred place and somehow connected with the religious ideas of the aborigines. There were many other isolated figures found at various places on the rocks, some of which were oftentimes repeated.[37]

Squier conducted his most significant archaeological expeditions to the islands of Pensacola and Zapatero in Lake Nicaragua in December 1849. He and his crew of Indian sailors made for the island of Pensacola on December 2 in search of the *piedras antiguas* of great size said to exist there. Squier found it strange that in all of his inquiries about antiquities to the *padres* (priests), *licenciados* (local officials), and "the best informed citizens" of Granada he had learned nothing about the existence of these monuments. He knew from his own experience, however, that more information about the location of antiquities was to be obtained from "bare-footed *mozos* [a *mozo* is an assistant, servant, or hired hand] than from black-robed priests."[38] Such was certainly the case in this instance, for at Pensacola, Squier and his crew found several elaborately sculptured monoliths that were partially hidden in the ground. The monuments were well proportioned, exhibited excellent workmanship, and were larger than any he had yet found. The faces of the stones were mutilated, and some appeared to have been purposely buried, a condition he again attributed to the actions of "Catholic zealots."

One of the Pensacola idols in particular made a deep impression on Squier. He thought it likely that the representation of the crouched figure with a large head and distended tongue found there had been connected with the rites of human sacrifice. "I readily comprehended the awe with which it might be regarded by the devotees of the ancient religion, when the bloody priest daubed the lapping tongue with the yet palpitating hearts of his human victims!" Oviedo y Valdez described the practice of human sacrifice during his visit to Nicaragua only a few years after the Spanish Conquest. Squier little doubted that the idols on the island of Pensacola had been associated with very rites described by Oviedo. He even imagined that they might have been

among the idols thrown to the ground by the hands of Gil Gonzales himself, when the cacique (hereditary chief) Nicaragua consented to be bap-
tized along with nine thousand of his subjects. It was then that the Spanish
conquerors erected the cross in place of the aborigines' fallen idols, whose
locations were gradually forgotten with the passage of time. [39] Three of the
statues from Pensacola are today located in the Church of San Francisco in
Grenada under the authority of the National Museum of Nicaragua. [40]

The next day Squier visited the uninhabited island of Zapatero (the Shoe-
maker), where he made his most significant archaeological discoveries.
There he found the remains of what he identified as an aboriginal temple
and fifteen statues, some of which were of imposing size and excellent workmanship. The figures were located amidst a group of stone mounds. All of
the statues at Zapatero were set upright and sketched by McDonough, while
Squier made a plan of the site showing the location of the statues relative to
the stone mounds or ruined teocalli. He attempted to excavate one of the
mounds, removing its stones to a depth of several feet. It appeared to be
composed entirely of stone and fragments of pottery that had been painted in
bright colors. The mounds did not appear to be arranged with any regularity
in respect to each other, nor was there any apparent design in the relative
positions of the monuments. Squier thought it quite likely, however, that
the idols no longer stood in their original locations. [41] He spent three days
at Zapatero with McDonough and their Indian laborers. He was certain that
other idols were to be found at different places on the island, but once again
the constraints of time and local conditions prevented them from pursuing
those investigations to his satisfaction. He believed, nevertheless, that he
had already made enough discoveries of antiquities in Nicaragua to form a
respectable volume. He half hoped, however, that he would soon be relieved
of his diplomatic post so that he could extend his fieldwork into Guatemala,
which remained his great desideratum. [42]

The idols on Zapatero were all skillfully carved from local sources of black
basalt. Squier's imaginative crew collectively called the statues *frailes* (friars)
but also assigned them individual names: "El Canon" (The Cannon), "Joro
bado" (The Humpback), "Ojos Grandes" (Big Eyes), and "Gardo" (The Fat).
The primeval beauty of the place where the monoliths were found moved
Squier to a flight of romantic fancy:

> The bushes were cleared away, and I could easily make out the positions
> of the ruined *teocalli*, and take in the whole plan of the great aboriginal
> temple. Over all now towered immense trees, shrouded in long robes of
> grey moss, which hung in masses from every limb, and swayed solemnly

in the wind. I almost fancied them in mourning for the departed glories of the place. In fact, a kind of superstitious feeling, little in consonance with the severity of philosophical investigation, began to creep over me. Upon one side were steep cliffs, against which the waters of the lake chafed with a subdued roar, and upon the other was the deep extinct crater, with its black sides and sulfurous lake; it was in truth a weird place, not unfittingly chosen by the aboriginal priesthood as the site of their strange and gloomy rites.[43]

Such passages shared the wonder of discovery with Squier's readers and to this day bristle with life.

Squier placed considerable archaeological significance on the idols recovered in his travels, especially those found on the islands of Pensacola and Zapatero. The similarity in design between some of those statues gave him pause to reflect about their probable origin and signification. One of the most remarkable of the idols at Zapatero, for example, was that of a humanlike figure whose head was surmounted with "a monstrous symbolical head" similar to those that sat atop the statues on Pensacola. "The resemblance to some of the symbolical heads in the ancient Mexican rituals cannot be overlooked; and I am inclined to the opinion that I shall be able to identify all these figures, as I believe I already have some them, with the divinities of the Aztec Pantheon." He was more specific on this point in a letter to Joseph Henry. The idols provided "conclusive collateral evidence" in support of the statement of Oviedo, who visited Nicaragua in 1529, that a large portion of the inhabitants of Nicaragua were Mexicans, belonging to the same stock as the Aztecs and nations living in the valley of Anahuac. "I was able at first glance, to recognize in some of these statues, the representations of several of the gods of the Mexican Pantheon. Among these was Tlalocthe, the God of Rain, and the second of the Aztec Triad who corresponded in his essential attributes with Vishnu of the Hindu Mythology."[44]

The style of workmanship exhibited by the monuments at Zapatero was the same in all of them, but each had such a marked individuality in its symbolic form that Squier thought them to be representations of deities possessing distinct attributes and holding particular positions within the religious system of their worshipers. He was no less struck by the representations of male and female genitalia on the statues and their probable symbolic significance. The idols "afford strong corroborative proof" of phallic worship among the aborigines of Central America. Squier found no reason to attribute the origin of the monoliths to anyone other than the Indian peoples who occupied Nicaragua at the time of the Spanish Conquest in 1522, but he was prepared to assign them a much higher antiquity. "They may differ somewhat amongst themselves in antiquity, for it is not to be supposed that they were all made at the same period. But there is no good reason for supposing, that they were not made by the nations found in possession of the country." The Spanish chroniclers' early accounts made it clear that the natives of Nicaragua had stone idols in their temples that were carved into different forms representing distinct deities. The same authorities also affirmed that even though the aborigines of Nicaragua differed significantly in their languages, customs, and origins, they were alike or closely affiliated in their religious conceptions.[45]

Squier also comments on the frequent appearance of what some early observers identified as the symbol of the Christian cross in the aboriginal iconography of Mexico and Central America. The head of one of the idols found on the island Zapatero formed a cross, a design feature shared by some of the other monuments at Zapatero. Stephens had also found the symbol represented in the monoliths at Palenque, an example of which Squier reproduced in *Nicaragua* for comparison to the appearance of the symbol on the idols at Zapatero. Squier thought it possible that the symbol denoted some kind of headdress, but he commented further on the presence of the cross in the aboriginal monuments of the New World. Catholic priests noted at the time of the Conquest that the sign of the cross was to be found among the native symbols of Yucatán and Central America, but they were entirely at a loss to account for its presence unless it was the vestige of an earlier but failed attempt to introduce Christianity. Botturini also reported the presence of crosses in the painted records of Mexico. Squier, however, saw no connection between the symbol of the cross in the New World and Christianity. Boturini and others had mistaken the aboriginal symbol for the Tonacaquahuitl (the tree of life) for the Christian cross. Native peoples represented the Tonacaquahuitl with tree branches surmounted by a bird, a symbol somewhat resembling a cross. The sign of the Tonacaquahuitl appeared in the design of aboriginal monoliths of Central America and in the painted records of Mexico because of the importance of the ideas associated with that symbol within native religions.[46]

Over the course of his investigations in Nicaragua, Squier sent the Smithsonian five large idols and other items in the hope that they would form the nucleus of a national archaeological museum worthy of comparison to those in Europe.[47] He regarded the establishment of such a museum to be a matter of some importance. As he observed to Joseph Henry in December 1850,

You know that I have long cherished the plan of forming a grand collection, which should illustrate the arts of the aboriginies [sic] of every part of the continent, but more particularly of our own country. Small and detached collections, such as individuals may be able to form, can serve no good purpose in the way of comparison and mutual illustration, and are always liable to be destroyed by accident, or dispersed, and, piece by piece, irretrievably lost. . . . It is a fact not at all creditable to us, that we have no public collection of this kind worthy to be mentioned, in the United States, while some of the museums of Europe are really rich in relics of aboriginal American art.[48]

Squier's sense of national mission dictated that the United States should have an archaeological museum "worthy of our age and country." He believed that the Smithsonian should actively seek to become the repository of a national archaeological collection and was doubtlessly disappointed that Henry did not share that opinion. Henry, however, was determined to keep the Smithsonian out of the museum business for as long as possible.

Squier proposed to number and catalog the idols and the other Central American materials he had sent to the Smithsonian during a planned visit to Washington in January 1851. What he described as "the finer specimens" of aboriginal art in Nicaragua were too large to be removed under existing circumstances, but he was confident that once steamers had successfully ascended the San Juan River to Lake Nicaragua, more monuments on the islands of the lake could be obtained without much difficulty. These would make interesting and important additions to the proposed Smithsonian collection of American antiquities. Two of the statues he sent to Smithsonian were from Zapatero Island in Lake Nicaragua, "where once existed one of the most imposing aboriginal temples of the country. Here, amongst the ruins of the teocalli or high places of the former inhabitants I have found fifteen entire statues, besides the fragments of many others; several broken sacrificial stones, &c. I was unable to remove but two of the smallest and rudest, but I have accurate drawings of all." The largest of the idols that Squier sent to the Smithsonian was carved from black basalt and recovered from Momotombita Island in Lake Managua, which also appeared to have been a sacred place of the aborigines. The statue with "the sphinx like head dress" was also from Momotombita. Several of the monoliths at that locality had been removed at various times and placed at the corners of Nicaraguan towns or sent abroad. "Within the recollection of persons now living, there were some twenty or thirty of these figures existing at one place on the island, arranged in the form of a square, the faces looking inward."

Nicaragua presented Squier with an immense laboratory for ethnological inquiry. The aborigines of Nicaragua and the other Central American states still represented the largest segment of the population. When the people of other races who had amalgamated with the Indians were included within that enumeration, they represented some three-fourths of the entire population. Most of the Indian groups in Nicaragua had adopted elements of European culture and were classified by Squier as "civilized." Many other tribes, however, resided in extensive tracts of unexplored territory and were generally known as "Indios Bravos." Those groups were characterized as being more or less "savage" and their numbers unknown. The more remote and little-known groups held great interest from an ethnological standpoint, for they were thought to retain habits that had little changed from what they had been prior to the Spanish Conquest. Even the Indians of Nicaragua that Squier classified as civilized, notwithstanding the fact that they had been interacting with inhabitants of European descent for centuries, did not exhibit as great an alteration in traditional lifestyles as might be expected. "Indeed, it is, in many respects, hard to say whether the conquerors have assimilated most to the Indians, or the Indians most to the Spanish." Native settlements were often located on ancestral sites, while the departments and other political subdivisions of Nicaragua generally corresponded with the ancient princi-palities of the aborigines. The prefects or leaders of those departments suc-ceeded the caciques, and the municipal authorities had only taken the places of the *guegues* (councils of tribal elders). The Spanish perpetuated many abo-riginal social and political institutions in Nicaragua after the establishment of the Council of the Indies at Seville in 1524, even as they had systemati-cally expunged and suppressed others during the initial trauma of the Con-quest. Some aboriginal ceremonies were also incorporated within the Cath-olic Church of Nicaragua in conformity with those conciliatory policies.[49]

More is the pity that such humane policies were not adopted sooner, for the Spanish Conquest of Nicaragua was initially as violent and devastating to its native inhabitants as it had been in Mexico and Peru. Fray Bartolomé de Las Casas, the bishop of Chiapas and the great defender of the Indians, visited Nicaragua and reported that the same cruelties were committed there by the soldiers of Cordova as were committed by those of Cortés and Pizarro. Pedro Arias de Avila, the governor of Darien, received much of the blame from Las Casas for the atrocities committed against the Indians, for it was he who ordered Cordova's conquest of Nicaragua. According to Las Casas, the enslavement of Indians in Nicaragua for shipment to Peru and Panama was one of the chief causes of the depopulation of the country. He estimated that half a million Indian inhabitants were removed from Nicaragua in the slave trade, a number that Squier believed to be greatly exaggerated. He thought that Las Casas's statement that from fifty to sixty thousand Indians had been killed during the Conquest of Nicaragua was possibly closer to the truth. [50] Regardless of the actual numbers, however, there can be little doubt that the depopulation of Nicaragua as chronicled by Las Casas in his *Apologetica historia de las Indias* was as traumatic and as lethal as it had been in Mexico and Peru.

Social conditions among the Indian population in Nicaragua during the Spanish entrada contrasted greatly with those observed by Squier in 1849 and 1850. He maintained that the Indians of Nicaragua enjoyed "equal privileges with whites" in the offices of church and state, but he also noted with apparent approval: "Yet the Indian retains his traditionary [sic] deference for the white man, and tacitly admits his superiority." Although he marveled at the lack of a rigid caste system in Central America, Squier clearly feared its implications. He deplored the fact that in some parts of Spanish America "unscrupulous partisans" were artfully inciting "a jealousy of caste." Such agitations had occurred in Guatemala and Peru, while in Yucatán they threatened "the entire extinction of the white race." Nicaragua had been mercifully spared such convulsions. If such sentiment existed in Nicaragua at all, Squier said, it was only in latent form. "This quiet, however, may be that of the slumbering volcano; and its continuance may depend very much upon the judicious encouragement of white emigration from the United States and Europe." [51] Squier encouraged immigration to Nicaragua as a means of increasing the proportional amount of Caucasians in the general population and of developing its latent economic potential through the investment of foreign capital. The racist assumptions that informed those views and his commitment to the colonizing mission of the United States in Central America sometimes spilled over into his ethnology and compromised its objectivity.

Squier's ethnology at other times was decidedly more empirical. Squier directed his inquiries into the geographical distribution, relations, languages, customs, and religious beliefs of the native peoples of Nicaragua at the problem of defining their "ethnical position" relative to the other aboriginal families of the American continent. He restricted his fieldwork almost entirely to the interior areas around Lake Nicaragua and Lake Managua, "a region unerringly marked out, by the circumstances of geographical position and physical conformation, as the theatre of vaster enterprises than human daring has hitherto conceived, or human energy yet attempted. Here nature has lavished her richest gifts, and assumed her most magnificent forms." The contrast of towering volcanoes and level plains, the scenic grandeur and scale of the interior lakes and rivers, and the unrivaled fertility of the soil and pleasantness of the climate made a profound impression upon him. In a word, the region possessed everything necessary to support the ancient societies that had once flourished there. Those who beheld that tableau of unsurpassed resources and natural beauty could more readily accept Las Casas's statement that the Nicaraguan interior had been one of the most populous areas of the American continent. [52] Oviedo had been no less taken than Squier with the fertility, climate, and natural resources of Nicaragua during his residence there in the sixteenth century. No other part of the Indies surpassed it, he said; it was truly "Mohammed's Paradise." [53] Squier beheld those very same vistas and described them with equal fondness.

Squier divided the aboriginal peoples of Nicaragua into two widely separated and possibly radically distinct families whose geographical distribution very nearly conformed to Nicaragua's natural provinces. His cultural geography emphasized the correlation between topographical and environmental considerations and characteristics of its aboriginal peoples, an approach that is similar to the concept of the cultural and natural area employed by later anthropologists. Squier characterized the tribes living along the alluvial areas and tropical forests of the Atlantic coast as being "rude," nomadic, and few in numbers. These groups subsisted primarily by hunting and fishing, had little or no agriculture, lacked civil organizations, practiced "a debased religion," and closely resembled the Caribs of the islands. Some of the descendants of the Moscos or Mosquito, a group he described as "wretched," had been "still further debased by the introduction of negro blood." The tribes on the Atlantic coast were hunters and gatherers, a social condition he attributed to the fact that the low-lying, subtropical conditions in the region made the development of agriculture very difficult. What Squier regarded as the higher cultures on the Pacific coast, by contrast, exploited the fertile soil and climate to develop into agricultural societies with large towns and complex religions. [54]

Squier identified the small population of Melchoras on the San Juan River as being of Carib stock and thought it more than likely that the Woolwas, Ramas, Toacas, and Poyas were of Carib origin too. The groups residing in the upland regions of the interior lakes and the Pacific slopes, by contrast, exhibited many characteristics in common with the semi-civilized nations of Mexico, Guatemala, and Yucatán. The groups inhabiting the narrow isthmus between Lake Nicaragua and the Pacific (the Rivas region), as well as upon the main islands of the lake, were those that most interested him. He considered the presence of those groups to be one of the more remarkable facts connected with the ethnology of the region. The inhabitants of the area "were Mexicans, speaking the ancient Mexican language, and having a civil and social organization, as also a system of religion, identical with those which prevailed among the Aztecs, and their affiliated nations."[55] Squier is first known to have stated his opinion that some of the aboriginal groups of Nicaragua were descended from the ancient Mexicans in a paper on the "Archaeology of Nicaragua" given before the New-York Historical Society on October 1, 1850.[56] He elaborated upon that theory in *Nicaragua* and in the *Transactions of the American Ethnological Society*. Squier believed his archaeological and ethnological investigations in Nicaragua provided conclusive evidence in support of that assertion. His thesis was supported by the testimony of the Spanish chronicler Oviedo, who resided in Nicaragua in the years immediately following the Spanish Conquest. The "Niquirans," according to Oviedo, lived between Lake Nicaragua and the ocean, spoke the Mexican language, and had the same customs and appearance as the natives of New Spain.[57]

Based upon the names and descriptions of Oviedo, Squier divided the aboriginal inhabitants of Nicaragua into two distinct families: the "semi-civilized" and the "savage" tribes. The former consisted of the Chorotegans (the Dirians, Nagrandans, and Orotinans), the Cholutecans and Niquirans (both of which he identified as Mexican colonies), and the Chondals (whom he described as approximating the savage tribes). The latter embraced the Waiknas (or Moscos), Melchoras, Woolwas, Toacas, Poyas, and other tribal groups located on the Caribbean Sea and to the east and south of the Gulf of Nicoya. Oviedo, Herrara, and Gomara identified the Chorotega as the original inhabitants and dominant family in Nicaragua, an aboriginal group that Squier accepted as probably being *autochthones*, or original inhabitants.[58]

Squier's study of Nicaraguan languages led him to the same conclusion regarding Mexican colonization. No vocabularies of Indian languages had been compiled prior to his arrival in Nicaragua, so he gathered them whenever possible. He obtained a vocabulary of some two hundred words from the Indians of Subtiaba near León in the northwest region of the country, and at another point he hired *mozos* to travel to the Indian pueblos of Jinotepec and Nindiri in Masaya to bring him the oldest residents who still retained any knowledge of the original language spoken in those communities. Squier obtained another vocabulary of approximately equal number from his Indian informants from Masaya, which was located one hundred miles south of León in the area immediately adjacent to that occupied by the Mexican (Nahual)-speaking Niquirans. Besides these he procured a few words and numerals from the Indians living on the Island of Ometepec in Lake Nicaragua. The Niquirans occupied the island, and the words he procured from the tribes yet living there coincided precisely with the Mexican. Indeed, the very name of this island, distinguished for its two high volcanic peaks, is pure Mexican: *Ome* (two) and *tepec* (mountain). Squier compiled a table of words for the various languages spoken in Nicaragua, and he inserted Mexican words to facilitate comparison with the Niquiran language. He noted, however, that the Niquiran language was really "Mexican" (Nahual) and differed from it in no essential respect except that the terminals tl or tli were contracted or omitted. Squier also obtained some of the grammatical rules and constructions of the Nagrandan language with the assistance of Francisco Diaz Zapata. [59]

That the Niquirans were of Mexican origin, said Squier, required no further proof than that exhibited by the surviving fragments of their language, which conclusively corroborated the testimony of the early Spanish chroniclers. No one had previously brought forward evidence in support of the Spanish accounts, however, which had rendered the authority of their observations tenuous or even doubtful. Robert G. Latham, in fact, stated in *The Natural History of the Varieties of Man* (1850) that evidence in support of a Mexican-Nicaraguan connection was in no way conclusive. [60] Squier, consequently, regarded this as one his most important contributions to knowledge: "In completing the evidence, and establishing incontestably that such a [Mexican] colony had existed in Nicaragua, at the period of discovery in the fifteenth century, I have the satisfaction of fixing one more and a very important point of departure in American Ethnological Inquiries." The American continent, like other areas of the globe, had been swept by migrations among its ancient population, affecting the conditions, relations, and intermixtures of its aboriginal inhabitants. "We have then presented to us the extraordinary phenomenon of a fragment of a great aboriginal nation, widely separated from the parent stock, and intruded among other and hostile nations; yet, from the comparative lateness of the separation, or some other cause, still retaining its original, distinguishing features, so as to be easily recognized." [61]

Squier doubted whether the causes of the migrations from Mexico to Nicaragua would ever be known, but he thought that tribal tradition might suggest a plausible scenario. In support of that supposition, he cited a tradition among the Niquirans recorded by the Fray Francisco de Bobadilla in 1528. The Niquirans informed Bobadilla that they had come from the northwest after being defeated by a hostile nation. They called the country of their nativity Ticomega Emaguatega, a place-name that corresponded with no aboriginal language with which Squier was familiar. The Niquiran tradition, however, appeared to Squier to receive strong corroboration from a Mexican tradition recorded by the Franciscan chronicler Fray Juan de Torquemada in his three-volume *Monarquia Indiana* (1615). According to that authority, the Ulmeques attacked two large Mexican nations living in Soconusco on the coast of Oaxaca near Tehuantepec at a very early date. It was said that the groups in Soconusco were the enemies of the Ulmeques before their settlement in that region, a circumstance from which Squier inferred that there had been an earlier migration of the same nations. That migration had probably been from the valley of Anahuac to Soconusco, when the Mexican nations fled the Ulmeques by migrating southward. Eventually they arrived in Nicaragua and established settlements or colonies among the region's original aboriginal population.

Torquemada further notes that some groups split off from the main body of the migrating Mexicans. Some are reported to have settled in Guatemala, where they established Mictlan (City of the Dead) and Yzcuitlan (City of the Rabbit), where, Squier noted, there still existed numerous place-names of Mexican (Nahua) origin. Torquemada specifically mentions the Cholultecans as one of the Mexican migrant groups that separated from the rest and settled on the Gulf of Nicoya. Squier believed that Torquemada meant to say the Gulf of Fornesca instead of Nicoya, for the name Cholulteca was still used there. Squier thought his opinion about the actual locations of the Cholutecans was supported by Torquemada's subsequent statement that some of the people among whom the refugee Mexicans had settled fled to Nicoya, which probably accounted for the then-existing divisions of the Chorotegans.[62] Squier's supposition about the origin of the Nahual-speaking peoples of Nicaragua is a plausible reading of the fragmentary evidence before him. It is also consonant with the subsequent opinion of scholars.

The early Spanish observers supposed that the Pipil Indians on the coast of San Salvador were also of Mexican origin and that they had arrived there contemporaneously with the colony in Nicaragua. Squier had no vocabularies available to him with which to test the correctness of that claim, but he noted that the names of the places they once occupied, or continued to occupy, were clearly Nahua: Istepec, Usulatan, Sesuntepec, Cuscutlan, Suchitltepec, Cojutepec, Cuyutitan, and Jilpango were all "unmistakably Mexican" in their origin. It had been suggested that the occurrence of those names might be accounted for by the presence of Nahual-speaking peoples who accompanied Pedro de Alvarado in his conquest of San Salvador, who gave those names to the places where they settled. Squier acknowledged that this was still an open question, but he was inclined to believe that a colony from Mexico had existed in San Salvador before the Spanish incursion.

Squier cited the tradition of a Mexican migration to Nicaragua recorded by the Mexican historian Fernando de Alva Cortés Ixtlilxochitl ([1568]–1648) in further support of his thesis. According to Ixtlilxochitl it was during the destruction of the Toltecan Empire in the year Cetecpatl (or 959 AD) that a surviving remnant of the Toltecs migrated south to Nicaragua. Squier hastened to note, however, that the traditions of the peoples themselves more closely resembled the account of Torquemada and were likely to be nearest the truth. It appeared that the Mexican colony in Nicaragua originated through a general migration by refugees fleeing persecution in the former homelands. Establishing authentic instances of such migrations was an important point of inquiry in determining the probable relationships and affinities that might exist between its various aboriginal families.

> That similar separations and migrations have occurred in the night of American history, seems undoubted; but at periods so remote, that the offshoots have lost their original features, or have retained them in a modified and obscured form, painful to the investigator, because suggestive of relations which it is impossible clearly to establish. . . . Enigmatical fragments like these, scattered over both the Northern and Southern Hemispheres, betoken a high antiquity for the American race.[63]

Squier allowed that the causes of those migrations and divisions would probably never be known, except to the extent that they could be inferred from analogies with the recorded history of the Old World. "For, after all, man, of whatever race, or however situated, is subject to the same laws, and guided by the same influences." There were those who variously attributed the state of separation existing among the American tribes at earliest knowledge – sometimes called "disruption" – to a defect in their physiological character, to extraordinary convulsions of nature like those said to have destroyed the legendary island of Atlantis, or to other unknown horrors so terrible that they had "darkened their intellects, and hardened their hearts, and drove them, flying from each other, far from the blessing of social life." To Squier, however, the separation and subdivision of the American race could more likely be attributed to long periods of time and continued migrations of individual tribes from one part of the continent to another. Did not the North American Indians provide abundant historical and archaeological evidence of their migrations? The history of the Indian tribes of New England and the mid-Atlantic states documented such movements, while the aboriginal monuments of the Mississippi Valley likewise provided evidence of ancient migrations "not of single tribes and petty nations, but of vast families of men."[64] It would be singular indeed if the causes of ancient migrations in Central America could not be attributed to similar conditions and occurrences.

The inhabitants of Nicaragua, according to Oviedo, differed widely in their customs but were similar in their religion. Squier greatly valued Oviedo's descriptions, which he regarded as fair approximations of the religious ideas

and practices existing there prior to the Conquest. The religion of the Nicaraguans as described appears to have closely resembled that of the Aztecs.
The names of their deities and the nature of their religious rights, including
the practice of human sacrifice, were, said Squier, "identical with those of the
Aztecs and their neighbors in the Valley of Anahuac."[65] The records preserved
by Oviedo shed much light on their religious beliefs and customs, especially
his transcript of a commission headed by the Fray Francisco de Bobadilla.
Pedro Arias de Avila, the governor of Nicaragua, commissioned Bobadilla
in 1528 to investigate the Indians' conditions and religion and to ascertain
how far they had been affected by the introduction of Christianity. Bobadilla
commenced his inquires among the Indians upon his arrival in the province
of Niquira on September 28, 1528. Squier quoted at length several of his
interviews with Nicaraguan caciques, elders, and priests. The descriptions
of aboriginal temples by Andres de Cereceda (spelled Cerezeda by Squier)
were of no less interest. Cereceda says that native temples were built of timber
and thatch and that nearby stood the *tezarit* (high places). Oviedo describes
these as conical or pyramidal structures that were ascended by steps. Human
sacrifices were sometimes made upon those high places, of which Cereceda
gives an explicit account. Squier believed that the "stone of sacrifice" and the
idols he had found on the Island of Zapatero were associated with precisely
such ceremonies.

Squier associated another Nicaraguan ritual observed by Oviedo with phallic worship. He believed that phallicism was more prevalent in the New World
than was generally supposed, providing the "rationale" for many religious
practices that could not otherwise be explained. According to Oviedo, the
Nicaraguans drew blood from their genitals and sprinkled it upon maize,
which was then distributed and solemnly eaten by the devotees of the ancient
religion. Robert Fowler has noted, however, that Oviedo was actually referring to the Chorotega, whereas the accounts of Francisco Lopez de Gomara
and Antonio de Herrera y Tordesillas imply that Oviedo was describing a
custom of the Nicarao. Squier perpetuated Gomara's mistaken attribution
in *Nicaragua* and in the *Transactions of the American Ethnological Society*.[66] Had
Squier realized that Oviedo was describing a Chorotega and not a Nicarao
ceremony, however, it would have in no way changed his views on the ceremony's significance as an expression of phallic ritualism in the New World.
"This scenical [sic] rite, under one form or another, may be traced through the
rituals of all the semi-civilized nations of America, in strict parallelism with
certain Phallic rites of the Hindus, and of those other numerous nations of
the old world which were devoted to a similar primitive religion."[67]

Squier was the first of several scholars to study the Pipil-Nicarao calendar and compare it to the calendar used by the Aztecs in Mexico. His brief analysis of the Nicaraguan calendar and its symbols appears at the end of his account on the archaeology and ethnology of Nicaragua in the third volume of the *Transactions* and is not present in the appendix or narrative chapters of *Nicaragua*. He believed that Bobadilla and other Spanish observers had obtained most, if not all, of their information about the calendar from the Niquirans (Nicarao), whom he identified as the "descendants of Mexicans." Bobadilla interrogated his native informants about the number of their festivals, "but either those festivals bore the names of the days of the month, or the Indians misunderstood the question; for they gave him the names of the twenty days of the month, which are the same as those of the Mexican calendar."

Squier presents a table showing the names of the days of the month as given to Bobadilla, the order in which he presents them, what Squier called their "true order," their equivalent names in Mexican (Aztec), and the conventional signs or symbols by which they were known. He copied the signs (animal heads and other symbols) from the Codex Mendoza, which is apparently a Spanish copy of an original pre-Columbian codex or painted record.[68] He had no doubt that the same system of reckoning time that existed among the Aztecs also existed in Nicaragua among the aboriginal groups of Nahua descent. The Aztec cycle known as the Xiuhmopilli ("the tying up of years") consisted of a series of fifty-two years and was represented by a sign representing a bundle of reeds. The Mexicans divided the cycle of fifty-two years into four periods of thirteen years each, each of which corresponded with a specific sign or symbol.[69] Squier reproduced the four signs and corresponding names of the Xiuhmopilli that represented each of the four divisions of thirteen years within the Mexican calendar. He did so without further comment, but there is no doubt that he believed the same divisions of time were used among Nicaraguan groups of Mexican descent. Squier's discussion of the Pipil-Nicarao calendar and his comparative table of the days of the month are still of interest to scholars in their efforts to reconstruct the Mexican sequence of days (see fig. 11).[70]

The fact that Squier presented his findings in a two-volume travelogue and an appendix may partly explain why his contributions to the archaeology and ethnology of Nicaragua have not received more recognition. One must work to retrieve the significant archaeological, ethnological, and ethnohistorical observations scattered across its discursive pages. The narrative qualities and length of *Nicaragua* stand in stark contrast to the scientific tone, style, and discipline of his Smithsonian monographs. But if we are prejudiced against the travelogue genre today that was certainly not the case in Squier's day.

True Order.	Order acc. to Oviedo.	Nicaragua.	Signs.	Mexico.	Significance.
1	9	Cipat,		Cipactli,	Sea animal.
2	10	Hecat,		Ehecatl,	Wind or air.
3	11	Cali,		CALLI,	House.
4	12	Quespal,		Cuetzpalin,	Lizard.
5	13	*Coat,*		Cohuatl,	Serpent.
6	14	Migiste,		Miquiztli,	Death.
7	15	Mazat,		Mazatl,	Deer.
8	16	Toste,		TOCHTLI,	Rabbit.
9	17	At,		Atl,	Water.

True Order.	Order acd. to Oviedo.	Nicaragua.	Signs.	Mexico.	Significance.
10	18	Izquindi,		Itzcuintli,	Dog.
11	19	Ocomate,		Ozomatli,	Ape.
12	20	Malinal,		Malinalli,	Grass.
13	1	Acato,		ACATL,	Reed.
14	2	Ocelot,		Ocelotl,	Tiger.
15	3	Oate,		Quauhtli,	Eagle.
16	4	Cozgacoate,		Cozcaquauhtli,	Bird.
17	5	Olin,		Ollin,	Movements of Sun.
18	6	Topecat,		TECPATL,	Flint.
19	7	Quiauvit,		Quiahuitl,	Rain.
20	8	Sochit,		Xochtli,	Flower.

11. Pipil-Nicarao calendar. Squier was the first of several scholars to study the Pipil-Nicarao calendar and compare it to that used by the Aztecs in Mexico. His discussion of the Pipil-Nicarao calendar and his comparative table of the "Days of the Month and Their Order" are still of interest to scholars in their efforts to reconstruct the Mexican sequence of days. (From Squier, "The Archaeology and Ethnology of Nicaragua," *Transactions of the American Ethnological Society* 3 (1853): 154–55.)

Contemporaries favorably compared *Nicaragua* to John Lloyd Stephens's *Incidents of Travel in Central America, Chiapas, and Yucatan*,[71] a work that doubtless served as Squier's model. The learned community both in the United States and in Europe recognized Squier as an authority on all subjects relating to Central America, and certainly no less so on its archaeology and ethnology. *Nicaragua* was reissued as *Travels in Central America* in 1853, while a revised, single-volume edition appeared under the original title in 1860.[72]

Squier himself never made extravagant claims for *Nicaragua*, once describing the work to Francis Parkman as "the greatest bore, and altogether the . . . most unsatisfactory thing which I ever encountered or undertook. It goes against the grain from first to last, and if the public doesn't damn it, I shall ever after despise the public. If so much had not been expended on it, I should throw it to the dogs. It is built as we build houses here, thin and lathy in a twinkling of a loon's eye."[73] A two-volume work of that length was, he admitted, a bit much, containing as it did "side slices in politics and other trash." The cost associated with writing and publishing *Nicaragua* put him in financial straits, forcing him to sell his coveted copy of Edward Kingsborough's nine-volume *Antiquities of Mexico* published at London between 1830 and 1848.[74]

Nicaragua possesses, nonetheless, many enduring qualities. Squier's narrative of his archaeological discoveries and his descriptions of the habits and customs of Indian peoples are related with all the warmth and allure of a fireside tale. The work reveals the qualities of character that so endeared him to friends. *Nicaragua* is Squier writ large upon the page. He was willing "to risk the imputation of vanity," he confessed, if the manner in which he had related his experiences would "awaken a true sympathy in the hearts of the American people, for their simple, but unfortunate friends and allies in Central America."[75] As Charles Eliot Norton so perceptively observed of the work and its irrepressible author, "It is a complete reflex of yourself, full of spirit, talent, animation, enthusiasm, & now & then come[s] in a little cock-a-doodle-doism."[76]

It is reasonable to assume that Squier could have contributed substantially more to the archaeology and ethnology of Nicaragua had he not been distracted by his diplomatic activities. His investigations there were conducted under difficult circumstances that gave little encouragement for the prosecution of large-scale archaeological investigations. The aboriginal idols and crumbling teocalli of Central America were largely hidden from view in tropical forests that could only be penetrated with great difficulty. Local Indian groups regarded these sites as the sacred places of their ancestors, for whom it was "a religious duty to hide from the profane view of an alien race." It would be a long time, Squier said, before these difficulties would be surmounted and Central America's ancient past would become better known. "Their investigation must be the gradual work of time, in which individuals can but partly assist." Immense works were rumored to exist in the district of Chontales, near the Indian town of Juygalpa on the northern shore of Lake Nicaragua, but diplomatic duties and other difficulties prevented him from seeking them out. His curiosity and sense of adventure were likewise tantalized by reports of sites in Honduras and in Salvador that were said to be equal in monumental grandeur to those at Copán. Once again he had no opportunity to visit them, although he hoped to do so in the near future. [77]

But what Squier did accomplish is far from insignificant. He recognized, however imprecisely, some of the archaeological frontiers in Nicaragua that were more clearly delineated and explained by later archaeologists. He similarly perceived the significance of external relations between the indigenous peoples of Nicaragua and their Mayan and Mexican neighbors to the North, even though he lacked sufficient evidence to pinpoint the sources and directions of those interactions and corresponding influences. The blending of cultures that occurred in the region at various points and its different configurations of ethnicity eluded him, [78] but he recognized borrowings, interregional influences, and conclusive evidence of migrations. Some of Squier's tribal classifications based upon linguistic evidence have proven correct and others incorrect, yet even his mistakes were reasonable readings of the cultural landscape based upon the minimal evidence available to him. William Duncan Strong, for example, acknowledged that Squier was the first investigator to provide linguistic and ethnographic information about the Indian tribes of Nicaragua, and that he did so at time when virtually nothing was known of those groups and the available evidence was entirely fragmentary. "The situation today," Strong lamented in 1940, "is little better." [79]

What was known of the antiquities of Central America before Squier's investigations in Nicaragua extended only to the northern portion of the region and was confined solely to the monuments at Copán in Honduras and at Quirigua, Quiche, and Quesaltenango in Guatemala. Squier's investigations gave the first indication of the general characteristics of the non-Mayan cultures located south of Guatemala. His conclusions regarding archaeological remains and the distribution and probable migrations of aboriginal populations were based on a small but significant sampling of geographical, archaeological, and ethnohistorical data. His methodology was consonant with the comprehensive approach taken in his earlier studies and with the work of later anthropologists. His observations on the existing condition, geographical distribution, and languages of Nicaragua's Indian peoples were original contributions to knowledge that are still of interest to archaeologists and ethnologists.

Squier was the first Central American scholar to recognize the importance of the observations made by the Spanish chroniclers regarding the linguistic similarities existing between the Aztecs of Mexico and the Nicarao of Nicaragua and to establish an affinity between some of them and the Nahuatl (Aztec) language of Mexico. His study of ethnographic data culled from sixteenth-century Spanish sources, the artifacts recovered in his expeditions, the comparative study of vocabularies, and the surviving fragments of traditions convinced him that there had been migrations into Nicaragua from the north or northwest before the arrival of the Spanish. Most scholars still concur in that opinion.[80] Though uncertain as to the causes of those migrations, he thought that the collapse of the Toltecs in Mexico might have resulted in their southward movement. Scholars today believe that this was actually a second stage in the "Mesoamericanization" of the region, but Squier's theory of a southern migration of Nahual-speaking peoples after the collapse of the Toltecs was essentially correct.[81]

The accuracy of the engravings of the stone idols figured in *Nicaragua* has been both criticized and defended. They were based on the drawings of James McDonough, who traveled with Squier throughout his residence in Nicaragua. Carl Bovallius, who studied the Nicaraguan statues in 1893 for the Swedish Society of Anthropology, contended that "some of Squier's figures do not quite agree with the originals."[82] Wolfgang Haberland, however, took both Squier and Bovallius to task, criticizing their drawings for their tendency to be "fanciful" and "sometimes completely incorrect."[83] Squier would have taken forceful exception to those criticisms, for he attested that McDonough's drawings were "faithful copies from nature, in which accuracy has been consulted, rather that than artistical [sic] effect."[84] A reexamination of those statues by John A. Strong in the summer of 1986 supports Squier's claims to accuracy against those of his detractors.[85] Strong argues that Squier was the more accurate scholar. The collection of prehistoric statues assembled for the Squier-Zapatera exhibition at the National Museum of Nicaragua in 1975 further supports that assessment. Jorge Eduardo Arellano noted in the exhibit's catalog exhibit that he sought to "do justice to the discoverer" by juxtaposing McDonough's drawings with photographs of the original statues, along with quotes from Squier's descriptions.[86] Strong's and Arellano's comparisons of the engravings in *Nicaragua* with the actual statues reveal nothing fanciful or seriously inaccurate about McDonough's drawings, notwithstanding the charges made by Bovallius and Haberland. Squier would be pleased to know that his explorations in Nicaragua have generated such enduring interest.

8. The Mind of Man

The Serpent Symbol and the Reciprocal Principles of Nature

The findings embodied in the comparatively obscure *Serpent Symbol* are critical in any assessment of Squier's anthropological thought. His interest in the origin and development of religious ideas and symbols crystallized in stages between 1846 and the publication, in 1851, of *The Serpent Symbol, and the Worship of the Reciprocal Principles of Nature in America* – the first and last number of his self-styled American Archaeological Researches series.[1] Squier noted the importance of this collateral line of investigation in *Ancient Monuments of the Mississippi*, in the appendix of *Aboriginal Monuments of the State of New York*, in an unpublished paper on the serpent symbol in America read before the American Ethnological Society in 1848,[2] and in a series of articles published in the *American Review* in 1848 and 1849. Squier considered *The Serpent Symbol* an extension of his Smithsonian monographs, and there is, indeed, a unifying set of ideas and themes that intimately connects them.

The train of thought developed in *The Serpent Symbol*, however, is a notably significant departure from the close and guarded factual descriptions of his Smithsonian monographs. Theory and conjecture were never absent in those works but were kept within bounds by the editorial control of Joseph Henry. Freed from Henry's restraining hand, Squier indulged himself in *The Serpent Symbol* in what his friend and reviewer Francis Parkman referred to as "a free spirit of philosophical inquiry."[3] The work is, indeed, by far his most philosophical and far ranging in subject matter. The ideas elaborated here are not divorced from the content of his Smithsonian monographs and early minor writings but read more as a series of shadow chapters to them. *The Serpent Symbol* is the fullest elaboration of Squier's views on the psychic unity of man, and it encapsulates many of the developmentalist assumptions of comparative ethnology in the mid-nineteenth century. *The Serpent Symbol* is Squier's study of the mind of man.

The origin of *The Serpent Symbol* dates to the discovery of the Serpent Mound at Brush Creek in Adams County, Ohio, in 1846. Squier was certain that the effigy mound at Brush Creek was the representation of a serpent and an egg in combination, a symbol found within the religions of the Old World.

He struggled from that time forward to explain the presence of the serpent and egg in the New World. John Russell Bartlett, secretary of the American Ethnological Society, regarded the "great serpent and egg" effigy as one of the most important discoveries yet made in American archaeology. "You are perhaps aware that the 'serpent and egg' are very prominent in the Hindu mythology," he wrote Squier, "but even with this striking analogy, I would not be so ready to jump to conclusions in connecting the American and Asiatic races as some are. I can only say, it is the most striking of any analogies yet discovered."⁴ Gliddon also took interest in "that Serpent's Egg-business," but he expressed concern about what Squier would make of it. He regarded it "as a very dangerous subject for *theorizing* upon, lest it should not be the Serpent and *the* egg! – so be cautious."⁵ Sage advice indeed. The effigy mound at Brush Creek needs interpolation. The earthwork is unquestionably the representation of a serpent, but is it actually swallowing or ejecting an egg? Could the "egg" be a representation of something else?

Squier enlisted Gliddon's knowledge of Oriental mythology and classical history in investigating the archaeological problems suggested by the serpent-and-egg effigy at Brush Creek. He asked Gliddon: "Do the *Serpent* and the *Egg*, separate or in combination, occur among the *Egyptian* symbols, and if they occur what signification was assigned to them? Was the *Serpent* in Egypt in any way associated with the worship of the sun and its attendant worship of the Phallus[?]" Gliddon responded with a fifteen-page disquisition on serpent symbolism in ancient Egypt, asking Squier "to excuse brevity." But again he sounded a note of caution. "No one has recognized more thoroughly than yourself . . . this harmonizing furor of uncritical observers to confound things distinct in origin as in nature, if presenting at first sight a suppositious resemblance to the vestiges of other Nations, other countries, other centres of man's civilization."

Gliddon worried about the conclusions that would follow the announcement of Squier's "Serpico-Ovine discoveries." Uncritical observers would surely embrace the discovery as evidence that the Mound Builders originated in Asia. The problem with serpent symbolism in antiquity, Gliddon noted, was its ubiquity: "The serpent is everywhere in the mythologies and cosmogonies of the East, and one cannot be assured that the Serpent of the Ophites (any more than that emitting [from] or encircling the *Mundane Egg*) was Egyptian rather than Jewish, Persian, or Hindustanic." Gliddon could not find the serpent and egg in combination on a single Egyptian monument, so he abstained from speculation. Neither could he find hieroglyphic evidence directly connecting phallic worship with the solar symbol of the serpent. Gliddon remained curious about Squier's "philosophy of *Eggs* & *Ser-*

pents," which he characterized as "the most beautiful and dangerous subject of your discoveries."[6]

By the time he concluded his investigations with Davis, Squier had become so preoccupied with this line of inquiry that he contemplated writing a book on the subject. He could not ignore, he informed Joseph Henry, the "connections existing between our Western Monuments and those of Central America, and incidentally with those of Southern Asia." His investigations in Ohio had led him to "an analysis of the religion and mythology of the Savage and Semi-Civilized nations of this continent, in connection with those primitive beliefs that have undergone so many modifications (yet retain their original features) in Asia." He regarded the results of those investigations to be "truly remarkable" and again stated his certainty that once completed they would bring new evidence to bear upon the "the origin and antiquity of the American race." Squier did not say what that evidence was or how it explained the origin and antiquity of American Indians. Something of an explanation of that position would be forthcoming in The Serpent Symbol, but it would be an ambiguous and sometimes even a contradictory one.

Those uncertainties stand in marked contrast to the confidence and enthusiasm Squier expressed in sharing his findings with Henry. "I speak with almost absolute certainty when I say that I have the key to the whole system of our aboriginal religion, North and South, and that I have identified not only the original purpose of the imposing monuments of Central America, but the very nature of the worship and the divinities to which they were dedicated."[7] Squier was uncertain whether he should embody those findings into the volume he was preparing for the Smithsonian, for they were based upon the discoveries that he and Davis had made jointly in Ohio. But owing to his open feud with Davis over their respective contributions to those investigations and authorship of the manuscript forthcoming from the Smithsonian, he wanted it known that conceptually those ideas were exclusively his own. Squier's "best friends" advised him to reserve those considerations for a separate volume under his name only, but he was reluctant to do so since he feared that he might never again have the opportunity to place his views on the subject before the public.

Squier's growing interest in pursuing these investigations beyond casual mention had prompted Henry to eliminate certain "theoretical matter" from the Squier-Davis manuscript just prior to its printing.[8] Squier complained to Samuel George Morton in September 1848 that the work had been "emasculated" by Henry's heavy-handed editing. He declared that he would thereafter remain free and clear of all "entangling alliances" with institutions: "I have danced to one turn in fetters – for the first and last time."[9] Henry further angered Squier due to his reluctance to underwrite the cost of extending Squier's investigations into other portions of the Mississippi Valley. Squier complained that he had not received a "red cent" of remuneration or reimbursement from the Smithsonian for the cost of his explorations, even though they had been willing enough to publish the results. "Rich men may possibly afford to be patronized," said Squier, but not he. He was determined that once his business with the Smithsonian was concluded "our paths will diverge at a very large angle."[10]

Squier's attitude toward Henry and the Smithsonian was unfortunate. His reputation as an archaeologist rests squarely upon the originality and disciplined nature of his two monographs published in the *Smithsonian Contributions to Knowledge*. He did, nevertheless, part company with the Smithsonian immediately after completing the second of those works. Henry allowed the truculent Squier to place much of the comparative and speculative materials he had excised from *Ancient Monuments of the Mississippi Valley* within the appendix of his second Smithsonian monograph, *Aboriginal Monuments of the State of New York*, published in 1851. There Squier compares the defensive structures of American aborigines with those of the Pacific Islanders and Celts; the sepulchral monuments in Mexico and Central America and those of the Old World; the aboriginal sacred enclosures or "temples" of North American Indians to those of Mexico, Central America, and Peru; similar religious sites of the Polynesian Islanders and Hindus; and the primitive temples of the British Isles. He also discusses the symbolism of temples. Those comparisons further document his interest in developing cross-cultural analogies as a means of interpreting archaeological evidence and in tracing supposed universals in the psychological development of man. Squier eventually elaborated those interests in *The Serpent Symbol*, where he made his most systematic and comprehensive comparison of the mind of man as illustrated by religious ideas, symbols, and customs from around the globe. Everywhere he looked in his study of religious symbolism he saw further evidence of the psychic unity of man.

The scope and design of *The Serpent Symbol* are much broader than its title suggests. An important objective of Squier's inquiries into the origin and character of archaeological remains was to gather information about the beliefs, customs, and arts of the aboriginal groups occupying the American continent at the time of the European discovery. Native religious conceptions and historical traditions held particular interest to him, since they might suggest the meaning of corresponding ideas within the symbolism of archaeological remains. He was convinced that the diligent study of the religious conceptions and traditions of American Indians would reveal corresponding ideas in the symbolism of their archaeological remains. These, in turn, he compared with analogous beliefs and antiquities in the Old World as a means of further inferring their probable meaning. His assumption was that when entirely distinct peoples were placed in similar circumstances they met their basic needs in similar ways, including their psychological need for symbols to communicate before the invention of writing. This again assumes the psychic unity of man. Human nature is constant and universal in its manifestations.

The worship of the sun, the phallic emblem, the serpent, and the egg occurred among ancient peoples in virtually ever quarter of the globe. Squier compared the religious beliefs and symbolism in the Old and New Worlds not to necessarily establish a connection or common origin but as a means of extrapolating what he saw as universal psychological principles that would explicate the symbolism of mute archaeological remains of peoples remotely separated by time, place, and origin. He referred to these commonalities in human thought as the reciprocal principles of nature, which expressed themselves through complexes of associated ideas, customs, and symbols as distinct societies passed through similar stages of development. The Serpent Symbol is an elaboration of these reciprocal principles and of the developmental stage through which all human societies had at one time passed. The development of this study from conception to completion was a tedious and tortuous experience for Squier, but one that reveals much about the methodology and philosophy of his researches. In The Serpent Symbol, Squier synthesizes and generalizes on a large scale.

A major impetus to Squier's interest in cross-cultural analogies was his correspondence with Edme-François Jomard, president of the Geographical Society of Paris and a member of the Institute of France. The European savant and the young American scholar philosophically discussed comparative ethnology and the natural history of man. Jomard published a detailed notice of the Squier-Davis investigations in the Bulletin de la Société de Geographie as early as December 1846, which was based on a letter written by Benjamin Silliman to the English geologist Dr. Gideon A. Mantell of London and published in Silliman's Journal of American Arts and Sciences. Jomard's account also cites a letter written to him by Squier on October 12, 1846, regarding the position of human remains and different types of burials found within the Ohio mounds. Jomard continued to give detached notices of Squier's investigations until their completion in 1848.[11] He was particularly interested in Squier's "sound" opinions on the state of American civilization when first known to Europeans and on the similarities exhibited between archaeological remains in the Old and New Worlds. Jomard believed that the archaeological remains in the New

World indicated that a higher state of civilization had once existed there than was encountered by the first European explorers. At the time of the European contact, Jomard asserted, groups in North America were found living in an uncultivated and semi-savage state in which the arts were forgotten and tradition itself was dead. He even regarded Mexico and Peru at the time of the Conquest to be but pale reflections of their former states of civilization. Squier's discoveries in the mounds of Ohio seemed to add further evidence in support of Jomard's theory of cultural declension. A higher state of civilization was suggested by the materials found in the mounds, some of which had been transported from distant locations through either extensive commerce or migrations. In either event, the presence of those exotic materials in Ohio mounds established the fact that a contemporaneous communication had occurred between the Great Lakes, the Allegheny Mountains, and the Gulf of Mexico during the era in which the mounds were constructed. [12]

Jomard was fascinated by the "coincidences in forms" existing between archaeological remains and the ethnological characteristics of ancient societies in both the Old World and the New. Those similarities did not necessarily appear to Squier as proof that the American race derived from Asia, as many assumed – an opinion with which Jomard fully concurred. Jomard and Squier both accepted the opinion of the German naturalist and explorer Baron Alexander von Humboldt (1769–1859) that human societies everywhere exhibited certain analogies. Humboldt, perhaps the most respected scientist of his day, succinctly stated the promise and peril of cross-cultural analogies in a series of questions that were well known to Squier and his contemporaries. As Humboldt noted in the first volume of his *Researches, Concerning the Institutions and Monuments of the Ancient Inhabitants of America* (1814),

> It would no doubt be absurd to suppose the migration of Egyptian colonies wherever pyramidal monuments and symbolical paintings are found; but how can we avoid being struck with the traces of resemblance offered by the vast pictures of manners, of arts, of language, and traditions, which exist at present among nations at the most remote distance from each other? Why should we hesitate to point out, wherever they occur, the analogies of construction in languages, of style in monuments, and of fictions in cosmogonies, although we may be unable to decide what were the secret causes of these resemblances, while no historical fact carries us back to the epoch of the communications, which existed between the inhabitants of different climates? [13]

Discovering "the secret causes" of those resemblances was an archaeological and ethnological problem to which Squier would dedicate several years of research and reflection. He greatly admired Humboldt and would later cite him in support of his own views on the similarities that naturally arose between peoples remotely separated by time and place.

It was in the essence of man to seek progress, Jomard believed, and progress was always achieved in human societies under favorable circumstances. Thus one may see similarities between the industries, fundamental ideas, and symbols of the African, the American, and the Asian without deriving the American race from the former or the latter. Man was a born imitator who throughout time and in all parts of the globe had copied natural forms and phenomena as a means of self-expression. Nature presented human societies with certain constant forms and identical phenomena that impressed themselves upon human imagination, furnishing the same raw materials or analogous models with which to meet basic human needs and stimulate intellectual progress. Thus one should not be surprised by similarities among people at the most distant points of the world. Jomard's belief in man's innate desire and capacity for intellectual progress resonated with Squier, who had made similar assertions during his lectures at Albany.

The same line of reasoning also explained differences among human cultures, which Jomard admitted were more numerous than similarities. Whereas nature presented uniformity in certain phenomena and forms throughout the globe, it by no means did so in all instances. Nature also manifests diversity across various localities. Differences in the arts, customs, and languages of peoples existed on different continents, placing the stamp of distinctiveness on human societies. But the single most important cause of similarities between men, despite their physical differences and diverse languages, was humankind's aptitude and need to know, the faculty of reflecting, and the ability to combine ideas in order to form a judgment. It was humankind's intellect – the "divine breath" – that animated and distinguished them from the brute and that everywhere produced certain elementary similarities in human thought. Where, therefore, was the necessity of explaining similarities between the nations of the globe through improbable theories that are repugnant to good sense? Jomard lamented that the branch of natural history that examined human varieties in the light of these considerations had been neglected for too long.

Such neglect invited investigation. Jomard's observations introduced Squier to a new line of research. The archaeological and ethnological problems that Squier addressed at length in The Serpent Symbol began to take shape during his correspondence with Jomard in 1846 and 1847 and became something of a preoccupation with him for several more years. Squier appropriately dedicated The Serpent Symbol to Jomard, whose correspondence with

Squier and interest in the comparative study of archaeological remains ultimately led to its production. Squier had conceptualized such a work during the writing of Ancient Monuments, which he considered but a prelude to a larger comparative work. [14] Ancient Monuments had no sooner been put to press, in fact, than Squier announced his intention of undertaking a comparative study of ancient remains in America and the Old World. [15] His diplomatic appointment delayed completion of the work, but he put the finishing touches on the manuscript soon after his return from Nicaragua. As he confided to Morton in February 1851: "Snake 'drags its slow length along,' and when published will probably be bought by three persons, read by two, and understood by one!" He was relieved that the work was nearing completion, "for the thing has been squirming in my head so long that I want to get rid of it." [16] Squier finally exorcised his snake-demon when The Serpent Symbol, and the Worship of the Reciprocal Principles of Nature in America made its appearance in April 1851. The publisher made no money on the book, prompting Squier to lament: "I must buy my own copies if I am foolish enough to want such a book." [17]

The Serpent Symbol at its worst is a poorly organized cut-and-paste elaboration of Squier's earlier writings, but at its best it is his most philosophical and original conception of aboriginal America. Squier recognized the disjointed nature of the work in the preface, citing his many other duties in apology for its literary flaws. Nonetheless, The Serpent Symbol is a remarkably original and bold attempt to discover the underlying principles of the aboriginal religions of America. The religious conceptions and historical traditions of American Indians, the iconography of their archaeological remains, and the study of analogous beliefs and antiquities in the Old World are all called to witness in its eclectic pages. The originality of the work is in its approach and the ambitiousness of its goals. Squier has the distinction of being the first writer to attempt a synthesis of the religious conceptions of the American Indian.

The primary purpose of The Serpent Symbol is to establish the "essential identity" in some of the fundamental religious conceptions of ancient peoples in the Old and New Worlds and to illustrate similarities in their manner of expression through symbolical systems. Squier's analysis encompasses archaeological remains and the known religious conceptions, historical traditions, and customs of American Indians. It was upon those "unimpeachable witnesses" that he based the "hypothetical conclusions" embodied in The Serpent Symbol. Squier investigated these subjects in the spirit of Humboldt, who remarked in the introduction to his Researches that "we shall be surprised to find, towards the end of the fifteenth century, in a world which we call new, those ancient institutions, those religious notions, and that style of building which seem in Asia to indicate the dawn of civilization." [18] Similarities between the archaeological remains and religious conceptions of the Old and New Worlds led some to speculate that there must have been "an original connection" or diffusion between them, a conclusion firmly grounded in "popular prejudice."[19]

Before that conclusion could be accepted as self-evident, it was first necessary to ask how similar conditions and similar mental, moral, and physical "constitutions" might result in institutions, religions, and archaeological remains of an analogous or "cognate type." Received opinion on the subject could not be accepted as conclusive, for at no previous time were the materials for the comparative study of man more abundant. Many of the "great collateral questions of natural science" had been answered in recent years, while geographic exploration had advanced knowledge about the religions, institutions, history, and customs of nations around the globe. Archaeologists could now make systematic comparisons among groups greatly separated by time and place and thereby evaluate "the relations" they sustained one to the other. "For no sciences are so eminently inductive," said Squier, "as Archaeology and Ethnology, or the sciences of Man and Nations; none which require so extensive a range of facts to their elucidation."[20] He reveals a breadth of learning in his attempt to elucidate those extensive facts, and in defining the ground upon which he was traveling he disavowed allegiance to any established theories or presumably self-evident truths. "In pursuing my investigations, I have sought only to arrive at truth, however much it may conflict with preconceived notions, or what are often called 'established opinions.' I have no system to sustain, no creed to defend; but [I] entertain as many hypotheses as there are possibilities, and claim to be ready to reject or accept according to the weight of evidence and the tendency of facts." There was clearly no concession to monogenism and biblical ethnology in that statement, but neither was there an endorsement of polygenism. Squier is characteristically cautious in *The Serpent Symbol* about matters relating to race and human origins.

Squier believed that the study of the religious conceptions and symbols of American Indians would lead to the same results as collateral investigations into physical anthropology, archaeology, and linguistics. All branches of ethnological inquiry demonstrated "the unity of the American race, and its radical difference in respect to all other families of the globe." When one distinguished between what was radically different in the physical characteristics, religions, and languages of American Indian groups and what was only incidentally different, it became apparent that the disparities were not differences of kind but of condition. Differences between the various divisions and families of the American race reflected interactions with specific environments over long periods of time. Squier saw a striking uniformity among American Indian groups when such conditional and circumstantial considerations were taken into account, a uniformity that bespoke a common origin and racial distinctiveness. The distinctive characteristics of the buffalo hunters of the plains, the fur-trapping and deer-hunting peoples of the East, and the agricultural and sedentary groups of the Southeast were thus incidental differences induced by different environments and not radical differences that denied the essential unity and distinctive character of American Indians as a type of mankind. [21]

Were it not for the efforts of scholars to reconcile the existence of the American Indian with the biblical account of creation (which required all branches of the human species to be derived from a single pair), Squier believed, the unity and distinctiveness of the American race would never have been called into question. But many persisted in the belief that American Indians were the descendants of one or more of the nations known in ancient history, and accordingly they directed their inquiries toward establishing which group or groups had been the progenitors of the American Indian. Squier would have none of Caleb Atwater's confident assertion that the more one studied the subject of American antiquities, the more evidence would be found establishing the truth of the Mosaic account of creation. "The discoveries of the Antiquarian throw a strong and steady light upon the scriptures, while the scriptures afford to the Antiquarian the means of elucidating many subjects otherwise difficult to be explained, and serve as an important guide in the prosecution of his investigations." [22] Archaeologists could not follow the evidence wherever it led in the face of such a priori assumptions.

Squier saw no need to harmonize the biblical account with America antiquities or to derive the American Indian from the lost tribes of Israel or any other hypothetical ancestors in the Old World. Those who persisted in doing so based upon the alleged proofs of analogy ignored a more plausible explanation, such as that made by the English theologian William Warburton (1698–1779) in his *Divine Legation of Moses* (1737, 1741). According to Warburton, they committed "the old, inveterate error, that a similitude of customs and manners, amongst the various tribes of mankind most remote from each other, must needs arise from some communication. Whereas human nature, without any help, will in the same circumstances always exhibit the same appearances." [23] Similarities between the customs and way of life among the various families of man did not establish an *ex post facto* connection or communication between them.

How far a comparative study of the religious conceptions and symbols of American Indians would go to confirm the results of physical anthropology and philology that established the radical distinctiveness of the American Indian remained to be seen. The results of Squier's own investigations convinced him, however, that their predominant religious ideas and symbols were rooted in the worship of the sun, or what should more properly be called the reciprocal powers of nature – a universal form of worship dating to the earliest periods of man's development. All ancient mythological systems were rooted in the worship of the sun and the veneration of nature. This could be traced in aboriginal America in its incipient, intermediate, and most advanced forms, passing from the Eskimo to the ancient societies of Mexico and Peru, where it most closely resembled the form that had developed in ancient India and Assyria.

The reciprocal principles of nature reflected psychological characteristics deeply ingrained in man's early religious beliefs and did not necessarily denote common origins for the various nations sharing them. Since man was morally and mentally everywhere the same and motivated by the same impulses and aspirations, it was not astonishing that he should manifest a "wonderful unity" in fundamental religious conceptions. Man's early religious beliefs were superficially unrelated but logically rooted in the first principle of nature: the worship of the sun as the giver of heat, light, and life.[24] Squier further explained these universal psychological principles through his philosophy of symbolism. In the absence of a written language or other means of conveying abstract ideas, the symbols of a people were invested with sacred and esoteric significance that continued long after their original meanings were forgotten or only dimly remembered.

Squier believed that the worship of the sun as an ideological system was closely connected to phallic worship. He saw evidence of phallicism in all ancient religions and speculated that it may have been their basis. While the egg sometimes symbolized the idea of procreation, procreation could also take the form of the phallus.[25] Squier deduced the essential elements of phallicism from the ancient religions of Asia and Europe as expressed in Ouranus and Gia, Osiris and Isis, and the lingam and yoni of Hindustan, which explained the rationale of its existence in the Old World. He then applied those same principles in explaining the probable nature of phallic symbols in the New World. Squier saw evidence of phallic symbolism in Stephens's descriptions of the ruins at Uxmal, where the ornamental cornices of public buildings were sculptures of *membra conjuncta in coitu*. He saw further evidence of phallic worship in Dupaix's observations on Mexican temples, in Juan de Batauzos's comments on the great square at the temple of the sun at Cuzco in his unedited history of the Incas in the library of the Escurial, and in Palacio's observations about the Indians of Honduras made in 1576. He also thought it likely that the monoliths at Copán were representations of phallic symbolism.[26] Squier seconded Gerard Troost's opinion that phallic worship had existed among the Mound Builders as illustrated by the sculptured sandstone images or figurines found during his investigation in Tennessee.[27] Those images show an erect penis, which Squier politely and formally Latinized as *membrane generationis virile in eretione.*

The Indians of Honduras, according to Herrera, worshiped the sun through two idols, one in the form of a women and the other a man. He made these same observations on the religious practices of aboriginal groups in San Salvador and Nicaragua. He noted that the natives of Nicaragua drew blood from the genital organs and sprinkled it on ears of maize before eating them in solemn ritual. Squier interpreted that ritual as worship of the life-giving power of the phallus. Herrara's descriptions of the idolatry of the Honduran and Nicaraguan tribes, said Squier, were confirmed by his own investigations in Nicaragua. Squier found carved monoliths or idols on the islands of Lake Nicaragua and Managua at what he believed were the sites of ancient temples. All of the idols were clearly delineated male and female figures, with the male genitals being in some instances preeminent by design. He interpreted the Nicaraguan idols as obvious representations of the reciprocal principles of nature. The ancient practice of phallic worship, like sun worship, was a natural and logical adoration of the creative powers and active principles of nature, and both practices were present among the religious conceptions of American Indians.[28]

The rationale of symbolism that explained representations of abstract religious ideas on the American continent also explicated the remains classified by Squier as "temple" mounds or sacred "high places."[29] Temple mounds were truncated pyramidal structures with graded ascents to their summits. They were present in the Ohio Valley but were most abundant at the Gulf of Mexico. Squier thought them to have been originally erected as sacred places or as sites for public buildings or temples. Bartram's accounts of his travels among the Creeks indicate that they built their temples and public buildings upon platform mounds of this type, which he attributed to the perpetuation of a custom of the earlier groups of mound-building Indians. It was known from Du Pratz's *History of Louisiana* that the Natchez used platform mounds in precisely the same way. Garcilaso de la Vega described similar structures among the Floridian tribes in his account of the de Soto expedition, which also contained a description of mound building among those groups. Squier invited comparison of the temple or pyramidal mounds of the United States described in *Ancient Monuments of the Mississippi* and the analogous teocalli of Mexico and Central America described by Stephens and Kingsborough, which seemed to have been built in association with the same religious principles. Squier saw the temple mounds of the Mississippi as the work of an earlier and ruder people, but they served the same purpose as the more elaborate brick and stone structures of Mesoamerica. At Copán, Palenque, Chichén Itzá, and Uxmal one found an almost identical combination of mounds, terraces, and pyramidal structures as were found in the Mississippi Valley. Squier specifically compared one of the larger terraced pyramidal structures at Uxmal to similar remains at Madison Parish, Louisiana, and to works in Washington County, Mississippi.[30]

Squier considered the practice of building temple mounds in America to be an indigenous invention, but he was nonetheless struck by perceived similarities between these temple mounds and similar structures in Asia. That the practice of building these temples or sacred high places was necessarily derivative he would not admit, but he qualified that opinion by adding that there was "not only a general identity between the American and Asiatic structures of this class, but there are detailed resemblances, which could hardly be the result of accident, and which go further than any monumental evidence to establish an original connection between the two continents."[31] The probability of such a connection was most clearly suggested by the ancient monuments of Central America, which were in a relatively better state of preservation and allowed the most detailed comparisons. Here he saw some extraordinary coincidences between Central American structures and the Buddhist monuments of India. While the temples of Central America bore a general similarity with those of Mexico, they also had many peculiar features all their own. The Central American temples described by Stephens and Catherwood, said Squier, exhibited a remarkable likeness to the Buddhist temples of southern India. At Palenque he saw small structures completely corresponding with the *dagobas* at Ceylon. He believed that a systematic investigation would show that the shape, interior structure, and purpose of the structures at Palenque exactly resembled those of Hindustan and the Indian archipelago.

It is difficult to harmonize those statements with Squier's opinion that the civilizations of Central America were indigenous and not derivative or intruded. Perhaps he saw the resemblances between the structures at Palenque and those of Hindustan and India as vestiges of an unknown period of contact, but if so he makes no effort to indicate whether the direction of diffusion was from Asia to America or vice versa. So guarded is he in such matters that he himself seems quite uncertain as to what he really means to suggest. Why such similarities could not be explained as independent inventions rooted in universal needs and impulses (as he asserts in all his writings) seems quite unfathomable. His opinion that architectural analogies suggest "an original connection" between Asia and America within the confines of a book that elaborates an alternative rationale for explaining such similarities upon psychological principles is a little like having one's cake and eating it too. It appears that in the lack of conclusive evidence one way or the other he wanted to keep his options open by hedging.

Squier took the same position regarding the presence of phallic worship in America. The practice of phallic worship could not necessarily be accepted as derivative, "for how naturally, in the mind of the primitive man, must the apparent cause of reproduction associate itself with his ideas of creation; and with the sun, as the obvious vivifier of the physical world, become the common symbol of the supreme creative power, whose existence is everywhere manifested!" Neither could it be denied, on the other hand, that coincidences in the arts, institutions, and religious practices of Asia and America – together with the prevalence of phallic worship on both continents – tended to support the possibility of a remote connection between the Old and New Worlds. Such resemblances did not establish such a connection as a certainty, but they did justify the conjecture. "But if we accept this hypothesis, how are we to determine whether the impression has been from Asia on America – or, as certain facts would imply, from America on Asia? So far as natural science reflects any light on the questions it seems to favor the latter alternative." [32] If the monogenists took comfort from Squier's willingness to consider the hypothesis of an ancient connection between Asia and America, they could take little pleasure in contemplating the possibility that the diffusion of ideas and practices had flowed from America to Asia. There was nothing in the existing evidence that positively established that these practices were derivative, but neither did the evidence refute the probability of a remote connection. The question simply could not be answered given the available evidence.

Squier would wrestle with that same conundrum in trying to explain the origin and meaning of the serpent symbol in America. Everywhere he looked he saw the symbol of the serpent. The astronomical serpent bearing the moon and stars is figured in the Mexican Codex at Dresden and peers forth in colossal dimensions in the ruins of Chichén Itzá. Squier found the serpent depicted upon the painted rocks at Managua in Nicaragua and in the Mexican sculptures at the Louvre. The sculptured stone rattlesnake tablets recovered from Clark's Work near Chillicothe and the remarkable Serpent Mound at Brush Creek in Adams County, Ohio, provided additional evidence of its ubiquity and significance as an aboriginal symbol. Squier was not prepared to speculate on whether the effigy mounds of Wisconsin were built by the same people as erected the mounds in Ohio, but he was intrigued by the presence of serpents represented in three effigy mounds in Iowa, which he figured in The Serpent Symbol. Squier interpreted the Serpent Mound at Brush Creek as the representation of a snake in the act of swallowing or ejecting an egg. The egg was a symbol of creation in the cosmologies of several early societies, while the serpent was a prominent symbol invested with various meanings that included the worship of the sun. He regarded the serpent and egg in combination to be an allusion to the act of creation and the life-giving properties of the sun as symbolized by the serpent, yet another illustration of his doctrine of the reciprocal principles of nature.[33]

The question of how the serpent came to symbolize the sun in the Old World was not easily answered, for it was often invested with meanings other than sun worship in early Eastern cosmologies. But there could be no question that it symbolized the sun among certain groups of American Indians. Squier's rationale of symbolism seemed to explain the phenomenon quite naturally. It was the characteristic behavior of the serpent that made it one of the most mysterious of all creatures. The serpent moved without feet seemingly by the power of its own spirit, and through its annual shedding of skin it appeared to possess the power of rejuvenation. How natural and logical it was that the snake would become an object of veneration. The annual shedding of skin associated the serpent with the idea of rejuvenation and a succession of forms as observed in the succession of the seasons. Thus the serpent came to symbolize the sun and the reproductive or creative power of the universe. Squier believed that the various manifestations of sun worship, phallic worship, and serpent worship in America were intimately related, if not absolutely identical in their underlying principles: "They are all forms of a single worship."[34]

Squier identified sun worship as the underlying principle of serpent symbolism and regarded it as the key to understanding the entire religious system of the Aztecs. The sun symbolized Tezcatlipoca, the principal deity of the Aztecs. A male and female serpent symbolized the great Aztec father and mother, and the feather-headed serpent Tonacatlecoatl was the "serpent sun." Chihuacohuatl, or the female serpent, was pictured with the feather-headed Tonacatlecoatl in the Codex Vaticanus.[35] A feathered serpent also symbolized Quetzalcoatl, the earthly son of Tonacatlecoatl. Squier planned to explore the classification of Aztec deities in a projected work on the "Mythological System of the Ancient Mexicans" that was to have appeared as the third number of his American Archaeological Researches series. There he proposed to show the conformity of Aztec religious beliefs to similar conceptions in the early cosmologies of the Old World.[36] The Aztec veneration of Tezcatlipoca as depicted in obsidian idols, for example, reminded Squier of the Assyrian veneration of Baal. Squier never completed the project, but he did give an account of the subject in the *New York Tribune* in November 1852.[37]

Squier drew attention to the prominence of serpent symbols in the sculptured ruins of Central America as seen in the colossal feathered-serpent heads in the Mayan ruins at Chichén Itzá. He believed that the ruins at Chichén Itzá had been a temple of Ku Kulcan, or Cuculcan, a Mayan deity that corresponded with the Aztec Quetzalcoatl. Squier believed that Ku Kulcan might, in fact, have been the Mayan name for Quetzalcoatl. The etymology of the name Ku Kulcan (which translated as "feathered-serpent God") gave Squier more evidence in support of that conclusion. The derivation of the name for the Mayan deity Kinchahan similarly corresponded with that of Tonacatlecoatl, the "sun serpent" of the Aztecs. The *caracol* structure at Chichén Itzá described by Stephens was also connected with serpent worship as evidenced by the presence of the entwined bodies of two gigantic serpents. Squier thought them to be allusive to the male and female serpent deities of the Aztecs. The remains of entwined serpents were also present among the ruins of Uxmal. Squier believed that the similarities between Aztec and Mayan beliefs, despite their modifications, derived from a common Toltecan root.[38]

The symbolism of the feathered serpent also manifested itself south of Mexico and Yucatán. Squier encountered it in Nicaragua on the shores of Lake Managua in the drawing of a coiled and feathered serpent painted in red on the smooth face of the adjacent cliff. More painted serpents were found on other rocks at this site, which Squier identified as being identical to those figured in the Dresden Codex copied by Kingsborough. The correspondence between the serpent drawings near Managua and those in the Dresden Codex seemed to confirm the speculations of Humboldt and others that the Codex had originated south of Mexico. Indians who accompanied Squier to the Managua site regarded the serpent drawing as a representation of the sun. A large figure of the sun and moon could be seen on the surrounding cliffs before the Nicaraguan earthquake of 1838, and when Squier examined the site in 1849, fragments of these representations could still be found in the fallen debris.[39]

Serpents, especially the rattlesnake, were esteemed by many groups of North American Indians, as recorded in the works of Bartram, Adair, Charlevoix, Heckewelder, Henry, and Carver. They were regarded as possessing supernatural powers, which Squier interpreted as the remote and subconscious vestige of an earlier belief that saw the serpent as the symbol of the "incorporeal powers" of the supernatural beings known as manitous. The Menominee, according to James, translated the Ojibwa word for manitou as *ahwahtoke* ("a snake"). [40] Other Algonquian peoples in the Great Lakes region regarded serpents as the symbol of an evil manitou, as described in the legends published by Squier and verified by the Ojibwa historian George Copway. Squier and Davis recovered sculptured sandstone tablets in the form of coiled rattlesnakes from Mound no. 1 at Clark's Work on Paint Creek, three of which were partially restored. The restored tablets showed that their heads had originally been ornamented with a feathered design similar to that commonly found in Mexico and Central America. Fragments of other tablets that had been broken and damaged by fire were recovered from the same mound, having been enclosed in copper sheets. [41] Those circumstances suggested that the tablets were greatly valued and perhaps sacred.

It was the specific combination of the serpent and egg at the Serpent Mound – the compound symbol that entered widely into the ancient Eastern cosmologies – that most intrigued and perplexed Squier. While he admitted that there was no distinct allusion to the serpent and egg in known cosmological ideas of the North American Indian, one could expect to find it, if anywhere, among the more elaborate mythological systems of Mexico and Central America. It was all the more regrettable, therefore, that the "barbarous zeal" of the Spanish had not only destroyed many of the Mexican pictorial records and monuments but also "distorted" the few native traditions they bothered to record. The destruction of those pictorial records and symbols left Squier precious little to work with concerning evidences of the existence of specific ideological conceptions like the serpent and egg in combination. While one could discern representations that were manifestly symbolic of aboriginal cosmology and mythology, no collateral and corroborated proofs could be recovered from the surviving traditions and pictorial records of Mexico and Central America that would confirm what logic and analogy suggested regarding their actual meanings. The only hint of the serpent-and-egg motif in the New World – other than the Serpent Mound at Brush Creek – was found in the sculptured serpent and egg discovered by Stephens among the monoliths at Copán. Squier hypothesized that the monoliths at Copán were connected with phallic worship, a kind of worship that had been illustrated by the serpent and the egg in other parts of the globe. Among the figures sculptured on the ruined temple of Zaya in Yucatán was the depiction of an indistinct animal carrying a globe upon its back. Squier thought that the animal was probably a serpent. The Algonquian tradition of a great serpent related to Squier by Copway likewise showed a "curious parallelism" with Old World allegories. [42]

Squier concluded that the serpent symbol had figured prominently in the religious systems and symbolic representations of aboriginal America, particularly among the populations of Mexico and Central America. The significance of the serpent symbol in America was "essentially the same with that which attached to it among the early nations of the old continent." The parallelism and uniformity he had identified in the elementary religious ideas and corresponding symbols of the Old and New Worlds led him irresistibly to ascribe to

> the emblematic SERPENT AND EGG OF OHIO a significance radically the same with that which was assigned to the analogous compound symbol among the primitive nations of the East. This conclusion is further sustained, as we have seen, by the character of some of the religious structures of the old continent, in which we find the symbolic serpent, and the egg or circle represented on a most gigantic scale. Analogy could probably furnish no more decisive sanction, unless by exhibiting other structures, in which not only a general correspondence, but an absolute identity should exist. Such an identity it would be unreasonable to look for, even among the works of the same people, constructed in accordance with a common design.[43]

It was then that Squier delivered his boldest stroke – one that gave monogenists another glimmer of hope and that polygenists doubtless looked upon with disapproval. He set caution aside for a moment in order to "hazard the suggestion that the symbolical Serpent and Egg of Ohio are distinctly allusive to the specific notions of cosmogony which prevailed among the nations of the East, for the reason that it is impossible to bring positive collateral proof that such notions were entertained by any of the American nations."[44] That statement had definite implications for the debate about human origins and led to three contending hypotheses. First, if the serpent symbol could be shown to be a parallel development in America, then there was no need to attribute its presence to contact or diffusion from the Old World – a position that fit with the arguments of Morton and the polygenists. Second, if the serpent symbol in America proved to be derivative, then the arguments of the monogenists would be greatly advanced. A third hypothesis argued that the diffusion of common ideas and practices did not necessarily establish a common origin but merely indicated a period of influential contact between peoples of separate origins during an era of their respective pasts.

Squier disclaimed a preference for any of those theories. He refused, in fact, to choose between them, although he clearly leaned toward the theory of separate origins. His purpose in writing The Serpent Symbol was not polemical but utilitarian. The explanatory model presented there is one of independent invention, not cultural diffusion. He saw no need to derive American Indians from any of the peoples or nations recorded in the Old Testament, and time and again in his writings he criticized popular theories that attempted to do so. He struggled to free American archaeology from the larger problem that Bruce G. Trigger has called the "the impasse of antiquarianism" – the need to connect prehistoric remains to written records and the known peoples of the past. [45] The presence of the serpent symbol in America, however, presented Squier with an anthropological problem that he never satisfactorily resolved. He understood the contending explanations, but one can see him struggling with trying to choose between independent invention and the hint of a connection and common origin.

The emphasis Squier placed upon uniformity in man's mental, moral, and physical faculties was a necessary counterbalance to the inordinate amount of unsound speculation and errors too often occasioned by feeble analogies. Similarities and coincidences, real or imagined, could not be uncritically accepted as proof of connections depending upon "communications remote or recent." Humboldt had cautioned wisely when remarking upon this very problem, and once again Squier called upon him in his concluding observations in The Serpent Symbol: "How rash to point out the group of nations on the old continent to which the Toltecs, Aztecs, Muyscas, and Peruvians present the nearest analogies; since these analogies are apparent in the traditions, the monuments, and customs which perhaps preceded the present divisions of Asiatics into Chinese, Hindus, and Mongols." [46] The aboriginal peoples that the Spanish encountered in the sixteenth century may well have been older than the oldest civilizations of the Old World.

But the presence of the serpent symbol in America, Squier confessed, presented no easy solution. He was clearly at a loss to satisfactorily explain it, even upon the principles he had himself so diligently and consistently elaborated. He easily understood how the annual shedding of a snake's skin might symbolize reproduction, time, or evil force (an evil manitou), but most of its occurrences were not readily accounted for unless they were essentially arbitrary. The fact that serpent symbolism in aboriginal America appeared to be essentially arbitrary imparted a special interest to its predominance on the American continent, especially in Mexico and Central America. Squier was treading upon dangerous ground here, just as Gliddon had warned.

> This fact also tends to establish a community of origin, or a connection or intercourse of some kind, between the primitive nations of the two continents; for it can hardly be supposed that a strictly arbitrary symbol should accidentally be chosen to express the same ideas and combinations of ideas, by nations of diverse origins and totally disconnected. Hence it is

that the serpent claims so large a portion of our attention; for the more numerous and decided the coincidences between its various symbolical applications, the more plausible the hypothesis of a dependence, at some period or other, between the people of the old and new worlds.[47]

Those who take interest in Squier's affiliation with the polygenists of the American School of Ethnology would do well to reflect upon the meaning of that passage. That Squier was receptive and even sympathetic to the doctrine of separate origins is undeniable, but he was not so doctrinaire a supporter as to reject the possibility that certain analogies, if submitted to the proper tests, might indicate connections more or less intimate between the ancient peoples of the Old and New Worlds during the remote recesses of the unrecorded past. Squier clearly regarded the serpent symbol in America as suggestive of just such a connection, but he readily admitted that speculation in this regard fell far short of the requirements of absolute proof. He was at least willing to entertain the possibility that serpent symbolism indicated a common origin, connection, or intercourse of some kind, even when submitted to critical scrutiny. Squier quoted the British Oriental scholar and antiquary Sir William Jones (1746–94) in support of his own position. As Jones once observed, even the most rigid proofs required of analogies did not preclude the possibility of a least some common origin.

> We cannot justly conclude by arguments, preceding the proof of fact, that one idolatrous people must have borrowed their deities, rites, and tenets from another; since gods of all shapes and dimensions may be framed by the boundless powers of imagination, or by the frauds and follies of men, in countries never connected; but when features of resemblance too strong to have been accidental are observable in different systems of polytheism, without fancy or prejudice to color them and improve their likeness, we can scarcely help believing that some connection has in immemorial time subsisted between the several nations which have adopted them.[48]

Squier believed this to be a reasonably safe position to maintain.

Squier's hypothesis of a remote connection between the Old and New Worlds neither proved monogenism nor disproved polygenism, for peoples of entirely distinct and separate origins could have had a period of influential contact at some point in the remote past. The fact that Squier openly entertained that possibility is precisely why the doctrinaire Gliddon regarded such speculations as being decidedly "dangerous." They did not refute the theory of separate origins, but they did introduce untidy anomalies and hypotheses that were not easily explained. Squier may well have been a convert to polygenism, but he was first and last a free thinker. There was no room for biblical ethnology in his vision of aboriginal America, but he was at least open to the possibility that there had been an influential connection between the Old and New Worlds in remote antiquity. That position neither proved nor disproved the doctrine of separate origins. It remained an open question whether the American Indians had originated as a distinct type of mankind in Asia and subsequently migrated to the New World or whether they had an autochthonous origin in the New World.

Squier had discussed the rudiments of these ideas in his earlier works, but he elaborated and extended them in *The Serpent Symbol* through supplemental materials drawn from wide array of sources. To attempt such a synthesis was as courageous as it was naive, as impossible as it was suggestive. Squier had taken the eighteenth- and nineteenth-century preoccupation with cultural analogies and given it his own twist, using the observations of Warburton, Jomard, and Humboldt as his ultimate authorities. The work also owes much to the currents of literary romanticism that left a deep impression on American thought in the mid-nineteenth century. The conjunction of the countervailing traditions of romanticism and empiricism in American archaeology and ethnology is well illustrated in Squier's thought, and in his generation there is perhaps none better. Oriental literature and the history of the early centers of civilization were much in vogue in literary and scientific salons and informed the entire romantic movement. Squier's initiation into a portion of that literature led him to see a "psychic unity" in human thought and what he perceived to be the universal principles that explained its operations a rationale of religious symbolism. He ransacked Coleman's *Hindu Mythology*, Tod's *Rajasthan*, and Savary's *Egypt* in search of symbols and associated beliefs and practices that might aid him in that endeavor. These works provided him with a philosophy of symbolism based on inherent psychological principles of human nature that were universal in their application. Squier's original contribution was to apply these concepts in his interpretation of the religious ideas and symbols of native peoples throughout the American continent.

Reviews of *The Serpent Symbol* were mostly favorable and noted the impressive extent of the author's research, the novelty of his views, and the philosophical spirit in which he approached his subject. The most substantive and flattering review appeared in the *Literary World*.[49] The anonymous writer noted that *The Serpent Symbol* added "concurrent testimony" to the unity and homogeneous character of the American race, confirming the researches of Morton in physiology and Duponceau in philology. Squier's comparative study of the religious conceptions, customs, and structures of the various

American nations established the fact that there was a singular uniformity in their religious views. Squier had delineated "the great leading principles of a common belief arising from a similarity of outward circumstances and the identity of psychological conformation." He had ably demonstrated how the deification of the physical attributes of nature among American Indians had passed through different developmental stages until it emerged in a conventional form of symbolism represented in their archaeological remains. The active principles of nature were expressed through the worship of the sun and the kindred principle of fire at their highest stage of development. Squier had demonstrated "in a learned and satisfactory manner" that this form of worship was practiced whether one examined the teocalli and high places of the Mexicans or the "altar" mounds of the Mississippi Valley.

The reviewer acknowledged that Squier had strengthened his conclusions regarding serpent worship by frequent reference to the works of European writers on the subject, but he thought that in many cases Squier had perhaps done so unnecessarily,

> for we think the facts and data collected by Mr. Squier give more support to the hypotheses of Stukeley and Deane than they can ever give to him. No subject has been more obscured by half learning, rash conjecture, and a craving for Biblical analogies, than this of the Worship of the Serpent; and we think that if it is ever thoroughly understood it will be by studying it from an American point of view exclusively, as on this continent its existence is a fixed fact, attested by monuments, and accounted for by the universal presence of the chosen symbol, the rattlesnake, to which species all the sculptures and pictured serpents of the Mexicans, Indians, etc., are referable.

The Serpent Symbol had initiated a new era in the study of American antiquities, and its author manifested "a wide range of information, remarkable in so young a writer, and more especially in one whose active career would have been sufficient for most men. Wherever Mr. Squier is on American ground he is strong, and much of his work partakes of the nature of original authority and is a specific addition to the existing stock of information." If any alterations to *The Serpent Symbol* could be recommended, it would be that Squier omit some of the analogies from the Old World, for they make him dependent on the opinions of English writers such as Bryant, Faber, and Maurice, who the reviewer said were utterly clueless about the true ends of ethnology and entirely ignorant of the means of achieving them. The London *Athenaeum* likewise expressed admiration for what Squier had attempted and his the breadth of learning. "He has proceeded with an enlarged, a liberal, and a learned spirit." *The Serpent Symbol* embodied an impressive range of research and presented original views on a previously unexplored subject. "We have been traveling over new ground with a new guide."[50]

Not all of Squier's contemporaries shared in that favorable opinion, however. Henry Rowe Schoolcraft was highly critical of *The Serpent Symbol*. A good deal of antipathy existed between Schoolcraft (the established ethnologist) and Squier (the arriviste), which was no doubt based on mutual jealousy and large egos. Squier's relationship with Schoolcraft has been perceptively characterized as a contest to see "which was to be dean of American ethnology."[51] Schoolcraft stated his unqualified disapproval of *The Serpent Symbol* and its author in the fourth volume of his *History of the Indian Tribes of the United States*, published in 1854. "Mr. Ephraim G. Squier, abruptly entered the field of American archaeology by a paper for the Smithsonian Institution for 1838 [1848], which created expectations of future promise. These are not sustained by his work on the serpent symbol, which there is no possibility of considering a contribution to American archaeology."[52] Schoolcraft gave no reason for that dictum but merely seemed satisfied to have stated it. Squier reported to Morton that Rev. Dr. Francis L. Hawks, a founder of the American Ethnological Society and a biblical ethnologist, considered *The Serpent Symbol* "a most adroit and dangerous attack on the Christian religion," an assertion that Squier found "rather cool in consideration of the fact that the Bible and Christianity were not even discussed."[53] Francis Parkman clearly had in mind Christian scholars like Hawks when he noted in his review of *The Serpent Symbol* that "the conclusions to which his [Squier's] investigations tend will prove to minds of a certain cast startling, bewildering, and painful, while thinkers of a different stamp will discover in them fresh proof of the fundamental truths of religion."[54] Squier's views on the need to eliminate matters of religious doctrine from archeological and ethnological inquiry clearly threatened the beliefs of biblical ethnologists like Hawks, but in truth Squier steered clear of theological disputes regarding the origins of American Indians and their antiquities whenever possible.

Later investigators of American Indian religions have also criticized *The Serpent Symbol*. Daniel G. Brinton noted the work's wide scope but claimed that it was written "in the interests of one school of mythology [only], and it the rather shallow physical one, so fashionable in Europe a century ago." Briton took exception to Squier's "sweeping generalization" that the religions of the American Indians were elementally the same and that all observable differences found among them were but modifications of sun or fire worship. "With this he combines the doctrine, that the chief topic of mythology is the adoration of the generative power; and to rescue such views from their materializing tendencies, imagines to counterbalance them with a clear universal monotheism." Brinton was unwilling to accept Squier's claim that "the grand conception of a Supreme Unity and the doctrine of the reciprocal principles existed in America in a well-defined and clearly recognizable form," or his related assertion that all American aboriginal religions were monotheistic. [55] "These are views which to-day probably have no defenders, [and] certainly not among those who have made a study of the scientific analysis of primitive religions."[56] Brinton's criticisms are eminently fair. Squier's view of native religions certainly reflects the intellectual fashion of the day. The romantic movement in American arts and letters and the preoccupations of the American School of Ethnology informed his archaeology in significant ways, and those influences are clearly reflected in The Serpent Symbol.

The significance of serpent symbolism in the religious conceptions and archaeological remains of American Indians remained a subject of absorbing interest among later investigators. Squier's approach to the subject, the themes he explored, and even some of his categories of analysis are found in later works, but with a surprising absence of recognition. Squier's effort to correlate archaeological symbols with known religious conceptions of American Indians became a basic anthropological approach to interpreting archaeological remains, but others who have gone over some of the same ground and arrived at similar conclusions have failed to acknowledge the priority of his pioneering work. Charles Clark Willoughby and Frederic Ward Putnam, who were undoubtedly familiar with The Serpent Symbol, make no mention of it in their collaborative work on "Symbolism in Ancient American Art." [57] And yet there they note that the art of the Mound Builders and that of the ancient Mexicans and Central Americans were closely related and in some instances appeared to be identical, and that serpent symbolism was often closely associated with sun worship.

Willoughby's views on the Serpent Mound at Brush Creek are similarly of interest in this regard. He disputed Squier and Davis's claim that their plan of the Serpent Mound was based upon an actual survey, suggesting it was merely a rough field sketch with little attempt at accuracy. Squier would have taken forceful exception to that assertion. He defended the accuracy of his survey of the Serpent Mound and his observations about serpent worship in America. He once bristled at the suggestion made in the London Athenaeum that more accurate surveys were needed before his views on serpent worship could be fully accepted. "Educated as a civil engineer," he wrote the editor of the Athenaeum, "I know what accuracy means." [58] Squier's work as a self-trained civil engineer and surveyor is not beyond criticism, but there seems to be no reason for assuming or asserting that his plan of the Serpent Mound is not based upon an actual survey – accurate or otherwise. Willoughby's criticism of Squier and Davis's plan of the Serpent Mound is tempered, however, by the fact that his own survey of the site was made in 1918, *after* Putnam had reconstructed the site owing to its rapid deterioration. The site was more intact in 1846 when Squier and Davis made their plan than when Willoughby made what is doubtless a more accurate survey.

When it came to interpreting the Serpent Mound, however, Willoughby's views had more in common with those of Squier than not. Willoughby too believed that the religious beliefs associated with elevated locations (Squier's sacred high places) probably determined the site chosen to build the Serpent Mound, which is located on an elevated headland overlooking Brush Creek. Willoughby also associated the Serpent Mound with sun worship and observed that its builders had kept "the ceremonial sun fires" on the oval enclosure (Squier and Davis's "egg") and its central altar of burnt stones. He thought the embankments protruding from the serpent's head were horns as found on the familiar horned serpent of Algonquian and Iroquoian tradition.[59]

Willoughby's interpretation of the effigy mound at Brush Creek as a horned serpent is certainly more plausible than attributing it to the mundane egg of Hindu mythology. Gliddon had served Squier well when he cautioned him against theorizing too much about the serpent and egg at Brush Creek lest it not be "*the* egg!" Given Squier's familiarity with horned serpents in Algonquian traditions and in the Walam Olum, it is not a little surprising that he did not arrive at Willoughby's conclusion himself. Willoughby's correlation of mythological beliefs and archaeological motifs went far beyond anything accomplished by Squier in *The Serpent Symbol*, but Squier's earlier efforts were far from insignificant. Putnam, for example, asked, as Squier had before him: "Will it be forcing fact to argue . . . that the oval embankment with its central pile of burnt stones in combination with the serpent, we have the three symbols everywhere regarded in the Old World as emblems of those [i.e. their] primitive faiths?"[60] Squier would have answered that question in the affirmative, but Putnam is strangely silent regarding Squier's earlier views on the subject.

Squier's interest in interpreting the religious concepts and symbols of American Indians occurred in an era when the subject was little valued. He made the case for the importance of such investigations, and *The Serpent Symbol* is the first book-length treatment to deal with the religion of American Indians in a serious manner. As Willoughby noted in 1936, "There is much to be learned through a comparative study of the mythical traditions of the Indians and the various archaeological remains constantly being brought to light. This phase of study has not received the attention it deserves."[61] Squier had said much the same thing in *The Serpent Symbol* and related writings during an earlier era of American archaeology. He raised many of the right questions even though he sometimes failed to arrive at the right answers. *The Serpent Symbol* is problematic because there are too many overconfident generalizations that are ultimately reduced to sun worship, phallicism, and monotheism, as Brinton noted in his criticism of the work. And yet Squier's interest in explaining cultural universals as expressions of the psychic unity of mankind, however inadequate on its own terms, was in line with the thrust of later anthropological research. The concept of the psychic unity of mankind subsequently received significant empirical substantiation based upon ethnographic and psychological evidence.[62] As Clifford Geertz observed in 1973, "The doctrine of the psychic unity of mankind, which so far as I am aware, is today not seriously questioned by any reputable anthropologist, is but the direct contradictory of the primitive mentality argument; it asserts that there are no essential differences in the fundamental nature of the thought process among the various living races of man."[63] Squier would have agreed with that statement too.

Squier's interest in demonstrating the psychic unity of man was rooted in the rational optimism of the Enlightenment. In his early writings he regarded social progress as a necessary consequence of universal natural laws, but in the mid- to late 1850s he came to question that assumption in regard to the mixed-race population of Central America. *The Serpent Symbol* is an expression of Squier's earlier and more optimistic view of human nature. Human societies progressed from primitive conditions to civilizations through a linear developmental sequence. The idea of progress in human history was equated with social, intellectual, and moral improvement leading toward greater human happiness. We have no such confidence in the inevitability of social progress today, but it was a potent bequest of the Enlightenment that continued to influence anthropological thought throughout the nineteenth century. "The period between 1725 and 1890," Fred W. Voget has noted, "was characterized by an overriding interest in tracing the history of mankind according to natural law. The development of ideas and social institutions from earliest times to the present was the primary objective."[64] It followed that societies at the same stage of development would meet their basic needs in a similar or parallel manner. Independent invention or parallel development was a logical outcome of the psychic unity of mankind.[65]

Such assumptions formed the basis of Squier's reasoning in *The Serpent Symbol*. He looked to comparative mythology as a means explaining similarities in fundamental religious ideas and symbols connected with the phenomena of nature among distinct peoples at similar stages of cultural development. The study of cognate beliefs and symbols through cross-cultural analogies illustrated these common psychological principles and might indicate either independent invention or cultural diffusion. As Voget has noted regarding the developmental ethnology of the period, "Comparative mythology disclosed the similarities in the fundamental ideas and identifications of natural forces by distant peoples which could be traced either to common human mental processes or to historic contact." [66] Such were precisely the problems with which Squier wrestled in *The Serpent Symbol*. That work is not mentioned in Voget's historical survey, but it is a classic elaboration of this fundamental aspect of developmentalist thought.

9. Nahua Nations and Migrations

*The Archaeology and Ethnology of Honduras
and San Salvador*

Squier returned to Central America in 1853 in pursuit of a clearly defined agenda. His enthusiasm for building an interoceanic canal across Nicaragua fizzled due to the difficulties associated with the proposed route and the enormous cost that would be involved in its construction. Squier now turned his attention to building a railroad across part of Nicaragua and Honduras. For the remainder of the decade he devoted himself almost exclusively to promoting the Honduras Interoceanic Railway. He was determined to continue his archaeological and ethnological investigations in the region, but again he found himself without the means to do so. His goals had clearly changed. As he observed in an autobiographical sketch written for Evert A. Duyckinck in 1854, "My present purpose is to make money" – a preoccupation he likened to a "Job-like captivity." [1] Squier temporarily set aside his books and papers to work on surveying the railway's proposed route and raising money from investors in England and France. His railway scheme never made him a man of independent means as he initially hoped, but it did allow him to live comfortably for the remainder of the decade.

Anthropology became a secondary consideration for Squier once he began promoting the Honduran railway project. Brantz Mayer, an officer of the American Ethnological Society and a promoter of Squier's investigations, thought he was "wasting a great deal of precious life on this project." Mayer knew Squier to be a man of great zeal, judgment, talent, and unbounded nerve and industry, but he could only regret that Squier was not working as hard to advance his scholarship as he was with his railroad scheme. [2] And yet Squier never entirely abandoned his researches. He conducted archaeological and ethnological investigations in Honduras and San Salvador (a province within the republic of El Salvador), [3] even though the promotion of his Honduras Railway scheme absorbed nearly all his time and was his sole means of income. He continued to collect native vocabularies and to compile ethnographic accounts of Central American Indian groups from sixteenth-century Spanish manuscripts. He hoped the railway project would establish him financially and enable him to pursue his scholarly proclivities unencumbered by debt, want, and worry. Squier lived in London for a considerable period of time, when he conveniently pocketed his strident Anglophobia while seeking British investors for the railroad. The Honduras Interoceanic Railway died a slow, agonizing death between 1859 and 1860, but not for want of effort on Squier's part. He embraced his entrepreneurial activities with same energy and buoyant optimism that characterized all of his interests and pursuits.[4]

Squier's surveying expeditions across Honduras presented him with the opportunity to examine archaeological remains and to collect Indian vocabularies. His vested economic interest in the railway colored his views on the population of Honduras and San Salvador, his support of white immigration to the region from America and Europe, and what he perceived to be the region's social and economic future. Just as his diplomatic mission and promotion of an American canal in Nicaragua influenced his political and anthropological writings between 1849 and 1853, his entrepreneurial activities as secretary of the Honduras Interoceanic Railway Company and corresponding political lobbying profoundly influenced the views expressed in Notes on Central America (1855) and its sequel, The States of Central America (1858). Squier's political and anthropological thought cannot be neatly segregated or compartmentalized, although he continued to be more objective in his treatment of some archaeological and ethnological subjects than of others. His Central American writings could be either polemical or scholarly depending upon his subject, purpose, and intended audience.[5] Both of these tendencies must be taken into account. His brief account of the Ruins of Tenampua, Honduras, Central America (1853), Collection of Rare and Original Documents and Relations, Concerning the Discovery and Conquest of America (1860), Monograph of Authors Who Have Written on the Languages of Central America (1861), and his little-known Observations on the Chalchihuitl of Mexico and Central America (1869) are notably detached from his entrepreneurial interests and activities in the region and lack the polemics associated with certain topics in his major writings on Central America. Criticisms of the more subjective and politicized aspects of Squier's anthropological writings on Central America are certainly justified, but to dwell only upon these aspects of his works suggests a lack of familiarity with the larger goals of his research in the region, the range and scope of his original contributions to knowledge, and the difficult circumstances under which his archaeological and ethnological fieldwork was conducted.[6]

Squier began to seriously entertain the idea of an interoceanic railway across the Isthmus of Tehuantepec in the autumn of 1852. The proposed Honduran route would be an alternative to traveling to California via the

Panama railroad. He proposed the construction of a railway that would cross the isthmus and terminate at the Bay of Fonseca, a route he was convinced would become a significant artery of trade. He learned that Spanish officials had found a passage between the oceans along the very line of the proposed railway as early as 1540. Squier's railway would run from Puerto Caballos on the Bay of Honduras 161 miles south across the isthmus to the Bay of Fonseca. The London *Athenaeum* acknowledged that his arguments in favor of that route were "weighty."[7] Squier argued in *Notes on Central America* that the Honduras railway could be constructed for less than seven million dollars, or half the cost of the Panamanian route. He projected, over-optimistically, that average revenues during the first four years of operation would be not less than two million dollars per year and that travel time between New York and California would be reduced by at least seven days.

The first order of business was to verify the feasibility of the railway project through a careful survey of the proposed route. Squier organized a reconnaissance party consisting of himself and Lieutenant W. N. Jeffers of the U.S. Navy, former professor of mathematics at the U.S. Naval Academy; Dr. S. W. Woodhouse, a member of the United States Expedition to the Colorado of California, who served as the mineralogist on the expedition; and D. C. Hitchcock, Squier's draftsman and artist. Squier's surveying party departed for Central America in February 1853 to survey the route of the proposed Honduran Interoceanic Railway. The crew began its fieldwork in April at the Bay of Fonseca. Jeffers made observations and barometric measurements across the entire isthmus, while Woodhouse ran a similar line from León de Nicaragua to the city of Comayagua in Honduras. Squier surveyed a third line from Comayagua to the town of Santa Rosa in the extreme western border of Honduras, and from Santa Rosa to the city of San Salvador within the state of the same name (present-day El Salvador). He continued his reconnaissance across the length of San Salvador from Sonsonate to the port of La Union.

The surveys made for the proposed railway presented Squier with the opportunity to make archaeological and ethnological investigations in Honduras and San Salvador. His examination of the ruins of Tenampua in the Department of Comayagua is particularly significant. He visited the site in June 1853 and communicated his observations to William W. Turner of New York, a member of the American Ethnological Society and the New-York Historical Society. Turner published the communication as *Ruins of Tenampua, Honduras, Central America*, an eight-page pamphlet taken from the *Proceedings of the Historical Society of New-York* in October 1853.[8] Squier later incorporated this account into *Notes on Central America*.[9] Squier found many traces of aboriginal populations on the great plain of Comayagua, but many of those remains had been greatly damaged and defaced by the Spanish conquerors and "bigots" as a means of obliterating native religious traditions and customs.[10] He examined aboriginal remains in the vicinity of Yarumela, Ljamini, and near the ruined town of Cururu. Those sites consisted of large pyramidal and terraced structures (often faced with stones), conical mounds of earth, and walls of stone. Stone carvings and painted vases were found within and near those remains. The largest archaeological sites were not found on the plain of Comayagua but in the lateral valleys or on the adjacent mesas (table lands of the mountains). Squier visited the aboriginal remains ruins at Calamulla, located on the road to the Indian town of Guajiquero; at Jamalteca, in the valley of that name; at Maniani, in the Espino Valley; at Guasistagua, near the village of that name; at Chapuluca, in the vicinity of Opoteca; and at Chapulistagua, in the valley located behind the mountains of Comayagua.

Squier visited all of those sites, but he found the ruins at Tenampua to be the most extensive and interesting. The remains at Tenampua were popularly known as Pueblo Viejo ("Old Town"). The ruins were situated upon the level summit of a high hill about twenty miles southeast of Comayagua, near the village of Lo de Flores. Walls of rough stone, terraced on the inside, varied in height from 6 to 15 feet and in base width from 10 to 25 feet. Traces of towers or buildings were also evident at various points of the site. Squier thought it one of the strongest places for defense he had ever seen. The site's most interesting features were the terraced mounds found on the eastern half of its level summit. The mounds were rectangular in shape and were made either of stone or of earth faced with stone. The sides of the structures conformed to the cardinal points, and their uncut stones were laid with great precision. Most of the smaller mounds were 20 to 30 feet square and from 4 to 8 feet in height. They occurred in groups and were arranged with an obvious design in relation to each other. The large pyramidal structures ranged in size from 60 to 120 feet in length, proportional width, and varying heights. They were terraced and usually had the ruins of steps on their western sides. Several rectangular enclosures of stone and a number of platforms and terraced slopes were also present.

Squier found other interesting features at Tenampua that seemed to correspond in the principles of their construction to other aboriginal sites in Mesoamerica. He thought it likely that the remains of the transverse walls that divided the great enclosure into rectangular spaces had been the foundations of houses. It seemed probable that the walls had supported wooden structures used by aboriginal priests or guardians of the great temple. According to the Spanish chroniclers, the cloisters of the priests and their attendants surrounded the court of the great temple of Mexico. Perhaps a similar usage had occurred at Tenampua. Squier also used analogy to infer the probable purposes of two long, parallel mounds. Each mound was 140 feet in length, 36 feet wide at the base, and 10 feet high at the center. The inner sides of the mounds faced each other and appeared to have three terraces, which rose like seats in an amphitheater. The lower terraces were 40 feet apart and were faced with huge flat stones. The outer sides of the mounds appeared to conform to the wall of the great enclosure and had probably supported three large buildings. The parallel mounds seemed to Squier to correspond in design to the parallel walls found by John Lloyd Stevens at Chichén Itzá and Uxmal in Yucatán. "Doubtless games, processions, or other civic or religious rights or ceremonies, took place between them, in the presence of priests or dignitaries who were seated upon the terraces on either hand."[11]

The form of the various stone mounds at Tenampua seemed to preclude the possibility that they were used as the foundations of dwellings. The principles of their construction suggested that they had been either altars or sites of temples, the counterparts of similar structures found in Guatemala, Yucatán, and Mexico and in a large class of mounds in the Mississippi Valley. Squier excavated but one of them, which was situated near the structure he denominated "the great temple." Most of the mound was constructed of mere earth, but the interior of the upper terrace was largely composed of ashes and great quantities of pottery fragments. He was able to recover enough of the fragments to surmise their original shape and the manner in which the pottery had been painted and ornamented. Some were flat like pans, while others were vases of various forms. All of them were painted with ornaments or "mythological figures." Fragments of obsidian knives were also present.[12] The paintings on the vases, he added, were identical to those of Palenque and Yucatán. "Some of them are exact counterparts of figures found the Dresden MS [Codex]."[13] Squier calculated that the remains of between three and four hundred terraced and truncated pyramids of various sizes were to be found at Tenampua, besides its enclosures. He thought it likely that the site had served both religious and defensive purposes. The rocky summit of the hill upon which the mounds were found and the thin and poor condition of the soil suggested that it had not been a fortified town or place of permanent residence.[14] He made no effort to further investigate this interesting site, presumably owing to the need to continue his survey of the railroad route.

Squier's reconnaissance for the proposed Honduras railway also took him to San Salvador. The aboriginal population of San Salvador presented him with another important field for ethnological inquiry. In San Salvador, as in Nicaragua, Squier encountered enigmatic fragments of aboriginal families that had become separated from their parent stocks and were living among Indians that differed from them in their customs, language, social organization, and religion.

> These *erratic* fragments – to adopt a geological term – in some instances present the clearest and most indubitable evidences of their origin and relationship, in an almost unchanged language, and in a civil and social organization, manners, and customs, little, if at all, modified from those of their distant progenitors. The inference from this would naturally be that their separation had been comparatively recent; yet these identities have been found to exist in cases where tradition fails to assign a cause or period for the disruption, or even or indicate the manner in which it took place. [15]

Squier found two fragments of "the true Nahual or Aztec stock" living among the earliest-known aboriginal inhabitants of Nicaragua and San Salvador. One of those groups occupied the principal islands of Lake Nicaragua and probably a portion of the country as far south as the Gulf of Nicoya. His accounts of the Nahual-speaking Nicaraguans in *Nicaragua* and in the third volume of the *Transactions of the American Ethnological Society* attempted to show in what respect their language had been modified or differed from that spoken by the Nahuals of Mexico. He gives an account of another and larger colony or fragment of Nahua origin in *Notes on Central America*. That group was located between Nicaragua and Guatemala, primarily in the state of San Salvador. Their descendants, notwithstanding the adoption of Catholicism, still retained their native language and many aboriginal manners and customs. The earliest Spanish chronicles attest to the existence of the Nahuals of San Salvador, but Squier was the first ethnologists to marshal evidence supporting the correctness of those accounts based on his own observations among existing groups. He first presented his findings in "Observations on an Existing Fragment of the Nahual, or Pure Mexican Stock in the State of San Salvador, Central America," a paper read before the American Ethnological Society in 1854 and reprinted in the *New York Tribune*. [16] He based those observations upon the comparison of a Pipil vocabulary he collected and the Aztec vocabularies recorded by the Spanish chroniclers. The similarities in vocabularies indicated that the Pipil of San Salvador were Aztec in origin, further enabling him to establish their linguistic boundaries.

Squier encountered the Nahual-speaking groups during his travels through San Salvador in 1853, when he visited each of its departments. San Salvador's aboriginal population had been modified by three centuries of contact with Europeans, as might be expected, but Squier also found Indian towns that retained elements of their aboriginal customs to a surprising extent. The native languages in most instances had fallen into disuse, but many aboriginal place-names had been preserved. Squier used those names to infer the range of territory over which the various aboriginal groups had formerly resided. In the district of Costa del Balsimo (the Balsam Coast), however, the aborigines continued to live in relative isolation. They still spoke their native language and retained many of their traditional rites and customs. Squier believed their habits had been only slightly modified from what they were at the time of the Spanish Conquest. The principal changes introduced among the Indian towns of the Balsam Coast stemmed from the trade of balsam and the adoption of Catholicism. Although they practiced the Catholic faith, Squier observed that many aboriginal rites had been incorporated into the ceremonies of the local church.

Squier described the condition of the Nahual-speaking Indians of San Salvador and then ventured to establish the extent of their territory at the period of the Conquest. Early Spanish authorities provide direct testimony on the subject, as did surviving Nahual names of rivers and other natural features. Pedro de Alvarado learned in 1524 of the existence of a people called the Pipiles who lived to the southwest of Guatemala on the coast of the South Sea. Alvarado led an expedition against the Pipiles in an effort to subdue them. He gave an account of the expedition in his second letter to Cortés, giving the names of the places where he had encountered the Pipiles. Many of the place-names mentioned by Alvarado, Squier noted, were still in use, making it possible to distinctly trace the route of his army. The principal town of the Nahua was called Cuscatlán, a name also applied to the language of the Pipiles at large. Herrera provides further evidence that Nahua, or Mexican-speaking Indians, occupied San Salvador. The name given to their county was Cuscatlán. Squier refrained from speculating on the origin of the Nahua of Nicaragua and San Salvador, but he did observe that "the hypothesis of a migration from Nicaragua and Cuscatlan to Anahuac is altogether more consonant with probabilities and with tradition than that which derives the Mexicans from the north. . . . We must look for the primitive country of the Nahuals to the south of Mexico."[17]

Squier was able to obtain a vocabulary of the dialect spoken on the Balsam Coast from an informant who lived in the Indian village of Chiltiapam. He also obtained a few additional words from an Indian living at Izalco near Sonsonate. Squier identified the language spoken on the Balsam Coast as being almost identical with the ancient Nahual or Mexican, indicating the differences existing between them in a comparative table.[18] The variations in words spoken by the Nahua of San Salvador from those in ancient Mexico were thought to be slight and probably attributable to phonetic inconsistencies on the part of the different Europeans who had recorded them. The Indian groups he encountered in the Comayagua Valley in Honduras and in central San Salvador presented new opportunities for the collection of vocabularies. Those groups received attention in an extended note to chapter 12 of his *Notes on Central America*,[19] which subsequently became the basis of a chapter on the Indians of Honduras in his *States of Central America*.

Squier's descriptions of the Lenca, Jicaque, and Guajiquero Indians of Honduras were the first to provide the outside world with accurate information about the conditions existing among those groups. Squier has been recognized as the first ethnological observer to correctly apply the name "Lenca" to the aboriginal inhabitants of the Comayagua Valley and to collect dialects of all four of the Lenca dialects.[20] Later investigators have only slightly adjusted the linguistic boundaries he established for the Lenca in *Notes on Central America*,[21] although later students of the language of the Jicaque Indians have argued that Squier incorrectly classified them as a Lenca group.[22] Squier obtained a short vocabulary of the dialect spoken at Opotero in Honduras from an Indian informant of that town whom Squier had met in Comayagua. He obtained another vocabulary when he visited the Indian town of Guajiquero in June 1853. He subsequently obtained a brief vocabulary from the town of Yamalanguira, located about six miles to the west of Intibucat and near the district of the ancient chiefs of Sensenti. He acquired a list of numerals used by the people of Similiton, along with a few words and phrases, from a resident of Tegucigalpa who as a youth had spent some time in Similiton.[23]

The difficulty of obtaining vocabularies in interviews with native informants in Honduras is indicated in Squier's account of his visit to the Indian town of Guajiquero. He spent a day there in June 1853 and gave a colorful of account of that visit in *Harper's New Monthly Magazine* in October 1859.

> If any one supposes that it is an easy task to elicit a satisfactory vocabulary from Indians incapable of comprehending your interest in the matter, and naturally disposed to think that you have a sinister purpose, I commend them to a trial in Guajiquero [located some thirty miles south of Comayagua]. Then there is the other difficulty of making them understand the abstract nature of many of your inquiries, which is so seldom effected that most vocabularies collected by travelers are almost valueless. . . . Unless the interrogator has a quick ear, and adroitly varies his questions so as to get at the elementary word, his vocabulary will be a strange jumble of phrases, of little use in comparative philology.[24]

Squier's observations on the Guajiquero Indians represent the only detailed account of that group made in the nineteenth century. The description of the dance he observed during his visit among the Guajiquero is of particular interest (see fig. 12).[25]

Squier identified at least four distinct aboriginal groups or families in Honduras based on their linguistic affinities. The first group was the Chortis of Sensenti, who belonged to the same group with the Quiches, the Kachiquels, and the Mayas and who occupied what became the Department of Gracias. The second group was the Lencas, who were, according to Squier, "less advanced in civilization" than the Chortis. The Lencas were also known as the Chontal and perhaps also included the Xicaques and Payas. They occupied what became the Department of San Miguel in San Salvador, Comayagua, Choluteca, Tegucigalpa, and parts of Olancho and Yoro in Honduras, including the islands of Roatan and Guanaja. The third group was made up of various tribes intervening between the Lencas proper and the inhabitants of Cariay, or what is now known as the Mosquito Shore. The fourth group was the tribes (or "savages," as Squier would have it) who lived on the Mosquito Shore, from near Carataska Lagoon southward to the Rio San Juan, whose language was entirely distinct from those spoken by the Indians in the interior.[26]

Squier's Central American writings are also noteworthy for the perspective they provide on his changing views on race. The fullest statement of his racial theory appears in Notes on Central America. Notwithstanding the fact that the racial thought of Samuel George Morton, Josiah Clark Nott, and George Robins Gliddon were formative influences on Squier's conclusions, his early writings on race are decidedly guarded and cautious. They are much less so in Notes on Central America. His remarks on the population of Central America and the presumed results of the free amalgamation of the races indicate how fully he had come to subscribe to the racist tenets of the American School of Ethnology. The relative numbers of Caucasians, Indians, and Ladinos (people of mixed ancestry) in Spanish America was a subject to which Squier devoted considerable attention. The demographic characteristics of the region, said Squier, largely explained (if they did not, in fact, determine) the conditions, capabilities, and destinies of the peoples of Central America. The European element in the population was decreasing in both absolute and relative numbers to those of the Indians, with Ladinos increasingly approaching the aboriginal type.[27] The decrease in the European element of the population would soon result in its absorption into the aboriginal population.

Central America, said Squier, appeared to provide "a striking illustration of the laws which have been established as the results of anthropological inquiries during the past fifty years." Neither statesmen nor political econo-

12. "Collecting a Vocabulary." Squier collected a vocabulary during his visit to the Guajiquero Indians of Honduras in June 1853. His observations represent the only detailed account of that group made in the nineteenth century. (From Squier, "A Visit to the Guajiquero Indians," *Harper's New Monthly Magazine*, October 1859, 615.)

mists could ignore those results or their implications for the moral and intellectual condition of the region's growing population. The more the various nations and races of Central America were brought into close contact, the more the nature and character of their social relations became considerations of immediate and practical significance.

> It may be claimed without hesitation that the wide physical, intellectual, and moral differences which all history and observation have distinguished as existing between the various families of man, can be no longer regarded as the consequences of accident or of circumstances; that is to say, it has come to be understood that their physical, moral, and intellectual traits are radical and permanent, and that there can be no admixture of widely-separated families, or of superior with inferior races, which can be harmonious, or otherwise than disastrous in its consequences.[28]

Such assumptions were widespread among American and European anthropologists in the mid-nineteenth century. The French ethnologist Joseph-Arthur de Gobineau argued in his four-volume *Essay on the Inequality of the Human Races* (1853–55) that the destiny of nations was determined by their racial composition. The mixing of superior and inferior races resulted in stagnation and corruption if the superior racial stock became too "diluted."[29]

Squier was clearly influenced by these ideas and had arrived at similar conclusions regarding the mixing of races in Central America. He was more directly influenced by the writings of Nott and Morton in that regard than by Gobineau, to be certain, but such racist assumptions were widespread in the transatlantic anthropological community. Nott had published a short essay on the mulatto as a hybrid in the *American Journal of the Medical Sciences* in 1843 in order to show that Caucasians and Negroes were distinct "species." He argued that dreadful biological consequences would result if whites and blacks were allowed to intermarry. His treatment of the subject interested Morton, who began a correspondence with Nott regarding racial matters that continued until Morton's death in 1851. Morton began his own inquiry into the question of hybridity in animals and plants and what it implied for the debate about human origins. He published an article on the subject in a contribution to the third volume of the *American Journal of Science and Arts* for 1847, and he continued to state his views on hybridity in the *Charleston Medical Journal*. More importantly, Nott elaborated upon the subject in *Types of Mankind* in 1854.[30] Squier found Nott's arguments about hybridity and the dangers of racial amalgamation persuasive, since they appeared to him to be based upon natural laws of racial distinctiveness.

Nott's views on racial hybridity among mulattoes are particularly instructive, not only for their chilling racism but for the influence they exerted on Squier's anthropological thought. Nott maintained that mulattoes were the shortest-lived of any class of the human race, were of intermediate intelligence between blacks and whites, and were less capable of withstanding fatigue and hardship. Mulatto women were particularly delicate and subject to a variety of chronic diseases. They were, he said, "bad breeders, bad nurses, liable to abortions, and . . . their children generally die young." When mulattoes intermarried they were less prolific than when they married a member of either of the parent races, and when black men married white women the children conformed more to the Negro type than when black women married white men. Both mulattoes and Negroes enjoyed extraordinary immunity from yellow fever. Nott made those remarks based on almost fifty years of residence among the white and black populations of South Carolina and Alabama. Twenty-five years of medical practice had convinced him of "the absolute truth" of those deductions as well as the inevitable results stemming from the intermixture of "the strictly *white* race (i.e. the Anglo-Saxon, or Teuton,) with the true *Negro*." [31] Hybridization produced congenitally defective offspring, and if racial amalgamation were not prevented or limited it would weaken society as a whole.

Squier was familiar with those views and applied them to the social conditions existing in Central America. Anthropological inquiry, he said, had established the existence of two laws of vital importance in their application to the interactions of men and nations. The first of these laws applied to the mixing of races. Whenever "a free amalgamation" occurred between two distinct stocks, the result was the absolute absorption of one into the other. What was generally denominated as "prejudice" against the mixing of races was, in reality, "a natural instinct." Echoing Nott's racial theory, Squier noted that the process of absorption became more rapid as the races brought into contact approximated each other in type and that it occurred in proportion to the size of the predominant group. "Nature perpetuates no human hybrids, as, for instance, a permanent race of mulattoes." That opinion owes more to Nott than to anyone else.

Second, "natural distinctions of race" and deeply ingrained racial "instincts" were intended "to perpetuate the superior races in their purity." Disregarding these natural laws could only lead to calamitous results. Nations could ill afford to be unmindful of "the wise designs of Nature" that explained the physical, intellectual, and moral conditions and capabilities of different races. "In other words, the offspring of such combinations or amalgamations are not only generally deficient in physical constitution, in intellect, and in moral restraint, but to a degree which often contrasted unfavorably with any of the original stocks."[32] The idea of the amalgamation of the races was anathema to many in the nineteenth century, and not just the members of the American School of Ethnology. Scientific attitudes toward hybridization, however, reinforced prejudice against mixed-bloods in society at large by painting a grim picture of biological deterioration – and even extinction.[33] The later maxim of geneticists that racial intermixture has certain genetic benefits for a given population would have been as abhorrent as it was inconceivable to the racial theorists of the nineteenth century.

The efficacy of those natural laws of race presumably explained much about the history, condition, and prospects of Central America. The "anarchical" governments of the region seemed to confirm the truth of Squier's racial propositions.

> In Central and South America, and Mexico, we find a people not only demoralized from the unrestricted association of different races, but also the superior stocks becoming gradually absorbed in the lower, and their institutions disappearing under the relative barbarism of which the latter are the exponents. If existing causes and conditions continue to operate, many years cannot pass before some of those countries will have relapsed into a state not far removed from that in which they were found at the period of the conquest.[34]

Squier accounted for the backwardness that Euro-American travelers commonly attributed to Mexican, Central American, and South American nations to the same problem: "a grand practical misconception of the just relations of the races." He held forth little hope for the future of Spanish America until the relationship between the races changed. "The Indian does not possess, still less the South Sea Islander, and least of all the negro, the capacity to comprehend the principles which enter into the higher order of civil and political organizations. His instincts and his habits are inconsistent with their development, and no degree of education can teach him to understand and practice them." This sounds more like Nott than Squier, but these words are Squier's indeed. He even qualified his earlier defense of the moral and intellectual capabilities of the North American tribes, now asserting that "under no circumstances had the North American Indians shown an appreciation of the value, or a dispossession to abide by the reciprocal obligations involved in a government of the people." Only the Cherokees had made social progress, a fact that Squier now entirely attributed to their being led by chiefs who were predominantly of European ancestry.[35] That was Nott's stated opinion and another of his views adopted by Squier. Squier placed a premium on the "industry, docility, and traditional deference to authority" exhibited by the

Indian families of Mexico and Central America. Any attempt to place them "on a political and social footing with the white man had entailed eternal anarchy, and threatens a complete dissolution of the political body."[36]

The corollary of Squier's racial determinism was his support of America's "Manifest Destiny" in Central America. He attributed American advances to

> the rigid and inexorable refusal of the dominant Teutonic stock to debase its blood, impair its intellect, lower its moral standards, or peril its institutions by intermixture with the inferior and subordinate races of man. In obedience to the ordinances of Heaven, it has rescued half a continent from savage beasts and still more savage men, whose period of existence has terminated, and who must give place to higher organizations and a superior life. Short-sighted philanthropy may lament, and sympathy drop a tear as it looks forward to the total disappearance of the lower forms of humanity, but the laws of Nature are irreversible. *Deus vult* – it is the will of God![37]

Squier had learned his lessons in racial determinism well. In the mid-nineteenth century, ethnocentrism translated into a kind of anthropological nationalism that affirmed the superiority of certain European peoples ("races") and a "Europocentrism" that assumed the superiority of Caucasians.[38] Squier reflected those attitudes toward race in his Central American writings.

Given those assumptions, it appeared that Central America's only hope for social progress was to stop the numerical decline of its white population. The number of Europeans living in the region should be increased through the encouragement of immigration or colonization, an idea Squier had earlier advanced in *Nicaragua*. The strategic location and abundant natural resources of Central America had much to offer potential colonizers, and Squier could easily envision the day when the United States or Great Britain might be tempted to seize the region by force. There is no question that his sympathies were with the prospect of the former and not the latter. Steps should immediately be taken to provide for the future of Central America as "the true mission" and "highest aim" of patriots and statesmen in the United States: "The enterprise of our people is setting in that direction in a full and increasing current."[39] Squier promoted the ideas of American immigration and colonization in Central America in order to advance his own economic interests in the Honduras Interoceanic Railway project, and those of the United States generally.

Anthropology, as Squier's comments forcibly remind us, has often been called upon to justify colonialism, dispossession, economic exploitation, and the maintenance of social hierarchy and deference. Such sentiments represent the most polemical and least useful aspects of Squier's Central American scholarship, but they speak volumes of about scientific and popular attitudes toward race in mid-nineteenth-century America. His invocation of the "natural laws" that should control social relations and the paternalistic policies of colonizing nations stand in stark contrast to his earlier and more reserved comments on race and its implications for government policy. Squier's intemperate and subjective comments were motivated by nationalism and self-interest, and they show how far he had moved intellectually toward the racial determinism of the American School and away from his earlier willingness to question some of its more pessimistic and gloomy assumptions. Squier had defended the intellectual and moral capacities of American Indians in 1849 and had marveled at the equality existing among the different races when he first arrived in Nicaragua that same year. He clearly had second thoughts, as least so far as the mixed population of Central America was concerned.

Squier's self-interest is also clear enough in his designs for the Carib Indians of Honduras. Squier valued the Caribs as a good and useful laboring population, such as would be needed in the construction of his proposed interoceanic railway.[40] If it were left to its own devices, however, he thought that the Indian element of the population promised little or nothing for Honduras's future development. An infusion of American entrepreneurship, however, might make a difference:

> with the introduction of an intelligent and enterprising people, their industry may probably be turned to good account. Frugal, patient, and docile, they have many of the best qualities of a valuable laboring population, and only lack direction to become an important means in the physical regeneration of the country. The Caribs certainly have shown great capacity for improvement, and at their present rate of increase must always be able to supply every industrial demand which may be created on the northern coast, where the climate is least favorable for the introduction of foreign labor.[41]

Such were the cold calculations of scientific racism, Manifest Destiny, and commercial interests in the mid-nineteenth century. Squier used the anthropological arguments of the American School to promote American immigration, colonization, and his own entrenched economic interests. As secretary of the proposed Honduras Interoceanic Railway and a promoter of American immigration and investment in the region, he was clearly a party concerned.

The success of Squier's *Notes on Central America* led to the publication of *The States of Central America* in 1858.[42] Whereas the former work dealt primarily with Honduras and San Salvador, the latter included additional chapters on Nicaragua, Costa Rica, Guatemala, Belize, the Bay Islands, and the Mosquito Shore. The States of Central America is a 783-page compendium presenting the most complete picture that had yet appeared of the region's geography, topography, climate, population, resources, commerce, and facilities for interoceanic communication. Squier continued his study of the archaeology and ethnology of the region in The States of Central America, amplifying some of the discussions in his earlier writings. Squier's note on the Indians of Honduras in chapter 12 of Notes on Central America, for example, here became a standalone chapter.[43] Most of his original contributions to knowledge to the archaeology and ethnology of the region were embodied in Nicaragua and Notes of Central America, but several themes emerge in The States of Central America that provide continuity with Squier's earlier works, denoting ongoing interests that he applies to the region as a whole.

Squier was particularly interested in how the geographical and topographical characteristics of Central America had influenced the character and destinies of its aboriginal population. The natural setting of the region was writ large in its past and in the condition of its existing population. When Central America first became known to the Spanish, it was occupied by two families of men whose different characteristics stood in bold relief. The high plateaus of the interior and the Pacific coast were home to numerous peoples who were far advanced in civilization and possessed a systematic religion and social organization. The Atlantic coast, by contrast, provided a comparatively meager existence to "savage tribes" who lived without fixed habitations or highly developed religious, social, and political systems. "It is impossible to resist the conviction that the contrasting conditions of these two great families were principally due to the equally contrasting physical conditions of their respective countries." Squier's correlation of natural and cultural provinces in The States of Central America owes much to his earlier discussions of the subject in Nicaragua and Notes on Central America.

Civilization could never have developed, Squier believed, under the adverse conditions existing on the Atlantic coast. It could only originate where favorable circumstances afforded some relief from the pressure of immediate and recurring wants. Civilization arose in relatively genial climates and with easily cultivated soils that provided a bounty of natural foods. Those were the conditions that enabled humans to devote a portion of their time to improvement.[44] Such were precisely the conditions existing upon the high plains of Honduras and Guatemala, where wide and fertile savannas supported maize agriculture and bountiful harvests. Squier thought it likely that maize was indigenous to those regions, from where it subsequently spread northward into Mexico and the southeastern region of what became the United States. Indeed, the languages and traditions of the various groups who once lived in those regions pointed to the plateaus of Guatemala as their original homeland.[45]

Nor was the achievement of civilization among the region's aboriginal population solely confined to Guatemala, even though little was then known of the antiquities and peoples who lived south of the Maya. Western Honduras was at the southeastern edge of the great Mayan civilization during the first millennium AD, and the ruins at Copán attest to the advanced stage of the country's population. The earliest records relating to the northwestern Honduras indicate that the region was occupied by what Squier called "civilized nations." Their chiefs were known as *Calel* or *Kalel*, and their language belonged to the same stock as the Quiche, Kachiquel, and Maya, suggesting that the Honduran groups in question belonged to "the same great family of semi-civilized nations which spread over Guatemala, Chiapas, and Yucatan."[46] Further evidence of those connections came from the ancient monuments of the district that corresponded in type with those at Ocosingo, Palenque, and Chichén Itzá. The ruins at Copán had their corresponding number in elaborately carved monoliths examined by Squier in the Chamelicon Valley of Honduras. Those at Palenque, by contrast, displayed elaborate bas-reliefs, suggesting that they belonged to a later and more advanced period of art. Most of the architectural remains in Guatemala and Yucatán were from structures built and occupied by the aboriginal population residing in the region at the time of the Spanish Conquest. The ruins at Copán, however, appeared to be an exception. Squier did not attribute them to the tribes living in the area during the sixteenth century. He based that conclusion upon the account of Guatemala written by the Licenciado Palacio in 1576, less than fifty years after the Conquest. Palacio described the ruins at Copán with great accuracy and had searched in vain among local elders to learn something of their origin.[47]

The States of Central America also gives an interesting account of archaeological remains recently discovered in the Department of Jutiapa in Guatemala. The site, known as the ruins of Cinaca-Mecallo, was located near the town of Comapa near the boundary of San Salvador and within the ancient province of Guazacapan. Squier did not make that discovery himself but learned of it from Señor Don José Antonio Urrita, the *cura* (priest) of Jutiapa. Urrita communicated to Squier his account of the remains, which first appeared in the London *Athenaeum* in December 1856. Squier incorporated Urrita's letter into his general comments on archaeology in *The States of Central America*.[48] Squier thought the ruins of Cinaca-Mecallo quite possibly were the remains of one of the fortified towns attacked by Alvarado. His observations on Urrita's account of the site indicate his ongoing interest in correlating linguistic affinities and the earliest known locations of tribal groups as a means of inferring their probable relationship to archaeological remains.

The province of Guazacapan at the time of the Spanish Conquest was located between the Quiche kingdom of the Kachiquels and the Nahuals of Cuscatlán in San Salvador. The Quiche spoke a dialect of the Tzendal language, the same family of the Mayan dialect, while the Nahuals (as identified by their name) spoke a dialect of the Mexican language. The people living in the middle ground or district between them (Jutiapa) spoke a mixed Tzendal-Nahual language. Urrita's letter attested to the fact that the native language spoken in Jutiapa was still a composite and had probably changed little. The Quiches, Kachiquels, and Mayas had attained the highest development in the arts and came closer to developing a written language than all the American families. Squier inferred from the character of the remains discovered at Guazacapan and the affinities of the language spoken there that their builders were of the same stock as the builders at Copán, Palenque, and Yucatán. He interpreted the intrusion of the Mexican language into the local dialect as evidence of a former colony or dominion in that district.

Squier continued his interest in the archaeology and ethnology of Central America throughout the 1860s, no longer as an explorer but as a compiler of manuscripts relating to the Spanish Conquest and a bibliographer of those who had written on the region's aboriginal languages. He never again undertook fieldwork in Central America after 1853, but he culled the archives of Spain looking for documents that described conditions among aboriginal populations when first known to the Spanish. Squier's collection of Spanish manuscripts consisted of extracts and copies of letters and reports of audiencias, bishops, governors, and other government officials relating to the civil and ecclesiastical administration of the Spanish provinces in Central America during the sixteenth century. The manuscripts were copied from originals in the Royal Academy of History at Madrid and other archival depositories.

Buckingham Smith, Squier's friend and secretary of the United States diplomatic legation in Madrid, copied a large portion of the manuscripts for Squier in 1856 and 1857. Squier acquired others during his years of travel in Central America, either by himself or through the aid of friends. He planned to translate and publish the manuscripts serially, but the proposed collection appeared in its first and only number in 1860 as a *Collection of Rare and Original Documents and Relations, Concerning the Discovery and Conquest of America*. Squier's own autographed copy of the *Collection* contained an eight-page prospectus of nineteen Spanish manuscripts he proposed to publish as part of that series at some point in the future. Charles B. Norton published the prospectus at New York in 1861.[49]

The first and only number of Squier's *Collection of Rare and Original Documents* contains the account of the Licenciado Dr. Don Diego Garcia de Palacio (d. ca. 1595), auditor of the Audiencia of Guatemala, written to the king of Spain in 1576.[50] Palacio's letter ccount describes the ancient provinces of Guazacapan, Izalco, Cuscatlán, and Chiquimula in the Audiencia of Guatemala, including an account of the languages, customs, and religious beliefs of the aboriginal inhabitants and the ruins at Copán. Squier published the document in the original Spanish together with his English translation, adding illustrative notes, maps, and a biographical sketch of Palacio. His translation is based on a manuscript copy of Palacio's relation made by the Spanish chronicler Munoz and deposited in the Royal Academy of History at Madrid. Buckingham Smith obtained and verified the manuscript copy from which Squier's Spanish text was taken.[51]

Henri Ternaux-Compans published a French translation of the account at Paris in 1840, but Squier found inaccuracies in that edition which rendered it unsuitable for critical scholarship. He attempted to avoid similar problems in his own translation by publishing it along with the original Spanish text, enabling readers to judge for themselves the accuracy of his translation. Herrera drew upon the relation of Palacio in several chapters of his *Fourth Decade*, but Squier found Herrera's abridgments and paraphrases to have been made carelessly. Sometimes they conveyed a meaning entirely different from that expressed in Palacio's original, while in other instances they omitted information of ethnological and archaeological interest without explanation. Squier's translation of the full text and his annotations supplied those omissions, which provided "another illustration of the necessity of following back the stream of American history to its source."[52] His efforts at ascertaining the reliability of his sources inspired his contemporaries' confidence in his works on Central America and distinguished his works from those based almost entirely upon secondary authorities.

Squier placed great value on Palacio's relation because he had himself traveled over much of the same country visited and described by its author. He could personally vouch for the accuracy of Palacio's accounts of the physical features and natural productions of the districts through which he traveled, a circumstance that inspired confidence in the reliability of those parts of the relation that could no longer be verified by personal observation. Palacio visited an area of Guatemala's Pacific coast located between the Michatoyat and Lempa Rivers, which run inland as far as the ruins at Copán and the city of Chiquimula. Most of his account relates to Cuscatlán, later San Salvador, which was then occupied by Nahual-speaking peoples of Mexican origin. The neighbors of the Nahua of Nicaragua spoke languages different from their own. No plausible account or tradition concerning the origin of the Nahua peoples of Central America was known, and the question of whether they were a colony from Anahuac in Mexico or were the parent stock that subsequently migrated north into Mexico represented an ethnological problem in which Squier took a serious interest.

Palacio's account is significant for its description of aboriginal religious customs and the ruins at Copán, especially when compared to the later accounts of Galindo[53] and Stephens and the drawings of Catherwood. Galindo, for example, erred in thinking that the ruins at Copán were the remains of the nearby town of the same name, which Hernando de Chavez had destroyed in 1530. Palacio's account clearly established that the ruins at Copán were of far greater antiquity. The local traditions concerning those remains obtained by Palacio said only that the same people who erected structures at Palenque and Uxmal had also constructed those at Copán. Squier regarded the hieroglyphics found on the altars and stone idols at Copán to be identical with those of Palenque and those found in aboriginal paintings. He thought the remains at Copán and Quirigua to be older than those at Ocosingo and Palenque, just as those sites were more ancient than the ruins at Quiche, Chichén Itzá, and Uxmal. Squier attributed all of those remains to the ancestors of the Indian peoples still living there when first known to the Spanish.[54]

Palacio's account is also important for its discussion of native dialects and their supposed relations.[55] Palacio gave Popoluca, Pipil, and Chontal as the dialects spoken in Guazacapan, Itzalco, and their immediate vicinity. Palacio's Pipil was the dominant language spoken from the Michatoyat River to the Lenpa River, including nearly all of the state of San Salvador. Squier identified the Pipil language as a dialect of the Nahual or Mexican language. It was still spoken in most of the Indian towns of that district but was known by the name of Nahual. The derivation of the term Pipil was unknown to Squier, and it did not appear to him that the people who actually spoke the language ever adopted the name themselves. The etymology of the term indicated that it meant "childish," "backward," or "provincial" and that it probably originated with the Mexican auxiliaries who fought with the armies of Alvarado. It was likely an expression of contempt used by the Mexicans for a language and people they considered their subjects or inferiors. The vocabularies Squier acquired from the Indians of that district in 1853 showed only slight variations from the Nahual language recorded in the dictionaries of the aboriginal languages of Mexico. He attributed the differences existing between them to inconsistencies in phonetic interpretation on the part of the people who recorded them – that is, different persons wrote down what they thought they heard. He had found that to be precisely the case with variations in the pronunciation of Nahual words in Nicaragua, where Mexican prefixes and suffixes of common words were sometimes omitted or contracted. [56]

According to Palacio, "The Mexican language is current among them, although their proper tongue is the *Populuca*." Squier identified Pipil as an "intruded" Mexican language and Populuca as the native language. Herrera corroborates Palacio's statement in his *Historia de las Indias Occidentales*, where he states that the natives of Guazacapan spoke Mexican, although they also spoke another language peculiar to themselves. "We may fairly infer from this and other testimony, that the district was occupied by a people, probably of the same family with the nation or group of nations vaguely denominated *Chontals*, who had either been brought more or less under the subjection of their *Nahual* neighbors, and [had] been compelled to adopt their language, or who had gained a knowledge of it, and assimilated in other respects with them, from long contact and association." [57] Squier doubted if the term *Chontal* was ever used to identify a particular language or dialect, thinking rather that it was a general designation for "savage" or "barbarian" applied indiscriminately by the Aztecs to the tribes living on the frontiers of their own territory. It was in this sense that the Spanish employed it in their accounts of exploration and conquest. [58]

Squier's interest in the native dialects of Central America next led to the compilation of his *Monograph of Authors Who Have Written on the Languages of Central America*, published in 1861. [59] Squier attached great importance to properly delineating the linguistic affinities and differences existing among the aboriginal groups inhabiting the region extending between the isthmuses of Tehuantepec and Darien and those residing in the Mexican provinces of Yucatán, Chiapas, Tabasco, and Soconusco. The presumed interactions and linguistic affinities of the Indian inhabitants of those locations presented an important field for archaeological and ethnological inquiry and speculation. The importance Squier placed upon that line of inquiry is quite apparent, as is the confidence with which he asserted his theory of migration and interaction between Central America and Mexico.

And there are many reasons for believing that it was here also [Central America], where Aboriginal Civilization reached its highest development, and whence it spread, in a modified form, to the northward as far as the mouth of the Panuco river, where it was reflected in what is known as the Mexican civilization. Nor is it impossible, at least there are a number of facts supporting such an inference, that the *Nahuals* or *Aztecs*, who attained a dominating position on the high plains of Anahuac, had their original seats in Central America, where we still find, in the States of Nicaragua and San Salvador, considerable fragments of the same stock.

It is Central America also, where we must look for the original seats and permanent establishments of the *Tulhuatecas*, who, under the name of *Toltecs*, figure so conspicuously in all speculations on the origin of Mexican or Aztec civilization. That the original *Tula*, *Tulha* or *Tollan* existed in the province of Chiapas near Ocosingo or Palenque, if it were not one of those ruined cities, scarcely admits of doubt; and it is equally certain, if not capable of demonstration, that the great semi-civilized family which, under the general name of Mayas in Yucatan, Quiches, Zutugiles and Kachiquels, etc., etc., in Chiapas and Guatemala, still constitutes the predominating population of those provinces, was precisely that which is vaguely known as *Toltec*.[60]

Squier entertained the possibility that Central America might have been the true source of Mexican civilization. Evidence that Mexican groups had migrated to Central America before the arrival of the Spanish was conclusive, but that very evidence suggested that similar but earlier movements might also have taken place from Central America to Mexico at remote but unknown periods of time. The various divisions or "families" that made up the aborigines of the American continent, Squier observed in 1860, had undoubtedly manifested the same kinds of migrations and dislocations associated with the histories of mankind around the globe. Interactions between Mexico and Central America had most likely followed an analogous pattern. Based on his reading of the archaeology of the two regions, Squier tentatively floated the suggestion that Mexico might have been colonized from Central America. He saw the imposing and extensive monuments of Central America as the zenith of artistic achievement on the American continent. The monumental remains of Mexico also reflected significant architectural skill, but he regarded what he called "the qualified civilization" of Mexico as "rather reflected than of original growth." The models or "types" of architectural remains found in Mexico were to be sought further to the south, "if, indeed, many of them do not owe their origin to colonies from the same direction."[61]

Squier believed that Mayan colonizers from Chiapas, Yucatán, and Guatemala had migrated to the Panuco River, where the Spanish knew them as the Huastecas. The Central American colony on the Panuco had sent forth their priests to instruct the tribes of Anahuac in their religion, government, and arts. It was then that Cuculcan, the great lawgiver of the Central Americans, became Quetzalcoatl. Squier even thought it possible that those colonizers had traveled as far north as the island of Cuba and perhaps even Hispaniola, but evidence in support of that hypothesis was inconclusive. He attributed the pictorial records of the ancient Mexicans, such as the Dresden Codex, and the sculptured tablets at Palenque and Copán to that same great aboriginal family. He little doubted that pictorial writing originated in Central America and was in whole or part hieroglyphic. If archaeologists were ever to determine the phonetic values of those glyphs, he observed, they must search for them in the ancient mother language, of which the Tzendal, Maya, Huasteca, Quiche, Kachiquel, Chorti, and Mam were only dialects. In the light of that theory, the study of native dialects in Central America assumed great ethnological and archaeological significance.[62]

It was by studying the existing dialects of Central American languages and by them alone that an approximation was to be gained of the ancient languages from which they developed. The original languages, said Squier, were "fossilized" in the engraved architecture of Palenque, Copán, and other Central American sites. He likened the relationship between the living languages of Central America and their ancient sources to that existing between the Coptic language and that of the ancient Egyptian. It was only by determining the "radixes" of the aboriginal languages of Central America that the hieroglyphics on its monumental architecture could be decoded.[63] Native languages were still spoken by a majority of the people of Yucatán and Guatemala and also by a considerable portion of the population in Chiapas and Tabasco. The Lancandones, Choles, and Manches occupying the unexplored region watered by the Usumasinta River spoke them exclusively. Those circumstances presented archaeologists and ethnologists with an important field of inquiry, for there was every indication that the languages and customs of those peoples would not only remain relatively intact but also become predominant within those localities.

> These countries are relapsing into their aboriginal condition, or rather under the domination of their aboriginal inhabitants, whose blood is fast washing out the infusions of the Spanish Conquest and European colonization; and the time seems not far distant, when the language of the Maya chiefs will become almost exclusive in Yucatan, and that of the old Kings of Quiche and Rabinal equally predominant in Vera Paz and the Altos of Guatemala. Such a result is inevitable unless prevented by some speedy and powerful interposition of other races, who shall regain all that Spanish power has lost and is losing.[64]

Squier little doubted that it was the destiny and true mission of the American republic to fill the void left by the decline of Spanish influence in Central

America. He also understood that American intervention and colonization would come with an ethnological price. The vestiges of aboriginal conditions existing in the provinces of Yucatán, Guatemala, Chiapas, and Tabasco would become less and not more ascendant with the arrival of American commercial interests and culture. Such was the inevitable price of the progress promoted by Squier and other American expansionists during the 1850s.

The native languages of Central America were worthy of study as aids to archaeological investigations, as were the unpublished Spanish manuscripts containing the surviving remnants of their grammars and vocabularies. Squier devoted significant time and effort to pursuing both lines of inquiry throughout the 1850s and 1860s. Although his interest focused on the fragments of the Nahual-speaking peoples in Nicaragua and San Salvador, groups that retained their language and many aboriginal traits but slightly changed, he attempted to classify all the aboriginal inhabitants into five linguistic groups: the Tzendal or Maya groups, the Nahuas or Aztecs, the Chontals, those he denominated as the relatively "savage" tribes, and the Indians of the isthmus. Squier's Tzendal or Maya group includes the Mayas, Quiches, Zutugils, Kachiquels, Pocomans, Lacandones, Mams, Manches, Choles, Itzaes, Chortes, Achis, and Zoques. Those groups inhabited nearly all of what became the provinces of Guatemala, Yucatán, Tabasco, Chiapas, probably Soconusco, and a small part of northwestern Honduras. The Nahuals or Aztecs occupied most of San Salvador, where they were known as the Pipil. They extended their range into Guatemala at least as far as the Rio Michatoyat and possibly further. The Nahuas also resided between Lake Nicaragua and the Pacific as far south as the Gulf of Nicoya in Costa Rica, including the islands of the lake and probably those of Gulf.

The Chontals, derived from the Mexican *Chontalli* ("stranger" or "foreigner"), were identified as being "a ruder people" than either the Tzendals or the Nahuas. Squier placed the Chontals in the central and southern areas of Honduras and the northern and western areas of Nicaragua. They included the Lencas, Payas, Uluas or Woolwas, Maribious, Taulepas, and possibly also the Chorotegans and Nagrandans. A group he classified as "relatively savage" closely resembled the Guaranis and Caribs of the eastern and northern regions of South America. They lived on the Atlantic coast and were scattered across Costa Rica, and included the Waiknas or Mosquito, the Talamancas, Buricas, Valienes, Tojares, and Urimanas. The Indians of the isthmus comprised Squier's fifth group. They represented a large number of tribes sharing similar conditions, characteristics, and perhaps also languages. They included the tribes inhabiting Veraguas (the Chiriqui), Panama, and Darien, about whose languages little was known. He largely based his classification, except in the case of the Tzendals and Nahuals, upon "contiguity and similarity of character, condition, and development."[65]

What most interested Squier was the language of the Tzendals, a language that had early become the subject of study by the Spanish. Those accounts provide philologists with more information about the language of the Tzendals, and their neighbors the Nahuas, than about all the other Central American groups combined. Spanish missionaries studied their forms of government, religion, and most especially their language in order to more rapidly convert them to Christianity. "The efforts of these Zealots, as recorded in the chronicles of the various Religious Orders, exhaust language and almost stagger belief, in recounting to us the rapidity with which they acquired the 'barbaras y disicillimas lenguas de lo Indios,' and the perfection they attained in them." The formal study of Indian languages, particularly the Kachiquel, began at the College of Santo Tomás (later San Carlos) in the city of Guatemala shortly after the Conquest. Indian languages were studied in the convents and religious orders, many of which became rivals in the study of Indian grammars and the laborious compilation of dictionaries.

Very few of the vocabularies, grammars, and dictionaries compiled by the Spanish religious orders had yet been published. Many had undoubtedly been lost, but Squier thought it likely that a considerable number still existed in church archives and other repositories. Here was a wide and potentially valuable field of investigation. His *Monograph of Authors Who Have Written on the Languages of Central America* was an aid to scholars in their search for those documents, a compilation that includes the collected vocabularies and works composed in the region's native dialects. Squier identifies the convents to which the various clerical writers belonged and constructs a chronology of their activities. He derived much of his information from the three-volume *Biblioteca Hispano-Americana Septentrional* compiled by Don José Mariano Beristain de Souza. Squier knew of but one copy of the work in existence, which was in the possession of Henry Stevens. Stevens, an American, lived in London, where he bought and sold books and was in some way connected with the British Museum. Francis Parkman introduced Squier to Stevens in 1851, describing him as "one of the sort commonly called 'smart fellers' with a considerable knowledge of the world, a great knowledge of books and libraries, and an eye to the main chance."[66] Stevens was a scholarly acquaintance worth knowing. He generously permitted Squier to use Souza's *Biblioteca* in the preparation of his own work. Squier collected the rest of the information through his own investigation of religious orders and political archives; his collation of the chronicles of Remesal, Vasquez, Cogolludo, Villiagutierre, and Juarros; and the biographical and other publications of the various religious orders.[67] The appendix to Squier's *Monograph of Authors* contains a list of books and manuscripts relating to the history, aborigines, and antiquities of Central America that pays ample testimony to the breadth and depth of his knowledge of those subjects.

An advertisement at the end of Squier's *Monograph of Authors* announces his plan of bringing forward a previously unpublished grammar composed by Bartolome Anleo circa 1660. Antonio Ramirez Utrilla copied Anleo's grammar in 1744 from the original manuscript, which was then in the possession of Antonio M. Betancur. Squier proposed to publish Anleo's grammar under the title of "Arte de Lengua Quiche, o Utlateca; Compusto por N. M. R. P. Fray Bartolome Anleo, Religioso Menor de N. S. Pe. San Francisco." The edition was to have contained about 250 pages and an introductory essay on the Quiche dialect by Squier. Only 150 copies were to be printed and issued to subscribers by C. B. Richardson and Company at New York and by N. Trubner and Company at London in October 1862. Squier informed the members of the American Ethnological Society in November 1860 that his forthcoming *Monograph of Authors* would be followed by the publication of a Quiche and Kachiquel grammar, which he identified as the two dialects spoken by the builders of Palenque and Copán.[68] Whether he intended to publish that account as part of his *Collection of Rare and Original Documents* or separately is unclear.

Squier made his last original contribution to the archaeology of Central America in a paper on the ornamental green stones known as *chalchihuitl*. The stones were round or oblong and were shaped into beads. They were greatly valued for personal ornamentation by the aboriginal inhabitants of Mexico and Central America. Squier regarded the workmanship exhibited by these stones to surpass any aboriginal works of art he had seen.[69] He gave an extended notice of them before the Lyceum of Natural History of New York in 1869 that was published by the Lyceum and appeared in the *American Naturalist* the following year.[70] Squier had in his possession a number of *chalchihuitl* that he acquired from the ruins of Ocosingo in Chiapas, not far from Palenque. The ornaments were worked from a variety of green stone that resembled emerald. The accounts of the early Spanish explorers and chroniclers make frequent mention of these stones, attesting to the value placed on them by the native populations of Mexico and Central America. Molina defined *chalchihuitl* in his *Vocabulario Mexicano* (1571) as *esmeralda baja*, an inferior kind of emerald. Native speakers, by contrast, knew emeralds proper as *quetzalitztli*. Squier believed the mineral composition of the *chalchihuitl* to be either nephrite or jasper.[71]

It is clear from the accounts of Bernal Diaz, Torquemada, and Sahagun that the ancient Mexicans attached great value to these stones. Fuentes, in his manuscript history of the old kingdom of Guatemala, observes that the Indians of Quiche wore headdresses resplendent with feathers and brilliant stones they called *chalchiguites*, a dialectal variation of the Mexican *chalchihuitl*. Palacio mentions these stones in his account of the Pipil Indians of San Salvador written in 1576, noting that they were worn on the wrists and ankles and were believed to ward off certain illnesses.[72] The pictorial records of Mexico and Central America show ornaments in the form of round or oblong beads that fit the descriptions of the *chalchihuitl* mentioned in written accounts. The inhabitants near the ruins of Ocosingo in Guatemala, where Squier had also found several of these green stones, knew them as *chalchichuites*. Squier attributed the slight variation in pronunciation to differences in dialect, leaving little doubt that he had obtained the specimens of the ornaments so prominently described by the Spanish chroniclers.

Examples of the *chalchihuitls* in Squier's collection are figured in the extracts of his observations published by the Lyceum of Natural History of New York. Many of the stones were perforated so they could be suspended and worn as personal ornaments. The most remarkable of the *chalchihuitls* is an engraved stone showing a figure sitting cross-legged upon a carved seat. His left hand rests upon his thigh and his right is raised to his breast, "as if in the act of giving benediction." The facial features resemble those found on other Central American sculptures. Ornaments are inserted into the lobes of the ears, and the head is adorned with a feathered headdress like that found on the monuments at Palenque and in aboriginal pictorial records. "The whole is almost an exact miniature copy of the large bas-relief found by Mr. Stephens in an inner chamber of one of the ruined structures of Palenque." Squier presented the sculptured figure at Palenque, which he presumed to be a representation of the god Cuculcan, to aid comparison with the engraved figure in his own collection.[73] Another of the engraved stones figured from Squier's collection is a perforated sphere or globe with "hieroglyphics" on three of its surfaces. Squier used the term *hieroglyphics* in its "popular sense," believing the designs to be "syllabo-phonetic or phono-syllabic" symbols.

Assessments of Squier's contributions as a Central Americanist have been mixed. He expressed the same nationalistic and expansionistic sentiments in *Notes on Central America* and *The States of Central America* that he had earlier expressed in *Nicaragua*. An anonymous reviewer of *Notes on Central America* wrote in the London *Athenaeum* in 1856 that ever since Squier's diplomatic appointment to Nicaragua in 1849 he had urged the American government, "more or less openly," to take possession of Central America. The reviewer found Squier's writings on Central America to be admirable in their presentation of facts but noted that they were unfortunately marred by the author's Anglophobic opinions. "Mr. Squier had no reason to quarrel with the attention accorded by the English to his facts, if not to his opinions – to that which made the literature, apart from the politics, of his book." Squier's English reviewer rightly identified him as an advocate of Manifest Destiny – the widespread assumption that is was the providential mission of the United States to colonize and have dominion over Central America – and noted that this belief colored both his reasoning and his statements of facts. His anthropology was no exception.

Squier had leveled his most severe comments against the British protectorate on the Mosquito Shore, but the *Athenaeum* acknowledged that at least some parties in Great Britain thought his hostility to the Mosquito protectorate was justified. Squier described the "Mosquito King" with unrestrained disgust, characterizing him as a ruler who would sell his crown for a quart of rum. He lampooned the burlesque spectacle of a potentate without shoes who paraded in ragged trousers. Squier's republican antipathy to monarchy was plain enough to his English readers, as was his resentment over the British government's willingness to pursue its commercial and territorial interests in Central America in defiance of the Monroe Doctrine. Squier's intemperate tone in *Notes on Central America* prompted the *Athenaeum* to call for moderation and conciliation in Anglo-American relations. "Above all things, we deprecate a menacing tone."[74]

Squier's polemical treatment of the Mosquito Indians has far more to do with politics, Anglophobia, and racial prejudice than objective scholarship, and it speaks volumes about the attitudes and assumptions of many nineteenth-century anthropologists. Squier shared Nott and Morton's view that racial hybridity produced an inferior offspring. Squier regarded the Mosquito Indians – a mixture of black, Indian, and white populations – as a decadent race. He contemptuously derided their claim to political sovereignty and thought them incapable of understanding and implementing the responsibilities of self-government. Squier had no kind words for the Mosquito in any of his writings, once referring to the Kingdom of Mosquito as "the stalking horse of British designs" and to the Mosquito themselves as "mongrel savages" and licentious drunkards who were doomed for extinction.[75] Squier's pronounced Anglophobia and disdain for the Mosquito prompted him to anonymously write *Waikna; or, Adventures on the Mosquito Shore*, a romantic novel published in 1855 under the pseudonym of Samuel A. Bard. There the Mosquito are further ridiculed and grossly caricatured.[76] *Waikna* was also the source of a sketch called "Something about the Mosquitos," which appeared in *Harper's New Monthly Magazine* that same year, also under the name of Samuel A. Bard.[77]

The "Mosquito King" George Augustus Frederic at length had a measure of revenge upon his detractor Samuel A. Bard, whose actual identity was never a secret. The English traveler Bedford Pim met King Frederic during his visit to the town of Bluefields in Nicaragua and noted in his account of that interview that he had found a copy of *Waikna* among Frederic's rather impressive library. Frederic remarked to Pim that before he had read the book "he could not have believed it possible for anyone to string together for any purpose such a pack of lies; especially when it was notorious that the author had never visited the Mosquito coast."[78] The influence of politics and ethnocentrism so evident in Squier's treatment of the Mosquito Indians has also received censure from those familiar with their history and culture.[79] It is not surprising that Squier would adopt a pseudonym for such a blatantly racist and polemical novel.

Squier's activities in Central America in the 1850s and his various writings promoted the rediscovery of Central America in the United States and significantly affected American and British attitudes and policies toward the region in the process. His *Notes on Central America* was the first work to present accurate geographical, historical, and political information about the region and its latent potentialities. Translations of the work immediately appeared in Spanish, French, and German, establishing Squier's reputation at home and abroad as the leading authority on Central America. As A. Curtis Wilgus observed of *Notes on Central America*, "No contemporary scholar could presume to understand the area unless he had read Squier's book. Indeed, Squier's contribution to the literature on the area was not to be equaled for several decades."[80] That is not to suggest that *Notes on Central America* is an entirely objective work when judged by the standards of Squier's day or of our own, for the author's social and political views form something of a running commentary of their own. But it did make him the most celebrated Central Americanist of his day.

The geographical and historical data embodied in *The States of Central America* received similar laurels. The London *Athenaeum* acknowledged in its review that Squier's knowledge of the region's history, geography, resources, population, and current conditions was unequaled by any of his contemporaries.[81] Squier continued to promote both scholarly and popular interest in Central America and its potential for economic development for years to come.[82] His study of the region's geography, archaeology, ethnology, and history began in 1849, and he continued to write on Central American subjects for both scholarly and popular audiences until 1870. Central America, said Squier, geographically approximated "the ancient idea of the centre of the world."[83] It connected the Northern and Southern Hemispheres, and its harbors were certain to someday beckon the trade of Europe and Africa on the east and Polynesia, Asia, and African on the west. The high mountain ranges, towering volcanoes, elevated table lands, scenic valleys, broad and fertile plains, extensive lakes and rivers, and exotic plants and abundant wildlife were all found in close proximity, presenting a panorama of natural grandeur that never fully relinquished its claim on his time, attention, and enthusiasm. He became the consul general of Honduras at New York in 1868, a position he held through the early 1870s, and brought forward his *Honduras Historical and Statistical* in 1870 – a reprint of the Honduran chapter of *The States of Central America*.

Squier's narratives of Central American travel and adventure frequently lapse into polemics and distortions regarding British designs and the character of the Mosquito Indians, while his racial theorizing about the nature and destiny of the region's population supported his economic interests and related desire to develop Central America through the promotion of white emigration from the United States and Europe. But Squier was also a close and careful observer of nature and of men. He consistently demonstrated critical scholarship in his study of archaeological remains, comparative vocabularies, and ethnohistorical accounts. He conducted his inquiries in those subjects, moreover, at a time when there were no authorities and few reliable sources of information. His original contributions helped to unravel the complex and problematic archaeology and ethnology of Honduras and San Salvador. One must acknowledge both the empirical and the polemical aspects of his writings.

Squier never tired of speaking about Central America as a region "of singular interest" for the geographer, naturalist, archaeologist, and ethnologist. "And lying, moreover, almost at our own doors, rich in its resources and tempting in its natural wealth, it must soon appeal to that restless spirit of enterprise and commercial activity which, not content with its past triumphs, longs for new conquests and a wider field of exercise."[84] Squier made that observation in his introduction to the English edition of Arthur Morelet's *Travels in Central America*, published at London in 1871. He was then nearing the end of his active days as a scholar, but he could well have been describing his own "restless spirit of enterprise" and ambitions in the region at an earlier day. His enthusiasm for Central America's past, present, and future never subsided.

10. Ancient Peru

An Indigenous Civilization

Squier made his final contribution to the development of American anthropology among the archaeological remains and native peoples of Peru and Bolivia. He served as a United States claims commissioner to Peru from 1863 to 1865, having once again sought a diplomatic post as a means of conducting archaeological fieldwork. Squier completed most of his diplomatic work during the first six months of his appointment and largely devoted the next eighteen months to surveying and photographing archaeological sites. He was not the apostle of American Manifest Destiny in Peru as he earlier had been in Nicaragua and Honduras. Keeping his diplomatic duties and archaeological activities within their proper spheres, he was a far more objective reporter in Peru than he had been in Central America. Squier conducted his archaeological explorations in Peru on a large scale and at his own expense, their cost far surpassing the meager funds he received for his diplomatic appointment.[1]

Squier presented the results of his fieldwork in Peru through a series of lectures between 1865 and 1867, in some remarks on the geography and antiquities of Peru published as an extract from the *Bulletin de la Société de Geographie* of Paris in 1868, and more extensively in a five-part series of illustrated articles on his explorations appearing in *Harper's New Monthly Magazine* between April and August 1868.[2] Squier further promoted interest in his investigations in a brief but significant account of Peruvian antiquities for the *American Naturalist* in 1870, and another on the geography and archaeology of Peru for the American Geographical Society published that same year.[3] The full range of his findings did not appear, however, until the publication of his long-awaited *Peru: Incidents of Travel and Exploration in the Land of the Incas* in 1877 – his magnum opus on the monumental architecture of an indigenous civilization.[4] Several of the engraved illustrations appearing in *Peru* are based on photographs taken for Squier by Augustus Le Plongeon or, later, by Squier himself under difficult and often exacerbating conditions.

Peru's ancient and largely unknown past offered a rich field of inquiry for the explorer and student of archaeology. As the American historian William

Hickling Prescott observed in the introductory essay to his monumental *History of the Conquest of Peru* (1847),

> The hand of the Conquerors, indeed, has fallen heavily upon these venerable monuments, and, in their blind and superstitious search for hidden treasure, has caused infinitely more ruin than time or the earthquake. Yet enough of these monuments still remain to invite the researches of the antiquary. Those only in the most conspicuous situations have been hitherto examined. But, by the testimony of travellers, many more are to be found in the less frequented parts of the country; and we may hope they will one day call forth a kindred spirit of enterprise to that which has so successfully explored the mysterious recesses of Central America and Yucatan.[5]

Squier saw himself as that "kindred spirit of enterprise" and was certain that great archaeological discoveries were yet to be made in the land of the Incas. When Prescott first published those words in 1847, Squier was concluding his investigations of Ohio mounds with Edwin Hamilton Davis. Prescott took a personal interest in those investigations and became one of Squier's most esteemed acquaintances. It was largely through the influence of Prescott and other eminent worthies that the Taylor administration had appointed Squier as a diplomat to Central America in 1849. Prescott's hope that the antiquities of Peru would one day be systematically explored resonated loudly with Squier, stoking an ambition that would one day lead him to cross and re-cross the Cordilleras in search of the ancient centers of Incan civilization. Many years would pass before he would be able to visit Peru, but when unexpected circumstances presented that opportunity in 1863 he embraced it with an earnest sense of personal mission.

Squier's earlier interest in the antiquities of Peru is not merely a matter of surmise or de facto assertion. Squier published an anonymous article entitled "Ancient Peru – Its People and Its Monuments" for *Harper's* in June 1853.[6] Squier later identified himself as the author of this account in the first installment of his five-part series on his explorations in the Andes published in *Harper's* for April 1868.[7] The attribution of authorship to Squier can be made, however, upon internal evidence alone. Here we find a significant continuity in thought, theme, approach, and language that connects this article to other writings by Squier published both before and after its appearance. The article is a popular piece and the sources of Squier's illustrations and descriptions are derivative, but his discussion, based on both manuscript sources and the most recent works on the subject of Peruvian antiquities, lacks neither substance nor originality. The article clearly indicates the set of assumptions he brought with him to Peru in 1863 and is a benchmark for what did and did not change as a result of his later explorations.

The *Harper's* article further reveals the lengths to which Squier had already gone to bring the subject of Peruvian art, architecture, *quippus* (knotted ropes used to record time), and religious systems under serious study at a comparatively early point in his researches. He specifically draws on the accounts of Fernando de Montesinos, Padre Joseph de Acosta, Garcilaso de la Vega, Antonio de la Calancha, Zarate, Sarmiento, Gomara, Pedro Pizarro, the Friar Niza, Pedro Cieza de Leon, Diego d'Alcobaca, and Padre Blas Valerio. The more recent observations of Don Mariano Rivero (director of the national museum at Lima), von Tschudi, Prescott, and Don Juan Nieto are also cited in this informed discussion of ancient Peru. By far the most important of the most recent accounts was Rivero and von Tschudi's *Antiguedades Peruana*, published in Spanish at Vienna in 1851.[8] The plans, views, and several descriptions of architectural remains and objects appearing in Squier's article are taken from Rivero and von Tschudi's lithographic plates. Nine of these engravings appear in Squier's *Peru*, published in 1877, but by that time he had enough original materials of his own to dispense with most of the earlier engravings and have new ones made from his own photographs and drawings.

When Squier published his first account of Peruvian antiquities in 1853, he little could have imagined that one day he would be able to fulfill his ambition of conducting original investigations in the land of the Incas. The exigencies involved in making a living had forced him to abandon his archaeological explorations throughout most of the previous decade. As he confessed in a brief but remarkably candid passage of *Peru*, the "inexorable circumstances, distracting occupations, and the thousand vicissitudes which make us what we are, and often prevent us from becoming what we might have been, interfered to defeat his hopes and aspirations."[9] Squier was forty-two years old in 1863, still robust and active but beginning to have problems with his vision. He had temporarily lost sight in one eye by that time and could only see imperfectly with the other. He had every reason to believe that he might go completely blind. Complete rest and an entire change of surroundings and occupation, his physician told him, might partially restore his failing vision, but rest did not come easily to Squier; it was not in his makeup. He was a man of seemingly endless energy and enterprise, driven by the personal demons of an incessant ambition.

It was then that Squier received word that a mixed commission to Peru was being formed to settle outstanding commercial claims and that his name had been brought forward as a possible appointment. Squier seized the day. He joined the commission and with great dispatch set about fulfilling a long-cherished desire of conducting explorations in Peru.[10] Quite remarkably, he later recovered nearly all of his sight amidst the frost, snow, and desolation of the Andes, but thereafter his eyes allowed him to work very little at night – a time he usually devoted to concentrated work.[11] Squier's failing vision redoubled his determination to conduct fieldwork in Peru before the light of the world left him entirely. He was keenly aware that his diplomatic appointment to Peru probably presented his last opportunity to undertake original archaeological explorations. A man on a mission he most certainly was.

Squier's diplomatic commission instructed him to settle outstanding commercial claims between the United States and Peru arising from the mining and export of guano.[12] Negotiating the adjustment of those claims was not the most exciting mission on the face of it, but it was one he certainly turned to good advantage. His diplomatic status and reputation as an archaeologist put him in contact with influential people who were in a position to aid him in his travels. In contrast to his earlier experience in Nicaragua, he allowed nothing to divert him from his main purpose of surveying and photographing Peruvian antiquities. Squier's diplomatic appointment to Peru was not nearly as significant as his earlier assignment in Nicaragua, either on its own terms or in the influence it had on his anthropological thought, but it was nonetheless indispensable as a means to a larger end, and it provided yet another example of the marriage of diplomatic appointments and scientific exploration in the nineteenth century.

Squier believed he had covered more ground than any previous explorer during his travels in Peru. His archaeological expeditions first took him to the coastal region of Peru between the Cordillera and the Pacific Ocean – from Tumbes to Cobija. There he visited the large ruins of Pachacamac, Grand Chimú, and Cajamarquilla as well as numerous lesser-known but equally interesting sites in the valleys of Santa, Nepena, Casma, Chillon, Rimac, Canete, Pisco, and Arica. He traveled inland from the port of Arica across the Cordillera into Bolivia and the remarkable remains at Tiahuanaco. Striking northward he reached the great terrestrial basin of Lake Titicaca and its eight sacred islands. The Inca traced their origin to those islands and invested them with great religious significance.

Squier believed himself to be the only explorer to have ever completely traversed Lake Titicaca, a natural wonder lying 12,500 feet above sea level. He and his entourage of field assistants and mules continued their journey northward over the great divide separating the waters flowing into Lake Titicaca from the headwaters of the Amazon. Traveling down the Valley of the Vilcanota, he came to the bolsones (high plains surrounded by mountains) and the ancient city of Cuzco – "the Rome of the New World" and the "Um-

bilicus" of the Incan cosmos. [13] Squier spent several months at Cuzco, where he conducted explorations in every direction within a radius of one hundred miles, continuing them as far as "the savage frontier" on the Atlantic declivity of the Andes. Steering northwest, he traveled along the approximate line of the former Inca road running from Cuzco to Quito. That route took him through Ayachucho (site of the ancient Inca town of Guamanga). He had almost reached Jauja when heavy rains forced him back down the slope to Lima. [14]

Squier went to Peru to study the Inca, but he soon discovered that other groups had made many advances before the ascent of Incan supremacy. He was particularly interested and impressed with the accomplishments of the Chimú and devoted an entire chapter of *Peru* to their art, customs, and religion. His descriptions of the distinctive styles and motifs found in the ornaments, implements, and pottery of the Chimú are not without interest. Some of these materials formed part of his own collection, while others were in the museum at Lima or in private collections. The Chimú and other coastal tribes were particularly accomplished in the manufacture of pottery. Squier illustrates several examples of Chimú pottery, the originals of which were either in his own collection or among those that either he or Le Plongeon photographed in private collections.

Squier was particularly intrigued by examples representing the human head, which not only suggested the probable physical features of the ancient peoples of the coast – the Yungas and Chinchas – but also indicated their hairstyle, types of headdress, and common forms of personal ornamentation. Squier was struck by how closely they seemed to conform to the physical type still seen among the existing Indian population of Peru. He dramatically illustrates that similarity in what appears to be an engraved version of a photograph (apparently taken by Le Plongeon) entitled the "Modern Peruvian Head." The illustration gives the profile of "a servant-boy" who, Squier tells us, had but "a slight infusion of Spanish blood." The subject's profile is shown in comparison with the profiles of two examples of pottery representing the heads of *huacas* (the personifications of spirit-beings or deities) that presumably imitated the prevailing physical type of the Chimú (see fig. 13).

What most intrigued Squier about examples of Chimú pottery were their design motifs and painted symbols. He saw in these motifs the representation of ideas and beings associated with the aboriginal religious beliefs of the region as related by the Spanish chroniclers. Squier restricted himself to presenting a "resume" of his findings on the subject, "always reserving the right to altar, modify, or abandon my present conclusions." The Spanish chroniclers give direct testimony that when the Inca Yupanqui conquered

13. The "Modern Peruvian Head." Wood engraving, 1877. Squier's engraving of the "Modern
Peruvian Head" is based on a photograph that was probably taken for Squier by Augustus
Le Plongeon, and possibly in Le Plongeon's photographic studio in Lima. Squier was struck
by how examples of Peruvian pottery exhibiting the human head resembled "the type" of
the existing Indian population, which served as the inspiration for this engraving and the
photograph on which it is based. (From Squier, *Peru*, 184.)

the Chimú they were worshiping animals and fishes. The Chimú are said to have abandoned those beliefs and to have adopted the form of sun worship practiced by the Inca. It is, perhaps, just as probable that the Inca had earlier adopted sun worship from other groups with whom they traded and eventually conquered or that cognate forms of sun worship developed separately among all the Peruvian groups. Be that as it may, however, the type of animal worship practiced by the Chimú was symbolic. The representations of animals found in their sculptures and on painted pottery embodied "a conception of the mind." The ideas that Squier summarizes regarding those conceptions owe much to the philosophy of symbolism elaborated in *The Serpent Symbol*, a work he neither mentions nor cites in *Peru* but which significantly informs his discussions of the religious symbolism found in Peruvian antiquities. Many articles of Chimú pottery, Squier hastened to note, had primarily served religious rather than secular or utilitarian functions, and he inferred their probably meaning along the same lines of inquiry perused in his earlier works.

Pottery vessels of this kind were *huaca* (sacred) and connected with religious and mortuary customs. The design motifs found on this class of pottery illustrated the religious symbolism and associated ideas of their makers. "And on them we do find representations, which from their clearly mythological character, close identity, and frequent recurrence, indicate that they originated in prevailing notions, and are exponents of a common system." The iconography of the Chimú indicated that they worshiped the powers of nature as manifested by the elements of earth, air, and water – the center of life and the place where it originates and ends. "In the absence of written language men employ signs and symbols to indicate their ideas and conceptions; and these symbols are usually obvious and easily intelligible."

Nothing was more obvious or more intelligible to the mind of early man than the elements and the powers of nature, representations of which were clearly evident in the iconography of the Chimú. Their symbols for water were the fish, the turtle, or the crab; for earth, the serpent and the lizard; and for air, the lightning or thunderbolt represented by a lance or spear. Squier hypothesized that the beings or deities associated with the three elements were depicted not only in conventional symbols but also by their particular style of headdress. [15] The Chimú and other coastal tribes practiced a form of worship he described as "little removed from fetishism." He took his evidence in support of that belief from the observations made by Padre Pablo Joseph de Arriaga, the Jesuit author of the *Extirpación de la Idolatría del Perú*, published at Lima in 1621. [16]

Squier's explorations on the Peruvian coast were not insignificant, but it was the Incan remains found in the highlands of Peru and Bolivia that intrigued him the most. Crossing the Cordilleras to the centers of Incan civilization was not an easy journey, but Squier undertook it with the same confidence, sense of adventure, and swaggering bravado that characterized his earlier explorations in Central America. He outfitted himself at Tacna in preparation for his travels among the Andes. There was only one way of reaching the interior from Tacna, and that was by mule. Squier and an *arrierro* (muleteer) named Berrios made the trip from Tacna to Puno in the company of their mules and two *mozos*. Squier's accoutrements for the trip made him a picturesque explorer. Heavily clothed and booted, he sported a broad-brimmed hat, a colorful *bufanda* (scarf), and a native-made poncho. A knife hung from his bootleg, large spurs jangled as he walked and tinkled as he rode, and a rifle hung conspicuously from the bow of his saddle. Such made up his equipment and that of his fellow adventurers in the mountains. One needed to be prepared for the long and difficult journey and to possess not a little of what the Spanish called *sabiduria* and Americans called "gumption" (see fig. 14). [17]

Squier plunged into the interior in high spirits – a curious pilgrim in search of the monumental remains left by the children of the sun. He examined the *chulpas* (stone burial towers) and other aboriginal remains at Acora, Quellenata, and Sillustani; at the hill fortress of Pucura; and in the basin of Lake Titicaca in the Collao region of the ancient Peruvian empire. He marveled at the skill of the Incan stonecutters and fitters, and accepted the common features of design and purpose found in their works as evidence of a common origin. The various forms of the *chulpas* indicated different eras of construction and progressive stages of development. Squier did not presume to determine what those eras and stages of development were, but he recognized their existence (see fig. 15).

Squier considered the fortress at Sacsahuaman, near the ancient Incan seat of Cuzco, to be as imposing a monument as any found elsewhere in the world, ranking with the pyramids as a testament to human ingenuity. He similarly referred to the megalithic ruins at Tiahuanaco in Bolivia as the Stonehenge and Carnac of the Americas. He remained an impassioned defender of the attainments of the ancient inhabitants of America against European savants who denied that a true "civilization" had ever developed in the New World. As he observed in the *American Naturalist* in March 1870: "Civilization is, of course, a relative term, and one to which nations who in this age go to war with one another may doubtless aspire, but to which the beneficent Incas, to say nothing of the Arcadian inhabitants of New Mexico, might lay good claim. Still, if megalithic monuments of any kind are evidences of civ-

14. "Equipped for the Cordillera." Wood engraving, 1868, 1877. Crossing the Cordilleras to the centers of Incan civilization was not an easy journey, but Squier undertook it with a sense of adventure and bravado. His accoutrements for the trip made him a picturesque explorer. (From Squier, "Among the Andes of Peru and Bolivia," *Harper's New Monthly Magazine*, April 1868, 545, and *Peru*, 239.)

15. Peruvian *chulpa* (burial tower). Squier considered the *chulpas* of Peru to be an indigenous invention. He noted that the different types of *chulpas* in the great terrestrial basin of Lake Titicaca probably reflected different eras of construction and that the "rude monuments" of unfinished stone on the plain outside Acora were the ruder prototypes of what later became elaborate and symmetrical *chulpas*. (From Squier, "Among the Andes of Peru and Bolivia," *Harper's New Monthly Magazine*, April 1868, 553, and *Peru*, 243.)

ilization, or even its first stages, Peru . . . can no longer be 'left out in the cold.' " [18]

Squier spent three weeks in an open boat on Lake Titicaca in the company of Antonio Raimondi, "a gentleman of high scientific attainments." Raimondi had devoted years to collecting reliable data about Peru, and he did so, said Squier, "with a zeal, intelligence, and industry impossible to be surpassed." Raimondi placed at Squier's disposal his survey and description of the ancient works of Huanuco Viejo, which Squier acknowledged as the contribution of a "laborious and conscientious antiquary." [19] Squier and Raimondi visited the eight islands of Lake Titicaca: Amantene, Taqueli, Soto, Titicaca, Coati, Campanario, Taquari, and Apunto. The largest of these is Titicaca, the sacred island of the Inca. The Inca traced their origin to the island, and their descendants still regarded it with "profound veneration."

According to Incan tradition, it was on the island of Titicaca that Manco Capac and Mama Oella, his sister and wife, started the conquests of tribes that established the Incan Empire. Manco Capac and his followers settled at Cuzco, which in time became the City of the Sun – the seat of the Incan empire and the center of its religion. Not far from the island of Titicaca is the island of Coati, a sacred place upon which stood the Palace of the Virgins of the Sun. Squier found the site to be one of the best-preserved and most remarkable remains of aboriginal architecture in America. The population around Lake Titicaca was almost entirely aboriginal. The Aymaras represented the largest part of the Indian population, while groups speaking the Quichua language were the smallest. Squier believed the ancestors of the Quichua to have been the dominant group within the empire established by Manco Capac, or the Inca proper. [20]

The journey from the coast to the soul of the Incan empire at Cuzco was long and weary but was more than worth the effort. Cuzco – "this lofty eyrie of aboriginal power" – was the place where the legendary Manco Capac began the earthly mission among the Inca entrusted to him by his father, the sun. Here he built his palace, and here too were some of the most impressive remains of Incan architecture. Looking down upon the site of Cuzco was the commanding presence of the great fortress of Sacsahuaman, "the most massive and enduring monument of aboriginal art on the American continent." The name Cuzco signified "the umbilicus, or navel," attesting to the central importance and dominating position of Cuzco within the Incan empire. The very construction of the ancient city and the arrangement of its divisions reflected "the polity" of the Incan state. Cuzco was "a microcosm of the empire" and a window into the lost world of the Inca. "In common with the country at large, it was divided into four quarters by four roads leading to the corresponding portions of the empire, which bore the general designation of Tihuantisuya, signifying the 'four quarters of the world.' " The four roads did not follow the true direction of the cardinal points; rather, in conformity with the local topography, they ran intermediately to the northeast and southeast and to the northwest and southwest. The northwestern division of Cuzco was called Chinchasuya and pointed to the Incan town of Quito; the southwestern quadrant of Cuntisuya faced the coastal regions of the empire; the road in the southeastern section of Collasuya led to Lake Titicaca; while Antisuya led to distant Inca frontier extending to the northeast.

Squier considered Cuzco the most interesting archaeological site in the Americas. He surveyed the site with the aid of two engineers, (J. P.) Davis and Church, an acknowledgment he makes in *Observations on the Geography and Archaeology of Peru* but curiously omits in *Peru*.[21] His map "Cuzco Ancient and Modern" is based on that survey, which indicates the locations of the Incan ruins and walls that were still standing. Enough of the Temple of the Sun remained to indicate its design and character. No less remarkable was the great fortress of Sacsahuaman. Squier's plan of the formidable structure provides a section of its walls, an overall plan of the site, a view of one of its salient angles, and the commanding view of the fortress as seen from "The Seat of the Inca." Everywhere he looked at Cuzco, Squier saw evidence of Incan greatness. The streets of the modern city followed the orientation of the old ones and were defined by long sections of Incan stone walls. The walls were cut and placed with a precision unsurpassed by any of the structures of Greece or Rome. Modern art, said Squier, might emulate, but could not surpass, the masonry skill of the Inca.[22]

The architectural remains of the Inca bore the imprint of an original and highly accomplished civilization that owed nothing to the outside world. The burial towers at Sillustani were entirely unique as an architectural form, and Squier was no less impressed with the fortress of Ollantaytambo on the Incan frontier than with the Antis of the Amazon. Many of the lines of the buildings at that site could still be accurately traced, and some were largely intact. Squier described the citadel at Ollantaytambo to Francis Parkman as nothing less than "a manual of labor and skill," and the positioning of its other defenses demanded the admiration of the military engineer.[23] Although the fortress at Ollantaytambo was less imposing than the Sacsahuaman at Cuzco, it was more complicated and equal in the skill of its design. Squier visited the site often during his two-week stay at Ollantaytambo, surveying and photographing the fortress's more important features. The structure stood on the spur of a snowy mountain, with its exterior walls zigzagging upward at right angles. The walls were approximately twenty-five feet high, were made of rough stones stuccoed on both sides, and had an inner shelf for the convenience of defenders. The Inca had built the structure with such skill and obvious design that it could well be mistaken for a medieval fortification in Europe.[24]

A subject that receives a significant amount of attention in *Peru* is the problem of archaeological treasure hunting. The practice was associated with traditions of searching for the lost treasure of the Inca and Chimú dating to the Spanish Conquest. One such seeker of legendary treasures was Colonel La Rosa, whom Squier described as "the most experienced, enthusiastic, and persistence treasure-hunter of Truxillo."[25] Searching for *tapadas* (treasures) had been a passion in Peru ever since Juan Gutierrez de Toledo began the practice almost three hundred year earlier. Squier had seen at London some years earlier a collection of articles said to have been obtained by La Rosa from the ruins of Chimú, Moche, and Viru. Squier learned that La Rosa had "confided" the collection to a person calling himself "Dr. Ferris," asking him to help with their disposal in London. Ferris, however, claimed to have discovered the items himself and sold them on his own account. A part of the collection went to the British Museum. George Folsom, a member of the American Ethnological Society and the New-York Historical Society, purchased the other portion, which he deposited in the collections of the historical society. Squier saw one of La Rosa's collections for sale on the antiquities market at Lima during his residence there, when he purchased the more remarkable items made of precious metals.

As a foreign traveler and archaeologist, Squier was, of course, part of the problem. He collected human crania from several sites, mummies at Pachacamac, and artifacts throughout his explorations in Peru. Some of these he recovered in his fieldwork and others he purchased at Lima. These he brought back with him to the United States as "trophies" of his travels. Nonetheless, Squier made a clear distinction between the interests and ends that had brought him to Peru and those of La Rosa. That distinction in some ways may be more apparent than real, even self-serving, but in other respects it was more than justified. The orientations and interests of Squier and La Rosa ran in different directions. They were compatible in some instances and incongruent in others.

The colonel is neither an archaeologist nor an antiquary, and had little care for the relics he obtained in his excavations, except in a mercantile sense. He had rather a contempt for pottery, and for implements or utensils in bronze. His interest in Chimú architecture was mainly in the way of finding hidden vaults and chambers; he cared nothing for arabesques or paintings; and his knowledge of the ancient modes of sepulture was limited to ascertaining where the rich and powerful were buried, and where ornaments of gold and silver were most likely to abound. In these directions he had become proverbially expert.

La Rosa showed little sympathy with Squier's interest in surveying, measuring, and mapping. He suspected that Squier too was in search of the legendary treasure of the Chimú and that all declarations to the contrary were but a pretext to disguise his true designs. He accompanied Squier on his reconnaissance of the ruins of Chimú not so much to assist him or ease his way, Squier suspected, as to guard against the possibility that Squier might discover the *peje grande* (the big fish) of lost Chimú treasure at the colonel's expense. Squier did not seek archaeological materials for their commercial value, and the wanton looting and destruction of sites and the selling of collections was not his business. He valued the materials he collected in Peru for what could be learned from them, and made every effort to document the localities and circumstances in which they were found. Afterward he either donated or sold those materials to museums in the United States instead of placing them on the nefarious antiquities market that existed then as now, where they would have fetched him a much handsomer price.

The tradition of treasure hunting was just as problematic at Tiahuanaco and Cuzco. Squier recorded a conversation with the *cura* (priest) at Tiahuanaco (whom he reported to have been quite drunk and not entirely coherent) that was symptomatic of the problem. When Squier began to interrogate the *cura* about the ancient ruins of the vicinity, he fell silent and drew Squier aside. He whispered that he knew all about the hidden treasures of the place and assured Squier that he could count on his assistance in finding them in return for a fair share of the spoils. "It was in vain I protested that we were not money-diggers. He could not conceive how any stranger should evince an interest in the 'vestiges of the Gentiles' not founded on the hope of discovering treasure among them." The lust for Incan treasure existed in all parts of the country.

And here I may mention that throughout all our explorations, in all parts of Peru, whether in the city or in the field, we were supposed to be searching for *tapadas*, and were constantly watched and followed by people who hoped to get some clue to the whereabouts of the treasures through our indications. Often, when engaged in surveys of fortifications or buildings, we found the marks left by us at night, to guide us in resuming our work in the morning, not only removed, but the earth deeply excavated below them. The ancient monuments of the country have suffered vastly more from the hands of treasure-seekers than from fanatic violence, time, and the elements combined. The work of destruction from this cause has been going on for three hundred years, and still actively continues. [26]

Squier knew whereof he spoke, and he would not be the last observer to lament the tragic consequences of treasure hunting in Peru. The tradition began when the Spanish discovered that the tombs of Inca leaders and nobles contained gold and silver. As Michael E. Moseley has noted, "Within a generation of the conquest, looting operations grew so large and financially rewarding that they became legally synonymous with mining. Ancient monuments were divided into claim areas with titles registered in notarial archives. Title holders established chartered corporations to mobilize massive work forces and systematically quarry ruins." The commercial exploitation of Peruvian antiquities has continued unabated from that day to this, "and the Andean Cordillera is probably the most intensively looted ancient center of civilization in the world." The result of "four centuries of monument-mining and ruin-quarrying" is that Peruvian archaeological materials are found in museums and private collections around the world, but too often with little information about where they were found and in what context. [27]

Treasure hunting at the Sacsahuaman – the remains of the fortress of Cuzco – had been no less destructive. Squier sympathized with the lament of Garcilaso de la Vega (1539?–1616), himself of Incan-Spanish descent, that the Spanish had not spared the fortress from destruction. The only three walls of the structure left standing were those they could not throw down. These solitary remnants were subsequently damaged, however, in searching for the golden chain of Huayna Capac that treasure hunters believed to be buried there. Squier noted that little had changed since Garcilaso recorded the tradition of buried treasure at Cuzco.

Three hundred years have not sufficed to eradicate the notion that enormous treasures are concealed within the fortress; nor have three hundred years of excavation, more or less constant, entirely discouraged the searchers for *tapadas*. In making our surveys of the fortress and of the Rodadero, often have we found, upon returning to our work in the mornings, the ground deeply excavated overnight where we had planted our little peg to determine the limit of our day's survey, and as a guide for resumption of our work. I doubt if, among all the people, high and low, whom I met in the Sierra, half a dozen could be found who, when questioned apart, would not testify to a belief that the investigation of ancient monuments was rather a clumsy pretext under which to carry on search[ing] for the chain of Huayna Capac or some other *tapada* of equal value.[28]

Squier doubted if a single foot of soil at the Sacsahuaman had escaped the diggings of treasure seekers. "Men were constantly busy there during the whole time of our stay. Perhaps our visit gave a new impulse to money-digging, or treasure-hunting, which, if called on to say, I should declare to be the principal occupation of the people of Peru. The time, labor, and money that have been spent in digging and dismantling ancient edifices would have built a railway from one end of the country to the other, given wharves to the ports, and, what is far more needed, sewers to the cities."[29]

Although Squier appropriated materials of cultural patrimony in Peru like many a foreign traveler before and after, he was a grave robber of a different sort. His interests centered on the stories that graves could tell – stories about agricultural laborers as well as of princes.[30] His explorations in Peru occurred within the context of American commercial intervention (he was there to diplomatically promote American economic interests), reminding us that archaeology has often been a concomitant of foreign intervention. The burden of archaeology's past in this regard is often a heavy one, and Squier certainly must assume his share, but as foreign explorer he is interesting in many ways. His unqualified admiration for the Incan achievement, his disdain for theories that derived their genius from foreign sources, and his observations on the problem of treasure hunting in Peru place him at an interesting juncture of exploitation and appreciation. The strident ethnocentrism and racial determinism so characteristic of his Central American writings is noticeably subdued (though not entirely absent) in Peru, where his buoyant optimism and sunny view of life make a welcome return. His primary interest was to study the antiquities and Indian peoples of Peru, not foreign investments, guano exports, or the centuries-old search for lost treasure.

Squier noted that with more time and adequate means at his disposal he could have greatly extended the field of his explorations. But so far as his primary purpose – illustrating Incan civilization through architecture – was concerned, he doubted that he would have obtained more than an accumulation of supplemental facts and illustrations. He informed Parkman in February 1866 that he was entirely satisfied with the scope and completeness of his explorations and entirely confident in the correctness of his findings.

> These materials will, I think, show not only that there were originally several detached and distinct civilizations in Peru, but that some of them antedated the Incas; while my observations on the geography and topography of the country will show how the Incas were enabled to establish

their extensive dominion, and how their expansive and astute policy was suggested and developed. My researches will, I think, correct many mistakes and exaggerations as regards ancient Peru, and enable us to form a rational and just estimate of the power and development of the most thoroughly organized, most wisely administered, and most extensive empire of aboriginal America. [31]

Squier returned from Peru in 1865 with a large archaeological collection illustrating the art and industry of ancient Peru: more than four hundred plans, sections, and elevations; about as many sketches and drawings; and a large number of photographs. [32] He placed great stock in his collection of Peruvian photographs, not only for their intrinsic value but also because of the extraordinary difficulty and expense involved in obtaining them. Accurately illustrating Peruvian antiquities based on surveys and photographs was a leading objective of his investigations from the start. "I carried with me the compass, the measuring-line, the pencil, and the photographic camera; knowing well that only accurate plans, sections, elevations, drawings, and views can adequately meet the rigorous demands of modern science, and render clear what mere verbal description would fail to make intelligible." [33] He claimed to have either made or supervised the making of all of the photographs that became the basis of several engraved illustrations appearing in *Peru*. That statement is not entirely false, but it is certainly less than candid, since Squier received invaluable assistance from Augustus Le Plongeon in photographing and surveying several archaeological sites in Peru.

Squier says in *Peru* that during his investigations of the ruins at Cajamarquilla "I was accompanied by a friend, who was both draftsman and photographer, and we intended to spend a week there, and bring away such plans and views as would give a clear notion of the singular and undescribed remains of the ancient city." Squier's friend is not named and is subsequently referred to in his narrative only as "Mr. P____" or "P____." There is no question that Augustus Le Plongeon (1825–1908) was the photographer and draftsman to whom Squier is referring. Le Plongeon lived in Lima from 1862 to 1870, where he had a commercial photographic studio. [34] He appears to have taken most, if not all, of the photographs of sites along the central and northern coast of Peru, while the photos of pottery in Squier's collection and in private collections at Lima were no doubt taken at Le Plongeon's photographic studio in Lima.

Squier's silence about Le Plongeon's contributions raises important ethical questions about the implicit or explicit understanding existing between them regarding their professional relationship. Did Le Plongeon take these photographs for hire, as Squier would seem to suggest, or did he take them for his own purposes without compensation, as Le Plongeon would later assert? The circumstances under which Le Plongeon took those photographs and the extent to which he worked for Squier and for himself are sketchy at best, but Le Plongeon's later views are clear enough. Writing in February 1878 to Stephen Salisbury Jr., a promoter of Le Plongeon's investigations at the American Antiquarian Society, Le Plongeon bitterly complained that Squier had published his photographs without his consent, acknowledgment, or compensation.[35] Not all of the accusations made in that letter, written more than a decade after the fact, can now be substantiated.

Le Plongeon made his complaints against Squier after reading A. H. Guernsey's review of Squier's *Peru* in *Harper's* for February 1877. Harper and Brothers illustrated Guernsey's review with some of the same wood engravings that appear in *Peru*. Le Plongeon stated that the illustrations appearing on pages 363 to 365 of the *Harper's* review were all taken from his own photographic plates. One of those illustrations was of the ruins at Cajamarquilla, twelve miles from Lima, which were located on land owned by Pablo Sacio (or Saio?), a good friend of Le Plongeon's who had introduced the photographer to Squier. Those remains were "photographed and surveyed by myself," said Le Plongeon, a claim that is no doubt partially true. Le Plongeon had worked as a surveyor in California until his departure for Peru in 1862, and he was quite capable of making surveys on his own. But the surveys in question would appear to have been made with and for Squier and not independent of him.

Le Plongeon may well have regarded his work with Squier as part of his own ongoing investigations, but that seems a stretch given the purpose of Squier's visit to Peru. Le Plongeon traveled with Squier to the Cajamarquilla ruins, photographed them, and either assisted Squier in surveying the site or conducted the survey by himself at his request. He also traveled with Squier to Chimú and Chan Chan near Trujillo, where he doubtless performed the same services. If such was the case, however, the work was again done with Squier and, as circumstantial evidence would suggest, for him. Le Plongeon said he had been photographing the ancient remains in Inca for nearly two years before Squier's arrival in July 1863. "I left San Francisco in 1862 for Peru in order to study the antiquities of that country." He claimed to have undertaken those investigations under the auspices of the Academy of Sciences of California, of which he said he had been a member since 1856. Le Plongeon doubtless had an interest in the archaeological remains of Peru before Squier's arrival, and he had probably already photographed several, but his contributions to

Squier's investigations were made at the latter's behest and not independent of them as he would later seem to suggest.

Le Plongeon wanted it known that he had been Squier's photographer, and he gave Salisbury an account of "the history of my scientific acquaintance with Squier" during his travels in Peru. He and Squier arranged to visit the sites on the coast together in order to photograph and survey them. They traveled in the company of a "Mr. Chamberlain" (Squier's "Mr. C____"), the purser on an American store ship at Callao and later a minister in Buffalo, New York. He stated that he was the only one involved in the investigations who knew photography. "I took, as a matter of course, my instruments and chemicals with me in order to illustrate my notes and keep an exact copy of the monuments, so they might be studied by antiquarians abroad." Le Plongeon said he spent two months on the coast with Squier and Chamberlain but then declined Squier's invitation to accompany him to the interior because he was in ill health and could not afford to abandon his clientele for such an extended period of time.

Le Plongeon claimed that his expenses during those excursions were not remunerated, but whether that means that Squier never paid him for his services as photographer at any time or only failed to compensate him for the expenses incurred on their expeditions is unclear. It is difficult to understand, however, why a commercial photographer – even one with a serious interest in archaeology – would work for Squier for nothing. Le Plongeon said it was he who taught Squier what little he knew of the art of photography during his residence in Lima, a claim that again seems quite probable. What is less likely is Le Plongeon's assertion that when Squier was ready to start for the interior Le Plongeon lent him his own photographic instruments – instruments he would have himself needed at his studio in Lima. That statement is contradicted, moreover, by Le Plongeon's letter to Squier in March 1865, which was written much closer to the time of the investigations than his later account to Salisbury. Le Plongeon then informed Squier that the photographic equipment used in their investigations, which he had left with a friend at Lima, was of better quality than his own for making large plates. He regretted that he did not have the money to purchase it for himself and that the equipment was being sold on Squier's account by a friend at Lima.[36] That would seem to corroborate Squier's statements that he had purchased costly photographic equipment expressly for the explorations.

Even more serious charges would be leveled against Squier. Le Plongeon claimed to have entrusted Squier with a large collection of negatives "representing the only collection of photographic views of the Peruvian monuments" as Squier was preparing to return to New York. He asked Squier to take them to Henry Anthony of New York for printing as a means of getting some benefit for his time and expenses as a photographer. Le Plongeon said he later learned from Anthony that Squier had brought him the negatives as requested but had taken them with him after they had been printed. Le Plongeon said this was the last he had heard or seen of them until he learned they were being used to illustrate Squier's book on Peru – a lapse of twelve years.

Le Plongeon further claimed that in 1873, when he had offered Harper Brothers a manuscript of his own work on Peru during a visit to New York, he learned that they were under contract with Squier to publish a work on the same subject. How Le Plongeon could have been surprised by that fact is difficult to fathom, however, since the purpose of Squier's visit to Peru was to conduct archaeological explorations and place the results before the world. But he was outraged that "my photos of the monuments on the coast are now published by Harper without even an acknowledgement of being my *gratuitous* work." It may well be that Squier did not seek Le Plongeon's authorization to use those materials because he did not regard them as belonging to anyone other than himself. If, in fact, the photographs had been taken with Squier, for Squier, and with Squier's photographic equipment, Squier might well have regarded the negatives as his own and not those of the photographer.

Le Plongeon was impressed with neither Squier's archaeology nor his ethics. He considered himself fortunate that noting worse than the loss of his photographs had resulted from his association with Squier, whom he also charged with having stolen archaeological materials from a private collection in Peru. "Little experience was indeed to be gain[ed] from such a man as Squier in scientific researches. I have seen him in the field of investigation. I know what he is worth; and my opinion of him is that he is a most unscrupulous and superficial man." Le Plongeon said he had not read Squier's work on Peru, but he thought Squier might at least have had the courtesy to send him a copy in partial payment for his negatives. He was certain that many pages of the work were "mere plagiarism," as was the case in his book on Nicaragua. Le Plongeon did not say from whom Squier had probably plagiarized in his work on Peru (possibly himself?) or from whom he had allegedly plagiarized in *Nicaragua*. Indeed, it was easier for him to make those charges than to prove them, as there is no evidence that either *Peru* or *Nicaragua* was the work of anyone other than Squier. Not all of Le Plongeon's accusations against Squier can be rejected out of hand, but the charge of plagiarism rings hollow.

It is simply impossible to now know what understanding or agreement, if any, existed between Squier and Le Plongeon at the time of the investigations.

As Lawrence G. Desmond has observed on this point, "Solid evidence yet remains to be uncovered which will prove or disprove Le Plongeon's assertions."[37] Le Plongeon had every reason to complain that his photographic contributions to the investigations had not been acknowledged. He was not the first to denounce Squier as an opportunist who occasionally manifested amnesia and loose ethics in acknowledging the contributions and assistance of others. But Le Plongeon's own motives and reputation urge caution in placing too much credence in his de facto accusations. He appears to have regarded Squier as a rival in archaeological investigations – a perception that was no doubt mutual – and to have deeply resented the recognition accorded Squier in the face of his own aspirations. Squier and Le Plongeon, it has been well said, were not entirely honest about their working relationship or their mutual photographic contributions.[38]

There seems little reason to doubt Le Plongeon's claim that he had taught Squier everything he knew about the art of photography. He apparently taught him well, for Squier later became his own photographer, less by design than by mishap. Writing to Frank Leslie from Lima in April 1864, Squier noted that "I now do my own photography 'wisely if not too well,' as you will see from the specimens sent to Mrs. S. . . . All my companions for the interior have backed out, and I am now going it alone."[39] Squier was not exactly going it alone, for he subsequently hired another anonymous photographer to accompany him to the highlands of Peru and Bolivia. Where he found him and under what circumstances is unknown. Squier's second photographer is also referred to in Peru only as "P." Two years later, after Squier returned from Peru, he told Parkman that his "drunken photographic assistant" had died on top of the Cordilleras, "where he will last forever." Squier claimed to have taken all the photographs in his collection after that untoward event (with the aid of an "obtuse" English manual of photography). He described photography as a process bedeviling enough to drive even "a more pious man than myself into hysterics of profanity" and regarded many of his Peruvian photographs less as works of art and more as the productions of "a poor devil" largely unacquainted with photographic process, who sometimes carried his water fifteen miles into the mountains only to have it freeze on the plates during the process of washing.[40]

Squier subsequently related the story of the death of his drunken photographer in the second installment of his series for Harper's in May 1868 and in his address before the Photographic Section of the American Institute of New York that same month, and he retold the tale with equal relish in Peru.[41] Squier and his small company of field assistants and mules had just reached Tiahuanaco near the center of the great terrestrial basin of Lake Titicaca and

Lake Aullages, a region he called the Tibet of the New World. There, at an elevation of 12,900 feet, the photographer fell seriously ill and died soon thereafter of unknown causes.

> I had provided myself with a complete and costly set of photographic apparatus, which I regarded as indispensable to success in depicting the ancient monuments; but I had little knowledge of the art, and must now become my own photographer, or lose many of the results of my labor. With no instruction except such as I could gain from Hardwick's "Manual of Photographic Chemistry," I went to work, and, after numerous failures, became tolerably expert. I had but a single assistant, Mr. H____ [Harvey], an amateur draughtsman, and only such other aid as I could get from my muleteer and his men, who were eager to conclude their engagement, and simply astounded that we should waste an hour, much more that we should spend days, on the remains of heathens.[42]

Squier's photographer and companion died before morning, "murmuring something in the Gaelic tongue, in which the endearing term of 'Mamma,' common to all languages, and sacred in all, was alone intelligible, and the last on his thin blue lips, – the password to a better world!" Squier found himself alone the next day, "encumbered with a bulky apparatus" and giving self-instruction in the mysteries of the collodion process and its inscrutable formulas.[43] The identity of the second "P." is unknown and perhaps unknowable. Some of the stereopticon views in the Squier photograph collection that were taken in the Andes are signed "E. G. S. Phot.," but most are unsigned and undated. It is possible that the oft-told story of his photographer's death is apocryphal, but that assumption seems unwarranted. Squier had every incentive to find another photographer and draftsman after Le Plongeon declined to travel with him into the interior, someone who could give a reasonable assurance that Squier would not return to Lima empty-handed. He became his own photographer by default and not by choice.

Squier returned from Peru with empty pockets but laden with abundant and significant materials. He was anxious to get his findings before the public and to recoup some of the considerable cost involved in his explorations. He brought with him some one hundred cases of Peruvian materials, consisting of pottery, worked metals, carved stone, and crania together with photographs, sketches, maps, and plans of archaeological sites. He initially used these materials to promote interest in his explorations through lectures. Squier gave an address on the "Geography and Topography of Southern Peru, Particularly the Great Terrestrial Basin of Lake Titicaca" before the American Geographical and Statistical Society in May 1865,[44] and he displayed some of his collection together with his maps, plans, drawings, and photographs of Cuzco before the members of the American Ethnological Society in July and December 1865. His drawings and photographs of Peruvian temples and tombs elicited astonishment and admiration among his audiences for the skill exhibited in their design and construction. His photographs also dramatically showed the inaccuracy of the early Spanish descriptions upon which the standard accounts of Peruvian antiquities had been based.[45]

Squier confided to Parkman that he was too poor to even buy books and that his fieldwork in Peru hand cost him sixteen thousand dollars over and above the living expenses he received from the U.S. government. Wanting to lecture at the Lowell Institute in Boston as a means of promoting his forthcoming "opus" on Peru, he solicited Parkman's help in getting an invitation. The prestige of lecturing at the Lowell Institute was something that Squier coveted greatly. His friend and confidant George Robins Gliddon gave twenty-four lectures on "Ancient Egypt" at the Lowell Institute in 1843 and 1844, and Edwin Hamilton Davis delivered four lecture there on the "Mounds and Earthworks of the Mississippi Valley" in 1853 and 1854.[46] Squier was positively incensed at the fact that the Lowell Institute had not invited him to lecture on the results of his investigations in Peru. "Had Prescott lived, who urged me often to go there," he wrote Parkman, "I should not be obliged to suggest such a thing to the people of Boston." Squier's Peruvian investigations were a matter of great pride, and his often-sensitive ego could not brook the prospect that the learned few might be indifferent to the importance of his discoveries.

Squier frankly confessed the wellspring of his ambition and angst to Parkman, displaying the biting sarcasm and invective he could mete out to those who, like the trustees of the Lowell Institute, were unfortunate enough to meet with his displeasure.

> You will not suspect me of vain-glory, when I tell you that no man ever brought home from any explorations whatever in America, the amount of material that I have done from Peru. . . . You know me well enough to be aware that I don't care "a continental d——n" for "figure heads" and mere names. But I do care for the appreciation of my contemporaries and I *did* work to get their good opinion and deserve it – especially in this long, weary, and costly exploration of Peru. But it seems that the wise men of the Lowell Institute prefer a rehash of what everybody outside of an Infant School knows about Pompeii – I expect to hear next – "ten lectures on the Alphabet, by Sylvanus Cobb," or whatever Cobb it may be, who got up a spelling book.

Squier became further provoked over his unsuccessful effort to examine Prescott's Peruvian manuscript materials, which Prescott's family rather coolly told him were "inaccessible." He did not take it well. "I wonder you can live in Boston," he told Parkman. "Here at least [in New York], one may go to the devil in a free, easy, and magnificent manner. He will not die of stint and narrowness." [47]

Squier half apologized to Parkman for his querulous and complaining letters about the Lowell Institute, but he restated his annoyance that the lecture series seemed incapable of promoting anything better than the "skimmings" from stale old books on Pompeii. Meanwhile, "there was a poor but not utterly incompetent devil in New York, working night and day to pay off the extravagances of his explorations in Peru, the very heart and center of a civilization far more wonderful than that of Rome, and before which Boston had paid tribute in the person of Prescott. I have audacity for everything and every body except my own affairs and myself." Squier wanted "an appreciative audience" and felt slighted that he had to work so hard to get one. [48] He claimed to have received several invitations to lecture at small lyceums, but he declined them because he did not want "to cheapen my materials." His findings were far too valuable and had cost him far too much in time, effort, and money to be announced to the world on the lyceum circuit. "I intend to talk to a purpose or not at all, having lost, if I ever had it, any ambition for notoriety." [49] It was the critical opinion of the few and not the curiosity of the many that Squier so assiduously sought to satisfy.

Parkman pushed the matter of inviting Squier to lecture with the trustees of the Lowell Institute by showing them the photographic proofs of Peruvian archaeological remains sent him by Squier. [50] Charles Eliot Norton, another of Squier's Bostonian friends, made similar entreaties on his behalf. The lobbying efforts of Parkman and Norton succeeded. Squier gave twelve evening lectures at the Lowell Institute on "The Inca Empire" in 1866 and 1867. [51] The content of Squier's Lowell lectures may be inferred from one of his letters to Parkman, where he outlines the progression of topics to be covered in the proposed lectures. He commenced with an examination of the physical geography of Peru and its influence on the development of the Inca, and then proceeded with an overview of what was known about the political, religious, and material aspects of Incan society at the time of the Spanish Conquest. He next allowed his auditors to vicariously experience the original centers of Incan development though his plans and photographs. He delineated the characteristics of the Inca at the beginning of their influence and raised the question of whether Incan civilization was in any way derivative of earlier societies. Such an inquiry involved the classification and description of the different types of remains found in Peru and a determination of what they revealed about the religion, defenses, and domestic life of their ancient architects. Squier concluded his comments with an outline of the distinctive traits of Incan political, religious, and artistic development at the zenith of their influence, contrasting them with those exhibited in earlier periods of development. He deduced those characteristics from his study of Inca traditions, the recorded observations of the Spanish chroniclers, and his own examinations of Incan archaeological remains. [52]

Squier's lectures at the Lowell Institute came to the attention of Dr. Jeffries Wyman, the curator of Harvard University's Peabody Museum of American Archaeology and Ethnology. Wyman had lectured at the Lowell Institute on "Comparative Anatomy" in 1840 and 1841 and again on "Comparative Physiology" in 1848 and 1849. [53] It is very likely that he was present at Squier's Lowell lectures. He certainly would have known of them. He also appears to have solicited the donation of some of Squier's Peruvian archaeological materials for the Peabody Museum, for Squier made a gift of seventy-five Peruvian crania and a Peruvian mummy to the museum in 1866. Squier gave the provenance of the crania in a letter to Wyman written at the time of the gift. What were usually called "Peruvian skulls," Squier noted, were not uncommon in archaeological cabinets, since they were easily obtained from the Indian cemeteries on the Peruvian coast. Crania from the interior of Peru, where Inca civilization had originated and developed, were less common due to the difficulty of penetrating the locations where they were found. The crania Squier donated to the Peabody Museum were from both the interior and the coast. He collected them with his own hands so as to leave no doubt as to the precise localities and circumstances in which they were found. The skulls from the interior were of the Aymaras on Lake Titicaca, as well as the Quichua, and those from the coast represented every coastal family from Ecuador to Chili. Squier carefully noted on each skull the exact location from which it came. It is reported that in addition to his donation of crania Squier also presented the museum with a collection of archaeological and ethnological specimens that he had presumably obtained in Peru, except for those made of gold and silver. [54]

Wyman made comparative measurements of fifty-six of the Peruvian skulls Squier donated to the museum, calculating cranial capacity, circumference, length, breadth, height, the indexes of those measurements, the frontal and parietal arches, the longitudinal arch, and the zygomatic diameter. He presented the results of those measurements for six crania recovered from the *chulpas* (stone burial towers) near Lake Titicaca, fourteen skulls from Casma, sixteen from Amacavilca, seven from Grand Chimú, fourteen from Pachacamac, five from Cajamarquilla, and four from Trujillo. Wyman presented his findings on the Peruvian skulls in his "Observations on Crania" appearing in the *Fourth Annual Report of the Peabody Museum of American Archaeology and Ethnology*. Squier included Wyman's observations and seven tables of comparative measurements in the appendix of *Peru*.[55] Wyman's measurement clearly show that the Peruvian crania obtained by Squier illustrate the two types of artificial distortion commonly found in Peruvian skulls. Those from the *chulpas* and other locations near Titicaca had long skulls, and those from almost all other localities represented in the collection had been broadened and shortened by the flattening of the occipital bone. It was further evident that some crania had been artificially distorted more than others, a condition that would skew conventional means of measurement unless allowances were made for such variations.

Wyman's observations and conclusions on this point are significant and speak directly to one of the leading problems confronting physical anthropologists in the mid- to late nineteenth century. Were the variations in the breadth and length of skulls among various American aboriginal groups natural differences or entirely artificial? Peruvian crania, such as the Aymara Indian skull described and figured in Squier's *Peru*, were particularly notable for being elongated. Squier obtained the cranium near, but not from, the *chulpas* in the vicinity of Palca, and it represented "a fine specimen of the Aymara skull, artificially distorted and lengthened."[56] Wyman's measurements of Squier's Peruvian crania established that variations in skull type were beyond all doubt artificially induced. He rejected the idea advanced by Daniel Wilson in the second volume of his *Prehistoric Man* that dolichocephalic skulls among the Peruvians occurred naturally, and he endorsed those of J. Barnard Davis that they were artificial (see fig. 16).[57]

Wyman's most telling observation regarded differences in the internal capacity of crania existing between Peruvian skulls and those of aboriginal groups in North America. The average capacity of the fifty-six Peruvian crania measured by Wyman closely approximated that indicated by Samuel George Morton and by Charles D. Meigs in his memoir on Morton's work.[58] The average was considerably less than that of the supposedly barbarous tribes of North America and almost exactly the same as that of the Australians and Hottentots as given in the measurements of Morton and Meigs. The average internal capacity of Peruvian skulls was likewise smaller than that obtained by J. Barnard Davis from a larger number of measurements. That difference represented a conundrum within the racial theory of Morton and his disciples Josiah Clark Nott and George Robin Gliddon. The Peruvians had developed complex civil and religious institutions and made notable advances in the

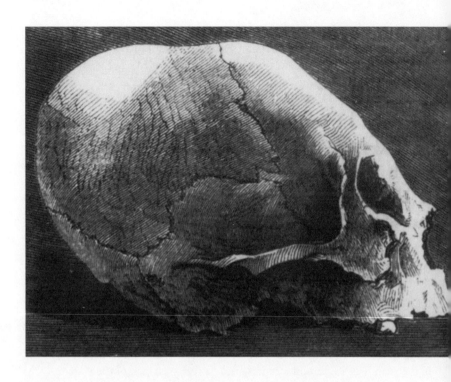

16. Aymara skull from Totora. Several groups of American aborigines artificially compressed or flattened the cranium, as evidenced in this Aymara skull from Totora. The question of whether variations in the breadth and length of skulls among various American aboriginal groups were natural differences or entirely artificial generated considerable debate among anthropologists in the nineteenth century. Peruvian crania were particularly notable for being artificially distorted and lengthened, such as the Aymara Indian skull described and figured in Squier's *Peru*. (From Squier, "Among the Andes of Peru and Bolivia," *Harper's New Monthly Magazine*, April 1868, 553, and *Peru*, 244.)

arts and sciences. Peruvian pottery, textiles, metallurgy, roads, aqueducts, and architecture exhibited intellect and skill yet were the work of a people with a smaller brain than that possessed by "a race [people] whose social and religious conditions are among the most degraded exhibited by the human race." Wyman's characterization of the "degraded" social conditions and beliefs of North American Indians reflects period attitudes to be certain, but his next comment gave the coup de grâce to the racial theory of Morton and the American School of Ethnology as well as to the contradictory results following from their attempts to use brain size as a means of accounting for differences in cultural achievement among the various races.

> All this goes to show, and cannot be too much insisted upon, that the relative capacity of the skull is to be considered merely as an anatomical, and not as a physiological characteristic; and unless the quality of the brain can be represented at the same time as the quantity, brain-measurement cannot be assumed as an indication of the intellectual position of races any more than of individuals. From such results, the question is very naturally forced upon us whether comparisons based upon cranial measurements of capacity, as generally made, are entitled to the value usually assigned them.

Wyman's cranial measurements and observations must have given Squier pause for reflection, even though he presented them in the appendix of *Peru* without comment. Squier himself had questioned the certainty of Morton's views on the alleged intellectual and moral inferiority of American Indians in 1849, when he passionately defended their capacity for progress against the charges of those who denied it. Subsequently, however, he came to accept the racial theories of the American School as a justification for American Manifest Destiny in Central American and for his own diplomatic and entrepreneurial activities in the region. He must have perceived that the bedrock of assumptions and biases on which the racial theory of the American School had been built was beginning to crumble. The racial theorists of the American School had recognized that in the case of the ancient Peruvians (who had presumably belonged to Morton's Toltecan division of the American race), brain size did not correlate with intellectual capacity and cultural achievement. They tried to explain that discrepancy by equating it to differences in the posterior lobes of the brain, which allegedly were more developed among the Peruvians and other Toltecan groups within Morton's arbitrary classification. The larger concern of the American School, however, was in determining the relative position of the various races within society. That concern and its corresponding biases skewed their findings to a significant degree. They had, as Wyman so clearly indicates, linked purely anatomical differences with a broader range of physiological characteristics, and they had further compounded the problem by linking these to what were presumably racially determined cultural traits and capacities for progress. Stephen Gould could well call Morton's calculations of racial inferiority "the mismeasure of man."[59]

The most curious skull obtained by Squier in Peru was that presented to him by a Señora Zenito, a member of one of the older families at Cuzco who was known for her hospitality to foreign travelers and her collection of Peruvian antiquities. The skull had been taken from an Incan cemetery in the valley of Yucay, but by whom and under what circumstances Squier did not say.[60] Le Plongeon actually asserted that Squier robbed the cranium from "Mrs. Centeno's [Squier's Señora Zenito] collection," returning it only after being tracked down by a party acting on her behalf.[61] The frontal bone of the skull shows unmistakable evidence that the Peruvians had knowledge of a surgical procedure known as trepanning, or trephining, where a small section of the skull is cut and removed in order to relieve pressure on the brain caused by an injury or a pathological condition affecting the brain. The Neolithic peoples of Europe, North Africa, and parts of Asia used similar procedures. Trepanning among American aborigines either originated independently or arrived through emigration from Asia. Evidence of the practice in the Americas is most frequently found in the highlands of Peru and Bolivia.[62]

Squier submitted the cranium to the opinion of the French surgeon and physical anthropologists Paul Broca, who gave a paper on the subject before the Anthropological Society of Paris. Broca's account of the then-singular find appeared in the *Journal of the Anthropological Society of Paris* in July 1867,[63] which Squier reprinted in full in the *Journal of the Anthropological Institute of New-York* for 1871–72 and excerpted in the appendix of *Peru*. In a letter accompanying the cranium, Squier informed Broca: "This skull was taken from an Incan cemetery in the valley of Yucay, twenty-four miles east of Cuzco, Peru. The cemetery is within one mile of the 'Baths of the Incas,' a favorite resort of the ruling family or race – their 'country-seat,' in fact. There is no doubt of its ante-Columbian date. The evidence of its authenticity is complete."[64] Broca presented evidence that the procedure of trepanning exhibited in this skull had been practiced during life, by a process entirely different from that practiced in European surgery. Broca concluded that "there was in Peru, before the European epoch, an advanced surgery, and this idea, an entirely new one, is not without interest in American anthropology." Trepanning was an ancient surgical procedure among Indo-European cultures, but this was the first known instance of the practice by an American aboriginal culture. The procedure implied a diagnosis of the condition from which the subject was suffering, regardless of whether the diagnosis was right or wrong. There was no way of deducing how widespread the practice was from a single skull, but the skull did provide further evidence of the advances in knowledge made by an indigenous civilization before the arrival of the Spanish.

The scope of Squier's investigation in Peru was impressive and the results were significant. He positively ached to get them before the public, but he was frustrated at every turn by the demands of other responsibilities that incessantly tugged at his sleeve. He did not have the luxury of devoting himself exclusively to writing or to preparing the numerous illustrations necessary to make the subject intelligible and useful. Work on the larger manuscript moved at a painfully slow pace. He had too much work to do as a contributing editor for Frank Leslie, and he was again having problems with his vision.[65] Very few of his surveys had been delineated since his return from Peru. Other exigencies of a private and tragic nature intervened to delay progress on the work even further. Squier experienced a complete mental breakdown in July 1874. He was declared a lunatic by an examining commission of physicians the following month and was temporarily institutionalized. Squier partially but never entirely recovered from his mental disorder. Although he spent his remaining years as a ward of his brother Frank, he did regain enough energy and good humor to return to the long-overdue task of preparing his Peruvian materials for publication. But the appearance of *Peru* in 1877 was only made possible with the assistance of his brother and keeper Frank. The work is E. G.'s from start to finish, but Frank's assistance in helping him arrange and revise the manuscript after 1874 was absolutely essential to its eventual publication.

Peru: Incidents of Travel and Exploration in the Land of the Incas is a remarkable achievement consisting of 599 engaging pages and 295 supporting illustrations. It is a travelogue on the model of *Nicaragua* and not an archaeological monograph like *Ancient Monuments of the Mississippi Valley*. It is difficult to compress a work of such breadth and depth and still do it justice, but a few topics and themes in *Peru* make important connections with some of his early writings and more fully frame the dimensions of his anthropological thought. Squier recognized that some of the prehistoric remains in Peru predate those of the Inca, and he saw a developmental sequence of unknown duration indicating that the ancient civilizations of Peru (he sometimes spoke in the singular and sometimes the plural) were separate, distinct, and of an indigenous origin. He made no effort to date the remains, but noted that they were very old and had been constructed in different eras and for different purposes. Squier compared the stone structures of the ancient Peruvians to the cromlechs, dolmens, and Druidical sun circles of Scandinavia, Great Britain, and France and to similar remains found in northern and central Asia. He did so not to suggest a connection of any kind but rather to employ analogy as a means of establishing that the works in Peru and Bolivia were similar to those of the Old World in antiquity, design, and purpose. The antiquities of Peru bespoke the presence of a society that had arrived at the same stage of development as those that had constructed similar structures in the Old World. Squier did not doubt that the antiquities of Peru were constructed by the progenitors of the natives encountered there at the time of the Spanish Conquest, or by other aboriginal groups that had preceded them in occupying the same area. He first stated in the *American Naturalist* for March 1870 that all Peruvian architecture was "indigenous, gradually developed and not intruded." The later structures found there had most certainly developed in situ from the earlier and more simplistic forms and had not been derived from anywhere else.[66] All the additional evidence presented in *Peru* gave further testimony to the correctness of that opinion.

Squier's conclusions regarding the origin and development of Peruvian civilization were logical inferences based on his fieldwork and related research into ethnohistorical sources. He believed that numerous tribes had existed in the remote periods of Peru's past, groups that eventually consolidated by interacting and interblending over a long period of time. The Inca ultimately became the dominant group and the others their subjects. The French naturalist Alcide Dessalines Orbigny (1802–57), whom Squier regarded as one of the ablest writers on the subject, divided the indigenous population of the Incan empire into two groups in his *l'Homme Americain* (1840): the Quichuas and the Aymaras. Orbigny thought those groups to be of the same stock, speaking dialects or variations of a common language. Squier, however, was not prepared to accept that generalization. The differences existing between those groups were too great to be attributed solely to the effects of climate and physical environment acting upon a localized and largely homogeneous population. He suggested that those differences amounted to "distinctions of race" (i.e., they belonged to different aboriginal families or groups of cognate tribes).

The Quichuas and Aymaras were, indeed, Indians, and both South American Indians, as distinguished from the aborigines of North America. But they differed from each other as widely as the Germans differ from the French; and both differed widely from the present degenerate natives of the coast. There was indeed, a certain blending of the various families, or races, and a certain predominance of the Quichua language, which was that of the Incas; but this was less than can be reconciled with the accounts which we have of the persistent and energetic efforts of the Incas to assimilate all the peoples who fell under their sway.[67]

The Incan language and culture largely submerged the linguistic and other cultural differences of their subjects, but one could still assume the existence of earlier and significant differences.

Squier believed that the assimilation of distinct groups ("races," as he often said) by the Inca explained the existence of contradictory and apparently irreconcilable historical traditions among the indigenous peoples of Peru. Native traditions merged together over time as a consequence of intertribal interactions and consolidations. The Inca borrowed traditions from those over whom they had dominion, and those groups in turn adopted Inca legends as their own. Eventually it became difficult to determine "where the history of one race ended and that of the other began." Those circumstances went a long way toward explaining the differences in the Inca lineage given by Garcilaso de la Vega and that by Fernando de Montesinos in his *Memorias Antiquas, historiales y politicas del Peru* (1627). Garcilaso identifies 14 Inca rulers, whose successive dynasties began in the eleventh century, but Motesinos says that 101 rulers reigned back to within five hundred years of the deluge. "In other words, it seems evident that the legendary history of the various principalities, if we may so style them, which went to make up the Inca empire is one thing, and that of the empire itself is quite another. The former is very ancient, going back, probably, as far into antiquity as that of any other people of the globe, while the latter is comparatively modern."[68]

Squier showed great interest in the aboriginal religious traditions of Peru and the persistence with which they were perpetuated, but he was decidedly more skeptical about the accuracy of the historical traditions. It was the manner and circumstances in which they had been recorded that bothered him. Incan informants may not have related their traditions fully or accurately to the Spanish chroniclers, who themselves may not have entirely understood or faithfully recorded what they were being told. The *quippus* (knotted ropes) used to perpetuate Incan historical traditions were, in Squier's opinion, equally problematic, "a very clumsy and inadequate contrivance for perpetuating dates and numbers." They were at best aids to memory whose precision in measuring time was questionable. "Even if they had a proper numerical significance (and this is by no means certain), they were in every other respect inferior to the rudest pictured symbols of our North American Indians, and still far inferior to the painted records of the Mexicans, or the probably syllabo-phonetic writings of the aborigines of Central America."[69]

Students of the *quippus* may take exception to Squier's characterization of their value as historical records, but his critical attitude toward the integrity, authenticity, and accuracy of the Inca traditions recorded by the Spanish cannot be easily dismissed.[70]

Thus it was that the study of the architectural remains of Peru assumed such importance. In the absence of written records and reliable traditions, they were mute but unimpeachable witnesses of a remote and largely hidden past. What approximate date could be assigned to the ancient monuments of Peru was an important but difficult question to answer. "They were, of course, the results of gradual development; they are the later mile-stones of progress. But where are the anterior mile-stones – where the antecedent monuments marking the stages of development?" The absence of earlier architectural forms or prototypes might suggest to some that these works were built, or at least inspired, by a more developed people who had immigrated to Peru from one of the older and distant centers of civilization. Someone from the Old World must have taught the Peruvians what they knew. Peruvian civilization under that view might be regarded as being intruded and imitative. But Squier found no evidence to support the theory of contact and diffusion among the ancient remains of Peru.

There were, on the contrary, many evidences in Peru of an earlier and comparatively ruder culture predating the rise of the Inca, one that gradually developed over time and ultimately produced an indigenous civilization. Together with the elaborate remains at Tiahuanaco, for example, Squier found remains that seemed to be almost the exact counterparts of Stonehenge in England and Carnac in Brittany – works that were assigned a very remote antiquity in the history of the world. The sun circles at Sillustani, similarly, were found "in the very shadow" of some of the most elaborate and wonderful architecture of aboriginal America. They could not from their outward appearance be distinguished from similar structures in England, Denmark, and Tartary – a combination of characteristics and circumstances that probably bespoke an equally remote antiquity. The fact that few traces of earlier Peruvian towns and structures had been found did not support the supposition that Incan civilization was comparatively recent and "implanted." The physical characteristics of the Incan homeland and the circumstances in which the empire developed explained the relative absence of the earlier structures or prototypes of the more elaborate edifices of later date.

The topography of the Incan realm explained the problem to Squier's complete satisfaction. The amount of land suitable for habitation and farming in Peru was small and the size of the population living under Incan rule "redundant." Space was at a premium, a condition giving every incentive to removing the older structures of their ancestors and replacing them with larger and more elaborate buildings needed by a growing population. The Inca were a progressive but utilitarian people. "The only modern nation that, in its polity, its aggressiveness, its adaptation, and, above all, its powers of assimilation, as well as its utter disregard of traditions and of monuments, [is] at all comparable to the Incas is our own. Does the most ancient of cemeteries stand in our way? Do we respect monuments if they interfere with our notions of utility?"[71] Squier thought it remarkable that so many evidences of a remote antiquity had actually survived in Peru, where the needs of the people necessitated the use of every inch of arable and habitable land and placed a premium on utilitarian values.

Squier made no effort to assign dates or eras to Peruvian civilization or for the origin of the Peruvians themselves. He was certain that the monuments were very old, and possibly as ancient as monuments of similar character found in the Old World, but how old he could not say. There was, moreover, positively no evidence that at any known period of human history the progenitors of the Peruvians had migrated from abroad or had derived their civilization from any other than native sources. "Even if it be assumed that the whole human family sprung from a single pair, and that their original seat was in the highlands of Armenia, whence they have overspread the globe, still it remains true that the period of their advent in Peru antedates all human record. The attempt to make them Hindoos because *inta* is the Quichua name for the sun, and *India* has the same meaning in Hindostanee, is simply absurd."[72]

That the civilization of the ancient Peruvians was indigenous was beyond reasonable doubt. Whether one followed its traces in the *bolsones* of the mountains or in the valleys descending to the coast, it everywhere presented peculiar and distinctive characteristics. That fact remained unchanged whether one assumed the unity or the diversity of humankind. Any similarities existing between the monumental architecture of Peru and that found in other parts of the globe did not imply a connection or a communication. As Squier noted regarding Incan architecture of Cuzco, "Architectural progress must be made through the same steps and over the same road in all countries; and primitive architecture, as primitive ideas, must have a likeness."[73] All peoples passed through the same stages of development at some point in their respective pasts. That developmentalist assumption was a constant in all phases of Squier's anthropological career.

Squier has the distinction of being the first archaeologist to advance the idea that the indigenous architecture of Peru had developed in stages over a long but indeterminate period of time. He could not positively date Peruvian archaeological remains, but he did recognize that some of the sites he surveyed and photographed predated those of the Inca. He noted that the different types of chulpas in the great terrestrial basin of Lake Titicaca probably reflected different eras of construction. He observed that the plain outside Acora was covered with many "rude monuments," structures consisting of small circles and squares of unfinished stones standing upright in the ground. The slabs sometimes overlapped and formed chambers with openings. "They are almost identical in appearance and character, with the cromlechs of Europe, and might be transferred to Brittany or Wales, and pass for structures contemporaneous with the thousand rude monuments of antiquity found in those regions." A closer examination of the structures at Acora convinced Squier that they had originated as burial places. They were, in fact, the ruder prototypes of what later became elaborate and symmetrical chulpas. [74] "For his time," Michael Moseley has observed, "this was an innovative insight, although chronological matters were not a significant theme of his work." Squier's narrative of his explorations in Peru, moreover, possessed "unusually high standards of archaeological mapping and description." [75]

Not all of the investigators who have revisited the sites described and figured in Peru would entirely concur in that opinion. Charles Fletcher Lummis retraced some of Squier's footsteps as a photographer on the Adolf F. Bandelier expedition to Peru and Bolivia in 1892 and 1893. Lummis visited Tiahuanaco, located in the Andean Cordillera near the shore of Lake Titicaca, near the end of the expedition on September 20, 1893, where he photographed and measured stone carvings and architectural remains. Lummis carried with him a copy of Squier's Peru, making notations and comments directly on the engravings and in the margins. He corrects the dimensions given by Squier for the monuments at Tiahuanaco and notes inaccuracies in his descriptions of the site. Lummis notes that the idealized engravings in Squier's Peru exaggerate the size of the monuments. Compare, for instance, Squier's illustration of the "Lesser Monolithic Door-Way" at Tiahuanaco with Lummis's photograph of the same. Squier similarly exaggerated the size of the larger monolithic gateway as represented in Peru. [76]

Gordon R. Willey, himself no stranger to Peruvian archaeology, has pointed out that Squier's drawings are of "fair accuracy" but that his building plans can only be regarded as approximations: "Either the originals were made at too small a scale, the reduction for publication was too great, or both." He also found Squier's background research on the history and ethnohistory of the Spanish Conquest and the Incan state to be "relatively perfunctory" but noted that those subjects were of secondary interest to Squier. It can certainly be said, however, that Squier dug more deeply into the ethnohistory of Peru than has been generally acknowledged. His use of the observations made by Padre Pablo Joseph de Arriaga in *Extirpación de la Idolatria del Peru* (1621) in his interpretation of the religious ideas and archaeological remains is a case in point. His primary concern was, indeed, to describe archaeological sites and artifacts, a task he performed in a relatively thorough manner, but he certainly recognized the value of the early Spanish chroniclers in helping him interpret his findings. He was consistent in this regard in his approach to archaeological and ethnological problems in all phases of his anthropological career. Although his work is more descriptive than analytic in relative terms, Squier certainly undertook an analysis of religious ideas and practices in Peru culled from ethnohistoric sources and analyzed what they probably suggested for the interpretation of archaeological remains – an informed and relatively sophisticated approach given the dearth of knowledge then existing.

Squier perceived the implications of observable differences in the archaeological record of Peru – a record that was still largely hidden from view. He recognized the existence of several separate and distinct civilizations, some of which were older than the civilization of the Inca. Archaeologists only gradually reconstructed the complex cultural history of Peru's prehistoric past over the course of the twentieth century, and their work is still far from complete. It would be asking too much to expect Squier to have sorted this out himself or to have accomplished much more than he actually did. His work was but a beginning for Peruvian archaeology, but not an insignificant one. "He did this well and, above all, he did it interestingly." The archaeological reporting in *Peru* was best praised, said Willey, as being "good for its time."[77]

Keith McElroy's comparative study of the engravings in *Peru* and the photographs and drawings on which they are based shows that in some instances the engravers "took considerable liberties while fabricating the final images," while in others they remained remarkably faithful. The problem of relativity in the accuracy of the engravings used in Squier's publications on Peru is explained by the circumstances in which they originated and the problems inherent in the engraving process of the period. Different engravers made the 295 illustrations appearing in *Peru* at different times and for different purposes between 1853 and the publication of that work in 1877.[78] Some engravers were more skilled than others, but equally important is the fact that the incipient art of making impressions on wood directly from photographic negatives or positives was an imprecise process. Remaining true to the scale, detail, and orientation of drawings, surveys maps, and photographs was a constant challenge for engravers.

The question of accuracy is particularly crucial in scientific illustration, and for those authorities who, like Squier, consistently touted the accuracy of their fieldwork. Squier's site plans, maps, and views are not in all instances inaccurate – quite the contrary, in fact – but in some cases details of potential importance to archaeologists investigating a particular site can be present in source materials but either missing or altered in the engravings on which they are based. Squier had the good fortune of working with some of the best illustrators and engravers of his day, but his work was in no way immune to the problems inherent in the engraving process that sometimes skewed the accuracy of plans and views of archaeological sites. Instances of discrepancies between engravings and original field sketches and photographs are numerous enough in the history of American anthropology to make going to the photographic and manuscript sources a laborious but imperative component of critical method. Squier was painfully aware of the problem as it applied to his own materials, referring in 1868 to the engraver as "that costly assassin of all life and truth in a picture."[79]

Squier's fieldwork in Peru allowed him to speak about the archaeology of that country with greater authority than any of his predecessors or contemporaries. He was an informed and curious traveler, but he was well aware that the unanswered questions connected with the origin and development of Peruvian civilizations awaited the attentions of those who would certainly follow in his footsteps. "The field thus, and in a thousand other ways, opened to us is a wide one; and I may confidently trust that my researches and explorations furnish many valuable aids for its further investigation. It is not too much to hope that patient labor in this department will enable some future student to reconstruct for us the vanished empire of the Incas. What we already know is enough to awaken the desire to know more."[80] Whatever the shortcomings of his work, Squier did, indeed, awaken the desire of many to know more. He eagerly gathered a vast array of facts relating to the country, its peoples, and its ancient past. He found himself at the conclusion of his investigations "surrounded by my trophies of travel, on the deck of a steamer in the harbor of Callao, homeward-bound, brown in color and firm in muscle."[81] Squier could take pardonable pride in what he had accomplished, and savor a moment of contentment on the long journey home.

11. The Science of Men and Nations

Ephraim George Squier and the American School of Ethnology

Squier's relationship with the American School of Ethnology began in 1846 and effectively continued until the end of his active days as a scholar. His association with Samuel George Morton, Josiah Clark Nott, and George Robins Gliddon has received considerable attention from historians, since each of them took a deep personal interest in Squier's investigations, promoted them, and used Squier's archaeological evidence to bolster his own racial theories. The arguments advanced in their writings profoundly influenced Squier in his thinking about race and human origins, and by the 1850s they led him to question some of his earlier assumptions. Morton, Nott, and Gliddon continued to correspond with Squier until their respective deaths in 1851, 1857, and 1873, while Squier, the youngest member of the American School, lived on until 1888. Squier's relationship with the American School and his efforts to accommodate himself to the implications of its racial theory provide a useful framework in which to assess the distinct junctures of his remarkable career.

The question of race and equality in antebellum America was a potent one. The ideal of human equality and the realities of race relations embodied the two faces of the American Janus: the uplifting ideals and promise of American democracy and its tragic failings and paradoxical realities. The political debate over democracy and slavery in the United States had its corollary among ethnologists. Racial theorists debated over the presumably inherent characteristics and capabilities of the different races and over what those traits seemed to imply about human origins and broader issues concerning race relations. The antagonistic principles sustaining that debate were rooted in conflicting views of human nature. One view allowed for human perfectibility and progress (an inheritance of the Enlightenment), while the other argued for the existence of inherently inferior and presumably irredeemable races, primarily and conveniently restricting perfectibility to Caucasians. Those opposing views of human nature, William Stanton has noted, represented "a war of ideas" – a true "battle between science and the American Dream."[1] The earlier and more optimistic views of human perfectibility existed concurrently with the newer and darker assumptions of racial determinism. Those conflicting views of human nature were contested and in some instances reformulated within the anthropological thought of specific writers. [2]

In the early and mid-nineteenth century, the idea of race and assumptions about racial inferiority reflected prejudices deeply seated within Western thought. The physical anthropology of the period in particular reinforced those assumptions and attitudes by advancing confident generalizations based on presumably immutable differences between the races. [3] Racial prejudice informed all aspects of social relations, political theory, and scientific thought. It informed American Indian policy, the debate over the abolition of slavery, and American foreign policy. Scientific racism shaped the arguments of the leading proponents of Manifest Destiny, providing them with "a rationale for the failure of American Indian policy and a justification for the seemingly ruthless appropriation of both Indian and Mexican lands." [4] It also gave Squier a justification for American intervention in Central America. Advocates of the importance of ethnology in the mid-nineteenth century touted its claims to attention as an applied science, the presumed lessons of which should guide the actions of philanthropists, naturalists, and statesmen. Did the observable physical differences among the various races translate into racially determined moral and intellectual traits? What lessons did ethnological science offer concerning the relative positions of the races within "the social scale"? [5]

The moral and political implications of those interests and concerns were many. Ethnologists openly debated questions of racial equality, perfectibility, and destiny and self-assuredly offered their findings as blueprints for adjusting and regulating social relations. Polemicists intruded ethnology into defenses of slavery and arguments against philanthropic efforts to reform American Indian policy. The self-consciously "new" science of ethnology in the 1840s and 1850s piously laid claim to empirical truths, but too often it stood upon a weak foundation of anecdotal evidence and racial stereotypes. Scientific attitudes toward race in the period both reflected and shaped the assumptions and attitudes of American society as a whole. Anthropological debates over the alleged inferiority and superiority of races were part of a larger social discourse about the very nature of American democracy itself, forcibly reminding us of the problems inherent in the social construction of scientific "truths." The racial determinism of the American School of Ethnology is particularly instructive in this regard. The correlation of differences in human anatomy and physical appearance with alleged differences in intellectual and moral capacity was a hallmark of the racial theory of the

American School and was the basis of scientific arguments used to maintain the privileged social and political positions of Caucasians at the expense of darker-skinned peoples.

The vexed question of human origins was the great ethnological problem of the early and mid-nineteenth century. Did the different races have a common origin (monogenism) or separate origins (polygenism)? Were the different races actually distinctive species of the genus *Homo sapiens*? Were racial characteristics immutable, or did they change over time? The orthodox Christian view assumed the unity of man and argued that all humans had descended from Adam and Eve in less than six thousand years. Polygenists assumed the diversity of man and argued that each of mankind's different types or races had a separate origin.[6] Polygenists enjoined the debate with new fervor in the 1840s and 1850s as the study of geology, paleontology, and archaeology presented new evidence that shattered received opinion about the antiquity of man. Humankind was far older than biblical chronology allowed, and as new evidence accumulated it was growing older every day. The various races of man were, indeed, older than the oldest human records and had remained physically unchanged for at least four thousand years – and probably much longer. The great debate between the monogenists and polygenists in the 1840s and 1850s informed the works of all the members of the American School, including those of its most cautious and guarded member – Ephraim George Squier.

The results of archaeological and ethnological investigations in the United States by the mid-nineteenth century had attracted considerable attention both at home and abroad. Luke Burke, editor of the London *Ethnological Journal*, recognized Morton in September 1848 as "the father of American Ethnology" and collectively referred to the works of Morton, Nott, Gliddon, and Squier as comprising "the School of American Ethnologists."[7] Morton's disciples Nott and Gliddon echoed those words in their collaborative and combative *Types of Mankind*, published in 1854, where they self-consciously acknowledged Morton as the founder of "the American School of Ethnology."[8] *Types of Mankind* was a festschrift to Morton, who died in 1851. The mantle of leadership then fell upon the shoulders of his acolytes Nott and Gliddon, who were fearless in advancing Morton's racial theories together with their own.

Nott and Gliddon first met during Gliddon's lectures on Egyptian archaeology at Mobile in 1848. "He is a kind hearted fellow," Nott wrote Squier, "and one of the most obliging men I ever met – He deserves far more credit than he receives, for though not as profound as some, he has gathered a vast body of valuable material." Through his lectures and the publication of

Ancient Egypt, Gliddon had disseminated "more valuable knowledge than any man living."[9] He recognized his own strengths and limitations, and once he candidly told Squier: "I am a *lecturer* and not an Author. If I publish my stores I cut my own throat." Gliddon had a wife and a son to support, and lecturing was far more lucrative than writing books. He could make more money in a single course of lectures than he could ever make by publishing books, while lecturing also freed him from the cupidity of cheating publishers.[10]

No one was more attuned to the broader implications of the racial theory of Morton, Nott, and Gliddon than Squier, who embraced American archaeology and ethnology with the same infectious enthusiasm and sense of national mission that characterized all of his pursuits. He and the other members of the American School articulated a generally recognized need for a more comprehensive and integrated approach to the study of man. Squier first did so in an article on "American Ethnology" appearing in the *American Review* for April 1849, where he noted that "the study of man, physiologically and psychically, is confessedly the noblest which can claim human attention."[11] Ethnology was, above all else, a practical pursuit that should inform all aspects of social, civil, and religious organization. Inquiry into how basic human wants, capabilities, impulses, and ambitions were affected by circumstances held great implications for the policies of statesmen, reformers, and all who were leaders of men. "The study of man, in this comprehensive sense, constitutes the science of Ethnology. The elements of this science are the results, the ultimates of all other sciences; it begins where the rest stop." Philologists, anatomists, archaeologists, geographers, and historians were all allies of the ethnologist in examining the affinities of humanity and determining the ancestral seats, migrations, and "the interblendings of the primary divisions and families of men." The science of ethnology, said Squier, "presupposes a general high attainment in all other departments of knowledge. It is essentially the science of the age; the offspring of that prevailing mental and physical energy which neglects no subject of inquiry."[12]

It was a matter of pride with Squier, ever the nationalist, to acknowledge the original contributions made by American investigators to the infant science of ethnology. "Nor is the circumstance surprising; for nowhere else on the globe is afforded so wide and so favorable a field for researches of this nature. Nowhere else can we find brought in so close proximity, the representatives of races and families of men, of origins and physical and mental constitutions so diverse." American Indians, Africans, and Caucasians lived cheek by jowl in the United States, rendering it one vast ethnological laboratory where theories of race and social relations were to be tested. "For these reasons, we claim that Ethnology is not only the science of the age, but also that it is, and must continue to be, to a prevailing extent, an *American science*."[13] Questions concerning the origin and affinities of American Indians in particular were "a constant stimulus" to ethnological investigation.

> Do we seek to know the course and progress of development among a people separated from the rest of the world, insulated physically and mentally, and left to the operation of its own peculiar elements? The inquirer must turn to America, where alone he can hope to find the primitive conceptions, beliefs and practices of an entire[ly] original people, in no considerable degree modified or impaired by the adventitious circumstances of intermixture and association. Do we desire to discover the results which must follow from the blending of men of different races and families? Do we inquire in what consists the superiority of certain families over others; to what extent they may assimilate with, to what repel each other, and how their relations may be adjusted so as to produce the greatest attainable advantage to both? The practical solution of these problems can only be found in America, where alone exist the requisite conjunctions. [14]

It is clear from this passage that Squier, like most of his contemporaries, fully believed in the existence of superior and inferior races. His assumptions were distinctly shaped by the racial tenets of the American School, but there was a larger current of racial prejudice against non-Caucasians in American society that both encouraged the racial theorizing of the American School and received encouragement from its scientific arguments.

Squier was the silent partner of the American School in many ways. He was far too cautious to openly take a stand on the racial issues confronting nineteenth-century America, but there can be no doubt that the racial theories of Morton, Gliddon, and Nott profoundly influenced his anthropological thought. Historians have noted Squier's relationship with the American School, but far more is known about how the other members of the American School used Squier's findings to support their own racial arguments than about how their works influenced Squier. Squier's views on race changed significantly between 1848 and 1858. The view of human nature and the faith in human perfectibility he expressed at the beginning of his anthropological career were more in keeping with the opinions of Albert Gallatin, an apostle of Enlightenment thought and another of his major intellectual mentors.[15] By the 1850s, however, Squier had come to embrace the more pessimistic view of human nature based on the assumptions of racial determinism. Morton and Nott's views on racial hybridity, for example, informed Squier's views of the presumably deleterious effects arising from the free amalgamation of races in Central America. Whereas Squier made an impassioned defense of the intellectual and moral capabilities of American Indians in 1849, he had incorporated the dogmas of Morton, Nott, and other racial theorists into the views expressed on race and Manifest Destiny in *Nicaragua* (1852), *Notes on Central America* (1855), and *The States of Central America* (1858). Some of his earlier statements are contradicted by his later ones, discrepancies that mark the distance traveled in his thinking about race between those distinct junctures of his career.

Morton's craniological investigations were by far the most important of those influences. Squier regarded the views on the origin, connections, and "essential peculiarity of the American race" embodied in Morton's *Crania Americana* (1839) and related minor writings to be established scientific truths, and he had no patience for those who continued to speculate on the subject of ethnology as if nothing had been determined. Morton concluded that the cranial conformation of the American Indian was "radically distinct" from that exhibited by any other division of the human family. The American race differed essentially from all others, including the Mongolian. Feeble analogies of language, political organization, religious ideas and customs, and the arts represented nothing more than casual or colonial communication with Asiatic nations. Even these analogies could probably be accounted for, as Humboldt had suggested, by coincidences arising from similar wants and needs in nations inhabiting similar latitudes. The American nations, with the notable exception of the polar tribes, were of one race and one species, but they existed in two great divisions or families that resembled each other in physical characteristics but differed in their intellectual and moral capacities. The cranial remains of the ancient Mound Builders belonged to the same race, but probably to the Toltecan family or division.[16]

The manifest gradations in complexion and physical type existing among the aboriginal families of the American continent were not differences of kind but of circumstances. As Squier noted on this point, when "we separate what is radical from what is incidental, or the result of circumstances, it will be found that these diversities are superficial, and that elementarily the various natives of the continent exhibit identities of the most striking kind. . . . And if we can point to no other race on the globe which has exhibited so many modifications, it is because there is no other which in its infancy, and before it was able to overcome or control natural influences, was so widely disseminated and subjected to so many vicissitudes."[17] Morton recognized that many differences existed among the American aborigines in the far reaches of the northern, central, and southern regions of the American continent, but he attributed all of them directly to the peculiar affects of their respective environments. History provided many examples of how changes in circumstances could result in notable differences "not only among nations of the same race, but of the same family." Such analogies likewise explained the differences existing among the different aboriginal families of the American continent. Squier accepted Morton's evidence and arguments that American Indians were essentially homogeneous and peculiar in their physical features, which identified them as "a separate people." [18] The physical uniformity evident in both ancient and modern aboriginal crania, moreover, was conclusive evidence that the Mound Builders and the Indians belonged to the same indigenous and distinct race.

Morton's findings on the physical characteristics of American Indians challenged conventional explanations as to how they had come to people the New World. Morton's physical anthropology presented scholars with a means of liberating American archaeology and ethnology from the leaden thrall of the biblical account of creation, "of deriving all varieties of the human species from a single pair on the banks of the Euphrates." There was no need to assume that American Indians were descended from one or more of the nations mentioned in the Old Testament. They may well have originated in the New World as true autochthons, or in Asia from whence they subsequently migrated at an early date. In either event, they were still a radically distinct race whose origins could not be accounted for by connecting them with history or biblical ethnology. Assigning the Indians a Jewish origin was the most common theory, as writers elaborated on similarities between the customs and habits of the Indians and those found in scriptural accounts of the ancient Hebrews. Edward Kingsborough, author of *Antiquities of Mexico*, was one such authority. Kingsborough derived the aboriginal population of America from the ten lost tribes of Israel, which were carried away by the King Salmanazer of Assyria. John Delafield entertained a variation of that theory in his *An Inquiry into the Origin of the Antiquities of America*. Delafield derived the semi-civilized nations of America from the Cuthites, which Scripture tells us built the monuments of Egypt and Indostan. [19] Squier dismissed such hypotheses as "absurd" and "impossible." The architects of such theories failed to acknowledge that "a coincidence in circumstances" would result in resemblances between distinct peoples at similar stages of development. Their arguments were based on what was "conditional and changing, instead of what is fixed and radical." [20]

Squier saw further evidence of the radical distinctness of the America race in the linguistic studies of Albert Gallatin, who had amassed extensive and valuable materials relating to the languages of North American Indians. Even though Gallatin assumed a common origin for all of mankind, his philological inquiries attested that the aboriginal languages of North America were sui generis and similarly peculiar. American Indian languages greatly differed in vocabularies and dialects, but their construction and grammatical forms were essentially the same. Those uniformities taken together with the similarity of physical type indicated "a general, though not perhaps universal, common origin." [21] Comparison of the structure and character of the aboriginal languages of the American continent with those in other parts of the globe provided the strongest evidence of their "essential peculiarity." Gallatin concluded that the dialectical modifications and different vocabularies existing among the various divisions of the American race could only have developed across a long span of time. If it was necessary to derive the American race from the Old World, Squier noted, the migration must have occurred in remote antiquity. [22]

Squier regarded Gallatin's conclusions to be just as fatal to popular notions about the origin of American Indians as was Morton's physical anthropology. As Squier observed, "The doctrine of a diversity of origin in the human race, although gathering supporters daily, has yet so few open advocates, and is generally esteemed so radical a heresy, that investigations in this, as in many other departments of science, hesitate in pushing their researches to their ultimate results. The discussion of this question cannot, however, be long postponed, and it is not difficult to see in what manner it will be determined." [23] That was as close as the cautious Squier ever came to publicly advocating the doctrine of polygenism. Although clearly leaning toward the doctrine of separate origins, the ultimate heresy for a clergyman's son, he stopped just short of an outright endorsement.

Privately, Squier was more candid in expressing his views on the vexed question of human origins. As he confided to Morton, "The public mind is very nearly prepared to receive the unqualified Truth; and if the doses are skillfully administered it will one day come to be very well purged of chronic prejudice and malignant ignorance." He even proposed the establishment of an American archaeological and ethnological journal on the model of Burke's *Ethnological Journal* in London, which would be the vehicle for discussing the "established truths" of ethnological inquiry. Squier balked at his colleagues' suggestion that the proposed journal should be merged or affiliated with the *Transactions of the American Ethnological Society*, for he believed that the society's orthodox members were not prepared to hear the unvarnished truth. What he sought was an independent journal that could be a medium of "sound opinion and truth," one that would be prepared to contradict popular prejudice and to "shock long visaged divines" such as those found among the more conservative members of the American Ethnological Society. Squier regarded the society as by far the most liberal of any similar organization in the United States, but it was still comprised of doctors of divinity and other members "who really believed in a devil, that the world was made in six days of twenty four [hours] each, and that Muses unto the Pentateuch [the first five books of the Old Testament]."[24]

Squier also proposed to Nott the establishment of an "Archaeological Review," which the latter thought to be "a capital idea." He would support it in any way, including the submission of articles. A "New Archaeological and Infidelical Journal," said the cheeky Nott, would be a valuable outlet for scientific truths and good sport besides. Squier also broached the subject of the proposed journal with J. G. M. Ramsey of Tennessee, and he continued to entertain the "nebulous notion" of an American archaeological and ethnological journal as the debate on human origins continued over the next decade. His efforts were continually sidetracked, however, by the demands of other affairs. He even went so far as to draft a prospectus for the proposed journal in 1859, one he circulated among friends but did not make public. Such a journal would be a valuable outlet for the research of those who found themselves in the predicament of expounding "good-for-nothing" subjects such as archaeology and ethnology.[25]

Although Squier greatly admired Morton's research, he was not so slavish a disciple as to be uncritical of all his opinions. He deferred to Morton entirely in his conclusions on the physical characteristics of American Indians, but he held serious reservations – at least initially – about Morton's opinions on their presumed intellectual faculties and moral traits. Morton characterized American Indians as an intellectually and morally inferior race that was incapable of improvement. Squier begged to differ. The extent to which American Indians had been bedeviled and defiled throughout the history of Indian-white relations made assertions of the moral superiority of Caucasians ring rather hollow in the light of their own deeds toward Indians. Squier was not yet willing to declare American Indians a doomed race, and he was willing to defend them against their detractors. His faith in "the power of mental development" would not allow him to accept the notion that American Indians were incapable of social progress. To do so would be to "deny that in his higher nature man is capable of infinite progression."

In fact, Squier saw evidence to the contrary among various groups of American Indians. He admired the artistic and intellectual attainments of Central American groups and regarded the aboriginal art of the region to be equal in the scale of artistic development to that of Hindustan and Egypt. He seconded the opinion of James Cowles Prichard, author of *Researches into the Physical History of Man*, on the truly remarkable intellectual achievement of the ancient Mexicans. A people who had developed a calendar more accurate than that of the Greeks and had precisely calculated the length of the solar year could not be said to be lacking in intelligence. Squier saw that same capacity for progress in the League of the Iroquois and in the social and political institutions of the ancient Peruvians. The sedentary and agricultural Zuni and Moqui Indians of New Mexico, he argued, more nearly approached the "the poetical ideal of Arcadian simplicity and happiness" than any other group known to history.[26] Could they too be said to be lacking in intelligence?

Squier also denied the charge that American Indians had failed to "profit" from their contact with other races. The example provided by the southeastern or so-called civilized tribes disproved this claim, for their way of life could not be said to be in any respect inferior to that of their white neighbors on the frontier. He championed the character and achievement of Indian peoples as strongly as he condemned the moral transgressions of their white oppressors.

> When the Indians shall be treated as human beings, and not as wild animals; when they shall be relieved from the contaminations of unprincipled hunters and traders, and the moral charlatanism of ignorant and narrow-minded missionaries; when we shall pursue towards them a just, enlightened, and truly Christian policy; then, if they shall exhibit no advancement, and ultimately reach a respectable rank in the scale of civilization, it will be quite time enough to pronounce upon them the severe sentence of a deficient intellect and an unhallowed heart – dead to sympathy, and incapable of higher developments. Till then, with the black catalogue of European wrongs and oppressions before him, and the grasping hand of powerful avarice at his throat, blame not the American Indian if he sternly and gloomily prefers utter extinction to an association with races which have exhibited to him no benign aspect, and whose touch has been death.[27]

The rhetoric of moral indignation expressed in this passage is reminiscent of Squier's earlier days as a reform-minded journalist and lecturer at Albany. His faith in the power of mental development and in mankind's unlimited capacity for social advancement, so evident in his Albany lectures, did not exclude American Indians. Those beliefs had no place in Morton's clinical assessment of the Indian's mind and character and were far more consonant with Gallatin's ethnology than with Morton's.

Squier found it by no means clear that a reversal of circumstances under which allegedly "fierce" and "mild" races were placed would not transform the "destructive savage into the mild agriculturalist, and the peaceable tiller of the soil into the fierce and predatory nomad." That conviction and line of reasoning led him to question some of Morton's characterizations of the intellectual and moral traits of American Indians. Deceitfulness, aggressiveness, indolence, and improvidence were allegedly the leading character traits of American Indians, said Morton, while intellectually they were widely perceived as being incapable of abstract reasoning. More than two centuries of living in proximity of Europeans had supposedly affected few modifications among American Indians, whose social condition remained largely unchanged. The exceptions were the nations that fell within Morton's semi-civilized "Toltecan family," whose attainments in the arts and sciences contrasted sharply with the intellectual poverty he assigned the tribes within his "Barbarous family" of the American race. Morton believed that the Toltecan and Barbarous families of American Indians possessed entirely different intellectual capabilities. The former had shown itself capable of developing a civilization, while the latter exhibited "an abasement" rooted in a degraded state of barbarism that defied all efforts at intellectual advancement.

Nott and Squier first learned of each other's ethnological interests through their mutual friend Gliddon, and they began a long correspondence in August 1848. "I have long had my eye upon you," said Nott, "and have been waiting anxiously the results of your labor." He was keenly interested in how far back Squier pushed the probable era of the mounds, "for chronology to me is every thing." Nott had established chronologies for the Bible, Egypt, China, and India, and he looked to Squier to give the coup de grâce to the venerable "He brayist [sic], Moses." Nott claimed to have no quarrel with religion so long as it was kept in its proper sphere and clear of the path of science, but he categorically denied the authority of the Pentateuch in scientific matters concerning the origin of mankind. [28] The infidel Nott wrote Squier that he would tell his lecture audiences about "that sinner Squier who has the hardihood to assert that the Indians were making potato hills in [the Mississippi] Valley before Eve was convicted and punished for stealing apples." [29] *Ancient Monuments of the Mississippi Valley* was certain to secure for Squier a prominent place in posterity. "You have opened a glorious field for fame and will reap your reward in honor if not money – Your name will be coupled with Morton[']s for the future." [30]

In December 1848, at the University of Louisiana at New Orleans and before the state legislature, Nott gave two lectures on the biblical and physical history of man that had "knocked their eyes so wide open that I am told some of the ungodly have never slept since." He wanted to publish an expanded version of the lectures at either Philadelphia or New York, since the publishers he had already approached would not touch it "upon conscientious grounds." They objected to Nott's arguments for the diversity of the races and the "modern" origin of the Old Testament. Nott claimed that he did not advance any doctrine that he could not support directly from the Bible and that he had ignored all "infidel authorities." His lectures on "Niggerology" were eagerly sought after in the South, and given the state of political concerns over the issue of slavery he was certain that they would sell well in the North too if he could only find a willing publisher. He sought Squier's help in finding him one in New York. Nott had never written to please the crowd, he told him, but only for the advancement of truth. He knew he would be abused for his views, but science would benefit from the discussion. The New York publishing house of Bartlett and Welford published Nott's lectures in 1849, no doubt at the suggestion and with the encouragement of Squier.

Nott's lectures gave a public nod to the beneficial influences of Christianity on the world and approvingly noted that the great advances made in philology, archaeology, and biblical criticism had led to enlarged and more rational religious views. But no free-thinking person could deny that the diversity of races was demonstrated by the civil and the physical history of man no less than by the ethnography, geography, cosmology, and chronology of the Bible itself. Whether one studied ancient Egypt, China, or the Mound Builders of America, the ancient diversity of the races stood boldly forth on the pages of the human past. Nott argued that the Old Testament originated one thousand years *after* Moses and was, comparatively speaking, of modern origin. His lectures also gave a résumé of the history of alphabetic writing, the Hebrew language, and the canonical texts of the Old Testament. Nott drew upon evidence for the diversity of the human races from the New Testament as well. The four evangelists knew no geography beyond the Roman Empire, no national history beyond that of their contemporaries, and nothing of the existence of America, Australia, and Oceania. His purpose in establishing these facts was not to wage war against the Christian faith but rather to firmly oppose all dogmas that conflicted with the findings of science. Nott repeatedly noted that he did not draw upon "infidel" writers in support of his arguments but only cited learned and authoritative theologians. He was contemptuous, however, of those "pious souls" who abused him for his views, even though they themselves did "not know in what language the Bible was written."[31]

Nott defended his views on the ancient and scriptural chronology of man in a contribution to the *Southern Quarterly Review* for November 1850.[32] There he took on his critics in the *Southern Presbyterian Review* (conducted by an association of ministers in Columbia, South Carolina) for a hostile review of his *Two Lectures on the Connection between the Biblical and Physical History of Man*. The review of that work by the Reverend Dr. Howe denounced Nott as an "assailant of religion" whose opinions were "dangerous to religion, morality, and law."[33] Nott answered that his anthropological interests were a natural extension of his medical training and practice and nothing more. He was a man of science, not an assassin of religious principles. He pursued his investigations as a physician and scientist because of their intrinsic importance and certainly not through a love for the theological disputes that anthropology seemed to inevitably occasion. The discoveries made by Egyptian archaeologists in recent years challenged commonplace assumptions about the unity of races and needed to be heard. The resistance of certain clerical authorities to those findings compelled him to write on the subject of human chronology regardless of opposition. He had little interest in biblical criticism per se and had turned his attention to the subject only as a means of advancing ethnological science against the biblical arguments consistently used against it. He doubted not that the Bible had advanced civilization, happiness, and was a force for good. Matters of religious *doctrine*, however, were an entirely different matter, for they tended to confuse more than clarify the positive aspects of the Christian faith.[34]

In *Two Lectures*, Nott's purpose was not to subvert the Christian faith but to "cut the natural history of man loose from the Bible," and in order for him to do so it was first necessary to debunk the scriptural authority of the Old Testament regarding human origins and antiquity. He enlisted the opinions of theologians who held that the books of the Old Testament were of uncertain authenticity, interpolated long after the fact, and lacking in historical accuracy. The original intent of the Old Testament authors was almost exclusively to write the history of the Hebrews from the generations of Shem (son of Noah) down to Abraham. The Old Testament mentions other peoples that were known to Hebrews only incidentally, and it was never meant to be a literal explanation for the origins of all mankind. Nott continued to set his face against those who denied the credibility of such evidence, or, for that matter, believed that the acceptance of the doctrine of separate origins made one an infidel: "We find nothing in the Pentateuch which would induce us to believe that its author knew or cared anything about the Unity or Diversity of races, and should be most happy here to drop all farther allusion to the Bible, but that the nature of the subject forbids it. . . . We have before said that we can see no reason (if the ethnology of Genesis is untenable) why the Almighty may not have created, at different points, a hundred pairs of human beings, as well as one."[35] The irreconcilability of the physical history of man with the ethnography, geography, genealogies, and chronology of the book of Genesis had to be demonstrated before the claims of scientific inquiry could be impartially judged. The Old Testament was too bound by time, place, and cosmology to ever explain the history of the entire world, something which its creators had never intended to do.

Nott found further evidence of remote antiquity and an indigenous origin for American aborigines in Squier and Davis's *Ancient Monuments*, a work he credited with linking American Indians to world history, "which has long been a desideratum."[36] Based on Morton's physical anthropology and Squier and Davis's archaeology, Nott identified the Mound Builders as pre-Mexican Toltecs. According to Clavigero, the Toltecs had migrated to Anahuac (Mexico) from the north in AD 648 and abandoned the country in 1051. Although those dates were most certainly approximations and open to challenge, they were probably not so inaccurate as to deny that the Toltecs were an ancient people. The assumption that the Mound Builders were pre-Mexican Toltecs of the same race as the ancient Mexicans, Central Americas, and Peruvians established an even remoter chronology for the Mound Builders: "Is there not every reason to infer that these migrations *begin* where the history of the Mound Builders *ends?*"[37] The known migrations of the Toltecs had occurred from the seventh to the twelfth centuries AD, so who could doubt that they made earlier migrations in their distant homeland in the north? The Toltec–Mound Builder association was an erroneous one, but it was logical given its underlying assumptions. Even if Nott could have been persuaded that the Mound Builders were not Toltecs, however, it would not have changed his opinion on their antiquity and indigenous origin. Whatever the ethnic affinities of the Mound Builders, they were still an ancient people whose existence could not be accounted for by biblical ethnology or the written records of antiquity.

Gliddon began promoting interest in Squier's investigations in England and on the Continent through correspondence as early as June 1847.[38] He continued to do during his visit to England in September and October 1848, bringing with him communications from the leading practitioners of ethnology in the United States and several copies of their recent works. As Nott observed to Squier, "Gliddon is a good hearted fellow and does not forget kindnesses as most people do. He *will* make us great men in Europe, whether we want it or not."[39] Nott knew his man well. Gliddon was generous to a fault with friends and ever ready to do them service. He had brought with him a letter from Squier to Luke Burke of the *Ethnological Journal* and proof sheets of Squier and Davis's *Ancient Monuments*. Delighted at the prospect of becoming a correspondent of the "eminent and ardent cultivators of our science in America," Burke used his influence to promote interest in the work of American ethnologists among his readers. Burke and Gliddon had several long and pleasant conversations at the office of the *Ethnological Journal* on the work of American ethnologists, especially on Squier's investigations of the mounds. "I am greatly deceived," Burke wrote Squier, "if the bones which you disturb were not alive before Egypt was heard of. If such be the fact, what must be the importance of your *labours!*" He was most curious to learn Squier's views on the subject, and he solicited contributions to the *Ethnological Journal* from Squier and his American colleagues.[40] As Gliddon informed Squier from Bayswater, England, in October 1848: "Enfin, dear Squier, you are now fairly launched – few have appeared in the world of science with your auspices."[41]

The fourth issue of the *Ethnological Journal* contained a review essay by Burke entitled "The Progress of Ethnology in the United States."[42] Gliddon asked Squier to have it reprinted in the *Literary World*, to call attention to it in the press, and to send copies to Morton, Pickering, and Nott.[43] Burke intended to use the *Ethnological Journal* to make archaeology as free of religious dogma as geology, astronomy, and other sciences. He was delighted to learn that ethnologists in the United States were conducting original investigations and were willing to present their findings "irrespective of conventional prejudice." America was one of the most interesting ethnological regions on the globe, and its archaeology held particular importance for polygenists such as Burke. The New World was proving to be not so new after all. Indisputable archaeological evidence revealed that humans had been living there since time immemorial. Squier and Davis's findings suggested to Burke that the era of the Mound Builders was older than that of the architects of the stone monuments of Central America. The antiquity of the mounds was still a matter of surmise, but they were manifestly ancient. The question was, how old were they? Was America one of the earliest centers of human civilization? What secrets were yet to be revealed about the hidden past of aboriginal America and its interesting remains of antiquity?[44]

Burke, perhaps presuming too much, observed that it was a "gratifying fact" that all the leading practitioners of the science of ethnology were "advocates of the doctrine of a plurality of Human Races." Whether acceptance of that tenet in all instances also implied a belief in a plurality of *origins* he was not prepared to say, but he suspected that the unpopularity of that opinion led many of those who held it to either express it cautiously or remain prudently silent. He praised Nott for being one of the few men of science who was bold enough to advocate the doctrine openly. Nott heartily approved of the aims of the *Ethnological Journal* and the boldness of its editor. "If such things as this can be printed and praised in the Country where Lawrence was put in prison for an offense twenty five years ago," he wrote Squier, "the thing is out – Moses must walk quietly back and take his seat among the lesser heathen Gods." Nott likened his first reading of the *Ethnological Journal* to a religious experience. The "Gospel according to Luke Burke" gave form to vague ideas that had been coursing through his thoughts for some time. Burke had conceived and implemented much of the same plan of attack as he against the arguments of the orthodox concerning the origin of man, "but mine is even bolder than his as I attack the authenticity of the Pentateuch directly and quote 'all the parsons this side of Hell' to sustain me." If the authority of the Old Testament were destroyed, then the entire field of study would be theirs. [45] Squier had no taste for Nott's public attacks on the Old Testament (his clergyman father may well have disowned him if he had), but he was decidedly in sympathy with Nott's views on the absolute necessity of removing matters of religion from scientific inquiry.

The fullest expression of the racial theory of the American School appeared in 1854 with the publication of Nott and Gliddon's *Types of Mankind*. Nott and Gliddon were the pugilists of the American School, and *Types of Mankind* was most definitely a fighting book. The question of how human antiquity and diversity could be explained if *all* races had a common origin, as related in the book of Genesis, grew more urgent as the new science of ethnology marched forward. Were the various physical characteristics of the races evidence of permanently fixed traits as well as of separate origins? Nott and Gliddon answered in the affirmative to both questions. As Nott asserted in the introduction to *Types of Mankind*: "Whether an original diversity of races be admitted or not, the *permanence* of existing physical types will not be questioned by any Archaeologist or Naturalist of the present day. Nor, by such competent arbitrators, can the consequent permanence of moral and intellectual peculiarities of types be denied. The intellectual man is inseparable from the physical man; and the nature of the one cannot be altered without a corresponding change in the other." [46]

Nott's statement is, of course, a non sequitur. One can admit permanence in physical type without accepting a consequent permanence in moral and intellectual characteristics. The coupling of permanent physical characteristics with correspondingly fixed moral and intellectual traits does not follow, but it was nonetheless a central tenet of scientific racism. The different types of mankind do have biologically inherited physical characteristics that are unquestionably of ancient origin. But the assignment of inherent moral and intellectual traits is a mere cultural construction, and not the scientific delineation of immutable organic laws determining human destiny. Such calculations of race tell us far more about the assumptions and attitudes of the ethnologists of the era than about the actual subjects they were studying so intently.

The question of the equality and perfectibility of races became a practical consideration in social relations and governmental policies. Defenders of slavery as a domestic institution of the South could marshal seemingly unassailable arguments to counter the agitations of abolitionists. If the genetic constitution of blacks rendered them inherently incapable of exercising the political and social rights and liberties enjoyed by Caucasians, then it could be argued that slavery was a benign institution. "The immense evils of false philanthropy are becoming too glaring to be longer overlooked. While, on the one hand, every true philanthropist must admit that no race has a right to enslave or oppress the weaker, it must be conceded, on the other, that all changes in existing institutions should be guided, not by fanaticism and groundless hypothesis, but by experience, sound judgment, and real charity."[47] If the moral and intellectual character of races was permanently fixed and some races were inherently inferior or superior to others, then the prescriptions of social reformers that ignored such characteristics were doomed to failure.

The antiquity of man could not be accounted for by the Mosaic account of creation or by the Hebrew chronology and genealogies. Egyptian civilization flourished four thousand years before Christ, but it would have required a far longer period of time to reach that stage of development. Lepsius estimated the era of Menes to be 3893 BC, while his computation of the Hebrew chronology approximated the time of Abraham to be 1500 BC. American Indians, moreover, were building earthen mounds at an indeterminate but remote period of antiquity, and one that might well have predated Abraham's arrival in Palestine. Geological, anatomical, archaeological, historical, and linguistic evidence led inexorably to but one conclusion among polygenists, clerical objections to the contrary notwithstanding: humankind had not *one* but *several* distinct origins, during which the physical, psychological, and moral characteristics of the radically distinct races were permanently established. Such a gloomy pronouncement relegated a good portion of humanity to the category of irredeemable races. Lest philanthropists object to such cold sentiments, Nott and Gliddon noted that racial conflict was written into the warp and woof of the human past. "Looking back over the world's history, it will be seen that human progress has arisen mainly from the war of races. All the great impulses which have been given to it from time to time have been the results of conquests and colonizations. Certain races would be stationary and barbarous for ever, were it not for the introduction of new blood and novel influences; and some of the lowest types are hopelessly beyond the reach even of these salutary stimulants to melioration."[48]

The most authoritative advocate of the orthodox view of the unity of the human races was Dr. James Cowles Prichard, whose monumental *Researches into the Physical History of Man* appeared in three editions in 1813, 1826, and 1847. Prichard's work had a profound impact on anthropological thought.[49] Each edition repositioned his defense of the unity of humankind relative to new arguments raised against it. Nott and Gliddon's *Types of Mankind* was, in large measure, an answer to Prichard's "special pleading" for the unity of the races and his defense of the book of Genesis. Nott and Gliddon mustered evidence demonstrating that the existing races were physically distinct long before Abraham had arrived in Egypt and that their peculiar characteristics had remained fixed and unchanged. Did this not identify them as distinct species? "The grand battle between science and dogmatism, on the primitive origin of races, has now commenced. It requires no prophetic eye to foretell that science must gain, and finally, triumph." All attempts to reconcile science and theology on the question of human origins were futile. Nott and Gliddon made no apologies for the inconvenience their ethnological treatise created for orthodox views on the unity of races, no matter how objectionable or odious they might be to the friends of Moses. "The broad banner of science is herein nailed to the mast."[50]

Nott had published his views on the unity of the races four years earlier in *Two Lectures on the Connection between the Biblical and Physical History of Man*. There he remarked that if the unity of the human race was admitted, there were but three suppositions that would account for the diversities found in the white, black, and intermediate colors of skin: first, a miracle or direct act of the Almighty changed one type of man into another; second, the types of man resulted from the gradual affects of climate, diet, and way of life; or third, racial differences must be attributed to congenital or accidental variations.[51] In the absence of any evidence in support of miracles, Nott dismissed the first hypothesis from further consideration. Prichard advanced the second and third scenarios in his *Physical History of Man*, but both were refuted, Nott maintained, by the mass of facts pointing to separate origins. Nott also answered those who attempted to defend the unity of the human species by asserting the intellectual equality of the dark and white races. History had been ransacked for examples of such equality, he said, but they were nowhere to be found. "Can any one [re]call the name of a full-blooded Negro who has ever written a page worthy of being remembered?"[52] Nott saw no reason to modify those earlier opinions; he believed them to be further confirmed by the evidence and arguments brought forth in the combative pages of *Types of Mankind*.

Nott and Gliddon saw the aboriginal inhabitants of America as providing equally compelling proof against the unity of man. Although it was customary to refer to the American continent as the New World, recent scientific investigations had established beyond reasonable doubt that the New World was geologically, botanically, zoologically, and anthropologically a very old one. Louis Agassiz had identified some of the world's oldest geological features on the American continent, while the English geologist Charles Lyell estimated that the Mississippi River had been running its course for more than one hundred thousand years.[53] If that was true, the question naturally arose as to whether America's aboriginal inhabitants were contemporary with the earliest known races of the Old World. Was it not reasonable to infer that American aborigines had inhabited the Western Hemisphere at least five thousand years ago? If the distinct flora and fauna of the Old and New Worlds had existed contemporaneously, why could not their equally peculiar races of men have done the same? "All facts, and all analogy war against the position that America should have been left by the Creator a dreary waste for thousands of years, while the other half of the world was teeming with organized beings."[54]

The conclusion to be drawn from these circumstances was that American Indians had originated in the New World. The physical characteristics of American aborigines were entirely independent of all climatic and physical influences. The vast geographical distribution of American Indians embraced a variety of climates, yet withal they still exhibited a prevailing physical type. Variation of type occurred within certain geographical limits throughout that range, but all retained a distinct and unifying family resemblance that differed from all other races of the globe. As Charles Pickering observed in *Races of Men and Their Geographical Distribution* (1848), the diversity of races inscribed in the remote past could not be entirely attributed to differences in climate: "The existence of races, it should be observed, is a phenomenon independent of climate. All the physical races that occur in cold regions can be traced by continuity to the Tropics; where, moreover, we find other races in addition."[55] Races had historically changed climates without losing their distinct physical types; more importantly, they had retained those traits despite admixture with other races.

The polygenists found such evidence as indisputable proof that American Indians, like all other primeval divisions of the human race, were of indigenous origin. As Nott and Gliddon observed, "The Natural History of the American aborigines runs a close parallel with that of races in other countries. We have made but two divisions [the Barbarous and the Toltecan families]; but it is more than probable that each of these families, instead of originating in a single pair, have originated in many."[56] That was certainly Morton's opinion, though it mattered little whether the different families of

American Indians were descended from a single pair of progenitors or many. All the tribes bespoke a common and indigenous origin; they were so alike in their physiognomy, intellect, moral habits, and archaeological remains as to denote a race that was *"aborigine,* distinct and separate from all others."[57]

As for supposed similarities between American Indians and Mongols – another popular theory that derived the Indians from Asia – Nott and Gliddon argued that the radical differences in language alone should provide sufficient proof against such a connection. American Indians all spoke dialects of languages that were peculiar to themselves and entirely distinct from all others. If the Mongols had preserved their entire language in Asia for five thousand years, they should have also retained at least part of it during their isolation in the New World. If Mongolians had peopled the New World, where were the vestiges of a former connection?

> No *trace* of Mongol language can be found in the American languages. If they brought a language to this country, it is clear that they have lost it, and acquired that of some extinct race which preceded them. It will be conceded that a colony, or a nation, could never lose its language so completely, unless through conquest and amalgamation; in which case they would adopt another language. But, even when a language ceases to be spoken, some trace of it will continue to exist in names of individuals, rivers, places, countries, etc. The names of Moses, Solomon, David, Lazarus, Isaac and Jacob, are still found among the Jews every where, though the Hebrew language has ceased to be spoken for more than 2,000 years. And the names Mississippi, Missouri, Orinoka, Ontario, Seneca, Alabama, and a thousand other Indian names, will live for ages after the Red man is mingled with the dust. They have no likeness to any other [language] in the Old World.[58]

The American race was peculiar and distinct from all others, but it did manifest internal distinctions that could not be explained by the influence of climate. Morton accounted for those differences by dividing American Indians into two great divisions: "The Toltecan and the Barbarous Tribes." Though altogether arbitrary, this distinction was deemed necessary by its proponents to account for differences existing *within* the racial type of America Indians. Those differences were seen as residues or reflections of the combined effects of wars, migrations, and amalgamations that occurred during remote prehistoric times among the ethnically distinct but racially kindred peoples of the American continent. Events of the prehistoric past had "disturbed and confused nature's original work; and we must now deal with masses [of the America race] as we find them."[59] The tribes in Morton's

Toltecan-Barbarous divisions were said to differ in their moral and intellectual traits – differences that were allegedly confirmed by their equally distinct cranial confirmations. Morton arrived at that conclusion after examining 338 Indian skulls, in which the tribes he classified as Totlecan and Barbarous were nearly equally represented.

The presumed intellectual and moral differences existing between Morton's Toltecan and Barbarous families of the American race represent the assumptions upon which his racial theory rested, as well as its elaboration by Nott and Gliddon. Morton's Toltecan family consisted of the "semi-civilized nations" of Mexico, Peru, and Bogotá. There was every reason, argued Nott and Gliddon, to suppose that the Mound Builders of the Mississippi Valley were also of the Toltecan family. [60] Morton had made that association in *Crania Americana* based on conformity of skull type, noting that skulls removed from North American mounds more nearly approximated Peruvian crania than any other. Incongruent with the idea of attributing superior moral and intellectual capabilities to the Toltecan tribes, however, was the singular fact that the internal capacity of their skulls was smaller than that of the so-called Barbarous groups. The Peruvians possessed a brain smaller that of the Shawnee and Iroquois, who presumably were among the Barbarous tribes that had driven the Mound Builders into exile from the Mississippi Valley. "The semi-civilized communities seem, at all times, to have been hemmed in, and pressed upon, by the more restless and warlike barbarous tribes, as they are at the present day." Just as the Comanche and Apache tribes were warring against the Indians living in northern Mexico, so too, presumably, had the Barbarous tribes of prehistoric times encroached upon the semi-civilized Mound Builders.

Morton was at a loss in accounting for the smaller brain size among the supposedly more advanced tribes of his Toltecan family. The craniological principle that the size of brain was a measure of intellect seemed to be in error. Among Morton's disciples, however, the exception was more apparent than real. Morton's unknown "something" that explained this disparity was a supposed difference existing in the posterior part of the brain (the intellectual lobes) found in the Toltecan and Barbarous families. J. S. Phillips made that attribution in the appendix to Morton's work on the "Physical Type of the Americans" that was published after Morton's death. An explanation for such an incongruity could also be found in George Combe's "Phrenological Remarks" made in the appendix to Morton's *Crania Americana*.

Phillips's attempt to solve the problem of how presumably barbarous and uncivilized tribes could possess larger brains than the semi-civilized tribes clearly shows the influence of phrenology on physical anthropology in the mid-nineteenth century, as well as racist assumptions upon which both were sometimes based.

> The prevailing features in the character of the North American savage are, stoicism, a severe cruelty, excessive watchfulness, and that coarse brutality which results from the entire preponderance of the animal propensities. These so outweigh the intellectual portion of the character, that it is completely subordinate, making the Indian what we see him, a most unintellectual and uncivilized man. The intellectual lobe of the brain in these people, if not borne down by such overpowering animal propensities and passions, would have doubtless been capable of much greater efforts than any we are acquainted with, and have enabled these barbarous tribes to make some progress in civilization. This appears to be the cerebral differences between the Mexicans and Peruvians on the one hand, and the barbarous tribes of North America on the other. . . . The intellectual lobe of the brain in the two former is at least as large as in the latter, the difference in volume being chiefly confined to the occipital and basal portions of the encephalon; so that the intellectual and moral qualities of the Mexicans and Peruvians, (at least as large, if not larger, than those of the other group) are left more free to act, being not so subordinate to the propensities and violent passions. This view of the subject is in accordance with the history of these two divisions, Barbarous and Civilizable. . . . Viewed in this light, the apparent contradiction of a race with a smaller brain being superior to tribes with large brains, is so far explained, that the volume and distribution of their respective brains appear to be in accordance with such facts of their history as have come to our knowledge.[61]

The correlation of cranial characteristics with moral and intellectual traits makes it abundantly clear how anatomists used physical differences in race to explain what are actually cultural differences, which were not, in fact, racially determined in the first instance. Cranial characteristics alone were inadequate to explain what were presumably racially based and fixed moral and intellectual capabilities. The refusal to see cranial type and cultural achievement as independent variables resulted in an all-inclusive racial determinism, and one that grossly distorted and misrepresented human diversity.[62] It served the social agendas of Caucasians far better than it served science. Only after anthropology freed itself from those socially derived constructions of race could anthropologists attribute cultural differences to causes other than race.

The findings of Morton and Phillips provided a possible explanation for the fate of the presumably Toltecan Mound Builders. The example of large-brained but intellectually inferior Indian groups subjecting their smaller-brained but intellectually superior neighbors seemed to explain the fate of Toltecan peoples in the prehistoric past. Nott stated that scenario as follows:

> Who can doubt that similar occurrences had been going on over this continent for many centuries, or even thousands of years? There are scattered over North America countless tumuli, which, it is believed, were built by races [racial families or subgroups of American Indians, i.e., tribes or closely affiliated groups of tribes] different from the savage tribes found around them by the whites, and an impenetrable oblivion rests upon these works. There are many reasons for believing that these races were identical with, or closely related to, the Toltecs; and may have been driven South, or exterminated, by more savage and warlike races, like the Iroquois. The traditions of the Mexicans point to the North as their original country . . . we must infer that a succession of events was going on for ages, during ante-historic times, similar to those we find in the pages of written history. Human nature never changes, else it would cease to be human nature. [63]

Had the ancient and presumably Toltecan Mound Builders been driven South, where they ultimately produced the civilizations of Mexico? Some, at least, were prepared to entertain that very possibility.

No lesser a figure than the eminent naturalist Louis Agassiz also argued that both the different races of men and different species of animals had originated separately at different parts of the globe. Agassiz first expressed that opinion in the *Christian Examiner* in March 1850, bringing down upon himself a firestorm of protest. "The Orthodox are at him in consequence," Francis Parkman told Squier, "raising a great outcry about impiety, and attacking him with texts of Scripture. If they could, they would serve him as the Church served Galileo." [64] Agassiz's observations were as compelling to the polygenists as they were repugnant to those whom Nott once disdainfully labeled "theological naturalists." The truth of the matter, said Nott, was with Agassiz, who observed that American Indians and other distinct races could not be derived from a common origin. Agassiz elaborated his position on the diversity of human origins in the *Christian Examiner* in July 1850. There he noted that both the diversity of human languages and zoological evidence derived from analogies between animals and men indicated that

> these races did not originate from a common stock, but are only closely allied as men, endowed equally with the same intellectual powers, the

same organs of speech, the same sympathies, only developed in slightly different ways in the different races, precisely as we observe the fact between closely allied species of the same genus among birds. There is no ornithologist who ever watched the natural habits of birds and their notes, who has not been surprised at the similarity of intonation of the notes of closely allied species, and the greater difference between the notes of birds belonging to different genera and families. . . . And why should it be different with men? Why should not the different races of men have originally spoken distinct languages, as they do at present, differing in the same proportions as their organs of speech are variously modified? And why should not these modifications in their turn be indicative of primitive differences among them? It were [i.e., would be] giving up all induction, all power of arguing from sound premises, if the force of such evidence were to be denied.[65]

Nott and Gliddon thought such arguments were unanswerable and invited Agassiz to contribute an essay on the subject in their forthcoming work on ethnology. Agassiz's contribution offered additional zoological and ethnological evidence in support of Morton's ethnological views on the primitive diversity of man. He called attention to the "close connection" existing between the geographical distribution of animals and men and attempted to establish that the natural boundaries of different animals originally coincided with those of the different types of mankind.[66] Agassiz's study of the geographical distribution of plants, animals, and humans led him to see natural relations existing between the different types of man and the plants and animals inhabiting the same regions. "The coincidence between the circumscription of the races of man, and the natural limits of different zoological provinces, characterized by peculiar [and] distinctive species of animals is one of the most important and unexpected features in the natural history of mankind, which the study of the geographical distribution of all the organized beings now existing upon earth has disclosed to us." Here was the key to understanding "the very origin of the differences existing among men," for it established that physiologically humans were "modified by the same laws as that as animals." The organic differences existing among various species of animals must likewise apply to man.[67]

Agassiz suggested that mankind had not sprung from a single pair of humans, nor had each race necessarily originated from different pairs. It was more likely that the different types of that mankind were "created in nations," within the various zoological provinces they inhabited when first known to history.[68] Barthold George Niebuhr had expressed a very similar opinion on human diversity, one that Nott drew upon as corroborating evidence in support of Agassiz:

> These great national races have never sprung from the growth of a single family into a nation, but always from the association of several families of human beings. . . . By this I explain the immense variety of languages among the North American Indians, which it is absolutely impossible to refer to any common source, but which, in some case, have resolved themselves into one language, as in Mexico and Peru, for instance; . . . I believe, farther [sic], that the origin of the human race is not connected with any given place, but is to be sought everywhere over the face of the earth; and that it is an idea more worthy of the power and wisdom of the Creator, to assume that he gave to each zone and each climate its proper inhabitants, to whom that zone and climate would be most suited, than to assume that the human species has degenerated in such innumerable instances.[69]

The publication of *Types of Mankind* in 1854 had the anticipated effect on the defenders of the unity of man. Gliddon wanted to answer his detractors with an archaeological critique in the New York press that would "blow the orthodox to the devil." He sought Squier's assistance in getting him a forum in which to defend his views, as well as Squier's editorial assistance in crafting a reply. Gliddon had heard that Rev. Frances Hawks of the American Ethnological Society was about to come out against *Types of Mankind* in *Putnam's Magazine*. "If he does," said the pugnacious Gliddon, "tell Putnam that I'll lay him stiff, as I owe him for 12 years of back-biting." Hawks epitomized for Gliddon the problem facing ethnologists generally and everything that was wrong with the American Ethnological Society specifically. He was a monogenist, a clergyman, and an officer of the American Ethnological Society who could not separate ethnology from his Christian assumptions. Gliddon imagined that Squier's followers in the American Ethnological Society would be glad to turn the parsons out of their ranks if Squier would but lead the way. He suggested that Squier play the part of "mischief maker" by drawing Hawks out at the society's next meeting by moving a vote of thanks to the publishers of *Types of Mankind*. Gliddon hoped that such a vote would provoke Hawks enough to resign his membership. If Squier would set things in motion, Gliddon would be only too happy to join in the fun. "Depend upon it the 'Ethnogs' must fight, this time. You must split the Society, and then our side can go ahead at once."[70]

Squier balked at Gliddon's suggestion of forcing a monogenist-polygenist division among the society's members, but he did help his friend by defending *Types of Mankind* in an anonymous review for the *New York Herald*.[71] It is unclear how much of the review originated with Gliddon and how much was written by Squier. Gliddon sent him a puff about the book that he had written himself, which he asked Squier to promote for him in the press. Internal evidence suggests, however, that Squier substantially rewrote whatever Gliddon had sent him. The introduction and conclusion of the review are quite Squiresque, even to the point that certain phrases echo those found in the some of Squier's earlier writings, while some portions of the body of the review stylistically and substantively seem less so. Some writers have attributed this anonymous review to Squier and others to Gliddon himself.[72] Gliddon's reaction to the review, together with the internal evidence, suggests that Squier wrote most it. That is the attribution made here.[73]

Nott and Gliddon's *Types of Mankind*, said Squier, was a remarkable contribution to the eminently "American science" of ethnology and a worthy successor to the works of Morton. The authors boldly presented the doctrine of the original diversity of man not as a "hypothesis to be sustained, but as a result which is demonstrated." Squier admired the authors' courageous and fearless refusal to privilege orthodox views in the face of contradictory scientific evidence. The arguments they advanced were as fatal to the Mosaic account of creation and biblical chronology as was the indisputable evidence of geology. Only the incredulous could hereafter insist upon the unity of mankind given such evidence. Ethnological science marched inexorably forward in the pursuit of "truth" and the correction of error, even when confronted by "the lions of bigotry, superstition, and ignorance."

The arguments advanced by Nott and Gliddon exposed the inconsistencies of orthodox views on the origin and antiquity of man, as well as the untenability of holding to both the "vulgar chronology" and the doctrine of the unity of man. They could not, said Squier, have it both ways:

> If the chronology which places the date of the creation of man six thousand years ago be true, and the existing types of men have been unchanged for five thousand years, then the diversity which men present must have arisen in the four thousand years after the creation, and the causes which produced them have thenceforward ceased to act! Such are the absurdities in which "orthodoxy" involves its blind followers.

Those of an unquestioning faith would most certainly denounce the authors of *Types of Mankind* as infidels, but its conclusions reflected the results of scientific inquiry unencumbered by the suppositions required by religious orthodoxy. It uttered what many ethnologists believed was actually true but were reluctant to say openly. *Types of Mankind* was the "response of the Watchman" – of the "earnest student" to the leading scientific questions of the day – and embodied the leading results of "modern ethnographic science" as it was known. The work would have great influence and would "produce a profound and permanent impression on the public mind."

A grateful Gliddon responded to Squier's review in characteristic fashion: "You are, by God, the pluckiest man I ever knew." He credited Squier with having thoroughly grasped the subject and thought his review a "perfection of critiques" and a "vindication of science."[74] Nott thought Squier's review to be "altogether the best thing I have ever seen from your pen."[75] Gliddon was so pleased with the review that he invited Squier to be coauthor of a planned sequel to *Types of Mankind*.[76] Squier would have been a good recruit, for his powers of declamation were considerable, his knowledge far ranging, and his authority as coauthor of *Ancient Monuments* considerable. But he had no taste for public frays with the clergy over points of religion and science, and he was too busy promoting his Honduras Interoceanic Railway project to be of service.

Gliddon later became Squier's agent in the ill-fated scheme and died of a sudden illness in Panama on November 16, 1857, while returning to the United States from Honduras. Thousands of Americans died of fever in Panama as they crossed the isthmus between the Atlantic and Pacific coasts in the 1850s during the high tide of migration to California in the 1850s. Gliddon appears to have been one of the many unfortunates who died of the Panama fever. He was buried in the "American Cemetery" at Panama, and his grave was marked with an enclosure and a marble slab that Squier had sent there by way of the American consul. Squier visited the grave of his old friend while en route to Peru in 1863. He arranged to have Gliddon's remains sent to Philadelphia in the care of Gliddon's friend and publisher J. B. Lippincott, who had the late and lamented Gliddon reinterred in Philadelphia's Laurel Hill Cemetery.[77] Gliddon was, perhaps, Squier's closest friend and confidant.

Predictably, *Types of Mankind* caused a stir in the ranks of the American Ethnological Society, but it did not generate the schism hoped for by Gliddon. Brantz Mayer of Baltimore, another member of the society and a firm supporter of Squier's researchers, also objected to *Types of Mankind*, but upon entirely different and more essential grounds. Mayer found the work a useful résumé of archaeological discoveries in Egypt, but its organization was "somewhat chaotic" and obtuse, requiring a reader at several junctures to cry "let there be light!" Too many writers were involved in its production, and Morton's unedited papers seemed completely out of place if not context. The work begged for an editor and an index of its jumbled contents.

Mayer was entirely at a loss to describe the authors' treatment of American subjects, and he was impatient with their preoccupation with craniology at the expense of archaeology. After reading such a ponderous tome, he told Squier, "Who would suppose that our continent had a monumental history, or anything but an osteological one? I begin to think that the bone and skull theory, tho' very good, is rather so as a system of confirmation than origination. We want the result of the mind that dwelt in the skull and moved in the bones, and this we find in the monumental remains."[78] Daniel Wilson would later object in a similar manner to the "scientific dogma" that had arisen around Morton's craniology.[79] The all-encompassing generalizations arising from the biological determinism of Morton, Nott, and Gliddon have not aged well.

Squier continued his correspondence and friendship with Nott after Gliddon's death. The growing crises over slavery and the threat of secession made it difficult, but they still shared an interest in ethnology. Squier's relationship with Nott is curious given their opposing views on slavery. Nott on several occasions declared his opposition to slavery as a matter of principle (slavery was a bane to mankind, all things being equal), but he consistently defended its existence as a domestic institution of the South that conformed with the presumed findings of ethnological science (all things were not equal when dealing with the capabilities of allegedly inferior races). The prospect of emancipation was as abhorrent to Nott as the perpetuation of slavery was to Squier. There can be no doubt that Squier held strong antislavery opinions, even though he never embraced abolitionism as a political movement per se. Northern Whigs like Squier recognized the intractable nature of slavery as a political issue that posed the single greatest threat to their existence as a national political party and to the perpetuation of the Union. Whigs understood that the abolitionists' bid for a third party would hurt them in the presidential election of 1844. Voters who might otherwise align themselves with the Whig Party because of their distaste for slavery were likely to cast their ballots for abolitionists instead of Whigs. Leaders of the Whig Party, on the other hand, also greatly feared the consequences of moving too far in the direction of the abolitionists.[80] Southern Whigs were certain to bolt the party in that eventuality, while those in the North who opposed the extension of slavery into the territories but accepted its existence in the South might be equally alienated.

In some of his lectures at Albany, Squier declared the institution of slavery to be incompatible with republican principles and a curse on the body politic. As coeditor of the *Hartford Journal* he opposed the annexation of Texas in the belief that it would preserve and extend the curse of slavery. He and his fellow

Whigs acknowledged that the Constitution protected slavery where it already existed, but they made no allowance for its extension under the guise of annexation.[81] Squier also appears to have concurred with the opinion of those Whigs who saw the annexation of Oregon as a necessary "counterpoint" on the part of non-slave states to offset the political advantage given the slave states by the annexation of Texas.[82] Squier further expressed his disgust with the institution of slavery when he declined a journalistic position at Baltimore in 1845 because he refused to live in the presence of slaves.[83] He fully expected that a struggle with the South over the issue of slavery would one day come, but he wanted no further concessions to be made even if it meant a peaceful or a forceful division of the Union.[84]

As the issue of extending slavery into the territories continued to agitate the nation in 1848, Squier declared that " 'Free Soil' is my rallying cry. *Free Soil*, [even] if the Union falls! I had rather see the Mississippi run blood, than that the American Union should longer stand before the world as the *Propagandist of Slavery* – the forger of chains for the new bond men!"[85] Americans could not allow the reputation of the republic to be indefinitely tarnished by the perpetuation of slavery. Eight years later, when he was convinced that the nation was "trembling on the verge of Civil War," Squier hoped that when the dissolution of the Union finally came it would be an amicable one and that the two nations could peacefully coexist. He thought it far more likely, however, that the deteriorating state of relations between the North and South would soon lead to "hostility and warfare." Squier attributed the worsening condition of the Union to southern intransigence and arrogance: "The South is absolutely anti-republican, hostile to the key principles of all liberty, despotic, arrogant, ignorant, and blood-thirsty." He confessed that he had a "precious poor opinion of niggers, or any of the darker races," but "a still poorer one of slavery."[86] Politics could never have been the basis of Nott and Squier's long friendship and mutual respect.

Nott visited Squier in New York sometime before 1861, when the two correspondents at long last discussed their ethnological interests face-to-face. Nott later recalled that during his visit Squier had jokingly admonished the "the 'damd grinning bluster, bravado' &c of Southern people – [and] thought they could not be kicked into resistance by black republicans & were incapable of any effort beyond grinning." Nott had politely demurred from the opinion of his congenial host and informed Squier that by denying the South the right of secession the North was forcing the issue of resistance and was about to bring about "a terrible upheaval." He assured Squier in May 1861 that southerners were quite capable of fighting Yankees: "The Southern people would rise up as one man & resist it [the imposing attitude of the

North regarding secession] with the old spirit of '76 – The declaration of Independence is the chart by which the Anglo-Saxon race sails – this doctrine [the right of secession] is repeated in every one of the State constitutions, & the Southern people will see all the whites & blacks on the globe slaughtered before they will yield this point." The Lincoln administration's attitude and policies toward the secession and the restoration of the Union would not end the crisis but rather ensure war. "Certainly, you do not expect to conquer us & make us vassals! – This idea is too absurd to be entertained by any sane mind, that comprehends the Anglo Saxon character." [87]

The coming of war led to Nott and Squier's temporary estrangement. Ethnologists broke ranks during the Civil War, as did Americans in all walks of life. The social order that Nott had known and defended in the South before the war gave him little comfort afterward. The war went hard on his personal fortunes and turned his world upside down. The medical school he had worked so hard to establish at Mobile closed at the end of its second session as the students and faculty went off to war. Nott was among them. He served as a surgeon and medical inspector in Bragg's Second Corps of the Army of Mississippi. He lost one of his two sons in the war, saw his property destroyed, and witnessed – what must have been a mocking spectacle – his former medical school converted to a training school for freedmen. Nott wrote Squier in December 1865 and shared his dismay and disgust at the changes that had been brought about by the South's defeat: "I confess it does not increase by love for the Government when I pass by every day or two & see two or three hundred Negroes racing through and tearing every thing to pieces – The chemical laboratory is occupied by negro cobblers." [88]

Nott's exasperation with the social engineering of the Freedman's Bureau at length prompted him to leave the South – not the South he had once known but the one he had come to despise. The South was no longer a suitable place in which "gentlemen" could live. He had decided "to leave the Negroland to you damd Yankees" and recoup his fortunes elsewhere. He first moved to Baltimore in 1867 but found it to be the most intellectually stultifying and unprogressive community he had ever seen: "no scientific association, no medical society even, no journal, no concert of action." He next moved to New York City, which he found more compatible with his temper and interests, describing it to Squier as a city "without morals, without political scruples, without religion, and without *niggers*." Nott soon established his own medical practice in New York, joined the American Ethnological Society, and renewed his friendship with Squier. He was among those who joined Squier in 1869 and 1870 in the movement to reorganize the society as the Anthropological Society of New-York. Nott's failing health forced him to abandon his medical practice, sell his books, forget ethnology, and return to Mobile in the hope that rest and a change of climate might restore his health. He died there in the spring of 1873.[89]

Squier's affiliation with the American School of Ethnology informed his anthropology for more than thirty years and likewise affected his relationships with other members of the American Ethnological Society. Squier began his association with the society in 1846 and was its most active and important member throughout the 1850s and 1860s. His impatience and frustration with those members who refused to free themselves of the Bible in the study of man, and who even opposed the discussion of unorthodox views at the society's meetings, had prompted him in September 1848 to propose the establishment of an American "Archaeological and Ethnological Journal" on the model of Burke's *Ethnological Journal*.

Eventually, Squier's frustration with certain members of the society led him to attempt its reorganization and revitalization as the short-lived Anthropological Institute of New-York between 1869 and 1871.[90] Charles C. Jones Jr., William H. Thomson, John G. Shea, Henry T. Drowne, Josiah Clark Nott, Alexander J. Cotheal, and Charles Rau joined Squier in that effort. The American Ethnological Society was established in 1842, essentially under the auspices of Albert Gallatin. Gallatin's home became a salon for ethnological discussions, and his purse paid for the first two volumes of the *Transactions of the American Ethnological Society*, published in 1845 and 1848. The society's reputation as a learned society rested primarily on the authority of those two volumes. Gallatin's death in 1849 was crippling blow to fortunes of the society, which entered a period of decline shortly thereafter. It published the first part of the third and final volume of its highly regarded *Transactions* in 1853,[91] only one volume of some disjointed numbers of the *Bulletin* for 1860–61, and a few fugitive papers.

Matters worsened for the society in the late 1860s. Of the forty-seven resident members named in its last published membership list, twenty-five were either deceased or had moved from the city. The number of corresponding or honorary members was unknown, its archives had largely disappeared, and it was entirely without means. The society's interests and activities had fallen behind all similar societies in Europe, and it had lost the authority it once commanded. It had become preoccupied, said Squier, "with 'holy stones' and such rubbish . . . and [the] apparent sanction of bold impostures." Those wishing to end that state of affairs gathered at a regular meeting of the society on May 11, 1869. Squier, Alexander J. Cotheal, J. A. Spencer, Josiah Clark Nott, and Charles C. Jones Jr. were appointed a special committee to report on the best means of reorganizing the society along lines more in accord with developments among anthropological, ethnological, and archaeological societies in Europe.

The committee took the newly consolidated ethnological and anthropological societies of London as its model. "By the consolidation of the Ethnological Society of London with the Anthropological Society of the same capital, the designation 'Ethnological' had ceased to apply to any society of importance in Europe, and the term 'Anthropological' had been accepted instead." The new name was more comprehensive and better reflected the fact that the study of man required "the cooperation of naturalists as well as archaeologists, anatomists as well as antiquaries." Squier submitted the committee's report and resolutions on November 17, 1869, and the American Ethnological Society was formally dissolved and succeeded by the Anthropological Institute of New-York on March 9, 1871. The new institute was incorporated on March 20, with Squier as president, George Gibbs and Josiah Clark Nott as vice-presidents, and Edwin Hamilton Davis as a member of the executive committee.

The new organization was needed, said Squier, because "Anthropology, which is only a more comprehensive name for the Science of Man than Ethnology, has really risen to the rank of a recognized science. It is no longer hazy speculation; its area is no longer the waste field into which pretenders, half-schooled philosophers, vague theorists, and Jonathan Oldbucks of all sorts, may shove their inconsequent rubbish." Sadly, the American Ethnological Society had contributed nothing to those developments. An organization was needed that could promote "a wider and deeper investigation of the character and true relations of the varieties and races of mankind than had ever existed before. . . . But this investigation must be made *ab initio*, or rather in a purely abstract scientific sense. It can not be done by men who, for any reason or motive, bring into the study the element of faith, or adhesion to dogmas or creeds of any kind whatever. These subtle elements of depression of scientific inquiry have been, to a certain degree, the ruin of this Society."[92] Squier could remember when the question of human unity could not even be discussed at the society's meetings without offending some of its members, and when all attempts to introduce it were immediately protested. In matters pertaining to scientific inquiry, Squier asserted, "The item of faith must be entirely eliminated."[93]

Contemporary developments within the anthropological community of Europe were further explained by Dr. M. Paul Broca (1824–80), secretary-general of the Anthropological Society of Paris and professor of medicine at the University of Paris, in an address given before the Anthropological Society of Paris. Squier published the address in the *Journal of the Anthropological*

Institute of New-York as a further elaboration of its purpose.[94] Broca was most interested in the physical characteristics of man and in the guidance anatomy and craniology offered in studying the natural history of man. He regarded anatomy as "the only sure foundation of natural history."[95] Comparative osteology of the human races required representative collections, thus pointing to the importance attached to craniological museums in Europe. Savants in Europe were methodically advancing their researches in prehistoric archaeology and paleontology, and each new discovery further demonstrated the antiquity of man and suggested new lines of investigation. The Anthropological Society of Paris, for example, added prehistoric, paleontological, and zoological anthropology to the branches of study that were defining the emerging discipline of anthropology in Europe. "Now, what is the chief aim of anthropology," Broca asked, "if it be not the natural history of man – that is to say, the anatomy and biology of man?"

Broca noted that there were parallel developments between the American Ethnological Society in New York, founded in 1842, and the Ethnological Society of London, established that same year. In the face of new developments, neither society had distanced itself from the older and more fragmented ethnology. As Broca saw the problem, by "dividing ethnology from natural history" the societies deprived themselves of the aid of scholars schooled in the rigorous methods of scientific observation. The rise of anthropological science in both societies had appealed to some members, but it had repelled those who clung tenaciously to the old ethnology. The introduction of anatomy and natural history into the time-honored pursuits of the Ethnological Society of London eventually resulted in a schism not unlike that which occurred within the ranks of the American Ethnological Society. The dissenting members of the Ethnological Society of London founded the Anthropological Society of London on February 24, 1863, and subsequently launched the *Anthropological Review*. The rival entities consolidated in 1870 as the Anthropological Society of London. Those parallels were not lost on Squier, who had participated in similar events and discussions within the American Ethnological Society throughout the 1850s and 1860s. It is not surprising that he modeled the Anthropological Institute of New-York on the recently consolidated Anthropological Society of London.

Anthropological studies in Europe received further impetus from the establishment of the International Congress of Anthropology and Prehistoric Archaeology. The idea for such a congress originated with M. Gabriel Mortillet at a meeting of the Society of Natural Sciences held at Spezia, Italy, in September 1865. Mortillet proposed to the antehistoric section of the society the creation of an International Paleontological Congress. The society adopted the proposal, and the congress first met at Neufchâtel, France, in September 1866. The next congress was held in Paris in August 1867 under the new name of the International Congress of Anthropology and Prehistoric Archaeology. The Paris congress coincided with the Exposition Universelle, to which many American and European countries sent delegations. Both Squier and John Russell Bartlett attended the Paris congress. Squier served as a vice-president of the congress and a delegate of the American Ethnological Society, while Bartlett attended both as a delegate of both the American Ethnological Society and the American Antiquarian Society. [96] Squier's participation in the congress had doubtless spurred his interest in reorganizing the American Ethnological Society.

Squier's aspirations for the short-lived Anthropological Institute of New-York were never realized. It would be left to the next generation of anthropologically trained archaeologists and ethnologists to institute the kind of studies that he had endeavored to promote at an earlier day. Squier began his archaeological researches in 1845 firmly rooted within the tradition of romantic antiquarianism, but his archaeological thought continued to develop over the next thirty years. The influence of European ideas and approaches to the study of prehistory played an important part in the process, as he made a concerted effort to keep abreast of archaeological and ethnological investigations in Europe. Bruce G. Trigger has called attention to what he calls "the impasse of antiquarianism" – the need to connect prehistoric remains to written records and the known people of the past. [97] Biblical ethnologists attempted, and often insisted, on doing just that. Squier struggled to free the American Ethnological Society from the assumptions of biblical ethnology, and when that failed he formed the Anthropological Institute of New-York, the first such society established in the United States. The heat of the monogenist-polygenist debate about human origins had, by that time, largely subsided. Darwin's theory of biological evolution was emerging as the new scientific paradigm. Polygenist arguments were not entirely silenced, but the doctrine of separate origins was no longer the most viable explanation of human diversity. [98]

Squier's historical reputation as an anthropologist rests upon several grounds. The originality of his researches, his attempt to bring order to the collection and organization of anthropological data, his affirmations of the need for establishing more exacting standards of inquiry, and his hostility toward unsubstantiated speculation were distinguishing characteristics of his scholarship. As he observed in 1848,

Archaeology and Ethnology now rank among the sciences, and researches in either department should be conducted in a spirit of the most rigid criticism. The day for conjecture and mere speculation is past, and he who has dreamed away any portion of his life in one or both, has no right to complain when his air-built fabrics are overthrown. The path to truth is direct, and its announcement needs no circumlocution. If to arrive at it, it be necessary to demolish the stronghold of prejudice and ignorance, the student, like the engineer of the inexorable railway, must raze their foundations, regardless of the complaints of the one, or the unintelligible mutterings of the other.[99]

Even though he was not a trained scientist himself, Squier sought to place American archaeology and ethnology on a more scientific footing. He wanted to rid the field of "the shallow hypotheses and absurd conjectures of pretenders" that seemed endemic, for no subjects called forth a more unbridled and fevered speculations than that of American aborigines and antiquities. Archaeology and ethnology should be purged of "charlatans and fools" and its "George Joneses and Josiah Priests, – an array unmatched for its complacent ignorance and stupid assurance."[100] Squier's efforts to sweep the "reveries" of idlers and charlatans from the field of American anthropology continued to the end of his productive days as a scholar. He remained particularly hostile toward groundless but popular theories of the European colonization of prehistoric America, relishing his role as hoax-hunter and "fool-killer" extraordinaire in demolishing their claims to serious attention.[101] He had little patience for those who uncritically accepted sensational finds such as the Grave Creek stone and the Newark "Holy Stones" as significant archaeological discoveries. As Squier noted in 1870, "To *hoax* is eminently an American proclivity or habit, a kind of friskiness not without a tinge of mischief, and always reckless, which pervades our society far and wide, and which is gratified by creating what is called 'a sensation.'"[102] The infant sciences of American archaeology and ethnology had no abler advocate than Ephraim George Squier (see fig. 17).

17. E. Geo. Squier, 1871. Cabinet photograph, Rockwood & Co., New York. Signed and dated. Squier led the attempt to reorganize and revitalize the American Ethnological Society as the short-lived Anthropological Institute of New-York between 1869 and 1871. The *Journal of the Anthropological Institute of New-York* appeared in one volume only in 1872, with Squier as the contributing editor. (National Portrait Gallery, Smithsonian Institution, Washington DC. Reprinted with permission.)

Epilogue

Insanity and the "Eclipse of Genius"

The private sphere of Squier's life, unlike the public one, is difficult to fathom. The richness and fullness of the latter overshadows the former almost entirely. His work was his life, whether it was journalism, the Honduras Interoceanic Railway, anthropological research, or his activities as an officer of the American Ethnological Society. As revealing as his writings are of most of his political and social views, Squier carefully guarded his personal life. A notable exception to that statement was his divorce from Miriam Squier in 1873 and his temporary bout with insanity the following year. His mental disorder ended his active days as a scholar and resulted in the sale of his cherished library and archaeological collection. He was temporarily committed to an asylum in 1874, and after his release he remained a ward of his brother Frank until his death in 1888. With Frank's help he was able to oversee the publication of his Peruvian materials in 1877, but he remained a shadow of his former self. Squier's last years are a tragic epilogue to a brilliant career.

Ephraim George Squier and Miriam Florence Follin (1836–1914) were married in Providence, Rhode Island, on October 23, 1857. Squier's friend Henry Bowen Anthony, editor of the *Providence Journal* and a former governor of Rhode Island, arranged the wedding. [1] It is unclear precisely when and where E.G. and Miriam first met, but in announcing his engagement to his parents on September 10, 1857, he informed them that he had known Miriam and had corresponded with her for more than three years. [2] Miriam's uncle Augustus Follin was an agent of the Honduras Interoceanic Railway from late 1853 through 1856, and it is likely that the two first became acquainted during that time and in that connection.

Miriam was an intriguing woman – well educated, worldly, a polished writer, and every bit as ambitious and capable as Squier. She was born in New Orleans in 1836, the daughter of Charles Follin and Susan Danforth. [3] Her father provided Miriam with a formal education that included private tutoring in French, Spanish, Italian, German, and Latin. The family later moved to New York, where the eighteen-year-old Miriam married David Charles Peacock. The marriage soon ended in separation. After a brief stint in the theater as "Minnie Montez," the stage sister of Lola Montez, the twenty-one-year-old Miriam became Mrs. Ephraim George Squier.

A new dynamic entered into the Squier marriage when both E.G. and Miriam joined the New York publishing empire of Frank Leslie (1821–80). The failure of the Honduras Interoceanic Railway in 1860 had once again left Squier without a sustainable income. He was first and last a journalist, a profession in which he had considerable experience and which always promised steady work. On September 21, 1861, Squier became managing editor of *Frank Leslie's Illustrated Newspaper*, a sensational paper that at the time boasted a readership of 200,000.[4] Squier edited the two volumes of *Frank Leslie's Pictorial History of the Civil War* in 1861 and 1862, and he continued to edit *Leslie's Illustrated Newspaper* until his departure for Peru in 1863. After he returned from Peru in 1865, Squier resumed his editorial work on the illustrated newspaper.

Miriam became the editor of *Frank Leslie's Lady's Magazine* in 1863 and editor of the *Frank Leslie's Chimney Corner* in 1865.[5] She was Leslie's constant companion both at work and in public, and by degrees she became estranged from Squier. The Squier marriage appears to have entered into a period of difficulty after Frank Leslie left his wife, Sarah Ann Welham Leslie, in 1860. It was then that Leslie rented rooms in the Squiers' Thirty-ninth Street home in New York City.[6] Leslie hired Squier as the editor of the *Illustrated Newspaper* the following year, and thereafter Squier's private and business affairs became hopelessly muddled. E.G.'s marriage would ultimately become a casualty of the strange triangular relationship that developed between the Squiers and Leslie, but their business and personal relations appear to have remained amicable for some time. Leslie initiated divorce proceedings against his wife in December 1866, discontinued them in February 1867, and resumed them in January 1868, only to again discontinue the action in May 1869. When Leslie finally obtained a divorce in 1872, his attentions toward Miriam took a more serious turn, as did hers toward him.[7]

Problems in the Squier marriage may have begun during or shortly after the couple's residence in Peru, but details about the nature of their relationship at that time are spotty at best. The Squiers arrived at Callao aboard the Vanderbilt steamer *Valparaiso* on July 3, 1863, in the company of James Mackie, another member of the U.S. Claims Commission. They resided at the Hotel Maury and at the American Legation house until the conclusion of E.G.'s diplomatic affairs.[8] Miriam left Peru in November 1863, while Squier continued his archaeological explorations into the highlands of Peru and Bolivia. Miriam gave an account of her impressions and experiences at Lima in *Frank Leslie's Chimney Corner* in June 1865 and in *Harper's New Monthly Magazine* in December 1866. [9] Neither the coldness and dampness of Lima nor the open sewers of its streets held much appeal for her, but she did find much of interest in the local festivals and customs. Her separation from Squier at that time may have contributed to their estrangement and encouraged her to gradually turn her attentions and affections away from Squier and toward Leslie.

Miriam's presence at Lima is, interestingly enough, nowhere mentioned in the pages of Squier's highly discursive *Peru*. It was not germane to his purposes to do so, to be certain, but there could be another reason why he passed her over in silence. Squier published *Peru* in 1877, four years after his divorce in May 1873 and three years after Miriam married Frank Leslie in July 1874. There is no question that he was still bitter about the entire affair, and there are, curiously, but two surviving letters from Miriam to Squier of which I am aware. Only one of them is among Squier's personal papers, [10] yet in announcing their engagement to his parents in 1857 he told them that he and Miriam had corresponded for more than three years before their marriage. Other letters from Miriam of a later date must have at one point existed, and their absence in Squier's personal papers would suggest that he made a conscious effort to eliminate her from his memory. His silence about Miriam's companionship in *Peru* may be attributable to the same motive and to the same avenging hand.

Problems in the Squier marriage appear to have first become public knowledge when E.G. and Miriam traveled with Leslie to the Paris Exposition in February 1867. Upon arriving in Liverpool, Squier was arrested for an outstanding debt owed a Liverpool creditor in connection with his former Honduras Interoceanic Railway scheme. He was detained, suffered the ignominy of spending ten days at Lancaster Castle (a debtor's prison), and declared bankruptcy. [11] The *Liverpool Courier* reported that a passenger aboard the *Australasian* had sent a telegram to Liverpool while at Queenstown, informing Squier's creditor that he was about to arrive at Liverpool en route to Paris. [12] The informant's identity is uncertain, but suspicion clearly falls upon Leslie or Miriam, and possibly both.

Only someone intimately familiar with Squier's business dealings could have sent that telegram, for the debt in question was more than a decade old. Both Leslie and Miriam possessed such knowledge. Squier was convinced that Leslie had done the deed. Miriam's biographer, Madeline B. Stern, shared that opinion, stating that the "identity of the 'fellow-passenger' is clear enough." [13] The inference that Leslie wanted Squier out of the way so he could romance his wife is plausible but entirely circumstantial. If one assumes that Leslie sent the telegram, it is unclear whether he acted alone or in concert with Miriam. It was later alleged in Leslie's divorce proceedings from Sarah Ann Leslie and in the press that illicit relations between Miriam and Leslie began on that trip. Squier consistently defended Miriam, and his own pride, against the sting of those rumors and accusations. What E.G.'s relationship with Leslie and Miriam was like after the Liverpool incident can only be surmised, but clearly the Squiers' tempestuous marriage was anything but stable from that time forward.

Squier continued to work for Leslie in some capacity until 1873, but apparently he no longer edited the *Illustrated Newspaper* after 1868. Much of the ardor and self-confidence of his earlier years had already begun to dissipate, and he confessed to his parents in 1869 that what he longed for most was "quiet." Squier's tastes, habits, and pursuits had long ago distanced him from his family, but he prophetically noted that when his troubles and reverses finally broke him down he might someday need the shelter of his brother Frank's home and the good cheer of Frank's wife and family.[14] It is difficult to imagine how Squier coped with the tangled web of deceit that soon followed. He could not have been oblivious to the mutual attentions of his wife and Leslie, or insensitive to the gossip and rumor that must have swirled around them in the fashionable circles of New York society. His marriage had become one of convenience, running more, perhaps, on inertia than affection and commitment. Squier's thoughts and innermost feelings about the situation are not known, but the bitterness he expressed in later years suggests that he felt used and betrayed and was growing increasingly despondent.

At the start of 1873, Squier contemplated leaving journalism altogether so that he could devote himself to preparing his manuscript materials on Peru for publication.[15] The results of his investigations in Peru had yet to be presented in full or in a suitable manner, even though it had been eight years since his return to the United States. Those plans were forestalled, however, when his unstable relationship with Miriam reached critical mass. On April 25, 1873, Squier received a summons to answer Miriam's complaint of adultery. Her attorneys were with the firm of Hilton, Campbell, and Bell. Squier was the defendant and Miriam the plaintiff in the divorce case of *Squier v. Squier*. Miriam accused E.G. of several acts of adultery. On or about March 28, 1872, at a house kept by Lizzie A. Rice at 27 East Twenty-seventh Street, Squier allegedly committed adultery with a woman whose name was unknown to Miriam. Other acts of adultery were reputedly committed with a woman known as "Gypsy" on or about April 1, April 4, and April 5, 1872, and allegedly at other times besides between January 1 and June 17, 1872. Miriam further charged Squier with having an adulterous relationship with Lizzie A. Rice and other women whose names she did not know on various occasions between June 17, 1872, and April 24, 1873, at 106 West Thirty-first Street. Miriam denied any connivance or consent in those relationships and stated that she had not lived with Squier since her discovery of his alleged adultery.

Miriam's accusations were formally presented during a special term of the Superior Court of the City, held at the City Court House of New York on May 2, 1873. Squier neither appeared before Miriam's attorneys nor answered the court's summons. The court then referred the matter to Thomas Boese, counselor at law, to report to the court all the material facts relating to Miriam's complaint. Boese, the sole referee in the case, found on May 30, 1873, that all the allegations contained in Miriam's complaint were true and that Miriam was entitled to a divorce.

The testimony given by Matthew L. Morgan was particularly damaging. Morgan, an artist, testified that at Squier's invitation he went to "an assignation house" at 27 East Twenty-seventh Street in order to sketch for Squier a women of "very fine form." After Squier's request to close the house to other visitors was granted, an "elaborate supper" was prepared. Squier and Morgan were invited upstairs after supper, where two girls stripped off all their clothing and Morgan sketched them in the nude. One of the girls, named "Gypsy," reportedly sat naked upon Squier's lap, indicating by her conversation that she had slept with him. Matthew reported that Squier "was on familiar terms with all the women, and was apparently well acquainted with them." Squier accompanied Morgan to the door at about 2 AM, having told the women in the parlor that he intended to return and to stay the night. Squier allegedly informed Morgan that he was a frequent visitor.

The sworn testimony of De Witt Clinton Hitchcock, Squier's artist and roommate, was equally incriminating. Hitchcock had known Squier since 1852, had worked as an illustrator for Harper and Brothers and for Frank Leslie, and had roomed with Squier at the Stevens Apartment House in New York since April 1873. One night, after the two of them had attended the theater, Squier proposed that they go to a "house of prostitution" at 44 West Sixteenth Street. Upon arriving at the door, Squier asked for a girl named "Indiana," whom he greeted as an old acquaintance. Squier informed Hitchcock of his plans to spend the night with Indiana, at which time Hitchcock returned home alone. Squier did not return to his apartment until 8 AM, when he informed Hitchcock that he had slept with Indiana. Squier also told him of a girl named "Gypsy" who had a "splendid form" and lived at an assignation house at 27 East Twenty-seventh Street; Squier boasted that he had also slept with her. After visiting the house with Squier, Hitchcock reported: "He showed me the girl's arm and was very free with her person." The two friends also visited the establishment of Lizzie Rice at 106 West Thirty-first Street in April 1873. There were several women present, all of whom, Hitchcock testified, Squier appeared to know.

Justice William R. Curtis read Boese's report on May 30, 1873. He found that the material facts and allegations made in the report were "in all things confirmed" and decreed the Squiers' marriage to be dissolved. The justice further ruled that it was lawful for Miriam to remarry but that it was unlawful for Squier to do so until Miriam's death. The court granted the decree of divorce on May 31, 1873.[16] In a letter, Squier told Miriam's attorney Douglas Campbell that he was thankful that the divorce had gone quickly and quietly, but he maintained that the entire affair "was rotten from the core and can be broken down from foundation to dome by a single wave of my hand." He said he was satisfied that the result was the best for all parties, and knew that it was for him, but added, menacingly, "There is but one chance in a hundred that it [the settlement] will be regretted or disturbed by me. Unless that *single* contingency occurs, my mouth is sealed not in anger, but out of regard for her reputation and the future I hope is in store for her. But if that hundredth contingency shall occur here or abroad, and then no single continent can hold us both." Squier's cryptic reference to "that *single* contingency" was not explained. It might have been his insistence that matters remain private or that Miriam and Leslie not marry. By not contesting the divorce, Squier believed he had "surrendered every consideration of pride and manhood," but his continued silence was conditional. He would not disturb matters so long as matters remained discreet and confidential. His admonition about discretion and leaving matters as they stood, he told Campbell, was "not a threat but a *warning!*" He would not allow his disgrace to be flung in his face throughout the city of New York.[17]

The events that soon followed Squier's divorce suggest that it had taken more from him than his wife – it had also broken his spirit. Two months later he bequeathed his estate and property to his brother Frank. Squier's dispatches and drafts of treaties relating to his diplomatic missions to Central American and Peru, along with his scrapbooks, library, archaeological collections, manuscripts, and personal papers, were part of the bequest. He appointed Frank, his longtime friend Henry B. Anthony, and Malcolm Campbell of New York as the executors of his estate.[18] His troubles were just beginning, however, for on July 13, 1874, Miriam married Frank Leslie. The date of their marriage corresponds almost to the day with the time when Squier began to become mentally unhinged. The two events may have been coincidental, but according to Squier's brother they were inextricably linked. One may speculate on that connection, but the fact remains that Squier's temporary loss of sanity occurred less than a month after Miriam married Leslie.

Concern over Squier's rapidly deteriorating mental state led family and friends to seek professional help. In August 1874, at his brother Frank's request, Justice Charles Donohue of the New York City Court established a commission to inquire into the state of Squier's sanity. Squier was then living under the care and custody of his brother, who testified on August 5, 1874, that E.G. no longer demonstrated reason or understanding. He had been in that condition for better part of the previous month and was incapable of caring for himself or managing his affairs. Dr. A. A. Smith, Squier's personal physician, corroborated Frank's testimony, declaring Squier to be "unsound of mind and understanding." Smith confirmed that Squier had been under his daily care during that time, noting that Squier had difficulty remembering persons, places, and events and was occasionally delusional. He sometimes thought he was in various countries or cities, insisted that the streetcars passing by his residence were "falling waters," and no longer recognized family and friends. Smith thought it unlikely that Squier would ever recover the full extent of his mental faculties, and he agreed that E.G. was no longer able to manage his personal affairs and property.

Dr. Meredith Clymer, president of the Neurological Society of New York and formerly surgeon general of the U.S. Army, concurred with Smith's opinion in every particular. Clymer had known Squier for the past five years, and he became a consulting physician at the request of Squier's friends. He acknowledged that he had also been in attendance upon Squier for the previous three weeks. Clymer stated that during some of his visits the patient actually believed he was in Central America and that at other times he became completely incoherent and irrational in his conversation about the events he imagined were occurring around him. One moment he imagined himself in Central America and the next at Saratoga or just returning from the Hudson. Clymer considered Squier to be entirely incapable of reason and only slightly aware of reality.

The petition of Frank Squier and the supporting affidavits of Drs. Smith and Clymer presented a compelling picture of a disoriented and dependent person. Justice Charles Donohue of the New York Supreme Court declared on August 18, 1874, that Ephraim George Squier was "a lunatic, not having lucid intervals," and entrusted his care, custody, and estate to his brother Frank and his father, Joel. [19] A panel of twenty-four jurors assembled on that date confirmed the inquest's findings. The panel found no signs of "lucid intervals" since approximately July 14 but declared the cause of Squier's insanity as "unknown." At Frank Squier's request, Justice Donohue committed Squier to the Sanford Hall Asylum on August 11.

Squier's certification and commitment as a lunatic was, indeed, a melancholy affair. Those who knew him as a journalist, anthropologist, or diplomat felt a deep sense of personal loss at the sad news. The *New York Herald* characterized Squier's "mad vagaries" as nothing less than an "Eclipse of Genius," attributing his disorder to "over study." [20] Squier most certainly did study, but it was rumored in other papers that the cause of Squier's mental condition was Leslie's marriage to Miriam. The *Brooklyn Union* observed: "Recently the marriage of Mr. Leslie to the divorced wife of Mr. Squier was announced, which, it is reported, had some melancholy effect in ending his journalistic career." [21] Speculation that Squier's mental deterioration was directly attributable to his divorce quickly made the rounds. [22] Some observers saw no reason to doubt the press reports attributing Squier's insanity to Miriam's remarriage. [23] Almost a decade later, the chatty *Town Topics* stated matters even more bluntly: "He was cast into a madhouse, and his successor sat down to enjoy life and love at the hearth he had polluted." [24] Whether that accusation was true or not, Squier undoubtedly felt betrayed when his friend, employer, and fellow lodger married his once beloved "Minnie."

That was certainly the opinion of Squier's brother, who witnessed the entire affair firsthand. Frank stated unequivocally that his brother's divorce and mental breakdown were related: "I consider the circumstances which had produced my brother's lunacy had [also] produced the [Leslie] marriage & the two things together – they were one thing – the same things." [25] The evidence bearing upon that contention neither confirms nor refutes it, but Frank's personal testimony certainly suggests that the two events were more than merely coincidental. Miriam and Leslie were married on July 13, 1874 – one day before Squier's mental disorders were said to have begun. Frank Squier could well say under those circumstances that it was his brother's divorce and Miriam's marriage to Leslie that had brought about his brother's mental condition. [26]

Squier spent several months at the Sanford Hall Asylum, a private facility in Flushing on Long Island, where his physical and mental health gradually began to improve. With the worst of his affliction behind him, he began corresponding again by October 1874. He thought he would soon be as good as ever and was anxious to bring his travels in Peru before the public, a work already in an advanced stage of preparation. He prudently declined to either attempt or to promise too much, but he was determined to see the manuscript published. His Peruvian explorations had cost him much in money and effort, and as he grew more confident in his recovery he became increasingly eager to resume writing. Squier described himself to his parents as "an improved man" and thought his complete recovery would soon follow. No longer bothered by "disordered fancies," he was willing to patiently await his restoration to an active and purposeful life. Squier confessed to Frank that he yearned to again "feel himself a part of the moving world, even while resting on my oars," and thought his afflictions were at last behind him. He expressed surprise at the patience with which he bore his confinement at Sanford Hall, where he cheerfully awaited the day when he could return to working on his papers and manuscripts.[27] Squier continued his recovery and left Sanford Hall in late 1874 or early 1875, when he once again took up residence with Frank and his family in Brooklyn. Squier regained his sanity, but he would never again be self-sufficient. His work as an anthropologist was now behind him.

The sale, in 1874, of Squier's archaeological collection to the American Museum of Natural History, where it had been deposited for an indefinite period of time, offers further evidence that his researches were behind him.[28] Archaeological materials that were formerly part of Squier's personal collection, and acquired at various phases of his career, are today in the American Museum of Natural History at New York and in the Peabody Museum of American Archaeology and Ethnology at Harvard. Edwin Hamilton Davis sold most of the materials recovered in Ohio during his explorations with Squier to William Blackmore of Liverpool and London in 1864, notwithstanding Squier's claim to half ownership. The memorandum of agreement between Davis and Blackmore makes no mention of Squier, who was then conducting archaeological explorations in Peru. Blackmore displayed his collection at the Blackmore Museum in Salisbury after it opened in 1867. The British Museum purchased the Ohio materials in the Davis Collection in 1931, and they remain there today as part of the North American Indian collections.[29]

More than any other, the event that announced the effective close of Squier's career was the sale of his cherished library. Bangs, Merwin, and Company sold the Squier library and manuscript collection at public auction in New York on April 24, 1876. Few private collections in the United States rivaled Squier's library, which paid ample testimony to the range and depth of the interests and accomplishments that had earned him international recognition as a scholar. Squier's library consisted of 2,034 items at the time of its sale. The books, manuscripts, maps, drawings, engravings, and photographs in the collection related mostly to Central America, Peru, and the general subject of American antiquities. The American bibliographer Joseph Sabin judged the Central American portion of Squier's library superior to any other then in existence. Several of the books bore Central American imprints and were almost entirely unknown outside their place of publication. Parting with such a collection under any circumstances would have been difficult for Squier, but its sale in 1876 was itself part of the personal tragedy that followed his temporary bout with insanity in 1874. The books, manuscripts, photographs, and drawings in that collection represented the labor of an extraordinarily productive lifetime.

Among the more significant items were volumes of newspapers and pamphlets relating to the political history of Central America, works on the proposed Central American canal, copies of Squier's own works in various languages, bound volumes of *Frank Leslie's Illustrated Newspaper*, a series of bound transcriptions of sixteenth-century manuscripts relating to Central America copied from Spanish repositories, manuscript maps and printed maps relating to Spanish America, several engravings, original drawings by Frederick Catherwood of architectural remains in Yucatán, a large and significant collection of photographs mostly relating to his explorations in Peru, volumes of the *Jesuit Relations*, and several books from the library of Alexander von Humboldt.[30] Squier greatly admired Humboldt and sought to emulate him as a world traveler and author. Humboldt's views on the natural causes explaining similarities or analogies between peoples remotely separated by time and place significantly influenced Squier's own writings. Squier must have been genuinely flattered, and perhaps somewhat fulfilled, when Sabin expressed the opinion that Squier's capacity for research and writing was unsurpassed since the time of Baron von Humboldt.[31]

Hubert Howe Bancroft of San Francisco purchased the Central American materials in the Squier collection as a valued addition to his own library. The books and manuscripts in the Squier collection, said Bancroft, were "by far the best in existence, better than he himself [apparently meaning Squier] could again make even if he had twenty more years in which to attempt it." The purchase added greatly to Bancroft's holdings, "but the number was not commensurate with the rarity and value of the books."[32] The University of California at Berkeley acquired the Bancroft library, including the Squier materials, in 1907. An examination of the acquisition records and index cards relating to Bancroft's purchase of the Squier materials attests to the accuracy of Bancroft's statement about their historical value. They clearly indicate, moreover, the titles that Squier had hoped to add to his *Collection of Rare and Original Documents and Relations*, which had appeared in its first and last number in 1860. Squier went to considerable lengths to identify and publish reliable Spanish and other European manuscript sources on the aboriginal peoples of the American continent. He was among those who suggested in 1856 that the Smithsonian publish, in the original Spanish, Castanede's and Jarramillo's accounts of the Spanish expeditions to New Mexico between 1540 and 1542. Their accounts provide the earliest trustworthy information on the condition of the native groups encountered by the Spanish, groups who were reported to be industrious agricultural peoples living in peaceful communities and speaking diverse languages. Such accounts would be of great interest to American ethnologists in their efforts to understand the affinities of the different groups of American aborigines. [33] While in Europe in 1859, Squier made a considerable effort to obtain copies of manuscript materials in European archives. He copied a manuscript relating to the Saguenay Indians below Quebec while visiting the British Museum, one of the lost manuscripts of Boturini while at Paris, and also a "Mexican School Book on History" written on native Maguey paper illustrating the aboriginal method recording historical events and chronology with hieroglyphics and drawings. [34]

In 1877, with his brother's help, Squier was finally able to complete and publish his long-awaited *Peru*, and in 1880 he published a pamphlet on *Honduras and British Honduras*. [35] The light of reason returned to him, even though he would remain a shadow of his former self. It was then that Squier broke his strange silence about his divorce and the relationship between Miriam and Frank Leslie. The final chapter relating to that sordid affair unfolded by a circuitous and seemingly unlikely route, but one that ultimately began with Squier. The Leslies made a two-month tour of the West between April 10 and June 7, 1877, traveling in the company of twelve editors, journalists, and artists. Accounts of the excursion appeared in *Leslie's Illustrated Newspaper* between April 1877 and May 1878 as a series of illustrated articles entitled "Across the Continent." Miriam gave her own account of the journey in *California: A Pleasure Trip from Gotham to the Golden Gate*, published in December 1877. [36] There she made some disdainful remarks about conditions in the silver-mining town of Virginia City, Nevada. "To call a place dreary, desolate, homeless, uncomfortable, and wicked is a good deal," she wrote, "but to call it God-forsaken is a good deal more, and in a tolerably large experience of this world's wonders, we never found a place better deserving the title than Virginia City." [37] Local architecture, she noted, consisted of a fine hotel and few substantial stone and brick buildings, but they were the exception. The more numerous frame houses were "as loosely and carelessly put together as a child's card house." The city was lawless and funerals frequent. The population consisted mostly of men, with very few women except for those of "the worst class." Every other house was a drinking or gambling saloon, where audacious-looking women spoke openly with those who passed by or entertained guests inside. Two policemen accompanied the Leslie entourage, not as an honor guard or a courtesy but as "a most necessary protection." [38]

Miriam would pay dearly for those comments, although she could not possibly have imagined the tempest they would provoke. Rollin M. Daggett, editor of Virginia City's *Daily Territorial Enterprise*, was determined to have a measure of revenge for her uncharitable comments on local society. Daggett apparently had journalistic connections with Squier, who was then living with his brother and apparently supplied Daggett with the incriminating information about Miriam's early life and first marriage, which was contained in the Peacock Judgment Roll recorded in the New York Supreme Court. Miriam's alleged extramarital relations with Leslie and the scandal of the Squier divorce added extra piquancy to Daggett's attack. Only Squier or his brother could have provided such intimate and detailed knowledge of Miriam's life, especially its more delicate episodes. Or at least that is the conclusion reached by Madeline Stern, Miriam's biographer, after some superior sleuthing. There is no reason to dissent from her conclusion. Indeed, it is significant to note that a transcript of the Peacock Judgment Roll is in the Squier Family Papers of the New-York Historical Society. The opportunity to cause the Leslies public embarrassment for the humiliations and disappointments of Squier's own marriage and divorce apparently proved too much for E.G. to resist. It is possible that a disgruntled Leslie employee, one of Squier's friends, or even his brother could have provided Daggett with the sordid details found in the Peacock Judgment Roll, but even then Squier would have been the indirect source. The details are simply too intimate and too complete to have been known by anyone else.

Daggett made the origin and purpose of the piece crystal clear. "In order to show the character of the authoress," he wrote, "we sent to New York and had the history of the Leslie family written out, together with the certified records of courts in which Mrs. Leslie figured in the past." The account that follows appears as a letter to the editor of the *Enterprise* from an anonymous source.

In giving you an account of Mr. and Mrs. Frank Leslie, I may as well commence by saying that there is no love between us, but I will try and "set down naught in malice," but give you the tale as it is, and give you only those things I do know. To show up this couple it is only necessary to tell the truth, as nothing that could be said about them would be one half as damaging as the truth. I think there is nothing in this statement but can be fully proven. I have known Mrs. Leslie for twenty years and over, and I first knew Mr. Leslie eighteen years ago. I have lived with both of them, and have done and received many favors from both, but in the end have received more damage than can be ever blotted out by all the favors they gave or ever can give. They have set aside all the laws of God and man, and there is nothing in their lives which will indicate that they had any fear of either. Their own selfish ends have been their only thoughts, and the connection of Leslie with the press has kept him from being exposed long ago. The press of New York have never written him up, and if he is ever shown up, it will be done by some out-of-town party, like the ENTERPRISE. I leave the last with them, requesting that they do not use the name of young Follin, for the sake of his family, and that this shall be at least partly rewritten, and that my name shall in no way be brought out. [39]

Daggett honored his informant's request for anonymity and, apparently, his request that it be partially rewritten. However, no one familiar with the details of Squier's marriage, divorce, and professional relationship with Leslie can for a moment doubt that Squier was Daggett's nameless source. Only Squier could have provided the information contained in that account. Both the internal evidence and the materials found in the Squier Family Papers at the New-York Historical Society confirm that Squier was the anonymous source of the exposé and that he probably wrote it too. He decided that it was time to break his long silence about Leslie and his former wife, and he was determined to have the last word.

The certified court records printed in the Enterprise were those relating to the annulment of Miriam's marriage to David Charles Peacock in 1856. The records of the annulment proceedings were collectively filed in the court as the Peacock Judgment Roll, a transcript of which is among the Squier Family Papers at the New-York Historical Society. That is undoubtedly the transcript that Daggett printed verbatim at the end of Squier's anonymous excoriation of the Leslies. It is interesting to note that this transcript is certified as having been made on July 19, 1873, by Charles E. Loew, clerk of the City and County of New York and clerk of the New York Supreme Court. That is seven weeks after the May 31 divorce decree in the case of Squier v. Squier and one year before Miriam married Frank Leslie. Clearly, Squier planned to use the document against Miriam at some point should it prove necessary or desirable to do so. That he did not to do so before 1878 is largely attributable to the onset of mental illness. When Daggett "sent to New York" in 1877 or 1878 for the history of the Leslies, Squier's illness had passed. The return of lucidity, the desire for revenge, and Daggett's invitation to publicly embarrass the Leslies was simply too great for Squier to resist.

Daggett pulled no punches in his assault on Miriam's character. The front page of the Enterprise for July 14, 1878, reads: "OUR FEMALE SLANDERER. MRS. FRANK LESLIE'S BOOK SCANDALIZING THE FAMILIES OF VIRGINIA CITY – THE HISTORY OF THE AUTHORESS – A LIFE DRAMA OF CRIME AND LICENTIOUSNESS – STARTLING DEVELOPMENTS." Daggett reprinted his excoriation as a twenty-four-page pamphlet entitled TERRITORIAL ENTERPRISE EXTRA. CONTAINING A FULL ACCOUNT OF "FRANK LESLIE" AND WIFE. [40] Few details of the "strange and eventful history" of Mrs. Frank Leslie were spared in the denunciation. Her birth out of wedlock, her marriage to Peacock, her interlude on the stage as Lola Montez, her extramarital activities with Leslie, and her divorce from Squier were trotted out for public view. According to the Enterprise, Miriam and Frank Leslie had thrown Squier away like an old toy: "Squiers [sic] was put [to] one side and spent a dog's life." He soon turned to hard drinking as a means of drowning his sorrows and coping with the notoriety of the Squier-Leslie living arrangements. The Enterprise accused Miriam and her accomplices of concocting the charges of adultery against Squier as a means of obtaining grounds for divorce:

> She planned a grand dinner, which was to be given at a disreputable house in West Twenty-seventh street, to which the demi monde of the city were to be invited. Leslie artists were to be "upon the spot"; sketches were to be made, and it was all to be illustrated in the highly moral paper published by Frank Leslie, Esq., called the Days Doings. They all went. Squiers [sic] was made drunk; fell into the hands of one of the girls called "Gipsey" [sic], just as it had been arranged by our lady. Within one week a divorce suit was commenced against him. He was too much broken in mind to appear, having at that time the seeds of disease, not fully developed in his brain, but which afterwards brought him to the edge of the grave, and left him a helpless wreck for the rest of his days.

Whether such collusion actually occurred is unknown, but the court found the case against Squier to be a strong one. It did not help that he refused to appear in court or to defend himself against the charges, regardless of their truth or falsity.

Squier at length had exacted a measure of revenge against the Leslies. The bitterness and humiliation stemming from Miriam's marriage to Leslie had finally gotten the better of him. It does not appear that the Leslies ever responded to the scurrilous charges made in the Enterprise, but Frank Leslie did buy every copy of the paper he could find in an effort to control the damage. He also hired a detective to identify Daggett's anonymous New York informant. [41] But there could have been no doubt in Miriam's mind as to whom that person was. Only Squier or his brother could have provided Daggett with such intimate details about Miriam's life – details she had previously managed to hide.

Squier spent the final decade of his life uneventfully, and apparently comfortably, in his brother's Brooklyn home. In September 1878 he confessed to his parents that he had begun to feel the approach of age but was otherwise fine.[42] He periodically rallied himself to answer a letter, but by the 1880s Frank was handling most of his correspondence. Squier recovered from his bout with mental illness, but he never regained his once redoubtable energy and enormous capacity for work. He passed the next eight years in relative silence. His library and archaeological collection were gone, as was the ambition that had once driven him forward in all of his various enterprises. Most of the personal papers and manuscripts that so readily attest to his many activities and interests were still in the care and custody of his brother, but for Squier they had largely served their purpose. He died at Frank's home on April 17, 1888, at age sixty-seven.[43] Squier's life was fuller and more celebrated than most, and the force of his personality left an indelible impression on those who knew him. He was vain and ambitious and seldom brooked a rival, but his many friends valued his gregariousness, wit, and charm. He made several enemies in life but far more friends.

American anthropology at the time of Squier's death had already passed him by and was well on its way to becoming a specialized and integrated profession. Not only were the avocational anthropologists of Squier's generation passing from the scene, but later investigators had already overthrown the common stock of many of their assumptions and assertions. And yet Squier in many respects is no worse for the comparison. He is among a handful of investigators whose individual interests and activities collectively defined American anthropology from the 1840s to the 1870s. The *Baltimore American* noted of Squier in 1874 that his scholarship and activities in the American Ethnological Society had greatly advanced the development of American anthropology, while his popular writings and lectures had promoted a general appreciation of American archaeology among the public.[44] That is a fitting legacy for Squier, whose archaeological and ethnological writings, both popular and scholarly, appeared in a not insignificant stream between the appearance of *Ancient Monuments of the Mississippi Valley* in 1848 and *Peru* in 1877. His body of work significantly contributed to the development of American archaeology and ethnology as incipient fields of scientific inquiry, an ongoing process that made a faltering but significant beginning in the mid-nineteenth century.

For a biographer, Squier is both a delight and a nightmare – there are so many materials with which to work, so many interests and activities that must be taken into account, and so many fascinating personalities that must be linked together within the confines of an exceedingly busy life. Few individuals have documented their exploits and adventures through such extensive collections of correspondence, manuscripts, books, pamphlets, and contributions to periodicals. It has been well said that a bibliography of Squier's writings is a better biography of his life than will ever be written. [45] That is undoubtedly true. Squier's motto, "Ten to One the Feather Beats the Iron," reflects the literary ambitions and love of writing that sustained him from age nineteen onward as an extraordinarily gifted and prolific writer. It is my hope that this study has contributed to a better understanding of his contributions to the development of American anthropology, which, after all, occupied but one corner of a very crowded life.

A NOTE ON ARCHIVAL SOURCES

At the time of his death in 1888, Squier left a mass of correspondence and manuscripts in the possession of his brother and executor Frank Squier. The sheer volume and scope of these materials lends powerful testimony to his accomplishments in various endeavors. And yet they represent only the remains of a larger collection that existed before the sale of Squier's library in 1876. His papers, manuscripts, photographs, and personal copies of his own books eventually found their way into several archives by both direct and indirect routes. Many of the items sold in 1876 changed hands over the years among private collectors and were eventually either donated or sold to the different repositories that today possess collections of Squier materials. The archival sources relating to Squier's archaeological and ethnological inquiries are essential in tracing the development of American anthropology from the mid-1840s to the early 1870s.

The Library of Congress acquired the largest number of Squier manuscripts in 1905 as a gift from Frank Squier. Additions to the collection were made through subsequent donations, purchases, and transfers between 1941 and 1994. William Gates donated additional Squier materials to the Library of Congress in 1941, which were further supplemented in 1948 by a purchase of Squier papers in the possession of Richard S. Wormser. The Squier Papers at the Library of Congress include approximately 2,500 items dating from 1841 to 1884, with most of the material dating from 1846 to 1874. These materials include correspondence, diplomatic documents, and business records relating to the Honduras Interoceanic Railway; lectures on archaeology and ethnology; and articles, bibliographic notes, drawings, and scrapbooks of newspaper clippings that represent the single most important collection of Squier papers.

Squier's general correspondence at the Library of Congress dates from 1841 to 1888 and, taken together with his Book File (1848–77), is particularly important in documenting his contributions to archaeology and ethnology. The collection further consists of some five hundred pages of manuscript notes and drafts of *Ancient Monuments of the Mississippi Valley* (1848), fifty pages of plates for the engravings in that work, drafts of the first ten chapters of *Nicaragua* (1852), drafts of *The Serpent Symbol*, and some five hundred pages of manuscript notes relating to the archaeology of Central America, descriptions of Central American Indians, aboriginal vocabularies and languages of Mexico and Central America, Mexican and Central American drawings or pictographs, notes on serpent symbolism and the origin of phallic worship, extracts from sixteenth- and seventeenth-century sources relating to the exploration of the

American continent, and an unpublished "Memoir on the didactic paintings and the figurative writings of the ancient Mexicans."[1]

Squier may well have intended to publish that manuscript as part of his projected works on the Mexican calendar and the mythological system of the ancient Mexicans. He never completed those projects, which he intended to publish as part of his American Archaeological Researches series, of which *The Serpent Symbol* was the only number ever published. A collection of thirty-nine manuscript maps of Central America and Peru by Squier are also among the materials in the Geography and Map Division of the Library of Congress. The Library of Congress acquired the Squier maps, along with related field notes, in 1909 from Dr. Stewart Culin of the Brooklyn Institution of Arts and Sciences. The collection received its first notice in the *Quarterly Journal of the Library of Congress* in 1972.[2] Squier delineated the maps during his diplomatic, archaeological, and entrepreneurial undertakings in Nicaragua between 1849 and 1850, in Honduras between 1853 and 1854, and in Peru between 1863 and 1865.

Important collections of Squier letters and documents are in the Squier Family Papers and the Ephraim George Squier Papers of the New-York Historical Society. These are separate but related collections. The Squier Family Papers consist of four boxes, which primarily contain letters from Squier to family members and other documents directly concerning him. Correspondence and manuscript materials relating to his father, Joel Squier (1798–1891), and his brothers, Charles Wesley Squier (1836–69) and Frank Squier (1840–1908), are also part of the Squier Family Papers. The letters from Squier to his parents in the Squier Family Papers are invaluable for the insights they provide into his personality and multifaceted activities. The Squier Family Papers also provide details regarding his temporary insanity in 1874 and of his last years with his brother Frank. The Ephraim George Squier Papers proper at the New-York Historical Society consist of eight bound volumes with two boxes of manuscript bibliographies and notes compiled by Squier's nephew Frank Squier between 1938 and 1950. The Squier Papers contain certificates of membership in learned societies; official diplomatic correspondence, dispatches, and documents; a scrapbook relating to his activities in Nicaragua between 1849 and 1850; and correspondence from 1857 to 1859 relating to the Honduras Interoceanic Railway. Squier's letters and documents are available on microfilm as the Ephraim George Squier Papers of the New-York Historical Society, but the microfilm does not always clearly distinguish between the two collections. It is sometimes still necessary to consult the boxes and bound volumes of the originals for correct citations.

Manuscript materials relating to Squier's anthropological career are also present in the Ephraim George Squier Papers at the Latin American Library of Tulane University in New Orleans. This collection includes materials from 1835 to 1872, most of which date from between 1849 and 1872. The Middle American Research Institute of Tulane University purchased the collection from William Gates in 1924, who had purchased the materials in 1917. The collection includes correspondence dating between 1835 and 1871, portions of manuscripts and notes used in preparing Squier's major and minor writings on Central America, publishing contracts, unpublished "Notes on Central American Indians," and a manuscript on "Universal Primitive Religion." The Tulane collection contains notes used in the preparation of *Peru*, pencil and ink drawings of various archaeological sites and artifacts, and an extensive collection of photographs of Honduras and Peru from the 1850s and 1860s.

The photographs in the collection mostly consist of stereopticon views of Peruvian landscapes and archeological remains taken in 1863 and 1864. The photographs were sold in 1876 as part of Squier's library and were subsequently acquired by the Middle American Research Institute.[3] The collection also includes clippings of articles and book reviews from American, British, and French newspapers and periodicals that Squier had collected throughout his active years as a scholar. Many of the press clippings report on the proceedings of ethnological societies, museums, and various subjects relating to the archaeology and ethnology of North America, Central and South America, and Asia.[4] The Squier Papers at the Latin American Library of Tulane University are available on microfilm with a printed guide. Squier's photographs were not microfilmed for inclusion in the microfilm edition of the collection, but copies are available from the Latin American Library.

The Ephraim George Squier Papers at the William L. Clements Library of the University of Michigan has forty-six items dating from 1818 to 1886. This is a miscellaneous collection of correspondence consisting primarily of letters sent to Squier. Most of it relates to his various diplomatic appointments. The finding aid for the collection says that it contains "the manuscript" of Squier and Davis's *Ancient Monuments of the Mississippi Valley*, but an earlier edition of the guide makes no mention of its existence. The manuscript is not, in fact, a part of the collection. The Clements Library has a copy of the Bartlett and Welford edition of *Ancient Monuments* that has the notation "author's own copy," which may account for the confusion. The only manuscript drafts of *Ancient Monuments* of which I am aware are those in the Squier Papers at the Library of Congress. The final version of the manuscript as published by the Smithsonian Institution has never been found. The woodcut engravings used to illustrate *Ancient Monuments* perished in the Smithsonian fire of 1865, and it is possible that the draft of the manuscript that was actually printed was lost at the same time.

Smaller but significant collections of Squier letters and manuscripts have found their way into other repositories. The Harry E. Huntington Library in San Marino, California, has several hundred items relating to Squier's entrepreneurial activities between 1852 and 1858 in the Honduras Interoceanic Railway Company, but the collection is not significant in terms of his contributions to anthropology. A small collection of Squier manuscript materials circa 1845–70 are also in the Ephraim George Squier Papers at the Western Reserve Historical Society in Cleveland, Ohio. The collection consists of an address book, pocket diaries, memoranda books, and other bound and unbound notes (some in Spanish) kept by Squier. Also present are plates showing prehistoric earthworks in Ohio, Indiana, Kentucky, Louisiana, South Carolina, and Wisconsin; some of Squier's writings, such as a proof copy of an article on "Notices of the minor departments of aboriginal art"; approximately forty-five pages of notes on the Inca Empire; and a 283-page manuscript copy of a "A Trip to Salvador," which describes a journey from La Union in San Salvador to San Vicente.

The Squier Papers at the Indiana Historical Society (1838–1905) are part of the Manuscript Collections Department of the William Henry Smith Memorial Library.[5] They consist of three manuscript boxes of letters, printed articles, transcripts, newspaper clippings, miscellaneous scrapbooks, and notebooks. Almost all of the letters were written to Squier and date from 1842 to 1874. Two of the notebooks relate to writings on archaeology, and a scrapbook, circa 1847, is entitled "Mss on American Antiquities." A number of drawings and maps of archaeological sites and transcripts of correspondence from Squier to Francis Parkman dating from 1849 to 1868 are also present. Eli Lilly donated the materials to the Indiana Historical Society in 1958 together with seventy books by Squier and twenty-two by others that were Squier's personal copies. The clippings and notes that were contained between the pages of these books have been removed and placed in folders. The manuscript materials primarily relate to Squier's diplomatic and entrepreneurial activities in Central America and his journalistic work for Frank Leslie. The correspondence in this collection is not extensive, but it contains significant details about little-known corners of a crowded and very public life. A portion of the collection has been microfilmed.

The Ephraim George Squier Papers at the American Antiquarian Society in Worcester, Massachusetts, contain a folder of letters dating from 1847 to 1848 relating to the Squier-Davis investigations and their request for financial assistance. It includes letters from Edwin Hamilton Davis to John Davis and

Samuel Foster Haven as well as Haven's report on his fact-finding tour to the scene of the Squier-Davis investigations in Ohio. The collection contains maps and surveys of archaeological sites together with sketches of artifacts as part of incoming letters from both Squier and Davis. The collection is particularly important for documenting Davis's active interest in the investigations and the ultimately unsuccessful effort by both he and Squier to secure the society's financial assistance. This correspondence should be read together with Davis's letters to Squier in the Library of Congress and letters from both Squier and Davis to Samuel George Morton in the Morton Papers of the Library Company of Philadelphia. Collectively they are essential for understanding the Squier-Davis association and the mutual contributions of each.

Other important letters relating to Squier's archaeological investigations in the 1840s and 1850s are in the Joseph Henry Papers at the Smithsonian Institution Archives, which also include copies of outgoing correspondence. Letters from Edwin Hamilton Davis to Henry dating from the 1840s through the 1870s are also present in the Henry Papers. A smaller number of letters from Davis to Charles Rau and Spencer Baird written in the 1880s are in other record groups of the Smithsonian Institution Archives. Edwin Hamilton Davis Jr. and his sister Betsy B. Davis donated their father's portfolio of watercolor drawings to the archives of the Smithsonian Institution's Bureau of American Ethnology in 1928, which today forms part of the National Anthropological Archives of the Smithsonian Institution. See "Sketches of Monuments and Antiques; Found in the Mounds, Tombs and Ancient Cities of America: Arranged, Classified, and Described by Edwin Hamilton Davis, A.M., M.D." (New York, 1858). The title page of the Davis portfolio is dated 1858, but some sheets were added at a later date.

Letters relating to Squier's archaeological fieldwork in Ohio and New York are among the John Russell Bartlett Papers at the John Carter Brown Library in Providence, Rhode Island, and the Samuel George Morton Papers of the Library Company of Philadelphia. The Morton Papers are particularly important. It should be noted, however, that the manuscript collections of the Library of Philadelphia, including the Morton Papers, are physically housed at the Historical Society of Pennsylvania through a reciprocal agreement regarding books and manuscripts. The Morton Papers include letters from both Squier and Davis relating to their research activities. This collection, like the Squier Papers at the American Antiquarian Society, further documents Davis's interest and involvement in the investigations. A microfilm edition of the Squier and Davis letters present in the Morton Papers is available from the Historical Society of Philadelphia, but it incorrectly identifies the letters as the Squier-Davis Papers of the Historical Society of Pennsylvania instead of the Morton Papers of the Library Company of Philadelphia. The Library Company of Philadelphia should be credited in citations of these letters.

Squier letters are also found in the Charles Eliot Norton Papers at the Houghton Library of Harvard University and in the Francis Parkman Papers at the Massachusetts Historical Society in Boston. Transcripts of original letters from Squier to Parkman in the Parkman Papers at the Massachusetts Historical Society are in the Squier Papers at the New-York Historical Society and the Squier Papers at the Indiana Historical Society. Parkman's letters to Squier were compiled and published by Don Carlos Seitz as *Letters from Francis Parkman to E. G. Squier: With Biographical Notes and a Bibliography of E. G. Squier* (1911). The Squier-Parkman correspondence is important and should be brought together in an annotated edition. Squier's letters to Parkman are particularly revealing of his activities, interests, and ambitions over several decades.

Squier's collection of sixteenth- and seventeenth-century Spanish manuscripts was sold as part of his library in 1876. Buckingham Smith, the former secretary of the legation of the United States to Spain, gathered a large portion of the materials for Squier from various Spanish archives and repositories. Squier acquired others during his travels in Central America, either directly himself or through the good offices of friends. It was his intention to translate and publish the manuscripts in a series entitled *A Collection of Rare and Original Documents and Relations, Concerning the Discovery and Conquest of America*. He never completed the project as designed, but he did manage to publish one of manuscripts. The letter written by Don Diego Garcia de Palacio, auditor of the Audiencia of Guatemala, to the King of Spain in 1576 appeared in 1860 as the first and only number of the proposed series.[6] Hubert Howe Bancroft purchased the Central American materials in the Squier collection, including the manuscripts. The University of California at Berkeley acquired the Bancroft library, including the Squier materials, in 1907.

Squier corresponded widely with scholars, business associates, and government officials in the United States, Europe, and Central America. No attempt has been made to locate fugitive letters in the personal papers of Squier's many and far-flung acquaintances. Those letters no doubt exist, and several of them may well relate to his archaeological and ethnological interests. A list of Squier's published works relating to archaeology and ethnology appears in the accompanying bibliography.

NOTES

Abbreviations

DFP   Duyckinck Family Papers. Manuscripts and Archives Division, New York Public Library.

JRBP   John Russell Bartlett Papers. John Carter Brown Library, Brown University. Providence, Rhode Island.

SFP   Squier Family Papers. New-York Historical Society. New York, New York.

SGMP   Samuel George Morton Papers. Library Company of Philadelphia. Philadelphia, Pennsylvania.

SPAAS   Ephraim George Squier Papers. American Antiquarian Society. Worcester, Massachusetts.

SPIHS   Ephraim George Squier Papers. Indiana Historical Society. Indianapolis, Indiana.

SPLAL   Ephraim George Squier Papers. Latin American Library, Tulane University Library. New Orleans.

SPLC   Ephraim George Squier Papers. Library of Congress. Washington DC.

PROLOGUE

1. See C. S. Rafinesque, "Anthropology: The Fundamental Base of the Philosophy of Human Speech, or Philology and Ethnology," *Atlantic Journal* 1, no. 2 (1832): 48–54.

2. Luke Burke, ed., introduction to the *Ethnological Journal* 1 (June 1848): 1–2; see also Josiah Clark Nott and George Robins Gliddon, *Types of Mankind: Or, Ethnological Researches, Based on Ancient Monuments, Paintings, Sculptures, and Crania of Races* (Philadelphia: Lippincott, Grambo, 1854), 49, on ethnology's leading characteristics and claims to attention.

3. E. G. Squier, "American Ethnology: Being a Summary of Some of the Results Which Have Followed the Investigation of this Subject," *American Review*, n.s., 3 (April 1849): 385–98.

4. See Terry A. Barnhart, "Toward a Science of Man: European Influences on the Archaeology of Ephraim George Squier," in *New Perspectives on the Origins of Americanist Archaeology*, ed. David L. Browman and Stephen Williams (Tuscaloosa: University of Alabama Press, 2002), 87–116.

5. William Stanton, *The Leopard's Spots: Scientific Attitudes toward Race in America, 1815–1859* (Chicago: University of Chicago Press, 1960), 10.

6. See E. G. Squier, "The Monumental Evidence of the Discovery of America by the Northmen Critically Examined," *Ethnological Journal* 1 (December 1848): 313–25; and C. A. Adolf Zestermann, *Memoir on the European Colonization of America in Ante-Historic Times, with Critical Observations Thereon, by E. G. Squier* (London: Bateman and Hardwicke, 1851), a pamphlet reprinted from the proceedings of the American Ethnological Society, April 1851.

7. Barry Alan Joyce, *The Shaping of American Ethnography: The Wilkes Exploring Expedition, 1838–1842* (Lincoln: University of Nebraska Press, 2001), 2.

8. Joan Mark, "Towards an Organized Community of Anthropologists," in *Four Anthropologists: An American Science in Its Early Years* (New York: Science History Publications, 1980), 5–13; Sally Gregory Kohlstedt, *The Formation of the American Scientific Community: The American Association for the Advancement of Science, 1848–1860* (Urbana: University of Illinois Press, 1976), x.

9. See the following works by John Higham: *From Boundlessness to Consolidation: The Transformation of American Culture, 1848–1860* (Ann Arbor: The Clements Library, 1969) and "The Matrix of Specialization," in *The Organization of Knowledge in Modern America, 1860–1920*, ed. Alexandra Oleson and John Voss (Baltimore: Johns Hopkins University Press, 1979), 3–18.

10. Nott and Gliddon, *Types of Mankind*, ix.

11. *Anthropological Review* 6 (1868): lxxix–lxxxiii. The notice is a premature obituary of Josiah Clark Nott, who did not die until 1873. One can imagine the great pleasure it gave Nott to read of his own death. He could only have been pleased, however, with the prominent place that the *Anthropological Review* assigned him in the history of anthropology.

12. James B. Griffin commented on this aspect of the archaeology of Squier and Davis in his introduction to the 1973 reprint of *Ancient Monuments of the Mississippi Valley* by AMS Press for Harvard University's Peabody Museum of Archaeology and Ethnology. See *Antiquities of the New World, Early Explorations in Archaeology*, vol. 2, *Ancient Monuments of the Mississippi Valley* (New York: AMS Press, 1973), viii–ix. There he notes Squier and Davis's use of historic accounts of American Indian groups and other non-European cultures to interpret archaeological evidence, "thus following an accepted anthropological pattern of interpretation." Squier made extensive use of cross-cultural analogies in all of his subsequent works.

13. Gordon R. Willey and Jeremy A. Sabloff, *A History of American Archaeology*, 2nd ed. (San Francisco: Freeman, 1980), 1.

14. John A. Garraty, *The Nature of Biography* (New York: Knopf, 1957), ix.

15. David B. Davis, "Some Recent Directions in Cultural History," *American Historical Review* 73 (February 1968): 705.

16. Jacob Gruber, "In Search of Experience: Biography as an Instrument for

the History of Anthropology," in *Pioneers of American Anthropology: The Uses of Biography*, ed. June Helm (Seattle: University of Washington Press, 1966), 6; see also Douglas Givens, "The Role of Biography in the History of Archaeology," in *Rediscovering Our Past: Essays in the History of American Archaeology*, ed. J. E. Reyman (Brookfield VT: Avebury, 1992), 51–66.

17. Regna Darnell, ed., *Readings in the History of Anthropology* (New York: Harper and Row, 1974), 2.

18. As Jennifer L. Croissant has noted regarding the history of archaeology in her "Narrating Archaeology: A Historiography and Notes toward a Sociology of Archaeological Knowledge," in *It's about Time: A History of Archaeological Dating in North America*, ed. Stephen E. Nash (Salt Lake City: University of Utah Press, 2000), 186–206.

19. See Regna Darnell, *Invisible Genealogies: A History of Americanist Anthropology* (Lincoln: University of Nebraska Press, 2001), xvii–xxvi, 1–30; and Irving A. Hallowell, "The History of Anthropology as an Anthropological Problem," *Journal of the History of the Behavioral Sciences* 1 (1965): 24–38.

20. Herbert Butterfield, *The Whig Interpretation of History* (London: G. Bell and Sons, 1931). Several historians have elaborated upon the distortions arising from presentism in history, but priority must be given to Butterfield's seminal discussion of the problem.

21. David Hackett Fischer, *Historians' Fallacies: Toward a Logic of Historical Thought* (New York: Harper and Row, 1970), 135.

22. See Thomas S. Kuhn, *The Structure of Scientific Revolutions* (Chicago: University of Chicago Press, 1962).

23. See George W. Stocking Jr., *Race, Culture, and Evolution: Essays in the History of Anthropology* (New York: Free Press, 1968), and his "On the Limits of 'Presentism' and 'Historicism' in the Historiography of the Behavioral Sciences," *Journal of the History of the Behavioral Sciences* 1 (1965): 211–17.

24. Christopher Chippendale, " 'Social Archaeology' in the Nineteenth Century: Is It Right to Look for Modern Ideas in Old Places?" in *Tracing Archaeology's Past: The Historiography of Archaeology*, ed. Andrew L. Christenson (Carbondale: Southern Illinois University Press, 1989), 23.

25. Regna Darnell and Stephen O. Murray, "Series Editors' Introduction," in Darnell, *Invisible Genealogies*, xiii.

26. Christenson, *Tracing Archaeology's Past*, x; see also Robert L. Schuyler, "The History of American Archaeology: An Examination of Procedure," *American Antiquity* 36 (1971): 383–409.

27. Bruce G. Trigger, "The Coming of Age of the History of Archaeology," *Journal of Archaeological Research* 2, no. 1 (1994): 125.

28. On the pervasive influence of Franz Boas and his students as a problem

in the history of American anthropology, see Darnell, *Invisible Genealogies*, 33–67; Donald McVicker, "Prejudice and Context: The Anthropological Archaeologist and Historian," in Christenson, *Tracing Archaeology's Past*, 113–26; and Bruce G. Trigger, "Writing the History of Archaeology: A Survey of Trends," in *Objects and Others: Essays on Museum and Material Culture*, ed. George W. Stocking Jr. (Madison: University of Wisconsin Press, 1985), 225.

29. Trigger, "Coming of Age," 125–26.

30. Thomas G. Tax, "The Development of American Archaeology, 1800–1879" (Ph.D. diss., University of Chicago, 1973), 1–2.

31. Willey and Sabloff, *History of American Archaeology*, xi.

1. LITERARY AMBITIONS

1. Frank Squier, "Ephraim George Squier, 1821–1888," SFP; Terry A. Barnhart, "Ephraim George Squier," in *American National Biography*, ed. John A. Garraty and Marc C. Carnes (New York: Oxford University Press, 1999), 20:519–20.

2. Squier to parents, West Poultney, [Vermont], June 30, 1839, SFP. Ephraim's school and living expenses between 1836 and 1846 are documented in Joel Squier, Account Book (1836–83), SFP. See also School Scrapbook, Troy Academy, 1839–1840, and John Neuman to Frank Squier, Poultney, August 20, 1874, SPIHS.

3. Squier to parents, Albany, December 30, 1841, SFP.

4. [James D. Whelpley], "Mr. E. G. Squier: Charge d'Affaires, Central America," *American Review*, n.s., 6 (October 1850): 347–48; Squier to the editor, *London Athenaeum*, December 7, 1869.

5. E. G. S., "To the Public" and "Prospectus of the Literary Pearl," *Literary Pearl*, November 18, 1840, 7, 8.

6. Mrs. E. C. Stedman, "Lines to the Literary Pearl," *Literary Pearl*, December 30, 1840, 52.

7. Squier's earliest-known published work is a poem entitled "Spring," which appeared in James H. Chappell's *Philadelphia Visiter* 6, no. 5 (May 1840): 113.

8. See Joel Munsell to Squier, Albany, November 6, 1843, and two undated letters, SPIHS.

9. [E. G. Squier], "Our Corner," *Lady's Cabinet Magazine*, January 1842, 204; Squier to Evert A. Duyckinck, New York, September 5, 1854, DFP; M. E. Hewitt to Squier, New York, February 28, 1842, SPIHS; E. C. [Stedman] to Squier, Cedar Brooks [New Jersey], July 28, 1841, SPLC.

10. E. G. S., "What's in a Name? – Impromptu," *Lady's Cabinet Magazine*, August 1841, 173.

11. Frank Squier, ed., "A Collection of Books by Ephraim George Squier,"

typescript catalog (New York, 1939), 35, Archives – Library Division, Ohio Historical Society, Columbus.

12. E. G. Squier, "Introduction," *Poet's Magazine*, April 1842, i.

13. Squier, "Introduction," ii.

14. E. G. Squier, "The Past," *New York State Mechanic*, April 8, 1843, 156. This poem originally appeared in Joel Munsell's *Northern Light*.

15. Squier to Evert A. Duyckinck, New York, September 5, 1854, DFP.

16. [Squier], "Our Corner," 205.

17. A scrapbook (1839–46) in the Ephraim George Squier Papers at the Indiana Historical Society contains poems by Squier (see box 2, folder 3). The Ephraim George Squier Papers at Tulane University likewise contain twenty-three undated poems by Squier (see Group IV. Miscellaneous, box 2, folders 27–48, Poetry by Squier). He may have continued to write poetry for his own edification for several more years.

18. Squier to parents, Albany, December 30, 1841, SFP

19. "Declaration," *New York State Mechanic*, December 4, 1841, 13; "To Our Readers – The Mechanics," *New York State Mechanic*, July 23, 1842, 69; "The Present Condition of the Millions," *New York State Mechanic*, March 25, 1843, 141.

20. "The State Mechanic and State Prison System," *New York State Mechanic*, November 20, 1841, 2; "Our Objects," "State Prisons," and "State Prison Contracts," *New York State Mechanic*, December 18, 1841, 6, 7; Scrutator, "State Prison Labor," *New York State Mechanic*, December 4, 1841, 10–11; "Legislative Action on the Prison Question," *New York State Mechanic*, December 4, 1841, 13; "Mechanics State Convention," *New York State Mechanic*, December 11, 1841, 18–19.

21. Squier to parents, Albany, October 23, 1843, SFP; J. Hochstasser, M. Hawes, E. G. Squier, J. Munsell, and J. Easterly, "Report of the Committee appointed to visit the Sing Sing Prison," in *Documents in Relation to State Prison Competition* ([Albany], 1843).

22. D. C. Bloomer, "Social Reform," *New York State Mechanic*, February 18, 1843, 98–99.

23. Squier to parents, Albany, January 3, 1843, SFP.

24. Squier to parents, Albany, June 24, 1842, May 23, 1843, SFP; Squier to Evert A. Duyckinck, September 5, 1854, DFP.

25. E. G. Squier, "Two Lectures on the Origin and Progress of Modern Civilization," Albany, 1841–1842, MS, SFP.

26. Squier to parents, Albany, June 24, 1842, SFP.

27. E. G. Squier, "The Laboring Classes of Europe and America," *New York*

State Mechanic, February 18, 1843, 97–98, March 18, 1843, 129–30, March 25, 1843, 137, April 1, 1843, 146–47, April 15, 1843, 162–63.

28. E. G. Squier, "Lecture on the Condition and True Interests of the Laboring Class of America," *The Working Man's Miscellany* (Albany: The Offices of the New York State Mechanic and Cultivator; New York: The Office of the New York Tribune, 1843).

29. Squier, "Two Lectures on the Origin and Progress of Modern Civilization." Robert E. Bieder cites François Guizot's popular *History of Civilization* as the source of ideas that Squier developed in these lectures. I have been unable to verify that connection, but it is certainly plausible. The first English translation of Guizot's work appeared in 1837, and by 1841 it had appeared in three editions in the United States and three in England. It is likely that Squier would have had access to the work at Albany, where it is known that he was drawing upon materials in local libraries in preparation for his lectures for the New York Mechanics' Association. Bieder, "Ephraim George Squier and the Archaeology of Mental Progress," in his *Science Encounters the Indian, 1820–1880: The Early Years of American Ethnology* (Norman: University of Oklahoma Press, 1986), 106–7.

30. Squier, "Two Lectures on the Origin and Progress of Modern Civilization," 47–48.

31. Squier, *Working Man's Miscellany*, 11–12.

32. [E. G. Squier], "Literary Notices," *Lady's Cabinet Magazine*, August 1841, 178–79.

33. Squier, *Working Man's Miscellany*, 12.

34. Squier, *Working Man's Miscellany*, 12.

35. Squier, *Working Man's Miscellany*, 12.

36. [Whelpley], "Mr. E. G. Squier," 348.

37. Squier to parents, Albany, June 24, 1842, October 23, 1843, SFP.

38. E. G. S., "Letter from New York," *New York State Mechanic*, December 17, 1842, 29–30; Squier, *Working Man's Miscellany*, 13. On Leggett's political journalism see Richard Hofstadter, "William Leggett, Spokesman of Jacksonian Democracy," *Political Science Quarterly* 58 (1943): 581–94.

39. E. G. S., "Poughkeepsie," New York, December 4, 1842, *New York State Mechanic*, December 10, 1842, 22.

40. Squier, *Working Man's Miscellany*, 3; Squier, "Laboring Classes," March 18, 1843, 130.

41. Squier, *Working Man's Miscellany*, 8; Squier, "Laboring Classes," April 1, 1843, 146–47.

42. Squier, *Working Man's Miscellany*, 7; Squier, "Laboring Classes," April 1, 1843, 147.

43. Squier to Evert A. Duyckinck, New York, September 5, 1854, DFP.

44. "To the Mechanic," *New York State Mechanic*, November 26, 1842, 5; "Mr. Squier's Lecture," *New York State Mechanic*, January 21, 1843, 69; "Dying Confessions," *New York State Mechanic*, June 17, 1843, 219; Squier to parents, Albany, June 24, 1842, SFP.

45. G. Tradescent Lay, *The Chinese as They Are: Their Moral and Social Character*, ed. E. G. Squier (Albany: George Jones, 1843), iii–iv. Lay published the original and substantially larger edition at London in 1841. Squier omitted several of Lay's chapters and greatly condensed and rearranged those retained on Chinese arts and sciences, medical practices, and the activities of Protestant missionaries. Lay based his work on his experiences as a resident of Canton.

46. Squier to parents, Albany, January 3, 1843, SFP.

47. Squier to parents, Hartford, December 13, 1843, SFP.

48. Squier to parents, Hartford, April 5, 1844, SFP; "Introductory," *Hartford Journal*, November 1, 1843.

49. E. G. S., "The South," *New York State Mechanic*, April 30, 1842, 182–83; "Review of Tariff Report," *New York State Mechanic*, May 21, 1842, 206; [Whelpley], "Mr. E. G. Squier," 348.

50. Ethan Squier to E. G. Squier, Knowles Ville, December 3, 1843, SFP; [Whelpley], "Mr. E. G. Squier," 348.

51. "The Whip in the Right Hands," *Hartford Journal*, May 29, 1844; "The Course of Our Opponents," *Hartford Journal*, June 25, 1844.

52. "Organize! – Organize!! Young Men's Clay Clubs," *Hartford Journal*, November 9, 1843; "To Clay Clubs," *Hartford Journal*, January 18, 1844; "Organization," *Hartford Journal*, June 11, 1844; "To the Whigs of Connecticut," *Hartford Journal*, June 20, 1844; "Proceedings of the State Convention of Clay Clubs," *Hartford Journal*, July 10, July 11, 1844; "Opening of the Campaign," *Hartford Journal*, August 17, 1844; "Ho for New Haven!" *Hartford Journal*, August 29, 1844.

53. Squier to parents, Washington, April 28, 1844, SFP; "For Baltimore," *Hartford Journal*, April 7, 1844; "Editorial Correspondence, Baltimore, May 1, 1844," "Whig National Convention," and "The Great Whig Young Men's Convention," *Hartford Journal*, May 4, 1844; and "Editorial Correspondence, Baltimore, May 3, 1844," *Hartford Journal*, May 6, 1844.

54. Squier to Evert A. Duyckinck, New York, September 5, 1854, DFP.

55. Squier to parents, Hartford, January 18, February 6, 1845, SFP.

56. [E. G. Squier], "Editor's Table," *Lady's Cabinet Magazine*, August 1841, 182.

57. Squier to parents, Albany, June 24, 1842, SFP.

58. Squier to parents, Albany, December 30, 1841, May 23, 1843, and Joel Squier to Ephraim George Squier, Broadalbin, [New York], April 15, 1844, SFP.

59. E. [Ethan] Squier to Ephraim George Squier, West Gaines, [New York], December 18, 1845, Ephraim George Squier Papers, William L. Clements Library, University of Michigan, Ann Arbor.

60. E. G. Squier, "The Days of Our Sunny Youth: A Song," *Hartford Journal*, November 18, 1843. Originally published in the *Orion Magazine*.

2. IN SEARCH OF THE MOUND BUILDERS

1. "To the Patrons of the Gazette," *Scioto Gazette*, May 1, 1845; *Scioto Gazette*, August 21, 1845; [Whelpley], "Mr. E. G. Squier," 349; Squier to parents, Chillicothe, July 20, 1845, SFP; Squier to Edward A. Duyckinck, New York, September 5, 1854, DFP. The August 21 edition of the *Gazette* is the first to cite "E. G. Squier, editor." It was announced in the May 1 edition, however, that arrangements had been completed whereby he was to begin editorship of the paper effective that date.

2. Squier to Munsell, Chillicothe, June 12, 1845. Squier's letter is in the possession of Mr. John W. Kincheloe III of Meredith College in Raleigh, North Carolina. I am indebted to Mr. Kincheloe for providing me with a copy of the letter. His account of this important letter appears in John W. Kincheloe, "Yours Very Respectfully, E. G. Squier," *Ohio Archaeologist* 48 (November 1998): 4–12.

3. Squier to parents, Chillicothe, July 20, 1845, SFP.

4. Squier to Munsell, Chillicothe, June 12, 1845, in Kincheloe, "Yours Very Respectfully," 6.

5. Davis to Henry, New York, January 5, 1876, Joseph Henry Papers, Smithsonian Institution Archives, Washington DC.

6. Henry Howe, "Some Recollections of Historic Travel," *Ohio Archaeological and Historical Quarterly* 2 (March 1889): 441. Howe described Squier as "one of the most audacious spirits" he had ever encountered. "He had a talent for management and notwithstanding his insignificant presence could make his way everywhere, with no fear of power, station, or weight of intellect and character."

7. Biographical sources on Davis in this and the following paragraph are E. H. Davis, "Antiquities of Ohio," September 4, 1833, Commencement Address Announcement, Kenyon College, and Genealogy and Record of Edwin Hamilton Davis, both in Edwin Hamilton Davis Collection, Ross County Historical Society, Chillicothe, Ohio; Davis to James McCormick, New York, November 20, 1853, MSS VF 3911, Cincinnati Historical Society, Cincinnati Museum Center; "Death of Dr. Edwin H. Davis," *New York Daily Tribune*, May 16, 1888, 4; "Dr. Edwin Hamilton Davis," *Proceedings of the American Antiquarian Society*, n.s., 5 (October 1888): 368–69; and Howe, "Some Recollections of Historic Travel," 442.

8. Davis to John Davis, Chillicothe, February 22, 1847, SPAAS.

9. Davis to James McCormick, New York, November 20, 1853, MSS 3911, Cincinnati Historical Society, Cincinnati Museum Center.

10. Davis to John Russell Bartlett, Chillicothe, May 25, 1846, JRBP; Davis to Samuel George Morton, Chillicothe, October, 26, 1845, and May 18, 1846, SGMP.

11. Davis to Hildreth, Chillicothe, May 24, 1846, Samuel P. Hildreth Papers, vol. 6, Dawes Memorial Library, Marietta College, Marietta, Ohio.

12. Caleb Atwater, "Description of the Antiquities Discovered in the State of Ohio, and Other Western States," *Archaeologia Americana: Transactions of the American Antiquarian Society* 1 (1820): 110, 110n, 111, 121.

13. Silliman to Squier, New Haven, December 26, 1845, SPLC.

14. See Richard C. Taylor, "Notes Respecting Certain Indian Mounds and Earthworks in the Form of Animal Effigies, Chiefly in the Wisconsin Territory, U.S.," *American Journal of Science and Arts* 34, no. 1 (1838): 88–104; S. Taylor, "Description of Ancient Remains, Animal Mounds, and Embankments, Principally in the Counties of Grant, Iowa, and Richmond, in Wisconsin," *American Journal of Science and Arts* 44 (1843): 21–40; and C. G. Forshey, "Description of Some Artificial Mounds on Prairie Jefferson, Louisiana," *American Journal of Science and Arts* 49 (1845): 38–42.

15. Charles Wilkes, *Narrative of the United States Exploring Expedition during the Years 1838, 1839, 1840, 1841, 1842*, 5 vols. (Philadelphia: Lea and Blanchard, 1845). On the work of the United States Exploring Expedition see Joyce, *The Shaping of American Ethnography*, esp. chap. 6, "Ethnography and the Legacy of the Expedition," 144–61; William R. Stanton, *The Great United States Exploring Expedition of 1838–1842* (Berkeley: University of California Press, 1975); and David B. Tyler, *The Wilkes Expedition: The First United States Exploring Expedition, 1838–1842* (Philadelphia: American Philosophical Society, 1968).

16. John C. Frémont, *Report of the Exploring Expedition to the Rocky Mountains in 1842 and to Oregon and North California in the Years 1843–1844*, 28th Cong., 2nd sess., Senate Doc. 11 (Washington DC: Government Printing Office, 1845), 7–693.

17. "Preface," *Transactions of the American Ethnological Society* 1 (1845): ix–x; "Preface," *Transactions of the American Ethnological Society* 2 (1848): viii; and John Russell Bartlett, "Progress of Ethnology: An Account of Recent Archaeological, Philological, and Geographical Researches," *Transactions of the American Ethnological Society* 2 (1848): appendix, 3–8.

18. See William H. Goetzmann, *Exploration and Empire: The Explorer and the Scientist in the Winning of the American West* (New York: Knopf, 1966) and *Army*

Exploration in the American West, 1803–1863 (New Haven: Yale University Press, 1959).

19. Davis to James McCormick, New York, November 20, 1853, MSS 3911, Cincinnati Historical Society, Cincinnati Museum Center.

20. Davis to Hildreth, Chillicothe, May 24, 1846, Hildreth Papers; Davis to John Russell Bartlett, Chillicothe, May 25, 1846, JRBP; Davis to Samuel George Morton, Chillicothe, October 26, 1845, May 18, 1846, Samuel George Morton Papers, Historical Society of Pennsylvania, Philadelphia.

21. Squier to parents, Chillicothe, July 20, 1845, and Columbus, November 26, 1845, SFP; Benjamin Silliman, "On the Mounds and Relics of the Ancient Nations of America," *American Journal of Science and Arts*, 2nd ser., 2 (November 1846): 246.

22. Squier to parents, Chillicothe, March 10, 1846, SFP.

23. Squier to John Collins Warren, Hartford, July 6, 1846, SFP (a transcript of an original letter in the Massachusetts Historical Society).

24. Henry Rowe Schoolcraft, "Observations Respecting the Grave Creek Mound," *Transactions of the American Ethnological Society* 1 (1845): 369–420; Gerard Troost, "An Account of Some Ancient Remains in Tennessee," *Transactions of the American Ethnological Society* 1 (1845): 355–65.

25. "Preface," *Transactions of the American Ethnological Society* 1 (1845): iii, ix, x; "Preface," *Transactions of the American Ethnological Society* 2 (1848): vii, viii.

26. Davis to Squier, Chillicothe, June 14, 1846, SPLC; Squier to parents, Hartford, June 29, 1846, SFP.

27. Squier to parents, Hartford, June 29, 1846, SFP.

28. Benjamin Silliman Jr. to Squier, New Haven, July 6, 1846, SPLC; Squier to Joel Squier, New York, July 9, 1846, SFP.

29. Sources for this and the following paragraph are Davis to Squier, Chillicothe, June 9, 14, 15, July 3, 1846, SPLC.

30. Davis to Squier, Chillicothe, July 7, 1846, SPLC.

31. Sources for this and the following paragraph are John C. Warren to Squier, Boston, August 30, 1846, SPLC; Squier to parents, Chillicothe, November 2, 1846, SFP; Squier to John Russell Bartlett, Chillicothe, September 21, 1846, JRBP; Samuel Foster Haven to Squier, Worcester, August 28, 1846, SPLC; [Samuel Foster Haven], "Account of the American Antiquarian Society," MS, n.d., SPAAS.

32. Squier and Davis sent brief progress reports to the *American Journal of Science and Arts* during that period of renewed activity. The purpose of the communications was to keep public attention focused on the investigations until the American Ethnological Society published its findings. See E. G. Squier, "On the Discoidal Stones of the Indian Mounds," *American Journal of Science and Arts*,

2nd ser., 2 (November 1846): 216–18; Squier, "Pipestone of the Ancient Pipes in the Indian Mounds," 2 (November 1846): 287; Squier, "Hieroglyphical Mica Plates from the Mounds," 4 (November 1847): 145; Squier, "Miscellaneous Intelligence," 4 (November 1847): 439–40; E. H. Davis, "Footprints and Indian Sculpture," 3 (May 1847): 286–88.

33. Bartlett to Squier, New York, September 10, November 13, 1846 SPLC.

34. Squier to parents, Chillicothe, November 2, 1846, Columbus, December 9 and 19, 1846, January 28, 1847, SFP; *Journal of the House of Representatives of the State of Ohio*, vol. 65 (Columbus, 1847), 15.

35. John Teesdale to Squier, Columbus, November 22, 1846, SPLC.

36. Squier's editorial support for the repeal of the black codes in Ohio was later recalled in the *Scioto Gazette*. See an untitled notice in the *Gazette* of a visit that Squier made to Chillicothe in 1871. *Scioto Gazette*, August 2, 1871.

37. Squier to Samuel George Morton, Chillicothe, December 1, 1846, Columbus, January 4, 1847; Squier to Benjamin Silliman, Columbus, December 16, 1846, Benjamin Silliman Papers, Historical Society of Pennsylvania, Philadelphia; Squier to parents, Columbus, December 30, 1846, SFP.

38. Joel Squier to E. G. Squier, Esperance, [New York], July 13, 1846, Squier Papers, William L. Clements Library.

39. John Russell Bartlett to Squier, New York, September 10, 1846, SPLC; Morton to Squier, Philadelphia, December 8, 1846, SGMP; M. W. Dickeson, "An Account of Researches and Discoveries Amongst the Tumuli and Earthworks of Mississippi and Louisiana" and "A Catalogue of Antiquities in the Collection of M. W. Dickeson," *Transactions of the American Ethnological Society* 2 (1848): ix; Bartlett, "Progress of Ethnology," 8–13.

40. Davis to Squier, Chillicothe, December 24 and 29, 1846, SPLC.

41. Dickeson exhibited his celebrated archaeological collection at the Agricultural Fair held at Washington, Mississippi, in July 1842, at another Agricultural Fair at Natchez, and at Washington College. He showcased the artifacts and lectured on American archaeology throughout the country in 1852 together with an imposing panorama of the Mississippi Valley painted by John J. Egan in 1850. Egan's panorama illustrated Indian mounds on the Ohio and Mississippi Rivers and romanticized depictions of Indian life. The Dickeson collection later comprised the Indian cabinet of the City Museum of Philadelphia. He subsequently combined his archaeological and natural history collections for display at another Philadelphia museum as the Dickeson Collection of Arts and Sciences. Dickeson opened his own museum at Philadelphia in the winter of 1867–68, but the venture quickly proved a failure. He also exhibited his archaeological collection in the Main Exhibition Building during the United States Centennial Exposition at Philadelphia in 1876. Dickeson's

archaeological collection and Egan's panorama are in the collections of the Free Museum of Science and Art at the University of Pennsylvania. Stewart Culin, "The Dickeson Collection of American Antiquities," *Bulletin of the Free Museum of Science and Art of the University of Pennsylvania* 2 (January 1900): 114n.

42. Squier to Morton, Columbus, January 4, 1847, SGMP.

43. Squier to Bartlett, [New York], September 21, 1846, JRBP.

44. Sparks to Squier, Salem, Massachusetts, February 19, 1847, SPLC. Gallatin suggested that Squier garner support for the idea of additional investigations by issuing a prospectus of the proposed work that bore the endorsements of scholars familiar with his investigations. Squier solicited Morton's opinion regarding Gallatin's suggestion of funding the work by subscription. Squier to Morton, Columbus, January 16, 1847, draft copy, SPLC.

45. Marsh to Squier, Washington DC, February 23, March 6, 1847, SPLC.

46. Henry to Squier, Princeton, April 3, 1847, SPLC.

47. Harriette Knight Smith, *The History of the Lowell Institute* (Boston: Lamson, Wolffe, 1898), 50. Another source says that Gliddon gave seven lectures at Boston in the winter of 1842 and 1843. [Luke Burke], "Progress of Ethnology in the United States," *Ethnological Journal* 2 (September 1848): 173. It may be that Gliddon lectured in Boston on more than one occasion or that Burke was actually referring to his expanded course of lectures given at Lowell Institute in 1843 and 1844. Gliddon also lectured at New York in the winter of 1842. Frederick Catherwood to Gliddon, September 20, 1842, SPIHS. Gliddon continued to lecture throughout a good portion of the country until his death in 1858.

48. Samuel George Morton, *Crania Aegyptiaca; Or, Observations on Egyptian Ethnography, Derived from Anatomy, History, and the Monuments* (Philadelphia: John Penington; London: Madden and Co., 1844).

49. Sources for this and the following two paragraphs are "Egypt – Mr. Gliddon," *Scioto Gazette*, February 24, March 3, and March 31, 1847; "Lectures on Egyptian History and Antiquities," *Scioto Gazette*, May 5, 1847; Gliddon to Squier, Pittsburgh, March 15, and Cincinnati, April 23, 1847, SPLC; [Burke], "Progress of Ethnology in the United States," 170–71, 173–74; and George Austin Allibone, ed., *A Critical Dictionary of English Literature and British and American Authors*, vol. 1 (Philadelphia: J. B. Lippincott, 1900), 678.

50. Bartlett to Squier, February 8, 1847, SPLC.

51. Gliddon to Squier, Cincinnati, April 23, 1847, SPLC.

52. Gliddon to Squier, [Cincinnati], April 28, 1847, SPLC.

53. [Burke], "Progress of Ethnology in the United States," 173. William Stanton gives an account of the American School and Squier's cautious association with its members in *The Leopard's Spots*, particularly his chapter entitled "No Inconsiderable Antiquity," 82–89.

54. Gliddon to Squier, Philadelphia, June 8, 1847, SPLC.

55. Davis to Squier, Chillicothe, June 12, 1847, SPLC.

56. Davis to Morton, Chillicothe, October 26, 1845, May 18, 1846, and Squier to Morton, Chillicothe, December 1, 1846, SGMP; Squier to Bartlett, Chillicothe, September 21, 1846, JRBP.

57. Squier to Morton, Chillicothe, June 10, 1846, SGMP; Morton to Squier, Philadelphia, December 8, 1846, SPLC.

58. Squier to Morton, Chillicothe, April 6, 1847, SGMP.

59. Morton to Squier, Philadelphia, April 10, 1847, September 25, 1848, SPLC; Samuel George Morton, "On an Aboriginal Cranium Obtained by Dr. Davis and Mr. Squier," *Proceedings of the Philadelphia Academy of Natural Sciences* 3, no. 9 (1847): 212–13.

60. Davis to Morton, Chillicothe, October 26, 1845, SGMP. See Samuel George Morton, *An Inquiry into the Distinctive Characteristics of the Aboriginal Race of America* (Boston: Tuttle and Dennett, 1842). Morton published a second edition of this pamphlet at Philadelphia in 1844.

3. ARCHAEOLOGY AND THE SMITHSONIAN INSTITUTION

1. Sources for this and the following paragraph are Joseph Henry, "Report of the Secretary of the Smithsonian Institution to the Board of Regents, December 8, 1847," *Report of the Board of Regents of the Smithsonian Institution*, January 6, 1848, U.S. Senate, 30th Cong., 1st sess., Miscellaneous Doc. no. 23, 173, 175, 181, 184, 188; and Joseph Henry, "Organization of the Smithsonian Institution," *Proceedings of the American Association for the Advancement of Science* 1 (September 1848): 88.

2. Joseph Henry, "Programme of Organization of the Smithsonian Institution," in *Report of the Board of Regents of the Smithsonian Institution*, 173. Henry presented the plan of organization to the Board of Regents on December 8, 1847.

3. See Curtis M. Hinsley Jr., *Savages and Scientists: The Smithsonian Institution and the Development of American Anthropology, 1846–1910* (Washington DC: Smithsonian Institution Press, 1981).

4. Henry's salutary influence on the work of Squier and Davis has often been noted. See Hinsley, *Savages and Scientists*, 34–37; Tax, "The Development of American Archaeology," 173, 194, 202–3; and Wilcomb E. Washburn, "Joseph Henry's Conception of the Purpose of the Smithsonian Institution," in *A Cabinet of Curiosities: Five Episodes in the Evolution of American Museums*, ed. Whitfield J. Bell (Charlottesville: University of Virginia Press, 1967), 153.

5. Squier to Bartlett, Columbus, January 24, 1847, JRBP; Bartlett to Squier, New York, February 8, 1847, SPLC; Squier to parents, Princeton, May 15, 1847,

and New York, May 30, June 9, 1847, SFP; "Preface," *Transactions of the American Ethnological Society* 2 (1848): vii–viii; [Haven], "Account of the American Antiquarian Society."

6. *Proceedings of the American Antiquarian Society, 1812–1849* (Worcester MA: American Antiquarian Society, 1912), 516, 518, 530; Davis to Squier, Chillicothe, June 27, 1847, SPLC; [Haven], "Account of the American Antiquarian Society."

7. Jared Sparks to Squier, July 20, 1847, SPLC.

8. Haven to Squier, Worcester, August 12, 1847, SPLC.

9. Haven to Squier, August 12, 1847.

10. Gallatin to Henry, New York, June 16, 1847, SPLC; Edward Robinson, John R. Bartlett, and William W. Turner, "Report of the Evaluative Committee of the American Ethnological Society," New York, June 12, 1847, SPLC. The committee report is accompanied by supporting letters from Marsh and Morton.

11. Henry to Squier, Princeton, June 23, 1847, SPLC.

12. Gliddon to Squier, Philadelphia, May 31, 1847, SPLC.

13. Davis to Squier, Chillicothe, June 12, 27, August 2, 1847, SPLC.

14. See "American Archaeology," *Literary World*, September 18, 1847, 158.

15. Davis to Squier, Chillicothe, September 22, 1847, SPLC.

16. Squier to Davis, New York, September 30, 1847, SPLC.

17. E. G. Squier, *Observations on the Aboriginal Monuments of the Mississippi Valley* (New York: Bartlett and Welford, 1847). Although the title page of this pamphlet says it is taken from the *Transactions of the American Ethnological Society*, the second volume of the *Transactions* in which it appears was not published until 1848. Bartlett and Welford issued the pamphlet edition in late 1847 before the printing and binding of the second volume of the *Transactions* had been completed.

18. Before the appearance of the account for the American Ethnological Society, the article that Squier prepared for Benjamin Silliman had also appeared under Squier's name only. E. G. Squier, "Observations on the Uses of the Mounds of the West, with an Attempt at their Classification," *American Journal of Science and Arts*, 2nd ser., 3 (May 1847): 237–48. Here Davis receives passing mention as an "associate" in research, but Squier gives no further notice of him or his contributions to the investigations. A third article based on Squier-Davis research also later appeared under Squier's name only. E. G. Squier, "Observations on the Fossils, Minerals, Organic Remains, etc. Found in the Mounds of the West," *Edinburgh New Philosophical Journal* 44 (October 1847–April 1848): 141–44. This account was taken from a paper Squier read

before the American Geologists and Naturalists Society at Boston in September 1847. Davis is ignored completely.

19. Davis to Charles Rau, New York, February 17, 1882, Smithsonian Institution Archives.

20. Squier to Henry, New York, December 31, 1847, SPLC.

21. The source for this and the following paragraph is Davis to Haven, October 27, 1847, SPAAS.

22. Locke gave Squier permission to use his published surveys in January 1847. Locke surveyed the Fort Ancient site located on the east bank of the Little Miami River in Warren County, Ohio, in 1842. He considered that survey to be as accurate as any made by professional engineers. Locke to Squier, [Cincinnati], Medical College of Ohio, January 24, 1847, SPLC. The Philadelphia lithographer Duval made the lithographic map based upon Locke's delineation of his survey, which originally appeared in the papers of the American Association of Geologists and Naturalists in 1843. Squier and Davis made some slight additions to Locke's map to better indicate some of the site's more important features and published it along with Locke's description. See plate VII of Squier and Davis, *Ancient Monuments*, 18–21. The authors also published three of Locke's surveys of effigy mounds in Dade County, Wisconsin, one of which he made jointly with Richard C. Taylor. See plates XLI and XLII of Squier and Davis, *Ancient Monuments*, 127–29. Although the year or years in which Locke made these surveys is not given, they were probably made in 1839 or 1840. Locke gave an account of these remains in his "Report on the Mineral Lands of the United States" that he presented to Congress in 1840. See John Locke, "Earthwork Antiquities in Wisconsin," in *Mineral Lands of the United States* (Washington DC: Government Printing Office, 1844).

23. James McBride, "Survey and Description of Ancient Fortifications Situated in Butler County, Ohio," *Journal of the Historical and Philosophical Society of Ohio* Part 1 – volume 1 (1838): 104–11.

24. McBride to Charles Whittlesey, Hamilton, Ohio, December 27, 1839, vol. 9, and McBride to De Hass, Columbus, October 18, 1845, vol. 9, James McBride Letters, MSS qM119L RFM, Cincinnati Historical Society, Cincinnati Museum Center.

25. McBride to John W. Erwin, Columbus, June 14, 1846, vol. 12, and McBride to Davis, Columbus, June 30, September 30, 1846, vol. 12, McBride Letters. These are copies of outgoing letters.

26. McBride to Squier, Hamilton, December 1, 1847, SPLC.

27. McBride to Squier, Hamilton, December 22, 1847, SPLC.

28. McBride to Charles Whittlesey, Hamilton, December 9, 1840, vol. 9, McBride Letters; Henry Howe, *Historical Collections of Ohio*, vol. 1 (Columbus:

Henry Howe and Son, 1889), 34; L. H. Everts, *Combination Atlas Map of Butler County, Ohio* (Philadelphia: L. H. Everts, 1875), 27.

29. See Squier, *Observations on the Aboriginal Monuments of the Mississippi Valley*, "Fortified Hill, Butler, County, Ohio, J MC BRIDE 1836," plate 2, facing p. 18; and Squier, "Observations on the Aboriginal Monuments of the Mississippi Valley," plate 2, facing p. 146.

30. J. W. E. to the editor, *Cincinnati Gazette*, December 30, 1847.

31. McBride to Squier, Hamilton, January 25 and 27, 1848, and Marsh to Squier, Washington, January 7, 1848, SPLC. McBride informed Squier after the publication of *Ancient Monuments* that he was completely satisfied with the credit he received for his contributions to the work. Only then did he request the return of his surveys, drawings, and field notes. McBride to Squier, Hamilton, March 19, 1849, SPLC.

32. Squier and Davis published the survey and incorrectly attributed it to Whittlesey instead of Curtis. See James L. Murphy, "Authorship of Squier and Davis' Map of the Marietta Earthworks: A Belated Correction," *Ohio Archaeologist* 27, no. 3 (1977): 20–21.

33. W. W. Mather, ed., *First Annual Report on the Geological Survey of the State of Ohio* (Columbus: Samuel Medary, 1838), 22; "Report of Mr. Whittlesey," in *First Annual Report*, 104–6; "Mr. Whittlesey's Report," *Second Annual Report* (same bound volume), 43.

34. "Report of Mr. Whittlesey," 105–6.

35. "Report of Mr. Whittlesey," 106.

36. Whittlesey to McBride, Hamilton, December 4, 1839, vol. 9, McBride Letters; Charles Whittlesey, "Descriptions of Ancient Works in Ohio," *Smithsonian Contributions to Knowledge*, vol. 3 (Washington DC: Smithsonian Institution, 1852), 5; "Ancient Earth Forts of the Cuyahoga Valley, Ohio," *Tracts of the Western Reserve and Northern Ohio Historical Society* no. 5 (1871): 4.

37. Squier to Whittlesey, New York, October 9, 1847, Ephraim George Squier, Miscellaneous Letter, Manuscripts and Archives Division, New York Public Library.

38. Whittlesey to Squier, Clinton, Summit County, December 6 and 20, 1847, SPLC. Whittlesey wrote Squier after the publication of *Ancient Monuments*, informing him that the acknowledgments of his investigations in that work were satisfactory and met his expectation of "full justice." Whittlesey to Squier, December 11, 1848, SPLC. Whittlesey later published several additional surveys of sites in northern Ohio, which are an important supplement to those published by Squier and Davis. See Whittlesey, "Descriptions of Ancient Works in Ohio."

39. Marsh to Squier, Washington, January 7, 1848, SPLC.

40. Henry to Squier, Washington, n.d., Henry Papers.

41. Henry to Asa Gray, Washington, January 10, 1848, in Nathan Reingold, ed., *Science in Nineteenth-Century America: A Documentary History* (New York: Hill and Wang, 1964), 159.

42. Henry to Squier and Davis, Washington, February 16, 1848, SPLC.

43. Squier to Henry, New York, February 21, 1848, SPLC.

44. Squier to Henry, February 21, 1848.

45. Squier to parents, New York, March 18, 1848, SFP.

46. An act of Congress stipulated that $240,000 be spent on the construction of buildings at the Smithsonian in order to adequately accommodate the scientific collections of the United States Exploring Expedition. Henry, who wanted to keep the Smithsonian out of the museum business as much as possible, lamented that so large an amount of money had been appropriated for buildings. Henry, "Organization of the Smithsonian Institution," 89.

47. Gliddon to Squier, Philadelphia, May 31, June 8, 1847, SPLC.

48. Henry to Squier, Washington, May 13, 1848, SPLC.

49. Squier to Henry, New York, June 8, 1848, SPLC.

50. E. G. Squier, A.M., and E. H. Davis, M.D., *Ancient Monuments of the Mississippi Valley: Comprising the Results of Extensive Original Surveys and Explorations, Smithsonian Contributions to Knowledge*, vol. 1 (Washington DC: Smithsonian Institution, 1848). Bartlett and Welford at New York and J. A. and U. P. James at Cincinnati published separate editions of the work from the same type, woodcuts, and lithographic plates. The separate editions cost $10.00.

51. A vague discussion of arbitration and "suits" between Squier and Davis is contained in Squier to Bartlett, Syracuse, October 26, November 7, 1848, and Buffalo, November 12, 1848, and Davis to Bartlett, Chillicothe, November 10, 1849, JRBP; and P. Woodbury to Squier, New York, September 20, November 14, 1849, May 3, 1850, SPLC. Years later Davis informed Charles Rau that he had recovered the papers and affidavits in the case of Squier against Davis claiming half ownership of the archaeological collection resulting from their explorations. The papers, said Davis, contained the true history of their relative contributions to the investigations and the expenses involved in conducting them. Davis to Rau, New York, December 12, 1883, Charles Rau Correspondence, Smithsonian Institution Archives. It is quite possible that court or attorneys' records of the suits still exist, but the whereabouts of the papers that were at one time in Davis's possession (if they are still extant) is unknown. The litigation between Squier and Davis appears to have been settled out of court.

52. Squier to Bartlett, Syracuse, October 26, November 7, 1848, Buffalo, November 12, 1848, and León, Nicaragua, May 7, 1850, JRBP.

53. See "Ethnographic Map of the Mound-Areas of North America," Sheet

no. 7 of Edwin Hamilton Davis's "Paintings and Drawings of Antique Objects Found in the Mounds, Tombs, and Ancient Cities of the Americas: Arranged, Classified, and Described by Edwin Hamilton Davis, AM, MD, New York, 1858," National Anthropological Archives, Smithsonian Institution; and E. H. Davis, "On Ethnological Research: A Communication from Dr. E. H. Davis, of New York," *Annual Report of the Smithsonian Institution for 1866* (Washington DC: Government Printing Office, 1867), 370–71. The communication is a letter from Davis to Henry, New York, December 1, 1865. See also Sheets 3 to 6 of Davis's "Paintings and Drawings."

54. Davis to Morton, Chillicothe, June 3, 1849, SGMP.

55. Davis's complaints and grievances against Squier are stated in Davis to Henry, Chillicothe, September 21, 1848, May 8, 1849, Henry Papers; Davis to Bartlett, Chillicothe, April 17, November 10, 1849, JRBP; Davis to Morton, Chillicothe, June 3, 1849, SGMP; Davis to James McCormick, New York, November 20, 1853, MSS 3911, Cincinnati Historical Society, Cincinnati Museum Center; Davis to Samuel Foster Haven, [New York], March 29, 1858, SPAAS; Davis to Henry Rowe Schoolcraft, New York, April 5, 1858, Schoolcraft Papers, Library of Congress; and Davis to Charles Rau, New York, December 12, 1883, Charles Rau Papers, Smithsonian Institution Archives.

56. Davis to James McCormick, New York, November 20, 1853, MSS 3911, Cincinnati Historical Society, Cincinnati Museum Center.

57. Earlier accounts of Davis's contributions to the Squier-Davis investigations are Terry A. Barnhart, "Of Mounds and Men: The Early Anthropological Career of Ephraim George Squier" (Ph.D. diss., Miami University, Oxford, Ohio, 1989); and Barnhart, "A Question of Authorship: The Ephraim George Squier–Edwin Hamilton Davis Controversy," *Ohio History* 92 (1983): 52–71.

58. Davis to Bartlett, Chillicothe, October 27, 1846, JRBP. Squier also noted that Davis's medical practice only occasionally allowed him to participate in the excavations and surveys, although Squier consistently minimized all of Davis's interests and contributions, fairly or otherwise. Squier to Marsh, New York, January 8, 1848, SPLC.

59. Davis's subsequent collecting interests and activities as a resident member of the American Ethnological Society from the late 1850s to the late 1860s are documented in the brief notices of the society's proceedings appearing in the *Historical Record*, in the *Bulletin of the American Ethnological Society* (September 1860–January 1861), and in the *Bulletin* for the years 1861 and 1862 and for January, February, and March 1863. The society published the *Bulletin* of its proceedings for September 1860 to January 1861, but it is unclear whether it published the *Bulletin* for the remainder of 1861 and for 1862 and part of 1863 or merely printed and distributed it among its members. A printed and

unbound copy of the *Bulletin* for those years is in the archival collections of the Johnson-Humrickhouse Memorial Museum at Coshocton, Ohio, in the museum's Newark "Holy Stones" file. It is almost a certainty that other unbound or bound copies are also extant. I am indebted to Dr. Bradley T. Lepper of the Ohio Historical Society for providing me with an unbound copy of the *Bulletin of the American Ethnological* for 1861 to 1863, which he found as part of his own research into the history of the Newark Holy Stones.

4. INTERPRETING THE MOUND BUILDERS

1. Squier and Davis, *Ancient Monuments*, xxxiii–xxxiv.

2. Squier to Morton, Columbus, January 16, 1847, SGMP.

3. Squier to Morton, January 16, 1847.

4. See, e.g., James Madison, "A Letter on the Supposed Fortifications of the Western Country," *Transactions of the American Philosophical Society* 6, no. 26 (1804): 132–42.

5. Squier and Davis, *Ancient Monuments*, 7, 139, 142; E. G. Squier, *Observations on the Uses of the Mounds of the West, with an Attempt at Their Classification* (New Haven: B. L. Hamlen, 1847), 3–4.

6. Squier and Davis, *Ancient Monuments*, 47–48.

7. Squier and Davis, *Ancient Monuments*, 49.

8. Squier and Davis, *Ancient Monuments*, 304.

9. Squier and Davis, *Ancient Monuments*, 97.

10. Squier and Davis, *Ancient Monuments*, 98.

11. See also E. G. Squier, "A Monograph on the Ancient Monuments of the State of Kentucky," *American Journal of Science and Arts*, 2nd ser., 8 (July 1849): 1–14. Squier's account is based on the "confused notes" of Rafinesque, who devoted considerable attention to subject of American antiquities before his death in 1840. See Charles Boewe, ed., *John D. Clifford's "Indian Antiquities" [and] Related Material by C. S. Rafinesque* (Knoxville: University of Tennessee Press, 2000). The Rafinesque material appears in four appendices together with Boewe's explanatory notes. See also Boewe's *C. S. Rafinesque and Ohio Valley Archaeology* (Barnardsville NC: Center for Ancient American Studies, 2004).

12. Squier and Davis, *Ancient Monuments*, 76–77, 103, 173; plate XVIII facing p. 52 and fig. 9, p. 53; plate XXV facing p. 67 and fig. 14, p. 69; plate XXVI facing p. 73 and fig. 17, p. 74; and plate XXVIII facing p. 78.

13. Squier, *Observations on the Uses of the Mounds of the West*, 13, fig. 4; Squier, "Observations on the Aboriginal Monuments of the Mississippi Valley," 170–71, fig. 4.

14. See Thaddeus Mason Harris, *Journal of a Tour into the Territory Northwest of the Allegheny Mountains* (Boston: Manning and Loring, 1805), 158–76; Atwater,

"Description of the Antiquities Discovered in the State of Ohio," 244–67; and Samuel P. Hildreth, "Pyramids at Marietta," *American Pioneer* 2 (June 1843): 243–45.

15. Hildreth, "Pyramids at Marietta," 244.

16. Squier and Davis, *Ancient Monuments*, 119–20; see also Squier to Samuel George Morton, Columbus, January 4, 1847, SGMP.

17. See Gregory A. Waselkov and Kathryn E. Holland Braund, eds., *William Bartram on the Southeastern Indians* (Lincoln: University of Nebraska Press, 1995).

18. A ninety-four-page manuscript copy of the Bartram manuscript, including its five pen tracings, is in the National Anthropological Archives of the Smithsonian Institution. See William Bartram, "Observations on the Creek and Cherokee Indians," Philadelphia, December 15, 1789, United States National Museum Catalog Number 173,683, Accession Number 31,588. J. Woodbridge Davis, son of Edwin Hamilton Davis, made the copy sometime before its donation to the National Museum in 1898. It is based on another copy found in his father's papers. J. Woodbridge Davis to Thomas Wilson, New York, February 11, 1898, National Anthropological Archives, Smithsonian Institution. The original Bartram manuscript may no longer be extant.

19. These excerpts, with additional illustrations, also appear in E. G. Squier, *Aboriginal Monuments of the State of New York: Comprising the Results of Original Surveys and Explorations, With an Illustrated Appendix*, Article IX of Smithsonian Contributions to Knowledge, vol. 2 (Washington DC: Smithsonian Institution, 1851), 135–40. See also E. G. Squier, *The Serpent Symbol, and the Worship of the Reciprocal Principles of Nature in America*, American Archaeological Researches no. 1 (New York: Putnam, 1851), chapter 3, "The Sacred 'High Places,' or Teocalli of America," note E, 94–97.

20. E. G. Squier, "Observations on the Creek and Cherokee Indians," *Transactions of the American Ethnological Society* 3, pt. 1 (1853): 1–81.

21. William Bartram, *Travels through North and South Carolina, Georgia, East and West Florida* (Philadelphia: James and Johnson, 1791).

22. Squier and Davis, *Ancient Monuments*, 120.

23. Squier and Davis, *Ancient Monuments*, 120–23.

24. Squier and Davis, *Ancient Monuments*, 143n; Squier, "Observations on the Aboriginal Monuments of the Mississippi Valley," 158n. See also Squier's comments on mounds of more recent origin in *Aboriginal Monuments of the State of New York*, 106–9.

25. Squier and Davis, *Ancient Monuments*, 123.

26. Wailes to Squier, Washington, Mississippi, September 22, 1846, February 26, 1847, SPLC.

27. Squier and Davis, *Ancient Monuments*, xxxvii, xxxvi, 219n.

28. Squier and Davis, *Ancient Monuments*, plate XXXVIII facing p. 108. Morris's descriptions of these works appear on pp. 110–13.

29. Morris to Squier, Mount Sylvan Academy, Lafayette County, Mississippi, March 30, June 3, August 2, August 10, and October 2, 1847, SPLC.

30. Ramsey to Squier, Mecklenburg, Tennessee, September 14, 1848, January 1, 1849, SPLC.

31. Troost, "An Account of Some Ancient Remains in Tennessee," 355–65.

32. Hammond to Squier, New York, September 11, 1847, and Silver Bluff, South Carolina, April 20, 1848, SPLC.

33. Hawks to Squier, New Orleans, April 20, 1848, SPLC.

34. Morton to Squier, Philadelphia, December 23, 1848, SPLC.

35. Marsh to Squier, Washington DC, July 3, 1848, SPLC.

36. Haven to Squier, Worcester, July 18, 1848, SPLC.

37. Sparks to Squier, Cambridge, July 30, 1848, SPLC.

38. Squier and Davis, *Ancient Monuments*, 104n.

39. Squier and Davis, *Ancient Monuments*, xxxiii, 118n.

40. Norton to Squier, Cambridge, Massachusetts, February 5, 1849, and Squier to Norton, New York, February 7, 1849, SPLC. This a copy of an outgoing letter.

41. Squier to Morton, New York, September 27, 1848, SGMP.

42. Squier to Morton, New York, December 28, 1848, SGMP.

43. See Culin, "The Dickeson Collection of American Antiquities," 113–33. Culin's account is an abstract of Dickeson's partially completed manuscript on American antiquities and a manuscript catalog of his collection.

44. Atwater, "Description of the Antiquities Discovered in the State of Ohio," 125.

45. Squier and Davis, *Ancient Monuments*, 145–46, 166; Squier, *Observations on the Uses of the Mounds of the West*, 7, 8; Squier, "On the Discoidal Stones of the Indian Mounds," 216.

46. Squier and Davis, *Ancient Monument*, 188, 242.

47. Squier and Davis, *Ancient Monument*, 153, 246–47.

48. Davis to Squier, Chillicothe, June 9, 1846, SPLC; Squier and Davis, *Ancient Monuments*, 242, 251–52, 254, 260.

49. See Henry W. Henshaw, "Animal Carvings from Mounds of the Mississippi Valley," *Second Annual Report of the Bureau of Ethnology*, 1880–'81 (Washington DC: Government Printing Office, 1883), 123–66.

50. E. G. Squier, "American Antiquities," *Scioto Gazette*, October 23, 1845.

51. Davis to Morton, Chillicothe, October 26, 1845, SGMP.

52. Squier and Davis, *Ancient Monuments*, 273.

53. M. Lewis Clark to Squier, St. Louis, June 8, 1848, SPLC.

54. Schoolcraft, "Observations Respecting the Grave Creek Mound," 386–97. Schoolcraft's views on the Celtic origin of the Grave Creek inscription were essentially the same as those earlier advanced by Carl Christian Rafn of the Royal Society of Northern Antiquaries. See *Memoires de la Société Royale des Antiquaries du Nord, 1840–1843* (Copenhagen: Au Secretariat de la Société, 1844), 125. Edme-François Jomard, however, saw a north African origin and attempted to show the resemblance between the Grave Creek inscription and characters in the ancient Libyan and Numidian alphabets. That was the same conclusion independently arrived at by William B. Hodgson of Savannah, Georgia, a former U.S. consul at Tunis. See Edme-François Jomard, *Seconde Note sur une Pierre Gravee trouvee dans un ancien tumulus Americain* (Paris: Benjamin Duprat, [1845]); and William B. Hodgson, *Notes on Northern Africa, the Sahara, and the Soudan* (New York: Wiley Putnam, 1844), 44–47. Jomard's first notice of the Grave Creek inscription appeared in Eugene A. Vail's *Notice sur les Indiens de l'Amerique du nord* (Paris: Arthus Bertrand, 1840), 37n.

55. Henry R. Schoolcraft, *Incentives to the Study of the Ancient Period of American History* (New York: Press of the Historical Society, 1847), 8, 11–14, 19.

56. Davis to Samuel Foster Haven, Chillicothe, September 20, 1847, SPAAS; Gliddon to Squier, Philadelphia, May 31 and June 8, 1847, SPLC. See also Nott and Gliddon, *Types of Mankind*, 652–53, and their *Indigenous Races of the Earth* (Philadelphia: J. B. Lippincott, 1857), 181n.

57. Gliddon to Squier, Philadelphia, April 16, 1851, SPLC.

58. Squier and Davis, *Ancient Monuments*, 274.

59. Squier to Morton, New York, September 18, 1847, SGMP.

60. Controversy over the origin and meaning of the Grave Creek inscription continued long after Squier pronounced it a fraud. See Terry A. Barnhart, "Curious Antiquity? The Grave Creek Controversy Revisited," *West Virginia History* 46, nos. 1–4 (1985–86): 103–24.

61. Squier, "Observations on the Aboriginal Monuments of the Mississippi Valley," 200n (dialogue), 204, 206n.

62. Davis to Bartlett, Chillicothe, October 28, 1846, JRBP.

63. Squier and Davis, *Ancient Monuments*, 277.

64. Davis to Morton, Chillicothe, October 26, 1845, May 18, 1846, and Squier to Morton, Chillicothe, December 1, 1846, SGMP; Squier and Davis, *Ancient Monuments*, 148, 153n, 163, 164, 168.

65. The quotations in this and the following paragraph are taken from Squier and Davis, *Ancient Monuments*, 288–89.

66. Samuel George Morton, *Crania Americana: Or, A Comparative View of the Skulls of Various Aboriginal Nations of North and South America* (Philadelphia: J. Dobson; London: Simpkin, Marshall, 1839), iii, 219–23, and plates 51–55.

67. Morton, *Crania Americana*, 292, 230.

68. Morton, *Crania Americana*, 6, 63, 83.

69. Troost, "An Account of Some Ancient Remains in Tennessee," 356–57, 359.

70. Squier and Davis, *Ancient Monuments*, 289–90, and Table A, "Comparative Measurements of Crania," 291. The authors gave Morton's mean measurements of eight mound crania as compared to his measurements of their own Scioto Valley skull and those of other skulls previously attributed to "the race of the mounds." See Table B, "Comparative View of Mean Cranial Measurements," 292.

71. Ales Hrdlicka, "Physical Anthropology in America: An Historical Sketch," *American Anthropologist*, n.s., 16 (October–December 1914): 520.

72. Robert Silverberg, *Ancient Mound Builders of America: The Archaeology of a Myth* (Greenwich CT: New York Graphic, 1968), 109. Silverberg misunderstood Squier and Davis on this point and thus found it "a little puzzling, in view of Morton's enthusiastic support for and praise of Squier and Davis, to find that their book employs his statistics while largely rejecting his conclusions" (129–30). Squier and Davis made no such rejection.

73. Jane Buikstra, "Contributions of Physical Anthropologists to the Concept of Hopewell: A Historical Perspective," in *Hopewell Archaeology*, ed. David S. Brose and N'omi Greber (Kent OH: Kent State University Press, 1979), 220–33.

74. Squier and Davis's celebrated Mound Builder skull is no. 1512 in the cranial collection of the Academy of Natural Sciences of Philadelphia. It has since been identified as an aged and slightly deformed brachycephalic cranium of a male Adena Indian. The Grave Creek skull, which Squier and Davis also accepted as an original mound cranium, is also that of an Adena Indian. William S. Webb and Charles E. Snow, *The Adena People* (Knoxville: University of Tennessee Press, 1954), 261, 263.

75. Davis to Morton, Chillicothe, October 26, 1845, SGMP; "American Ethnological Society," *Historical Magazine* 3 (December 1859): 364. See Morton, *An Inquiry into the Distinctive Characteristics of the Aboriginal Race of America*.

76. Squier and Davis, *Ancient Monuments*, 301.

77. Squier and Davis, *Ancient Monuments*, 301.

78. Squier and Davis, *Ancient Monuments*, 10, 50, 60, 89, 304–6.

79. Squier and Davis, *Ancient Monuments*, 14, 16, 305–6.

80. Squier, "American Antiquities."

81. Nott to Squier, September 7, 1848, SPLC. An account of Nott's intellectual relationship with Squier is given by Reginald Horsman in *Josiah Clark Nott*

of Mobile: Southerner, Physician, and Racial Theorist (Baton Rouge: Louisiana State University Press, 1987).

82. See David Levin, *History as Romantic Art* (Stanford CA: Stanford University Press, 1959).

83. Henry, "Organization of the Smithsonian Institution," 88; Joseph Henry, "Explanations and Illustrations of the Plan of the Smithsonian Institution," *American Journal of Science and Arts*, 2nd ser., 6 (November 1848): 306, 314; William J. Rhees, ed., "The Smithsonian Institution: Documents Relative to Its Origin and History," *Smithsonian Miscellaneous Collections* 17 (Washington DC: Smithsonian Institution, 1879), 197, 966, 971; "Great American Work," *Literary World*, September 23, 1848, 680; "Literary News," *Southern Literary Messenger*, July 1848, 456.

84. Henry to Squier, Princeton, June 28, 1848, SPLC.

85. [Theodore Dwight Woolsey], "Monuments of the Mississippi Valley," *New Englander and Yale Review* 7 (February 1849): 95.

86. [Woolsey], "Monuments of the Mississippi Valley," 107, 109.

87. "Western Mound Builders," *Literary World*, October 28, 1848, 768.

88. [Charles Eliot Norton], "Ancient Monuments of the Mississippi Valley," *North American Review* 68 (April 1849): 466–96. Norton identifies himself as the author of the review in Norton to Squier, Cambridge, February 5, 1849, SPLC.

89. [Norton], "Ancient Monuments," 466, 492–93.

90. [Norton], "Ancient Monuments," 493.

91. [Norton], "Ancient Monuments," 494.

92. Squier to Parkman, New York, March 20, 1849, Transcript, SFP. The original of this letter is among others from Squier to Parkman in the Massachusetts Historical Society. As a result of Norton's review of *Ancient Monuments*, he and Squier maintained a long friendship. They were first introduced by Parkman, who was initially concerned that their views would not prove "in all respects congenial – as his education has been rather of the strict and precise sort – yet you will find him a capital fellow and well able to appreciate all you have done." Owing to Norton's influence in literary circles, Parkman recommended him as an "acquaintance worth having." Parkman to Squier, 1849, and Boston, March 15, 1849, in Don Carlos Seitz, ed., *Letters from Francis Parkman to E. G. Squier: With Biographical Notes and a Bibliography of E. G. Squier* (Cedar Rapids IA: Torch Press, 1911), 19–20.

93. [Burke], "Progress of Ethnology in the United States," 170, 177, 184.

94. [Burke], "Progress of Ethnology in the United States," 184.

95. M. Jomard, "Decouvertes recentes sur les bords du scioto," *Bulletin de la Société de Geographie*, 3rd ser., 6 (1846): 226–34; Jomard, "Sur Les Antiquities Americaines: Recement Decouvertes (Lettre a M. Squier), Paris, December 29,

1847," *Bulletin de la Société de Geographie*, 3rd ser., 9–10 (1848): 333–37; Jomard, "Lettre de M. Georges Squier a M. Jomard . . . Sur Les Antiquities Americaines Et La Montagne De Brush Creek," *Bulletin de la Société de Geographie*, 3rd ser., 9–10 (1848): 283–88; and Jomard, "Description D'Un Ancien Ouvrage Appele Le Serpent Sur Les Bords De La Riviere Brush-Creek, Etat De L'Ohio (Extrait)," *Bulletin de la Société de Geographie*, 3rd ser., 9–10 (1848): 288–90.

96. Quoted in Seitz, *Letters from Parkman to Squier*, 12.

97. A. Morlot, "On the Copper Age in the United States," *Proceedings of the American Philosophical Society* 9 (November 1862): 111, 114.

98. See Henshaw, "Animal Carvings from Mounds of the Mississippi Valley," 123–66.

99. See Cyrus Thomas, *The Circular, Square, and Octagonal Earthworks of Ohio* (Washington DC: Government Printing Office, 1889), 21; Thomas, "Report on the Mound Explorations of the Bureau of Ethnology," *Twelfth Annual Report of the Bureau of Ethnology, 1890–91* (Washington DC: Government Printing Office, 1894), 27, 604–10. On the correction of the Squier-Davis surveys, see 454–68 and 472–93. A defense of the surveys of Squier and Davis and a criticism of Thomas's "minimizing tendencies" appear in Stephen Denison Peet, "The Ancient Monuments of the Mississippi Valley," *American Antiquarian* 12, no. 2 (1890): 116–17. See also the various criticisms of Squier and Davis in Gerard Fowke, *Archaeological History of Ohio: The Mound Builders and Later Indians* (Columbus: Ohio Archaeological and Historical Society, 1902), 55–186. Fowke's detractions of Squier and Davis and other early writers of note produced a negative reaction. See Stephen Denison Peet, "Criticism of Fowke's Book," *Ohio Archaeological and Historical Publications* 11, no. 1 (1902): 139–43; in the same issue, see also J. P. MacLean, "Fowke's Book Reviewed," 143–48, and E. O. Randal, "Archaeological Agitation," 160–61.

100. Ephraim George Squier and Edwin H. Davis, *Ancient Monuments of the Mississippi Valley*, edited with an introduction by David J. Meltzer (Washington DC: Smithsonian Institution Press, 1998).

5. REVISITING THE MOUNDS

1. Squier to Bartlett, New York, February 1, 1848, JRBP.

2. Henry to Squier, Princeton, September 30, 1848, Washington, December 16, 1848, and George Henry Moore to Squier, New York, October 20, 1848, SPLC; *Fourth Annual Report of the Smithsonian Institution*, 1849, 31st Cong., 1st sess., Senate, Miscellaneous Doc. no. 120 (Washington DC: Printers to the Senate, 1850), 11. Squier received an additional fifty dollars from the Smithsonian for superintending the publication of the resulting manuscript. Squier

to Henry, letter drafts, December 23, 1848, January 1, 1849 [misdated 1848], SPLC.

3. An earlier account of those investigations is Terry A. Barnhart, "The Iroquois as Mound Builders: Ephraim George Squier and the Archaeology of Western New York," *New York History* 77 (April 1996): 125–50.

4. Griffin noted this feature of Squier's archaeology in regard to his investigations with Davis in Ohio, but the extent to which Squier continued this methodology in his investigations in New York has not been fully appreciated. See Griffin's introduction to Squier and Davis, *Ancient Monuments of the Mississippi Valley* (1973), vii–ix.

5. De Witt Clinton, *A Memoir on the Antiquities of the Western Parts of the State of New-York* (Albany: J. W. Clark, 1818) (Clinton read his address before the Literary and Philosophical Society of New-York on November 13, 1817); John V. N. Yates and Joseph W. Moulton, *History of the State of New-York*, vol. 1, pt. 1 (New York: A. T. Goodrich, 1824); James Macauley, *The Natural, Statistical, and Civil History of the State of New York*, vol. 2 (New York: Gould and Banks, 1829); Henry Rowe Schoolcraft, *Notes on the Iroquois* (Albany: Erastus H. Pease, 1847).

6. Squier and Davis, *Ancient Monuments*, xxii, 1n, 42, 44, 46.

7. Squier, *Aboriginal Monuments of the State of New York*, 11.

8. C. F. Hoffman to [Peter] Wilson, New York, October 12, 1848, SPIHS; Edward Robinson to Moses Bristole, New York, October 17, 1848, Frederick De Peyster to Charles G. Myers, New York, October 18, 1848, and Luther Brandish to Squier, New York, October 23, 1848, SPLC.

9. Thomas T. Davis to Selah Matthews, Syracuse, November 6, 1848; Orsamus H. Marshall to August Porter, November 14, 1848; Moses Long to E. P. Smith, Rochester, November 16, 1848; August Porter to Squier, Niagara Falls, November 18, 1848; Janus Clark to [W. W.] Turner, Lancaster, November 21, 1848; O. Turner to Squier, Buffalo, December 17, 1848; W. [Mc]Bride to Squier, Black Rock, December 22, 1848; J. H. Clark to Squier, Manlius, January 23, 1849; and Justice Eddy to Squier, Jefferson County, New York, February 28, 1849; all letters are found in SPLC.

10. Morgan to the Board of Regents, November 13, 1848, in *Second Annual Report of the Regents of the State University of New York, on the Condition of the State Cabinet* (Albany: Weed, Parsons, 1849), 90–91; Squier to Morgan, New York, December 14, 1848, Lewis Henry Morgan Papers, University of Rochester Library; Morgan to Squier, Rochester, December 22, 1848, March 5, 1849, SPLC.

11. Discussion of the map appears in Morgan to Squier, Rochester, December 22, 1848, January 18, March 5, 1849, and Henry to Squier, Smithsonian Institution, February 20, 1849, SPLC; Squier to Morgan, New York, March 20, 1849, Morgan Papers, University of Rochester Library; Thomas H. Bond et al.

to unknown party, Albany, March 27, 1849, JRBP; and *Literary World*, April 7, 1849, 316.

12. Parkman to Squier, Boston, May 13, November 18, 1849, in Seitz, *Letters from Parkman to Squier*, 22, 27. Parkman initially confused Morgan with Orsamus Holmes Marshall (1813–84) in regard to the proposed publication of a map of the Iroquois country. Marshall shared Morgan's interest in documenting Iroquois place-names and would have been equally up to the task of making such a map. Parkman later reviewed Squier's *Aboriginal Monuments of the State of New York* and Morgan's *League of the Iroquois* together. See Francis Parkman Jr., "Indian Antiquities in North America," *Christian Examiner*, 50 (May 1851): 417–28.

13. See Lewis Henry Morgan, "Map of Ho-De-No-Sau-Nee-Ga, or Territories of the People of the Long House in 1720," in his *League of the Ho-de-no-sau-nee or Iroquois*, ed. Herbert M. Lloyd, 2 vols. (New York: Dodd, Mead, 1901), 46 and appendix A, no. 1: "Schedule Explanatory of the Indian Map," 127–39. Morgan had been at work on this map for several years. It gives the aboriginal names of villages, natural features, the "ancient localities" of the Iroquois, and the routes of their principal trails. Sage and Brother published the original edition of *League of the Iroquois* at Rochester in 1851. Joseph Henry valued Morgan's opinion regarding ethnological mapping and published his recommendations in the Smithsonian *Annual Report* for 1861. See Lewis H. Morgan, "Suggestions Relative to an Ethnological Map of North America," *Annual Report of the Board of Regents of the Smithsonian Institution for 1861* (Washington DC: Government Printing Office, 1862), 397–98.

14. Squier to Bartlett, Buffalo, November 12, 1848, JRBP.

15. E. G. Squier, "Report upon the Aboriginal Monuments of Western New York," *Proceedings of the New-York Historical Society* (January 1849): 41–61. Squier gave his report before the society on January 2, 1849.

16. E. G. Squier, *Aboriginal Monuments of the State of New York: Comprising the Results of Original Surveys and Explorations, With an Illustrated Appendix*, Article IX of *Smithsonian Contributions to Knowledge*, vol. 2 (Washington DC: Smithsonian Institution, 1851), 100 pages and 14 lithographic plates of survey maps. There has been much confusion about the year in which the Smithsonian actually published this work. It is often incorrectly cited as 1849, when the manuscript was submitted to the Smithsonian and accepted for publication, rather than 1851, when it was published.

17. E. G. Squier, *Antiquities of the State of New York: Being the Results of Extensive Original Surveys and Explorations, with a Supplement on the Antiquities of the West* (Buffalo: George H. Derby, 1851). The pagination and sometimes the text in this edition differ from that found in the *Smithsonian Contributions to Knowledge*.

The privately printed edition is cited here only where revisions further elucidate important points of inquiry. In these instances, citations appear as *Antiquities of the State of New York*.

18. Squier to Bartlett, Buffalo, November 12, 1848, JRBP.

19. Squier, *Aboriginal Monuments of the State of New York*, 10–12; Squier to Bartlett, Syracuse, October 26, November 7, 1848, JRBP; Squier to parents, New York, December 8, 1848, SFP.

20. Squier, *Aboriginal Monuments of the State of New York*, 12–13, 18, 75–80.

21. Squier to Bartlett, Syracuse, November 7, 1848, JRBP.

22. Squier, *Antiquities of the State of New York*, 125. Squier's comments on implements and ornaments are greatly expanded in the privately printed edition.

23. *Second Annual Report of the Regents of the State University of New York*, 10–11; *Third Annual Report of the Regents of the University of the State of New York, on the Condition of the State Cabinet of Natural History, and the Historical and Antiquarian Collection* (Albany: Weed, Parsons, 1850), 10, 15, 55–56.

24. Squier, *Aboriginal Monuments of the State of New York*, 67–74.

25. The source for this and the following two paragraphs is Squier, *Aboriginal Monuments of the State of New York*, 82–84.

26. See Schoolcraft, *Notes on the Iroquois*, 442; Morgan, *League of the Iroquois*, 1:305–6; O. H. Marshall, "Champlain's Expedition of 1615 against the Onondagas," *Magazine of American History* 1 (January 1877): 2, 13; and Francis Parkman to Squier, Boston, November 18, 1849, in Seitz, *Letters from Parkman to Squier*, 27.

27. Whether the name Gah-kwas (or Kahkwas) referred to the Erie or to the Neutral Indians has been a source of controversy. The designation is problematic since both the French and the Huron sometimes applied the name of a particular village to an entire tribe. The Erie were located on the southeastern shore of Lake Erie, west of the Seneca, and the Neutral peoples were on the northern shore. Little is known of these seventeenth-century groups other than their affinity with northern Iroquoian cultural patterns. Marian E. White, "Neutral and Wenro," in *Handbook of North American Indians*, ed. Bruce G. Trigger, vol. 15 (Washington DC: Smithsonian Institution, 1978), 411, and see 412 for her "Erie."

28. Squier, *Aboriginal Monuments of the State of New York*, 83.

29. Squier, *Aboriginal Monuments of the State of New York*, 83–85.

30. Whittlesey to Squier, [Cleveland, Ohio], February 27, 1849, SPLC.

31. Charles Whittlesey, "On the Evidences of the Antiquity of Man in the United States," *Proceedings of the American Association for the Advancement of Science* 17 (August 1868): 279.

32. Squier, *Aboriginal Monuments of the State of New York*, 81.

33. Squier, *Aboriginal Monuments of the State of New York*, 99.

34. Squier, *Aboriginal Monuments of the State of New York*, 107.

35. E. G. Squier, "Historical and Mythological Traditions of the Algonquins, with a Translation of the 'Walum-Olum,' or Bark Record of the Lenni-Lenape," *American Review*, n.s., 3 (February 1849): 273, 292.

36. Morgan to Squier, Rochester, March 5, 1849, SPLC.

37. Morgan to the Board of Regents, November 13, 1848, *Second Annual Report of the Regents of the State University of New York*, 90–91.

38. Morgan, *League of the Iroquois*, 2:5, 5 n. 1, 8–9, 12.

39. Morgan to Squier, Rochester, March 5, 1849, SPLC.

40. Morgan, *League of the Iroquois*, 1:46, 161. Morgan recorded a Seneca and Onondaga tradition connected with a burial mound near Geneva (2:90n).

41. O. H. Marshall, "The Niagara Frontier," in *The Historical Writings of the Late Orsamus H. Marshall* (Albany: Joel Munsell's Sons, 1887), 277–78. Marshall read this account before the Buffalo Historical Society on February 27, 1865.

42. William A. Ritchie, *The Pre-Iroquoian Occupations of New York State* (Rochester: Rochester Museum of Arts and Sciences, 1944), 2. Ritchie seems confused on what to make of Squier's findings on this point. Elsewhere he states that Squier "correctly related them [mound structures] to the 'Mound Builders' of Ohio," thus contradicting both himself and Squier. William A. Ritchie, *The Archaeology of New York State* (Garden City NY: Natural History Press, 1965), 213.

43. Another early account of works in western New York is [Theseus] Apoleon Cheney, "Ancient Monuments in Western New York," *Contributions to the Thirteenth Annual Report of the Regents of the University on the State Cabinet of Natural History of the State of New York* (Albany: C. Van Benthuysen, 1860). Cheney's account gives the results of the explorations he conducted in 1859 at previously unexplored sites in Cattaraugus and Chautauqua Counties bordering Lake Erie. Cheney concluded that the earthworks in this section corresponded with those found elsewhere in the state and in northern Ohio. He thought the greater regularity of their outlines, however, more nearly resembled those found in the Mississippi Valley. Squier thought otherwise.

6. THE BURDEN OF PROOF

1. E. G. Squier, "Ne-She-Kay-Be-Nais, or the 'Lone Bird,' " *American Review*, n.s., 2 (September 1848): 255–59; Squier, "Manabozho and the Great Serpent: An Algonquin Tradition," *American Review*, n.s., 2 (October 1848): 392–98; and Squier, "Historical and Mythological Traditions of the Algonquins," 273–93. A typographical error in the original makes the pagination of this account read as pages 273 to 293, but it should be pages 173–93 to be in sequence with the

February 1849 number of the *America Review*. The pagination is retained here as it appears in the original.

2. Squier, "Historical and Mythological Traditions of the Algonquins," 275.

3. Squier, "Ne-She-Kay-Be-Nais," 256.

4. Squier, "Historical and Mythological Traditions of the Algonquins," 275.

5. Squier, "American Ethnology," 393.

6. Squier, "Ne-She-Kay-Be-Nais," 255.

7. Squier, "Manabozho and the Great Serpent," 392.

8. John Howard Payne, "Cherokee Manuscript," as cited in Squier, "Manabozho and the Great Serpent," 393 and n. The John Howard Payne Papers relating to the Cherokee are now part of the Edward E. Ayer Collection at the Newberry Library, Chicago.

9. Schoolcraft, *Notes on the Iroquois*, 270.

10. Thomas L. McKenney, *Sketches of a Tour to the Lakes, [and] of the Character and Customs of the Chippeway Indians, and of Incidents Connected with the Treaty of Fond Du Lac* (Baltimore: Fielding Lucas, Jr., 1827), 302–5; John Tanner, *A Narrative of the Captivity and Adventures of John Tanner (U.S. Interpreter at the Sault de Ste. Marie) during Thirty Years Residence among the Indians in the Interior of North America*, ed. Edwin James (New York: G. and C. and H. Carvill, 1830), 351.

11. Pierre-Jean de Smet, *Oregon Missions and Travels over the Rocky Mountains in 1845 and 1846* (New York: E. Dunigan, 1847), 347, 352, 353.

12. Henry Rowe Schoolcraft, *Algic Researches, Comprising Inquiries Respecting the Mental Characteristics of the North American Indians*, vol. 1 (New York: Harper and Row, 1839), 134.

13. Squier, "Manabozho and the Great Serpent."

14. Squier, "Manabozho and the Great Serpent," 398.

15. Prince Maximilian on the Mandan tradition of the serpent-being as cited by Squier in "Manabozho and the Great Serpent," 398. Squier's source is Prince Maximilian, *Travels in the Interior of North America*, trans. H. E. Loyd (London: Ackermann, 1843).

16. Squier, "Historical and Mythological Traditions of the Algonquins," 273, 292. Squier's views on a Natchez-Toltecan connection are based on Morton, *Crania Americana*, iii, 65, 157, 160–62; Morton, *An Inquiry into the Distinctive Characteristics of the Aboriginal Race of America*, 17; and Morton, "Some Observations on the Ethnology and Archaeology of the American Aborigines," *American Journal of Science and Arts*, 2nd ser., 2 (July 1846): 5–6, figs. 2 and 3. Similar commentary on the Natchez and possible connections with the Mexicans and Central Americans appears in James H. McCulloh Jr., *Researches, Philosophical and Antiquarian, Concerning the Aboriginal History of America* (Baltimore: Fielding Lucas, Jr., 1829), 69, 149–73, 271.

17. Squier, "Historical and Mythological Traditions of the Algonquins," 274.

18. Squier, "Historical and Mythological Traditions of the Algonquins," 274.

19. Benjamin Smith Barton, *New Views of the Origin of the Tribes and Nations of America*, 2nd ed. enlarged (Philadelphia: John Bioren, 1798), iv–v, xii–xv.

20. McCulloh, *Researches, Philosophical and Antiquarian*, 225.

21. William Hickling Prescott, *History of the Conquest of Mexico*, vol. 1 (New York: Harper and Brothers, 1843), 59.

22. Tod's *Rajasthan*, 1:538, cited in Squier, "Manabozho and the Great Serpent," 392n.

23. Squier, "Historical and Mythological Traditions of the Algonquins." William Beach reprinted Squier's account in his *Indian Miscellany: Containing Papers on the History, Antiquities, Arts, Languages, Traditions, and Superstitions of the American Aborigines* (Albany: J. Munsell, 1877), 9–42. It also appears in the appendix of Samuel G. Drake's *Aboriginal Races of North America* (New York: Hurst, 1880), 718–36.

24. Constantine S. Rafinesque, *The American Nations: or, Outlines of Their General History, Ancient and Modern*, vol. 1 (Philadelphia: C. S. Rafinesque, 1836), 122, 124, and an "Additional Note" on 160.

25. See Charles E. Boewe, "The Manuscripts of C. S. Rafinesque (1783–1840)," *Proceedings of the American Philosophical Society* 102 (December 1958): 590–95, and his *Fitzpatrick's Rafinesque: A Sketch of His Life with Bibliography* (Weston MA: M and S Press, 1982). The Historical Department of Iowa at Des Moines originally published Thomas Jefferson Fitzpatrick's *Rafinesque* in 1911. Boewe's revised and enlarged edition of this work is the point of departure for all research into the extensive writings of Rafinesque on all subjects.

26. See C. S. Rafinesque, *The Ancient Monuments of North and South America*, 2nd ed. rev. (Philadelphia, 1838), a twenty-eight-page pamphlet. The work originally appeared as "The Ancient Monuments of North and South America, Compared with Those of the Eastern Continent," *American Museum of Science, Literature, and the Arts* 1 (September 1838): 10–23.

27. See Paul Weer, "Brantz Mayer and the Walum Olum Manuscript," *Proceedings of the Indiana Academy of Science* 54 (1944): 44–48.

28. Squier, "Historical and Mythological Traditions of the Algonquins," 275.

29. Rafinesque, *American Nations*, 1:122, 151 n. 3.

30. Squier, "Historical and Mythological Traditions of the Algonquins," 275.

31. John Heckewelder, "An Account of the History, Manners and Customs

of the Indian Nations Who Once Inhabited Pennsylvania and the Neighboring States," *Transactions of the Historical and Literary Committee of the American Philosophical Society* 1 (1819): 118.

32. George Henry Loskiel, *History of the Mission of the United Brethren among the Indians in America*, trans. Christian Ignatus La Trobe (London: Burlinghouse, 1794), 25. The original German edition of this work appeared in 1788. Loskiel's *History* contains valuable information but must be used with caution. That portion dealing with Lenape beliefs and customs is based on a manuscript sent to Loskiel by the Moravian missionary David Zeisberger in 1779 and 1780, which is based on Zeisberger's own firsthand experiences and observations. Zeisberger's account is less filtered. See Earl P. Olmstead, *Blackcoats among the Lenape: David Zeisberger on the Ohio Frontier* (Kent, Ohio: Kent State University Press, 1991), 87, 178–79, 261 n. 2.

33. Squier, "Historical and Mythological Traditions of the Algonquins," 277.

34. Paul Weer curiously states that Squier submitted the Walam Olum manuscript to an educated Delaware for authentication, but he does not cite any evidence in support of that statement in an otherwise well-documented analysis. Squier himself never made any such claim, and there is no indication that he ever consulted the Delaware. He did submit the manuscript to the opinion of George Copway, but he makes no mention of having consulted the Delaware. It appears that Weer either incorrectly assumed that Copway was a Delaware or else confused Squier with Daniel G. Brinton, who did, in fact, consult with Delaware speakers. Paul Weer, "History of the Walam Olum Manuscript and Painted Records," in *Walam Olum, or Red Score: The Migration Legend of the Lenni Lenape or Delaware Indians; A New Translation, Interpreted by Linguistic, Historical, Archaeological, Ethnological, and Physical Anthropological Studies* (Indianapolis: Indiana Historical Society, 1954), 265.

35. David M. Oestreicher, "Unmasking the Walam Olum: A Nineteenth-Century Hoax," *Bulletin of the Archaeological Society of New Jersey* no. 4 (1994): 21, 35–36 n. 18. Copway describes how the Ojibwa carved sacred records on pieces of bark and wood, which were then buried in the ground for safekeeping by tribal guardians. See George Copway, *Traditional History and Characteristic Sketches of the Ojibway Nation* (London: C. Gilpin, 1850), 128, 131–32. His Ojibwa pictographs appear on 132–34. B. F. Mussey and Company of Boston published an edition of this work in 1851.

36. Squier, "Historical and Mythological Traditions of the Algonquins," 277.

37. Loskiel, *History of the Mission of the United Brethren*, 34.

38. Jonathan Carver, *Travels through the Interior Parts of North America in the Years 1766, 1767, and 1768* (London: J. Walter 1778), 381.

39. Squier, "Historical and Mythological Traditions of the Algonquins," 281.

40. Pierre-François Charlevoix, *Journal of a Voyage to North-America*, vol. 2 (London: R. and J. Dodsley, 1761), 142–43.

41. Alexander Henry, *Travels and Adventures in Canada and the Indian Territories, between the Years 1760 and 1776* (New York: I. Riley, 1809), 37, 110, 168.

42. Heckewelder, "Account," 246, 308.

43. Squier, "Historical and Mythological Traditions of the Algonquins," 286.

44. Sir Alexander Mackenzie, *Voyages from Montreal, on the River St. Laurence, Through the Continent of North America, . . . in the Years 1789 and 1793* (London: T. Cadell, Jr. and W. Davies, 1801), 113.

45. See Stephen Williams, "The Strait of Anian: A Pathway to the New World," 10–29, and "From Whence Came Those Aboriginal Inhabitants of America?" 30–59, both in Browman and Williams, *New Perspectives*.

46. Samuel Foster Haven, *Archaeology of the United States: Or Sketches, Historical and Bibliographical, of the Progress of Information and Opinion Respecting Vestiges of Antiquity in the United States*, vol. 8 of *Smithsonian Contributions to Knowledge* (Washington DC: Smithsonian Institution), 1856), 159.

47. Acosta's work first appeared in English in 1604. For his notion of polar land bridges see José de Acosta, *Naturall and Morall Historie of the East and West Indies* (London: Privately Printed for Edward Blount and William Aspley, 1604), 64–71.

48. Squier, "Historical and Mythological Traditions of the Algonquins," 290.

49. Loskiel, *History of the Mission of the United Brethren*, 24.

50. Squier, "Historical and Mythological Traditions of the Algonquins," 291.

51. Heckewelder, "Account," 47–51.

52. Heckewelder, "Account," 388. Squier may first have learned of Heckewelder's recording of this tradition by reading Morton, *Crania Americana*, 230, 292.

53. John Lawson, *A New Voyage to Carolina: Containing the Exact Description and Natural History of That Country, Together with the Present State Thereof and a Journal of a Thousand Miles Traveled Through Several Nations of Indians, Giving a Particular Account of Their Customs, Manners, etc.* (London: Privately Printed for the Author, 1709), 170.

54. Payne, "Cherokee Manuscript," cited in Squier, "Historical and Mythological Traditions of the Algonquins," 292–93.

55. Squier, "Historical and Mythological Traditions of the Algonquins," 293.

56. The source of this and the following two paragraphs is Schoolcraft to Squier, Washington DC, February 16, 1849, Manuscripts and Archives Division, New York Public Library. The letter is reproduced in full in Clinton Alfred Weslager's *The Delaware Indians: A History* (New Brunswick NJ: Rutgers University Press, 1972), appendix 2, 470–72.

57. See Regna Darnell, *Daniel Garrison Brinton: The "Fearless Critic" of Philadelphia* (Philadelphia: Department of Anthropology, University of Pennsylvania Monograph no. 3, 1988); and Darnell, "Daniel Brinton and the Professionalization of American Anthropology," *Proceedings of the American Ethnological Society* (1974): 69–98.

58. Daniel G. Brinton, *The Lenape and Their Legends: With the Complete Text and Symbols of the Walam Olum, A New Translation, and an Inquiry into Its Authenticity*, Brinton's Library of Aboriginal American Literature no. 5 (Philadelphia: D. G. Brinton, 1885), v–vi.

59. Brinton, *The Lenape and Their Legends*, v, 87, 88, 156, 159.

60. Brinton, *The Lenape and Their Legends*, 158–59.

61. Brinton, *The Lenape and Their Legends*, 155.

62. The materials Squier used to publish his account of the Walam Olum are in the Squier Papers at the Library of Congress. See "Archaeology," box 1. I have had no opportunity to compare them with the Rafinesque manuscript.

63. Brinton, *The Lenape and Their Legends*, 163, 220n, and his *Aboriginal American Authors and Their Productions* (1883; Chicago: Checagou Reprints, 1970), 21.

64. Weslager, *The Delaware Indians*, 85–86.

65. Herbert C. Kraft, *The Lenape: Archaeology, History, and Ethnography* (Newark: New Jersey Historical Society, 1986), xiv, 7.

66. "Premier Supplement a l'Examen analytique," 266, Archives Institut de France, Paris. Rafinesque sent the fourteen-page supplement to his unpublished Prix Volney essay on Algonquian languages and dialects to A. I Silvestre de Sacy of the Prix Volney Committee. The supplement is dated December 24, 1834, and is cited in David M. Oestreicher, "Roots of the Walam Olum: Constantine Samuel Rafinesque and the Intellectual Heritage of the Early Nineteenth Century," in Browman and Williams, *New Perspectives*, 60, 290 n. 3, and in Oestreicher's "Unmasking the Walam Olum," 14–15. The existence of Rafinesque's unpublished Prix Volney essay and the appended supplement was unknown until their discovery in the archives of the Royal Institute of France by Joan Leopold in 1982 and their identification the following year by

Jean Rousseau. The most thorough discussion of Rafinesque's essay and the circumstances surrounding its discovery are found in Charles Boewe, "The Other Candidate for the 1835 Volney Prize: Constantine Samuel Rafinesque" in Joan Leopold, ed. *The Prix Volney: III Contributions to Comparative Indo-European, African, and Chinese Linguistics* vol. 2, *Early-Nineteenth Century Contributions to General and Amerindian Linguistics: Duponceau and Rafinesque* (Dordrecht, The Netherlands: Kluwer Academic Publishers, 1999). A revised and more accessible version of Boewe's analsysis of Rafinesque's Volney Prize essay appears in his *Profiles of Rafinesque* (Knoxville: University of Tennessee Press, 2003).

67. Weslager, *The Delaware Indians*, 84–85.

68. Charles Boewe, "The Walam Olum and Dr. Ward, Again," *Indiana Magazine of History* 83 (December 1987): 348.

69. August C. Mahr, "Walam Olum, I, 17: A Proof of Rafinesque's Integrity," *American Anthropologist* 59 (1957): 705–8.

70. See Tanner, *Narrative*, 351–62; and Brinton, *The Lenape and Their Legends*, 152. David M. Oestreicher provides examples of Rafinesque's "theft" of pictographs from Tanner's *Narrative* and their use in the Walam Olum in "The Anatomy of a Hoax: The Dissection of a Nineteenth-Century Anthropological Hoax" (Ph.D. diss., Rutgers University, New Brunswick NJ, 1995), 130, 144–46, 172–77, 184–86, 193–98. Others have also commented on the similarity between the Midewiwin symbols of the Ojibwa appearing in the appendix of Tanner's *Narrative* and the pictographs of the Walam Olum. See Evan M. Maurer, *The Native American Heritage: A Survey of North American Indian Art* (Chicago: Art Institute of Chicago, 1977), 141–42; and Frederick J. Dockstader, *Indian Art in America* (Greenwich CT: New York Graphic Society, 1967), 223.

71. Kraft, *The Lenape*, 5, 7, 248 n. 25.

72. Oscar Williams, ed., *A Little Treasury of American Poetry* (New York: Scribner, 1948), xv. Some of Rafinesque's pictographs and translations appear on pages 3–9.

73. See Andrew Wiget, *Native American Literature* (Boston: Twayne Publishers, 1985), 44–69, who describes the Walam Olum as the beginnings of a written language; and Alan R. Velie, ed., *American Indian Literature, an Anthology* (Norman: University of Oklahoma Press, 1979), 93–135, for the Walam Olum and Velie's discussion of it. The Walam Olum also appears in George W. Cronyn, ed., *The Path of the Rainbow: An Anthology of Songs and Changes from the Indians of North America* (New York: Liveright, 1934), 35–37. Cronym writes: "This famous, the only written (pictograph) historical record extant among the Eastern tribes, is included as an example of the Saga element in Indian literature" (37n). Cronyn's anthology was originally published in 1918, with later editions appearing in 1972 and 1991. See also William M. Clements and Frances M.

Malpessi, eds., *Native American Folklore, 1879–1979: An Annotated Bibliography* (Athens: Ohio University Press, 1984).

74. See, e.g., David McCutchen, *The Red Record: The Wallam Olum; The Oldest Native North American History*, translation and annotation by David McCutchen (Garden City Park NY: Avery, 1993).

75. William W. Newcomb Jr., *The Culture and Acculturation of the Delaware Indians, University of Michigan Museum of Anthropology, Anthropological Papers No. 10* (Ann Arbor: University of Michigan Museum of Anthropology, 1956), 5; and Newcomb, "The Walam Olum of the Delaware Indians in Perspective," *Texas Journal of Science* 7 (March 1955): 57–63.

76. See Oestreicher, "Roots of the Walam Olum," 60–86. See also his "Unraveling the Walam Olum," *Natural History* 105, no. 10 (1996): 14–21; "The Anatomy of a Hoax"; "Text Out of Context: The Arguments That Sustained and Created the Walam Olum," *Bulletin of the Archaeological Society of New Jersey* no. 50 (1995): 31–52; and "Unmasking the Walam Olum," 1–44.

77. See Rafinesque, "Ancient Annals of Kentucky," in Humphrey Marshall, *The History of Kentucky*, 2nd rev. ed., vol. 1 (Frankfort: Geo. S. Robinson, 1824), 31–33.

78. C. S. Rafinesque, *A Life of Travels and Researches* (Philadelphia: Printed for the Author by F. Turner, 1836), 74.

79. Brinton, *The Lenape and Their Legends*, 154.

80. Weer, "History of the Walam Olum Manuscript and Painted Records," 243–72. See also Weer's "Provenience of the Walam Olum," *Proceedings of the Indiana Academy of Science* 51 (1941): 55–59.

81. William Barlow and David O. Powell, " 'The Late Dr. Ward of Indiana': Rafinesque's Source of the Walam Olum," *Indiana Magazine of History* 82 (June 1986): 185–93.

82. Boewe, "The Walam Olum and Dr. Ward, Again," 344–59.

83. C. S. Rafinesque, "Philology. First Letter to Champollion, on Graphic Systems of America, and the Glyphs of Otolum or Palenque, in Central America," *Atlantic Journal* 1, no. 1 (1832): 4. See also, in the same issue, "Philology. Second Letter to Champollion on the Graphic Systems of America, and the Glyphs of Otolum or Palenque, in Central America. – Elements of the Glyphs," 40–44.

84. Rafinesque, *Ancient Monuments of North and South America*, 28.

85. C. S. Rafinesque, *The Good Book, and Amenities of Nature, or Annals of Historical and Natural Sciences* (Philadelphia: Printed for the Eleutherium of Knowledge, 1840), 69.

86. See Rafinesque, *Ancient History, or Annals of Kentucky; with a Survey of the Ancient Monuments of North America* (Frankfort, Ky., 1824), appendix I, "Enumer-

ation of the Sites of Ancient Towns and Monuments of Kentucky, etc.," 33–37. Rafinesque's pamphlet *Ancient History, or Annals of Kentucky* originally appeared as the introduction to Humphrey Marshall's *History of Kentucky*, 1:ix–xii, 13–47. Rafinesque's appended enumeration of archaeological sites is given on pages 41–45 of Marshall.

87. Squier and Davis, *Ancient Monuments*, xxxvi; plate IX. no. 3, facing p. 24; plate XII, facing p. 31; plate XIII, facing p. 35; plate XIV, nos. 3 and 4, facing p. 36; plate XXXII, no. 6, facing p. 91; plate XXXIII, facing p. 93; and plate XXXVIII, no. 1, facing p. 108. See also E. G. Squier, "A Monograph of the Ancient Monuments of the State of Kentucky," *American Journal of Science and Arts* 8 sec. s. no. 22 (July 1849), 1–14.

88. See Charles Stout and R. Barry Lewis, "Constantine Rafinesque and the Canton Site, a Mississippian Town in Trigg County, Kentucky," *Southeastern Archaeology* 14 (Summer 1995): 83–90. Rafinesque made the plan and description of the site in 1833. Stout and Lewis have verified the accuracy of most of Rafinesque's description and map.

89. Charles Boewe, ed. *John D. Clifford's "Indian Antiquities,"* [and] *Related Material by C. S. Rafinesque* (Knowville: University of Tennessee Press, 2000), 146n, 151n. The Rafinesque material appears in four appendices together with Boewe's explanatory notes, which will go a long way toward granting Rafinesque his due as an early investigator of archaeological sites in the American Southeast. Boewe further corrects the record regarding the significance of Rafinesque's archaeological contributions in his pamphlet *C. S. Rafinesque and Ohio Valley Archaeology* (Barnardsville NC: Center for Ancient American Studies, 2004).

90. Boewe, *Clifford's "Indian Antiquities,"* xxvi, 137 n. 24. Boewe further observes (137 n. 24): "It is even more inexcusable that they [Squier and Davis] also remained ignorant of Rafinesque's published descriptions of Kentucky archaeological sites," even though the authors specifically noted that Rafinesque had published "several brief papers" relating to antiquities of the Mississippi Valley. Clearly Squier and Davis were not ignorant of those papers, since they made passing mention of them. It was not germane to their purpose to enter into a discussion of Rafinesque's earlier writings (copies of which may not have been in their possession), but it was germane to publish, with due credit, the original Rafinesque site plans that were in their possession in order to make their work as comprehensive as possible.

91. The jacket of Boewe's *Clifford's "Indian Antiquities"* – which possibly should not be attributed to the author – states even more strongly (and, unfortunately, even more incorrectly) that "Rafinesque's contribution [to archaeology] has also been neglected because it was pillaged by another well-known scholar,

E. G. Squier, who gave no credit to his source." Squier, quite to the contrary, credited Rafinesque's contributions repeatedly. See Squier and Davis, *Ancient Monuments*, xxxiii, xxxvi, 26, 31n, 35–36, 77, 93, 108n, 117n, and 175n and 176n.

92. Squier and Davis, *Ancient Monuments*, 194. Boewe notes that "Squier had silently lifted this drawing, probably from an unpublished Rafinesque manuscript ('Ancient Monuments of North and South America') then in his possession but now at the University of Pennsylvania." Boewe, "The Walam Olum and Dr. Ward, Again," 351 n. 21. Boewe states his case against Squier's use of the Rafinesque manuscripts in even stronger terms in his *C. S. Rafinesque and Ohio Valley Archaeology*, 11–14 and 18. Here he says that Squier "plagiarized" and committed "petty intellectual pilferage" in his use of the Rafinesque manuscripts, and that "it is hard to escape the conclusion that Squier filched many of Rafinesque's discoveries as well as several of his papers." Squier acknowledged that he was publishing original Rafinesque materials both in *Ancient Monuments of the Mississippi Valley* and in his article on aboriginal sites in Kentucky that appeared in the *American Journal of Science and Arts* in July of 1849. That hardly constitutes plagiarism, pilfering, or filching. Nonetheless, Boewe ably demonstrates Squier's "ham-handed use" of Rafinesque's site plans, and that the originals are more accurate than the engraved versions published by Squier in *Ancient Monuments of the Mississippi Valley*.

93. C. F. Rafinesque, "Three Letters on American Antiquities, Directed to the Honorable Thomas Jefferson, Late President of the United States. First Letter. On the Alleghawian Records," *Kentucky Reporter*, August 16, 1820; "Second Letter. Description of the Alleghawian Monuments," *Kentucky Reporter*, August 23, 1820; and "Third Letter. On Some Alleghawian Implements, &c," *Kentucky Reporter*, September 6, 1820.

94. Squier, "A Monograph of the Ancient Monuments of the State of Kentucky." Rafinesque's second letter to Jefferson appears on pages 8 and 11–12.

95. John D. Clifford (1779–1820) of Lexington, Kentucky, associated circular and ovular earthworks with sun worship and representations of the "mundane egg" of the Hindus in his second and third letters on "Indian Antiquities" that appeared in the *Western Review and Miscellaneous Magazine* in October and November 1819, respectively. Clifford believed that the Mound Builders were descended from the Hindus. The letters are reprinted in Boewe, *Clifford's "Indian Antiquities,"* 12, 19. Rafinesque, a friend and companion of Clifford's, most certainly would have been familiar with that opinion. Whether Clifford borrowed the idea from Rafinesque or vice versa in unknown, but they may well have arrived at the opinion independently, as Squier probably did also.

96. See Victor Wolfgang von Hagen, "Rafinesque, the Unnatural Naturalist," *Natural History* 56 (1947): 296–303.

97. The most recent study is Charles Boewe, *Profiles of Rafinesque*. Most of the attention has centered on Rafinesque's numerous contributions as a naturalist, where he has been both hailed as a misunderstood genius and condemned as a charlatan. A sampling of reaction to Rafinesque by his contemporaries and later scholars is found in Boewe, *Fitzpatrick's Rafinesque*, "Bibliotheca Rafinesquiana," 263–323. See also the bibliographical references in Boewe's *Mantissa: A Supplement to Fitzpatrick's Rafinesque* (Providence RI: M and S Press, 2001).

98. Haven, *Archaeology of the United States*, 39–41, 41n; Brinton, *Lenape and Their Legends*, 150–51; R. J. Farquharson, "Phonetic Elements in American Languages," *American Antiquarian* 1 (January 1879): 136–38; and Justin Winsor, ed., *Narrative and Critical History of America*, vol. 1 (Boston: Houghton Mifflin, 1889), 424.

99. Stephen Williams, *Fantastic Archaeology: The Wild Side of North American Prehistory* (Philadelphia: University of Pennsylvania Press, 1991), 98.

100. Boewe, *Clifford's "Indian Antiquities,"* 135–36 n. 15. See also Boewe's "The Fall from Grace of That 'Base Wretch' Rafinesque," *Kentucky Review* 7 (Fall–Winter 1987): 39–53.

7. IDOLS AND INDIANS

1. E. G. Squier, "Ancient Monuments in the Islands of Lake Nicaragua, Central America," *Literary World*, March 9, 1850, 233–35, March 16, 1850, 269–70, and March 23, 1850, 304–5. Leo Deuel reprinted most of this account in his *Conquistadors without Swords: Archaeologists in the Americas* (New York: St. Martin's Press, 1977).

2. Ephraim George Squier, *Nicaragua: Its People, Scenery, Monuments, and the Proposed Interoceanic Canal*, 2 vols. (New York: D. Appleton; London: Longman, Brown, Green, and Longman, 1852); E. G. Squier, "Observations on the Archaeology and Ethnology of Nicaragua," *Transactions of the American Ethnological Society* 3, pt. 1 (1853): 84–158 [hereafter cited as "Observations"]. *Nicaragua* remains a sourcebook on the geography, archaeology, ethnology, and history of Nicaragua, notwithstanding the social views and ethnocentrism of its author, and has been reprinted several times in English and Spanish editions.

3. Squier, *Nicaragua*, vol. 2: appendix, "Aborigines of Nicaragua." Chapter 1 of the appendix is entitled "Aboriginal Nations of Nicaragua; Their Geographical Distribution; Their Geographical Distribution; Languages, and Monuments," 305–39; chapter 2 is entitled "Civil, Political, and Social Organization; Manners, Customs, and Religion," 340–62. See also *Nicaragua*, 1:284–95.

4. John Lloyd Stephens, *Incidents of Travel in Central America, Chiapas, and Yucatan*, 2 vols. (New York: Harper and Brothers, 1841).

5. Squier, letter draft, New York, February 21, 1849, SPLC.

6. Squier to Francis Parkman, New York, March 20, 1849, SFP. The letters from Squier to Parkman cited here are photostats of the letters in the Squier Family Papers, New-York Historical Society. The originals are in the Massachusetts Historical Society.

7. On at least two occasions Squier reluctantly stated his plans to vote for Van Buren during the election. Squier to parents, New York, July 5, September 17, 1848, SFP. Squier stated surprise on receiving news of his diplomatic appointment. He knew that several prominent individuals had made application on his behalf, but he had not been overly hopeful of his chances. That statement is contradicted, however, by his letter to Parkman, and it appears to have been false modesty designed for the benefit of his parents. Squier to parents, Hartford, April 2, 1849, and Washington, April 5, 1849, SFP.

8. "Diplomatic Appointments," *National Intelligencer*, April 19, 1849.

9. Hammond to Squier, Washington DC, April 20, 1848, SPLC.

10. Governmental attitudes and policies regarding scientific inquiry in the early and mid-nineteenth century are discussed in George H. Daniels, *American Science in the Age of Jackson* (New York: Columbia University Press, 1968), and in portions of A. Hunter Dupree, *Science in the Federal Government: A History of Policies and Activities to 1940* (Cambridge: Belknap Press of Harvard University Press, 1957). On the relationship between the federal government and the United States Exploring Expedition, see Joyce, *The Shaping of American Ethnography*; Stanton, *The Great United States Exploring Expedition*; and Tyler, *The Wilkes Expedition*.

11. Squier, letter draft, New York, February 21, 1849, SPLC. This appears to be the draft of a letter Squier sent to those whose aid he hoped to enlist in securing a diplomatic post.

12. That Squier initially sought a diplomatic appointment to Guatemala is well documented. Regarding his "Guatemala scheme" see Parkman to Squier, Boston, March 15, 1849, in Seitz, *Letters from Parkman to Squier*, 20; Squier to unknown correspondent, New York, February 21, 1849, John M. Clayton to Squier, Washington, April 2, 1849, and John L. Stephens to H. Chatfield, New York, April 9, 1849, SPLC; John L. Stephens to Don Laturnino Ginocha, April 9, 1849, Stephens to El Cura Alcantara, New York, May 9, 1849, and Stephens to Don Nar Cisso Payes, New York, May 9, 1849, SPIHS (the spelling of Spanish names in these letters is uncertain); and "Diplomatic Appointments," *National Intelligencer*, April 19, 1849.

13. Few subjects captured the public imagination in 1848 more than California gold. Squier brought historical perspective to the clamor over California in an article on the earlier Spanish quest for a northern El Dorado. See E. G. S.,

"Gold Hunting in California, in the Sixteenth Century," *American Review*, n.s., 3 (January 1849): 84–88, where he manifests an early interest in the Spanish colonization of the Americas and a familiarity with sixteenth-century Spanish records and maps.

14. Squier to parents, San Juan de Nicaragua, June 8, 1849, SFP.

15. Squier, *Nicaragua*, 1:xvii–xviii, xxi.

16. Squier, *Nicaragua*, 1:8. That sense of national mission again found expression during Squier's first meeting with the affable and well-traveled bishop of León, Don George de Viteri y Ungo. "It was with something, I thought, of the spirit of prophecy, that the Bishop swept his hand around the horizon and said, 'We want only an infusion of your people, to make this broad land an Eden of beauty, and the garden of the world.' " *Nicaragua*, 1:247.

17. Squier, *Nicaragua*, 1:56–57.

18. Squier, *Nicaragua*, 1:70.

19. The significance of Squier's diplomatic and archaeological activities in fostering political, economic, and cultural change within Nicaragua is noted in David. E. Whisnant, *Rascally Signs in Sacred Places: The Politics of Culture in Nicaragua* (Chapel Hill: University of North Carolina Press, 1995), esp. chap. 2, "Rascally Signs in Sacred Places: The Politics of Cultural Change in the Nineteenth Century," 54–106, and chap. 7, "Looting the Past: The Removal of Antiquities from Nicaragua in the Nineteenth Century," 273–312.

20. Squier to parents, San Juan de Nicaragua, June 8, 1849, SFP.

21. White to Squier, New York, March 29, April 4, 1949, SPLC; Clayton to Squier, Washington DC, May 1, 1849, in William R. Manning, ed., *Diplomatic Correspondence of the United States: Inter-American Affairs, 1831–1860*, vol. 3 (Washington DC, 1933–36), 38, 50.

22. Parkman to Squier, Boston, May 13, 1849, in Seitz, *Letters from Parkman to Squier*, 21. Squier received much the same advice from Charles Eliot Norton, a mutual friend of himself and Parkman. Norton cautioned Squier to drop politics and keep to literature, for it was there that fame and happiness was to be found. Norton to Squier, Shady Hill, [Massachusetts], October 1, 1852, SPLC.

23. Parkman to Squier, Boston, October 15, 1849, and Parkman to Squier, Boston, October 3, 1851, in Seitz, *Letters from Parkman to Squier*, 23, 38.

24. Squier to parents, San Juan, June 8, 1849, Squier to parents, Grenada, June 23, 1849, and Squier to Parkman, León, September 15, 1849, SFP.

25. Squier, *Nicaragua*, 1:303–27, 402–11, 2:33–68.

26. The following account of Squier's archaeological expedition to the island of Momotombita in Lake Managua is based on Squier, *Nicaragua*, 1:301–3, 310–17.

27. Squier, *Nicaragua*, 1:314.

28. Parkman to Squier, November 18, 1849, in Seitz, *Letters from Parkman to Squier*, 25.

29. Squier, *Nicaragua*, 1:280.

30. Squier, *Nicaragua*, 1:280–81. Squier initially says that the Indians of Subtiaba brought him four statues at León, but elsewhere in *Nicaragua* (1:317) he says two. He provides engravings of three statues from Subtiaba, so it is likely that he received four as initially related in his narrative.

31. Squier to Henry, New York, December 2, 1850, in *Fifth Annual Report of the Board of Regents of the Smithsonian Institution* (Washington DC: Government Printing Office, 1851), appendix no. 2, 78–80.

32. Squier to Parkman, León, September 15, 1849, SFP. An extract of a letter from Squier to the American Ethnological Society also states that mozos in Nicaragua hailed Americans as "Sons of Washington." *Literary World*, October 27, 1849, 350. The phrase also appears in the address made to Squier by the delegates of the Indian Pueblo of Subtiaba. Squier, *Nicaragua*, 1:281.

33. Squier, *Nicaragua*, 1:282–84, 2:312; Squier, "Observations," 99.

34. Squier, *Nicaragua*, 1:294–95.

35. Squier, *Nicaragua*, 1:320–25.

36. Squier, *Nicaragua*, 1:402, 405–7, 407 n. 1. See plate I, figs. 1 and 2, "Painted Rocks of Managua," and plate II, "Painted Rocks of Managua," facing p. 409.

37. Squier, *Nicaragua*, 2:22–27. "Sculptured Rocks of Masaya," plates I and II of *Nicaragua*, 2: facing pp. 24 and 25 and "View of the Quebrada de las Inscripciones," 25.

38. Squier, *Nicaragua*, 2:33–35; Squier, "Ancient Monuments in the Islands of Lake Nicaragua," 233.

39. Squier, *Nicaragua*, 2:37–38, 40.

40. John A. Strong, "The Contributions of Ephraim George Squier to the Archaeology of Central America," paper presented to the Midwestern Archaeological Conference at Ohio State University, Columbus, Ohio, October 17, 1986, 7–8.

41. Squier, *Nicaragua*, 2:41–58.

42. Squier to parents, León, December 10, 1849, SFP.

43. Squier, *Nicaragua*, 2:55–56; Squier, "Ancient Monuments in the Islands of Lake Nicaragua," 305.

44. Squier to Henry, New York, December 2, 1850, in *Fifth Annual Report of the Board of Regents of the Smithsonian Institution*, 78–80.

45. Squier, *Nicaragua*, 2:65, 68, 335–36; Squier, "Observations," 121–22.

46. Squier, *Nicaragua*, 2:58–59, 337–38.

47. *National Intelligencer*, February 16, 1850; Squier to Henry, New York, December 2, 1850, in *Fifth Annual Report of the Board of Regents of the Smithsonian Institution*, 78–80. Although Squier's account says he sent six monuments from Nicaragua to the Smithsonian in addition to those he shipped via San Juan de Nicaragua, the *Eighth Annual Report* says he sent five large stone idols along with several smaller nondescript objects, probably fragments of other monoliths. A "B. Blanco" of New York paid the cost of shipping the three largest idols to the Smithsonian via Cape Horn. "American Antiquities," *Eighth Annual Report of the Board of Regents of the Smithsonian Institution, 1853* (Washington DC: A. O. P. Nicholson, 1854), 195.

48. Squier to Henry, New York, December 2, 1850, in *Fifth Annual Report of the Board of Regents of the Smithsonian Institution*, 78–80.

49. Squier, *Nicaragua*, 1:291; Squier, "Observations," 85–86.

50. Squier, "Observations," 91–93.

51. Squier, *Nicaragua*, 1:294; Squier, "Observations," 93.

52. Squier, *Nicaragua*, 1:xix; Squier, "Observations," 94.

53. Oviedo as quoted in Paul F. Healy, *Archaeology of the Rivas Region, Nicaragua* (Waterloo, Ontario: Wilfred Laurier University Press, 1980), 10.

54. Squier, "Observations," 95.

55. Squier, "Observations," 95–96.

56. E. G. Squier, "Archaeology of Nicaragua," *Literary World*, October 19, 1850, 314–15.

57. Squier, "Observations," 96.

58. Squier, "Observations," 97–98. On the Chorotega see Herbert J. Spinden, "The Chorotegan Culture Area," *Proceedings of the International Congress of Americanists* (1924–25): 529–45.

59. Squier, *Nicaragua*, 1:282–83, 2:20, 22, 312; Squier, "Observations," 99, 100–101.

60. Robert G. Latham, *The Natural History of the Varieties of Man* (London: van Voorst, 1850).

61. Squier, *Nicaragua*, 2:328–29; Squier, "Observations," 114–15.

62. Squier, *Nicaragua*, 2:329–30; Squier, "Observations," 115–16.

63. Squier, *Nicaragua*, 2:330–31; Squier, "Observations," 117–18.

64. Squier, *Nicaragua*, 2:331–32; Squier, "Observations," 118–19.

65. Squier, "Observations," 133–34.

66. Fowler, *The Cultural Evolution of Ancient Nahua Civilizations*, 242; Squier, *Nicaragua*, 2:360; Squier, "Observations," 144–45.

67. Squier, "Observations," 145.

68. Frank E. Comparato, ed., *Observations on the Archaeology and Ethnology of Nicaragua by Ephraim George Squier* (Culver City CA: Labyrinthos, 1990), 2 n.

5. Comparato's edition of Squier's article in the third volume of the *Transactions of the American Ethnological Society* (1853) retains Squier's explanatory notes and adds valuable notes of his own.

69. Squier, "Observations," 153–58. Squier's table of the "Days of the Month and Their Order" for the Nicaraguan calendar appears on pages 154–55, and the four signs and names of the Xiuhmopilli on page 158. An early expression of Squier's interest in the Mexican calendar is his "Some New Discoveries Respecting the Dates on the Great Calendar Stone of the Ancient Mexicans, with Observations on the Mexican Cycle of Fifty-Two Years; by E. G. Squier, New York," *American Journal of Science and Arts*, 2nd ser., 8 (March 1849): 153–57.

70. See, e.g., Fowler, *The Cultural Evolution of Ancient Nahua Civilizations*, 237–38. Table 13–1 of Fowler, "Comparison of Nicarao and Aztec day names," gives the Nicarao day names in the calendar, their equivalents in the Aztec *tonalpohualli*, and their translation in English. Fowler's table follows the work of Squier, Eduard Seler, Samuel K. Lothrop, and Miguel Leon-Portilla.

71. Evert A. Duyckinck and George Duyckinck, *Cyclopaedia of American Literature*, vol. 2 (Philadelphia: Baxter, 1881), 673.

72. E. G. Squier, *Nicaragua: Its People, Scenery, Monuments*, rev. ed. (New York: Harper and Brothers, 1860).

73. Squier to Parkman, New York, May 30, 1851, SFP.

74. Squier to Peter Force, New York, October 11, 1851, Peter Force Papers, William L. Clements Library, University of Michigan. It is unclear whether Squier sold at that time one, several, or all nine volumes of Kingsborough's *Antiquities of Mexico*. He repurchased whatever he sold, however, for his library contained all nine volumes at the time of its sale in 1876. Entry 595 of Joseph Sabin, ed., *Catalogue of the Library of E. G. Squier* (New York: Charles C. Shelley, 1876), 77–78.

75. Squier, *Nicaragua*, 1:xvii.

76. Norton to Squier, January 19, 1852, SPLC.

77. Squier, *Nicaragua*, 2:333–34; Squier, "Observations," 120–23.

78. See Doris Stone, "Synthesis of Lower Central American Ethnohistory," in *Handbook of Middle American Indians*, vol. 4, *Archaeological Frontiers and External Connections*, ed. Gordon F. Eckholm and Gordon R. Willey, gen. ed. Robert Wauchope (Austin: University of Texas Press, 1973), 209–33.

79. William D. Strong, "Anthropological Problems in Central America," in Clarence Hay et al., *The Maya and Their Neighbors: Essays on Middle American Anthropology and Archaeology* (New York: D. Appleton-Century, 1940), 383.

80. Squier, *Nicaragua*, 2:331. See Paul F. Healy, *Archaeology of the Rivas Region, Nicaragua* (Waterloo, Ontario: Wilfred Laurier University Press, 1980), 21–34;

and Samuel K. Lothrop, "Archaeology of Lower Central America," in *Handbook of Middle American Indians*, gen. ed. Robert Wauchope, vol. 4, *Archaeological Frontiers and External Connections*, ed. Gordon F. Eckholm and Gordon R. Willey (Austin: University of Texas Press, 1966), 180–201.

81. Healy, *Archaeology of the Rivas Region*, 339.

82. Carl Bovallius, *Nicaraguan Antiquities* (Stockholm: P. A. Norsted, 1886), 2.

83. Wolfgang Haberland, "Stone Sculptures from Southern Central America," in *The Iconography of Middle American Sculpture* (New York: Metropolitan Museum, 1970), 144.

84. Squier, *Nicaragua*, 1:xxi–xxii.

85. J. A. Strong, "The Contributions of Ephraim George Squier to the Archaeology of Central America."

86. Jorge Eduardo Arellano, "La Collection, Squier-Zapatera," *Boletin Nicaraguense de Bibliographia y Documentacion*, nos. 32–33 (Managua, Nicaragua: Banco Central de Nicaragua, 1979), 5.

8. THE MIND OF MAN

1. E. G. Squier, *The Serpent Symbol, and the Worship of the Reciprocal Principles of Nature in America*, American Archaeological Researches no. 1 (New York: Putnam, 1851). Squier announced that four additional titles in the American Archaeological Researches series were either prepared or in advanced stages of completion: "The Archaeology and Ethnology of Central America," "The Mexican Calendar," "The Mythological System of the Ancient Mexicans," and "The Semi-Civilized Nations of New Mexico." He never completed those works, but he did publish articles and read papers on those subjects.

2. E. G. Squier, "Serpentine Temples of the United States, with Observations on the Use of the Serpent Symbol in America, particularly in Mexico and Central America," an unpublished paper read before the American Ethnological Society, *Transactions of the American Ethnological Society* 2 (1848): ix.

3. [Francis Parkman], "The Serpent Symbol," *Christian Examiner* 51 (July 1851): 140.

4. Bartlett to Squier, New York, November 13, 1846, SPLC.

5. Gliddon to Squier, Philadelphia, September 21, 1847, SPLC.

6. Gliddon to Squier, Charleston, November 21, 1847, Philadelphia, July 16, 1847, and Bayswater, England, October 20, 1848, SPLC.

7. Squier to "My Dear Sir: – ," letter draft, New York, December 6, 1847, SPLC. Internal evidence shows Joseph Henry to have been the intended recipient of this letter. Since this is a draft it is possible that Squier never sent the

letter, but even so it clearly indicates the direction in which his investigations were heading.

8. Henry to Squier and Davis, Washington DC, February 16, 1848, SPLC.

9. Squier to Morton, New York, September 27, 1848, SGMP.

10. Squier to Morton, New York, December 28, 1848, SGMP.

11. M. Jomard, "Decouvertes recentes sur les bords du Scioto," *Bulletin de la Société de Geographie*, 3rd ser., 6 (1846): 226–34; Jomard, "Sur Les Antiquities Americaines: Recemment Decouvertes (Lettre a M. Squier), Paris, December 29, 1847," *Bulletin de la Société de Geographie*, 3rd ser., 9–10 (1848): 333–37; Jomard, "Lettre de M. Georges Jomard . . . Sur les Antiquities Americaines et la Montagne Serpent de Brush-Creek," *Bulletin de la Société de Geographie*, 3rd ser., 9–10 (1848): 283–88; and Jomard, "Description d'un Ancien Ouvrage Appele le Serpent Situe sur les Bords de la Riviere Brush-Creek, Etat de l'Ohio (Extrait)," *Bulletin de la Société de Geographie*, 3rd ser., 9–10 (1848): 288–90. The Squier-Jomard correspondence continued at least until 1859. Jomard was particularly interested in the inscribed stone tablet recovered during the excavation of the Grave Creek mound in 1838.

12. This and the following three paragraphs are based on Jomard, "Sur Les Antiquities Americaines: Recemment Decouvertes (Lettre a M. Squier), Paris, December 29, 1847," 333–37.

13. Alexander von Humboldt, *Researches, Concerning the Institutions and Monuments of the Ancient Inhabitants of America*, vol. 1 (London: Longman, Hurst, 1814), 147–48. Humboldt appears to have been no less impressed with Squier's researches than Jomard and other European savants. "With Dr. Morton's *Crania Americana*," he is reported as saying, "the work of Mr. Squier constitutes the most valuable contribution ever made to the archaeology and ethnology of America." Humboldt as quoted in Seitz, *Letters from Parkman to Squier*, 12. Squier later acquired several volumes from Humboldt's library. Sabin, *Catalogue of the Library of E. G. Squier*, 254–60.

14. Squier and Davis, *Ancient Monuments*, xxxviii.

15. "The Western Mound Builders," *Literary World*, October 28, 1848, 768n.

16. Squier to Morton, New York, February 12, 1851, MPLC.

17. Squier to Peter Force, New York, March 16, 1851, Force Papers.

18. Humboldt, *Researches*, 1:2.

19. Squier, *Serpent Symbol*, viii, ix.

20. Squier, *Serpent Symbol*, ix.

21. Squier, *Serpent Symbol*, 14–16. See Note A to chapter 1 of *Serpent Symbol*, 22–35, which continues an earlier discussion of this subject that first appeared as part of Squier's "American Ethnology."

22. Atwater, "Description of the Antiquities Discovered in the State of Ohio," 250–51.

23. Bishop William Warburton, *Divine Legation of Moses*, vol. 3 (London: T. Tegg, 1741), 991, as cited by Squier in *Serpent Symbol*, 17–18, and in "American Ethnology," 390n.

24. Squier, *Serpent Symbol*, 18–20.

25. Squier, *Serpent Symbol*, 38.

26. Squier's discussion of the practice of phallic worship in America is found in *Serpent Symbol*, 46–52.

27. Troost, "An Account of Some Ancient Remains in Tennessee," 361.

28. Squier, *Serpent Symbol*, 56–57.

29. See Squier's discussion of the rationale of symbolism associated with this class of remains in the appendix of *Aboriginal Monuments of the State of New York*.

30. Squier, *Serpent Symbol*, 72, 76, 76n. In figures 2, 3, 5, 6, and 7 of *Serpent Symbol*, Squier compares the pyramidal or "temple" mounds of the United States with the pyramidal structures of Mexico and Central America.

31. Squier, *Serpent Symbol*, 83. Squier continues the discussion of these similarities on pages 83–89.

32. Squier, *Serpent Symbol*, 89.

33. Squier, *Serpent Symbol*, 145–46, 154.

34. Squier, *Serpent Symbol*, 157–58, 158n.

35. Squier, *Serpent Symbol*, 163–65, 175–76.

36. Squier, *Serpent Symbol*, 180–81.

37. See E. G. Squier, "Aztec Picture Writing," *New York Tribune*, November 24, 1852. Entry no. 41 of Frank Squier's catalog of Squier's printed works notes that he was preparing for publication a manuscript entitled "The Hieroglyphics of Mexico, an Exposition of their Nature and Use," a project he never completed. Frank Squier, "A Collection of Books by Ephraim George Squier," 9.

38. Squier, *Serpent Symbol*, 202, 204, 208, 211–12, 214.

39. Squier, *Serpent Symbol*, 222.

40. Squier, *Serpent Symbol*, 223.

41. Squier, *Serpent Symbol*, 223–24.

42. Squier, *Serpent Symbol*, 224–27.

43. Squier, *Serpent Symbol*, 251.

44. Squier, *Serpent Symbol*, 251–52.

45. Bruce G. Trigger, *A History of Archaeological Thought* (Cambridge: Cambridge University Press, 1989), 70.

46. Humboldt, *Researches*, 1:25.

47. Squier, *Serpent Symbol*, 254.

48. Sir William Jones, *On the Gods of Greece, Italy, and India* (1785), in Jones's *Works* vol. 1, p. 229. As cited in Squier, *The Serpent Symbol*, 254n.

49. "American Archaeological Researches," *Literary World*, May 3, 1851, 353–54. The following quotes are taken from this source.

50. "American Archaeological Researches, No. 1 – The Serpent Symbol, and the Reciprocal Principles of Nature in America," *Athenaeum*, July 26, 1851, 800.

51. John V. Murra, ed., *American Anthropology: The Early Years* (St. Paul: West, 1976), 18.

52. Henry Rowe Schoolcraft, *History of the Indian Tribes of the United States*, vol. 4 (Philadelphia: Lippincott, 1854), 116.

53. Squier to Morton, Providence, Rhode Island, May 4, 1851, SGMP.

54. [Parkman], "The Serpent Symbol," 140–41.

55. Squier, *Serpent Symbol*, 111, 151, 154.

56. Daniel G. Brinton, *The Myths of the New World: A Treatise on the Symbolism and Mythology of the Red Race of America*, 3rd ed., rev. (Philadelphia: David McKay, 1896), 56.

57. Frederic Ward Putnam and Charles C. Willoughby, "Symbolism in Ancient American Art," *Proceedings of the American Association for the Advance of Science* 44 (1896): 3–23.

58. E. G. Squier to the editor, New York, December 7, 1869, "Serpent Worship in America," *Athenaeum*, December 25, 1869, 872.

59. Charles C. Willoughby, "The Serpent Mound of Adams County, Ohio," *American Anthropologist* 21 (April–June 1919): 153–63. See also his "The Cincinnati Tablet: An Interpretation," *Ohio State Archaeological and Historical Quarterly* 45 (July 1936): 257–64. Willoughby identified the anthropomorphic figure on the Cincinnati tablet as two four-horned or plumed serpents facing each other in opposition. He saw a close connection between Wathatotarho of the Iroquois, the serpent being on the Cincinnati tablet, and the "cognate being" in Mexican iconography. "That they are all variants of the same sinister being seems evident" (264).

60. Frederic Ward Putnam, "The Serpent-Mound of Ohio," *Century Magazine* 39 (1890): 871.

61. Willoughby, "The Cincinnati Tablet," 264.

62. See Clyde Kluckhohn, "Universal Categories of Culture," in *Anthropology Today*, ed. A. L. Kroeber (Chicago: University of Chicago Press, 1953), 507–23; and A. L. Kroeber, *Anthropology* (New York: Harcourt, Brace, 1923), 573.

63. Clifford Geertz, *The Interpretation of Cultures* (New York: Basic Books, 1973), 62.

64. Fred W. Voget, *A History of Ethnology* (New York: Holt, Rinehart, and Winston, 1975), 41. Voget traces the influence of the Enlightenment idea of

progress as natural law on the developmentalist school of nineteenth-century anthropology on pages 41–310, where he identifies two phases of developmentalism: one from 1725 to 1840 and the other from 1840 to 1890. See also Robert E. Bieder, "Albert Gallatin and Enlightenment Ethnology," in his *Science Encounters the Indian*, 16–54.

65. Trigger, *History of Archaeological Thought*, 55–59; Marvin Harris, *The Rise of Anthropological Theory: A History of Theories of Culture* (New York: Thomas Y. Crowell, 1968), 34–35, 37–39; J. S. Slotkin, ed., *Readings in Early Anthropology* (New York: Werner-Gren Foundation, 1965), 423, 445.

66. Voget, *A History of Ethnology*, 43.

9. NAHUA NATIONS AND MIGRATIONS

1. Squier to Duyckinck, New York, September 5, 1854, DFP.

2. Mayer to Squier, Baltimore, October 10, 1854, SPLC.

3. Use of the name San Salvador in the following pages is understood to mean the present-day republic of El Salvador. San Salvador is both the capital of El Salvador and the name of the province in which it is located. Squier's archaic usage of the name San Salvador is retained in order to avoid the confusion of using El Salvador in the narrative and "San Salvador" in direct quotes from Squier and the titles of his writings. The provinces of Sonsonate and San Salvador had earlier developed separately under Spanish rule. An independent state of San Salvador existed during the short-lived Central American Federation of the 1820s and 1830s following independence from Spain. It became the site of the federal capital in 1834. The republic of El Salvador was officially named in 1841, but it was only provisionally known as El Salvador until 1856. San Salvador has been the capital of El Salvador since 1841, except for the period from 1854 to 1859 when it was rebuilt after a devastating earthquake.

4. On Squier's entrepreneurial activities in Honduras, see Charles Lee Stansifer, "E. George Squier and the Honduras Interoceanic Railroad Project," *Hispanic American Historical Review* 46 (February 1966): 1–27, and his "The Central American Career of E. George Squier" (Ph.D. diss., Tulane University, 1959), chap. 4, "Promoter: The Honduras Interoceanic Railway Project," 85–131.

5. Stansifer has made a critical distinction between Squier's work as a Central American publicist and scholar. See "The Central American Career of E. George Squier," chap. 5, "Author: Central American Publicist," 132–60, and chap. 6, "Author: Central American Scholar," 161–87.

6. Michael D. Olien, e.g., incorrectly says that "His archeological endeavors totaled only four one day outings." Olien, "E. G. Squier and the Miskito: Anthropological Scholarship and Political Propaganda," *Ethnohistory* 32, no. 2 (1985): 115. He also says nothing about the valuable ethnographic information

embodied in the two-chapter appendix to *Nicaragua* or the actual results of his archaeological and ethnological fieldwork in Nicaragua, Honduras, and San Salvador.

7. "Notes on Central America," *Athenaeum*, February 9, 1856, 162, an anonymous review of Squier's *Notes on Central America,Particularly in the States of Honduras and San Salvador* (New York: Harper Brothers; London: Trubner, 1855).

8. E. G. Squier, *Ruins of Tenampua, Honduras, Central America* (New York: New-York Historical Society, 1853), an eight-page pamphlet taken from the "Proceedings of the Historical Society of New-York, October 1853." Squier's letter to William W. Turner from Comayagua, Honduras, is dated June 18, 1853. A copy of the pamphlet is in the Library of Congress.

9. Squier, *Notes on Central America*, 123–29.

10. Squier, *Ruins of Tenampua*, 2.

11. Squier, *Notes on Central America*, 127–28.

12. Squier, *Notes and Central America*, 128; Squier, *Ruins of Tenampua*, 7.

13. Squier, *Ruins of Tenampua*, 8.

14. Squier, *Notes on Central America*, 129.

15. Squier, *Notes on Central America*, 328.

16. E. George Squier, "Observations on an Existing Fragment of the Nahual, or Pure Mexican Stock in the State of San Salvador, Central America," *New York Tribune*, April 13, 1854.

17. Squier, *Notes on Central America*, 349.

18. Squier, *Notes on Central America*, "Table 3. Comparative Table of Nahual Vocabularies," 351–52.

19. Squier, *Notes on Central America*, "Aborigines of Honduras," 378–85.

20. Dorothy Hughes Popenoe, *The Ruins of Tenampua, Honduras* (Washington DC: Smithsonian Institution, 1936), 571; Daniel G. Brinton, *The American Race: A Linguistic Classification and Ethnographic Description of the Native Tribes of North and South America* (Philadelphia: D. McKay, 1901), 160.

21. Doris Stone, "The Archaeology of Central and Southern Honduras," *Papers of the Peabody Museum of Archaeology and Ethnology, Harvard University* 49, no. 3 (1957): 116–17.

22. Victor W. von Hagen, *The Jicaque (Torrupan) Indians of Honduras*, Indian Notes and Monographs no. 53 (New York: Museum of the American Indian, 1943), 74; Edward Conzemius, "The Jicaque of Honduras," *International Journal of American Linguistics* 2 (January 1923): 163.

23. Squier, *Notes on Central America*, 379.

24. E. G. Squier, "A Visit to the Guajiquero Indians," *Harper's New Monthly Magazine*, October 1859, 615.

25. Stansifer, "Central American Career of E. George Squier," 178. Squier's

description of the dance he observed during his visit among the Guajiquero is quoted in Stone, "The Archaeology of Central and Southern Honduras," 10–12; and Hubert Howe Bancroft, *Native Races of the Pacific States of North America*, vol. 1 (New York: D. Appleton, 1875), 737–39.

26. Squier, *Notes on Central America*, 385.

27. Squier, *Notes on Central America*, 51.

28. Squier, *Notes on Central America*, 54–55.

29. Joseph-Arthur de Gobineau as cited in Trigger, *History of Archaeological Thought*, 111–12.

30. Josiah Clark Nott, "The Mulatto[,] A Hybrid – Probable Extermination of the Two Races If the Whites and Blacks Are Allowed to Intermarry," *American Journal of the Medical Sciences* 6 (1843): 252–56; Samuel George Morton, "Hybridity in Animals and Plants, Considered in Reference to the Question of the Unity of the Human Species," *American Journal of Science and Arts*, 2nd ser., 3 (1847): 39–50, 203–12, and published separately as a pamphlet (New Haven: B. L. Hamlen, 1847); Morton, "Additional Observations on Hybridity in Animals, and Some Collateral Subjects; being a Reply to the Objection of the Rev. John Backman," *Charleston Medical Examiner* 5 (1850): 755–805; Morton, "Notes on Hybridity Designed as a Supplement to the Memoir on that Subject in the Last Number of this Journal," *Charleston Medical Examiner* 6 (1851): 145–52; and Nott, "Hybridity of Animals, Viewed in Connection with the Natural History of Mankind," in Nott and Gliddon, *Types of Mankind*, 372–410.

31. Nott and Gliddon, *Types of Mankind*, 373.

32. Squier, *Notes on Central America*, 54–55.

33. See Robert R. Bieder, "Scientific Attitudes towards Mixed-Bloods in Early Nineteenth-Century America," *Journal of Ethnic Studies* 8 (Summer 1980): 17–30.

34. Squier, *Notes on Central America*, 55–56.

35. Squier, *Notes on Central America*, 56–57.

36. Squier, *Notes on Central America*, 57.

37. Squier, *Notes on Central America*, 58.

38. Paul A. Erickson, "The Origins of Physical Anthropology" (Ph.D. diss., University of Connecticut, 1974), 7.

39. Squier, *Notes on Central America*, x, 58.

40. Squier, *Notes on Central America*, 214.

41. Squier, *Notes on Central America*, 218.

42. E. G. Squier, *The States of Central America; Their Geography, Topography, Climate, Population, Resources, Productions, Commerce, Political Organization, Aborigines, etc.* (New York: Harper and Brothers, 1858). University Microfilms issued a facsimile of the original in 1970.

43. Cf. "Aborigines of Honduras" (*Notes on Central America*, 378–85) with chap. 13 of *States of Central America*, 241–56.

44. Squier, *States of Central America*, 22.

45. Squier, *States of Central America*, 23.

46. Squier, *States of Central America*, 241.

47. Squier, *States of Central America*, 242–44.

48. Señor Don José Antonio Urrita to Squier, Jutiapa, Guatemala, January 8, 1856, in Squier to the editor, "Discovery of Additional Monuments of Antiquity in Central America," *Athenaeum*, December 13, 1856, 1535–36. Squier reprints this account in *States of Central America*, 341–44.

49. Frank Squier, "A Collection of Books by Ephraim George Squier," 14.

50. E. G. Squier, ed., *Collection of Rare and Original Documents and Relations, Concerning the Discovery and Conquest of America. Chiefly from the Spanish Archives.* No. 1 (New York: Charles B. Norton, 1860). Also published at Albany by Joel Munsell the same year. No. 1 contains *Carta dirijida al rey de Espana, por el Licenciado Dr. Don Diego Garcia de Palacio, oydor de la real Audencia de Guatemala, Ano 1576*. Another edition of Palacio's account appeared in 1985. The German naturalist Alexander von Frantzius (1821–77) published a German edition of Palacio's letter in 1873, making numerous notes on the geography and natural history of Central America. Frank E. Comaparto brought forward the most recent and authoritative edition Palacio's relation in 1985, which is based on Squier's translation and notes published in 1860. Comparato's edition retains Squier's explanatory notes and those appearing in the 1873 edition by Frantzius, and it adds valuable annotations of his own. See Comparato, ed., *Letter to the King of Spain by Licentiate Dr. Don Diego Garcia de Palacio* (Culver City CA: Labyrinthos, 1985).

51. Squier, *Collection of Rare and Original Documents*, 3n.

52. Squier, *Collection of Rare and Original Documents*, 105 n. 6.

53. Don Juan Galindo, "The Ruins of Copan in Central America," *Archaeologia Americana: Transactions and Collections of the American Antiquarian Society* 2 (1836): 543–50. Galindo was a former governor of the province of Peten. He submitted a similar communication to the Royal Society of London.

54. Squier, *Collection of Rare and Original Documents*, 3–11.

55. Squier, *Collection of Rare and Original Documents*, 100–105 n. 3.

56. Squier, *States of Central America*, 338.

57. Squier, *Collection of Rare and Original Documents*, 102.

58. Squier, *Collection of Rare and Original Documents*, 113–15 n. 22.

59. Squier, *Monograph of Authors Who Have Written on the Languages of Central America, and Collected Vocabularies or Composed Works in the Native Dialects of That Country* (New York: C. B. Richardson, 1861).

60. Squier, *Monograph of Authors*, iv–v.

61. E. G. Squier, "Ancient Monuments of the United States," *Harper's New Monthly Magazine*, May 1860, 738.

62. Squier, *Monograph of Authors*, v–vi.

63. Squier, *Monograph of Authors*, vi.

64. Squier, *Monograph of Authors*, vii.

65. Squier, *Monograph of Authors*, ix–xi.

66. Parkman to Squier, Boston, November 3, 1851, in Seitz, *Letters from Parkman to Squier*, 39.

67. Squier, *Monograph of Authors*, xv.

68. "Proceedings. – November 1860," *Bulletin of the American Ethnological Society* (September 1860–January 1861): 35. A copy of the advertisement announcing Squier's plan to publish Anleo's grammar is in box 10, folder 3, SPLC.

69. Squier, *Collection of Rare and Original Documents*, 110–11 n. 15.

70. E. G. Squier, *Observations on the Chalchihuitl of Mexico and Central America* (New York: Extract from the Annals of the Lyceum of Natural History of New York, 1869); Squier, "Observations on a Collection of Chalchihuitls from Mexico and Central America," *American Naturalist* 4 (May 1870): 171–81.

71. See the discussion of *chalchihuitl* in Joseph E. Pogue, "The Turquois: A Study of Its History, Mineralogy, Geology, Ethnology, Archaeology, Mythology, Folklore, and Technology," *Memoirs of the National Academy of Science* 12 (1915): 105–9.

72. Palacio in Squier, *Collection of Rare and Original Documents*, 55.

73. Squier, *Observations on the Chalchihuitl*, 11–12, figs. 2 and 3.

74. "Notes on Central America," *Athenaeum*, February 9, 1856, 161.

75. Squier to the editors of the *New-York Courier and Enquirer*, Leon de Nicaragua, January 5, [1850], SPLC; Squier, *Notes on Central America*, 48, 210.

76. Samuel A. Bard, *Waikna; or, Adventures on the Mosquito Shore* (New York: Harper and Brothers; London: Low and Company, 1855); "Saml. A. Bard to the editor, New York, November 18, 1855," *Athenaeum*, December 15, 1855, 1467.

77. Samuel A. Bard, "Something about the Mosquitos," *Harper's New Monthly Magazine*, September 1855, 456–65.

78. Bedford Pim and Berthold Seeman, *Dottings on the Roadside, in Panama, Nicaragua, and Mosquito* (London: Chapman and Hall, 1869), 271.

79. See Olien, "E. G. Squier and the Miskito," 111–33. On the political leadership of the Miskito Indians see Olien, "The Miskito Kings and the Line of Succession," *Journal of Anthropological Research* 39, no. 2 (1983): 198–241.

80. A. Curtis Wilgus, introduction to Ephraim George Squier, *Notes on Central America; Particularly the States of Honduras and San Salvador* (New York: Praeger, 1969), vii. Wilgus's introduction contains many factual errors regarding

Squier's life, but it does an excellent job of showing the importance of *Notes on Central America* as an early and oft-cited sourcebook. The work's scientific and descriptive value earned Squier's international reputation as the nineteenth century's preeminent authority on Central America.

81. "The States of Central America," *Athenaeum*, June 25, 1859, 835.

82. See, e.g., E. G. Squier, "The Unexplored Regions of Central America," *Historical Magazine* 4 (March 1860): 65–66, a paper read before the New-York Historical Society in January 1860.

83. Squier, *States of Central America*, 17.

84. E. Geo. Squier, introduction to *Travels in Central America, Including Accounts of Some Regions Unexplored since the Conquest, from the French of the Chevalier Arthur Morelet, by Mrs. M. F. Squier. Introduction and Notes by E. Geo. Squier* (London: Trubner, 1871), xii.

10. ANCIENT PERU

1. Squier's travels and experiences in Peru have remained a subject of interest. See the following works by Mariana Mould de Pease: "De bibliotecas y experiencias personales: Ephraim George Squier y los orígenes del coleccionismo peruano," in *El Hombre y los Andes*, vol. 1, ed. Javier Flores Espinoza y Rafael Varón Gabai (Lima: Fundación telephonica y Universidad Católica, 2002), 125–43; "Observaciones a un observador: Hurgando en el tintero de George Ephraim Squier," in *Etnographía e historia del mundo andino: Continuidad y cambio*, ed. Shozo Masuda (Tokio: Universidad de Tokio, 1986), 35–107; and "Ephraim George Squier y suvision del Perú" (B.A. thesis, Lima, Pontificia Universidad Católica del Perú, 1981). See also Estuardo Nuñez, *Viajeros de Tierra Adentro, 1860–1900* (Gainesville: School of Inter-American Studies, University of Florida, 1960), "Ephraim George Squier (1821–1888)," 25–34.

2. E. G. Squier, "Quelques Remarques sur la Geographie et les Monuments du Perou, par E. G. Squier," *Extrait du Bulletin de la Société de Geographie, Janvier 1868* (Paris: Impr. De E. Martinet, 1868); and the following articles from *Harper's New Monthly Magazine:* "Among the Andes of Peru and Bolivia: I – Over the Cordillera," April 1868, 545–66; "Among the Andes of Peru and Bolivia: II – Tiahuanaco – The Baalbec of the New World," May 1868, 681–700; "Among the Andes of Peru and Bolivia: III – The Sacred Islands," June 1868, 16–33; "Among the Andes of Peru and Bolivia: IV – The City of the Sun," July 1868, 145–65; and "Among the Andes of Peru and Bolivia: V – Fortresses and Gardens," August 1868, 307–32.

3. E. G. Squier, *Observations on the Geography and Archaeology of Peru* (London: Trubner, 1870), a paper read before the American Geographical Society in February 1870 and published as a pamphlet by Trubner; Squier, "The Primeval

Monuments of Peru Compared with Those in Other Parts of the World," *American Naturalist* 4 (March 1870): 1–17.

4. E. George Squier, *Peru: Incidents of Travel and Exploration in the Land of the Incas* (New York: Harper and Brothers, 1877).

5. William H. Prescott, *History of the Conquest of Peru, with a Preliminary View of the Civilization of the Incas*, vol. 1 (New York: Harper and Brothers, 1847), 159–60. Squier's personal copy of this work contained numerous handwritten notes. Entry 106 of Sabin, *Catalogue of the Library of E. G. Squier*, 148.

6. [Ephraim George Squier], "Ancient Peru – Its People and Its Monuments," *Harper's New Monthly Magazine*, June 1853, 7–38.

7. Squier, "Among the Andes of Peru and Bolivia: I," 545. The work also appears as entry 45 of Frank Squier, "A Collection of Books by Ephraim George Squier," 10.

8. Eduardo Mariano de Rivero Ustariz and Johan Jacob von Tschudi, *Antiguedades Peruana*, 2 vols. (Vienna: Imprenta Imperial de La Corte y del Estado, 1851). Both this original Spanish edition and Francis Hawks's English translation (New York, 1853) were in Squier's library. He also possessed an English manuscript translation of the original Spanish edition. It is unclear whether Squier made the translation himself, as Joseph Sabin would seem to indicate, or whether it was the translation made by Hawks that simply came into Squier's possession after Hawks's translation was published. Entries 1146 and 1148 of Sabin's *Catalogue of the Library of E. G. Squier*, 160.

9. Squier, *Peru*, 2.

10. Squier, "Among the Andes of Peru and Bolivia: I," 545–46.

11. Squier to Parkman, New York, January 12, 1866, SFP.

12. The papers relating to Squier's work on the commission are in Ephraim George Squier, "Claims Brought before the United States and Peru Mixed Claims Commission, 1863–1864," Harvard Law School Library, Harvard University. The collection includes claims brought by U.S. citizens before the commission, established by the Everett-Osma Agreement, relating to contract violations, illegal seizures of property and goods in the guano industry, false imprisonment, and charges of embezzlement by members of the commission.

13. Squier to Parkman, New York, February 6, 1866, SFP.

14. Squier, *Peru*, 3–4; Squier, *Observations on the Geography and Archaeology of Peru*, 1–2.

15. Squier, *Peru*, 170–86.

16. Squier's interpretation and application of the ethnographic observations made in Arriaga's *Extirpación de la Idolatria del Peru* appear in *Peru* on pages 63, 91, and 187–92.

17. Squier, *Peru*, 234–36, 238–39.

18. Squier, "Primeval Monuments of Peru," 8–9, 11, 12n.

19. Squier, *Peru*, 216, 358, 552; and Squier, *Observations on the Geography and Archeology of Peru*, 6–7, 12. See Antonio Raimondi, *El Peru*, vol. 1, pt. 1 (Lima: Imp. Del Estado, calle de La Rifa, Num. 58, 1874).

20. Squier, *Observations on the Geography and Archeology of Peru*, 8–10.

21. J. P. Davis of Massachusetts served in 1863 and 1864 as the government engineer of Peru. The identity of Church is unknown to me, but he probably worked in Peru in a similar capacity. Davis surveyed the Guano Islands (a corruption of the Quichua *huanu*) and reported on the extent of the guano deposits found there. While making borings and excavations in the guano on South Guanape Island, Davis found the remains of a building, pottery, and a wooden idol. An account of his discovery appears in Squier's "Antiquities from the Guano or Huanu Islands of Peru," *Journal of the Anthropological Institute of New-York* 1 (1872–72): 47–56.

22. Squier, *Peru*, 424–28; Squier, *Observations of the Geography and Archaeology of Peru*, 21–23.

23. Squier to Parkman, February 20, 1866, SFP.

24. Squier, *Peru*, 498–99. A detailed account of this structure is given in J. Ogden Outwater Jr., "Building the Fortress of Ollantaytambo," *Archaeology* 12 (Spring 1969): 26–32.

25. The following account of La Rosa and Squier's visit to the ruins of Chimú is taken from Squier, *Peru*, 116–20.

26. Squier, *Peru*, 270–71.

27. Michael E. Moseley, *The Incas and Their Ancestors: The Archaeology of Peru* (London: Thames and Hudson, 1992), 16–17.

28. Squier, *Peru*, 479.

29. Squier, *Peru*, 480–81.

30. See the following articles by Squier from *Frank Leslie's Illustrated Newspaper*: "Tongues from Tombs; or the Stories That Graves Tell, Number 2 – A Plain Man's Tomb in Peru," March 27, 1869, 21–22; "Tongues from Tombs; or the Stories That Graves Tell, Number 3 – Agricultural Laborers and the Princes of Chimu," June 12, 1869, 204–6; "Tongues from Tombs; or the Stories That Graves Tell, Number 4 – Grand Chimu and New Granada," June 19, 1869, 221–22.

31. Squier to Parkman, New York, February 6, 1866, SFP.

32. More than two hundred photographs relating to Squier's fieldwork in Peru and his related publications are today in the Ephraim George Squier Papers of the Latin American Library at Tulane University. How much of the original collection is still intact is not known.

33. Squier, *Peru*, 3–4.

34. Keith McElroy, "The History of Photography in Peru in the Nineteenth Century: 1839–1876" (Ph.D. diss., University of New Mexico, Albuquerque, 1977), 528–31; see also his *Early Peruvian Photography: A Critical Case Study* (Ann Arbor: UMI Research Press, 1985), which is a revision of the author's doctoral dissertation.

35. The following account is based on Le Plongeon to Stephen Salisbury Jr., Belize, February 19, 1878, Salisbury Family Papers, American Antiquarian Society, Worcester, Massachusetts.

36. Le Plongeon to Squier, Lima, March 28, 1865, SPLC.

37. Lawrence Gustave Desmond, "Augustus Le Plongeon: Early Maya Archaeologist" (Ph.D. diss., University of Colorado at Boulder, 1983), 53. Le Plongeon's association with Squier is examined on pages 51–54, and his work as a surveyor, land speculator, photographer, and physician in California from 1849 until his departure for Peru in 1862 is documented on pages 32–43.

38. Keith McElroy, "Ephraim George Squier: Photography and the Illustration of Peruvian Antiquities," *History of Photography* 10 (April–June 1986): 108.

39. Squier to Leslie, Lima, April 28, 1864, SPIHS.

40. Squier to Parkman, New York, February 6, 1866, SFP.

41. Squier, "Among the Andes of Peru and Bolivia: II," 682; Oscar G. Mason, "Discussions of the Photographical Section of the American Institute," in *Twenty-ninth Annual Report of the American Institute of the City of New York for the Year 1868–1869* (Albany: Argus, 1869), 1089; C. W. H., "New York Correspondence," *The Philadelphia Photographer*, June 1868, 196; and Squier, *Peru*, 272–73.

42. Squier, *Peru*, 273. Squier identifies Harvey (an amateur draftsman of limited experience) in "Among the Andes of Peru and Bolivia: II," 682.

43. Mason, "Discussions of the Photographical Section," 1089; C. W. H., "New York Correspondence," 196; Squier, *Peru*, 273.

44. An acknowledgment of thanks from the American Geographical and Statistical Society dated May 16, 1865, for a lecture on the "Geography and Topography of Southern Peru, Particularly the Great Terrestrial Basin of Lake Titicaca" is in the Squier Papers at the New-York Historical Society.

45. "The American Ethnological Society," *Historical Magazine* 9 (July 1865): 227–28 and (December 1865): 379.

46. Smith, *The History of the Lowell Institute*, 50, 56; see also Edward Weeks, *The Lowells and Their Institute* (Boston: Little, Brown, 1966).

47. Squier to Parkman, New York, January 12, 1866, SFP. Squier discusses the preparation of his Peruvian materials for lecture and publication in Squier to Parkman, New York, February 6, 1866, SFP

48. Squier to Parkman, New York, January 28, 1866, SFP.

49. Squier to Parkman, New York, February 20, 1866, SFP.

50. Parkman to Squier, Boston, January 18, February 2, 1866, in Seitz, *Letters from Parkman to Squier*, 42, 43–44; Squier to Parkman, New York, January 28, 1866, SFP.

51. John Amory Lowell to Squier, Boston, February 21, 1866, and Squier to Parkman, New York, February 23, 1866, SFP; Smith, *The History of the Lowell Institute*, 63. Squier also lectured at the New-York Historical Society, where he spoke on "The City of the Sun, Cuzco, the Capital of the Inca Empire" on January 10, 1867. A notice of that is in the Squier Papers at the New-York Historical Society and in R. W. G. Vail, *Knickerbocker Birthday: A Sesqui-Centennial History of the New-York Historical Society, 1804–1954* (New York: New-York Historical Society, 1954), 131.

52. Squier to Parkman, New York, February 6, 1866, SFP.

53. Smith, *The History of the Lowell Institute*, 49, 53.

54. Jeffries Wyman, "Report of the Curator," *First Annual Report of the Peabody Museum of American Archaeology and Ethnology* (Cambridge: John Wilson and Son, 1868), 6–7. The report states that the Squier donation consisted of seventy-five Peruvian crania, but it does not specify the other contents of the archaeological and ethnological collection that Squier presented to the museum.

55. The following account is based Squier's excerpts of Wyman's observations found in the appendix of *Peru*, 580–85, which includes his seven tables of comparative measurements.

56. Squier, *Peru*, 244.

57. See Daniel Wilson's observations of the American cranial type and artificial distortion in his *Prehistoric Man: Researches into the Origin of Civilisation in the Old and the New World*, vol. 2 (Cambridge: Macmillan, 1862), especially those relating to brachycephalic and dolichocephalic skulls and the influence of compression. His comments on Peruvian crania appear on pages 224, 235, 257–58, 266, and 284. On the opinion of John H. Blake see pages 70, 113, and 225 and on that of J. Barnard Davis pages 281, 306, and 314.

58. See Charles D. Meigs, *Memoir of Samuel George Morton, MD, Late President of the Academy of Natural Sciences of Philadelphia* (Philadelphia: T. K. and P. G. Collins, 1851).

59. See Stephen Jay Gould's *The Mismeasure of Man* (New York: Norton, 1981) for a devastating deconstruction and critique of Morton's methodology.

60. Squier, *Peru*, 456–57, 577. The skull is figured on page 457.

61. Le Plongeon to Salisbury, Belize, February 19, 1878, Salisbury Family Papers.

62. A further investigation of the subject of trepanning is given in Ales Hrdlicka, "Trepanation among Prehistoric People, Especially in America," *Ciba Symposium* 1, no. 6 (1939): 170–77.

63. Paul Broca, "Cas singulier de trepanation chez les Incas," *Journal of the Anthropological Society of Paris* 2 (July 1867): 403.

64. Paul Broca, "Trepanning among the Incas," *Journal of the Anthropological Institute of New-York* 1 (1871–72): 72, 74, 75. The skull is figured on page 71. Excerpts of Broca's account also appear in Squier's *Peru*, appendix A, 577–80.

65. Squier to Parkman, New York, February 6 and 20, 1866, and March 2, 1868, SFP.

66. Squier, "Primeval Monuments of Peru," 2, 14.

67. Squier, *Peru*, 570.

68. Squier, *Peru*, 570–71.

69. Squier, *Peru*, 571.

70. An early but still valuable analysis of the subject is Leland L. Locke, *The Ancient Quipu or Peruvian Knot Record* (New York: American Museum of Natural History, 1923).

71. Squier, *Peru*, 575.

72. Squier, *Peru*, 576.

73. Squier, *Peru*, 434.

74. Squier, *Peru*, 351.

75. Moseley, *The Incas and Their Ancestors*, 18.

76. Christopher B. Donnan, "Lummis at Tiahuanaco," *The Masterkey* 47 (July–September 1973): 85–93. An account of Lummis's examination and documentation of remains on the Peruvian coast is given in Keith McElroy, "Photography and Adobe: Charles Lummis in Peru," *The Masterkey* 55 (April–June 1981): 45–53. Lummis's annotated copy of *Peru* and his Peruvian photographs are in the Charles Fletcher Lummis Papers at the Southwest Museum Library in Los Angeles.

77. Gordon R. Willey, introduction to E. George Squier, *Peru: Incidents of Travel and Exploration in the Land of the Incas, Antiquities of the New World, Early Explorations in Archaeology*, vol. 9 (New York: AMS Press, Inc. for the Peabody Museum of Archaeology and Ethnology, 1973), ix–x.

78. McElroy documents the origin and lineage of the 295 engravings that ultimately comprised Squier's *Peru* in "Ephraim George Squier," 108–11.

79. C. W. H., "New York Correspondence," 199; Mason, "Discussions of the Photographical Section," 1092.

80. Squier, *Peru*, 572–73.

81. Squier, *Peru*, 567.

11. THE SCIENCE OF MEN AND NATIONS

1. Stanton, *The Leopard's Spots*, vii, 2.

2. Bieder's *Science Encounters the Indian* relates these developments to the

broader currents of American intellectual history through his analysis of the writings of Albert Gallatin, Samuel George Morton, Henry Rowe Schoolcraft, Ephraim George Squier, and Lewis Henry Morgan.

3. See Earl W. Count, "The Evolution of the Race Idea in Modern Western Culture during the Period of the Pre-Darwinian Nineteenth Century," *Transactions of the New York Academy of Natural Sciences*, 2nd ser., 8 (February 1946): 139–65; and Herbert H. Odum, "Generalizations on Race in Nineteenth-Century Physical Anthropology," *Isis* 58 (Spring 1967): 5–19.

4. Reginald Horsman, "Scientific Racism and the American Indian in the Mid-Nineteenth Century," *American Quarterly* 27 (May 1975): 153; see also Horsman's larger study *Race and Manifest Destiny* (Cambridge: Harvard University Press, 1981).

5. Nott and Gliddon, *Types of Mankind*, 49; Luke Burke, introduction to the *Ethnological Journal* 1 (June 1848): 1–2.

6. The origins of polygenist arguments are presented in Slotkin, *Readings in Early Anthropology*. Marvin Harris compares monogenist and polygenist assumptions and conclusions in the eighteenth and nineteenth centuries in *The Rise of Anthropological Theory*, chap. 4, "Rise of Racial Determinism," 80–107.

7. [Burke], "Progress of Ethnology in the United States," 173.

8. Nott and Gliddon, *Types of Mankind*, 87.

9. Nott to Squier, Mobile, August 19, 1848, SPLC.

10. Gliddon to Squier, London, March 8, 1849, SPLC.

11. Squier, "American Ethnology," 385.

12. Squier, "American Ethnology," 385.

13. Squier, "American Ethnology," 386.

14. Squier, "American Ethnology," 386.

15. See Bieder, "Albert Gallatin and Enlightenment Ethnology," 16–54.

16. Morton, *Crania Americana*, 260.

17. Squier, "American Ethnology," 388.

18. Squier, "American Ethnology," 388.

19. See Edward Kingsborough, *Antiquities of Mexico* (London, 1831–48); and John Delafield, *An Inquiry into the Origin of the Antiquities of America* (New York: Colt, Burgess, 1839).

20. Squier, "American Ethnology," 390.

21. Albert Gallatin, "Notes on the Semi-Civilized Nations of Mexico, Yucatan, and Central America," *Transactions of the American Ethnological Society* 1 (1845): 10.

22. Squier, "American Ethnology," 391.

23. Squier, "American Ethnology," 392.

24. Squier to Morton, New York, September 27, 1848, SGMP.

25. Nott to Squier, Mobile, August 19, September 30, 1848, and J. G. M. Ramsey to Squier, Mechlenburg, Tennessee, January 1, 1849, SPLC; Squier to Francis Parkman, New York, August 11, 1859, SFP. The latter is a transcript of an original letter in the Francis Parkman Papers at the Massachusetts Historical Society.

26. Squier, "American Ethnology," 398.

27. Squier, "American Ethnology," 398.

28. Nott to Squier, Mobile, August 19, 1848, SPLC.

29. Nott to Squier, Mobile, September 30, 1848, SPLC.

30. Nott to Squier, Mobile, February 14, 1849, SPLC.

31. Nott to Squier, Mobile, February 14, 1849, SPLC; Josiah Clark Nott, *Two Lectures on the Connection between the Biblical and Physical History of Man* (New York: Bartlett and Welford, 1849), 5–23.

32. Josiah Clark Nott, "Ancient and Scripture Chronology," *Southern Quarterly Review*, n.s., 2 (November 1850): 385–426.

33. Nott, "Ancient and Scripture Chronology," 386.

34. Nott, "Ancient and Scripture Chronology," 386–88, 390.

35. Nott, "Ancient and Scripture Chronology," 392, 405.

36. Nott, "Ancient and Scripture Chronology," 386.

37. Nott, "Ancient and Scripture Chronology," 412. Nott continues his discussion of the antiquity and indigenous origin of the Mound Builders through page 416.

38. Gliddon to Squier, Philadelphia, June 8, 1847, SPLC. Gliddon specifically mentions Birch, Bunsen, Lepsius, Setroune, Walsh, and Pauthier. He also solicited the aid of Morton Hunt, his brother-in-law and the editor of the *London Spectator*, in promoting interest in the work of American ethnologists.

39. Nott to Squier, Mobile, September 30, 1848, SPLC.

40. [Burke] to Squier, London, [September 1, 1848], SPLC. Burke's undated letter accompanied a note from Gliddon to Squier dated September 1, 1848.

41. Gliddon to Squier, Bayswater, [England], October 20, 1848, SPLC.

42. [Burke], "Progress of Ethnology in the United States," 169–85.

43. Gliddon to Squier, [London], Office of the *Ethnological Journal*, September 1, 1848, SPLC.

44. [Burke], "Progress of Ethnology in the United States," 170, 184.

45. Nott to Squier, Mobile, September 7, 1848, SPLC.

46. Nott and Gliddon, *Types of Mankind*, 50.

47. Nott and Gliddon, *Types of Mankind*, 52.

48. Nott and Gliddon, *Types of Mankind*, 53.

49. See James Cowles Prichard, *Researches into the Physical History of Man*, ed. George W. Stocking Jr. (Chicago: University of Chicago Press, 1973).

50. Nott and Gliddon, *Types of Mankind*, 60–61.

51. Nott, *Two Lectures*, 24; see also his "Unity of the Human Race," *Southern Quarterly Review* 9 (1846): 1–56.

52. Nott, *Two Lectures*, 31.

53. Charles Lyell, *A Second Visit to the United States of North America*, vol. 2 (New York: Harper and Brothers; London: John Murray, 1849), 188.

54. Nott and Gliddon, *Types of Mankind*, 274; Josiah Clark Nott, "Aboriginal Races of America," *Southern Quarterly Review* 8 (July 1853): 59, 62–63.

55. Charles Pickering, *The Races of Men, and Their Geographical Distribution*, vol. 9 of the Report of the United State Exploring Expedition (Philadelphia: C. Sherman, 1848), 12.

56. Nott and Gliddon, *Types of Mankind*, 283.

57. Morton to Squier, Philadelphia, December 8, 1846, SPLC.

58. Nott, "Aboriginal Races of America," 64–65.

59. Nott, "Aboriginal Races of America," 65.

60. Nott, "Aboriginal Races of America," 66.

61. Phillips cited in Nott, "Aboriginal Races of America," 68–69.

62. The methodological and theoretical aspects of Morton's physical anthropology are demolished in Gould, *The Mismeasure of Man*.

63. Nott, "Aboriginal Races of America," 70–71.

64. Parkman to Squier, Boston, April 2, 1850, in Seitz, *Letters from Parkman to Squier*, 29. The *Princeton Review* castigated Agassiz for his position that the human race had not descended from a single pair but from various stocks. See also "Unity of the Human Family," *Episcopal Reader*, June 22, 1850, 49.

65. Louis Agassiz, as cited in Nott, "Aboriginal Races of America," 74–75; in Nott and Gliddon, *Types of Mankind*, 282; and in Nott and Gliddon, *Indigenous Races of the Earth*, xv. A full statement of Agassiz's position on multiple centers of creation for animals and humans is found in his "Geographical Distribution of Animals," *Christian Examiner* 48 (March 1850): 181–204, and "The Diversity of Origin of the Human Races," *Christian Examiner* 49 (July 1850): 110–45.

66. Louis Agassiz, "Sketch of the Natural Provinces of the Animal World and Their Relationship to the Different Types of Man," in Nott and Gliddon, *Types of Mankind*, lviii–lxxvi.

67. Agassiz, "Sketch of the Natural Provinces," lviii.

68. Nott, "Aboriginal Races of America," 76.

69. Chevalier Bunsen, *Life and Letters of Barthold George Niebuhr* (New York, 1852), cited in Nott, "Aboriginal Races of America," 77n.

70. Gliddon to Squier, Philadelphia, April 6, 9, 10, 13, and 23, 1854, SPLC.

71. [E. G. Squier], "Notices of New Books: Science of Men and Nations, Types of Mankind," *New York Herald*, April 23, 1854.

72. In *The Leopard's Spots*, William R. Stanton attributes authorship of the review to Squier upon what appear to me to be sufficient grounds. Reginald Horsman, however, says in his biography *Josiah Clark Nott of Mobile* that Gliddon wrote his own review, which Squier obligingly arranged to have published in the *New York Herald*. He attributes the review exclusively to Gliddon and believes that Nott too was incorrect in attributing it to Squier.

73. See Gliddon to Squier, Philadelphia, April 24, August 31, 1854, and Nott to Squier, Mobile, April 30, 1854, SPLC; and the internal evidence of the review itself.

74. Gliddon to Squier, Philadelphia, April 24, August 31, 1854, SPLC.

75. Nott to Squier, Mobile, April 30, 1854, SPLC.

76. Gliddon to Squier, Philadelphia, August 31, 1854, SPLC.

77. Squier, *Peru*, 17–19.

78. Mayer to Squier, Baltimore, April 3, 1854, SPLC.

79. Wilson, *Prehistoric Man*, 2:205.

80. Ethan Squier to Ephraim George Squier, Knowles Ville, [Connecticut], December 3, 1843, SFP.

81. "Tyler, Treason, and Texas," *Hartford Journal*, May 24, 1844; "Resolutions on the Annexation of Texas," *Hartford Journal*, June 14, 1844.

82. James Dixon to Squier, December 11, 1845, SPIHS.

83. Squier to parents, Hartford, January 18, February 6, 1845, SFP.

84. Squier to parents, Chillicothe, March 10, 1846, SFP.

85. Squier to Joel Squier, New York, September 17, 1848, SFP.

86. Squier to parents, New York, October 30, 1856, SFP.

87. Nott to Squier, Mobile, May 3, 1861, SPLC.

88. Nott to Squier, Mobile, December 5, 1865, SPLC.

89. Nott to Squier, Mobile, January 12, 1866, Baltimore, May 28, 1868, and New York, May 26, October 7, 1872, SPLC.

90. The following account is based on E. G. Squier, "Report," *Journal of the Anthropological Society of New-York* 1 (1871–72): 16–17, 20.

91. A fire claimed most but not all of the third volume, which was republished in 1909. Franz Boas, "The American Ethnological Society," *Science*, January 1, 1943, 7.

92. Squier, "Report," 16.

93. Squier, "Report," 17.

94. Dr. M. Paul Broca, "The Progress of Anthropology in Europe and America," *Journal of the Anthropological Society of New-York* 1 (1871–72): 22–42.

95. Broca, "The Progress of Anthropology," 27, 29, 34, 35.

96. John Russell Bartlett, "Report of Hon. John R. Bartlett," *Proceedings of the American Antiquarian Society*, no. 49 (April 29, 1868): 51–79; Bartlett, "Au-

tobiography," MS, 80–94, JRBP; and *Congres Internationale D' Anthropologie et D' Archaeologie Prehistoriques, Compte Rendu de la 2me session, Paris, 1867* (Paris, 1868), 8. See also Frank Leslie, *Paris Universal Exposition, 1867. Reports of the United States Commissioners. Report on the Fine Arts* (Washington DC: Government Printing Office, 1868). American bibliographer Joseph Sabin attributed the authorship of this report to Squier and not to Leslie.

97. Trigger, *History of Archaeological Thought*, 70–72.

98. See George W. Stocking Jr., "The Persistence of Polygenist Thought in Post-Darwinism Anthropology," in his *Race, Culture, and Evolution*, 42–68.

99. Squier, "Monumental Evidence," 326.

100. Squier, "American Ethnology," 398.

101. See Zestermann, *Memoir on the European Colonization of America*; E. G. Squier, "Ancient Monuments of the United States," *Harper's New Monthly Magazine*, May 1860, 778, and July 1860, 178; Squier, "Archaeological Impostures," *American Naturalist* 4 (July 1870): 319–20; Squier, "The Arch in America," *Journal of the Anthropological Institute of New-York* 1 (1871–72): 78; Squier, "Report," 16, 18.

102. Squier, "Archaeological Impostures," 319–20.

EPILOGUE

1. The notice of their marriage appeared in the *Providence Journal*, October 23, 1857.

2. Squier to parents, New York, September 10, 1857, SFP.

3. Biographical information about Miriam is taken from Madeline B. Stern, *Purple Passage: The Life of Mrs. Frank Leslie* (1953; reprint, Norman: University of Oklahoma Press, 1971).

4. "The Publisher of Frank Leslie's Newspaper to the Public," *Frank Leslie's Illustrated Newspaper*, September 21, 1861, 289.

5. Frank Luther Mott, *A History of American Magazines, 1850–1865*, vol. 2 (Cambridge: Harvard University Press, 1957), 452n, 456, 461.

6. The *New York City Directory, 1861–1873*, shows Leslie boarding with E.G. and Miriam at their Thirty-ninth Street house. Rumors of scandal regarding the assignment of rooms within the Squier household and contradictory testimony about who owned what and who paid for what are found in the *Virginia City, Nevada, Territorial Enterprise Extra: Containing A Full Account of "Frank Leslie" and Wife* (Virginia City, 1878), 7–8. This is a reprint of the *Daily Territorial Enterprise*, July 14, 1878, 1. See also *Frank Leslie, Appellant v. Miriam F. Leslie, and Others, Respondents*, New York Court of Appeals, vol. 13 (1883), 45, 114, 164, 172–73, 347 [hereafter cited as *Leslie v. Leslie*]; and "The Chronicler, Tales of To-Day," *Town Topics*, March 27, 1886, 13.

7. *Frank Leslie v. Sarah Ann Leslie*, New York Common Pleas, Hall of Records. Both E.G. and Miriam gave testimony in the case.

8. A list of passengers arriving on the *Valparaiso* appears in the Lima newspaper *El Comercio*, July 3, 1869, 2.

9. Mrs. E. G. Squier, "The Ladies of Lima," *Frank Leslie's Chimney Corner*, June 3, 1865, 12–13, and "Santa Rosa of Lima," *Harper's New Monthly Magazine*, December 1866, 89–94.

10. Miriam wrote a somewhat scolding letter to Squier at London on March 22, 1867, while he was in debtor's prison at Liverpool. She hoped that "the cruel hours" he had spent there would teach him a lesson: "that money is the all in all of our existence. What is intellect or position without it?" The letter is among the papers relating to Frank Leslie's contested will. See *Leslie v. Leslie*, 359–60. The other letter is a teasing one she wrote after her return from Peru. See M. Squier to E. G. Squier, New York, April 12, 1864, SFP. Stern discusses these letters in *Purple Passage*, 42–43 and 48.

11. Documents relating to Squier's imprisonment for debt in Lancaster Castle in 1867 and his declaration of bankruptcy in England are in the Squier Family Papers of the New-York Historical Society.

12. *Liverpool Courier*, March 13, 1867, press clipping, SFP. Squier's arrest was also reported in the *New York Herald*, April 1, 1867.

13. Stern, *Purple Passage*, 221.

14. Squier to parents, New York, September 1, 1869, SFP.

15. Squier to parents, New York, January 4, 1873, SFP.

16. Attorneys pled the case of Miriam Florence Squier against Ephraim George Squier in the Superior Court of the City of New York in May 1873. The court issued affidavits and took the depositions of witnesses between May 25 and May 29 and granted the decree of divorce on May 31, 1873. See Superior Court of the City of New York, Divorce Records, vol. 35, pages 169–84. The records are archived at the Supreme Court, New York County, New York, New York, in the Old Records Division of the New York County Clerk's Office [hereafter cited in the text as *Squier v. Squier*].

17. Squier to Campbell, New York, June 5, 1873, SFP.

18. [E. G. Squier], "Last Will and Test. Of Ephraim George Squier," July 30, 1873, SFP.

19. William Walsh, Clerk, Supreme Court, "In the Matter of E. George Squier a Lunatic," Commission to [the] Committee [of Inquisition], August 18, 1874, SFP.

20. "Eclipse of Genius: A Distinguished Archaeologist Insane," *New York Herald*, August 18, 1874.

21. "Sad End of a Journalist," *Brooklyn Union*, August 17, 1874, SFP.

22. *Providence Journal*, August 19, 1874, SFP.

23. "Too Bad," unidentified press clipping, [ca. August 18, 1874], SFP.

24. "The Chronicler, Tales of To-Day," *Town Topics*, March 27, 1886, 14.

25. *Leslie v. Leslie*, 315.

26. That was also the opinion of Squier's nephew Frank Squier Jr. Frank Squier, ed., "A Collection of Books by Ephraim George Squier," 1.

27. Squier to Harper Brothers, Sanford Hall, Flushing, Long Island, October 21, 1874, Squier to Frank Squier, Sanford Hall, Flushing, Long Island, October 29, 1874, Squier to parents, Sanford Hall, Flushing, Long Island, November 18, 1874, and Squier to Frank Squier, [Sanford Hall, Flushing, Long Island], November 18, 1874, all in SFP.

28. *Nation*, December 17, 1874, SFP.

29. The circumstances leading to Davis's decision to sell the artifacts to William Blackmore in 1864 appear in Terry A. Barnhart, "In His Own Right: Dr. Edwin Hamilton Davis and the Davis Collection of American Antiquities," *Journal of the History of Collections* 16 (May 2004): 59–87, and in his "An American Menagerie: The Cabinet of Squier and Davis," *Timeline* 2 (December 1875–January 1986): 2–17.

30. See Sabin, *Catalogue of the Library of E. G. Squier*, i–ii, 229–32, 258. The Sabin catalog has entries for the 2,034 items sold at public auction, which included 64 manuscripts. The original Catherwood drawings were of archaeological remains at Copán, Uxmal, Chichén Itzá, and Tulum. Henry Stevens, an American book merchant in London connected with the British Museum, apparently purchased the Humboldt volumes that became part of Squier's library. A note regarding a missing volume of Humboldt's seven-volume *Nova Genera et Species Plantarum* accompanying entry 1980 of the Sabin catalog states that "the present owner holds Mr. Henry Steven's written promise to supply it in the same style as the others."

31. Sabin, *Catalogue of the Library of E. G. Squier*, i.

32. Hubert Howe Bancroft, *Literary Industries* (New York: Harper and Brothers, 1891), 103–4, 354, 358–60. An enumeration of the sixteenth- and seventeenth-century Spanish manuscript materials and printed works formerly belonging to Squier is found on p. 359. See also John Walton Gaughey, *Hubert Howe Bancroft: Historian of the West* (Berkeley: University of California Press, 1946), 76, 88. An annotated version of the Squier library auction catalog at the Bancroft identifies the items purchased by Bancroft. Most of the documents have annotations signed by Buckingham Smith in 1856–57, and sometimes also by Martin Fernandez de Navarrete or his assistant. The annotations certify the locations of the original documents. George P. Hammond, ed., *A Guide*

to the *Manuscript Collections of the Bancroft Library*, vol. 2 (Berkeley: University of California Press, 1972), 232.

33. Edward Robinson, Hermann E. Ludewig, E. Geo. Squier, and William B. Hodgson, "Communication Relative to the Publication of Spanish Works on New Mexico," *Tenth Annual Report of the Board of Regents of the Smithsonian Institution* (Washington DC: A. O. P. Nicholson, 1856), 307–9.

34. "Ethnological Society," *Historical Magazine* 3 (May 1859): 147. See Squier, "Specimen of the Montagnais Language of Lower Canada: From the British Museum," *Historical Magazine* 7 (September 1863): 268–69.

35. E. G. Squier, *Honduras and British Honduras* (New York: Scribner, 1880).

36. Mrs. Frank Leslie, *California: A Pleasure Trip From Gotham to the Golden Gate* (New York: Carlton, 1877). B. De Graaf published a facsimile of the original 1877 New York edition at Nieuwkoop in 1972, with an introduction by Madeline B. Stern.

37. Mrs. Frank Leslie, *California*, 277.

38. Mrs. Frank Leslie, *California*, 277–78, 280.

39. *Territorial Enterprise Extra. Containing a Full Account of "Frank Leslie" and Wife* (Virginia City, Nev., 1878), 3–4. The part of the account chronicling Squier's marriage to Miriam and their scandalous divorce consistently misspells his name as "Squiers": "Mrs. Squiers," "E. G. Squiers," and "the Squierses." That could be a simple misspelling on Daggett's part, a consistent typographical error, or a thinly veiled attempt to make it appear that Squier was not, in fact, the author of the letter to the editor of the *Enterprise* and the source of information about Miriam's past.

40. *Daily Territorial Enterprise*, July 14, 1878, 1. Madeline B. Stern provides an account of the Leslies' extravagant and well-publicized trip in her "Mrs. Leslie Goes West," *Book Club of California Quarterly News Letter* (Fall 1959): 77–80.

41. Stern, *Purple Passage*, 95–96.

42. Squier to parents, Brooklyn, September 11, 1878, March 9, 1881, SFP.

43. "Death of E. G. Squire [*sic*]: The Close of the Archaeologist's Career after a Long Illness," *New York Times*, April 18, 1888, p. 8, col. 3. News of Squier's death came as no surprise to his family, who knew that he had been seriously ill for some time. Joel Squier to Frank Squier, Chatham Center, April 20, 1888, SFP.

44. "The News," *Baltimore American*, August 19, 1874, SFP.

45. Seitz, *Letters from Parkman to Squier*, 15.

A NOTE ON ARCHIVAL SOURCES

1. Speech, Article, and Book File, ca. 1848–77, box 7, Reference Notes, SPLC. A guide to the Squier Papers at the Library of Congress is Jerry E. Patterson and

William R. Stanton, "The Ephraim George Squier Manuscripts in the Library of Congress: A Check List," *Papers of the Bibliographical Society of America* 53 (1959): 309–26, although their index makes occasional errors concerning the number of letters written by certain correspondents and their inclusive dates. A more complete finding aid is "The Papers of Ephraim George Squier, Manuscript Division, Library of Congress," a typed manuscript collection guide prepared by Michael Musick in October 1969. Joseph Sullivan and T. Michael Womack revised Musick's guide in 1997 as "A Register of the Ephraim George Squier Papers in the Library of Congress." Researchers should begin their investigation of the collection with that register. A microfilm edition of most of these papers is available by either loan or purchase.

2. John R. Hebert, "Maps by Ephraim George Squier: Journalist, Scholar, and Diplomat," *Quarterly Journal of the Library of Congress* 29, no. 1 (1972): 14–31. Hebert's account includes a bibliography of the Squier Map Collection in the Geography and Map Division of the Library of Congress.

3. Several lots of photographs of ancient Peruvian pottery, ruins, and native peoples were sold as part of Squier's library. See entries 1778, 1780, 1797, and 1804 in Sabin, *Catalogue of the Library of E. G. Squier*, 231–32.

4. Michael Forest Fry, "Ephraim George Squier Papers, Collection Guide," typescript, Latin American Library, Tulane University, February 1981, 1–20.

5. Charles Latham processed the Ephraim George Squier Papers at the Indiana Historical Society in April 1989 and May 1994. A description of the scope and content of the collection is available from the society's Manuscript Collections Department at the William Henry Smith Memorial Library, which includes a box and folder inventory.

6. The manuscript copies of the original Spanish relations and documents once in Squier's possession appear as entries 719 to 783 of Sabin's *Catalogue of the Library of E. G. Squier*, 96–107.

The Anthropological Writings of Ephraim George Squier

The following bibliography represents the works of Ephraim George Squier relating in whole or part to the subjects of American archaeology and ethnology. It includes both his major and minor writings. Squier wrote for both scholarly and popular audiences, a demarcation less clearly defined in his day than in ours, and some of his more popular works contain important information that is not available elsewhere. The relevant works of Squier's predecessors and contemporaries and the subsequent opinions of historians are fully referenced in the endnotes and are not replicated here. A larger listing of Squier's writings reflecting all of his manifold interests and activities is Frank Squier, ed., "A Collection of Books by Ephraim George Squier. His Own Copies with Some Recently Acquired Additions, And a Few Books by Others," a typed manuscript catalog compiled at New York in March 1939. Two boxes of manuscript bibliographies and notes compiled by Frank Squier between 1938 and 1950 are part of the Ephraim George Squier Papers of the New-York Historical Society.

The Frank Squier catalog contains valuable annotations. The ninety-one items listed there are the books, pamphlets, and contributions to periodicals that were in Squier's library at the time of its sale. Joseph Sabin prepared that list when Bangs, Merwin, and Company sold the Squier library at public auction in New York on April 24, 1876. Frank Squier's catalog makes important corrections to Sabin's list and also supplies omissions. So far as anthropological subjects are concerned, however, I have found several contributions to periodicals not listed in Frank Squier's entries. These articles appear in the following bibliography, which is the most complete list of Ephraim George Squier's anthropological writings that has been compiled to date. Other fugitive contributions to periodicals and newspapers relating to archaeology and ethnology will no doubt be found.

"American Antiquities." *Scioto Gazette*, October 23, 1845.

"On Discoidal Stones of the Indian Mounds." *American Journal of Science and Arts*, 2nd ser., 2 (November 1846): 216–18.

"Pipestone of the Ancient Pipes in the Indian Mounds." *American Journal of Science and Arts*, 2nd ser., 2 (November 1846): 287.

"Observations on the Uses of the Mounds of the West, With an Attempt at Their Classification." *American Journal of Science and Arts*, 2nd ser., 3 (May 1847): 237–48.

Observations on the Uses of the Mounds of the West, With an Attempt at Their Classification. New Haven: B. L. Hamlen, 1847.

"Observations on the Fossils, Minerals, Organic Remains, etc., Found in the Mounds of the West." *Edinburgh New Philosophical Journal* 44 (October 1847–April 1848): 141–44.

"Hieroglyphical Mica Plates from the Mounds." *American Journal of Science and Arts,* 2nd ser., 4 (November 1847): 145.

Observations on the Aboriginal Monuments of the Mississippi Valley. New York: Bartlett and Welford, 1847.

"Observations on the Aboriginal Monuments of the Mississippi Valley." *Transactions of the American Ethnological Society* 2 (1848): 131–207. The article appeared as a pamphlet of the same title published by Bartlett and Welford of New York in 1847.

"Ne-She-Kay-Be-Nais, or the 'Lone Bird,' an Ojibway Legend." *American Review: A Whig Journal of Politics, Literature, Art, and Science,* n.s., 2 (September 1848): 255–59.

"Manabozho and the Great Serpent, an Algonquin Tradition." *American Review: A Whig Journal of Politics, Literature, Art, and Science,* n.s., 2 (October 1848): 392–98.

"New Mexico and California: The Ancient Monuments, and the Aboriginal, Semi-Civilized Nations of New Mexico and California." *American Review: A Whig Journal of Politics, Literature, Art, and Science,* n.s., 2 (November 1848): 503–28.

Ancient Monuments of the Mississippi Valley: Comprising the Results of Extensive Original Surveys and Explorations by Ephraim George Squier and Edwin Hamilton Davis. *Smithsonian Contributions to Knowledge.* Vol. 1. Washington DC: Smithsonian Institution, 1848.

Ancient Monuments of the Mississippi Valley: Comprising the Results of Extensive Original Surveys and Explorations by Ephraim George Squier and Edwin Hamilton Davis. New York: Bartlett and Welford; Cincinnati: J. A. and U. P. James, 1848.

Ancient Monuments of the Mississippi Valley by Ephraim George Squier and Edwin Hamilton Davis. Edited with an introduction by David J. Meltzer. *Smithsonian Classics of Anthropology.* Washington DC: Smithsonian Institution Press, 1998. Includes an index and bibliography prepared by David J. Meltzer.

Ancient Monuments of the Mississippi Valley by Ephraim George Squier and Edwin Hamilton Davis. *Antiquities of the New World. Early Explorations in Archaeology.* Vol. 2. New York: AMS Press for Harvard University's Peabody Museum of Archaeology and Ethnology, 1973. With an introduction by James B. Griffin, vii–ix.

Bibliography

"Lettre de M. Georges Squier a M. Jomard . . . Sur Les Antiquities Americaines Et La Montagne de Brush Creek." *Bulletin de la Societe de Geographie* 9–10 (1848): 283–88.

"The Monumental Evidence of the Discovery of America by the Northmen Critically Examined." *Ethnological Journal* 1 (December 1848): 313–26.

"Historical and Mythological Traditions of the Algonquins, with a Translation of the 'Walum-Olum,' or Bark Record of the Lenni-Lenape." *American Review: A Whig Journal of Politics, Literature, Art, and Science*, n.s., 3 (February 1849): 273–93.

"Some New Discoveries respecting the Dates on the Great Calendar Stone of the Ancient Mexicans, with Observations on the Mexican Cycle of Fifty-Two Years; by E. G. Squier, New York." *American Journal of Science and Arts*, 2nd ser., 8 (March 1849): 153–57.

"American Ethnology: Being a Summary of Some of the Results Which Have Followed the Investigation of this Subject." *American Review: A Whig Journal of Politics, Literature, Art, and Science*, n.s., 3 (April 1849): 385–98.

"A Monograph of the Ancient Monuments of the State of Kentucky." *American Journal of Science and Arts*, 2nd ser., 8 (July 1849): 1–14.

"Report upon the Aboriginal Monuments of Western New York." *Proceedings of the New-York Historical Society* (January 1849): 41–61.

"Ancient Monuments in the Islands of Lake Nicaragua, Central America," *Literary World*, March 9, 1850, 233–35, March 16, 1850, 269–70, and March 23, 1850, 304–5.

"Archaeology of Nicaragua." *Literary World*, October 19, 1850, 314–15.

Squier to Joseph Henry, New York, December 2, 1850, in *Fifth Annual Report of the Board of Regents of the Smithsonian Institution*. Washington DC: Government Printing Office, 1851. Appendix no. 2, 78–79.

Aboriginal Monuments of the State of New York: Comprising the Results of Original Surveys and Explorations: With an Illustrative Appendix. Article IX of *Smithsonian Contributions to Knowledge*. Vol. 2. Washington DC: Smithsonian Institution, 1851.

Antiquities of the State of New York: Being the Results of Extensive Original Surveys and Explorations, with a Supplement on the Antiquities of the West. Buffalo: Geo. H. Derby, 1851.

"Observations on the Memoir of Dr. Zestermann, relating the Colonization of America in Pre-Historic Times." In C. A. Adolf Zestermann, *Memoir on the European Colonization of America in Ante-Historic Times, with Critical Observations Thereon, by E. G. Squier*, 20–32. From the proceedings of the American Ethnological Society, April 1851. London: Bateman and Hardwicke, 1851.

Bibliography

The Serpent Symbol, and the Worship of the Reciprocal Principles of Nature in America. Archaeological Researches no. 1. New York: Putnam, 1851.

"Aztec Picture-Writing." *New-York Tribune,* November 24, 1852. Notice of a paper read by Squier at a meeting of the American Ethnological Society.

Nicaragua: Its People, Scenery, Monuments, and the Proposed Inter-Oceanic Canal. 2 vols. New York: D. Appleton, 1852. London: Longman, Brown, Green, and Longman, 1852.

Nicaragua: Its People, Scenery, Monuments, and the Proposed Inter-Oceanic Canal. Revised, single-volume ed. New York: Harper and Brothers, 1860. Reprint, New York: AMS Press, 1973.

Nicaragua, Sus Gentes Y Paisajes. Trans. Luciano Cuadra. Managua: Editorial Nueva Nicaragua, 1989. Includes a prologue, "Ephraim George Squier (1821) Y Su Obra," by Jorge Eduardo Arellano, 9–11, and a "Nota Traductor" by Luciano Cuadra, 13–14. Spanish edition of Squier's *Nicaragua* originally published at New York in 1852.

Nicaragua, Sus Gentes Y Paisajes. Coleccion Viajeros no. 1. Trans. Luciano Cuadra. Ciudad Universitaria "Rodrigo Facio," Costa Rica: Editorial Universitaria Centroamericana (EDUCA), 1970. Based on the single-volume edition of *Nicaragua* published at New York in 1860.

"Observations on the Archaeology and Ethnology of Nicaragua." *Transactions of the American Ethnological Society* 3, pt. 1 (1853): 84–158.

"Observations on the Creek and Cherokee Indians by William Bartram, with Prefatory and Supplemental Notes by E. G. Squier." *Transactions of the American Ethnological Society* 3, pt. 1 (1853): 1–81.

"Ancient Peru – Its People and Its Monuments." *Harper's New Monthly Magazine,* June 1853, 7–38.

Ruins of Tenampua, Honduras, Central America. New York: New-York Historical Society, 1853. An eight-page pamphlet taken from the "Proceedings of the Historical Society of New-York, October 1853."

"Observations on an Existing Fragment of the Nahual, or Pure Mexican Stock in the State of San Salvador, Central America." *New-York Tribune,* April 13, 1854. Notice of a paper read by Squier before the American Ethnological Society.

Notes on Central America: Particularly the States of Honduras and San Salvador. New York: Harper and Brothers, 1855. Reprint, New York: Frederick A. Praeger, 1969, with an introduction by A. Curtis Wilgus. Reprint, New York: AMS Press, 1971.

"Some Critical Observations on the 'Literature of American Aboriginal Languages.'" *New York Daily Tribune,* January 22, 1858.

The States of Central America: Their Geography, Topography, Climate, Population, Re-

sources, Productions, Commerce, Political Organizations, Aborigines, etc. New York: Harper and Brothers; London: Sampson Low, Son, 1858. University Microfilms at Ann Arbor, Michigan, issued a facsimile of the original New York edition in 1970.

"Les Indiens Xicaques du Honduras." *Nouvelles Annales des Voyages* (November 1858): 133–36.

"A Visit to the Guajiquero Indians." *Harper's New Monthly Magazine*, October 1859, 602–19.

"Ancient Monuments of the United States." *Harper's New Monthly Magazine*, May 1860, 737–53, June 1860, 20–36, and July 1860, 165–78.

"The Unexplored Regions of Central America." *Historical Magazine* 4 (March 1860): 65–66. A paper read before the New-York Historical Society in January 1860.

Editor. *Collection of Rare and Original Documents and Relations, Concerning the Discovery and Conquest of America. Chiefly from the Spanish Archives. Number 1.* New York: Charles B. Norton, 1860. Albany: Joel Munsell, 1860. Contains the *Carta dirijida al rey de Espana, por el Licenciado Dr. Don Diego Garcia de Palacio, oydor de la real Audencia de Guatemala, Ano 1576.*

Monograph of Authors Who Have Written on the Languages of Central America, and Collected Vocabularies or Composed Works in the Native Dialects of That Country. New York: C. B. Richardson; Albany: Joel Munsell, 1861.

"Specimen of the Montagnais Language of Lower Canada: From the British Museum." *Historical Magazine*, September 1863, 268–69.

"The Aboriginal Graphic Systems of America." *American Phrenological Journal* 10 (January 1867): 18–21.

"Quelques Remarques sur la Geographie et les Monuments du Perou, par E. G. Squier." *Extrait du Bulletin de la Societe de Geographie, Janvier 1868.* Paris: Impr. De E. Martinet, 1868. A 28-page pamphlet.

"Among the Andes of Peru and Bolivia: I – Over the Cordillera." *Harper's New Monthly Magazine*, April 1868, 545–66.

"Among the Andes of Peru and Bolivia: II – Tiahuanaco – The Baalbec of the New World." *Harper's New Monthly Magazine*, May 1868, 681–700.

"Among the Andes of Peru and Bolivia: III – The Sacred Islands." *Harper's New Monthly Magazine*, June 1868, 16–33.

"Among the Andes of Peru and Bolivia: IV – The City of the Sun." *Harper's New Monthly Magazine*, July 1868, 145–65.

"Among the Andes of Peru and Bolivia: V – Fortresses and Gardens." *Harper's New Monthly Magazine*, August 1868, 307–32.

"Serpent Worship in America." *Athenaeum*, December 25, 1869, 872. E. G. Squier to the editor, New York, December 7, 1869.

Bibliography

Observations on the Chalchihuitl of Mexico and Central America. New York: Extract from the Annals of the Lyceum of Natural History of New York, 1869.

"Tongues from Tombs; or the Stories that Graves Tell. Number 1 – The Mounds of the United States." *Frank Leslie's Illustrated Newspaper*, March 20, 1869, 5–6.

"Tongues from Tombs; or the Stories that Graves Tell. Number 2 – A Plain Man's Tomb in Peru." *Frank Leslie's Illustrated Newspaper*, March 27, 1869, 21–22.

"Tongues from Tombs; or the Stories that Graves Tell. Number 3 – Agricultural Laborers and the Princes of Chimu." *Frank Leslie's Illustrated Newspaper*, June 12, 1869, 204–6.

"Tongues from Tombs; or the Stories that Graves Tell. Number 4 – Grand Chimu and New Granada." *Frank Leslie's Illustrated Newspaper*, June 19, 1869, 221–22.

"Tongues from Tombs; or the Stories that Graves Tell. Number 5 – Central America." *Frank Leslie's Illustrated Newspaper*, June 26, 1869, 236–38.

"Tongues from Tombs; or the Stories that Graves Tell. Number 6 – Central America and Yucatan." *Frank Leslie's Illustrated Newspaper*, July 10, 1869, 269–70.

"Tongues from Tombs; or the Stories that Graves Tell. Number 7 – Mexico." *Frank Leslie's Illustrated Newspaper*, July 17, 1869, 285–86.

"Tongues from Tombs; or the Stories that Graves Tell. Number 8 – The Egyptians." *Frank Leslie's Illustrated Newspaper*, July 24, 1869, 300–302.

"Observations on a Collection of Chalchihuitls from Mexico and Central America." *American Naturalist* 4 (May 1870): 171–81.

Observations on the Geography and Archaeology of Peru. London: Trubner, 1870. 27 pp. A paper read before the American Geographical Society in February of 1870 and published as a pamphlet by Trubner.

"Archaeological Impostures." *American Naturalist* 4 (July 1870): 319–20.

"The Primeval Monuments of Peru Compared with Those in the Other Parts of the World." *American Naturalist* 4 (March 1870): 1–17.

Honduras: Descriptive, Historical, and Statistical. London: Trubner, 1870. Republished, with some revisions, from Squier's *States of Central America* (1858). Reprint, New York: AMS Press, 1970.

Introduction and notes to Arthur Morclet. *Travels in Central America: Including Accounts of Some Regions Unexplored since the Conquest.* Translated from the French of the Chevalier Arthur Morelet, by Mrs. M. F. Squier. London: Trubner, 1871.

"The Arch in America." *Journal of the Anthropological Institute of New-York* 1 (1871–72): 78–80.

"Report." *Journal of the Anthropological Institute of New-York* 1 (1871–72): 15–20.

Bibliography

"American Antiquities." In *The American Cyclopaedia: A Popular Dictionary of General Knowledge*, ed. George Ripley and Charles A. Dana, 1:393–401. Rev. ed. New York: D. Appleton, 1873.

Peru: Incidents of Travel and Exploration in the Land of the Incas. New York: Harper and Brothers; London, Macmillan, 1877.

Peru: Incidents of Travel and Exploration in the Land of the Incas. Antiquities of the New World. Early Explorations in Archaeology. Vol. 9. New York: AMS Press, for the Peabody Museum of Archaeology and Ethnology, 1973. Includes an introduction by Gordon R. Willey, vii–x. This reprint maintains the pagination and index of the original 1877 edition.

Un Viaje Por Tierras Incaicas: Cronica e una expedicion arqueologica (1863–65). Contains an introduction by Juan de Dios Guevara, ix–x, and a prologue by Raul Porras Barrenechea, xi–xiii. La Paz, Bolivia: Editorial Los Amigo del Libro, 1974. From the original edition published at New York by Harper and Brothers in 1877.

Honduras and British Honduras. New York: Scribner, 1880.

INDEX

Page references in italics indicate illustrations.

Aboriginal Monuments of the Mississippi Valley, 58, 352n17

Aboriginal Monuments of the State of New York (1851): appendix of, 112–14, 190; findings in, 112; publication of, 103, 106, 365n16; subsequent opinions on, 116–17

Aboriginal Races of North America, 126, 128

aboriginal vocabularies and languages of Central America: affinities of and differences between, 234–37; classification of, 237–38; Squier's study of, 164, 165, 176, 219, 221, 223, 333

Acosta, José de, 133, 371n47

Agassiz, Louis: and human origins, 299, 303–5, 400n64, 400n65, 400n66

Algic Researches, 122, 136

Algonquian traditions, 118–19, 122

Alligewi, 91, 99. *See also* Tallegwi

Alvarado, Pedro de, 178, 220, 231, 233

American Academy of Arts and Sciences, 38, 40

American anthropological community, 3–4

American Antiquarian Society, 37–38, 53–55, 314

American Association for the Advancement of Science, 4, 340n8

American Atlantic and Pacific Ship-Canal Company, 158–59

American Ethnological Society, 4, 37, 52, 53, 55, 60, 104, 106, 151, 219, 288–89, 305, 307, 310–12, 313, 314, 316, 380n32

"American Ethnology," 284

"American family." *See* "American race"

American Geographical and Statistical Society, 265, 395n44

American Indians: antiquity of, 179, 189, 205; Squier's defense of artistic and intellectual attainments of, 289–90; theory of indigenous origin of, 96, 294, 299–300

American Institute, Photographic Section of, 264, 395n41

American Journal of Science and Arts, 34, 38, 40, 145, 146, 147, 191, 224, 382n69

American Nations, 126, 128, 148

American Naturalist, 239, 244, 251, 274

American Philosophical Society, 147

"American race" (period use of term), 70, 83–84, 91, 93, 286, 300–301

American Review, 118, 126, 187, 284, 367n1, 378n13

American School of Ethnology, 3, 4, 5, 206, 210; origin of phrase, 283; racial theory of, 296–305; Squier's relationship with, 47–48, 222, 226, 228, 271–72, 281, 284–86, 291–92, 294–96, 305–14

Anahuac, 294

analogies: Squier's use of cultural, 5, 65, 73, 78, 103, 179, 112–13, 190, 191–92, 207, 340n12

"Ancient Annals of Kentucky," 143, 148

Ancient History, or Annals of Kentucky, 374n86

Ancient Monuments of North and South America, 145, 369n26

Ancient Monuments of the Mississippi Valley (1848): analysis of artifacts in, 82–88; comparative analysis of mounds and enclosures in, 73, 75, 76–77; manuscript drafts of and plates of engravings in, 333, 335–36; reviews of, 97–100; scope of, 70–71; subsequent opinion on, 100–101

"Ancient Monuments of the United States," 109

"Ancient Peru – Its People and Its Monuments," 245–46

Anleo, Bartolome, 239, 391n68

Annals and Antiquities of Rajasthan, 125

Anthony, Henry Bowen, 317, 322

Anthropological Institute of New-York, 4, 310–14, 316

Anthropological Review (of London), 5, 313, 340n11

Anthropological Society of London, 313

Anthropological Society of Paris, 272, 312

anthropology: four-field approach to, 4;

Index

anthropology: four-field approach (*cont.*) idea of and early development, 1–2, 4–5, 312–13; problems with history of, 5, 10, 11

Antiguedades Peruana, 246

Antiquities of Mexico, 287

Antiquities of the State of New York, 365n17

Archaeologia Americana: Transactions and Collections of the American Antiquarian Society, 347n12, 390n53

Arellano, Jorge Eduardo, 186

Arriaga, Joseph de, 250, 279

Athenaeum (of London), 208, 210, 216, 230, 241–42

Atlantic Journal, 145

Atwater, Caleb, 31, 32, 34, 54, 196

autochthons (use of term), 176, 207, 287

Avila, Gil Gonzales de, 169

Avila, Pedro Arias de, 164, 173, 180

Aymara Indians, 254, 274; skull from Totora, 269, 270

Aztec: calendar, 181, 182, 382n69, 382n70; religious beliefs, 88, 121, 122–23, 201–2; symbolism of, in Nicaragua, 170, 176, 180, 181, 182–83

Bancroft, Hubert Howe, 326, 338, 404n32

Bandelier, Adolf F., 278

Bangs, Merwin, and Company, 325

"barbarous" (period use of term), 9, 42, 49, 91

Bard, Samuel A. (pseudonym of E. G. Squier), 241–42

Bartlett, John Russell, 37, 40–41, 46, 53, 55, 82, 102, 106, 107, 188, 314, 347n17; and Welford, 58, 292, 352n17, 355n50

Barton, Benjamin Smith, 125

Bartram, William, 77–78, 108, 113, 136, 198, 358n18

Beach, William, 126, 369n23

Beauchamp, William M., 116

Bering Strait, 133, 143

biblical ethnology, 3, 96, 195, 196, 207, 209, 287, 293–94, 314

Biblioteca Hispano-American Septentrional, 238

Bieder, Robert E., 344n29, 386n64, 389n33, 397n2

biography, 6–7

black codes, 41, 349n36

Blackmore, William, 325

Blackmore Museum, 325

Blanding, William, 75

Boas, Franz, 9, 10

Bobadilla, Fray Francisco de, 166, 177, 180, 181

Boewe, Charles, 142, 144, 357n11, 369n25, 372n66, 375n89, 375n90, 376n91, 376n92

bone burials, 77, 108

Boturini Benaducci, Lorenzo, 171, 327

Bovallius, Carl, 186

Brébeuf, Jean de, 108

Brinton, Daniel Garrison: and criticism of *Serpent Symbol*, 209–10; and Walam Olum, 137–39, 148

British Museum, 325

Broca, Dr. M. Paul, 272, 312–13

Brooklyn Union, 324

Bulletin de la Societe de Geographie, 100, 191, 244, 392n2

Bulletin of the American Ethnological Society, 311

Bureau of American Ethnology, 11, 100–101

burial mounds: of Ohio, 35, 53, 71–72, 82–83, 92–93, 101, 352n18; of western New York, 108, 109, 110. *See also* mounds

Burke, Luke, 1, 99, 283, 288, 294–96, 311

Burns, John, 126, 129, 139

Butterfield, Herbert, 8, 341n20

California: gold rush, 155; sixteenth-century gold hunting in, 378n13

Campbell, Douglas, 322

Campbell, Malcom, 322

Carver, Jonathan, 132

Catherwood, Frederick, 233, 326

Catlin, George, 35, 130

Cayuga Indians, 110

Central America: amalgamation of races in, 222, 224–26, 285–86; American interests in, 154–55, 157–58; development of civilization in, 229–30, 234; social conditions in, 155, 174; as source of Mexican civilization, 235–36; white emigration to, Squier's support of, 174, 215, 227, 228

Cereceda, Andres de, 189

chalchihuitl, 239–40

Champollion, Jean-François, 145

Channing, William Ellery, 20

Index

Index

Index

Index

Stanton, William R., 2, 339n5, 347n15, 350n53, 401n72
State University of New York at Albany, 105, 106, 108
States of Central America (1858), 215, 228–29, 242
Stephens, John Lloyd, 35, 151, 152, 184, 218, 233
Stern, Madeline B., 319, 328, 403n10
Stocking, George W., Jr., 341n23
Strong, John A., 186, 380n40
Strong, William Duncan, 185
Subtiaba, 161, 164–65, 166, 167, 176, 380n30, 380n32
Sullivant, Joseph, 63
sun worship, 72, 78, 88, 119, 122, 123, 147, 166, 197, 201, 209, 210, 211, 250
symbolism: of archaeological remains in the Mississippi Valley, 73; of circular and square design of earthworks, 78; rationale of, 190, 191, 197, 198, 201, 207, 208, 210, 358n29

Tallegwi (Allegwi, Alligewi), 133, 134, 135, 143
Tanner, John: captivity narrative of, 122, 130, 142, 373n70
Taylor, Richard C., 34, 353n18
Taylor, S., 34
Tax, Thomas Gilbert, 11, 342n30, 351n4
Tenampua: ruins of, 216–18
Ternaux-Compans, Henri, 232
Territorial Enterprise Extra, 330, 402n6, 405n39
Tezcatlipoca, 201–2
Thomas, Cyrus, 101, 363n99
Tiahuanaco, 278
Ticomega Emaguatega, 177
Tod, James, 125
Toltecan-Barbarous family division within Morton's classification of the American race, 42, 91–92, 114
Toltecs, 179, 186, 235, 294, 301, 303
Tonacaquahuitl (tree of life), 171
Tonacatlecoatl ("Serpent Sun"), 121, 122, 201, 202
Tonawanda Island (Niagara River), 108, 109
"Tongues from Tombs; or the Stories That Graves Tell," 394n30
Torquemada, Fray Juan de, 177–78

Town Topics, 324
Traditional History and Characteristic Sketches of the Ojibway Nation, 131
Transactions of the American Antiquarian Society, 34, 150, 176, 181, 401n91
Transactions of the American Ethnological Society, 37, 39–40, 288, 311, 347n17, 381n68; Bartram manuscript published in, 77; pamphlet edition of, 58, 352n17
Transactions of the American Philosophical Society, 135
Travels in Central America, 243
Travels in the Interior of North America, 123
Travels through North and South Carolina, Georgia, East and West Florida, 77
trepanning, 272–73, 396n62
Trigger, Bruce G., 10, 205, 341n27, 342n28, 342n29
Troost, Gerard, 37, 80, 92, 198
Tschudi, Johan Jacob von, 246
Turner, William W., 55, 106, 216
Two Lectures on the Connection between the Biblical and Physical History of Man, 292, 293, 298
"Two Lectures on the Origin and Progress of Modern Civilization," 20–21
Types of Mankind, 224, 283, 296–99, 305–6; Squier's anonymous review of, 306–7
Tzendal Language, 231, 238

Ulmeques, 177–78
Urrita, Don José Antonio, 230–31
U. S. Exploring Expedition, 35, 152, 347n15, 355n46

Vail, Eugene A., 360n54
Vanderbilt, Cornelius, 158
Vega, Garcilaso de la, 121, 198, 246, 258, 275
Victorino, 160
Vocabulario Mexicano (1571), 239
Voget, Fred W., 212, 213

Waikna; or, Adventures on the Mosquito Shore, 241
Wailes, Benjamin L. C., 78, 79
Walam Olum, 118, 126–29, 140; mnemonic symbols of, 127, 128; Schoolcraft's views on, 136–37; Squier's views on, 129, 130, 148
Walam Olum, or Red Score, 140

In the *Critical Studies in the History of Anthropology* series

Invisible Genealogies: A History of Americanist Anthropology
Regna Darnell

The Shaping of American Ethnography: The Wilkes Exploring Expedition, 1838–1842
Barry Alan Joyce

Ruth Landes: A Life in Anthropology
Sally Cole

Melville J. Herskovits and the Racial Politics of Knowledge
Jerry Gershenhorn

Leslie A. White: Evolution and Revolution in Anthropology
William J. Peace

Rolling in Ditches with Shamans:
Jaime de Angulo and the Professionalization of American Anthropology
Wendy Leeds-Hurwitz

Irregular Connections: A History of Anthropology and Sexuality
Andrew P. Lyons and Harriet D. Lyons

Ephraim George Squier and the Development of American Anthropology
Terry A. Barnhart

The Final Years of Ruth Benedict: Beyond Relativity, Beyond Pattern
Virginia Heyer Young